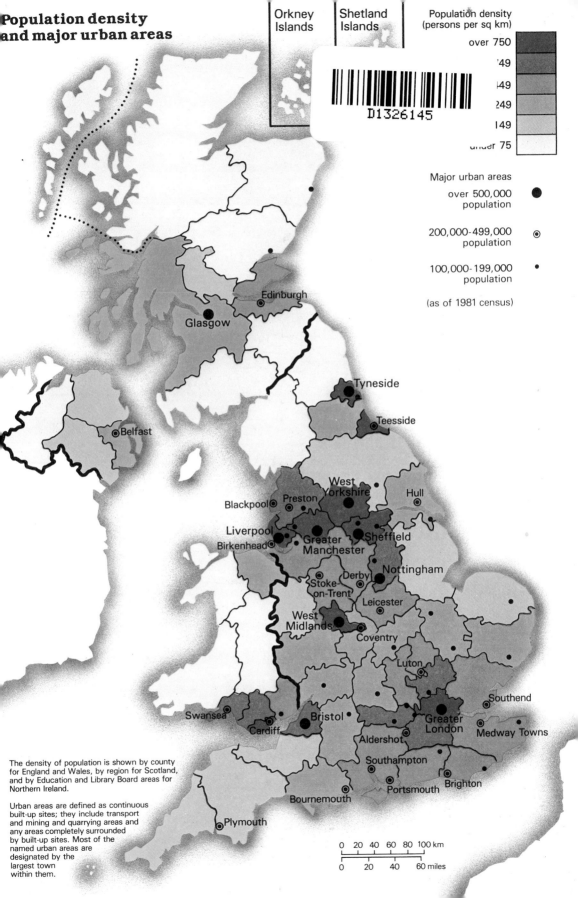

Population density and major urban areas

Orkney Islands

Shetland Islands

Population density (persons per sq km)

over 750	
'49	
149	
249	
149	
under 75	

D1326145

Major urban areas

over 500,000 population ●

200,000-499,000 population ◉

100,000-199,000 population •

(as of 1981 census)

Edinburgh

Glasgow

Belfast

Tyneside

Teesside

West Yorkshire

Blackpool · Preston

Hull

Liverpool · Greater Manchester · Sheffield

Birkenhead

Stoke-on-Trent · Derby · Nottingham

Leicester

West Midlands

Coventry

Luton

Southend

Swansea

Bristol

Greater London

Cardiff

Aldershot

Medway Towns

Southampton

Brighton

Bournemouth

Portsmouth

Plymouth

The density of population is shown by county for England and Wales, by region for Scotland, and by Education and Library Board areas for Northern Ireland.

Urban areas are defined as continuous built-up sites; they include transport and mining and quarrying areas and any areas completely surrounded by built-up sites. Most of the named urban areas are designated by the largest town within them.

0	20	40	60	80	100 km

0	20	40	60 miles

BRITAIN 1987

Corrections

Chapter 12—Manufacturing and Service Industries
p. 258. The last line should read:
40 per cent of Scotch whisky output. Over 80 per cent of all Scotch whisky

Chapter 19—Overseas Trade
p. 380. In Table 40 the visible trade balance for 1981 should be £3,360 million
(without minus sign).

BRITAIN

1987

AN OFFICIAL HANDBOOK

BRITAIN

1987

AN OFFICIAL HANDBOOK

Prepared by the Central Office of Information

LONDON: HER MAJESTY'S STATIONERY OFFICE

HMSO BOOKS

HMSO publications are available from:

HMSO Publications Centre
(Mail and telephone orders only)
PO Box 276, London, SW8 5DT
Telephone orders 01-622 3316
General enquiries 01-211 5656
(queuing system in operation for both numbers)

HMSO Bookshops
49 High Holborn, London, WC1V 6HB 01-211 5656 (Counter service only)
258 Broad Street, Birmingham, B1 2HE 021-643 3757
Southey House, 33 Wine Street, Bristol, BS1 2BQ (0272) 24306/24307
9-21 Princess Street, Manchester, M60 8AS 061-834 7201
80 Chichester Street, Belfast, BT1 4JY (0232) 238451
13a Castle Street, Edinburgh, EH2 3AR 031-225 6333

HMSO's Accredited Agents
(see Yellow Pages)

and through good booksellers

Obtainable in the United States of America
from Bernan Associates,
9730–E George Palmer Highway
Lanham, Maryland 20706

ISBN 0 11 701291 2

Contents

Diagrams

Maps

Photographs

Acknowledgments for use of photographs appear on p 469.

Front cover: The City of London, centre of Britain's financial services industry.

Introduction

Britain 1987 is the thirty-eighth official handbook in the series; it has been prepared by the Central Office of Information on behalf of the Foreign and Commonwealth Office. The handbook is widely known as an established work of reference and is the mainstay of the reference facilities provided by British information services in many countries. It is sold by Her Majesty's Stationery Office throughout the world.

Britain 1987 describes many features in the life of the country, including the workings of the Government and other major institutions. It does not attempt an analytical approach to current events.

Care should be taken when studying British statistics to note whether they refer to England, to England and Wales (considered together for many administrative and other purposes), to Great Britain, which comprises England, Wales and Scotland, or to the United Kingdom (which is the same as Britain, that is, Great Britain and Northern Ireland) as a whole.

The factual and statistical information in *Britain 1987* is compiled with the co-operation of other government departments and agencies, and of many other organisations. Sources of more detailed and more topical information (including statistics) are mentioned in the text and a guide to official sources is given in Appendix 2.

The text, generally, is based on information available up to August 1986.

Reference Services
Overseas Publications and Foreign Languages
Central Office of Information, London.

1 Land and People

Introduction

Britain comprises Great Britain (England, Wales and Scotland) and Northern Ireland, and is one of the 12 member states of the European Community. Its full name is the United Kingdom of Great Britain and Northern Ireland.

Historical Outline

The word Britain derives from Greek and Latin names probably stemming from a Celtic original, which is also reflected in the name of the region of north-western France ('Brittany' in English) settled by migrants from Britain in the fifth and sixth centuries AD. Although, in the prehistoric time-scale, the Celts were relatively late arrivals in the British Isles (following cultures which had produced such notable monuments as the stone circles of Avebury and Stonehenge) it is only with them that Britain emerges into recorded history, and the term Celtic is often used rather generally to distinguish the early inhabitants of the British Isles from the later Anglo-Saxon invaders.

Following sorties by Julius Caesar in 55 and 54 BC, Britain was occupied by the Romans in the first century AD and an ordered civilisation was established under their rule for two or three hundred years except in the territory north of Hadrian's Wall (the wall across northern England planned by Hadrian, Roman Emperor from 117 to 138 AD) and in some western areas. Christian missionaries arrived not only in Roman Britain but also in Scotland and Ireland.

England and Wales

The final Roman withdrawal in the fifth century, however, followed a long period of increasing disorder during which there began raids on the island from northern Europe—mainly by peoples traditionally described as Angles (from Schleswig), Saxons and Jutes. It is from the Angles that the name England derives. In the following two centuries the raids turned into settlement and the establishment of a number of small kingdoms (with the Britons, or Celts, maintaining an independent existence in the areas now known as Wales and Cornwall). Among these kingdoms, more powerful ones which claimed over-lordship over the whole country were established, first in the north (Northumbria), then in the central area (Mercia) and finally in the south (Wessex). However, the rise of Wessex in the ninth century under the leadership of Alfred the Great (849–99) was contemporaneous with further raids and settlement from Europe, in this case by the Vikings from Scandinavia. In the tenth century the Wessex dynasty defeated the invading Danes and established a wide-ranging authority in England. A second wave of Danish invasions, however, led to the establishment of a Danish dynasty in England between 1017 and 1042, when the Wessex line was restored.

The last successful invasion of England took place following a disputed succession when Duke William of Normandy (a duchy established by the Vikings and owing only nominal allegiance to the French king) enforced his claims by defeating the English at the Battle of Hastings in 1066. There was considerable settlement by Normans and others from France, French became the language of the nobility for the next three centuries and the legal and, to some extent, social structure was influenced by that which prevailed across the Channel. The monarchy established by William and his successors was (except in intervals of civil war) considerably more effective in administrative and military terms than its predecessors and it began to establish its authority over increasingly wide areas of the British Isles. This policy was pushed forward with most energy by Edward I (1272–1307). His most lasting success was in Wales, the main stronghold into which the Britons had retreated. With the death in battle in 1282 of the Welsh Prince Llywelyn the royal authority became firmly established there. Edward gave his own heir the title of 'Prince of Wales' which has subsequently been bestowed upon the eldest son of the sovereign. The rising led by Owain Glyndŵr at the beginning of the fifteenth century showed strong continuing Welsh national feeling but a new dimension to the situation was provided by the accession to the English throne in 1485 of Henry VII of the Welsh House of Tudor. Wales was politically assimilated to England under the Act of Union in 1535.

Scotland

A more difficult problem concerned relations between England and Scotland. Hadrian's Wall had proved no insurmountable barrier between the Romans and their northern neighbours, and far-reaching expeditions both by the Romans into Scotland and by the Scottish people known as Picts into England took place. In the sixth century the Scots from Ireland or 'Scotia' settled in the area of Scotland now known as Argyll. Lothian was English in population, and Welsh Britons moved north from the invading English into Strathclyde. A united kingdom, under the Scots king Kenneth MacAlpine, emerged in the ninth century while Scotland, like England, was endeavouring to defend itself against the Vikings. The establishment of a powerful monarchy in England, however, especially after the Norman Conquest in the eleventh century, was to pose an intermittent but considerable threat to Scottish independence throughout the Middle Ages and well into the sixteenth century.

The eventual unification of the crowns reflected the fact that, as a result of the Reformation (a process which occupied most of the sixteenth century), old national antagonisms had become less important than religious differences. Following the death of the childless Elizabeth I in 1603, the Protestant James Stuart, James VI of Scotland (son of Mary, Queen of Scots, whose grandmother was a sister of Henry VIII), ascended the English throne as James I. England, Wales and Scotland were henceforth known as Great Britain. Apart from the union of the monarchies, however, England and Scotland remained separate during the seventeenth century, except for an enforced unification by Oliver Cromwell early in the period of the Commonwealth (1649–60) after he had defeated royalist forces in Scotland. By the beginning of the following century political and economic arguments for a closer union were apparent in both countries. Eventually, in 1707, both sides agreed on the formation of a single parliament for Great Britain although Scotland retained its own system of law and church settlement. The Union was put under strain when Queen Anne died in 1714 and George, Elector of Hanover (descended from a daughter of James I), succeeded the Stuarts on the British throne. 'Jacobite' rebellions, aiming to restore the Stuarts to the British throne, took place in 1715 and 1745 but were unsuccessful.

Ireland

In Ireland, out of a patchwork of Celtic and pre-Celtic peoples similar to that in Britain, a number of kingdoms had emerged before the Christian era; any supremacy established by one over the others in the following 1,000 years was of a temporary nature. In cultural matters Ireland compared favourably with most of Europe during the Dark Ages and Christianity survived in Ireland when it had been displaced for the time being in England by Anglo-Saxon invaders. Ireland, however, did not escape the incursions of the Vikings, who dominated the country during the tenth century.

In 1169 Henry II of England launched an invasion of Ireland, the overlordship of which he had been granted by the Pope, who was anxious to bring the Irish church into full obedience to Rome. A large part of the country came under the control of Anglo-Norman magnates but their descendants tended to assimilate to their new country and little direct authority was exercised from England during the Middle Ages.

The Tudor monarchs showed a much greater tendency to intervene in Ireland. Henry VIII's assumption of the title of King of Ireland in 1541 arose from his desire to apply the Reformation settlement and thereafter the religious issue was to produce far-reaching consequences. The determination to establish royal authority in Ireland was strengthened during the reign of Elizabeth I by the fear that the country might be used by Philip of Spain in his efforts to subjugate England, and a series of campaigns was waged against Irish insurgents. The main focus of the resistance was the northern province of Ulster and, with its collapse in 1607, Ulster became an area of settlement by immigrants from Scotland and England. (There was settlement by immigrants elsewhere in Ireland, though on a lesser scale.)

The English civil war of 1642 to 1652 led to further risings in Ireland which were crushed by Cromwell. The restoration of the monarchy in 1660 was followed by the accession of the Roman Catholic James II to the throne in 1685, and there was more fighting after his deposition three years later in favour of his nephew and son-in-law, the Protestant William of Orange and his wife Mary.

During most of the eighteenth century there was an uneasy peace and towards its end various efforts were made by British governments to achieve stability. In 1782 the Irish Parliament (dating from medieval times) was given legislative independence; the only constitutional tie with Great Britain was the Crown. The Parliament represented, however, only the privileged Anglo-Irish minority, who had obtained possession of most of the agricultural land, and Catholics were excluded from it. Against the background of an abortive rebellion in 1798 and the prospect of intervention by France (with which Great Britain was at war between 1793 and 1815) the Irish Parliament was induced to vote for union with what, from 1801, was to be the Parliament of the United Kingdom of Great Britain and Ireland.

The 'Irish question' continued as one of the major problems of British politics during the nineteenth century. In 1886 the Liberal Government introduced a Home Rule Bill which would have given an Irish Parliament authority over most internal matters while reserving to Britain control over external affairs. This led to a split in the Liberal Party and the failure of the Bill. It was not until 1914 that Home Rule was enacted by the Government of Ireland Act. Its implementation was, however, prevented both by the threat of armed resistance on the part of the Protestant majority in Ulster and by the outbreak of the first world war.

A nationalist uprising in Dublin in 1916 was suppressed, but with the end of the first world war a guerrilla force known as the Irish Republican Army (IRA) began operations against the British administration. In 1921 a settlement was reached under which six of the nine counties of the province of Ulster received their own Parliament, but remained represented in and subject to the supreme authority of the British Parliament, while the remainder of Ireland as the Irish Free State (later to become the Irish Republic) became a self-governing state outside the United Kingdom of Great Britain and Northern Ireland.

Channel Islands and Isle of Man Although the Channel Islands and the Isle of Man are not part of the United Kingdom, they have a special relationship with it because of the antiquity of their connection with the Crown. The Channel Islands were integrated into the Duchy of Normandy in the tenth and eleventh centuries and have been territories of the Crown since the Norman Conquest. The Isle of Man was under the nominal sovereignty of Norway until 1266 when it was ceded to Scotland, subsequently passing to the Earls of Derby for a period but eventually coming under the direct administration of the Crown in 1765. Today the territories are Crown dependencies, with their own legislative assemblies and systems of local administration and of law, and their own courts. The British Government is responsible for their defence, their international relations and, ultimately, their good government.

The position of the Channel Islands and the Isle of Man in the European Community is broadly that the islands remain outside the Community except for customs purposes and for certain aspects of the Common Agricultural Policy. Community provisions relating to the free movement of people and services do not apply.

The Four Lands

In the following pages there are brief descriptions of a number of aspects of social, economic and political life for each of the four countries, England, Wales, Scotland and Northern Ireland, with some additional material on the political situation in Northern Ireland. (Statistics on the four lands are contained in Table 1.)

ENGLAND

England is predominantly a lowland country. There are upland regions in the north (the Pennine Chain, the Cumbrian mountains and the Yorkshire moorlands) and in the south west in Devon and Cornwall. For the most part, however, the country is undulating or flat and, in the south, crossed by low ranges of hills including the Cotswolds and the Kent and Sussex Downs. The greatest concentrations of population are in the London and Thames estuary areas, the West Yorkshire and north-west industrial cities, the midlands conurbation around Birmingham, the north-east conurbations on the rivers Tyne and Tees, and along the Channel coast.

The Church of England, which was separated from the Roman Catholic Church at the Reformation, is the Established Church in England, with privileges balanced by certain duties which it must fulfil; the Sovereign must always be a member of the Church and appoints its two archbishops, 24 bishops and some other senior clergy.

Government

England has no government minister or department exclusively responsible for its central administration of domestic affairs, in contrast to Wales, Scotland and Northern Ireland. Instead, responsibility is shared among a number of government departments, whose responsibilities in some cases also cover aspects of affairs in Wales and Scotland. There are 523 Members of Parliament for England in the House of Commons, and arrangements are made for the discussion of regional affairs. Traditionally, of the two major political parties, the Conservatives find their support chiefly in suburban and rural areas, while the Labour Party derives its main support from urban industrialised areas. In the 1983 election England returned 362 Conservative Members of Parliament, 148 Labour, 10 Liberal and 3 Social Democrat. Local government is administered through a two-tier system of counties subdivided into districts, except in London, where local government is the responsibility of 32 borough councils and the Corporation of the City of London. A major reorganisation of local government was implemented in April 1986 when the Greater London Council and the metropolitan county councils of Greater Manchester, Merseyside, South Yorkshire, Tyne and Wear, West Midlands and West Yorkshire were abolished and most of their functions transferred to London borough and metropolitan district councils.

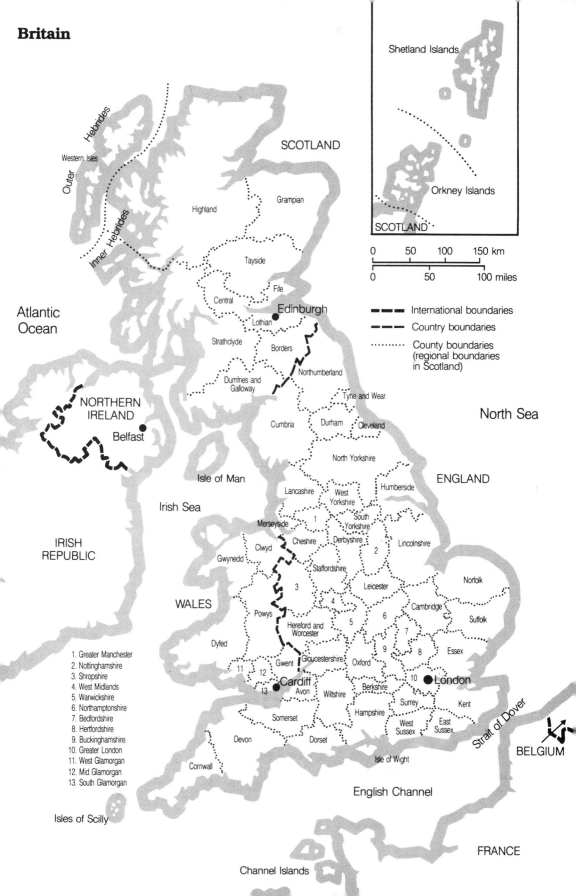

Britain

Shetland Islands

SCOTLAND

Orkney Islands

SCOTLAND

| 0 | 50 | 100 | 150 km |

| 0 | 50 | | 100 miles |

▬ ▬ International boundaries
— — Country boundaries
.... County boundaries
(regional boundaries
in Scotland)

Hebrides

Western Isles

Outer

Inner Hebrides

SCOTLAND

Highland

Grampian

Tayside

Fife

Central

Edinburgh

Lothian

Borders

Strathclyde

Dumfries and
Galloway

Northumberland

Atlantic
Ocean

NORTHERN
IRELAND

Belfast

North Sea

Tyne and Wear

Cumbria

Durham

Cleveland

Isle of Man

North Yorkshire

ENGLAND

Irish Sea

Lancashire

West
Yorkshire

Humberside

IRISH
REPUBLIC

Merseyside

1

South
Yorkshire

Cheshire

Derbyshire

2

Lincolnshire

Clwyd

Gwynedd

Staffordshire

3

Leicester

Norfolk

WALES

Powys

4

5

6

Cambridge

Suffolk

Hereford and
Worcester

7

Dyfed

9

8

Essex

Gwent

Gloucestershire

Oxford

11

12

10

London

13

Cardiff

Avon

Berkshire

Wiltshire

Surrey

Kent

Somerset

Hampshire

West
Sussex

East
Sussex

Strait of Dover

BELGIUM

Devon

Dorset

Isle of Wight

Cornwall

English Channel

Isles of Scilly

FRANCE

Channel Islands

1. Greater Manchester
2. Nottinghamshire
3. Shropshire
4. West Midlands
5. Warwickshire
6. Northamptonshire
7. Bedfordshire
8. Hertfordshire
9. Buckinghamshire
10. Greater London
11. West Glamorgan
12. Mid Glamorgan
13. South Glamorgan

Table 1: General Statistics

	England	Wales	Scotland	Northern Ireland	United Kingdom
Population ('000, mid-1984 estimate)	46,956	2,807	5,146	1,578	56,488
Area (sq km)	130,439	20,768	78,783	14,120	244,110
Population density (persons per sq km)	361	135	65	111	239
Gross domestic product (£ per head, 1984)	4,708	3,975	4,432	3,615	4,616
Employees in employment ('000, June 1985)	18,136	908	1,955	463	21,461
Percentage of employees in: (June 1985)					
agriculture, forestry and fishing	1·5	2·5	2·1	2·1	1·6
energy and water supply	2·7	5·3	3·9	1·9	2·9
manufacturing	26·5	22·8	22·3	22·4	25·8
construction	4·3	5·0	5·9	4·9	4·5
service industries	65·1	64·4	65·6	69·2	65·3
Unemployment rate (per cent, June 1986)	11·2	14·2	13·6	18·7	11·7
Average gross weekly earnings (£, all full-time men, April 1985)	193·3	179·1	189·7	172·0	192·4[a]
Identifiable public expenditure[b] (£ per head, 1984–85)	1,761	1,927	2,210	2,676	1,836

[a] Great Britain only.
[b] Excluding borrowing by nationalised industries and some other public corporations.

Eight 'standard' regions in England are delimited principally for statistical purposes: South East, East Anglia, South West, West Midlands, East Midlands, Yorkshire and Humberside, North West and North. They play no part in local government and do not always coincide with the regional units adopted by central government departments.

The legal system of England comprises on the one hand a historic body of conventions, known as 'common law' and 'equity', and on the other, parliamentary and European Community legislation. Common law stems from the work of the king's judges after the Norman Conquest of 1066 who sought to bring together into a single body of legal principles the various local customs of the Anglo-Saxons. Great reliance was placed on precedent, and the practice of reporting on cases commenced in the thirteenth century. Equity law derives from the practice of petitioning the king's Chancellor in cases not covered by common law. The English legal system is therefore distinct from many of those of Western Europe which have codes deriving from Roman law. The Habeas Corpus Act 1679 is a fundamental statute forbidding imprisonment without trial.

The Economy   Up to the eighteenth century the English economy was mainly agrarian and the chief manufacture was wool cloth. London as the capital city, and a major port and mercantile centre, and the textile areas (East Anglia, south-western England and West Yorkshire) were the most populous and prosperous regions. In the late eighteenth and nineteenth centuries, however, rapid growth took place in the midlands, the north west, west Yorkshire and the north east, where the coalfields and iron ore deposits permitted Britain to become the first industrialised nation, basing its wealth on coalmining, on the manufacture of iron and steel, heavy machinery and textiles, on shipbuilding and on trade. London enhanced its position with the growing strength of the economy but East Anglia and the west country, remote from areas of industrial development, were affected by agricultural depression, and entered a period of relative decline.

In the twentieth century, the second period of industrialisation, based on new sources of energy, new manufacturing industries and new forms of transport, has continued to change the broad pattern of regional and industrial development in England. In the 1920s and 1930s the northern industrial centres saw their traditional industries weakened owing to fluctuations in world trade and competition from other industrialising countries and, in some cases, from substitute products. London, its surrounding counties and the West Midlands generally benefited from the newer, more mobile, industries. These included chemicals (such as pharmaceuticals, dyes, plastics and artificial fibres), electrical and electronic engineering, vehicle manufacture, aircraft building, instrument engineering, aluminium and rubber manufacture and a wide range of consumer goods, including processed food, drink and tobacco products as well as durables.

In the second half of the century economic and population growth has tended to favour smaller towns and rural areas, particularly those in the South West and East Anglia. A number of industrial areas (in the North, the North West, Yorkshire and Humberside and the West Midlands) have suffered over the last decade as a result of the decline in manufacturing employment. Through its regional industrial policy the Government aims to reduce regional disparities in employment opportunities by making investment incentives available in the areas of greatest need, including those which have been dependent on declining industries. Measures also exist to revive economic activity in inner urban areas.

East Anglia, still largely agricultural, has been the fastest-growing English region in both population and employment since the 1960s. Particular growth points have been Peterborough, the east coast ports (which, besides benefiting from relative proximity to the northern European Community countries, have in some cases become important bases for the development of gas resources in the southern North Sea) and nine towns receiving population overspill from London. Food processing, agricultural machinery, vehicle engines and electronic and instrument engineering are the strongest industries, and the service sector has been growing in Cambridge, Ipswich and Norwich.

Greater London and the industrial cities of the West Midlands, the North West, Yorkshire and Humberside and the North continue to represent the largest concentrations of manufacturing industry. London is an important area for products of all kinds including food and drink (especially brewing), instrument engineering, electrical and electronic engineering, clothing, furniture and printing. Of importance in the surrounding south-eastern counties are oil refining (along the Thames and near Southampton), pharmaceuticals, pumps, valves and compressors, instrument engineering, electronics (particularly in Berkshire and Hertfordshire, and around Chelmsford), motor vehicles, aerospace, building materials, timber, paper and plastics products. There is diversity, too, in the North West, with significant activity in food processing (especially grain milling, bread, flour confectionery and biscuits), chemicals, textile machinery, insulated wires and cables, computers (Manchester being one of the largest centres in the country), motor vehicles, aerospace, clothing, glass making (with the world's largest flat glass maker, Pilkington, in St Helens), paper and rubber products. Lancashire is the centre of the cotton and allied textile industries.

The characteristic manufactures of the West Midlands are metals (steel tubes, iron castings and non-ferrous metals), machine tools, electrical engineering, motor vehicles, carpets, pottery (with over 80 per cent of Britain's ceramics industry located in Staffordshire) and rubber production. Of the other regions, Yorkshire and Humberside has important shares of cocoa, chocolate and confectionery production, iron and steel, machine tools, textile machinery, woollen and worsted goods (producing about two-thirds of Britain's wool textiles), carpets, clothing and glass containers. The North has general chemicals, iron and steel, process plant, marine engineering, and clothing; the East Midlands has steel tubes, iron castings, over two-thirds of Britain's hosiery and knitted goods industry, and footwear; and the South West has food processing (especially dairy products), aerospace and paper products.

In agriculture, the number of mixed holdings has been falling, as part of a general tendency towards greater specialisation. Dairying is most common in the west of England, where the wetter climate encourages the growth of good grass; sheep and cattle are reared in the hilly and moorland areas of northern and south-western England; and arable farming, pig and poultry farming and horticulture are concentrated in the east and south. Horticulture is also important in the West Midlands. Forestry is mainly found in the North, South East and South West regions. The principal fishing ports are on the east coast and in the South West.

England has plentiful energy resources in its coalfields and has access to offshore oil and gas reserves. About 60 per cent of Britain's deep-mined coal is produced in the East Midlands and Yorkshire coalfields, the former being the most productive in the country. The electricity grid of England and Wales is one of the largest interconnected power networks under unified control in the Western world. The world's first large-scale nuclear power station was established at Calder Hall in Cumbria in 1956, while substantial investment in reprocessing capacity is being undertaken nearby. Other nuclear power stations are on coastal sites, including eight around the coasts of southern England. Important mineral deposits in England include aggregates for the construction industry (sand, gravel and crushed rock), industrial minerals (including clay, salt from the North West and china clay from Cornwall), tin ore, also from Cornwall, and iron ore from the East Midlands and Humberside. Water resources include the Kielder Reservoir (Northumberland), one of Europe's largest man-made lakes.

A motorway network has been constructed in England since the 1950s and comprises four long-distance arterial routes linking London and the cities of the midlands, the North and North West and the South West, the London orbital route (the last stages of which should be completed in 1986), and over 30 shorter motorways. Inter-city travel has been improved by the introduction of high-speed rail services which are among the best in the world in speed, frequency and comfort. Many ports have been equipped to deal with new developments in shipping (such as container ships) and to take account of changes in the nature of trade brought about by the increase in oil traffic through North Sea ports and the growing proportion of trade with the continent of Europe. In January 1986 the British and French governments jointly announced their decision to facilitate the construction of a fixed link across the Channel in the form of twin single-track rail tunnels to carry through rail services, linking Britain directly with the European rail system, and a drive-on, drive-off vehicle shuttle service using specially designed shuttle trains. Construction could begin in 1987 and the tunnel could be in operation in 1993. The major airports are Heathrow (the busiest international airport in the world) and Gatwick, both serving London, and Manchester, Luton and Birmingham. A decision was made in 1985 to develop Stansted as London's third airport.

Employment in service industries has accounted for an increasing share of total employment in recent years, expansion being particularly marked in financial and business services. London is one of the world's leading centres of banking, insurance and other financial services. Decentralisation of some office services from the capital has led to a growth of office employment in the South West and East Anglia in particular. London and the surrounding counties account for much of advertising and market research activity, more than half of all services offered by research establishments (other than those attached to businesses), half of central government services and a significant proportion of non-food wholesale distribution in England. After London and the South East, the North West, with its main centre in Manchester, has the next most important concentration of service industries. Tourism, catering and the leisure industries have also expanded. Over half of expenditure by overseas visitors in Britain takes place in London, while the South West is the most popular region for domestic tourism. Each region has its own particular attraction for tourists. For example, a number of areas including Northumberland and Cumbria (whose peaks include Scafell, England's highest point, at 978 m, 3,210 ft) have hills and lakes which attract walkers, climbers and riders.

Cultural and Social Life

Cultural life in England takes so many forms that a brief summary can only attempt to suggest its variety. London alone has about 100 theatres, including some 40 in the 'West End', together with fringe and suburban theatres, about a dozen major centres for music concerts, ballet and opera, four major art galleries, a dozen major museums (with over 80 smaller galleries and museums), some 400 public libraries, and over 140 West End, local and independent cinemas, and other leisure facilities include discotheques, bingo halls, amusement arcades, ice and roller skating rinks and swimming pools. With its ceremonial occasions, palaces, other historic buildings and shops, London is also one of the world's leading tourist centres. About 15 attractions (Westminster Abbey, the Tower of London, Madame Tussaud's—an exhibition of waxworks of famous people—the London Zoo, Kew Gardens and the major museums and art galleries) each receive more than a million visitors a year.

Because of its size and its position as the capital city, London is not representative of the rest of England, but much the same broad range of cultural interests is reflected in many other cities and towns. The English Tourist Board lists some 1,230 art galleries, museums and similar institutions in the rest of England. Distinctive features of the northern industrial cities are special social clubs, working men's clubs, which attract well-known entertainers. In addition, many rural or outdoor recreations are strongly supported and there is active interest in numerous games and sports, many of them having been devised in England.

The English love of gardens and landscapes is associated with a tradition of sightseeing visits to the many country houses, gardens and unspoilt rural and coastal areas. There are seven national parks, two forest parks, some 32 designated 'areas of outstanding natural beauty', about 150 country parks approved by the Countryside Commission, 550 'outstanding conservation areas', 620 km (385 miles) of designated heritage coastline and 1,900 historic buildings and gardens listed by the English Tourist Board. Newer developments include the opening of safari and wildlife parks and of 'theme' parks devoted, for example, to maritime history, which offer a diversity of entertainments as well. Many regions and towns have associations with the great English writers and artists, such as William Shakespeare, William Wordsworth, Arnold Bennett, Charles Dickens, the Brontë sisters, Thomas Hardy, Thomas Gainsborough and John Constable.

WALES

Wales is a country of hills and mountains with extensive tracts of high plateau and shorter stretches of mountain ranges deeply dissected by river valleys. The highest mountains are in Snowdonia in the north west; the highest peak is Snowdon (1,085 m, 3,560 ft). The lower-lying ground is largely confined to the relatively narrow coastal belt and the lower parts of the river valleys. The main areas of settlement are in the southern valleys and coastal areas, where two-thirds of the population live. The chief urban centres are Cardiff, Swansea, Newport and Wrexham. Wales is a principality; Prince Charles, the heir to the throne, was invested by the Queen with the title of Prince of Wales at Caernarfon Castle in 1969 when he was 20.

The country has its own Welsh language, spoken (according to the 1981 census) by 19 per cent of the population, chiefly in the rural north and west. The Welsh name of the country is Cymru. Measures adopted since the 1960s have helped to revive the use of the language, which is of Celtic origin and closely resembles Breton, spoken in Brittany in France. They include recognising the equal validity of Welsh with English in law courts, the encouragement of bilingual education in schools, and the extended use of Welsh for official purposes and in broadcasting. Welsh-language television programmes are transmitted in Wales by Sianel 4 Cymru (Channel 4 Wales).

There is no established church in Wales, the Anglican church having been disestablished in 1920 following decades of pressure from adherents of the more evangelical Methodist and Baptist persuasions. Methodism in particular had spread rapidly in Wales in the eighteenth century, assuming the nature of a popular movement among Welsh speakers and finding strong support later in industrial communities.

Government

The country returns 38 Members of Parliament and there are special arrange-ments for the discussion of Welsh affairs. For the last 60 years the industrial communities of Wales have tended to support the Labour Party in elections, ensuring a Labour majority in Wales. In the 1983 election 20 Labour, 14 Conservative, 2 Plaid Cymru (Welsh Nationalist) and 2 Liberal members were returned. Substantial administrative autonomy is centred on the Secretary of State for Wales, who is a member of the Cabinet, and has wide-ranging responsibilities relating to the economy, welfare services and the provision of amenities. The headquarters of the administration is the Welsh Office in Cardiff, which also has an office in London. In 1979 proposals for the establishment of an elected Welsh assembly in Cardiff to take over policymaking and executive powers from central government were rejected in a referendum held in Wales. Local government is exercised through a system of elected authorities similar to that in England, and the legal system is identical with the English one.

The Economy

The south Wales coalfield was developed during the latter part of the industrial revolution in the second half of the nineteenth century, creating populous urban centres which drew labour from the rural areas and from England and Ireland.

However, the economy was narrowly based, mainly on coal, iron, steel and tinplate, and contracted sharply during the 1920s and 1930s, resulting in severe employment problems and substantial emigration.

Notable features of the past three decades have been the continuing contraction of coalmining and iron and steel production (although Wales still accounts for about one-third of Britain's steel production), the advent of a more diverse range of manufacturing industries and the growth of service industries. Wales is developing as an important centre for electronics in Britain and several new high-technology businesses in electronics and related industries have been established. Inward investment by overseas companies (especially Japanese and United States high-technology concerns) has been considerable, and there are over 200 overseas-owned or associated firms in Wales, employing about 50,000 people and accounting for around one in five jobs in the manufacturing sector. South Wales remains the principal industrial area but new industries and firms have also been introduced on the smaller coalfield in north-east Wales, around Wrexham and Deeside, again to offset the decline in the older, basic industries which previously dominated the area. Light industry has also been attracted to the towns in the rural areas in mid- and north Wales and an important refinery complex has developed around Milford Haven, which is one of Britain's major oil ports.

Agriculture occupies about 80 per cent of the land area, the main activities being sheep and cattle rearing in the hill regions and dairy farming in the lowlands. Wales accounts for about 11 per cent of forest area in Britain and over 20 per cent of Forestry Commission timber production.

Wales produces about 7 per cent of Britain's deep-mined coal and 14 per cent of opencast production, including all of its anthracite. The biggest pumped-storage power station in Europe is at Dinorwig, while there are nuclear power stations at Wylfa and Trawsfynydd. Wales exports about a third of its water supply to England.

Good communications exist in the south with motorway links across the Severn Bridge to southern England and the midlands, and high-speed rail services to a number of destinations in England, while the main road along the north Wales coast is being upgraded.

There has been expansion in financial and business services, in the tourist and catering trades and in some areas of public administration. With its coastal resorts (which include Tenby, Saundersfoot, Rhyl, Llandudno, Colwyn Bay, Porthcawl and Barry), and the attractions of three national parks (Snowdonia, the Brecon Beacons and the Pembrokeshire Coast), as well as other areas of picturesque hill, lake and mountain country, Wales attracts many tourists, especially for outdoor holidays.

Cultural and Social Life

There is much literary, musical and dramatic activity in Wales and there is a National Library and National Museum. Welsh literature is one of the oldest in Europe. The country is well known for its choral singing and the Welsh National Opera has an international reputation. The special festivals of Wales, known as eisteddfodau, encourage Welsh literature and music. The largest is the Royal National Eisteddfod of Wales, held annually, entirely in Welsh, and consisting of competitions in music, singing, prose and poetry. The town of Llangollen has extended its eisteddfod to include artists from all over the world in the annual International Musical Eisteddfod. Famous modern Welsh artists have included the opera singers Sir Geraint Evans and Dame Gwyneth Jones, the poet Dylan Thomas and the actor Richard Burton. The politicians David Lloyd George (former Prime Minister) and Aneurin Bevan were noted orators in a strong Welsh tradition. An active local press includes a number of Welsh language publications. Great interest is aroused by the annual rugby football competition in which sides representing Wales, England, Scotland, Ireland and France take part.

Health services are provided mainly under the National Health Service, administered by the Welsh Office, while personal social services and education (except at university level) are provided mainly through the local authorities. Educational provision is similar to that in England except for the use of Welsh in some schools, particularly in the Welsh-speaking, largely rural, areas. The collegiate University of Wales, founded in 1893, comprises seven member institutions.

SCOTLAND

Scotland may be divided broadly into three areas: the sparsely populated highlands and islands in the north, accounting for just over half the total area of the country; the central lowlands, containing three-quarters of the population and most of the industrial centres and cultivated farmland; and the Southern Uplands, containing a number of hill ranges, which border on England. The highest mountains are the Grampians in the central highlands, with Ben Nevis (1,342 m, 4,406 ft) the highest peak. The chief cities are the capital Edinburgh, the main industrial centre Glasgow, and the two regional centres Aberdeen and Dundee.

The period from 1750 onwards has seen considerable and continuous emigration of Scots to England and overseas. However, the rate slowed markedly in the 1970s as the offshore oil and gas industries developed and there was inward migration to the north east of Scotland, although the large outflow of people from Strathclyde has continued, but at a lower level. In the mid-nineteenth century, as Scotland industrialised rapidly, there was large-scale immigration from Ireland.

The period from 1750 until the beginning of the twentieth century was also one of stability and economic progress and of achievements in many fields. Among the famous men to emerge were David Hume, Robert Burns, Sir Walter Scott, Adam Smith, Robert Adam, James Watt, John MacAdam, Lord Kelvin, Alexander Graham Bell and James Clerk Maxwell.

The Church of Scotland, which became the established church in 1690, has complete freedom in all matters of doctrine, order and discipline. It is a Protestant church which is Presbyterian in form, being governed by a hierarchy of church courts, each of which includes lay people.

Government

There are special arrangements for the conduct of Scottish affairs within the British system of government and separate Acts of Parliament are passed for Scotland where appropriate. In the 1983 general election the 72 Scottish seats in the House of Commons were apportioned as follows: 41 Labour, 21 Conservative, 5 Liberal, 3 Social Democrat, and 2 Scottish National. Since 1959 Scotland, like Wales, has had a majority of Labour Members of Parliament. Administrative tasks relating to a wide range of economic and social functions are the responsibility of the Secretary of State for Scotland, a member of the Cabinet, working through the Scottish Office, with its administrative head-quarters in Edinburgh and an office in London. A proposal for an elected assembly for Scotland, on which a referendum was held in 1979, failed to gain the support of the required 40 per cent of the electorate, even though a majority of those voting gave it their approval.

Local government generally operates on a two-tier basis broadly similar to that in England and Wales but established by separate legislation. The three islands councils (for Orkney, Shetland and the Western Isles) are single-tier authorities.

The principles and procedures of the Scottish legal system (particularly in civil law) differ in many respects from those of England and Wales, stemming, in part, from the adoption of elements of other European legal systems, based on Roman law, during the sixteenth century.

The Economy Scotland has experienced the same pressure on its traditional industries as the north of England and Wales. The regional policies of successive governments and investment by overseas companies have both made significant contributions to the growth of modern, technologically based industries, and Scotland's economic structure is now broadly similar to that of Britain as a whole.

Engineering remains a major industry, accounting for over a quarter of the manufacturing workforce, but there has been a significant trend towards lighter engineering products and rapid expansion in electronics (including microelectronics). By mid-1985 an estimated 280 plants were employing some 44,000 workers, one of the biggest concentrations of the electronics industry in Western Europe. Scotland accounts for over 50 per cent of Britain's output of integrated circuits and for 15 per cent of European output.

Another significant economic development in recent years has been the substantial expansion of offshore-related industries following the discovery of oil and gas under the northern North Sea. Some 100,000 jobs have arisen directly or indirectly as a result of North Sea activities. Many of these jobs reflect overseas investment solely related to the development of North Sea resources, but oil and gas developments have stimulated other industries including engineering and chemicals, reinforcing Scotland's position in the chemicals industry, especially petrochemicals; the first phase of a major new plant at Mossmorran (Fife) was opened in 1984. Traditional industries, such as coal, steel and shipbuilding, have experienced a long-term decline in employment, but are still important contributors to the Scottish economy. Other traditional manufactures, such as high-quality tweeds and other textiles, and food and drink products, remain important. There are about 100 whisky distilleries in Scotland and the industry is a major export earner.

Northern and north-east Scotland (particularly Aberdeen) have benefited most from offshore developments. However, Strathclyde, by far the most populous region, has experienced serious industrial decline and population loss, particularly in Glasgow. In the remainder of the central belt and in the five new towns (East Kilbride, Glenrothes, Livingston, Irvine and Cumbernauld) trends have been generally more favourable. In Lothian the large concentration of financial and other service industries centred on Edinburgh has been a helpful influence.

Scotland has about one-third of Britain's total agricultural land, but 70 per cent of it consists of hill grazing for cattle and sheep. About 11 per cent of the agricultural area is used for crops, and 67 per cent of this is under barley. Scotland accounts for nearly half of Britain's forest area and for 40 per cent of public sector timber production; the bulk of new planting in Britain takes place in Scotland, much of it in the upland and mountain areas. Fishing remains an important activity; more than 65 per cent of total landings of fish in Britain are made by vessels based in Scotland.

Despite the advent of cheaper natural gas, Scotland still depends heavily on electricity; nuclear and hydro-electric generation supply a higher proportion of energy than in any other part of Britain. Large supplies of unpolluted water form a major resource.

Communications, both domestic and international, have improved in many areas, particularly in the north and north east, owing to the stimulus of the offshore oil industry and to road- and bridge-building programmes. The offshore oil industry has also encouraged expansion in financial and business services which have been traditionally strong in Scotland.

Tourism, which makes a significant contribution to the economy and to employment in Scotland as a whole, is estimated to generate, both directly and indirectly, nearly 100,000 jobs. Scotland's cultural and historic associations, its varied scenic beauty, and the opportunities for sport and recreation are particular attractions. Golf originated in Scotland, and courses at St Andrews, Gleneagles, Turnberry and Prestwick are internationally renowned. Skiing is growing in importance, with centres at Aviemore, Glenshee, Glencoe and the Lecht, and further developments are planned.

Cultural and Social Life

A vigorous cultural life in Scotland has as its highlight the annual Edinburgh International Festival, one of the world's leading cultural events. Notable performing arts bodies are the Scottish National Orchestra, Scottish Opera, Scottish Ballet, Scottish Chamber Orchestra, Scottish Baroque Ensemble and the BBC Scottish Symphony Orchestra. Scotland possesses excellent collections of the fine and applied arts, notably in the National Galleries of Scotland, the Royal Museums of Scotland and the City of Glasgow Museum and Art Galleries (including the Burrell collection, opened in 1983).

A language of ancient Celtic origin, Scots Gaelic is spoken by some 80,000 people mainly in the islands and north west of Scotland. It is the indigenous language, with its own literary background. Scottish people in the lowlands have for centuries spoken Scots (or Lallans), a derivative of the Northumbrian dialect of Old English, which has its own recognised literary tradition and has seen a revival in poetry in recent times.

An active press includes six national daily morning newspapers, six local evening newspapers and three national Sunday newspapers. There are also some 140 local weekly newspapers published in Scotland. Articles in some papers are printed in Gaelic. Television programmes are produced by BBC (Scotland) and by three independent companies, covering the highland, lowland and border regions. BBC Radio Scotland covers most of the population and there are five 'community' services in the highlands and islands, two of them mainly in Gaelic, and two in the borders. Independent radio stations provide services for Edinburgh, Glasgow, Dundee/Perth, Aberdeen, Ayr and Inverness.

Local authorities are responsible for the provision of most education, except at university level. Secondary education in Scotland is almost completely organised on comprehensive lines: colleges of further education are administered by education authorities while independent bodies administer higher education institutions and colleges of education. There are eight universities, of which four (St Andrews, Glasgow, Aberdeen and Edinburgh) were established in the fifteenth and sixteenth centuries, while the other four have been established since 1964. The educational tradition has been particularly strong in Scotland, helping many Scots to positions of eminence in the arts and sciences.

Over 50 per cent of Scotland's housing has been built since 1945, only Northern Ireland having a larger percentage. Scotland has a high proportion of housing rented from public authorities (almost 50 per cent compared with a national average of less than 30 per cent), although in recent years there has been a noticeable growth in owner-occupied housing as in the rest of Britain.

NORTHERN IRELAND

Northern Ireland is at its nearest point only 21 km (13 miles) from Scotland. It has a 488-km (303-mile) border in the south and west with the Irish Republic. At its centre lies Lough Neagh, Britain's largest freshwater lake (381 sq km, 147 sq miles). Many of the principal towns lie in valleys leading from the Lough, including the capital, Belfast, which stands at the mouth of the river Lagan. The Mourne Mountains, rising sharply in the south east, include Slieve Donard, Northern Ireland's highest peak (852 m, 2,796 ft).

Just under two-thirds of Northern Ireland's population are descendants of Scots or English settlers who crossed to north-eastern Ireland mainly in the seventeenth century; most belong to the Protestant faith, and have a traditional loyalty to the maintenance of the union with Great Britain. The remainder, over a third, are Irish in origin and mainly Roman Catholic; many of them are nationalist in political opinion, favouring union with the Irish Republic.

Government
Background to Civil Disturbances

Northern Ireland is part of the United Kingdom, but for 50 years from 1921 it had its own devolved Parliament in which the mainly Protestant Unionists consistently formed the majority and therefore constituted the Government after successive elections. Nationalists, who are predominantly Roman Catholic, resented this domination and their effective exclusion from political office. Although substantial advances for the whole population were achieved in social welfare and economic development, during the late 1960s an active and articulate civil rights movement emerged. Reforms were made but sectarian disturbances developed, which required the introduction of the Army in 1969 to support the police in keeping the peace. Subsequently, sectarian divisions were exploited by the actions of terrorists from both sides, but most notably by the Provisional Irish Republican Army who claimed to be protecting the Roman Catholic minority.

Direct Rule and Political Initiatives

Despite the Northern Ireland Government's substantial reform programme, the inter-communal violence continued and the United Kingdom Government concluded that the best hope of ending terrorism and achieving political progress would be for the United Kingdom Parliament and Government to take over responsibility for law and order in Northern Ireland. The Northern Ireland Government felt unable to accept this and resigned, and in 1972 direct rule began, with a United Kingdom Cabinet minister responsible for the functions previously exercised by the Northern Ireland Government.

Several attempts have been made to secure a stable and effective devolved government supported by both sides of the community. A new constitution which devolved powers to an elected legislative assembly, and a 'power-sharing' executive representing all sections of the community, encountered Protestant 'loyalist' opposition culminating in a general strike in 1974; in 1976 an elected constitutional convention failed to agree on a system of government that would command widespread acceptance; in 1978 a planned framework for a form of devolution to consolidate common ground among the political parties was rejected; and in 1980 there was a political conference and extensive discussions. In 1981 the appointment of a Northern Ireland Council to advise the Secretary of State was proposed but rejected by the political parties in Northern Ireland.

In October 1982 elections took place to a new 78-member Assembly. The Assembly was given responsibility for making proposals for devolving powers on a basis which would command widespread acceptance throughout the community. In the mean time, it performed scrutinising and consultative functions, commenting upon draft legislation and initiating reports on such matters as industry and education. Some members refused to take their seats on election. The unionist parties, who had a majority in the Assembly, decided not to fulfil the Assembly's statutory functions in March 1986 in protest at the Anglo-Irish Agreement (see p 16), and in June the Government decided that the present Assembly should be dissolved but at the same time expressed the hope that a future Assembly would play a responsible part in Northern Ireland.

The Government's policy continues to be based on two fundamental principles. First, that there will be no change in Northern Ireland's constitutional status as part of the United Kingdom without the consent of a majority of people in Northern Ireland. This is in accordance with internationally accepted principles of democracy: it is also reflected in the Anglo-Irish Agreement. A 'border poll' in 1973 showed that a clear majority wished Northern Ireland to remain part of the United Kingdom, and in subsequent elections parties which support that position have continued to receive the majority of votes. Secondly, the Government continues to believe that a devolved form of administration would best meet Northern Ireland's needs: but it will establish new structures of devolved government only if they are acceptable to both parts of the community.

Northern Ireland returns 17 members to the United Kingdom Parliament.

The Anglo-Irish Agreement

The United Kingdom attaches importance to co-operation with the Irish Republic and in November 1985 an Anglo-Irish Agreement was concluded between the two Governments. The Agreement aims to promote peace and stability in Northern Ireland, to create a new climate of friendship and co-operation between the peoples of the United Kingdom and the Republic of Ireland and to improve co-operation in combating terrorism. It commits both the United Kingdom and the Irish Governments in international law to the principle that Northern Ireland shall remain part of the United Kingdom for as long as that is the wish of a majority.

The Agreement established an Intergovernmental Conference through which the Irish Government can put forward views and proposals on specified matters affecting Northern Ireland affairs in so far as those matters are not the responsibility of a devolved administration in Northern Ireland, and where cross-border co-operation can be promoted in the interests of both countries. Matters discussed include avoidance of discrimination; relations between the security forces and the minority community; the administration of justice; extradition and prison regimes; cross-border co-operation on security; economic and social matters; human rights; electoral arrangements; and the use of flags and emblems and of the Irish language. The conference has no executive role or decision-making powers. There is no derogation from the sovereignty of either the United Kingdom Government or the Irish Government as a result of the Agreement; each retains full responsibility for the decisions and administration within its own jurisdiction.

Human Rights and Security Policy

Since the present disturbances began, the Government has paid considerable attention to protecting human rights in Northern Ireland. The United Kingdom is a signatory to the European Convention on Human Rights and allows the right of individual petition. Legislation passed in 1973 outlaws discrimination by public bodies, including the Government, on the grounds of religious belief or political opinion. Discrimination in employment by both public and private employers is also illegal and the Fair Employment Agency has been established to investigate complaints and enforce fair practices. The independent Standing Advisory Commission on Human Rights advises the Government on the effectiveness of these measures and on other human rights issues.

While terrorism continues, certain emergency powers are in force. These include special powers of arrest in respect of certain serious crimes; non-jury courts to try those offences; and the proscription of organisations involved in terrorism. There has been much concern, however, to reconcile these powers as far as possible with respect for individual liberties: the measures are temporary, need regular renewal by Parliament and have been subject to independent review, most recently in 1984. Most traditional rights, including the freedom of the media and the right to prosecute the security forces if they exceed their authority, remain in force. There is also an independent police complaints board. Northern Ireland's legal system, and the safeguards it enshrines, is broadly similar to that in England and Wales.

The use of violence as a means of overcoming political differences has been condemned by the overwhelming majority of people living in Northern Ireland and, although terrorism continues, the level of violence is much lower than some years ago. The police take the primary role in maintaining order; the Army's task is one of assisting the civil authorities, and the number of soldiers on service has been considerably reduced. Security policy rests on the principle of fair and effective enforcement of the law by bringing terrorists to justice through the courts. They are tried for criminal offences and not for political beliefs. At the heart of the policy is a determination to develop the effectiveness of the police to the point where military involvement in the maintenance of law and order is no longer needed.

The Economy   The geography of Northern Ireland has played an important part in shaping its economic development. A situation on the western edge of Europe, with few indigenous mineral resources and only a small local market, has tended to favour the concentration of industry and population on the eastern seaboard close to trading links with the rest of the United Kingdom. Most of Northern Ireland's trade is with, or through, Great Britain. With certain exceptions, the parts of the region beyond the immediate influence of the industrialised area around Belfast have stayed predominantly rural, with generally small and often scattered communities relying mainly on farming.

Since the end of the second world war two dominant trends have been apparent in the economy. First, employment in the traditionally important industries (shipbuilding, linen and agriculture) has declined. Secondly, there has been growth in the numbers seeking work, reflecting the relatively high rate of natural increase of the population, which is only partly offset by migration. In an effort to counterbalance these factors and to promote growth, programmes within the broad framework of United Kingdom regional policy have been carried out to develop infrastructure and attract investment from within the country and from abroad. Despite the impact of the world-wide recession in the 1970s and continuing high rates of unemployment, there have been encouraging developments in manufacturing recently and, as part of the Government's industrial development policy, the promotion of small firms to create new jobs in manufacturing, crafts and services is meeting with success. The discovery of large deposits of lignite around Lough Neagh, which offer the prospect of cheaper electricity in the longer term, should also benefit industry.

Belfast has Britain's largest shipyard, and aerospace engineering is now one of Northern Ireland's biggest manufacturing industries. Other well-established industrial activities include the manufacture of textile machinery and a wide range of engineering products, tobacco and clothing. There has also been extensive development in vehicle components, oil-well equipment, electronics, telecommunications equipment, carpets and synthetic rubber. The linen industry is enjoying a revival (farms are experimenting with growing flax) and food processing and packaging is seen as a source of new employment.

Agriculture (predominantly livestock and products) is still an important industry, accounting for almost a tenth of civil employment (including the self-employed), over three times the proportion in Britain as a whole.

To meet the special problem of unemployment rates that are persistently higher than in any of the other standard regions of Britain, successive governments have offered more generous incentives than are available in the rest of the country to encourage new investment both from within Britain and from overseas, and assistance to mitigate high energy costs. The establishment of 'enterprise zones' in Belfast and Londonderry and the designation of Aldergrove airport as a 'freeport' serve as additional incentives to investment. Northern Ireland's productivity and industrial relations records compare favourably with those in the country as a whole. Altogether more than 400 manufacturing projects which have been assisted are still in production, including some 100 from outside Northern Ireland.

The modern diversification of the economy has helped to stimulate output, productivity and incomes, and has assisted in narrowing the gap between living standards in Northern Ireland and those in the rest of the United Kingdom. Gross domestic product per person, which tends to be depressed in Northern Ireland relative to the country as a whole, has nonetheless risen from just under two-thirds of the British average in 1963 to almost three-quarters. Average earnings are more than nine-tenths of the national average.

The principle underlying Northern Ireland's financial relations with the rest of the country is that it has parity, both of taxation and services, with England, Scotland and Wales. To maintain social services at the level of those in Great Britain, to meet the cost of security measures, and to compensate for the natural disadvantages of geography and lack of resources, the United Kingdom Government's subvention to Northern Ireland in 1985–86 was nearly £1,600 million.

Cultural and Social Life

In day-to-day social life Northern Ireland is in many ways similar to the rest of the United Kingdom. For thousands of visitors (863,000 in 1985), as well as for local people, Northern Ireland's landscape and natural features, its cultural traditions and festivals continue to offer special attractions. For many North Americans the land from which their forebears emigrated (a number of United States presidents have been descended from Northern Ireland families) has a unique interest. The story of this contribution to American life, the history of Northern Ireland, and aspects of its culture—from the dialects and strong literary tradition (poets like Louis MacNeice and Seamus Heaney have inter-national reputations) to the songs and dances and folk art—are recorded in the Ulster–American Folk Park, the Ulster Museum and the Ulster Folk and Transport Museum.

The Arts Council of Northern Ireland is a major contributor to cultural life, which encompasses classical and traditional music, opera, literature and poetry, drama, ballet and the visual arts. The annual Belfast Festival at Queen's University is the second largest international festival in Britain. Among musicians who have achieved international distinction are the flautist James Galway and the soprano Heather Harper; the pianist Barry Douglas won the International Tchaikovsky Competition in Moscow in 1986.

The National Health Service provides both hospital and practitioner services, and health and personal social services correspond fairly closely to those in the rest of the United Kingdom, although the administrative framework is different. While publicly maintained schools are open to children of all religions, in practice, Protestants and Roman Catholics are for the most part educated in separate schools, although there is one publicly maintained integrated school and a small number of independent integrated schools. Contrary to develop-ments in the rest of the United Kingdom, emphasis on the comprehensive principle in secondary schools has been very small. Links between the two universities and industry are well developed. Housing and the improvement of the urban environment have presented problems for the authorities, but considerable progress has been made, notably in Belfast, and home ownership is increasing significantly. Major new town centre developments are taking place in Belfast, Londonderry and other towns which provide greatly improved shopping facilities. Planning and conservation arrangements are much like those in the rest of the country.

Distinctive local programmes are broadcast and there is a local press; national radio and television networks are received, however, and the national press is sold widely. Sport has an important role in the community, and many world-class sportsmen and sportswomen have come from Northern Ireland, including the boxer Barry McGuigan and the snooker player Dennis Taylor.

Physical Features

Britain constitutes the greater part of the British Isles, a geographical term for a group of islands lying off the north-west coast of mainland Europe. The largest of the islands is Great Britain (the mainlands of England, Wales and Scotland). The next largest comprises Northern Ireland and the Irish Republic. Off the southern coast of England is the Isle of Wight and off the extreme south west are the Isles of Scilly; off north Wales is Anglesey. Western Scotland is fringed by the large archipelago known as the Hebrides and to the north east of the Scottish mainland are the Orkneys and Shetlands. All these have administrative ties with the mainland, but the Isle of Man in the Irish Sea and the Channel Islands between Great Britain and France are largely self-governing, and are not part of England, Wales, Scotland or Northern Ireland.

Britain's area is some 244,100 sq km (94,250 sq miles), of which nearly 99 per cent is land and the remainder inland water. This is about the same size as the Federal Republic of Germany, New Zealand or Uganda, and half the size of France. It is just under 1,000 km (some 600 miles) from the south coast to the extreme north of Scotland and just under 500 km (some 300 miles) across in the widest part. There are numerous bays and inlets and no place in Britain is as much as 120 km (75 miles) from tidal water. The prime meridian of 0° passes through the old observatory at Greenwich (London).

The seas surrounding the British Isles are shallow, usually less than 90 m (50 fathoms or 300 ft), because the islands lie on the continental shelf. To the north west along the edge of the shelf the sea floor plunges abruptly from 180 m (some 600 ft) to 900 m (about 3,000 ft). The shallow waters are important because they provide breeding grounds for fish. The warming effect on the air of the North Atlantic current is magnified as its water spreads across the shelf.

Britain has a generally mild and temperate climate. The prevailing winds are south-westerly and the weather from day to day is mainly influenced by depressions moving eastwards across the Atlantic. The weather is subject to frequent changes but to few extremes of temperature. It is rarely above 32°C (90°F) or below −10°C (14°F). Near sea-level in the west the mean annual temperature ranges from 8°C (46°F) in the Hebrides to 11°C (52°F) in the extreme south west of England; latitude for latitude it is slightly lower in the east. The mean monthly temperature in the extreme north, at Lerwick (Shetland), ranges from 3°C (37°F) during the winter (December, January and February) to 11°C (52°F) during the summer (June, July and August); the corresponding figures for the Isle of Wight, in the extreme south, are 5°C (41°F) and 16°C (61°F). The average annual rainfall is more than 1,600 mm (over 60 inches) in the mountainous areas of the west and north but less than 800 mm (30 inches) over central and eastern parts. Rain is fairly well distributed throughout the year, but, on average, March to June are the driest months and September to January the wettest. The distribution of sunshine shows a general decrease from south to north, a decrease from the coast inland, and a decrease with altitude. During May, June and July (the months of longest daylight) the mean daily duration of sunshine varies from five hours in northern Scotland to eight hours in the Isle of Wight; during the months of shortest daylight (November, December and January) sunshine is at a minimum, with an average of an hour a day in northern Scotland and two hours a day on the south coast of England.

The Social Framework

The way of life of the people of Britain has been changing rapidly in the second half of the twentieth century. As in many other countries underlying causes include a lower birth rate, longer expectation of life, a higher divorce rate, widening educational opportunities, technical progress and a higher standard of living.

POPULATION

With 56·6 million people in 1985, Britain ranks about fifteenth in the world in terms of population. This compares with 38·2 million in 1901, about 9 million at the end of the seventeenth century and some 2 million at the end of the eleventh century. Early figures are based on contemporary estimates, but from the beginning of the nineteenth century relatively plentiful and reliable information is available. Most of it comes from two main sources: the regular flow since 1837 of statistical information based on compulsory registration of births, marriages and deaths, and the censuses taken regularly every ten years since 1801 (because of war there was no census in 1941). The most recent was in April 1981. After 1975 the population fell slightly for about three years, for the first time (other than in war) since records began, reflecting a temporary decline in the birth rate. Since then the upward trend has been resumed, except for a slight decline in 1982. Projections for the future suggest that population growth will take place at a low rate. Britain's total population is expected, on mid-1985 projections, to be 56·8 million in 1991, 57·7 million in 2001 and 58 million in 2011.

Birth Rates

In 1985 there were 752,000 live births in Britain, 22,500 more than in 1984, which outnumbered deaths (666,900) by 85,100. The total period fertility rate (an indication of the average size of family) remains below the level of 2·1 required for the replacement of the population, although it increased to 1·80 in 1985 from 1·77 in 1984.

Several factors may have contributed to the relatively low birth rate. Contraception has become more widespread and effective, making it easier to plan families, and voluntary sterilisation of men and women has also become more common. An appreciable proportion of pregnancies (in 1984 about 37 per cent of those conceived outside marriage and 7 per cent of those conceived within marriage) are ended by legal abortion.

The postponement of conception within marriage coupled with a trend towards later marriage has led to an increase, to 26, in the average age at which women have their first child in marriage. Another feature is the current preference for smaller families than in the past, especially two-children families, which has led to a significant decline in the proportion of families with four or more children.

Mortality

At birth the expectation of life for a man is about 70 years and for a woman 76 years compared with 49 years for men and 52 years for women in 1901. The improving health of the population has mainly had the effect of increasing young people's chances of reaching the older age groups. Life expectancy in the older age groups has increased relatively little.

The general death rate has remained about the same for the past 40 years, at about 12 per 1,000 population. However, there has been a considerable decline in mortality at most ages, particularly among children and young adults. The infant mortality rate (deaths of infants under one year old per 1,000 live births) was 9·6 in 1984; neonatal mortality (deaths of infants under four weeks old per 1,000 live births) was 5·7 in 1984; and maternal mortality is about 0·1 per 1,000 live births.

The causes of the decline in mortality include better nutrition, rising standards of living, the advance of medical science, the growth of medical facilities, improved health measures, better working conditions, education in personal hygiene, and the smaller size of families. Deaths resulting from infectious diseases (notably tuberculosis) have virtually disappeared. Deaths caused by circulatory diseases (including heart attacks and strokes) now account for nearly half of all deaths, the next largest cause of death being cancer (responsible for nearly one-quarter of deaths).

Marriage and Divorce

During the last 20 years there has been a marked change in the pattern of marriage. In 1972 there were 480,300 marriages in Britain, but by 1982 the number had declined to 387,000, with a subsequent increase to 393,249 in 1985. Of the population aged 16 or over in England and Wales in 1985, 61 per cent were married, 25 per cent single, 9 per cent widowed and 5 per cent divorced. The trend of the 1960s towards earlier marriage was reversed at the beginning of the 1970s, since when there has been a slow increase in the average age for first marriages, which in England and Wales is now nearly 26 for men and nearly 24 for women. In 1985 remarriages (of one or both parties) accounted for about 36 per cent of all marriages in England and Wales, compared with about 20 per cent in 1971 and 15 per cent in 1961. Some 12 per cent of all marriages in 1985 were remarriages where both partners had been divorced.

The divorce rate has been increasing steadily and in 1985 about 13 decrees of divorce were made absolute for every 1,000 married couples in England and Wales, compared with two per 1,000 in 1961. The rates are lower in Scotland and Northern Ireland. In 1985 about 160,300 divorces were granted in England and Wales; the proportion granted to wives was about 72 per cent. The average age of people at the time of divorce in England and Wales is now about 37 for men and 35 for women.

Another feature, common to many other Western European countries, has been a considerable increase in cohabitation. Nearly one-quarter of women in Great Britain marrying during the period 1979 to 1982 where the marriage was the first for both parties had lived with their husbands before marriage (compared with 8 per cent in the early 1970s) and about 12 per cent of non-married women aged 18 to 49 were cohabiting during 1983–84. Cohabitation occurs more frequently for separated or divorced women than for single women. There is some evidence of a growing number of stable non-married relationships in that half of illegitimate births (which now account for more than 19 per cent of live births in Britain compared with 6 per cent in 1961) are registered by both parents.

Age and Sex Structure

Although the total population has remained relatively stable in the last decade, there have been noticeable changes in the age and sex structure, including a decline in the proportion of young people under 16 and an increase in the proportion of elderly people, especially those aged 85 and over. The estimated age distribution of the British population in mid-1985 was roughly as follows: under 16 years, nearly 21 per cent; 16–64, 64 per cent; and 65 and over, 15 per cent. Some 18 per cent of the population were over the normal retirement ages (65 for men and 60 for women), compared with 15 per cent in 1961.

In mid-1985 there were an estimated 29 million females and 27·6 million males in Britain, representing a ratio of over 105 females to every 100 males. There are about 6 per cent more male than female births every year. Because of the higher mortality of men at all ages, however, there is a turning point, at about 51 years of age, at which the number of women exceeds the number of men. This imbalance increases with age so that there is a preponderance of women among the elderly.

Distribution of Population

The population density is about 239 per sq km, which is relatively high in comparison with most other countries. England is the most densely populated with 361 people per sq km (with Greater London having a density of 4,283 people per sq km), and Scotland the least densely populated with 65 people per sq km, while Wales and Northern Ireland have 135 and 111 people per sq km respectively.

Table 2 gives figures for some of Britain's largest urban areas. About half of the population lives in a belt across England, with south Lancashire and West Yorkshire at one end, the London area at the other, and the industrialised midlands at its centre. Other areas with large populations are: the central lowlands of Scotland; north-east England from north of the river Tyne down to the river Tees; south-east Wales; the Bristol area; and the English Channel coast from Poole, in Dorset, eastwards. Less densely populated areas are the eastern fringes of England between the Wash and the Thames estuary, and the far south west. Most of the mountainous parts, including much of Scotland, Wales and Northern Ireland and the central Pennines, are very sparsely populated.

Since the nineteenth century there has been a general trend, especially in London, for people to move away from the congested urban centres into the suburbs. The 1981 census recorded that only in the remoter rural areas had the rate of population growth been higher in the 1970s than in the 1960s. There has also been a geographical redistribution of the population from Scotland and the northern regions of England to East Anglia, the South West and the East Midlands. Another feature has been an increase in the rate of retirement migration, the main recipient areas (where in some towns the elderly can form over one-third of the population) being the south coast of England and East Anglia.

Table 2: Size and Population of the Main Urban Areas, Mid-1985

	Area		Population (thousands)
	sq km	sq miles	
Greater London	1,580	609·7	6,767·5
Birmingham	264	102·0	1,007·5
Glasgow	198	76·3	733·8
Leeds	562	217·0	710·5
Sheffield	368	141·9	538·7
Liverpool	113	43·6	491·5
Bradford	370	142·9	463·5
Manchester	116	44·9	451·1
Edinburgh	261	100·6	439·7
Bristol	110	42·3	393·8
Coventry	97	37·3	312·2
Belfast	140	54·0	301·6
Cardiff	120	46·3	278·9

Migration

Traditionally, there is a net population loss from Britain due to migration to the rest of the world, but in 1985, when the inflow was 34 per cent higher than in 1984, there was a net gain of 97,000.[1] Between 1980 and 1985 some 1·24 million people left Britain to live abroad and about 1·20 million came from overseas to live in Britain, so that net emigration reduced the population by about 41,000. Of the 174,000 departing residents in 1985, 19 per cent left for Australia, Canada or New Zealand, 18 per cent for other Commonwealth

---

[1] International migration statistics used here exclude movements to and from the Irish Republic.

countries, 17 per cent for other European Community countries, 14 per cent for the United States and 10 per cent for the Middle East. Of the 270,000 new residents, 14 per cent came from Australia, Canada or New Zealand, 21 per cent from other Commonwealth countries and 20 per cent from other European Community countries. Many of those coming into Britain, as well as those going abroad, are British citizens.

Nationality

Nationality legislation is embodied in the British Nationality Act 1981, which came into force on 1 January 1983. Under this Act, citizenship of the United Kingdom and Colonies was replaced by three citizenships: British citizenship for people closely connected with Britain, the Channel Islands, and the Isle of Man; British Dependent Territories citizenship for people connected with the dependencies; and British Overseas citizenship for those citizens of the United Kingdom and Colonies who did not acquire either of the other citizenships. With one small exception, citizens of the United Kingdom and Colonies who had the right of abode in Britain when the Act came into force acquired British citizenship.

British citizenship is acquired automatically at birth by a child born in Britain if his or her father or mother is a British citizen or is settled in Britain. A child adopted in Britain by a British citizen is a British citizen. A child born abroad to a British citizen born, adopted, naturalised or registered in Britain is a British citizen by descent. The Act safeguards the citizenship of a child born abroad to a British citizen in Crown service, certain related services, or in service under a European Community institution. British citizenship may also be acquired by registration by certain children born in Britain who do not automatically acquire such citizenship at birth or born abroad to a parent who is a citizen by descent; by British Dependent Territories citizens, British Overseas citizens, British subjects under the Act (three very limited categories) and British protected persons after five years' residence in Britain (except for people from Gibraltar, who may be registered without residence); and by naturalisation for Commonwealth citizens, citizens of the Irish Republic, and foreign nationals. The British Nationality (Falkland Islands) Act 1983 conferred British citizenship (with effect from 1 January 1983) on those Falkland Islanders who did not acquire it under the 1981 Act. For naturalisation, which is at the Home Secretary's discretion, five years' residence, good character and sufficient knowledge of English, Welsh or Scottish Gaelic are required except for the spouse of a British citizen, who needs only three years' residence and no language qualification. Most existing entitlements to registration (including those for Commonwealth citizens and Irish citizens settled in Britain since before 1973, and in certain circumstances that for women married to citizens of the United Kingdom and Colonies before 1983) are preserved for five years from 1 January 1983.

Special arrangements covering the status of British Dependent Territories citizens living in Hong Kong when the territory returns to the People's Republic of China in 1997 are made by the Hong Kong (British Nationality) Order 1986.

In 1985, 54,000 people acquired citizenship by naturalisation or registration in the United Kingdom.

Immigration

Immigration into the United Kingdom is controlled by the Immigration Act 1971 (as amended by the British Nationality Act 1981) and the Immigration Rules made in accordance with the Act. British citizens under the British Nationality Act 1981 and those Commonwealth citizens who had the right of abode before 1 January 1983 (when the 1981 Act came into force) have the right of abode and are not subject to immigration control. Those who do not have this right require permission to enter and remain in the United Kingdom, which is given in accordance with the rules. These, which are approved by Parliament and which may be changed from time to time, set out the requirements to be met by those seeking entry whether in a temporary capacity, for example as students or visitors, or with the intention of taking employment or setting up in business or for settlement as the dependants of a person already settled in the United Kingdom. Nationals from certain countries require a visa before they can enter the United Kingdom. Other nationals subject to immigration control require entry clearance when coming to settle in the United Kingdom and in certain other circumstances. Visas and other entry clearances are normally obtained from the nearest British diplomatic post in a person's home country. Changes to the rules were implemented in 1985 to remove differences relating to the admission of husbands and wives coming for settlement and in 1986 to prevent child spouses under 16 living in the United Kingdom.

In accordance with the United Kingdom's obligations under the Treaty of Rome, European Community nationals do not require entry clearances nor are they subject to restrictions on their freedom to take or seek work. The United Kingdom similarly respects its obligations under the United Nations Convention and Protocol relating to the Status of Refugees.

In 1985, 55,400 people were accepted for settlement, some 4,400 more than in 1984. A third of these were from the South Asian sub-continent and over half were the wives and children of men settled in the United Kingdom.

THE ECONOMIC AND SOCIAL PATTERN

This section deals (to some extent in broad and informal terms) with social developments affecting many sections of the population.

The majority of people (some 97 per cent) live in private households (in families or on their own). The remainder include residents in hotels, and people in the armed services and in educational or other institutions. In 1984 just under four-fifths of people living in private households lived in a unit headed by a married couple.

Among many changes in household and family structure is the continuing fall in the average size of households in Great Britain from over four people in 1911 to 3·09 in 1961 and 2·59 in 1984. The fall reflects a greater proportion of people living on their own (8 per cent) or in one-parent families, the increasing number of elderly people (more of whom are living alone), and the preferences of parents for smaller families. The trend towards smaller households (25 per cent of households consist of one person) is expected to continue and the number of one-person households is forecast to increase substantially in the next few years.

Housing and the Environment

A growing proportion of households, about 60 per cent, own or are buying their own homes, owner-occupation being higher among married couples than for single, divorced or widowed household heads. The number of owner-occupied dwellings rose from over 4 million in 1951 to 13·5 million in 1984. Four British households out of five live in houses rather than flats.

Nearly half of Britain's housing has been built since 1945. Recent housing developments have been concentrated in suburban areas. Many families now live in houses grouped in small terraces, or semi-detached or detached, usually of two storeys with gardens, and providing two main ground-floor living rooms, a kitchen, from two to four bedrooms, a bathroom, and one or two lavatories. Originally, many houses were located in 'ribbon development' along main roads, but in recent years housing estates have nearly always been sited away from main roads. In inner urban areas slum clearance and redevelopment have been major features of post-1945 public housing programmes. While high-rise flats were popular in the 1960s and 1970s, the emphasis in new building is now on low-rise, high-density designs, often incorporating gardens or patios.

Housing standards are continually improving; some 97 per cent of households in Great Britain have exclusive use of a bath or shower, and a similar proportion sole use of an inside lavatory (high percentages by international standards) while over 65 per cent have central heating.

An important influence on the planning of housing and services has been the growth of car ownership; about 61 per cent of households have the use of at least one car (or van), including 17 per cent with the use of two or more. Greater access to motorised transport and the construction of a network of modern trunk roads and motorways have resulted in a considerable increase in personal mobility and changed leisure patterns, and have influenced the design of housing estates and shopping areas. Most detached or semi-detached houses in new suburban estates have garages, and out-of-town shopping centres, which normally include large supermarkets, are usually planned for the motorist.

The growth in car ownership has brought very great benefits but also a number of problems, notably, in many towns and cities, increased congestion, noise and air pollution arising from motor vehicle emissions. Public transport, too, has been affected, and many services have been reduced or withdrawn, especially local bus and train services in rural areas. However, greater competition in express coach services has resulted in more long-distance and commuter coach services being provided.

There has been a steady reduction of the main atmospheric and freshwater pollutants that have been of concern in the past, producing dramatic improvements in, for example, the quality of the air in cities and the condition of major rivers, although various forms of pollution from traffic and industrial processes remain a problem in some areas. There is a high degree of concern for the environment, as shown by the growth in the number of organisations (especially voluntary societies) concerned with conservation.

Living Standards

Marked improvements in the standard of living have taken place during the twentieth century, but generally at a slower rate than in some other major industrialised countries. Although gross domestic product (GDP) per head fell in the early 1980s, Britain has experienced an economic recovery in the mid-1980s, and GDP is now at a record level, having risen by 3·6 per cent in 1985. Another feature of the economic improvement has been a substantial reduction in inflation, which from 1983 to 1985 ranged between about 4 and 7 per cent a year, compared with an average annual increase of 14·2 per cent between 1973 and the end of 1982, and was down to 2·4 per cent in mid-1986, the lowest rate since 1968.

Long-term trends in the pattern of expenditure show a substantial rise in expenditure on housing, televisions, telephones, electrical and some other durable goods, motor vehicles and entertainment, and in expenditure overseas. As real incomes have risen, the share of expenditure on food has fallen. Unlike in many other countries, the share devoted to tobacco continues to decline; an increasing number of people have stopped smoking for health reasons.

The general level of nutrition remains high. Over the last 20 years there have been substantial rises in the consumption of poultry, instant coffee, pork, margarine and processed (including frozen) vegetables, while home consumption per person of mutton and lamb, beef and veal, bread, potatoes, eggs, milk, butter, sugar, tea and some other foods has fallen. However, another feature has been an increase in the number of meals eaten away from home, either at work or in restaurants, and a growth in the consumption of food from 'take-away' and 'fast-food' shops. In addition, in the 1960s and 1970s the proportion of convenience foods eaten grew as women increasingly went out to work and had less time to prepare meals, and as the variety of prepared foods rose in line with the growth in ownership of refrigerators and freezers; there is some evidence of a

Availability of Certain Durable Goods

Per cent of households with goods

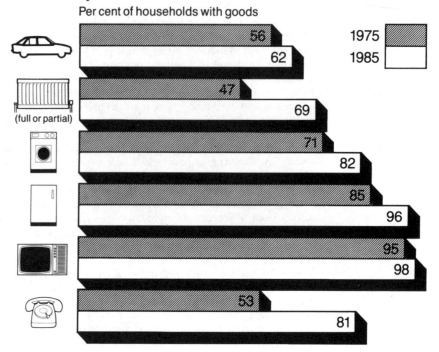

(full or partial)

	1975	1985
car	56	62
central heating (full or partial)	47	69
washing machine	71	82
refrigerator	85	96
television	95	98
telephone	53	81

more recent return to fresh foods, as well as growth in the popularity of health foods and slimming products.

Alcohol consumption has risen substantially since the 1950s and alcohol abuse has become a growing problem although the level is well below that in some other European Community countries. Beer remains much the most popular alcoholic drink. A high proportion of beer is drunk in public houses ('pubs'), which are a traditional social centre for many people, and in clubs. A notable development has been the increase in consumption of lager, now estimated to account for about two-fifths of the beer consumed. Consumption of light (table) wine has increased considerably in recent years, although there has been little change in the consumption of higher strength wines such as sherry and port. The pattern of spirits consumption has also been changing, with a decline in the consumption of whisky and gin, and higher consumption of some other spirits.

Ownership of many durable goods has been increasing and some goods, such as televisions, vacuum cleaners and refrigerators, are available in more than 90 per cent of households. Of durable goods shown in the diagram above, ownership of telephones, freezers and central heating systems is growing most rapidly; other durable goods which have grown in popularity include music centres and other audio equipment, video recorders and home computers.

The pattern of employment has altered considerably in recent years, with a substantial decline in employment in manufacturing industry being accompanied by a long-term increase in the numbers employed in service industries. The number of jobs in the economy has increased, but unemployment has also grown as demographic factors have contributed to a substantial increase in the population of working age. A recent feature has been a rapid growth in the number of self-employed, accounting in September 1985 for over 10 per cent of the workforce. Earnings from employment are the main source of income for most people; in 1984 wages and salaries accounted for 61 per cent of household income. The distribution of pre-tax income has remained relatively stable over a long period, the lower 50 per cent of income earners accounting for some 22 to 24 per cent of pre-tax income since 1949. However, the share of the top 1 per cent fell from 11 per cent in 1949 to 5·3 per cent in 1978–79, but increased to 6 per cent in 1981–82. Income before tax of the self-employed is less evenly distributed than total income, mostly because of the very large incomes of a small number of people, mainly professionals such as lawyers, accountants and doctors. The combined effect of the tax system and the receipt of benefits is to redistribute incomes on a more equal basis.

Wealth is much less evenly distributed, with the top 1 per cent of the population aged 18 or over owning about 21 per cent of marketable wealth, the top 10 per cent having 56 per cent and the top 50 per cent having 96 per cent. The inclusion of 'non-marketable' rights in occupational and state pension schemes reduces these shares substantially to around 11, 34 and 80 per cent respectively. Since the mid-1970s there has been little change in the distribution of marketable wealth or in that of marketable wealth plus occupational and state pension rights.

Women

Considerable changes have occurred in the twentieth century in the economic and domestic lives of women, due, in part, to the removal of almost all sex discrimination in political and legal rights. At the heart of women's changed role has been the rise in the number of women, particularly married women, at work. With later marriages and the availability of effective methods of family planning there has been a decline in family size. Women as a result are involved in child-bearing for a much shorter time and this, together with a variety of other factors which have made housework less burdensome, has made it possible for women with even young children to return to work.

Women comprise about two-fifths of the British labour force. Since the second world war the proportion of married women who work has grown to over 60 per cent of those between the ages of 16 and 60, and they now make up some 28 per cent of the labour force compared with 4 per cent in 1921. Many families have come to rely on married women's earnings as an essential part of their income. There is still a significant difference between women's and men's earnings but the equal pay legislation which came into force at the end of 1975 has narrowed the gap. Women's average hourly earnings, exclusive of overtime (for full-time employees), increased from just under two-thirds of those of men in 1970, to nearly three-quarters in 1985. Nevertheless, women's wages remain relatively low because women tend to work in lowly paid sectors of the economy and they work less overtime than men.

Equal Opportunities

These changes have been significant, but, because tradition and prejudice can still handicap women in their careers and personal lives, major legislation to help to promote equality was passed in the 1970s.

Under the Equal Pay Act 1970 as amended in 1984 (there is similar legislation in Northern Ireland), women in Great Britain are entitled to equal pay with men when doing work that is the same or broadly similar, or work which is of equal value. The Sex Discrimination Act 1975 makes discrimination between men and women unlawful in employment, education, training and the provision of housing, goods, facilities and services. Discriminatory advertisements which breach the Act are also unlawful. (Northern Ireland has similar legislation.) The Sex Discrimination Bill at present before Parliament will bring the Sex Discrimination Act 1975 into line with certain European Community directives, including one relating to the right of women to continue working until the same age as men in those occupations which have different retirement ages for men and women. In most cases complaints of discrimination are dealt with by industrial tribunals since they concern employment; others may be taken before the county courts in England and Wales or the sheriff courts in Scotland. The Equal Opportunities Commission was set up in 1975 (1976 in Northern Ireland under separate legislation) to enforce the Sex Discrimination Act and the Equal Pay Act. Its statutory duties are to work towards the elimination of discrimination and to promote equality of opportunity. The Commission advises people of their rights under both Acts and may give financial or other assistance to help individuals to conduct a case before a court or tribunal. It also has power to conduct investigations and to issue notices requiring discriminatory practices to stop. In addition, it keeps legislation under review and may submit proposals for amending it to the ministers concerned. The Commission seeks to make women more aware of the opportunities available to them and its information centre is a national source of material on all aspects of equality.

Ethnic and National Minorities

Britain has a long history of accommodating minority groups and in the last three hundred years or so a variety of people have settled in the country, some to avoid political or religious persecution, others seeking a better way of life or an escape from poverty.

The Irish have long made homes in Britain. Many Jewish refugees started a new life in the country towards the end of the nineteenth century and in the 1930s, and after 1945 large numbers of other European refugees settled in Britain. The large communities from the West Indies and South Asian sub-continent date principally from the 1950s and early 1960s. There are also sizeable groups of Americans, Australians, Chinese and various European communities such as Greek and Turkish Cypriots, Italians and Spaniards. More recently Ugandan Asians and refugees from Indo-China have settled in Britain.

In 1984, according to the results of a sample survey, the non-white population of Great Britain was nearly 2·4 million (just over 4 per cent of the total population) of whom about 40 per cent were born in Britain. Most of them share aspirations that are broadly similar to those of the British community as a whole and they enjoy full political and civic rights. Although the circumstances of many members of the ethnic minority communities are less fortunate than those of other groups (for example, they suffer disproportionately from unemployment and often live in poor housing in the older urban areas) and while they may experience racial discrimination there have been important advances over the last 25 years in employment and housing conditions, and many individuals have achieved distinction in their careers and in public life. The growth of Asian businesses has been a particularly noticeable development and there are numerous examples of enterprise among minorities to organise self-help.

The difficulties minorities face are being tackled by environmental and employment programmes in the inner cities, some of which benefit the whole community, while other projects, for example, in education and health, are directed towards meeting minorities' special needs. Although fewer children than formerly go to school with no knowledge of English, there are still many who have an insufficient grasp of the language. Language teaching is recognised to be of prime importance and various arrangements have been made for teaching English as a second language. For adults, classes at or outside their place of work are run by local authorities and voluntary organisations. Government grants are available to authorities with substantial ethnic minority groups towards the salaries of extra staff such as teachers, health visitors and interpreters.

The welfare of ethnic minorities and good relations between minorities and the local community are promoted by community relations councils and other voluntary bodies. In recognition of the tensions that can arise between the police and ethnic minorities, consultation between the police and the community has been made a statutory requirement and consultative committees have been set up in many areas. Policies for promoting equality of opportunity in a multiracial society in which all citizens receive equal respect are pursued against a background of legislation against discrimination.

Race Relations Act

The Race Relations Act 1976 makes discrimination unlawful on grounds of colour, race, nationality or ethnic or national origin in the provision of goods, facilities and services, in employment, training and related matters, in education, in housing and in advertising. It strengthened legislation passed in 1968 which, in turn, widened the scope of the first race relations legislation enacted in 1965. It also strengthened the criminal law on incitement to racial hatred which will be tightened up further by the Public Order Bill at present before Parliament.

The 1976 Act brought the law against racial discrimination into line with that against sex discrimination (see p 27), and gave complainants direct access to civil courts and, in the case of employment complaints, to industrial tribunals.

Commission for Racial Equality

The Commission for Racial Equality was established by the Race Relations Act 1976 with statutory duties to work towards the elimination of discrimination and to promote equality of opportunity and good relations between people of different racial groups. It has power to investigate unlawful discriminatory practices and to issue non-discrimination notices, requiring that such practices should cease. It has an important educational role and has issued a code of practice in employment. It is also the principal source of advice for the general public about the Race Relations Act and has discretion to assist individuals with their complaints.

The Commission supports the work of the 100 or so community relations councils, which are autonomous, voluntary bodies set up in most areas with a significant ethnic minority population to promote harmonious community relations at the local level. It makes grants towards the salaries of the community relations officers employed by the councils, most of whom also receive funds from their local authorities, and gives grants to ethnic minority self-help groups and to other projects run by or for the benefit of the minority communities.

Leisure Trends

Most people have considerably more free time, more ways in which to spend it and higher real incomes than had previous generations. Agreed hours of full-time work are usually from 35 to 40 hours a week, although many people actually work somewhat longer because of voluntary overtime. A large majority of employees work a five-day week.

The most common leisure activities are home based, or social, with visiting or entertaining relatives or friends and watching television among the most popular. Watching television is the main evening pastime for all except young men. Nearly all households have a television set and the population aged five and over spend on average some 20 hours a week watching programmes. Growing numbers are using video recorders to watch programmes at times other than their transmission; 21 per cent of households had a video recorder in 1984. Other popular pursuits include: listening to the radio, records or cassettes; reading; do-it-yourself home improvements such as house painting and decorating; going out for a meal or for a drink or to the cinema or to watch a sporting event; gardening; outings (such as visits to the countryside, seaside or to museums); photography; visits to social clubs and leisure centres; and social and voluntary work. About half the households in Britain have a pet, the most common being dogs (of which there are thought to be about 6 million in Britain) and cats (over 5 million).

Sports and other pastimes have grown in popularity, reflected by increasing membership of the main organisations concerned with outdoor activities, although for some sports, such as football, the number of spectators has been declining. Walking is the most popular sporting activity and is equally undertaken by men and women. Billiards/snooker and darts are the next most popular sports among men, followed by swimming and football, while swimming is the second most popular sporting activity for women, although an increasing number of women are participating in aerobics (keep-fit exercises) and yoga.

Holiday entitlements have increased for most full-time employees, and by the end of 1984 some 95 per cent of manual workers had a basic holiday entitlement of four weeks or more and 19 per cent five weeks or more. The number of holidays (of four or more nights) taken by British residents was 48·75 million in 1985 compared with 48 million in 1975; 15·75 million of these were taken abroad, well over half involving 'package' arrangements. More than four-fifths of overseas holidays were taken in other European countries, with Spain being the most popular destination; it received almost one-third of all British holiday-makers abroad. The next most popular destinations were France, Greece, Italy, the Federal Republic of Germany and Austria. The main holiday period is May to September when over 80 per cent of holidays in Britain and almost 70 per cent of holidays abroad are taken. An increasing number of people (20 per cent in 1985) take more than one long holiday each year, but a significant proportion take no holiday away from home.

2 Government

The United Kingdom constitution, unlike that of most other countries, is not contained in any single document. Formed partly by statute, partly by common law and partly by convention, it can be altered by Act of Parliament, or by general agreement to create, vary or abolish a convention. The constitution thus adapts readily to changing political conditions and ideas.

The organs of government are clearly distinguishable although their functions often intermingle and overlap. The legislature, Parliament, is the supreme authority. The executive consists of: (1) the Government—Cabinet and other ministers who are responsible for initiating and directing national policy; (2) government departments, which are responsible for national administration; (3) local authorities, which administer and manage many local services; and (4) public corporations responsible for operating particular nationalised industries or, for example, a social or cultural service, subject to ministerial control in varying degrees. The judiciary determines common law and interprets statutes, and is independent of both legislature and executive.

The Monarchy

The British people look to the Queen not only as their head of State, but also as the symbol of their nation's unity. The monarchy is the most ancient secular institution in the United Kingdom. During the last thousand years its continuity has only once been broken (by the establishment of a republic which lasted from 1649 to 1660) and, despite interruptions in the direct line of succession, the hereditary principle upon which it was founded has always been preserved. The royal title in the United Kingdom is: 'Elizabeth the Second, by the Grace of God of the United Kingdom of Great Britain and Northern Ireland and of Her other Realms and Territories Queen, Head of the Commonwealth, Defender of the Faith'. The form of the royal title is varied for those other member states of the Commonwealth of which the Queen is head of State,[1] to suit the particular circumstances of each. Other member states are republics or have their own monarchies.

The seat of the monarchy is in the United Kingdom. In the Channel Islands and the Isle of Man the Queen is represented by a Lieutenant-Governor. In the other member nations of the Commonwealth of which the Queen is head of State, her representative is the Governor-General appointed by her on the advice of the ministers of the country concerned and completely independent of the United Kingdom Government.

In the United Kingdom dependencies the Queen is usually represented by governors, who are responsible to the British Government for the good government of the countries concerned.

Succession, Accession and Coronation

The title to the Crown derives partly from statute and partly from common law rules of descent. Lineal Protestant descendants of a granddaughter of James I of England and VI of Scotland (Princess Sophia, the Electress of Hanover) are alone eligible to succeed, and although succession is not bound to continue in its

---

[1] The other Commonwealth countries of which the Queen is head of State are: Antigua and Barbuda, Australia, Bahamas, Barbados, Belize, Canada, Fiji, Grenada, Jamaica, Mauritius, New Zealand, Papua New Guinea, Saint Christopher and Nevis, Saint Lucia, Saint Vincent and the Grenadines, Solomon Islands and Tuvalu.

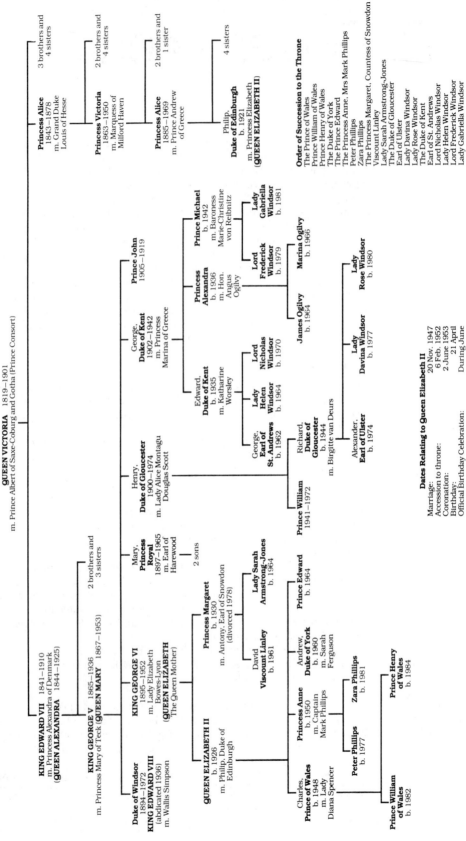

The Royal Family

From the reign of Queen Victoria to September 1986

QUEEN VICTORIA 1819–1901
m. Prince Albert of Saxe-Coburg and Gotha (Prince Consort)

Princess Alice 1843–1878
m. Grand Duke Louis of Hesse
3 brothers and 4 sisters

Princess Victoria 1863–1950
m. Marquess of Milford Haven
2 brothers and 4 sisters

Princess Alice 1885–1969
m. Prince Andrew of Greece
2 brothers and 1 sister

Philip, Duke of Edinburgh b. 1921
m. Princess Elizabeth (**QUEEN ELIZABETH II**)
4 sisters

KING EDWARD VII 1841–1910
m. Princess Alexandra of Denmark (**QUEEN ALEXANDRA** 1844–1925)

KING GEORGE V 1865–1936
m. Princess Mary of Teck (**QUEEN MARY** 1867–1953)
2 brothers and 3 sisters

Duke of Windsor 1894–1972
KING EDWARD VIII (abdicated 1936)
m. Wallis Simpson

KING GEORGE VI 1895–1952
m. Lady Elizabeth Bowes-Lyon (**QUEEN ELIZABETH** The Queen Mother)

Mary, Princess Royal 1897–1965
m. Earl of Harewood
2 sons

Henry, Duke of Gloucester 1900–1974
m. Lady Alice Montagu Douglas Scott

George, Duke of Kent 1902–1942
m. Princess Marina of Greece

Prince John 1905–1919

Prince William 1941–1972

Richard, Duke of Gloucester b. 1944
m. Birgitte van Deurs

Alexander, Earl of Ulster b. 1974

Lady Davina Windsor b. 1977

Lady Rose Windsor b. 1980

Edward, Duke of Kent b. 1935
m. Katharine Worsley

George, Earl of St. Andrews b. 1962

Lady Helen Windsor b. 1964

Lord Nicholas Windsor b. 1970

Princess Alexandra b. 1936
m. Hon. Angus Ogilvy

James Ogilvy b. 1964

Marina Ogilvy b. 1966

Prince Michael b. 1942
m. Baroness Marie-Christine von Reibnitz

Lord Frederick Windsor b. 1979

Lady Gabriella Windsor b. 1981

QUEEN ELIZABETH II b. 1926
m. Philip, Duke of Edinburgh

Princess Margaret b. 1930
m. Antony, Earl of Snowdon (divorced 1978)

David, Viscount Linley b. 1961

Lady Sarah Armstrong-Jones b. 1964

Charles, Prince of Wales b. 1948
m. Lady Diana Spencer

Prince William of Wales b. 1982

Prince Henry of Wales b. 1984

Princess Anne b. 1950
m. Captain Mark Phillips

Peter Phillips b. 1977

Zara Phillips b. 1981

Andrew, Duke of York b. 1960
m. Sarah Ferguson

Prince Edward b. 1964

Order of Succession to the Throne

The Prince of Wales
Prince William of Wales
Prince Henry of Wales
The Duke of York
The Prince Edward
The Princess Anne, Mrs Mark Phillips
Peter Phillips
Zara Phillips
The Princess Margaret, Countess of Snowdon
Viscount Linley
Lady Sarah Armstrong-Jones
The Duke of Gloucester
Earl of Ulster
Lady Davina Windsor
Lady Rose Windsor
The Duke of Kent
Earl of St. Andrews
Lord Nicholas Windsor
Lady Helen Windsor
Lord Frederick Windsor
Lady Gabriella Windsor

Dates Relating to Queen Elizabeth II

Marriage:	20 Nov. 1947
Accession to throne:	6 Feb. 1952
Coronation:	2 June 1953
Birthday:	21 April
Official Birthday Celebration:	During June

present line, it can be altered only by common consent of the member nations of the Commonwealth of which the Queen is Sovereign.

The sons of the Sovereign have precedence over the daughters in succeeding to the throne. When a daughter succeeds, she becomes Queen-Regnant, and the powers of the Crown are vested in her as though she were a king. While the consort of a king takes her husband's rank and style, the constitution does not give any special rank or privileges to the husband of a Queen-Regnant although in practice he fills an important role in the life of the nation, as does the Duke of Edinburgh.

The Sovereign succeeds to the throne as soon as his or her predecessor dies and there is no interregnum. He or she is at once proclaimed at an Accession Council to which all members of the Privy Council are summoned. The Lords Spiritual and Temporal (see p 36), the Lord Mayor and Aldermen and other leading citizens of the City of London are also invited.

The Sovereign's coronation follows the accession after a convenient interval. It is a ceremony which has remained essentially the same for over a thousand years, even if details have often been modified to conform to the customs of the time. It takes place at Westminster Abbey in London in the presence of representatives of the Houses of Parliament and of all the great public interests of the United Kingdom, of the Prime Ministers and leading members of the other Commonwealth nations, and of representatives of other countries.

Acts of Government

The Queen personifies the State. In law, she is head of the executive, an integral part of the legislature, head of the judiciary, the commander-in-chief of all armed forces of the Crown and the 'supreme governor' of the established Church of England. As a result of a long process of evolution, during which the monarchy's absolute power has been progressively reduced, the Queen acts on the advice of her ministers, which she cannot ignore. The United Kingdom is governed by Her Majesty's Government in the name of the Queen.

Within this framework, and in spite of a trend during the past hundred years towards assigning powers directly to ministers, there are still important acts of government which require the participation of the Queen. These include summoning, proroguing (discontinuing until the next session without disso-lution) and dissolving Parliament; giving royal assent to Bills passed by Parliament; appointing many important office holders, including government ministers, judges, officers in the armed forces, governors, diplomats and bishops and some other senior clergy of the Church of England; conferring peerages, knighthoods and other honours[1]; and remitting all or part of the penalty imposed on a person convicted of a crime. An important function is appointing the Prime Minister and by convention the Queen invites the leader of the political party which commands a majority in the House of Commons to form a government. In international affairs, the Queen as head of State has the power to declare war and make peace, to recognise foreign states and governments, to conclude treaties and to annexe or cede territory.

With rare exceptions (as when appointing the Prime Minister), those acts involving the use of 'royal prerogative' powers are nowadays performed by government ministers who are responsible to Parliament and can be questioned about a particular policy. It is not necessary to have Parliament's authority to exercise these powers, although Parliament has the power to restrict or abolish a prerogative right.

Ministerial responsibility in no way detracts from the importance of the Queen's role in the smooth working of government. She holds meetings of the

---

[1] Although most honours are conferred by the Queen on the advice of the Prime Minister, a few are conferred on her personal selection—the Order of the Garter, the Order of the Thistle, the Order of Merit and the Royal Victorian Order.

Privy Council, gives audiences to her ministers and other officials at home and overseas, receives accounts of Cabinet decisions, reads dispatches and signs numerous state papers; she must be informed and consulted on every aspect of national life; and she must show complete impartiality.

Such is the significance attached to these royal functions that provision has been made for a regent to be appointed to perform them should the Queen be totally incapacitated. The regent would be the Queen's eldest son, the Prince of Wales, then those in succession to the throne who are of age. In the event of the Queen's partial incapacity or absence abroad, there is provision for appointing Counsellors of State (the Duke of Edinburgh, the four adults next in line of succession, and the Queen Mother) to whom the Queen may delegate certain royal functions. However, Counsellors of State may not, for instance, dissolve Parliament (except on the Queen's express instructions), or create peers.

Ceremonial and Royal Visits

Ceremonial has always been associated with British kings and queens, and, in spite of the change in the outlook of both the Sovereign and the people, many traditional customs and ceremonies are retained. Royal marriages and royal funerals are marked by public ceremony, and the Sovereign's birthday is officially celebrated in June by Trooping the Colour on Horse Guards Parade. State banquets take place when a foreign monarch or head of State visits Britain; investitures are held at Buckingham Palace and the Palace of Holyroodhouse in Scotland to bestow honours; and royal processions add significance to such occasions as a State opening of Parliament, when the Queen drives from Buckingham Palace to Westminster. Each year the Queen and other members of the royal family visit many parts of the United Kingdom. Their presence at scientific, artistic, industrial and charitable events of national and local importance encourages nationwide interest and publicity. The Queen pays state visits to foreign governments, accompanied by the Duke of Edinburgh. She also undertakes lengthy tours in the other countries of the Commonwealth. Other members of the royal family pay official visits overseas, occasionally representing the Queen, and often in connection with an organisation or a cause with which they are associated.

Royal Income and Expenditure

About 85 per cent of all expenditure arising from the royal family's official duties is met by public departments. This includes the costs of the royal yacht, the Queen's Flight, travel by train and the upkeep of the royal palaces. Apart from this the Queen's public expenditure on staff and expenses incurred in carrying out official duties as head of State is financed from the Civil List, approved by Parliament. (In 1986 this was £4·1 million.) Her private expenditure as Sovereign is met from the Privy Purse, which is supplied mainly from the revenues of the Duchy of Lancaster[1]; and her personal expenditure as a private individual from her own personal resources. There are annual allowances approved by Parliament to other members of the royal family, though not to the Prince of Wales, who as Duke of Cornwall is entitled to the net revenue of the estate of the Duchy of Cornwall (he voluntarily surrenders a quarter of the revenue to the Exchequer). The Queen pays into the Exchequer a sum equivalent to that provided by Parliament in respect of certain members of the royal family.

Parliament

Parliament is the supreme legislative authority. Its three elements, the Queen, the House of Lords and the elected House of Commons, are outwardly separate,

---

[1] The Duchy of Lancaster is an inheritance which, since 1399, has always been enjoyed by the reigning Sovereign; it is kept quite apart from his or her other possessions and is separately administered by the Chancellor of the Duchy.

are constituted on different principles, and meet together only on occasions of symbolic significance such as the State opening of Parliament when the Commons are summoned by the Queen to the House of Lords. As a law-making body, however, Parliament usually requires the concurrence of all its parts.

Parliament can legislate for the United Kingdom as a whole, for any of the constituent parts of the country separately, or for any combination of them. It can also legislate for the Channel Islands and the Isle of Man, which are Crown dependencies and not part of the United Kingdom, having subordinate legislatures which make laws on island affairs.[1]

Free from any legal restraints imposed by a written constitution, Parliament is able to legislate as it pleases: generally to make, unmake, or alter any law; to legalise past illegalities and make void and punishable what was lawful when done and thus reverse the decisions of the ordinary courts; and to destroy established conventions or turn a convention into binding law. It can prolong its own life beyond the normal period without consulting the electorate.

In practice, however, Parliament does not assert its supremacy in this way. Its members bear in mind the common law and have tended to act in accordance with precedent and tradition. The validity of an Act of Parliament which has been duly passed, promulgated and published cannot be disputed in the law courts, but no Parliament would be likely to pass an Act which it knew would receive no public support. The system of party government helps to ensure that Parliament legislates with its responsibility to the electorate in mind.

As a member of the European Community, the United Kingdom recognises the various types of Community legislation, and sends 81 elected members to the European Parliament.

The Functions of Parliament

The main functions of Parliament are (1) to pass laws, (2) to provide, by voting taxation, the means of carrying on the work of government, (3) to scrutinise government policy and administration, particularly proposals for expenditure, and (4) to debate the great political issues of the day. In discharging these functions Parliament helps to bring the relevant facts and issues before the electorate. By custom, Parliament is also consulted before the ratification of all important international treaties and agreements, the making of treaties being, in theory at least, a royal prerogative exercised on the advice of the Government and not subject to parliamentary approval.

The Meeting of Parliament

A Parliament has a maximum duration of five years, but is often dissolved and a general election held before the end of this term. The maximum life has been prolonged by legislation in such rare circumstances as the two world wars. Dissolution and writs for a general election are ordered by the Queen on the advice of the Prime Minister.

The life of a Parliament is divided into sessions. Each usually lasts for one year—beginning and ending most often in October or November and interspersed with 'adjournments' at night, at weekends, at Christmas, Easter and the late (English) Spring Bank Holiday and during a long summer recess starting in late July or early August. The average number of 'sitting' days in a session is about 175 in the House of Commons and about 150 in the House of Lords. At the start of each session the Queen's speech to Parliament outlines the Government's broad policies and proposed legislative programme. Each session is terminated by prorogation. Parliament then 'stands prorogued' until the new

---

[1] The legislatures of the Channel Islands (the States of Jersey and the States of Guernsey) and the Isle of Man (the Tynwald Court) consist of the Queen, the Privy Council and the local assemblies. It is the duty of the Home Secretary, as the Privy Council member primarily concerned with island affairs, to scrutinise each legislative measure before it is submitted to the Queen in Council.

session opens (on occasions Parliament has been dissolved without prorogation). A short speech is made on behalf of the Queen summarising Parliament's work during the past session. An adjournment does not affect uncompleted business, but prorogation terminates nearly all parliamentary business, so that all public Bills not completed lapse, and must be reintroduced in the next session unless they are to be abandoned.

The House of Lords

The House of Lords consists of the Lords Spiritual and the Lords Temporal. The Lords Spiritual are the Archbishops of Canterbury and York, the Bishops of London, Durham and Winchester, and the 21 senior diocesan bishops of the Church of England. The Lords Temporal consist of (1) all hereditary peers and peeresses of England, Scotland, Great Britain and the United Kingdom who have not disclaimed their peerages, (2) all life peers and peeresses, and (3) those Lords of Appeal ('law lords') created life peers to assist the House in its judicial duties. Hereditary peerages carry a right to sit in the House (subject to certain disqualifications), provided the holder establishes his or her claim and is 21 years of age or over, but anyone succeeding to a peerage may, within 12 months of succession, disclaim that peerage for his or her lifetime. Disclaimants lose their right to sit in the House but gain the right to vote at parliamentary elections and to offer themselves for election to the House of Commons.

Temporal peerages, both hereditary and life, are conferred on the advice of the Prime Minister. They are usually granted either in recognition of service in politics or other walks of life or because the Government of the day wishes to have the recipient in the House of Lords. The House also provides a place in Parliament for men and women whose advice is useful to the State, but who do not wish to be involved in party politics.

In mid-1986 there were 1,175 members of the House of Lords, including the two archbishops and 24 bishops. The Lords Temporal consisted of 761 hereditary peers who had succeeded to their titles, 29 hereditary peers who have had their titles conferred on them (including the Prince of Wales), and 359 life peers, of whom 21 were 'law lords'. Of the total, 92 peers were not in receipt of a writ of summons and 136 peers were on leave of absence from the House (see below). Of the 114 Irish peers 47 were entitled to sit in the House of Lords because they were holders of an English, Scottish or United Kingdom peerage. Other Irish peerages which pre-date the union of Great Britain and Ireland in 1800 do not entitle their holders to membership of the House of Lords.

Not all peers with a right to sit in the House of Lords attend the sittings.[1] Peers who frequently attend the House (the average daily attendance is about 320) include elder statesmen and others who have spent their lives in public service. They receive no salary for their parliamentary work, but can recover expenses incurred in attending the House and certain travelling expenses (for which there are maximum daily rates).

The House is presided over by the Lord Chancellor, who takes his place on the woolsack[2] as *ex-officio* Speaker of the House. In his absence his place may be taken by a deputy speaker, a deputy chairman or, if neither is present, by a speaker chosen by the Lords present. The first of the deputy speakers is the Lord Chairman of Committees, who is appointed at the beginning of each session and takes the chair in all committees, unless the House decides otherwise. The Lord

---

[1] Some hereditary peers do not establish their claim to succeed and so do not receive a writ of summons entitling them to sit in the House. Lords may apply for leave of absence for the duration, or for the remainder, of a Parliament.

[2] The woolsack is a seat in the form of a large cushion stuffed with wool from several Commonwealth countries; it is a relic from the medieval period when wool was the greatest source of the country's wealth.

Chairman and the Principal Deputy Chairman of Committees are salaried officers of the House.

The permanent officers include the Clerk of the Parliaments who is responsible for the records of proceedings, including judgments, and for the promulgation of Acts of Parliament, and who is also the accounting officer for money voted to the House; the other Clerks at the Table who, with the Clerk of the Parliaments and the other officers and officials of the House, are collectively known as the Parliament Office; the Gentleman Usher of the Black Rod, who is also Serjeant at Arms in attendance upon the Lord Chancellor and is responsible for security and for accommodation and services in the House of Lords' part of the Palace of Westminster; and the Yeoman Usher who is Deputy Serjeant at Arms and assists Black Rod in his duties.

The House of Commons

The House of Commons is elected by universal adult suffrage and consists of 650 Members of Parliament (MPs). At present 27 are women. Of the 650 seats, 523 are for England, 38 for Wales, 72 for Scotland, and 17 for Northern Ireland.

General elections are held after a Parliament has been dissolved and a new one summoned by the Queen. When an MP dies or resigns[1] or is given a peerage, a by-election takes place. Members are paid an annual salary of £18,500 (from January 1987) and an allowance of £20,140 for secretarial and research expenses. They also have a number of other allowances, including travel allowances, a supplement for London members and, for provincial members, subsistence allowances and allowances for second homes. (For ministers' salaries, see p 49.)

The chief officer of the House of Commons is the Speaker, elected by MPs to preside over the House. Other officers are the Chairman of Ways and Means, and two deputy chairmen who act as Deputy Speakers, elected by the House on the nomination of the Government. They, like the Speaker, neither speak nor vote other than in their official capacity. The House is administered by a Commission chaired by the Speaker.

Permanent officers (who are not MPs) include the Clerk of the House of Commons, who is the principal adviser to the Speaker of the House on its privileges and procedures; his department has responsibilities relating to the conduct of the business of the House and its many committees. The Clerk is also accounting officer for the House. The Serjeant at Arms, who waits upon the Speaker, carries out certain orders of the House, is the official housekeeper of the Commons part of the building, and is responsible for its security. Other officers serve the House in the Library, the Department of the Official Report (*Hansard*), the Administration Department and the Refreshment Department.

Parliamentary Electoral System

For electoral purposes the United Kingdom is divided into constituencies, each of which returns one member to the House of Commons. To ensure equitable representation four permanent Boundary Commissions, one each for England, Wales, Scotland and Northern Ireland, make periodic reviews of constituencies and recommend any redistribution of seats that may seem necessary in the light of population movements or other changes. Their last recommendations were submitted to Parliament in 1982–83 and formed the basis for the constituencies in the 1983 general election.

Elections are by secret ballot. British citizens and citizens of other Commonwealth countries, together with citizens of the Irish Republic, may vote provided

---

[1] An MP who wishes to resign from the House can do so only by using the technical device of applying for an office under the Crown (Bailiff of the Chiltern Hundreds or Steward of the Manor of Northstead), ancient offices which disqualify the holder from membership of the House but which carry no salary and have no responsibilities.

they are aged 18 or over, resident in the United Kingdom, registered in the annual register of electors for the constituency and not subject to any disqualification. People not entitled to vote include members of the House of Lords, patients detained under mental health legislation, sentenced prisoners and people convicted within the previous five years of corrupt or illegal election practices. Service voters (members of the armed forces and their spouses, Crown servants and staff of the British Council employed overseas, together with their wives or husbands if accompanying them) may be registered for an address in a constituency where they would live but for their service.

Each elector may cast one vote, normally in person at a polling station. Service voters resident abroad and merchant seamen may vote by proxy or, if in the United Kingdom at the time of the election, by post. Electors who are physically incapacitated or unable to vote in person because of the nature of their work are also entitled to vote by post. The Representation of the People Act 1985 extends (from February 1987) the franchise to British citizens abroad for a period of five years after leaving the United Kingdom and extends the right to apply for an absent vote to all those who, including holidaymakers, cannot reasonably be expected to vote in person at the polling station.

Voting is not compulsory; nearly 73 per cent of a total electorate of some 42 million people voted in the general election of June 1983. The candidate who polls the most votes in a constituency is elected.

British citizens and citizens of other Commonwealth countries, together with citizens of the Irish Republic, may stand and be elected as MPs provided they are aged 21 or over and are not subject to any disqualification. Those disqualified include undischarged bankrupts; people sentenced to more than one year's imprisonment; clergy of the Church of England, Church of Scotland, Church of Ireland and Roman Catholic Church; peers; and holders of certain offices listed in the House of Commons Disqualification Act 1975. The latter include holders of judicial office, civil servants, some local government officers, members of the regular armed forces, or the police service, some members of public corporations and government commissions, and in addition British members of the legislature of any country or territory outside the Commonwealth. A candidate's nomination for election must be signed by two electors as proposer and seconder, and by eight other electors registered in the constituency. He or she does not require any party backing. A candidate must also deposit £500, which is forfeited if his or her votes do not exceed 5 per cent of those validly cast.

The maximum sum a candidate may spend on an election campaign is £3,240 plus 2·8 pence for each elector in a borough constituency or 3·7 pence for each elector in a county constituency. A candidate may post an election address to each elector in the constituency, free of charge. All election expenses, apart from the candidate's personal expenses, are subject to the statutory limit.

The Political Party System

The party system, existing in one form or another since the eighteenth century, is an essential element in the working of the constitution.

The present system relies heavily upon the existence of organised political parties, each laying policies before the electorate for approval. The parties are not registered or formally recognised in law, but in practice most candidates in elections, and almost all winning candidates, belong to one of the main parties.

For the last 150 years a predominantly two-party system has operated, and since 1945 either the Conservative Party, which can trace its origins to the eighteenth century, or the Labour Party, which emerged in the last decade of the nineteenth century, has held power. The Liberal Party, which last formed a government on its own in 1906–16, can also trace its origins to the eighteenth century, while the Social Democratic Party was formed in 1981 and made an alliance with the Liberal Party in the same year. Other parties include two nationalist parties, Plaid Cymru (founded in Wales in 1925) and the Scottish National Party (founded in 1934). In Northern Ireland there are a number of parties; the largest of those represented in the House of Commons are the Ulster Unionist Party, which was formed in the early part of this century, and the Democratic Unionist Party, founded in 1971 by a group which broke away from the Ulster Unionists.

The percentages of votes cast for the main political parties in the general election of June 1983 and the resulting distribution of seats in the House of Commons are given in Table 3.

Table 3: Percentages of Votes Cast, and Members Elected, in the 1983 General Election

Party	% of votes cast	Party	Members elected
Conservative	42·4	Conservative	397
Labour	27·6	Labour	209
Liberal–Social Democratic Alliance	25·4	Liberal	17
		Social Democratic	6
Others	4·6	Scottish National	2
		Plaid Cymru (Welsh Nationalist)	2
		Ulster Unionist (Northern Ireland)	11
		Democratic Unionist (Northern Ireland)	3
		Ulster Popular Unionist (Northern Ireland)	1
		Social Democratic and Labour (Northern Ireland)	1
		Sinn Fein (Northern Ireland)[a]	1
		Total	650

[a] The member of Sinn Fein (the political wing of the Provisional IRA) has not taken his seat.

Note: On 1 August 1986 the state of the parties (excluding the Speaker and his three deputies) was as follows: Conservative 391; Labour 208; Liberal 19; Social Democratic 7; Scottish National 2; Plaid Cymru (Welsh Nationalist) 2; Ulster Unionist 10; Democratic Unionist 3; Ulster Popular Unionist 1; Social Democratic and Labour 2; Sinn Fein 1.

The party which wins most seats (although not necessarily the most votes) at a general election, or which has the support of a majority of members in the House of Commons, usually forms the Government. By tradition, the leader of the majority party is asked by the Sovereign to form a government; and about 100 of its members in the House of Commons and the House of Lords receive ministerial appointments (including appointment to the Cabinet—see p 49) on the advice of the Prime Minister. The largest minority party becomes the official Opposition with its own leader and 'shadow cabinet'.

Leaders of the Government and Opposition sit on the front benches of the Commons with their supporters (the back-benchers) sitting behind them. Similar arrangements for the parties also apply to the House of Lords; however, Lords who do not wish to be associated with either the Government or the Opposition may sit on the 'cross-benches'. The effectiveness of the party system in Parliament rests largely on the relationship between the Government and the opposition parties. Depending on the relative voting strengths of the parties in the House of Commons, the Opposition might seek to overthrow the Government by securing its defeat on a 'matter of confidence'. In general, however, its aims are to contribute to the formulation of policy and legislation by constructive criticism; to oppose government proposals that it considers objectionable; to secure concessions on government Bills; and to increase public support and enhance its chances of electoral success.

The detailed arrangements of government business are settled, under the direction of the Prime Minister and the Leaders of the two Houses, by the Chief Government Whips in consultation with the Chief Opposition Whips. The Chief Whips together constitute the 'usual channels' often referred to when the question of finding time for debating some particular issue is discussed. The Leaders of the two Houses are primarily responsible for the direction of business and for providing facilities for the Houses to debate matters about which they are concerned.

Outside Parliament, party control is exercised by the national and local organisations. Inside Parliament, it is exercised by the Chief Whips and their assistants (chosen within the party) whose duties include keeping members informed of forthcoming parliamentary business, maintaining the party's voting strength by ensuring that members attend important debates, and conveying to the party leadership the opinions of back-bench members. The importance a party attaches to a vote on a particular issue is indicated to the MPs by the underlining (once, twice or three times) on the notice sent to them; failure to comply with a 'three-line whip' is usually seen as rebellion against the party's policy. Party discipline tends to be less strong in the Lords than in the Commons.

The Chief Government Whip in the Commons is Parliamentary Secretary to the Treasury; of the other Government Whips, three (one of whom is Deputy Chief Whip) are officers of the Royal Household, five hold titular posts as Lords Commissioners of the Treasury and five are Assistant Whips. Salaries are also paid to the Chief Opposition Whips in both Houses and to two of the Opposition Assistant Whips in the Commons. The Government Whips in the Lords hold offices in the Royal Household and act as government spokesmen.

Annual assistance from public funds helps opposition parties to carry out their parliamentary work at Westminster. It is limited to parties which had at least two members elected at the previous general election or one member elected and a minimum of 150,000 votes cast. The amount is: £1,500 for every seat won plus £3 for every 200 votes, up to a maximum of £450,000. Since 1945 there have been six Conservative and six Labour Governments and the great majority of members of the House of Commons have represented either the Conservative or the Labour Party.

Parliamentary Procedure

Parliamentary procedure is based on custom and precedent, partly formulated in standing orders governing details of practice in each House. The system of debate is much the same in the two Houses: the subject originates in the form of a motion (a proposal made by a member in order to elicit a decision from the House). When a motion has been moved, the Speaker proposes the question as the subject of debate. At the end of each debate the question may be agreed to without voting, or else is decided by a vote on a simple majority. The main difference between the two Houses is that in the Lords the office of Speaker carries with it no authority to check or curtail debate, such matters being decided by the general sense of the House, whereas in the Commons the Speaker has full authority to give effect, promptly and decisively, to the rules and orders of the House. The Speaker of the Commons must guard against abuse of procedure or infringement of minority rights; has discretion to allow or disallow

ROYAL OCCASIONS

The Queen and the Duke of Edinburgh –
a portrait taken by the Duke of York
to mark Her Majesty's sixtieth birthday
on 21 April 1986.

Below: The Duke and Duchess of York
driving to Buckingham Palace after their
marriage in Westminster Abbey on
23 July 1986.

ARCHITECTURAL HERITAGE

Little Moreton Hall, Cheshire

Background: Housesteads, Hadrian's Wall,
Northumberland

Craigievar Castle,
Grampian

Castle Coole,
Co. Fermanagh

Powis Castle, Powys

YOUNG PEOPLE

Children in the Tredworth Junior School, Gloucestershire, involved in multicultural studies. The school has over 200 pupils with 33 ethnic minorities represented.

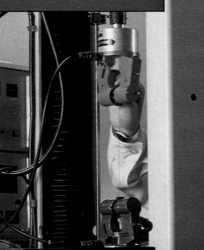

The Duke of Edinburgh's Award Scheme, which celebrated its thirtieth anniversary in 1986, enables young people to take part in activities in four areas: physical recreation (pictured here), community care, expeditions and the development of personal interests and social and practical skills.

In 1986–87 about 360,000 young people are expected to enter the Youth Training Scheme, which was first introduced in 1983. Here, a trainee works in a Scottish medical electronics company.

a closure motion (to end discussion so that the matter may be put to the vote); and has powers to check irrelevance and repetition in debate, and to save time in other respects. In cases of grave disorder the House can be adjourned or the sitting suspended by the Speaker. Voting in the Commons is under the direction of the Speaker, whose duty it is to pronounce the final result. In the event of a tied vote the Speaker gives the casting vote, but only in accordance with established conventions which preclude an expression of opinion on the merits of the question.

The voting procedure in the House of Lords is similar to that in the Commons, except that the Speaker or chairman has an original, but no casting, vote. Bills and subordinate legislation are in general allowed to proceed in the form before the House unless a majority votes to reject or amend them; on other motions the question is decided in the negative unless there is a majority in favour. When the House is sitting judicially (the Lords is the final court of appeal for civil cases in Britain and for criminal cases in England, Wales and Northern Ireland) the judgment under appeal is not changed if the votes are equal.

The Commons has a public register of MPs' financial interests. Members with a relevant pecuniary interest in a matter before the House, direct or indirect, must declare it when taking part in a debate, though to act as a disqualification from voting the interest must be direct, immediate and personal. In any other proceedings of the House or in transactions with other members or with ministers or civil servants, MPs must also disclose any relevant financial interest or benefit.

Proceedings of both Houses are public, except on extremely rare occasions; the minutes (in the Commons called Votes and Proceedings and in the Lords, Minutes of Proceedings) and the speeches (The Official Report of Parliamentary Debates, *Hansard*) are published daily. The records of the Lords from 1497 and of the Commons from 1547, together with the parliamentary and political papers of certain past members of the Houses, are available to the public on application to the House of Lords Record Office. Parliament is not normally televised, but proceedings are recorded and sound transmissions of some are made on television and radio, either live or recorded. A Parliamentary Sound Archive has been established. Debates on televising proceedings have taken place on several occasions and, most recently, in November 1985 the House of Commons voted against televising its proceedings. A televised broadcasting experiment of proceedings in the Lords began in early 1985 and in May 1986 the House authorised the televising to continue.

Legislative Proceedings

The law undergoes constant reform in the courts as established principles are interpreted, clarified or reapplied to meet new circumstances, but substantial changes are the responsibility of Parliament and the Government through the normal legislative process.

A draft law takes the form of a parliamentary Bill. Most Bills are public Bills involving measures relating to public policy, but there are also private Bills which deal solely with matters of individual, corporate or local interest. Hybrid Bills are public Bills which may in certain respects affect private rights, and their passage through Parliament is governed by a special procedure which allows those affected to make representations. Public Bills can be introduced, in either House, by a government minister or by a 'private' member. Most public Bills that become law are in practice sponsored by the Government.

Before a government Bill is finally drafted, there is normally considerable consultation with professional bodies, voluntary organisations and other agencies interested in the subject matter, such as major interest and pressure groups which aim to promote a specific cause. Proposals for legislative changes are sometimes set out in government 'White Papers' which may be debated in

Parliament before a Bill is introduced. From time to time consultative documents, sometimes called 'Green Papers', set out for public discussion government proposals which are still at a formative stage.

Bills must be passed by each House. As a rule government Bills likely to raise political controversy go through the Commons before the Lords, while those of an intricate but uncontroversial nature often pass through the Lords first. (Consolidation Bills are always introduced in the House of Lords.) A Bill with a mainly financial purpose is nearly always introduced in the Commons, and a Bill involving taxation must be based on resolutions agreed by that House, often after debate, before it can be introduced. If the main object of a Bill is to create a public charge, it can only be introduced by a minister or, if brought from the Lords, be proceeded with in the Commons if taken up by a minister, an arrangement which gives the Government considerable control over legislation.

At the beginning of each session private members of the Commons ballot for precedence in introducing a Bill on one of the Fridays specially allocated; the first 20 are successful. After the ballot a private member may also present a Bill after question time (see p 45), or seek to introduce a Bill under the 'ten minute rule' which allows two speeches, one in favour of and one against the measure, after which the House decides whether to allow the Bill to be brought in. Private members' Bills do not often proceed very far, but a few become law each session. If one secures a second reading, the Government usually introduces any necessary money resolution. Private members' Bills may be introduced in the House of Lords at any time, but the time that can be given to them in the Commons is strictly limited.

The process of passing a public Bill is similar in both Houses. The Bill receives a formal first reading on introduction, is printed, and after a while (between one day and several weeks depending on the nature of the Bill) is given a second reading after a debate on its general principles and merits. In the Commons a non-controversial Bill may be referred to a second reading committee to decide whether it should be read a second time. After a second reading in the Commons, a Bill is usually referred for detailed examination to a standing committee (see p 43). If the House so decides, the Bill may be referred to the whole House sitting in committee. The committee stage is followed by the report stage, during which further amendments may be considered. At the third reading a Bill is reviewed in its final form and may again be debated. The House may vote to limit the time devoted to examining a Bill by passing a government timetable motion, commonly referred to as a 'guillotine'. After the third reading a Commons Bill is sent to the Lords where it goes through broadly the same stages. In the Lords, after the second reading, a Bill is considered by a committee of the whole House unless the House takes the rare decision to refer it to a Public Bill Committee. It is then considered on report and read a third time; at all these stages amendments may be made. A Bill which starts in the Lords and is passed by that House is then sent to the Commons for all the stages there. Amendments made by the second House generally must be agreed by the first, or a compromise reached, before a Bill can become law.

Most government Bills introduced and passed in the Lords pass through the Commons without difficulty because of their non-controversial nature. However, if a non-governmental Lords Bill were unacceptable to the Commons it would generally not become law since no debating time would be allotted to it. The Lords, on the other hand, do not in general prevent a Bill insisted upon by the Commons from finally becoming law. Normally they either accept the Bill without changes, or amend and return it for consideration by the Commons, who frequently agree to the amendments made. In practice, the Lords pass without amendment Bills authorising taxation or national expenditure. A Bill that deals only with taxation or expenditure must become law within one month of being sent to the Lords, whether or not they agree to it, unless the Commons directs otherwise. If no agreement is reached between the two Houses on a non-financial Commons Bill (or an amendment to it) the Lords can in practice delay the Bill (with certain exceptions) for about 13 months. At the end of this time it may, in accordance with the Parliament Acts, be submitted to the Queen for royal assent, provided it has again been passed by the Commons. A Bill to lengthen the life of a Parliament would require the full assent of both Houses in the normal way.

The limitations on the power of the Lords, contained in the Parliament Acts 1911 and 1949, are based on the belief that the principal legislative function of the non-elected House nowadays is to act as a chamber of revision, complementing, not rivalling, the elected House.

When a Bill has passed through all its parliamentary stages, it is sent to the Queen for royal assent, after which it is part of the law of the land and known as an Act of Parliament. The royal assent has not been refused since 1707.

Private Bills, promoted by people or organisations outside Parliament (often local authorities) to give them special powers not granted by the general law, go through substantially the same procedure as public Bills, but most of the work is done in committee, where procedures follow a semi-judicial pattern: the promoter must prove the need for the powers or privileges sought and the objections of opposing interests are heard. Both sides may be legally represented.

Delegated Legislation

Delegated legislation, used to relieve pressure on parliamentary time, gives ministers and other authorities the power to regulate administrative details after a law has been passed. To minimise the risk that powers thus conferred on the executive might supersede or weaken parliamentary government, they are normally delegated to authorities directly responsible to Parliament. Moreover, the Acts of Parliament by which particular powers are delegated normally provide for some measure of parliamentary control over legislation made in carrying out these powers, for instance, by reserving to Parliament the right to affirm or annul the orders themselves. Certain Acts also require direct consultation with organisations affected before rules and orders can be made.

A joint committee of both Houses reports on the technical propriety of these 'statutory instruments'. In order to save time on the floor of the House, where statutory instruments may be considered, the Commons also uses standing committees to consider the merits of instruments, with any decisions reserved to the House.

Parliamentary Committees
Committees of the Whole House

Either House may resolve itself into a committee (of the whole House) to consider Bills in detail after their second reading. A committee of the whole House is presided over by the Chairman of Ways and Means (the Chairman of Committees in the House of Lords) or a deputy chairman.

Standing Committees

House of Commons standing committees include those which examine public Bills at the committee stage and, in certain cases, at the second reading and report stages; two Scottish standing committees; the Scottish Grand Committee; the Welsh Grand Committee; and the Northern Ireland standing committee. Ordinary standing committees have no distinctive names, being referred to simply as Standing Committee A, B, C, and so on, and are each appointed specially to consider a specific Bill. Each has between 16 and 50 members with a party balance reflecting as far as possible that in the House as a whole. The Scottish Grand Committee, which comprises all 72 Scottish members and 10 to 15 others (and may be convened in Edinburgh), considers the principles of Scottish Bills referred to it at second reading stage, the Scottish estimates and other matters concerning Scotland only. The Welsh Grand Committee, with all 38 Welsh members and up to five others, considers Bills referred to it at second reading stage, and matters concerning Wales only. The Northern Ireland committee considers matters relating specifically to Northern Ireland. A standing committee on regional affairs attended by any of the 523 members from the English constituencies is occasionally appointed to consider matters relating to the English regions. The Lords' equivalent to a standing committee, a Public Bill Committee, is rarely used.

Select Committees

In 1979 a new House of Commons select committee structure was set up in an attempt to provide closer examination of government departments and policies, and of the way ministers discharge their responsibilities.

This was in response to a recognition that Parliament was probably less effective a check on the executive than it had been for much of the nineteenth century. With the growth of mass political parties, the individual independence of many MPs has tended to become subordinated to party interests, and with the great extension of the range and complexity of central government activities, and the parallel growth of bureaucracy, MPs have a more difficult task in checking the actions of ministers and their departments.

The 14 committees examine the expenditure, administration and policy of the main government departments and related bodies. The Foreign Affairs Committee, for example, 'shadows' the work of the Foreign and Commonwealth Office, and there are select committees on Scottish and Welsh Affairs. The committees are constituted on a party basis, in approximate proportions to party strength in the House. Other regular committees include those on European Legislation, Defence, Public Accounts, Members' Interests, the Parliamentary Commissioner for Administration, and Sound Broadcasting. The Committee of Selection and the Standing Orders Committee have duties relating to private Bills, and the Committee of Selection also chooses members to serve on standing and select committees. A Liaison Committee considers general matters relating to select committees. On rare occasions a parliamentary Bill is examined by a select committee, a procedure additional to the usual legislative process—(an example of this which occurs every few years is the Armed Forces Bill).

In their scrutiny of government policies, the committees question ministers, senior civil servants and interested bodies and individuals. Through hearings and published reports, they bring before Parliament and the public a body of fact and informed opinion on many important issues, and build up considerable expertise in their subjects of inquiry.

In the House of Lords, besides the Appeal and Appellate Committees in which the bulk of the House's judicial work is transacted, there are two major select committees with several sub-committees on the European Communities and on Science and Technology. There are also select committees on House of Lords' Offices, Hybrid Instruments, Leave of Absence and Lords' Expenses, Personal Bills, Private Bills, Standing Orders, Privileges, Procedure, Selection and Sound Broadcasting and Television.

Joint Committees

Joint committees are also appointed in each session to deal with Consolidation Bills and delegated legislation. The two Houses may also agree to set up joint select committees on other subjects.

Party Committees

In addition to the official committees of the two Houses there are several unofficial party organisations or committees. The Conservative and Unionist Members' Committee (the 1922 Committee) consists of the back-bench membership of the party in the House of Commons. When the Conservative Party is in office, ministers attend its meetings by invitation and not by right, but when the party is in opposition, the whole membership of the party may attend meetings and the leader appoints a consultative committee which acts as the party's 'shadow cabinet'. The Parliamentary Labour Party is a corporate body comprising all members of the party in both Houses; when the Labour Party is in office a liaison committee acts as a channel of communication between the Government and its back-benchers in both Houses; when the party is in opposition the Parliamentary Labour Party is organised under the direction of an elected Parliamentary Committee which acts as the 'shadow cabinet'.

Other Forms of Parliamentary Control

The effectiveness of parliamentary control of the Government is a subject of continuing discussion, both inside and outside Parliament. Control is exercised finally by the ability of the House of Commons to force the Government to resign by passing a resolution of 'no confidence' or by rejecting a proposal which the Government considers so vital to its policy that it has made it a 'matter of confidence' or, ultimately, by refusing to vote the money required for the public service. In addition to the system of close scrutiny by select committees, the House of Commons offers a number of opportunities for a searching examination of government policy by both the Opposition and the Government's own back-benchers.

These include:

1. Question time when for an hour on Monday, Tuesday, Wednesday and Thursday, ministers answer MPs' questions. The Prime Minister's question time takes place on Tuesday and Thursday. Parliamentary questions are one means of eliciting information about the Government's intentions, as well as a way of airing, and possibly securing redress of, grievances brought to MPs' notice by constituents. MPs may also put questions to ministers for written answers, which are published in *Hansard*, the official report. (At question time in the House of Lords questions are addressed to the Government rather than to a particular minister.)

2. The right of MPs to use motions for the adjournment of the House to open discussions on constituency cases or matters of public concern. There is a half-hour adjournment period at the end of the business of the day; and immediately before the adjournment for each recess (Christmas, Easter, spring and summer), a full day is spent discussing matters raised by private members. Moreover, an MP wishing to discuss a 'specific and important matter that should have urgent consideration' may, at the end of question time, ask leave to move the adjournment of the House. If the Speaker accepts the terms of the motion, the MP asks the House for leave for the motion to be put forward. Leave can be given unanimously, or it can be given if 40 or more MPs support the motion or if fewer than 40 but more than ten support it and the House (on a vote) is in favour. Once leave has been given, the matter is debated for three hours, usually on the next day.

3. The 19 Opposition days each session when the Opposition can choose subjects for debate.

4. Debates on the occasion of the passage, three times a year, of Consolidated Fund or Appropriation Bills, when members can exercise their traditional right of 'raising grievances', on matters for which any minister is responsible, when voting the necessary supplies (money) for the Crown.

Procedural opportunities for criticism of the Government also arise during the debate on the Queen's speech at the beginning of a session, during debates or motions of censure for which the Government gives up part of its own time, and during debates on the Government's legislative proposals.

Opportunities for criticism and examination of government policy are provided in the House of Lords at daily question time, during debates on specific motions and in questions (which can be debated) at the end of the day's business as well as during debates on specific legislative proposals.

The main responsibilities of Parliament, and more particularly of the House of Commons, in managing the revenue of the State and payments for the public service are to authorise the taxes and duties to be levied and the various objects of expenditure and the sum to be spent on each. It also has to satisfy itself that the sums granted are spent only for the purposes which Parliament intended. No payment out of the central Government's public funds can be made and no taxation, charges or loans authorised, except by Act of Parliament, although interim payments can be made, within limits, from the Contingencies Fund. Scrutiny of public expenditure is carried out by House of Commons Select Committees (see p 44).

To keep the two Houses informed of European Community developments, and to enable them to scrutinise and debate Community policies and proposals, there is a select committee in each House (see p 44), and ministers make regular statements about Community business.

Parliamentary Commissioner for Administration

The Parliamentary Commissioner for Administration (the 'Parliamentary Ombudsman') investigates, independently, complaints of maladministration when asked to do so by MPs on behalf of members of the public. Powers of investigation extend to administrative actions by central government departments but not to policy decisions (which can be questioned in Parliament) nor to matters affecting relations with other countries. Complaints by British citizens arising from dealings with British posts overseas are open to investigation in some circumstances. The Commissioner has access to departmental papers and reports the findings to the MP who presented the complaint. The Commissioner is required to report annually to Parliament. In addition, he or she publishes details of selected investigations at quarterly intervals and may submit other reports where necessary. A Commons select committee has responsibility for overseeing the Commissioner's work.

Parliamentary Privilege

Each House of Parliament has certain rights and immunities to protect it from unnecessary obstruction in carrying out its duties. The rights apply collectively to each House and individually to each member.

For the Commons the Speaker formally claims 'their ancient and undoubted rights and privileges' at the beginning of each Parliament. These include freedom of speech; freedom from arrest in civil actions; exemption from serving on juries, attending as witnesses or serving as sheriffs; and the right of access to the Crown, a collective privilege of the House. Further privileges include the rights of the House to control its own proceedings (so that it is able, for instance, to exclude 'strangers' if it wishes), to pronounce upon legal disqualifications for membership and to declare a seat vacant on such grounds; and to penalise for breach of its privileges and for contempt.

The privileges of the House of Lords closely resemble those of the House of Commons.

The Privy Council

Until the eighteenth century, the Sovereign in Council, or Privy Council, was the chief source of executive power in the State. As the system of Cabinet government developed, however, the Privy Council became less prominent. Many powers were transferred to the Cabinet as an inner committee of the Council, and much of its work was handed over to newly created government departments, some of which were originally committees of the Privy Council.

Nowadays the main function of the Privy Council is to advise the Queen to approve Orders in Council (those made under prerogative powers, such as Orders approving the grant of royal charters of incorporation; and those made under statutory powers). Members of the Privy Council attending meetings at which Orders are made do not thereby become personally responsible for the policy upon which the Orders are based; this rests with the minister responsible for the subject matter of the Order in question, whether or not he or she was present at the meeting.

The Privy Council also advises the Crown on the issue of royal proclamations, some of the most important of which relate to prerogative acts (such as summoning or dissolving Parliament). The Council's own statutory responsibilities, which are independent of the powers of the Sovereign in Council, include powers of supervision over the registering bodies for the medical and allied professions.

Apart from Cabinet ministers, who must be Privy Counsellors and are sworn in on first assuming office, membership of the Council (retained for life except for very occasional removals) is accorded by the Sovereign on the recommendation of the Prime Minister to eminent people in independent monarchical countries of the Commonwealth. There are about 390 Privy Counsellors. A full Council is summoned only on the death of the Sovereign or when the Sovereign announces his or her intention to marry.

Committees of the Privy Council

There are a number of advisory Privy Council committees whose meetings differ from those of the Privy Council itself in that the Sovereign cannot constitutionally be present. These may be prerogative committees, such as those dealing with legislative matters submitted by the legislatures of the Channel Islands and the Isle of Man and with applications for charters of incorporation; or they may be provided for by statute as are those for the universities of Oxford and Cambridge and the Scottish universities.

The Judicial Committee of the Privy Council is the final court of appeal from the courts of the United Kingdom dependencies, courts of independent members of the Commonwealth which have not discontinued the appeal, courts of the Channel Islands and the Isle of Man, and certain other courts, some professional and disciplinary committees and ecclesiastical sources.

Administrative work is carried out in the Privy Council Office under the Lord President of the Council, a Cabinet minister.

Her Majesty's Government

Her Majesty's Government is the body of ministers responsible for the administration of national affairs.

The Prime Minister is appointed by the Queen, and all other ministers are appointed by the Queen on the recommendation of the Prime Minister.

The majority of ministers are members of the Commons, although the Government is also fully represented by ministers in the Lords. The Lord Chancellor is always a member of the House of Lords.

Composition

The composition of governments can vary both in the number of ministers and in the titles of some offices. New ministerial offices may be created, others may be abolished, and functions may be transferred from one minister to another.

Prime Minister

The Prime Minister is also, by tradition, First Lord of the Treasury and Minister for the Civil Service. The head of the Government became known as the Prime Minister during the eighteenth century. The Prime Minister's unique position of authority derives from majority support in Parliament and from the power to choose ministers and to obtain their resignation or dismissal individually. By modern convention, the Prime Minister always sits in the House of Commons.

The Prime Minister informs the Queen of the general business of the Government, presides over the Cabinet, and is responsible for the allocation of functions among ministers.

The Prime Minister's other responsibilities include recommending to the Queen a number of appointments. These include: Church of England archbishops, bishops and deans and some 200 other clergy in Crown 'livings'; high judicial offices, such as the Lord Chief Justice, Lords of Appeal in Ordinary, and the Lords Justices of Appeal; Privy Counsellors, Lords-Lieutenant and certain civil appointments, such as Lord High Commissioner to the General Assembly of the Church of Scotland, Poet Laureate, Constable of the Tower, and some university posts; and appointments to various public boards and institutions, such as the British Broadcasting Corporation, as well as various royal and statutory commissions. Recommendations are likewise made for the award of many civil honours and distinctions and of Civil List pensions (to people who have achieved eminence in science and the arts and are in some financial need). The Prime Minister also selects the trustees of certain national museums and institutions.

The Prime Minister's Office at 10 Downing Street (the official residence in central London) has a staff of civil servants who attend to the day-to-day discharge of the Prime Minister's numerous responsibilities. The Prime Minister may also appoint special advisers to the Office from time to time to assist in the formation of policies.

Departmental Ministers

Ministers in charge of government departments, who are usually in the Cabinet, are known as 'Secretary of State' or 'Minister', or may have a special title, as in the case of the Chancellor of the Exchequer.

Non-Departmental Ministers

The holders of various traditional offices, namely the Lord President of the Council, the Chancellor of the Duchy of Lancaster, the Lord Privy Seal, the Paymaster General and, from time to time, Ministers without Portfolio, may have few or no departmental duties and are thus available to perform any special duties the Prime Minister may wish to give them. In the present Government the Lord President of the Council, for example, co-ordinates the presentation of information on government policies and the Paymaster General is Minister for Employment in the Department of Employment.

Lord Chancellor and Law Officers

The Lord Chancellor holds a special position, being a minister with departmental functions and also head of the judiciary. The four Law Officers of the Crown are: for England and Wales, the Attorney General and the Solicitor General; for Scotland, the Lord Advocate and the Solicitor General for Scotland.

Ministers of State

Ministers of State usually work with ministers in charge of departments with responsibility for specific functions, and are sometimes given titles which reflect these particular functions. More than one may work in a department. A Minister of State may be given a seat in the Cabinet and paid accordingly.

Junior Ministers

Junior ministers (generally Parliamentary Under-Secretaries of State or, where the senior minister is not a Secretary of State, simply Parliamentary Secretaries) share in parliamentary and departmental duties. They may also be given responsibility, directly under the departmental minister, for specific aspects of the department's work. The Parliamentary Secretary to the Treasury and other Lords Commissioners of the Treasury are in a different category as Government Whips (see p 40).

Ministerial Salaries

The salaries of ministers in the House of Commons range from £30,760 a year (from January 1987) for junior ministers to £47,020 for Cabinet ministers. The Prime Minister receives £58,650 and the Lord Chancellor (from July 1986) £79,400.[1]

Ministers in the Commons, including the Prime Minister, receive a parliamentary salary of £13,875 a year (which is included in the above figures) in recognition of their constituency responsibilities and are entitled to claim the other allowances which are paid to all MPs (see p 37).[2]

The Cabinet

The Cabinet is composed of about 20 ministers chosen by the Prime Minister and may include departmental and non-departmental ministers. Its origins can be traced back to the informal conferences which the Sovereign held with leading ministers, independently of the Privy Council, during the seventeenth century. After the Sovereign's withdrawal from an active role in politics in the eighteenth century, and the development of organised political parties stimulated by successive extensions of the franchise from 1832 onwards, the Cabinet assumed its modern form.

The functions of the Cabinet are: the final determination of policies, the supreme control of government and the co-ordination of government departments. The exercise of these functions is vitally affected by the fact that the Cabinet is a group of party representatives, depending upon majority support in the House of Commons.

Cabinet Meetings

The Cabinet meets in private and its proceedings are confidential. Its members are bound by their oath as Privy Counsellors not to disclose information about its proceedings; although after Cabinet papers have been in existence for 30 years they may be made available for inspection in the Public Record Office. Diaries published by several former ministers have given the public an insight into Cabinet procedures in recent times.

Normally the Cabinet meets for a few hours once or twice a week during parliamentary sittings, and rather less often when Parliament is not sitting. To keep the amount of work coming before the Cabinet within manageable limits, a great deal of work is carried on through the committee system, which involves the reference of issues either to a standing Cabinet committee or to an *ad hoc* committee composed of the ministers primarily concerned. The committee then considers the matter in detail and either disposes of it or reports upon it to the Cabinet with recommendations for action. The present Cabinet has four standing committees: a defence and overseas policy committee and an economic strategy committee both under the chairmanship of the Prime Minister; and a home and social affairs committee and a legislation committee, both under the chairmanship of the Lord President of the Council. Sub-committees of the standing committees may be established. Membership and terms of reference of all Cabinet committees are confidential.

Non-Cabinet ministers may be invited to attend meetings on matters affecting their departments, and may be members of Cabinet committees. The Secretary of the Cabinet and other senior officials of the Cabinet Office also attend meetings of the Cabinet and its committees as appropriate.

The Cabinet Office

The Cabinet Office, headed by the Secretary of the Cabinet, under the direction of the Prime Minister, comprises the Cabinet Secretariat, the Central Statistical Office, the Management and Personnel Office and the Historical Section.

---

[1] These figures show the salaries to which the holders are entitled; however, the Prime Minister and the Lord Chancellor of the present Government have decided to draw no more than the salary payable to other Cabinet ministers.

[2] The Leader of the Opposition in the Commons receives a salary for the post, as well as a parliamentary salary; the Leader of the Opposition in the Lords also receives a salary.

The Cabinet Secretariat serves ministers collectively in the conduct of Cabinet business and operates as an instrument in the co-ordination of policy at the highest level.

The Central Statistical Office is concerned with the preparation and interpretation of the statistics necessary to support economic and social policies and management, and co-ordinates the statistical work of other departments.

The Management and Personnel Office is responsible for the management and organisation of the Civil Service and recruitment into it, training, efficiency, personnel management and senior appointments.

The Historical Section of the Cabinet Office is in the process of completing the official histories of the second world war, and is responsible for the preparation of official histories of certain peacetime events.

Ministerial Responsibility

'Ministerial responsibility' refers both to the collective responsibility which ministers share for government policy and actions and to ministers' individual responsibility to Parliament for their departments' work.

The doctrine of collective responsibility means that the Cabinet acts unanimously even when Cabinet ministers do not all agree on a subject. The policy of departmental ministers must be consistent with the policy of the Government as a whole. Once the Government's policy on a matter has been decided, each minister is expected to support it or resign. On rare occasions, ministers have been allowed free votes in Parliament on government policies involving important issues of principle.

The individual responsibility of a minister for the work of his or her department means that, as political head of that department, he or she is answerable for all its acts and omissions and must bear the consequences of any defect of administration, any injustice to an individual or any aspect of policy which may be criticised in Parliament, whether personally responsible or not. Since most ministers are members of the House of Commons, they must answer questions and defend themselves against criticism in person. Departmental ministers in the House of Lords are represented in the Commons by someone qualified to speak on their behalf, usually a junior minister.

Departmental ministers normally decide all matters within their responsibility, although on important political matters they usually consult their colleagues collectively, through the Cabinet or a Cabinet committee. A decision by a departmental minister binds the Government as a whole.

The responsibility of ministers for their departments is an effective way of keeping government under public control, for the knowledge that any departmental action may be reported to and examined in Parliament discourages the taking of arbitrary and ill-considered decisions.

On assuming office ministers must resign directorships in private and public companies, and must order their affairs so that there is no conflict between public duties and private interests.

Government Departments

Government departments are the main instruments for giving effect to government policy when Parliament has passed the necessary legislation, and for advising ministers. They may, and frequently do, work with and through local authorities, statutory boards, and government-sponsored organisations operating under various degrees of government control.

A change of government does not necessarily affect the number or general functions of government departments, although a radical change in policy may be accompanied by some organisational change.

The work of some departments (for instance, the Ministry of Defence) covers the United Kingdom as a whole. Other departments (like the Department of Employment) cover England, Wales and Scotland, but not Northern Ireland. Others, such as the Department of the Environment, are mainly concerned with affairs in England.

Some departments, such as the Department of Trade and Industry, maintain a regional organisation, and some which have direct contact with the public throughout the country (for example, the Department of Employment) also have local offices.

A department is usually headed by a minister. Certain departments in which questions of policy do not normally arise are headed by a permanent official, and a minister with other duties is responsible for them to Parliament. For instance, ministers in the Treasury are responsible for the Central Office of Information, Her Majesty's Stationery Office, HM Customs and Excise, the Inland Revenue and a number of small departments including the Treasury Solicitor's Department, the Royal Mint, and the National Investment and Loans Office. Departments generally receive their funds directly out of money provided by Parliament and are staffed by the Civil Service.

Non-Departmental Public Bodies

A number of bodies with a role in the process of government are neither government departments nor part of a department (in April 1985 the figure was 1,653). Known as non-departmental public bodies, but often popularly described as 'quangos' ('quasi-autonomous non-governmental organisations', although there is no precise definition of the term), they are of three kinds: executive bodies, advisory bodies and tribunals. Executive bodies normally employ staff and have their own budget; they consist of public bodies which carry out, among other duties, administrative, executive, regulatory and commercial functions. They operate typically within broad policy guidelines set by departmental ministers but are in varying degrees independent of government in carrying out their day-to-day responsibilities. Examples include the Arts Council of Great Britain, the British Council, the Commonwealth Development Corporation and the Commission for Racial Equality. Tribunals are a specialised group of judicial bodies which are akin to courts of law. They are normally set up under statutory powers which also govern their constitution, functions and procedure. Tribunals often consist of laymen, but generally have a legally qualified chairman. They tend to be less expensive, and less formal, than courts of law. Independently of the executive, tribunals decide the rights and obligations of private citizens towards one another or towards a government department or other public authority. Important examples are industrial tribunals, rent tribunals and social security tribunals. Tribunals usually consist of an uneven number of people so that a majority decision can be reached. Members are normally appointed by the minister concerned with the subject. Tribunals and advisory bodies do not normally employ staff or spend money themselves, but their expenses are paid by government departments concerned; a note on advisory bodies is set out below.

As a result of reviews of non-departmental public bodies undertaken in 1979 and subsequently, nearly 700 have been abolished or otherwise rationalised with an annual saving of £100 million at 1984 prices. Scrutiny of these bodies continues with a new programme to improve performance and value for money announced at the end of 1984.

Advisory Bodies

Many government departments are assisted by advisory councils or committees which undertake research and collect information, mainly to give ministers access to informed opinion before coming to a decision involving a legislative or executive act. In some cases a minister must consult a standing committee, but usually advisory bodies are appointed at the discretion of the minister.

The membership of the advisory councils and committees varies according to the nature of the work involved, and will usually include representatives of varying interests and professions.

In addition to the standing advisory bodies, there are committees set up by the Government to examine and make recommendations on specific matters. For certain important inquiries Royal Commissions, whose members are chosen for their wide experience and diverse knowledge, may be appointed. Royal Commissions examine written and oral evidence from government departments, interested organisations and individuals, and submit recommendations. The Government may accept the recommendations in whole or in part, or may decide to take no further action or to delay action. Inquiries may also be undertaken by departmental committees.

Government Information Services

Each of the main government departments has its own information division or directorate, public relations branch or news department staffed by professional information officers responsible for communicating their department's policies and activities to the news media and the public (sometimes using publicity services provided by the Central Office of Information—see p 53) and for advising their department on the public's reaction to them. The presentation of government policy is co-ordinated, at official level, by the Prime Minister's Press Secretary. As press adviser to the Prime Minister, the Press Secretary and other staff in the Prime Minister's Press Office have direct and constant contact with the parliamentary press through regular meetings with the Lobby correspondents (a group of political correspondents who have the special privilege of access to the Lobby of the House of Commons where they can talk privately to government ministers and other members of the House) and other day-to-day contacts. The Prime Minister's Press Office forms the accepted channel through which information about parliamentary business is conveyed to the media.

Distribution of Functions

An outline of the principal functions of the main government departments is given below. Departments are arranged in alphabetical order, except for the Scottish and Northern Ireland departments which are grouped at the end of the section and the Cabinet Office, which was described on p 49. Further information on the work of some departments is given in later chapters under the relevant subject headings.

DEPARTMENT	Main areas of responsibility
	The work of many departments listed on pp 52–5 covers the United Kingdom as a whole. Where this is not the case, the following abbreviations are used: (GB) for functions covering England, Wales and Scotland; (E, W & NI) for those covering England, Wales and Northern Ireland; (E & W) for those covering England and Wales; and (E) for those concerned with England only.
Ministry of Agriculture, Fisheries and Food	Policies for agriculture, horticulture and fishing (E & W); food policies.
Office of Arts and Libraries	General promotion of arts (GB); library and information services (E with advice to W and NI); national museums (E); public libraries and local museums (E); British Library (E); national heritage.

DEPARTMENT	*Main areas of responsibility*
HM Customs and Excise	Collecting and accounting for revenues of Customs and Excise, including value added tax; agency functions including controlling certain imports and exports and compiling overseas trade statistics.
Ministry of Defence	Defence policy and control and administration of the armed services.
Department of Education and Science	General promotion of education (E); the Government's relations with universities (GB); fostering civil science in Britain and internationally.
Department of Employment	Manpower policies, labour legislation, payment of unemployment benefit through local offices and issue of work permits to workers from overseas; health and safety at work; small businesses; tourism (GB); Race Relations Employment Advisory Service and policy for the Careers Service (E); international representation on employment matters.
Department of Energy	Policies for all forms of energy, including its efficient use and the development of new sources; the Government's relations with the nationalised energy industries and the Atomic Energy Authority.
Department of the Environment	Policies for planning, local government, new towns, housing, construction, inner city matters, environmental protection, water, the countryside, sport and recreation, conservation, historic buildings and ancient monuments (E); and Property Services Agency (GB).
Export Credits Guarantee Department	Provision of insurance for exporters against risk of not being paid for goods and services, and access to bank finance for exports; insurance cover for new investment overseas.
Foreign and Commonwealth Office	Conduct of Britain's overseas relations.
Department of Health and Social Security	National Health Service, personal social services provided by local authorities, and certain aspects of public health, including hygiene (E); the social security system (GB).
Home Office	Administration of law and order including criminal justice, police service, prisons and probation services; electoral matters; civil defence; fire services; licensing laws; approval of local authority by-laws; regulation of firearms and dangerous drugs (E & W). Gaming and lotteries (GB). Policies for immigration and nationality, race relations, broadcasting and sex discrimination. Responsibilities related to the Channel Islands and the Isle of Man.
Central Office of Information	Provision of publicity and other information services on behalf of government departments and a number of public agencies.
Board of Inland Revenue	Administration of the tax laws.

DEPARTMENT	*Main areas of responsibility*
The Law Officers' Department	Provision of advice to the Government on English law and representation of the Crown in appropriate domestic and international cases, both civil and criminal, by the Law Officers of the Crown for England and Wales—the Attorney General and the Solicitor General (E & W). The Attorney General is also Attorney General for Northern Ireland.
The Lord Chancellor's Department	Administration of the Supreme Court (Court of Appeal, High Court, Crown Court) and the county courts (E & W), together with certain other courts and tribunals, and all work relating to judicial and quasi-judicial appointments. Responsibility for promoting general reforms in the civil law and for operating the Legal Aid and Advice Scheme. (The Home Office has important responsibilities for the criminal law.)
Management and Personnel Office	(Part of the Cabinet Office.) Organisation, management and efficiency of the Civil Service (GB).
Ordnance Survey	Official surveying and mapping, including geodetic surveys and associated scientific work and topographic surveys covering all of Great Britain and some overseas countries.
Overseas Development Administration	Administration of financial aid to, and technical co-operation in, developing countries.
Parliamentary Counsel Office	Drafting of government Bills (except those relating exclusively to Scotland); advising departments on parliamentary procedure (E, W & NI).
Paymaster General's Office	Provision of banking services for government departments other than the Boards of Inland Revenue and Customs and Excise, and the payment of public service pensions.
Office of Population Censuses and Surveys	Administration of the Marriage Acts and local registration of births, marriages and deaths: population estimates and projections: compilation of health statistics: censuses (E & W). Surveys for other government departments (GB).
Procurator General and Treasury Solicitor's Department	Provision of a common legal service for a large number of government departments. Duties include instructing Parliamentary Counsel on Bills and drafting subordinate legislation: providing litigation and conveyancing services; and giving general advice on the interpretation and application of the law (E & W).
Her Majesty's Stationery Office	Provision to Parliament, government departments and certain public bodies of stationery, printing and related services; and publication and sale of government documents.
Office of Telecommunications	Monitoring of British Telecom and other public and non-public telecommunications operators.

DEPARTMENT	*Main areas of responsibility*
Department of Trade and Industry	Industrial and commercial policy, including: industrial innovation policy; international trade policy; commercial relations and export promotion; competition policy; company law; insolvency; consumer protection; and safety. Sponsorship of manufacturing and service industries (excluding transport industries); radio regulation (GB).
Department of Transport	Land, sea and air transport including sponsorship of the nationalised airline, rail and bus industries; airports; domestic and international civil aviation; shipping and the ports industry; navigational lights, pilotage, HM Coastguard and marine pollution; oversight of road transport (GB); motorways and trunk roads; and oversight of local authorities' transport planning (E).
HM Treasury	Broad economic strategy with particular responsibilities for public finance and expenditure, including control of manpower and pay in the Civil Service.
Welsh Office	Many aspects of Welsh affairs including health and personal social services; education, except for terms and conditions of service, student awards and the University of Wales; the Welsh language and culture; local government; housing; water and sewerage; environmental protection; sport; agriculture and fisheries; forestry; land use, including town and country planning; countryside and nature conservation; new towns, ancient monuments and historic buildings; roads; tourism; a range of matters affecting the careers service and the activities of the Manpower Services Commission in Wales; selective financial assistance to industry; the urban programme in Wales; the operation of the European Regional Development Fund in Wales and other European Community matters; non-departmental public bodies; civil emergencies; all financial aspects of these matters including Welsh rate support grant; and oversight responsibilities for economic affairs and regional planning in Wales.

| SCOTLAND | Scotland has its own system of law and wide administrative autonomy. The Secretary of State for Scotland, a Cabinet minister, has responsibility in Scotland (with some exceptions) for both formulating and carrying out policy relating to agriculture and fisheries, education, law and order, local government and environmental services, social work, health, housing, roads and certain aspects of shipping and road transport services. |

The Secretary of State also has a major role in the planning and development of the Scottish economy, and important functions relating to industrial development, with responsibility for financial assistance to industry, for the Scottish Development Agency, and the Highlands and Islands Development Board, the Scottish Tourist Board and for the work of the Manpower Services Commission and the Careers Service. The Secretary of State plays a full part in determining energy policy, particularly in relation to responsibility for the electricity supply industry in Scotland. He is also responsible for the government interest in a range of other functions from fire services to sport.

The distinctive features and the different conditions and needs of Scotland and its people are reflected in separate Scottish legislation on many domestic matters or else in special provisions applying to Scotland alone, inserted in Acts which otherwise apply to the United Kingdom generally.

The Secretary of State discharges his responsibilities principally through the Scottish Office's five departments, supported by Central Services (see p 56) and four smaller departments—the Department of the Registers of Scotland, the

Scottish Record Office, the General Register Office for Scotland and the Scottish Courts Administration.

United Kingdom government departments with significant Scottish responsibilities have offices in Scotland with delegated powers and work closely with the Scottish Office.

An outline of the main functions of the Scottish departments is given below.

DEPARTMENT	*Functions*
Department of Agriculture and Fisheries for Scotland	Promotion of the agricultural and fishing industries.
Scottish Development Department	Housing; roads; building control; water supplies and sewerage; environmental protection and the countryside; land-use planning; general policy relating to local government organisation; ancient monuments and historic buildings; certain transport functions.
Industry Department for Scotland	Industrial and regional economic development matters; energy; tourism.
Scottish Education Department	Education (excluding universities); student awards; libraries; museums and galleries; sport and recreation; the arts; social work services.
Scottish Home and Health Department	Central administration of law and order (including police service, criminal justice, legal aid and penal institutions); the National Health Service; fire, home defence and civil emergency services.
Central Services	Services to the five Scottish departments. These include the Office of the Solicitor to the Secretary of State, the Scottish Information Office, and Finance Divisions.
Lord Advocate's Department and Crown Office	Provision of legal advice to the Government on issues affecting Scotland and the principal representation of the Crown for litigation in Scotland by the Law Officers of the Crown for Scotland (the Lord Advocate and the Solicitor General for Scotland); control of all prosecution in Scotland.
Scottish Courts Administration	Organisation, administration and staffing of the courts and court offices; jurisdiction and procedure of civil courts; enforcement of judgments; and programme of Scottish Law Commission.
Other Administrative Departments	Department of the Registrar General for Scotland; Scottish Record Office; Department of the Registers of Scotland.

NORTHERN IRELAND

Between 1921 and 1972 Northern Ireland had its own Parliament and Government, subordinate to the Parliament at Westminster, but in 1972, following the resignation of the Northern Ireland Government, the British Government assumed direct responsibility with a United Kingdom Cabinet minister responsible for functions previously exercised by the Northern Ireland Government. Attempts have been made by successive governments to find a means of restoring devolved government to Northern Ireland on a basis that would command widespread acceptance throughout the community. The most recent attempt failed in June 1986 when the Northern Ireland Assembly, elected in 1982, was dissolved after it ceased to discharge its responsibilities of making proposals for the resumption of devolved government and of monitoring the work of the Northern Ireland departments. The Government expressed the hope that a new Assembly would be established which would contribute to the better government and administration of Northern Ireland.

The Secretary of State for Northern Ireland is the Cabinet minister responsible for Northern Ireland. Through the Northern Ireland Office he has direct responsibility for constitutional developments, law and order and security, and electoral matters. The work of the Northern Ireland departments, whose functions are listed below, are also subject to the direction and control of the Secretary of State.

DEPARTMENT	Functions
Department of Agriculture	Development of agricultural, forestry and fishing industries; administration of agricultural grant schemes; advisory service to farmers; agricultural research, education and training.
Department of Economic Development	Development of industry and commerce, as well as the administration of government policy in relation to tourism, energy, harbours and minerals; administration of an employment service and labour training schemes and assistance to industrial development, through the Industrial Development Board for Northern Ireland.
Department of Education	Central policy, co-ordination, legislation, oversight, and financial control of the five education and library boards and education as a whole from nursery to adult and continuing education, youth services, sport and recreation, cultural activities and community services and facilities including the improvement of community relations.
Department of the Environment	Housing (policy, programmes and finance); planning (regional strategy, development plans, development control and comprehensive development); construction and maintenance of roads, transport and traffic management, and motor taxation; water and sewerage; environmental protection; ordnance survey; collection of rates; historic monuments and buildings; maintenance of public records; and certain controls over local government.
Department of Finance and Personnel	Control of public expenditure; liaison with HM Treasury and the Northern Ireland Office on financial matters, economic and social planning and research; valuation and Lands Service; formulation of policy and co-ordination of arrangements for personnel management; general management and control of the Northern Ireland Civil Service.
Department of Health and Social Services	Health, personal social services and social security.

The Civil Service

The Civil Service is concerned with the conduct of the whole range of government activities as they affect the community, ranging from policy formulation to carrying out the day-to-day duties that public administration demands.

Civil servants are servants of the Crown. They are responsible to the minister in whose department they work for carrying out his or her policies. Ministers alone are answerable to Parliament for their policies and the actions of their staff (though civil servants may give evidence to parliamentary select committees on their minister's behalf). In the determination of policy the civil servant has no constitutional responsibility or role distinct from that of the minister. A change of minister, for whatever reason, does not involve a change of staff. (Ministers sometimes appoint special advisers from outside the Civil Service; the advisers are paid from public funds, but their appointments come to an end when the Government's term of office finishes, or when the Minister to whom the special adviser is appointed leaves the Government or moves to another appointment.)

Including part-time staff (two part-time officers being reckoned as equivalent to one full-time), in January 1986 there were around 597,000 civil servants (nearly half of them women), roughly half of whom were engaged in the provision of public services, such as paying sickness benefits and pensions, collecting taxes and contributions, running employment services, staffing prisons, and providing services to industry and agriculture. Just over a quarter were employed in the Ministry of Defence. The rest were divided between: central administrative and policy duties; service-wide support services, such as accommodation, printing and information; and largely financially self-supporting services, for instance, those provided by the Department for National Savings and the Royal Mint.

The total number includes about 99,000 'industrial' civil servants, mainly manual workers in government industrial establishments.

Over three-quarters of civil servants work outside London. As part of its policy of controlling the cost and size of the Civil Service and to improve its efficiency, the Government set a target in 1980 of reducing the number of civil servants by 14 per cent to 630,000 by April 1984. This was achieved as was the target for April 1985 (by when numbers had fallen to 599,000). It is planned to achieve a further reduction to 590,000 by April 1988 at which date the Civil Service will have been reduced by around one-fifth since 1979. At the same time reforms of all aspects of the management of government departments are being implemented to ensure improved management performance, in particular through the sharper accountability of individual managers based on clear objectives and responsibilities. These reforms include an experimental performance-related pay scheme, and other means to encourage and reward improved performance.

Northern Ireland has its own Civil Service and Civil Service Commission, modelled on its counterpart in Great Britain. Interchange of staff between the two Civil Services occurs to a minor extent only.

Central Management and Structure

Responsibility for central co-ordination and management of the Civil Service is divided between the Treasury and the Cabinet Office (Management and Personnel Office). In addition to its other functions, the Treasury is responsible for controlling Civil Service manpower, pay, pensions and allowances, while the Management and Personnel Office, which is part of the Cabinet Office and under the control of the Prime Minister, as Minister for the Civil Service, is responsible for the organisation, structure, management and overall efficiency of the Service. The function of official Head of the Home Civil Service is combined with that of Secretary to the Cabinet. At the senior levels of the Home Civil Service there is an open structure of unified grades which, with few exceptions, covers all posts whatever the nature of their duties. Grades 1, 2 and 3 replace the former grade titles of Permanent Secretary, Deputy Secretary and Under-Secretary while Grades 4, 5, 6 and 7 cover the senior levels of most occupational groups and classes down to Principal, Principal Scientific Officer, Principal Professional and Technology Officer and equivalent levels.

Below this the structure of the non-industrial Civil Service is based on a system of categories and occupational groups, which are the basic groupings of staff for the purposes of recruitment, pay and personnel management. These include the General Category (covering the Administration, Economist, Statistician, Information Officer and Librarian groups), the Science Category, the Professional and Technology Category (including architects, surveyors, electrical and mechanical engineers, graphics officers and marine services staff), and the Training, Legal, Police, Secretarial, Data Processing, Research Officer, Social Security, Security and Museum Categories. These 12 categories account for some 75 per cent of non-industrial staff. Work requiring specialist skill is always done by appropriately qualified individuals.

Personnel management policies encourage the deployment of staff so that talent can be used to the best advantage, and, with higher posts open to people of outstanding ability (whatever their specialist background or original method of entry into the Service), ensure that people with the necessary qualities can gain suitably wide experience to fit them for posts at the highest levels. The exchange of staff between the Civil Service and industry is also encouraged.

The Diplomatic Service

The Diplomatic Service, a separate service of some 4,650 or so people, provides the staff for the Foreign and Commonwealth Office and at United Kingdom diplomatic missions and consular posts abroad. Its functions include advising on policy, negotiating with overseas governments and conducting business in international organisations; promoting British exports and trade generally, administering aid, presenting ideas, policies and objectives to the people of overseas countries; and protecting British interests abroad.

The Service has its own grade structure, linked for salary purposes with that of the Home Civil Service, and conditions of work are in many ways comparable while taking into account the special demands of the Service, particularly of postings overseas. Members of the Home Civil Service and the armed forces, and individuals from the private sector, may serve in the Foreign and Commonwealth Office and at overseas posts on loan or attachment.

Recruitment and Training

Recruitment of staff to the middle and higher levels of the Home Civil Service and the Diplomatic Service is the responsibility of the Civil Service Commission which, in conjunction with departments, ensures that staff are selected solely on merit through fair and open competition. The selection of junior staff, such as those engaged in clerical and manual work, is undertaken by the departments.

For the Administration Group, the central part of the Home and Diplomatic Civil Services, entry is at three levels relating broadly to the academic achievements of: a second class honours degree, or better; GCE Advanced level; and GCE Ordinary level. The selection procedure for the highest of these levels (the Administration Trainee entry) comprises qualifying tests, followed by tests and interviews at the Civil Service Selection Board and an interview by the Final Selection Board. For the next level (the Executive Officer entry) selection involves qualifying tests followed by an interview. For the lower level (the clerical entry) selection is normally by interview of those holding the prescribed educational qualifications.

Entry to the professional and technical grades usually requires appropriate qualifications, and selection is on the basis of past record and by interview.

Most government departments employ full-time training officers and tutors to help to identify staff training needs and to organise training by the most appropriate methods (for example, formal courses or self-instruction). The Civil Service College provides training most efficiently undertaken centrally. Use is also made of external institutions.

Civil servants under the age of 18 may continue their education by attending courses usually for one day a week ('day release' schemes). Adult staff may be entitled to financial assistance to undertake, mainly in their own time, private studies leading to recognised educational or professional qualifications in approved subjects. There are also opportunities for civil servants to obtain fellowships for research in areas of interest both to themselves and to their departments.

Promotion and Terms of Service

Departments are responsible for promotion at all grade levels. Normally promotion is from grade to grade, but there can be accelerated promotion for staff who show exceptional promise. Promotion or appointment to Grades 1 and 2 and all transfers between departments at these levels are approved by the Prime Minister, who is advised by the official head of the Home Civil Service.

Terms of service for civil servants are generally governed by agreements between senior officials (the Official Side of the National Whitley Council) and representatives of the employees (the Trade Union Side of the National Whitley Council). For industrial civil servants, the negotiating body is the Joint Co-ordinating Committee of government industrial establishments.

Political and Private Activities

Civil servants are required to discharge loyally the duties assigned to them by the Government of the day of whatever political persuasion. For the Civil Service to serve successive governments of different political complexions it is essential that ministers and the public should have confidence that civil servants' personal views do not cut across the discharge of their official duties. The purpose of the rules which govern political activities by civil servants is to allow them the greatest possible freedom to participate in public affairs without infringing these fundamental principles. The rules are concerned with political activities liable to give public expression to political views, rather than with privately held beliefs and opinions.

The Civil Service is divided into three groups for the purposes of deciding the extent to which individuals may take part in political activities. The 'politically free' group, consisting of industrial staff and non-office grades, are free to engage in any political activity including adoption as a candidate for the United Kingdom or the European Parliament (although they would have to resign from the Service if elected). The 'politically restricted' group, which mainly comprises Principal and equivalent grades and above, are debarred from national political activities but may apply for permission to take part in local political activities. The 'intermediate' group, which comprises all civil servants not in either of the other two groups, may apply for permission to take part in national or local political activity, apart from candidature for the United Kingdom or the European Parliament.

Where required, permission is granted to the maximum extent consistent with the reputation of the Civil Service for political impartiality and the avoidance of any conflict with official duties. It is granted subject to a code of discretion requiring moderation and the avoidance of embarrassment to ministers.

Generally, there are no restrictions on the private activities of civil servants, provided that these do not bring discredit on the Civil Service, and that there is no possibility of conflict with official duties. For instance, a civil servant is required to seek permission before taking part in any outside activity which involves the use of official experience, or before accepting a directorship in any company holding a contract with his or her department.

Security

As a general rule the political views of civil servants are not a matter of official concern. However, no one whose loyalty is in doubt may be employed on work vital to the security of the State. For this reason certain posts are not open to those who are known to be members of communist or fascist organisations or of subversive groups, or associated with them in such a way as to raise legitimate doubts about their reliability, or to anyone whose reliability may be in doubt for any other reason.

Each department is responsible for its own internal security, advised as necessary by the Security Service. The Security Commission, if requested to do so by the Prime Minister after consultation with the Leader of the Opposition, may investigate and report on breaches of security in the public service and advise on changes in security procedure.

Local Government

A wide range of public services is provided by democratically elected local authorities throughout the United Kingdom. The gradual expansion of local services, particularly in the period between the late 1940s and mid-1970s, has inevitably led to a steady rise in local government expenditure and in its support from central funds. In recent years central government has sought to check this growth as part of a general policy of reducing public expenditure. Measures introduced to promote greater efficiency and cost-effectiveness include the holding back of central government grant from authorities spending above government targets, the prescription of maximum levels of spending and rates for selected high-spending authorities in England and Wales, the establishment in England and Wales of the independent Audit Commission to audit accounts and seek economical use of resources, and the encouragement given to local authorities to examine the scope for seeking competitive tenders for the provision of many of the services carried out by their own staff. In Scotland there is an independent Commission for Local Authority Accounts and similar action has been taken to control local authority expenditure. Moreover, since staff costs form such a significant part of public expenditure, local authorities have been urged to reduce staff levels. Local authorities in England, Wales and Scotland are now required to publish quarterly staffing levels for particular services.

The specific powers and duties of local authorities are conferred on them by Parliament, or by measures made under its authority. The actual administration, and the exercise of discretion within statutory limits, are the responsibility of the local authority. In the case of certain services, however, ministers have powers to secure a measure of national uniformity in the standard of a service provided, to safeguard public health, or to protect the rights of individual citizens. For some services the minister concerned has wide powers of supervision; for others there are strictly limited powers.

The main links between local authorities and the central government are: in England, the Department of the Environment, although other departments are concerned with various local government functions; in Scotland, the Scottish Office; in Wales, the Welsh Office; and in Northern Ireland, the Department of the Environment for Northern Ireland.

Principal Types of Local Authority

England and Wales (outside Greater London) are divided into 53 counties, within which there are 369 districts. All the districts and 47 of the counties—the 'non-metropolitan' counties—have independent, locally elected councils with separate functions. County authorities provide the large-scale local government services, while the district authorities are responsible for the more local ones (see p 63).

In Greater London (an area of about 1,580 sq km (610 sq miles) and a population of some 7 million) the local government authorities are the councils of 32 London boroughs and the Corporation of the City of London, while in the six metropolitan counties there are 36 district councils.

Until April 1986 Greater London and the metropolitan counties had their own councils but these were abolished by the Local Government Act 1985, which was designed to create a more effective, economical and accountable system by removing a tier of local government. As a result most of the functions previously carried out by the Greater London Council and the metropolitan county councils have been transferred to the London borough and metropolitan district councils. A small number of services (namely, waste regulation and disposal in certain areas; the police and fire services, including civil defence, and public transport in all metropolitan counties; and the fire service, including civil defence, in London) which require a statutory authority over areas wider than the boroughs and districts are now run by joint authorities composed of elected councillors nominated by the borough or district councils. Education in inner London is now the responsibility of a new, independent and directly elected authority (see p 64).

Special transitional bodies have been appointed to take responsibility for certain residual county council and Greater London Council matters. These include compensation, unassigned legal rights and liabilities and disposal of surplus property and, where appropriate, the management of debt and of the superannuation fund. The residuary bodies are required to prepare proposals to wind up their affairs as soon as practicable.

Within rural districts in England, parish councils or meetings are focuses for local opinion as bodies with limited powers of local interest. In Wales community councils have similar functions.

On the mainland of Scotland local government is on a two-tier basis: nine regions are divided into 53 districts, each area having its own elected council. There are three virtually all-purpose authorities for Orkney, Shetland and the Western Isles. Provision is also made for local community councils, although these are not local authorities.

The areas and electoral arrangements of local authorities are kept under review by the Local Government Boundary Commissions for England, Wales and Scotland.

In Northern Ireland 26 district councils are responsible for local environmental and certain other services. Statutory bodies, such as the Northern Ireland Housing Executive and area boards, are responsible to central government departments for the administration of major services such as housing, education and libraries, and health and personal social services. Regional services such as roads, water and sewerage, and planning, are the responsibility of central government, through the Department of the Environment for Northern Ireland.

Election of Councils

Local authority councils consist of a number of elected unpaid councillors presided over by a chairman. Councillors can claim a flat-rate attendance allowance or a financial loss allowance for performing council business; they are also entitled to travelling and subsistence allowances. Parish and community councillors cannot claim expenses for duties within their own areas.

In England, Wales and Northern Ireland each council annually elects a chairman and vice-chairman. Some districts have the ceremonial title of borough, or city, both granted by royal authority (in Northern Ireland by the Secretary of State). In boroughs and cities the chairman is normally known as the Mayor (in the City of London and certain other large cities, he or she is known as the Lord Mayor). In Scotland the chairman of the district council of each of the four cities is called the Lord Provost. No specific title is laid down for the chairmen of other councils, but some are known as conveners, while others continue to use the old title of 'provost'.

Elections for any form of local government normally take place every four years. Hitherto metropolitan district elections have been held for a third of the seats in each year when there were no county council elections. Non-metropolitan district councils may adopt the same procedure or opt for whole council elections every four years. London borough councils have whole council elections every four years.

In Scotland, local elections are held every two years, alternately for districts and for regions and islands authorities, so that all types of authority are elected for four years at a time.

Anyone is entitled to vote at a local government election in Great Britain provided he or she is aged 18 years or over, is a British citizen, other Commonwealth citizen, or a citizen of the Irish Republic, is not subject to any legal incapacity and is registered as a local government elector for the area for which the election is held. To qualify for registration a person must be resident in the council area on the qualifying date. In Northern Ireland there are slightly different requirements.

A candidate for election as councillor normally stands as a representative of one of the national political parties, or of some local interest, or as an independent. Candidates must be British citizens, other Commonwealth citizens or citizens of the Irish Republic and aged 21 or over. In addition, they must be registered as local electors in the area of the local authority to which they seek election; or have resided in or occupied (as owner or tenant) land or other premises in that area during the whole of the 12 months preceding the day on which they are nominated as candidates or, in that 12 months, have had their principal or only place of work there. No one may be elected to a council of which he or she is an employee, and there are a number of other disqualifications.

Local authority areas are generally divided into electoral areas for local council elections. Administrative counties in England and Wales are divided into electoral divisions. Districts in England, Wales and Northern Ireland are divided into electoral 'wards', returning one councillor or more. In Scotland the electoral areas in the regions and islands areas are called electoral divisions, each returning a single member; the districts are divided into wards, similarly returning a single member. For parish or community council elections in England and Wales, each parish or community, or ward of a parish or community, forms an electoral area which returns one member or more.

The procedure for local government voting in Great Britain is similar to that for parliamentary elections. Postal voting for such elections is being introduced in 1987. In Northern Ireland local government elections are held on the basis of proportional representation and electoral wards are grouped into district electoral areas.

**Functions and
Services**

Local authorities' functions are far-reaching. Some are primarily duties, others purely permissive.

Broadly speaking, functions in England and Wales are divided between county and district councils on the basis that county councils are responsible for matters requiring planning and administration over wide areas or requiring the support of substantial resources while district councils as a whole administer functions of more local significance.

English county councils are generally responsible for strategic planning, transport planning, highways, traffic regulation, consumer protection, refuse disposal, police and the fire service. Education, libraries and the personal social services are functions of county councils in non-metropolitan areas and of district councils in metropolitan areas. All district councils are responsible, for instance, for environmental health, housing, decisions on most planning applications, and refuse collection. They may also provide off-street car parks subject to the consent of the county council. Powers to carry out some functions—such as the provision of museums, art galleries and parks—are available at both levels; arrangements depend on local agreement.

In the metropolitan counties the district councils are responsible for the full range of services (apart from the police, the fire service and public transport and, in some areas only, waste regulation and disposal—see p 62). In Greater London the boroughs and the City Corporation are responsible for a similar range of functions but London's police force is directly responsible to the Home Secretary. Responsibility for passenger transport has been transferred to London Regional Transport and in inner London education is administered by the Inner London Education Authority, an independent and directly elected authority with the same name, functions and geographical coverage as its predecessor, which was an autonomous committee of the former Greater London Council. That Council was unique among local authorities in being responsible for land drainage for the greater part of its area ('the London excluded area') and flood protection, including the Thames Barrier. These responsibilities now rest with the Thames Water Authority.

In Wales the division of functions between county and district councils is much the same as that between county and district councils in non-metropolitan areas of England.

Local authorities in England and Wales may arrange for any of their functions to be carried out on their behalf by another local authority, other than functions relating to education, police, the personal social services and national parks.

In Scotland the regional and district authorities discharge local government functions in a way broadly similar to that of authorities in England and Wales. Orkney, Shetland and the Western Isles, because of their isolation from the mainland, have single, virtually all-purpose authorities.

In Northern Ireland, local environmental and certain other services, such as leisure and the arts, are administered by the district councils. Responsibility for planning, roads, water supply and sewerage services is exercised in each district through a divisional office of the Department of the Environment for Northern Ireland. Area boards, responsible to central departments, administer locally education, public libraries and the health and personal social services. The Northern Ireland Housing Executive, responsible to the Department of the Environment, administers housing.

Internal Organisation of Local Authorities   Local authorities can co-operate or share among themselves the discharge of their functions. They have considerable freedom to make internal arrangements for carrying out their duties. Most use the committee system, whereby policy and principle are decided in full council, and committees administer the various services. Parish and community councils in England and Wales are often able to do their work efficiently in full session although they appoint committees from time to time as necessary. Some councils have policy advisory or co-ordinating committees with powers to originate policy, subject to the approval of the full council. The powers and duties of local authority committees (which may be advisory or executive) are usually laid down in the council's standing orders.

A council may delegate to a committee or an officer any of its functions, except those in connection with raising loans, levying rates (see p 66), or making financial demands on other authorities liable to contribute; these are legally reserved to the council as a whole. An independent inquiry into the conduct of business in local authorities in Great Britain was completed in June 1986; the Government is considering its proposals.

Public Access

The public (including the press) are admitted to council, committee and sub-committee meetings, and have a right of access to agenda, reports and minutes of meetings and certain background papers. Local authorities may exclude the public from meetings and withhold these papers only in limited circumstances specified by legislation.

Officers and Employees

Nearly 3 million people are employed by local authorities in Great Britain. These include administrative, professional and technical staff, teachers, firemen, those engaged on law and order services, and manual workers. Nearly half of all local government workers are employed in the education service.

Although a few appointments must be made by all the authorities responsible for the functions concerned, councils are individually responsible within national policy requirements for determining the size, composition and deployment of their workforces. In Northern Ireland, each council must by law appoint a clerk of the council as its chief officer.

As a general rule, employees are of three kinds: heads of departments or chief officers; administrative, professional, clerical and technical staff; and manual workers. Senior staff appointments are usually made on the recommendation of the committee or committees particularly concerned; most junior appointments are made by heads of departments, who are also responsible for engaging manual workers. Appointments and engagements always conform to the council's set establishment, and committees are informed of appointments which they have not made themselves.

Pay and conditions of service for local authority staff are generally a matter for each council, although there are scales recommended by national negotiating machinery set up by the local authorities themselves.

Authorities differ in the degree to which they employ staff to carry out certain functions (for example, building work, street cleaning or refuse collection) or use private firms under contract. The Government's policy of promoting value for money is encouraging the use of private firms where there are resultant economies, and legislation is proposed to require authorities to open up further services to competition from the private sector. In the specific case of building and maintenance work, the Local Government, Planning and Land Act 1980 obliges authorities' direct labour organisations to bid for such work in open competition if they wish to undertake it.

Local Government Finance

In 1985–86 expenditure by local government in the United Kingdom was about £35,300 million, some 26 per cent of total public expenditure. Current expenditure amounted to some £31,300 million, and capital expenditure to about £4,000 million. Education accounts for about 40 per cent of the total. Most of the remainder is spent on law and order, housing and other environmental services, personal social services and transport.

Current Expenditure

Local government current expenditure in England and Wales is financed by a combination of central government grants and local rates (a tax based on property values). A few services such as the police, housing and transport and the urban programme for inner city areas receive specific central government grants towards their cost. However, most central government support for current spending is provided through the rate support grant. This has two elements, domestic rate relief grant, which is paid to rating authorities as a direct subsidy to domestic rates, and block grant. Block grant is a general grant which is designed to compensate for variations in the needs which local authorities have to provide for and for differences in the resources they may be able to raise in local rates. Each local authority's grant is, therefore, calculated to be sufficient for it to provide a similar level of service to that of other authorities while at the same time charging the same rate level. This system requires an assessment of each authority's need to provide services which takes account of over 60 different factors and characteristics of an authority's area and population.

Within this system, local authorities are free to decide on their overall level of spending and on their priorities between particular services. However, because of the need to control public expenditure, the methods for calculating an authority's entitlement to block grant have been amended in 1986–87 so that, for the majority of authorities, grant entitlement decreases as expenditure increases, thus providing an incentive for expenditure restraint. The previous system of setting expenditure targets for each authority has now been discontinued. The Government has power, subject to parliamentary approval, to fix upper limits on the rates of selected authorities whose spending it considers to be excessive. In 1986–87, 12 English authorities had an upper limit set on their rate levies.

In Scotland, the grant is distributed in three parts: the 'needs' element, designed to give most help to authorities whose spending needs are greatest; the 'resources' element, used to supplement the rate income of authorities whose rateable value per head of population falls below a standard figure, prescribed for each year; and the 'domestic' element, which compensates authorities for loss of rate income from reductions in rate poundage which they are required to give to householders. Local authorities are free to decide on their level of spending, but central government can make selective grant and rate reductions in the case of individual authorities planning excessive and unreasonable expenditure. Current expenditure guidelines are issued and the grant payable to authorities is reduced where the level of expenditure planned by authorities is in excess of the guidelines. The Government has power to set a general limitation on rates.

In Northern Ireland district councils receive central government grants comprising specific grants which assist with the financing of certain functions (for example, the acquisition of open space, and the provision of clean air) and certain capital projects (for example, leisure centres), and a general grant, which is paid by the Department of the Environment for Northern Ireland. The general grant compensates councils for loss of rate income arising from statutory derating of premises; it also contains a resources element which brings the rating resources of poorer councils up to a standard level determined by the Department.

Capital Expenditure

Local government capital expenditure (net of receipts) is financed mainly by borrowing with the remainder coming from grants and other income. The largest share in 1985–86—over 30 per cent in England and 40 per cent in Wales—goes to housing. Each local authority receives from the Government a capital expenditure allocation for the functions for which it is responsible. The allocation may be supplemented to some extent from capital receipts achieved by the authority. With other minor additions, these amounts constitute a ceiling on the authority's permitted capital expenditure for the year. They may normally be used for whatever services the authority wishes within its legal powers.

Rates

Rates are local taxes paid by the occupiers of land and property (with certain exceptions, see below) to meet part of the cost of local services. Each occupier's payment is calculated annually by the rating authority by multiplying the rateable value of a property (broadly equivalent to its annual rental value) by the rate poundage—an amount per £ of rateable value fixed by the authority according to its projected financial needs. Rateable values are assessed periodically, and there is a system of appeals for disputed assessments. Crown (government) property is not rateable but payments are made, based on values assessed by the Treasury Valuer, in place of rates.

Government grants reduce domestic rates below the levels paid by commercial concerns. Rating relief is available in certain circumstances on premises adapted for the use of the disabled. Agricultural land and buildings (apart from living accommodation) and places of religious worship are exempted from rates. Charities pay half the full rate on premises occupied for charitable purposes and may be given further relief by rating authorities, who can also reduce or remit the rates for a wide range of non-profit-making bodies. In England and Wales a maximum of 50 per cent of the full rate may be levied on empty non-domestic properties, with complete exemption for empty warehouses and industrial property. In enterprise zones, which have been set up in certain areas to foster industrial and commercial regeneration, commercial and industrial properties are exempted from paying rates for ten years.

In Scotland industrial (including freight transport) premises are rated at 60 per cent of net annual value. Most empty properties pay no rates.

Proposals for the reform of local authority finance in Great Britain, which are designed to strengthen local democratic accountability, were announced in January 1986. The main features are a national non-domestic rate, the proceeds of which would be distributed to local authorities in proportion to the number of adults; a phased replacement of domestic rates by a community charge which each authority would set and which would be payable by every resident adult; and a grant system that would compensate for differences in local authorities' needs and would provide additional help by way of a fixed sum per adult. If adopted, the new system would first be introduced in Scotland, beginning in 1989. Its introduction in England and Wales would follow a revaluation of non-domestic rates which is planned to be completed by 1990.

In Northern Ireland all industrial premises are fully derated as are commercial premises in enterprise zones. Certain other properties, such as freight transport and recreational premises, are partially derated.

Loans

Each year, local authorities receive a borrowing approval which enables them to raise loans under their general powers to finance capital expenditure up to the limit given in the approval. In Northern Ireland long-term borrowing by district councils is subject to central approval; in Scotland central approval is given to capital expenditure, not to loans.

Local authorities may raise long-term loans by means of private mortgages, issuing stock upon The Stock Exchange and bonds which may or may not be quoted on The Stock Exchange. Local authorities also have right of access to the Public Works Loan Board, financed by the Exchequer, or, in Northern Ireland, to the Consolidated Fund, for long-term borrowing to finance a proportion of their reckonable capital payments, and may borrow temporarily for a limited proportion of their current outstanding loan debt.

Control of Finance

Local councils normally have a finance committee to keep their financial policy under constant review. They must have their annual accounts audited by independent auditors appointed by the Audit Commission in England and Wales, or by the Commission for Local Authority Accounts in Scotland. In Northern Ireland this role is exercised by a local government audit section appointed by the Department of the Environment for Northern Ireland.

Local Government Complaints System

A complaints system for local government in England and Wales involves independent statutory Commissions for Local Administration comprising local commissioners (local government Ombudsmen). The English Commission has three local commissioners and the Welsh, one. In Scotland the statute provides for a single commissioner. All commissioners are responsible in their particular area for investigating citizens' allegations of injustice resulting from maladministration by local authorities. In normal circumstances, the Commissioners can only initiate an investigation at the request of a local councillor.

In Northern Ireland a Commissioner for Complaints deals with complaints alleging injustices suffered as a result of maladministration by district councils and certain other public bodies.

Fire Services

Every part of the United Kingdom is covered by a local authority fire service, which is subject to some general oversight by central government. Other than in Northern Ireland, where the fire service is financed wholly from central government funds, the cost is shared between local authorities and central government, the latter contribution through the rate support grant.

Each of the 64 fire authorities must by law make provision for fire-fighting, and maintain a brigade of sufficient strength to meet all normal requirements (in some parts of Scotland combined authorities provide fire cover). Other authorities also maintain fire brigades, for instance, the Army and Royal Air Force Departments of the Ministry of Defence; the Civil Aviation Authority at airports; and some large industrial and commercial concerns. These work in co-operation with the local authority fire services.

The Home Secretary and the Secretary of State for Scotland have central responsibility in England and Wales and in Scotland respectively. Central government is concerned mainly with ensuring the operational efficiency of brigades. Ministers have statutory powers to prescribe standards and general requirements on administrative and operational matters of service-wide significance. These include appointments and promotions, the provision of a central training institution, pensions and disciplinary matters. Their approval is also required for reductions in the fire-fighting establishments of fire brigades. Each minister is advised by a Central Fire Brigades Advisory Council, comprising the respective home departments, local authorities, fire service representative organisations and certain specialist advisers. In the home departments, inspectorates of fire services advise on operational and technical matters. Most fire brigades include part-time personnel who provide fire cover in less-densely populated areas in return for a retaining fee and call-out and attendance fee. Fire authorities also employ people for duties in controls, communications and mobilising and staff duties. There are about 40,000 full-time and 21,000 part-time operational members of fire brigades in Britain.

The standardisation of some equipment is encouraged, in order to assist compatibility when a fire is attended by more than one brigade. The principal types of fire-fighting appliances bought by fire authorities are based upon specifications approved by the Secretaries of State and issued in the form of advice by the Central Fire Brigades Advisory Councils. The specifications aim to describe the minimum standards required while allowing some freedom of design.

Each fire authority must appoint a Chief Fire Officer (Firemaster in Scotland) who exercises day-to-day control from brigade headquarters. Divisional officers in charge of the geographical areas into which most brigade regions are divided are responsible for mobilising forces. Constant communication is maintained between divisional and brigade headquarters and if additional resources are required to deal with an incident, neighbouring divisions, or a neighbouring fire brigade, are asked to provide assistance.

Fire Prevention

Fire authorities are concerned in some way with fire precautions in most buildings used by the public and have major responsibility for enforcing legislation concerning fire precautions. They must also make efficient arrangements for giving advice on fire prevention, restricting the spread of fires, and means of escape. Courses in fire prevention are held at the Fire Service College for fire brigade officers. In addition to their enforcement and advisory duties, brigades are also involved in education and publicity to promote fire safety, particularly in the home; the Home Office also promotes fire safety in the home. Central government is advised on prevention by the Joint Fire Prevention Committee of the Central Fire Brigades Advisory Councils, representing the fire service and central and local authorities.

Research

Research into health hazards to fire-fighters, fire prevention, fire-brigade organisation and fire-fighting equipment is conducted by the Home Office with the help of the fire services under the auspices of the Joint Committee on Fire Research of the Central Fire Brigades Advisory Councils. Individual research projects are undertaken by the Home Office Scientific Research and Development Branch or, under contract to the Home Office, by other government agencies, notably the Fire Research Station, which is part of the Building Research Establishment of the Department of the Environment, or by private consultants. The Fire Research Station is the principal organisation studying and investigating technical aspects of fire.

Special Services

Fire authorities have discretion to use their brigades and equipment in a variety of non-fire emergencies. These are known as 'special services' and include rail, road and aircraft accidents, collapse of buildings, flooding of premises, leakage of harmful gas or liquids and the rescue of people or animals from dangerous situations. Fire authorities are entitled to levy a charge for such services.

Fire Losses

The direct cost of damage to buildings and goods destroyed by fires in Great Britain in 1985 amounted to an estimated £450 million (consequential losses from the interruption of business are not included in this total). Most fires involving heavy losses occur when the premises are unattended; and fires are more likely to start in storage areas than in production departments. Industries which suffer most severely include engineering and electrical firms; textiles; food, drink and tobacco warehousing; chemical and allied industries; paper, printing and publishing firms; and retailing.

Fire Casualties

About 900 people, particularly the elderly and young children, die in fires every year (most of them at home) and about a further 11,000 suffer injury. Among the chief causes of fatal fires are ignition of upholstery, bedding and clothing by smokers' materials and by heaters.

3 Overseas Relations

Britain's overseas relations reflect both its traditional position as a major trading and maritime power whose people have settled throughout the world, and its concern to help to maintain peace and to secure world-wide economic and social progress through international co-operation. It has diplomatic relations with over 160 countries, and with about 20 of these has common security arrangements, principally through the North Atlantic Treaty Organisation. Commercial activities have helped Britain to maintain its position as a world financial centre. It has considerable overseas investments, imports over a third of its food and more than half of its raw material requirements, and exports account for over a quarter of its gross national product. Britain provides development assistance to over 120 independent countries as well as to its remaining dependencies.

In the belief that its overseas objectives can best be attained through co-operation with other nations on a regional or global basis, Britain is a member of some 120 international organisations ranging from the world-wide United Nations concerned with problems of world peace, international economic co-operation and social issues to regionally based and technically orientated bodies. In particular, it is a member of the European Community and is increasingly co-ordinating its overseas policies through the Community's political co-operation mechanism. As a member of the Commonwealth, Britain is a part of a representative cross-section of the international community, which has evolved from the British Empire (since 1945 Britain has progressively, and largely peacefully, dismantled its Empire and prepared nearly 50 countries for independence) and whose 49 members share a common language, common technical standards, similar systems of law and close professional, academic and commercial links.

Britain also has strong ties with the United States, including a common language and similar political and cultural traditions.

A long involvement in world affairs has given Britain both a vital interest and a firm belief in the maintenance of international order governed by respect for a generally accepted system of law. As a permanent member of the United Nations Security Council it makes support for the United Nations a central feature of its foreign policy.

Administration The general conduct of overseas relations is the responsibility of the Secretary of State for Foreign and Commonwealth Affairs acting through the Foreign and Commonwealth Office and over 200 British diplomatic posts overseas. The latter comprise embassies and high commissions in about 130 countries,[1] together with subordinate consulates-general and consulates, and missions at ten multilateral organisations. These posts, like the Foreign and Commonwealth Office, are staffed by members of the Diplomatic Service and locally engaged people. Excluding supporting administrative and communications services, the staff are employed on political and economic work, export promotion and other commercial matters, consular and immigration work, aid administration,

---

[1] A few embassies are accredited to more than one country; for example, the embassy at Dakar in Senegal is also accredited to Mauretania, Guinea, Guinea-Bissau, Mali and Cape Verde.

information and cultural work. Other departments which have a primary concern with overseas relations include the Ministry of Defence, the Department of Trade and Industry, the Treasury and the Overseas Development Administration (which is part of the Foreign and Commonwealth Office); but the involvement of most has increased in recent years with the growing dependence of domestic economic policy on international decisions and with Britain's membership of the European Community.

Where questions of overseas policy involve matters within the responsibility of other departments, the Foreign and Commonwealth Office formulates policy in consultation with the departments concerned. The balance of responsibilities is a matter of constant adjustment, and the department with the predominant functional interest, even though it may be primarily domestic, takes the lead. This is particularly so in policy concerning the European Community and international monetary matters. In the case of policy towards the Community, the Foreign and Commonwealth Office exercises its co-ordinating role at official level through the machinery of the Cabinet Office.

Other bodies whose work has an overseas dimension include the British Overseas Trade Board and the Export Credits Guarantee Department, which provide export services for industry; the Crown Agents for Oversea Governments and Administrations,[1] which helps to arrange purchases from British aid funds and appointments under technical co-operation programmes (as well as providing mainly purchasing and management services to overseas governments and institutions); and the British Council.

The British Council

The British Council, established in 1934, aims to promote overseas an enduring understanding and appreciation of Britain through cultural, educational and technical co-operation. The activities of the Council, which has staff in over 80 countries, include the teaching of English and the recruitment of British teachers for posts overseas; administering the Government's educational assistance and technical co-operation training programmes; fostering personal contacts between British and overseas people, especially in the educational, professional and scientific areas; running, or helping to maintain, libraries of British books and periodicals overseas and providing information through touring exhibitions and bibliographical services; and presenting overseas the best of British arts and culture. In Britain, the Council is concerned mainly with arranging programmes for professional visitors and with the placing, administration and welfare of overseas students. A basic principle is that the Council's work should be of benefit both to Britain and to the receiving country.

In 1985–86 the Council assisted 24,000 overseas students, trainees and visitors to come to Britain, and an average of 53,600 students at any one time were learning English in the Council and associated teaching centres overseas. Book issues made by the Council's 116 libraries around the world totalled 6·4 million from a library stock of 2·1 million. The Council handled over 700,000 inquiries about Britain.

About three-quarters of funds for the Council's total programme, which amount to an estimated £221 million in 1986–87, is provided by the Foreign and Commonwealth Office (including the Overseas Development Administration) and on its behalf the Council is responsible for the implementation of more than 30 cultural agreements with other countries. Overseas it acts as education adviser to Britain's diplomatic missions and is responsible for educational assistance in developing countries in which it is represented and for links and

---

[1] A public body established in 1833 to look after the financial and supply needs of British dependent territories, the Crown Agents have been reorganised with a view to their privatisation in due course.

exchanges in higher education which require official support. Increasingly, the Council is undertaking education projects paid for by overseas clients and is providing English classes abroad; it is estimated that these and other activities will amount to nearly £50 million in 1986–87.

Membership of the European Community

Britain joined the European Community on 1 January 1973 and its membership was endorsed in a national referendum in 1975. The other members are Belgium, Denmark, France, the Federal Republic of Germany, Greece, the Irish Republic, Italy, Luxembourg, the Netherlands, Portugal and Spain. Britain welcomes the accession of Portugal and Spain, which took place in January 1986.

The European Community consists of three communities set up by separate treaties: the European Coal and Steel Community (ECSC), the European Economic Community (EEC) and the European Atomic Energy Community (Euratom). The Community is the world's largest trading bloc, accounting for about a third of world trade. Designed to lay the foundations for a closer union between the peoples of Europe and to promote economic expansion by means of a common market and the gradual approximation of member states' economic policies, the Community has moved towards these objectives by abolishing internal tariffs and certain other trade barriers, establishing a common customs tariff, and making provision for the freer movement of labour, capital and services. Nearly half of Britain's trade is with the other member states. There are also common policies for agriculture and fisheries. Overseas countries having

The European Community

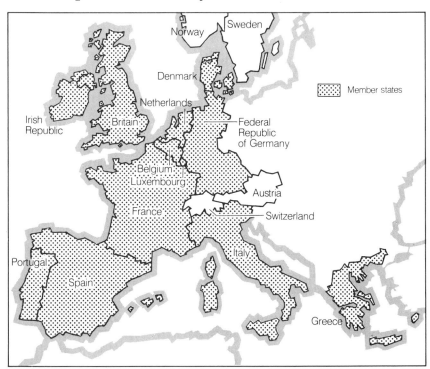

special links with Community member states are accorded preferential treatment in aid and the development of trade.

A common market for coal and steel is designed to ensure an orderly supply of these commodities to member states. The Coal and Steel Community's funds are raised by a levy on production, and investment grants are given to encourage the modernisation of the industries, for research, and for social measures to help to re-deploy coal and steel workers. Loans are also raised which promote workers' housing and aid capital investment.

One of the Community's aims is to co-ordinate member states' nuclear energy industries and their other peaceful nuclear activities. Since 1959 there has been a common market for all nuclear materials, and a control system prevents their diversion to purposes other than those declared. There is also a co-ordinated research programme in the peaceful uses of nuclear energy.

Community Institutions

The separate institutions established by the treaties for each of the three communities were merged in 1967. Each state has one representative on the Council of Ministers; in the other institutions Britain's representation is in line with that of France, the Federal Republic of Germany and Italy. English is one of the Community's official languages.

The Council of Ministers is the principal decision-making body for all major Community questions, member states being represented on it by foreign or other ministers as appropriate to the subject under discussion. The Presidency of the Council changes at six-monthly intervals. Most Council decisions are taken on the basis of a proposal by the Commission. Some issues may be decided by majority, or qualified majority, with votes weighted according to provisions in the Community treaties. Where very important interests of member states are involved, however, the Council's practice is to proceed on the basis of unanimity. The Community has agreed to improve decision-taking through more use of majority voting on internal market directives and other policies, while maintaining a member state's right to uphold a vital national interest by insisting on unanimity.

The Community's heads of State or of Government meet twice a year as the European Council, which considers both Community matters and those arising in the context of political co-operation. It discusses general Community problems and lays down guidelines and political direction for future work. When necessary, the Council addresses issues unresolved in the Council of Ministers, but Britain hopes that this will occur less frequently in future.

The Committee of Permanent Representatives (COREPER), composed of member states' ambassadors to the Community, assists the Council by preparing its meetings and co-ordinating the work of other subordinate bodies.

The Commission formulates policy proposals for submission to the Council of Ministers, promotes Community interests, attempts to reconcile national viewpoints and implements the provisions of the treaties and Community measures. Certain executive powers of decision are delegated to it, for example, in the areas of agricultural, trade and competition policy. It is composed of 17 commissioners (two from Britain) nominated by member governments. Each commissioner is responsible for one or more of the main Community activities. The Commission is pledged to act independently of national or sectional interests and to formulate its proposals and administer policy in the interests of the Community as a whole. Its proposals are made only after extensive consultation with officials of the national governments and with producers, trade unions, employers' associations and many others.

The Court of Justice interprets and adjudicates on the meaning of the treaties and of any measures taken by the Council of Ministers and Commission under them, hears complaints and appeals brought by or against Community institutions, member states or individuals, and gives preliminary rulings on questions referred to it by courts in the member states. As a court of final appeal, its procedure in such cases is broadly similar to that of the highest courts in member states; its rulings are binding on member countries, Community institutions and individuals. The Court consists of 13 judges assisted by six advocates-general who make reasoned submissions concerning cases brought before the Court to help it in its interpretation of Community law. In 1985 member states agreed to attach a court of first instance to the Court of Justice in order to provide for the more efficient disposal of the Court's growing workload.

The European Parliament is composed of 518 members, of whom 434 were directly elected in 1984; the 60 Spanish and the 24 Portuguese members are nominated at present but both countries have undertaken to hold elections. The Parliament's members (81 from Britain) sit according to party affiliation and not nationality. Elections to the Parliament are held every five years, the most recent in June 1984. The Parliament is consulted on and debates all major policy issues of the Community. Members may question the Council of Ministers and Commission, and have the power by a two-thirds majority to dismiss the Commission. The Parliament can also reject in its entirety the draft annual budget as presented by the Commission and approved by the Council. A formal conciliation procedure has been adopted for use in the event of disagreement between the Parliament and the Council of Ministers on matters with major budgetary or financial implications.

The European Court of Auditors examines all Community revenue and expenditure to see that it has been legally received and spent, and to ensure sound financial management. It draws up an annual report, and may submit observations on specific questions as the Community institutions request.

The Economic and Social Committee is a consultative body representing employers' organisations, trade unions and other interests, and is consulted by the Council of Ministers and the Commission during the formulation of policy.

Community policies are implemented by regulations, which are legally binding and directly applicable in all member countries; directives, which are binding, as to the result to be achieved, on member states to which they are addressed but allow national authorities to decide on means of implementation; decisions, which are binding on those to whom they are addressed (for example, member states, firms or individuals); and recommendations and opinions, which have no binding force. The Council can also indicate a general policy direction through resolutions.

In addition to, and separately from, the institutions operating within the Community framework established by treaty, the member states have set up machinery (now formalised in a draft treaty based on proposals submitted by Britain) under which they consult each other before taking up final positions on important questions of foreign policy. Known as political co-operation, these consultations include regular meetings of foreign ministers, monthly meetings of senior officials, and contacts at working level among those concerned with particular questions. In addition, the 12 foreign ministries are linked by a secure communications system and a small secretariat is being established in Brussels to assist the Presidency.

Finance

The Community is financed by a system of levies on agricultural imports, customs duties and the product of a notional rate of value added tax (VAT) levied on a Community harmonised basis at a rate at present not exceeding 1·4 per cent. These are known as 'own resources'.

Without some form of adjustment Britain's contributions under the system would be much higher than its receipts from Community policies, because the

Common Agricultural Policy absorbs about two-thirds of Community spending and Britain's agricultural sector is relatively small. This problem was foreseen during the accession negotiations, and Britain was given an assurance that, if unacceptable situations arose, the very survival of the Community would demand that its institutions found equitable solutions.

In 1980 the Community recognised that there was a problem for Britain and refunds were made for each year in the period from 1980 to 1983. In June 1984 the European Council (meeting in Fontainebleau) reached agreement on a fairer and more soundly based system for Britain's contributions, under which Britain obtains a rebate of 66 per cent of the gap between Britain's share of VAT payments and its share of Community expenditure. In addition, agreement has been reached on measures covering budgetary discipline and limitations on increases in agricultural spending.

The VAT ceiling of 1 per cent has been increased to 1·4 per cent for the Community as a whole, partly to meet the costs of enlargement.

In addition to agriculture, the Community budget includes spending on regional and social policies, projects concerned with research, energy, industry and transport, and aid to developing countries.

External Relations
Political Issues

Within the framework of political co-operation member states discuss a wide range of foreign policy issues. At the United Nations and in other international bodies their actions are closely co-ordinated and they vote together on most major issues. The cohesion of member states has played a key role in the process initiated at the 1975 Helsinki Conference on Security and Co-operation in Europe (see p 83), and especially in the setting up of the Conference on Confidence- and Security-Building Measures and Disarmament in Europe, which opened in Stockholm in January 1984. They are also pledged to continue seeking constructive, comprehensive and realistic dialogue with the Soviet Union and the countries of Eastern Europe, and they attach the highest importance to achieving effective arms control and disarmament agreements.

In July 1980, the European Council's Venice Declaration stated that a lasting solution to the problem of the Middle East required the mutual acceptance of two basic principles—the right of all countries in the area, including Israel, to secure existence within guaranteed borders and the right of the Palestinian people to self-determination. After Israel's invasion of Lebanon in 1982, Britain, France and Italy contributed to the multinational force deployed there from the end of that year until early 1984. Member states have consistently emphasised the importance to any future settlement of the complete withdrawal of foreign forces from Lebanon except for those whose presence is requested by the Lebanese Government, and the obligation on all parties to co-operate with the UN Interim Force in Lebanon. Member states have also followed with concern the conflict between Iran and Iraq and in February 1986 expressed their support for a UN Security Council resolution which called for an immediate ceasefire.

Member states are working closely to strengthen relations with Central America in order to support the efforts of the Contadora Group (Colombia, Mexico, Panama and Venezuela) to negotiate a comprehensive and verifiable peace agreement in Central America. In November 1985 a conference of foreign ministers from Community, Central American and Contadora countries met in Luxembourg to carry forward the dialogue initiated at a previous meeting in Costa Rica in 1984. It concluded with the signature of a Final Act recording agreement that the dialogue should be continued and developed, and of a co-operation agreement between the Community and the Central American countries and Panama providing for closer economic links and a substantial increase in Community aid to the region. Member states have made clear their conviction that the conflicts of the region cannot be resolved by armed force.

Member states have deplored the Soviet Union's continuing occupation of Afghanistan and continue to call for the immediate withdrawal of the occupying forces in order that a permanent settlement can be reached restoring the right of the Afghan people to self-determination.

In order to emphasise the importance they attach to the abolition of apartheid, member states have adopted a package of restrictive and positive measures towards South Africa. They have called for the release of all political prisoners, and an end to the ban on political parties and to discriminatory legislation in South Africa. Member states have also urged the South African Government to enter into a genuine dialogue with representatives of the black population, and in mid-1986 Britain's Foreign and Commonwealth Secretary, Sir Geoffrey Howe, visited Southern Africa on their behalf in an unsuccessful attempt to establish conditions in which such a dialogue could begin. Member states are also consulting with other industrialised countries on further measures which may be needed, including a ban on new investment in South Africa and a ban on coal, iron and steel imports. The Community has launched a programme of social and educational assistance to the black population of South Africa.

In response to growing evidence of state-supported terrorism by Libya and other countries, member states agreed early in 1986 to restrict the freedom of movement of Libyan diplomats, to reduce their number, to impose strict visa requirements on Libyans, and to reaffirm an export ban on arms or other military equipment to Libya. Britain broke off diplomatic relations with Libya in 1984 following the death of a policewoman in London caused by shots fired from the Libyan People's Bureau.

Trade

On most international trade matters the Council of Ministers agrees a common position, with the Commission speaking, and, where necessary, negotiating on behalf of the Community (for example, in the current preparations for a new round of multilateral trade negotiations within the General Agreement on Tariffs and Trade and for the renegotiation of the Multi-Fibre Arrangement). Association or co-operation agreements giving preferential access to Community markets have been concluded with most countries in the Mediterranean basin. Non-preferential co-operation agreements have been concluded with individual countries in South Asia and Latin America and also with two regional organisations—the Association of South East Asian Nations and the Andean Pact. Regular discussions covering trade and other matters are held with regional groupings of Latin American, Arab and South-East Asian countries.

The Community has also improved progressively its generalised scheme of preferences designed to benefit the poorest developing countries. The scheme provides duty-free access for almost all manufactured and semi-manufactured goods exported by developing countries and preferential access for agricultural products. The latest scheme started in 1981 and runs for ten years.

Aid

The third Lomé Convention, which governs aid, trade and co-operation between the Community and 66 developing countries in Africa, the Caribbean and the Pacific (ACP) was signed in December 1984 and came into force in May 1986. Over half the ACP countries are members of the Commonwealth. The Convention, which covers the period from 1985 to 1989, provides for aid and European Investment Bank lending of about £5,500 million, covering industrial and agricultural co-operation, a scheme designed to help stabilise the commodity export earnings of the ACP countries and assistance for ACP mineral producers whose production and income suffer from temporary disruptions beyond their control. It also offers duty-free access to the Community for ACP exports of all industrial and most agricultural goods, including privileged access for sugar, bananas, rum and beef. Emphasis is being placed on food production and on measures to prevent desertification. All British dependent territories (with the exception of Bermuda, Gibraltar and Hong Kong), together with the overseas territories of other Community members, are formally associated with the Community under provisions parallel to those of the Lomé Convention with similar aid and trade benefits.

Britain played a leading part in urging the Community to adopt an aid programme encompassing those developing countries (many of which are among the world's poorest) not covered by the Lomé Convention or having any other special relationship with the Community. The programme for these non-associated states has grown steadily since 1976 and was worth some £86 million in 1985. Priority is given to rural development and agricultural production in the poorest countries. In 1985 the Community spent some £330 million on food aid, of which Britain's share was about £77 million, much of which went to Africa. The British Government is pressing for improvements to the Community's food aid programme to make it more responsive to the real needs of recipients and to give higher priority to emergency relief.

Internal Policies   As a major trading nation, Britain believes that the Community's common market should be completed by removing the many barriers which still impede the movement of goods and services between member states. Since 1982 the European Council has emphasised the need for action along these lines on the grounds that European industry cannot become fully competitive in world markets unless the national markets of member states are closely integrated, and in 1985 the Community agreed on a target date of 1992 for the completion of a genuinely free internal market. In particular the British Government wants swift action to open up public purchasing to competition, the liberalisation of inland, sea and air transport services, full freedom of establishment for the professions, a European capital market and a liberalised European financial services industry capable of meeting competition from Japan and the United States.

The Common Agricultural Policy is designed to ensure food supplies at reasonable prices for consumers and a fair standard of living for farmers. Producers' returns are supported by a combination of charges on imports and internal support prices maintained by intervention buying where necessary. The Common Fisheries Policy, revised in 1983, governs access to coastal waters, conservation of stocks, the allocation of quotas among member states, and enforcement of these measures.

The European Social Fund assists areas of high unemployment by providing grants towards schemes of training, job creation and geographical mobility of workers. The European Regional Development Fund provides grants for industrial and infrastructure projects in the less-developed or industrially declining regions of the Community with the aim of reducing existing imbalances or preventing the creation of new ones. In 1985, Britain received £345 million (24 per cent of the resources) from the regional fund and £308 million (24 per cent) from the social fund. The British, Irish and Italian governments have made a number of proposals designed to promote enterprise and self-employment, flexible employment patterns and training, and to tackle long-term unemployment in the Community.

Britain also receives about a fifth of the lending of the European Investment Bank, which was set up in 1958 to provide finance on a non-profit-making basis for investment to develop the Community's less-favoured regions, to modernise industry and to help projects of common interest to two or more member states.

Community industrial policy includes measures designed to deal with the problems of the steel industry during its restructuring; temporary mandatory production quotas have been in force for several years in order to cut back production to the level of demand, thereby allowing economic price levels to be obtained. The Community is also involved in helping to create the right climate for high technology industries to flourish. The ESPRIT programme is bringing together many of the European computer companies in a common programme of research and development in information technology, while the nuclear fusion research project at Culham in Oxfordshire is designed to develop new energy sources. The EUREKA programme, launched in 1985 following a French initiative, is designed to encourage the development of new technologies in Community and other European countries.

The European Monetary System was established in 1979 to promote monetary stability in Europe. It consists of an exchange-rate mechanism, a monetary unit known as the European Currency Unit (ECU—based on a 'basket' of national currencies including sterling, the value of which is recalculated daily) which is used within the Community for budgetary and other purposes, and enlarged Community short- and medium-term credit facilities. The member states are also committed to the establishment of a European Monetary Fund. Britain has participated in the system from the outset, although not in the exchange-rate arrangements, and has deposited 20 per cent of its gold and dollar currency reserves with the European Monetary Co-operation Fund in exchange for ECUs. The Government intends that Britain should join the exchange-rate mechanism when conditions permit.

The Commonwealth

The Commonwealth is a voluntary association of 49 independent states with a combined population of over 1,100 million, about a quarter of the world total. Commonwealth members are a representative cross-section of nations at all stages of social and economic development. They include some of the richest and poorest members of the world community and also some of the largest and smallest. Their peoples are drawn from practically all the world's main races, from all continents and from many faiths. Britain participates fully in all Commonwealth activities and values it as a means of consulting and co-operating with peoples of widely different cultures and perspectives, thereby increasing international understanding, stability and peace, and contributing to more balanced global economic development.

The members are Antigua and Barbuda, Australia, Bahamas, Bangladesh, Barbados, Belize, Botswana, Britain, Brunei, Canada, Cyprus, Dominica, Fiji, The Gambia, Ghana, Grenada, Guyana, India, Jamaica, Kenya, Kiribati, Lesotho, Malawi, Malaysia, Maldives, Malta, Mauritius, Nauru, New Zealand, Nigeria, Papua New Guinea, Saint Christopher and Nevis, Saint Lucia, Saint Vincent and the Grenadines, Seychelles, Sierra Leone, Singapore, Solomon Islands, Sri Lanka, Swaziland, Tanzania, Tonga, Trinidad and Tobago, Tuvalu, Uganda, Vanuatu, Western Samoa, Zambia and Zimbabwe. Nauru and Tuvalu are special members, entitled to take part in all functional Commonwealth meetings and activities but not the two-yearly Commonwealth Heads of Government Meetings. The Queen is recognised as head of the Commonwealth; she is also head of State in 18 countries.

The origin of the Commonwealth lies in the gradual granting of self-government to the older-established British colonies (later known as the Dominions) in Australia, Canada, New Zealand and South Africa[1] where European settlement had occurred on a large scale. Their fully independent status in relation to Britain was legally formulated in the Statute of Westminster of 1931. The modern Commonwealth, comprising republics and national monarchies as well as monarchies under the Queen, was made possible by the

---

[1] South Africa ceased to be a member of the Commonwealth in 1961.

decision of India in 1949 to remain a member while becoming a republic. Since then, the great majority of Britain's former dependent territories have attained their independence and have voluntarily joined the Commonwealth.

Consultation

As a member of the Commonwealth, Britain participates in a system of mutual consultation and co-operation which benefits member countries and contributes to international understanding. It led, for instance, to the Commonwealth playing a significant role in the events leading to Zimbabwe's independence in April 1980.

Consultation takes place through diplomatic representatives known as High Commissioners, meetings of heads of Government, specialised conferences of other ministers and officials, expert groups, and discussions at international conferences and the United Nations. Trade and cultural exhibitions and conferences of professional and unofficial medical, cultural, educational and economic organisations are other ways in which frequent contacts are made.

Heads of Government usually meet every two years, most recently in Nassau in 1985; they will next meet in Canada in 1987. Proceedings are normally in private, which facilitates a frank and informal exchange of views. No votes are taken, decisions being reached by consensus. These meetings allow Prime Ministers and Presidents to discuss international issues and decide on collective initiatives. Common views on matters of major international concern are formulated and reflected in the communiqués issued at the end of the meetings. Occasionally, separate declarations are made on particular issues. These have included the 1971 Declaration of Commonwealth Principles, the 1977 Gleneagles statement, which commits member governments to take every practical step to discourage sporting contacts with South Africa, and the 1985 Accord on Southern Africa, which provides for measures designed to impress on South Africa the urgency of dismantling the apartheid system. Following the failure of Commonwealth and other attempts in 1986 to encourage the evolution of a political dialogue leading to the establishment of a non-racial and representative government, a mini-summit of Commonwealth leaders, meeting in London in August, agreed on the need for further measures against South Africa. Britain, while believing that economic sanctions would be counter-productive to promoting peaceful change, agreed to impose voluntary bans on new investment in, and the promotion of tourism to, South Africa, and to implement any European Community decision to ban the import of coal, iron and steel (see p 77).

With many small states among its members the Commonwealth has expressed concern about their security and development. At Nassau Commonwealth leaders called for action which would reduce the vulnerability of small states while not diminishing their status as independent, sovereign and equal members of the world community. British policy is to co-operate with other member states in order to increase the security of small nations by encouraging regional co-operation and by providing economic aid and technical assistance.

Finance ministers meet annually to discuss world economic problems, and in recent years have paid particular attention to the problems of development and the establishment of a fairer international economic order. Other meetings include those of agriculture, education, health and law ministers which take place every two or three years. Ministers of industry, labour and employment, trade and women's affairs also meet.

The Commonwealth Secretariat

The Commonwealth Secretariat, established in London in 1965 and financed by member states, is the main agency for multilateral communication between them. It is headed by a Secretary-General appointed by heads of Government and responsible to member states collectively.

The Secretariat promotes consultation, disseminates information on matters of common concern, and organises meetings and conferences, including those of heads of Government and of ministers. It co-ordinates many Commonwealth activities related to international economic, social and political affairs, including food production and rural development, the role of women in development, youth programmes, management development, science and technology, law and health. The Secretariat also administers the Commonwealth Fund for Technical Co-operation.

Because of its neutral position the Secretariat has been able to make its good offices available in cases of dispute, and has carried out, on request, special assignments requiring demonstrable impartiality.

Technical Co-operation

Britain plays an active part in the work of the Commonwealth Fund for Technical Co-operation, established within the Secretariat to provide technical assistance for economic and social development in Commonwealth developing countries, and contributes almost a third of its income. The Fund provides experts to undertake advisory assignments or fill specific posts and uses consultancy firms to make studies for governments. Its fellowships and training programme is of particular help in raising levels of technical, industrial, managerial and other skills, and makes wide use of training facilities within developing member countries for the benefit of other developing countries. It has a special programme to help countries develop their exports, another on food production and rural development and a small technical assistance group to give advice in key areas. An industrial development unit, the main executive agency of the Commonwealth Action Programme of Industrial Co-operation, investigates the feasibility of establishing new industries in developing countries and helps to prepare and initiate agreed projects.

Expenditure by Britain on bilateral technical co-operation with Commonwealth developing countries in 1985 was nearly £126 million, the greater part being spent on financing staff for service with Commonwealth governments and in financing training places in Britain for people from Commonwealth countries. In particular, Britain is a major contributor to the Commonwealth Scholarship and Fellowship Plan, a system of awards for people of high intellectual promise to study in Commonwealth countries other than their own. It was agreed in 1984 that the number of awards would be increased to about 1,700 of which Britain would provide some 800. In 1986, the Overseas Development Administration's Shared Scholarship Scheme, jointly funded by the Government, universities and polytechnics, was introduced to finance 150 new scholarships each year over a period of five years, the awards being open to private sector students from developing Commonwealth countries. Other assistance includes sending volunteers to serve overseas, consultancy services, the supply of training and research equipment and the provision of advice by British scientific and technical institutions. (Financial aid to Commonwealth developing countries totalled £443 million in 1985 and most received investment finance from the Commonwealth Development Corporation.)

Commonwealth Foundation and Other Organisations

The Commonwealth Foundation was established in 1966 and reconstituted as an international organisation in 1983. Financed by member governments, it promotes closer co-operation among professional and other non-governmental organisations within the Commonwealth. It has assisted over 30 Commonwealth professional associations, many of which it helped to establish, and has assisted in the creation and growth of many national ones; it has also supported 16 multidisciplinary professional centres.

The Commonwealth Institute, financed largely by the British Government, promotes knowledge about the Commonwealth through films, library services, lecture tours by members of the staff and study conferences for students; its headquarters in London has a permanent publicity exhibition depicting the life of member states, each country financing its own stand. The Royal Commonwealth Society, which is over 100 years old, is a centre for study and discussion, its library in London having one of the largest collections on the Commonwealth. The Society has branches in many countries.

In keeping with the fact that the Commonwealth is an association of peoples as well as governments, many unofficial organisations, professional bodies and voluntary societies provide machinery for co-operation. Professional bodies include associations of architects, doctors, engineers, journalists, lawyers, librarians, magistrates, museum curators, nurses, pharmacists, planners, surveyors and veterinary surgeons. Other organisations include the Commonwealth Parliamentary Association, which organises an annual conference of parliamentarians, the Commonwealth Press Union, the Commonwealth Broadcasting Association, the Commonwealth Youth Exchange Council, the Commonwealth Games Federation and the Commonwealth Arts Association.

DEPENDENCIES There are 15 remaining British dependent territories: Anguilla; Bermuda; British Antarctic Territory; British Indian Ocean Territory; British Virgin Islands; Cayman Islands; Falkland Islands; Gibraltar; Hong Kong; Montserrat; Pitcairn, Ducie, Henderson and Oeno; St Helena; St Helena Dependencies (Ascension, Tristan da Cunha); South Georgia and the South Sandwich Islands; and the Turks and Caicos Islands. They have a combined population of 5·5 million, of which 5·3 million live in Hong Kong. Few are rich in natural resources, and some are scattered groups of islands. There are no permanent inhabitants in the British Antarctic Territory, British Indian Ocean Territory or South Georgia and the South Sandwich Islands. Most dependencies have considerable self-government with their own legislature and civil service. Britain is generally responsible, through a Governor, for defence, internal security and foreign affairs.

It is Britain's policy to give independence to those dependencies that want it, and not to force it on those which do not. In the case of the Falkland Islands, which is the subject of a territorial claim by Argentina, the inhabitants wish to retain the link with Britain. The Government is committed to the defence of the Islanders' right to live under a government of their own choosing. The Islanders' right of self-determination is reflected in the new Falkland Islands Constitution, which came into effect in 1985.

Argentina and Chile have claims to territory which overlaps part of the British Antarctic Territory. Claims to territorial sovereignty in the Antarctic, however, are suspended by the provisions of the 1959 Antarctic Treaty.

Gibraltar is the subject of a territorial claim by Spain, which imposed border restrictions in the 1960s. Since the return of democracy to Spain, Britain and Spain have reached agreement on the method for handling their differences over Gibraltar, Spanish restrictions being lifted in February 1985. Britain wishes to see the development of practical co-operation between Gibraltar and Spain to the benefit of both peoples and remains committed to honouring the wishes of the people of Gibraltar as to their future.

In 1984 an agreement was signed between Britain and the People's Republic of China on the future of Hong Kong. Under the agreement, which was ratified by the two Governments in 1985, Britain will continue to be responsible for the administration of Hong Kong until 1997, when the territory will be restored to China. The Chinese Government will then establish a Hong Kong Special Administrative Region, which will enjoy a high degree of autonomy, except in foreign and defence affairs. It will be vested with executive, legislative and independent judicial powers and its government will be composed of local inhabitants. The laws currently in force in Hong Kong will remain basically unchanged, as will its present social and economic systems and its way of life. Private property rights and other rights and freedoms will be protected by law. These arrangements will remain in place for 50 years after 1997.

International Peace and Security

Britain is concerned to protect its territorial integrity and political independence, as well as the interests of its dependencies and of its allies, and pursues these objectives through a national security policy in which deterrence and defence are coupled with efforts towards removing or alleviating the causes of international tension and achieving balanced and verifiable international arms control and disarmament.

British defence policy is based on the North Atlantic Treaty Organisation (NATO)[1] which member countries regard as their guarantee of security, freedom and well-being, and as an important contributor to international peace and stability. The purpose of NATO is to enable its member countries to maintain peace with freedom. It pursues a strategy of deterrence, designed to convince any potential aggressor that the use of force, or the threat of it, carries risks far outweighing any likely advantage. At the same time NATO countries seek through international negotiations significant reductions in the level of nuclear and conventional forces.

Britain's defence resources are concentrated almost exclusively on key NATO tasks. However, the Government's defence policy is also designed to promote, whenever possible, British and more general Western interests outside the NATO area. In addition, Britain demonstrates its world-wide interests by periodic military deployments and exercises overseas; by supporting United Nations and other peacekeeping efforts; and by providing military assistance and training to a number of friendly countries.

East–West Relations

Britain seeks improvements in East–West relations based on a broader understanding and on the recognition that East and West have a common interest in peace and security at a lower level of weapons. The Government believes that both sides should avoid policies which risk provoking confrontation and should aim instead for mutual accommodation and co-operation while exercising restraint in the conduct of international relations both in Europe and in the rest of the world. This is explicitly recognised in the Final Act of the 1975 Helsinki Conference on Security and Co-operation in Europe, which states that European security has to be considered in the broader context of world security. Britain is committed to doing everything possible to reduce the risks of war and to avoid misunderstanding. The Government is following a policy of increased contacts at all levels with the Soviet Union and its allies, and welcomed the 1985 summit meeting in Geneva when the United States and the Soviet Union agreed to accelerate the pace of nuclear arms negotiations and seek better relations between their two countries through regular meetings. The Soviet Union's invasion of Afghanistan in December 1979 and its continued occupation of that country remain, however, an obstacle to improved relations.

Britain attaches great importance to the full and balanced implementation by all participants of the provisions of the 1975 Helsinki Final Act for increased stability in Europe and improved co-operation between the 35 European and North American signatory states. While not a legally binding document, the

---

[1] NATO's 16 member countries are Belgium, Britain, Canada, Denmark, France, the Federal Republic of Germany, Greece, Iceland, Italy, Luxembourg, the Netherlands, Norway, Portugal, Spain, Turkey and the United States. France and Spain do not participate in NATO's integrated military structure.

Final Act is a charter and code of behaviour for what the participants hope will in time become a more normal and open relationship between both governments and peoples in East and West. To this end it contains undertakings about security, respect for human rights, and co-operation in economic, humanitarian and other matters. Follow-up meetings took place in Belgrade (1977 to 1978) and Madrid (1980 to 1983), and a further follow-up meeting will be convened in Vienna in November 1986. As a result of the Madrid Conference, where it was decided that renewed efforts should be made to give full effect to the Final Act, an experts' meeting on the subject of human rights took place in Ottawa in 1985. This was followed by a cultural forum in Budapest later in the year. A meeting on human contacts took place in Berne in April 1986.

At the Conference on Confidence- and Security-Building Measures and Disarmament in Stockholm, which began in January 1984 at the behest of the Madrid Conference, Britain and its NATO allies have proposed a set of measures to build confidence and security in Europe by creating greater openness about normal military practices (for example, exercises) and thereby reducing the likelihood of an outbreak of hostilities by accident, misunderstanding or design.

Together with France, the United States and the Soviet Union, Britain is a signatory to the 1972 Quadripartite Agreement on Berlin, which reaffirms the four countries' rights and responsibilities there, and provides for greatly improved travel and communications facilities between West Berlin and the Federal Republic of Germany, the German Democratic Republic and East Berlin, and for the maintenance and development of the ties between West Berlin and the Federal Republic.

Arms Control and Disarmament

Britain is committed to the search for balanced and verifiable measures of arms control and disarmament, and has played a prominent part in multilateral disarmament negotiations. Britain is a participating state in the Conference on Disarmament at Geneva, in the Mutual and Balanced Force Reductions negotiations at Vienna, and in the Conference on Confidence- and Security-Building Measures and Disarmament at Stockholm; it also takes an active part in disarmament deliberations under the auspices of the United Nations.

Nuclear Weapons

Britain strongly supports the negotiations between the United States and the Soviet Union on nuclear and space arms, which began in Geneva in March 1985. It fully shares the agreed objective of working out effective agreements aimed at preventing an arms race in space and terminating it on earth, at limiting and reducing nuclear arms and at strengthening strategic stability. The British Government supports the latest proposals of the United States which involve, among other things, a 50 per cent cut in strategic nuclear missiles and the elimination within three years of all intermediate-range nuclear missiles. Britain's nuclear deterrent is a minimum force which will remain so after the introduction in service of the Trident system, and is very small in comparison with Soviet nuclear forces. The priority therefore is for reductions in the arsenals of the superpowers. None the less, Britain has made it clear that, if the US and Soviet strategic arsenals were to be very substantially reduced and there had been no significant increases in Soviet defences, Britain would review the position and consider how best it could contribute to arms control in the light of the reduced threat.

Britain has played a leading part in strengthening the regime of non-proliferation of nuclear weapons. It is a party to the most widely supported arms control agreement in existence, the 1968 Non-Proliferation Treaty, which is designed both to stop the spread of nuclear weapons by providing an assurance through international safeguards that nuclear facilities of non-nuclear-weapon states will not be used for making such weapons and to protect the right of all countries to use nuclear energy for peaceful purposes. Britain was the first nuclear-weapon state to conclude an agreement with the International Atomic Energy Agency, which administers the safeguards. Britain reaffirmed its full support for the Treaty at a review conference in 1985, and has been active in strengthening it by seeking the widest possible adherence. It has also undertaken not to use nuclear weapons against non-nuclear-weapon states which have internationally binding commitments not to manufacture or acquire nuclear explosive devices (except in the case of an attack on British interests by such a state in association with a nuclear-weapon state). Britain believes that limiting the security assurances to these states provides further support for nuclear non-proliferation.

Britain is also fully committed to progress towards a comprehensive, verifiable ban on all nuclear tests, and in recent years has tabled papers on verification at the Conference on Disarmament. However, solutions to verification problems need to be clearer before negotiations can be resumed.

The British Government thinks that the establishment of nuclear-weapon-free zones in certain parts of the world could contribute to regional security, to non-proliferation and to disarmament in general, provided that nuclear weapons do not already feature in the security of the region involved and all states concerned are prepared to participate on the basis of agreements freely entered into and in keeping with internationally recognised principles.

Two such nuclear-free zones have been established: the zone created by the 1967 Treaty of Tlatelolco in Latin America and that created by the 1985 Nuclear Free Zone Treaty in the South Pacific. Britain was the first nuclear-weapon state to ratify the two additional protocols in the Tlatelolco Treaty under which such states undertake to respect the aims and provisions of the Treaty, not to contribute to any violation of its terms, and not to use or threaten to use nuclear weapons against a contracting party. Britain is studying carefully the South Pacific Treaty and draft protocols similar to those in the 1967 Treaty before taking any decision on ratification.

Biological and Chemical Weapons

As a result of a British initiative, another category of weapons of mass destruction, biological weapons, is the subject of the 1972 Convention on Prohibition of the Development, Production and Stockpiling of Bacteriological (Biological) and Toxin Weapons and on their Destruction. A conference to review the Convention is to be held in Geneva in the autumn of 1986. Britain is also committed to achieving a comprehensive and verifiable world-wide ban on chemical weapons, having abandoned its chemical warfare capability in the late 1950s. In 1976 it tabled a draft treaty and in recent years has introduced a number of important working papers into the Conference. These have included detailed proposals on compliance, including a system of challenge inspection in cases of suspected non-compliance, the verification of non-production of banned chemicals, and measures to prevent misuse of civil chemical facilities.

Conventional Weapons

Conventional weapons are by far the largest component of national armouries and Britain has welcomed the completion of a UN study which emphasised the responsibility of all states to seek reductions in conventional forces. In particular, Britain believes in the value of regional agreements as a means of facilitating such reductions. In the Vienna negotiations, Britain, together with its NATO allies, is working for an agreement with the Warsaw Pact participants which would contribute to a more stable relationship and strengthen peace and security in Europe. This requires an approximate parity between NATO and Warsaw Pact forces in central Europe where the Warsaw Pact troops currently outnumber those of NATO by at least 200,000. Progress in the talks has been slight, mainly because of a long-standing disagreement over the size of Eastern forces in the reduction area. In an attempt to break the deadlock, the West tabled new proposals in December 1985 which accept reductions in the framework of a first-phase agreement without insisting on a prior agreement on force levels. These proposals, based on ideas put forward by Britain and the Federal Republic of Germany, provide for initial reductions of 5,000 US and 11,500 Soviet troops in central Europe, a subsequent collective commitment not to increase forces for three years in that area, and frequent inspections to ensure compliance.

Concerned about the rising scale of military expenditure in the world, Britain has supported proposals at the United Nations for the balanced and verifiable reduction of military budgets. Britain and its allies and partners have participated actively in developing a standardised system for reporting annual military expenditure to establish a basis for future comparison. Britain welcomes efforts to promote increased openness in the reporting of military expenditure and to this end has submitted figures on its military budget. British experts have taken part in a number of UN studies on aspects of arms control and disarmament.

Britain and the United Nations

Support for the United Nations and the purposes and principles of its Charter has been a cornerstone of British policy since 1945, for Britain sees a strong and effective United Nations as a means of pursuing and achieving many of its foreign policy objectives such as the peaceful resolution of disputes, disarmament and arms control, the protection of human rights and the promotion of the rule of law. It believes that all member states have a responsibility to ensure that the organisation's efforts are devoted to the furtherance of the principles enshrined in the Charter, and has suggested reforms to make it more effective.

Keeping the Peace

The maintenance of international peace and security was the primary purpose envisaged for the United Nations at the time of its establishment. Britain believes that it is appropriate for the United Nations, as the only forum in which almost the whole international community is represented, to seek to resolve disputes which threaten peace and stability whether on a regional or world scale. As a permanent member of the Security Council, Britain plays an active role in the Council's work and has sought to develop and improve its role in the peaceful settlement of disputes.

In 1985, for example, Britain expressed the belief that the Council should engage in more preventive diplomacy in an effort to help countries engaged in a dispute before it reached an acute stage. Britain proposed a new form of Council meeting of a private and formal nature which would include states engaged in the dispute under discussion but would minimise opportunities for propaganda. Britain has also put forward proposals for rationalising the work of the General Assembly.

Another British concern is that the United Nations should have an effective peacekeeping capacity. Britain contributes to the UN force in Cyprus and provides logistic support for the UN Interim Force in Lebanon.

Human Rights

Britain has consistently supported the efforts of the United Nations to promote human rights throughout the world through the establishment of internationally accepted standards. The UN Charter itself includes among the purposes of the United Nations the achievement of international co-operation in promoting and encouraging respect for human rights and fundamental freedoms for all without distinction as to race, sex, language or religion. Britain believes that this and the subsequent practice of the United Nations has established human rights as a legitimate matter for international concern and that the UN Charter imposes on member governments an obligation to co-operate with appropriate UN bodies in the pursuit of policies which promote human rights.

Fundamental human rights provisions are set out in the Universal Declaration of Human Rights proclaimed by the General Assembly in 1948, and in the two International Covenants (one on Economic, Social and Cultural Rights and the other on Civil and Political Rights) which impose legal obligations on those who ratify them and which came into force in 1976. Britain played a large part in their drafting and ratified the two Covenants in 1976. It also accepted the optional Article 41 of the Covenant on Civil and Political Rights recognising the competence of the Human Rights Committee established under this Covenant to receive and consider state complaints. (It is not party to the Optional Protocol to the Covenant which recognises the right of individuals to submit communications to the Committee; Britain recognises the right of individual petition under the European Convention on Human Rights.) Britain is also a party to other international instruments, including conventions on the elimination of racial discrimination and of discrimination against women (Britain deposited its instrument of ratification in April 1986), prevention of genocide, the abolition of slavery, the status of refugees and stateless persons, the political rights of women, and consent to marriage. In March 1985 Britain signed the UN Convention against Torture which was adopted with British support by the General Assembly in December 1984.

The adoption of conventions and covenants in itself is insufficient to secure the protection of human rights. It is up to states themselves to do that. Britain constantly urges states to adhere to those standards which have been agreed internationally as the basis of that protection. Britain has also supported the establishment of additional mechanisms such as the appointment of Special Rapporteurs or Representatives of the UN Commission on Human Rights to investigate human rights abuses in specific countries or globally.

Britain plays a leading part in the discussion of human rights in the various multilateral fora provided by the United Nations. In 1984 it was re-elected to the UN Commission on Human Rights for a further three-year term, and the British delegation will continue to build on the initiatives which it and other countries have taken there. Britain is also represented on the UN Sub-Commission on Prevention of Discrimination and Protection of Minorities, on the Human Rights Committee (which monitors the implementation of the provisions of the International Covenant on Civil and Political Rights by the parties to it), on the Committee on the Elimination of Racial Discrimination established under the Convention on the Elimination of All Forms of Racial Discrimination (to which a British expert was elected in January 1986), and on the UN Commission on the Status of Women.

Economic and Social Affairs

The UN Charter states that 'the promotion of the economic and social advancement of all peoples' is one of the principal aims of the United Nations, and an estimated 90 per cent of the organisation's efforts, in terms of resources and personnel, is now employed to this end. With the growing concern for the problems of development, the main emphasis has become increasingly the provision of direct assistance for member states. The UN system is now the largest single source of technical assistance for developing countries, as well as providing considerable emergency and relief aid and assistance for refugees. (The provision of capital assistance has been generally confined to the World Bank group and regional development banks whose operations are usually considered separately from those of the rest of the UN system.)

Successive British governments have affirmed their support for the functional and developmental work of the United Nations. Britain is the sixth largest contributor to the UN's regular budget, providing some £25·3 million, 4·67 per cent of the total, in 1985. In addition, it contributed some £9 million to the World Health Organisation, £4·7 million to the International Labour Organisation, £6·8 million to the Food and Agriculture Organisation and £6·3 million to the UN Educational, Scientific and Cultural Organisation. Britain provides considerable contributions to the UN's voluntary funds, donating £20 million in 1985 for the UN Development Programme, £15·5 million for the UN High Commissioner for Refugees, £5 million for the UN Relief and Works Agency for Palestinian Refugees, £8·4 million for the UN Children's Fund, £4·5 million for the UN Fund for Population Activities, and about £0·5 million for the World Food Programme.

In the deliberations of the governing bodies of the various agencies and programmes, Britain encourages the deployment of the resources towards the poorest countries and the poorest communities in the developing world. It also seeks to promote the most efficient use of UN development resources and improvements in the co-ordination, control and effectiveness of the system, in order to avoid unnecessary duplication by the various agencies.

In December 1985, Britain withdrew from the United Nations Educational, Scientific and Cultural Organisation (UNESCO). The decision followed a period of notice of withdrawal during which Britain worked within UNESCO to secure its reform. Although Britain supports the ideals and objectives contained in UNESCO's constitution, it has major doubts about the effectiveness with which the Organisation has been pursuing them. In particular, it considers that UNESCO is harmfully politicised, has been used to attack values it was designed to uphold, has suffered from inefficient management, implements certain programmes which contain meaningless studies and duplicate the work of other UN agencies, and in general lacks discrimination in its creation of activities.

Other International Organisations

Britain is a member of many other international organisations, including those concerned with the management of the world economy. It is a founder member of the International Monetary Fund, established in 1945 (along with the World Bank) to regulate the international financial system and to provide a source of credit for member countries facing balance of payments problems, and has welcomed the creation by the Fund of facilities to provide special assistance to developing countries experiencing financial or trading difficulties. It is a strong supporter of efforts under the General Agreement on Tariffs and Trade to liberalise further, and promote the growth of, world trade, and to improve the developing countries' participation in it.

Britain is also a member of the Organisation for Economic Co-operation and Development (OECD). An instrument for intergovernmental co-operation among 24 industrialised countries, the OECD's aims are to promote policies designed to achieve the highest sustainable economic growth and employment, and a rising standard of living in member countries while maintaining financial stability, and thus to contribute to the development of the world economy; to assist developing countries; and to contribute to the expansion of world trade on a multilateral, non-discriminatory basis in accordance with international obligations.

Other organisations to which Britain belongs or extends support are more restricted in their operations and include the regional development banks in Africa, the Americas and Asia and specialist technical, agricultural and medical institutions.

With 20 other nations Britain is a member of the Council of Europe, which aims to provide the widest possible European forum for the discussion of political, economic, social, cultural and scientific issues with a view to achieving greater unity between its members. Membership is open to any European parliamentary democracy which accepts the principles of the rule of law and the protection of human rights. The Council was responsible for the adoption in 1950 of the European Convention on Human Rights, to which Britain became a party in 1951. In 1985, with Britain's support, the Council adopted a declaration reaffirming its commitment to respect for human rights and calling upon all countries to comply fully with their international obligations in this area. In January 1986 Britain renewed its acceptance for a further five years of the optional articles of the Convention which recognise both the right of individual petition and the compulsory jurisdiction of the European Court of Human Rights.

Development Co-operation

The basic objective of Britain's aid programme is the promotion of sustainable, non-inflationary economic and social progress and the alleviation of poverty in developing countries. Britain's ability to support development overseas is dependent on the state of its own economy, and alongside development objectives, due weight is given to political, commercial and industrial considerations in the deployment of aid resources.

Official aid is only one aspect of Britain's support for overseas development. Private investment is also important and has benefited from the abolition of exchange controls in 1979. Britain is one of the world's largest overseas investors: in 1985 estimated net outward direct investment by British companies in developing countries amounted to £2,550 million out of a total of £6,680 million. Such investment is important not only because of the money provided but because of the transfer of skills, management expertise and the development of indigenous resources which accompany it. Trade, too, is vital, developing countries providing nearly a fifth of British imports in recent years.

Aid is also provided by voluntary societies which concentrate their activities in the poorest countries. Some of these societies' activities receive substantial support from the official aid programme.

Britain's aid represents part of a wider Western effort to help developing countries. In 1985 total net official development assistance disbursed by members of the Development Assistance Committee of the Organisation for Economic Co-operation and Development, comprising 18 main donor countries and the European Commission, amounted to $29,580 million. Members of the Organisation of Petroleum Exporting Countries provided $3,000 million and countries belonging to the Council for Mutual Economic Assistance (the Soviet bloc countries) an estimated $3,120 million.

Official and Other Flows

In 1985 total official flows[1] of aid amounted to some £1,478 million net, of which £1,181 million represented official development assistance and £297 million other official flows. Of the former, bilateral aid accounted for £663 million including technical co-operation funds of £257 million; some £518 million was provided through multilateral agencies. Repayments of capital and payments of interest on loans came to £89 million and £69 million respectively; another £24 million of capital repayments and £2 million of interest were cancelled.

Aid performance is commonly measured as a proportion of gross national

---

[1] 'Total official flows' is an international reporting concept. Its main component—official development assistance—is defined as official flows for development purposes with a grant (concessional) element of 25 per cent or more. The main British reporting concept is 'public expenditure on overseas aid' which differs from total official flows by excluding certain British flows which benefit developing countries but are not considered developmental, and by recording some contributions to multilateral agencies at a different time. All concepts can be measured before (gross) or after (net) deducting capital repayments.

product (GNP), particularly with reference to the two UN targets for resource transfers to developing countries: that net official development assistance should equal 0·7 per cent of GNP and that combined private and official flows should equal 1 per cent of GNP. Britain accepts in principle the first of these but is not committed to a timetable for reaching it. Successive governments have made it clear that progress must depend on Britain's economic condition and upon other calls on its resources. In 1985 net official development assistance amounted to £1,181 million, 0·34 per cent of GNP, close to the total 0·35 per cent for donor countries belonging to the Development Assistance Committee of the Organisation for Economic Co-operation and Development. Total net financial flows from Britain to developing countries amounted to £2,833 million, 0·81 per cent of GNP.

Bilateral Aid

Britain's aid programme began as part of the discharge of its responsibilities towards dependent territories, and the main emphasis remains on the Commonwealth, which includes among its members some of the world's poorest countries. In 1985, £822 million of gross public expenditure on overseas aid was disbursed bilaterally. Some £443 million (65 per cent of that directly allocated to countries) went to the Commonwealth, including £51 million to Britain's remaining dependencies, which are a first charge on the aid programme. Aid was disbursed regionally as follows: Africa £306 million; Asia £255 million; the Americas and the Caribbean £70 million; Oceania £22 million; and Europe £34 million. (A further £134 million was not allocable by region.)

The country receiving the largest amount (£106 million) was India. Other major recipients included Sudan, Bangladesh, Kenya, Indonesia, Ethiopia, Zambia and Zimbabwe. In line with the policy of concentrating aid on the poorest countries, £419 million of gross bilateral aid went to the poorest 50 developing countries (excluding states with a population under 100,000 and dependencies).

Financial Aid

Gross bilateral financial aid in 1985 totalled £508 million. Aid for individual projects totalled £357 million, the principal sectors supported being agriculture, fisheries and forestry (£76 million), manufacturing (£10 million), energy (£30 million), mining (£13 million), transport and communications (£26 million) and social and community services (£21 million). Non-project aid totalled £150 million, of which £49 million was for import financing, £28 million for food aid, £31 million for debt relief, £10 million for budgetary support and £33 million for disaster relief (some of these funds are channelled through the Overseas Development Administration's Disaster Unit which provides immediate assistance in disaster relief operations). About 77 per cent of financial aid was provided in grants and the rest in concessionary loans. Since 1975, development aid to the poorest countries (which include India, Bangladesh, Sri Lanka and many countries in Africa) has been on grant terms. In October 1984 these terms were extended to the majority of recipients of British financial aid, and simplified loan terms were introduced for those countries still not qualifying for grants. Britain has more than fulfilled the 1978 resolution of the United Nations Conference on Trade and Development on easing the terms of financial aid. Britain has concluded agreements to remove the burden of past aid loans worth about £1,000 million from 21 of the poorest countries, including India.

Financial aid is normally tied to the purchase of goods, equipment and services from Britain (51 per cent in 1985), although there may be a substantial element for local costs and foreign content in contracts financed from tied aid in appropriate cases. New loan but not grant commitments can be untied, if the recipient agrees, to the extent that goods can be purchased either from the poorest developing countries or from Britain.

Grants totalling £42 million were provided to 18 countries in 1985 under the Aid and Trade Provision, which is designed to match the mixed credit practices of other donors by providing aid in combination with export credits to support sound development projects which offer commercial opportunities to British exporters. In November 1985, the Government introduced a new soft loan facility under the Provision in order to respond to the preferences of certain developing countries and to counter the practices of competitors. Increased funds are being made available to enable British companies to double by 1988–89 the business won annually with the Provision. As a matter of general policy, however, the Government would like to see a reduction in the use of mixed credit by all exporting nations in the interests of more open competition and freer trade.

The Commonwealth Development Corporation is empowered to invest in Commonwealth countries which have achieved independence since 1948, the remaining British dependencies and certain non-Commonwealth countries. Its aim is to assist in the development of these countries' economies. By the end of 1985, the Corporation had invested some £640 million out of a total commitment of £907·7 million. Of this total, £437·1 million was in Africa, £235·3 million in Asia, £128·9 million in the Caribbean and Latin America and £102·9 million in the Pacific Islands. Commitments approved in 1985 totalled over £106 million, of which 72 per cent was allocated to agriculture, fisheries and forestry.

Technical
Co-operation

Technical co-operation, the transfer of specialised knowledge and skills from country to country, complements financial aid, expertise often being essential to the success of a programme of financial aid or investment. Expenditure on it has increased in recent years and was £278 million, 34 per cent of gross bilateral aid, in 1985. This included £64 million for the provision of expert personnel, including volunteers, £62 million for students and trainees in Britain and overseas, £18 million for research services and projects, £30 million for consultancy services, and £9 million for the provision of equipment and supplies.

At the end of 1985 there were 1,974 people financed by Britain (other than volunteers) working in developing countries, of whom 856 were engaged in the field of education, 325 in agriculture and allied fields, and 151 in health services. In addition, under the British Volunteer Programme there were 1,157 volunteers, mainly graduates or otherwise qualified, working in developing countries, the majority of them teaching. Recruitment, training and placing overseas is undertaken by four voluntary bodies (Catholic Institute for International Relations, International Voluntary Service, United Nations Association International Service and Voluntary Service Overseas), the bulk of their costs being met by the British Government.

Britain receives large numbers of students and trainees from developing countries. Some 12,150 were financed in 1985 under regional programmes of technical co-operation, by awards under the Commonwealth Scholarship and Fellowship Plan, and under British Council schemes. In early 1983 the Government decided to make an additional £46 million available (some outside the aid programme) over the next three years for the support of overseas students. A new scheme for students from Commonwealth developing countries was introduced in 1986 (see p 81).

To support development overseas, the Government maintains specialist scientific organisations (the Land Resources Development Centre, and the Tropical Development and Research Institute) and provides support for many others, including overseas units/divisions of the government-financed Transport and Road Research Laboratory, the Building Research Establishment, the

British Geological Survey, the Overseas Surveys Directorate of the Ordnance Survey, and of Hydraulics Research Ltd. These organisations provide specialist information, advice and experts for service overseas, and undertake field and laboratory research investigations.

Aid Evaluation

To ensure the most effective use of aid resources, the objectives and content of country aid programmes are determined through a systematic programming exercise which takes account of the circumstances of the recipient country, its development priorities, the activities of other donors, and what Britain can offer by way of expertise, goods and services. In addition, individual projects are carefully appraised before approval, monitored during progress against quantifiable targets and assessed in a project completion report, while a programme of special evaluation studies examines in more detail the achievements of particular projects and of special issues. The Overseas Development Administration also supports international studies of aid effectiveness.

Multilateral Aid

Britain is a major subscriber to the World Bank group of institutions—the International Bank for Reconstruction and Development, the International Development Association (IDA) and the International Finance Corporation. The resources of the IDA, which provides interest-free loans to developing countries unable to service loans on conventional terms, are replenished at roughly three-year intervals. The British commitment to its Seventh Replenishment (July 1984 to June 1987) is £401·5 million towards a total of $9,000 million. Negotiations for the Eighth Replenishment began in January 1986. Britain contributes to the resources of the Asian Development Bank, the Inter-American Development Bank, the Caribbean Development Bank and the African Development Bank. Its contribution to the United Nations Development Programme for 1985 was £21 million, and it is the largest source of expertise and the second largest of fellowships and equipment provided under the Programme. There is also a major British contribution to other UN agencies and programmes, and an increasing proportion of British aid is now channelled through the European Community's aid programme. Britain's commitment to the sixth European Development Fund established by the third Lomé Convention, covering the period from 1985 to 1989, is over £800 million at present exchange rates.

Voluntary Agencies

Voluntary agencies provided an estimated £140 million for work in developing countries in 1985, mainly on agriculture, health and nutrition, education projects, and emergency relief operations.

There are about 200 agencies in all, including church and missionary societies; among the best known are Oxfam, Christian Aid, War on Want, the Save the Children Fund, the British Red Cross Society and the Catholic Fund for Overseas Development. The funds are raised largely through regular donations and collections, legacies and trading activities and, particularly in response to specific emergencies, through appeals in the media. The Government co-operates with the agencies in various ways, especially in immediate post-disaster relief and rehabilitation operations and through its Joint Funding Scheme. Under this it meets half the cost of selected development projects undertaken by the agencies and aimed at helping the poorest. Such projects include community health, non-formal education, the improvement of food supplies, agricultural training, water supply and irrigation. Expenditure on the Scheme in 1985 was some £4·8 million.

Voluntary agencies' work on behalf of refugees overseas also receives official support.

**THE
INTERNATIONAL
ECONOMY**

Britain favours the continuing evolution of the existing world economic system with its free flow of trade and capital, and has defended the independence of efficient international institutions like the International Monetary Fund, the World Bank and the General Agreement on Tariffs and Trade. As constituted these institutions serve the vital interests of all nations and their work reflects the growing interdependence of developed and developing countries.

Britain also supports the important role of the International Monetary Fund in providing financial assistance, the level of which has recently been substantially increased, to help developing countries to carry out adjustment measures to overcome balance of payments difficulties.

The British Government recognises that the interests of developing and industrialised countries are mutual and that all will benefit if the problems of the world economy can be effectively tackled. Despite the recession Britain seeks to defend the open trading system. Although domestic priorities have obliged the Government to adopt restrictive measures in certain highly sensitive areas, it is conscious of their exceptional character. Moreover, as a member of the European Community, Britain has played a significant role in determining the nature of its trade arrangements, which are among the most liberal applied by industrialised nations. It took a major part in the negotiations on successive Lomé Conventions, both to safeguard the trading interests of Commonwealth developing countries and to ensure that reciprocal preferences would not be demanded from the developing countries. In addition, Britain has supported improvements to the Community's Generalised System of Preferences scheme, especially with regard to more liberal access into the Community for imports of manufactured and processed agricultural products and in its application to the poorest developed countries, particularly those in south Asia. Before entering the Community, Britain secured a commitment to expand and reinforce Community trade relations with the Commonwealth countries of Asia, and this has led to the conclusion of commercial co-operation agreements with India, Sri Lanka and Bangladesh. Britain remains committed to the objectives of the 1973 Tokyo Declaration, namely the further liberalisation of world trade through the progressive dismantling of tariff and non-tariff barriers, and within this, the provision of special and more favourable treatment for the developing countries where possible.

Britain has long recognised the importance of commodities to the economies of many developing countries and played a full part, in company with other European Community member states, in negotiating the commodities agreements called for by the United Nations Conference on Trade and Development in its 1976 resolution establishing the Integrated Programme for Commodities (IPC). It is a member of agreements covering rubber, cocoa and coffee, the purpose of which is to stabilise prices and supplies at levels just and remunerative to producers and equitable to consumers. It is also a member of an agreement for jute, largely concerned with research and development, and a similar agreement for tropical timber. Neither contains any economic provisions. As a member of the Community, Britain belongs to agreements covering wheat and olive oil designed to improve market conditions by consultations between producers and consumers, and the Community is a member of a purely administrative agreement for sugar. Britain ratified the Common Fund for Commodities, another element of the IPC, in 1981, and has agreed to contribute to the voluntary as well as to the obligatory part of its work. A substantial British contribution is made to the STABEX scheme operated by the Community which compensates commodity-producing Lomé Convention countries for shortfalls in commodity revenue.

4 Defence

The primary objectives of Britain's defence policy are to ensure the country's security, to preserve peace with freedom, and to enable it to pursue, by just and peaceful means, its legitimate interests both at home and abroad. Britain's policy is based on the North Atlantic Treaty Organisation (NATO), a defensive alliance whose collective strength provides each of its members with far greater security than any could achieve alone. Britain is fully committed to NATO and its strategy of deterrence and, in assigning directly or indirectly to NATO the vast majority of its forces and 95 per cent of its defence budget, makes a major contribution to the Alliance's deterrent capabilities. It also plays a full part in the Alliance's efforts, complementary to its defence preparations, to negotiate balanced and verifiable arms control agreements and to reduce tension so as to achieve a more just and lasting peace in Europe.

The defence budget for 1986–87 is nearly £18,500 million. In 1985 Britain's defence expenditure as a proportion of gross domestic product was an estimated 5·2 per cent, the highest in NATO after the United States and Greece, and, in absolute terms, larger than that of any other European NATO nation.

Within the budget, resources have been switched from manpower to equipment (Britain spends a higher proportion of its defence budget—some 45 per cent—on equipment than any other NATO country); manpower is being used with increased effectiveness, particularly by diverting personnel from non-operational support to front-line tasks; and measures are in hand to improve efficiency and value for money, especially through increased competition in the purchase of equipment.

Britain's defence programme is designed to ensure the most effective use of these resources in pursuit of its commitment to Western security, the main threat to which is posed by the nuclear and conventional forces of the Warsaw Pact. In recent years the structure and balance of the defence forces have been improved to increase their combat effectiveness and so enhance Britain's contribution to NATO. As a result of these improvements Britain also has the flexibility, as shown in the 1982 Falklands crisis, to respond quickly and effectively to challenges to its interests outside the NATO area.

Organisation and Management

The Ministry of Defence has been reorganised to improve policy formulation and to tighten control over the defence budget, while devolving responsibility for day-to-day management to the Services and the Procurement Executive.

The new structure contains a unified military/civilian Defence Staff responsible for defence policy and strategy, operational requirements and commitments; it reports to the Chief of Defence Staff and the Permanent Under-Secretary through a Vice-Chief of Defence Staff. An Office of Management and Budget reporting to a Permanent Under-Secretary is concerned with budgetary control and resource management. Each Service Chief of Staff reports through the Chief of Defence Staff to the Secretary of State on matters related to the fighting effectiveness, management, efficiency and morale of his Service. The management of the three Services is exercised through executive committees of the Service Boards, which are chaired by their respective Chiefs of Staff, and act in accordance with centrally determined policy objectives and budgets. The

Procurement Executive is headed by the Chief of Defence Procurement and a new post of Chief of Defence Equipment Collaboration has been established to promote collaborative procurement with allies and friendly nations.

A management information system has been introduced which enables ministers and senior management to scrutinise the activities, costs and efficiency of all areas of the Ministry. Increased awareness of the need to manage resources cost-effectively is being promoted, with managers becoming more accountable for the resources allocated.

NATO's Strategy

NATO's security policy is based on deterrence and defence, its aims being to prevent war or, should aggression occur, to respond at the right level to make the aggressor quickly cease his attack and withdraw. This strategy, called flexible response, is based on three key principles: a manifest determination to act jointly and to defend the Treaty area against all forms of aggression; a recognisable capability to respond effectively at all levels of aggression, and to escalate, if necessary, in order to convince the Warsaw Pact of NATO's resolve; and a flexibility that prevents the Soviet Union from predicting with confidence NATO's specific response to aggression but which would leave it in no doubt of the grave risk it would run in resorting to the use or the threat of force against the Alliance. These principles in turn are built on a combination of political will and military capacity. The latter comprises the following elements, which must be both visible and credible: adequate conventional forces deployed well forward to deter any Soviet non-nuclear attack; theatre nuclear forces to enhance deterrence by providing a link between conventional and strategic nuclear forces, and deterring the use of similar weapons by the other side; and strategic nuclear forces to provide the ultimate deterrent by having the ability to inflict unacceptable damage against a potential enemy, even after suffering a pre-emptive first strike.

In order to maintain the Alliance's defence and deterrent capacity, NATO members have agreed, among other things, to improve their conventional defences, including a doubling of funds for infrastructure projects such as airfield and port facilities and communications systems, an increase in ammunition stocks and the continued exploitation of new technology (including the co-ordination of research and procurement). NATO's intermediate-range nuclear forces are also being modernised. Britain is actively involved in these measures, and is also updating its own strategic nuclear capability.

The NATO allies have acknowledged the continuing Soviet threat to Western interests outside the NATO area and recognised the need, in the last resort, for those members with the means to do so to take action in consultation with their allies. At the same time, the NATO allies recognise the right of regional countries to self-determination and, as far as possible, to defend themselves. In the Government's view, these principles can best be satisfied through the provision of military assistance, including training courses in Britain, the loan of British Service personnel and the sale of defence equipment. Britain's commitment to these principles is also demonstrated by periodic deployments, exercises and the maintenance of a capability to intervene militarily in the last resort.

Britain's NATO Contribution

Britain's contribution to NATO is concentrated in areas where it can best help to maintain Alliance security, principally NATO's strategic nuclear deterrent and the defence of the Central Region of Europe, the Eastern Atlantic and English Channel, and the British 'home' base and its immediate approaches.

Britain's strategic forces, now equipped with improved Polaris missiles (to be replaced by a Trident force in the 1990s) represent an essential European element in NATO's deterrent strategy, by providing a second and independent centre of decision-making within the Alliance and an important insurance against any Warsaw Pact misconception that the United States would not be prepared to use its nuclear forces in Europe's defence. Britain has also committed its other nuclear systems to NATO, and is continuing to provide bases for ground-launched cruise missiles which, with Pershing II missiles, the United States began deploying in Europe from December 1983 in order to modernise NATO's intermediate-range nuclear forces.

Britain's decision to update its strategic deterrent has led to increased calls from some groups within the country for unilateral nuclear disarmament, both on the grounds of cost and as an example to others. While the Government understands the widespread concern regarding nuclear war, it believes such apprehensions to be misplaced so long as the policy of deterrence and efforts to relax East–West tensions, including the pursuit of arms control, which have helped to maintain peace in Europe for more than 40 years, are continued. It also believes that unilateral nuclear disarmament by Britain would not significantly alter the views on arms control of other states which possess, or may think of acquiring, nuclear weapons, and that such action would weaken NATO's ability to deter aggression in the face of the continuing Soviet nuclear and conventional threat.

Virtually all of the Royal Navy, the largest navy among the European NATO partners, is earmarked for assignment to the Alliance and permanent contributions are made to NATO's two standing naval forces, in the Atlantic and the Channel, and to its Mediterranean force when activated. The British Army of the Rhine (BAOR) and Royal Air Force (RAF) Germany are stationed in the Federal Republic of Germany. BAOR's combat element consists of three strong divisions, with supporting artillery; two divisions comprise three armoured brigades each and a third is made up of an armoured brigade, an air-mobile brigade and an infantry brigade (the latter being located in Britain in peacetime). A reinforcing division, comprising one regular and two Territorial Army brigades, is also located in Britain. On mobilisation, BAOR's peacetime strength of around 55,000 would be almost trebled by rapid reinforcement from Britain. Nearly all the RAF's combat and support aircraft are assigned to NATO. RAF Germany's 14 squadrons (two of helicopters) are equipped for strike/attack, reconnaissance, close support, air defence and air transport roles, while RAF Strike Command, which is based in Britain, provides forces for these and for the maritime patrol and anti-submarine warfare roles.

Britain also provides important elements of NATO's specialist reinforcement forces, including shipping and marine commando units forming the bulk of a British–Netherlands amphibious force, ground and air units for the Allied Command Europe Mobile Force, and several squadrons for NATO's Strategic Air Reserve.

Forces from all three Services are stationed at Gibraltar, which, positioned at the western entry to the Mediterranean, is an important base for NATO.

Europe and the Alliance

Britain's contribution to NATO is part of the wider effort which the European allies make to the defence of the West, including the protection of their common interests outside the NATO area. Since the security of each NATO member is inextricably linked to that of the others, substantial European forces are essential to the defence of the North American continent. There is no substitute for the United States' nuclear guarantee nor for North American forces stationed in Europe in peacetime; but, of NATO's ready forces in Europe, the European allies provide about 90 per cent of the manpower, 80 per cent of combat aircraft, 85 per cent of tanks and 95 per cent of artillery, as well as 70 per cent of the fighting ships in European and Atlantic waters. They also provide some 7 million men and women on active and reserve duties and are able to supply around 900 military facilities for United States forces and essential support requirements such as communications and transport. European members of the Alliance have on average increased their defence expenditure by 27 per cent in real terms between 1971 and 1983.

Britain and its European allies recognise the value of co-operation and collaboration by playing a full part in the Independent European Programme Group, a body committed to promoting intra-European arms collaboration and to facilitating a more balanced trade in armaments between Western Europe and North America, and in the Conference of National Armament Directors, the forum for defence equipment collaboration across the Atlantic. They also work together in the Eurogroup, formed following a British initiative in 1968, to improve the effectiveness of their contributions to the Alliance and to achieve better use of available resources through closer co-ordination. In addition, the Western European Union, which was created by the modified Brussels Treaty of 1954, was reactivated in 1984 to provide further impetus towards European security co-operation. The Treaty, which was signed by Belgium, Britain, the Federal Republic of Germany, France, Italy, Luxembourg and the Netherlands, also enshrines Britain's commitment to the stationing of British ground and air forces in the Federal Republic of Germany.

Outside the NATO Area

In support of other defence commitments, and with a view to playing a part in collective responses by the West to threats to its world-wide interests, Britain is maintaining and improving its ability to operate outside the NATO area without diminishing its central commitment to the Alliance. It has an airborne brigade which can move large numbers of men and their equipment to trouble spots should the need arise. British garrisons are maintained in Belize, Brunei, Cyprus, the Falkland Islands and Hong Kong. Britain also provides the largest national troop contingent to the United Nations Force in Cyprus as well as giving support for the United Nations Force in Lebanon. In addition it contributes a headquarters detachment to the Multinational Force and Observers in Sinai. Considerable effort is devoted to the provision of military assistance and training to a large number of friendly countries outside the NATO area, and Britain deploys its forces on visits and exercises in important areas.

Northern Ireland

Army units continue to provide support to the Royal Ulster Constabulary in its fight against terrorism in Northern Ireland. It has, however, been possible to reduce their numbers in recent years as the police have enhanced their capability for maintaining law and order in the face of the threat. Much of the Army's support to the police is provided by the Ulster Defence Regiment, comprising both full- and part-time members who are recruited locally.

THE ARMED FORCES
Personnel

The total strength of the armed forces, all volunteers, was 323,500 on 1 January 1986—68,200 in the Royal Navy and the Royal Marines, 162,100 in the Army and 93,100 in the Royal Air Force. The Ministry of Defence employs about 171,500 civilians (based in the United Kingdom).

The three women's Services, with a combined strength of 16,000, are integral parts of the armed forces, and servicewomen serve alongside servicemen in Britain and overseas, mainly in support roles.

Engagements for non-commissioned ranks range from 3 to 22 years, with a wide freedom of choice on the length and terms of service. Subject to a minimum period of service (varying from three to nine years, excluding training), entrants may leave at any time, at 18 months' notice. Discharge may also be granted on compassionate grounds, by purchase, or on grounds of conscience. Commissions, either by promotion from the ranks or by direct entry based on educational and other qualifications, are granted for short, medium and long terms. All three Services have schemes for school, university and college sponsorships.

Non-commissioned personnel receive basic training supplemented by further and specialist training throughout their careers. Study for educational qualifications is encouraged and Service trade and technical training, highly valued by industry, leads to nationally recognised qualifications for large numbers of Service personnel.

Commissioned ranks receive initial training at the Britannia Royal Naval College, Dartmouth; the Royal Military Academy, Sandhurst; or the Royal Air Force College, Cranwell. This is followed by specialist training, often including degree courses at university or Service establishments. Higher training for officers is provided by the Royal Naval College, Greenwich, the Army Staff College at Camberley, and the Royal Air Force Staff College at Bracknell. Selected senior officers and civilian officials from Britain and other countries attend the Joint Services Defence College, Greenwich, and the Royal College of Defence Studies, London, which provides the wider background necessary for those destined to fill higher appointments.

Operational training includes joint-Service and inter-allied exercises. Training is provided for the armed forces of allied, Commonwealth and other countries.

Reserve Forces   Reserve and auxiliary forces are an integral part of the armed forces. In addition to supplementing the regular forces on mobilisation with trained personnel able immediately to take their places either as formed units or as individual reinforcements, they form an important link between the Services and the civil community. Some members of these forces have a reserve liability following a period of regular service (regular reserve); others are volunteers who train in their spare time. Volunteer reserve forces include the Territorial Army, whose role is to reinforce the ground forces committed to NATO and help to maintain a secure home base in the United Kingdom; its strength is being increased to 86,000 over the remainder of the decade. Since 1985, a Home Service Force, linked to the Territorial Army and with an initial strength of about 5,000, has been established to assist in guarding important civilian and military installations on mobilisation. Other volunteer forces include the Royal Naval Reserve, the Royal Marines Reserve, the Royal Auxiliary Air Force and the Royal Air Force Volunteer Reserve. All have been expanded substantially in recent years or are planned to increase in strength in the near future. The Ulster Defence Regiment, with locally recruited and mostly part-time members, supports the police and the Army in Northern Ireland. On 1 January 1986 regular reserves totalled 209,700, and volunteer reserves and auxiliary forces 93,100. Cadet forces, which make a significant contribution to recruitment to the regular forces, totalled 144,700.

COMBAT
FORCES
Strategic
Nuclear Forces   The Royal Navy's Polaris force comprises four nuclear submarines, each of which can remain on underwater patrol for long periods and is capable of carrying 16 nuclear-armed Polaris missiles. The missile system, now incorporating improvements designed to penetrate anti-ballistic missile defences, will maintain the force's effectiveness until it is replaced in the mid-1990s by a Trident nuclear submarine force which will extend Britain's nuclear deterrent into the twenty-first century. The Trident programme, which will cost an estimated £9,869 million (at 1985–86 prices), is expected to account on average for about 3 per cent of the planned defence budget over the period of its procurement, and for about 6 per cent of the equipment budget.

Royal Navy General Purpose Combat Forces

Britain's naval forces, while capable of operating throughout the world when required, are concentrated in the Eastern Atlantic and English Channel where they constitute the majority of forces immediately available to NATO. They include three new Invincible-class anti-submarine warfare carriers, carrying Sea King anti-submarine and airborne early warning helicopters, Sea Harrier aircraft, and Sea Dart defence missile systems; 14 nuclear-powered attack submarines (with another four under construction or on order) equipped with torpedoes and the Sub-Harpoon anti-ship missile, and 13 diesel-powered submarines, soon to be replaced by the more powerful Upholder class; and about 50 destroyers and frigates for air defence, anti-submarine and general purpose duties. Most of these have weapon-carrying helicopters (the Lynx, Wasp or Wessex), and armaments installed include the Exocet surface-to-surface, Sea Wolf point air defence, Sea Dart area air defence and Sea Skua anti-ship missile systems, and the Ikara anti-submarine guided weapons system. There is also an amphibious capability comprising two assault ships, *Fearless* and *Intrepid*, supporting vessels and the Royal Marines. Other ships include about 40 mine counter-measures vessels, including 11 of the new Hunt and 12 of the River classes, and offshore patrol vessels for protecting fishing interests and oil and gas installations.

In coming years Britain's contribution to NATO's maritime defence will be based increasingly on an enhanced anti-submarine warfare element made up principally of nuclear-powered attack submarines and advanced diesel-electric conventional submarines, of which four have been ordered, one being under construction; a newly designed Type 23 frigate, the first of which will enter service at the end of the decade; and Nimrod maritime patrol aircraft equipped with Searchwater radar and armed with Harpoon anti-ship missiles and Sting Ray anti-submarine torpedoes. In addition, the surface fleet is being strengthened by the building of 14 multi-role Type 22 frigates; seven of these are already in service and the other seven are being constructed. New or improved weapons will include the Harpoon missile for the last of the Type 22 and for the new Type 23 frigates, the Spearfish heavyweight torpedo for submarines, the Sea Eagle anti-ship missile, and the development of the vertically launched Sea Wolf point-defence missiles and improvements to the Sea Dart surface-to-air missiles.

Army Combat Forces

Most of the Army's combat forces, consisting of BAOR and the forces stationed in Britain, have primary roles in support of NATO. Others are stationed overseas in support of treaty commitments.

All three armoured divisions in BAOR are equipped with the Chieftain or Challenger main battle tanks. The Challenger, fitted with Chobham armour to provide greatly improved protection, will equip, by 1990, six out of the planned 12 regiments stationed in Europe (an increase of four regiments since 1980). The war maintenance reserve will be strengthened with some of the Chieftains replaced in the front line by Challengers. Improvements for both tanks will be the fitting of thermal imaging sights and new 120-mm high-pressure guns. Tracked combat reconnaissance vehicles include Scorpion, a light tank with a 76-mm gun; Scimitar, a reconnaissance vehicle with a 30-mm cannon; and Striker, which mounts the Swingfire long-range anti-tank missiles. The primary tracked armoured personnel carrier for mechanised infantry is the FV432. The continuing purchase of the Saxon (a four-wheeled armoured personnel carrier) and the introduction later in the decade of the mechanised combat vehicle (Warrior) will increase the mobility of infantry. The crew-portable Milan anti-tank missile is deployed throughout BAOR (front-line and all regular and Territorial Army reinforcing battalions) and will be joined shortly by the man-portable light anti-tank weapon, LAW80. Lynx helicopters are fitted with an improved TOW long-range anti-tank weapon. A 155-mm gun, the SP70, will enter service around the turn of the decade, as will the Multiple-Launch Rocket System. Tactical nuclear support is provided by the Lance missile and dual-capable artillery. Integral air defence is based on the Rapier missile system, improved tracked versions of which are being introduced, and the Blowpipe and Javelin man-portable missiles. Important improvements in command, control and communication systems include the PTARMIGAN secure communication system now entering service in BAOR and a distributed data-processing system for field commanders (WAVELL); a computer-based artillery targeting system (BATES) is planned to enter into service by the end of the 1980s.

Royal Air Force General Purpose Forces

Phantom and Lightning aircraft, together with Rapier and Bloodhound surface-to-air missiles, provide Britain's air defence, assisted by Shackleton airborne early warning aircraft and the ground radars of the United Kingdom Air Defence Ground Environment system. The Tornado GR1 is replacing Jaguars in the strike/attack role and will, in due course, replace some Jaguars in the reconnaissance role. Harrier GR3s provide close air support to ground troops. Nimrod aircraft form part of Britain's anti-submarine warfare capability, their duties also involving long-range maritime patrol against surface ships, offshore surveillance and fishery protection. Improved Buccaneers will continue to be employed in an anti-ship role, armed with the Sea Eagle missile. Victor tankers, together with some converted Hercules aircraft, are used for in-flight refuelling. Tactical transport is provided by VC10 and Hercules aircraft, medium and light support being given by Chinook, Puma and Wessex helicopters. Sea King and Wessex helicopters perform search and rescue duties around the British Isles. Weapons in service include Skyflash, Sparrow, Sidewinder, Martel and Sea Eagle missiles, and guided and cluster bombs.

The Royal Air Force is undergoing a comprehensive re-equipment programme. Improvements to Britain's air defences include the replacement of the Lightning and some of the Phantom squadrons with seven squadrons of the air defence version of the Tornado aircraft; and replacement or modernisation of the radars and command, control and communications systems for the United Kingdom Air Defence Ground Environment. In addition, 72 Hawk trainer aircraft have been equipped with air-to-air missiles and cannon for local air defence. An increased air-to-air refuelling capability is being achieved with the introduction into service of converted VC10s and TriStars in the tanker role. The offensive power of the Royal Air Force has been substantially enhanced by the introduction into service of the Tornado GR1 (of which 220 have been ordered), and the procurement of some 80 of the new Harrier GR5, which will be delivered in 1988. All strike/attack and offensive support aircraft will be installed with advanced electronic warfare equipment to increase their ability to survive, and the Tornado GR1 will carry the British JP233 airfield attack weapon, ALARM (an all-British anti-radiation missile), and a Sky Shadow pod carrying electronic counter-measures equipment.

Defence Procurement

Responsibility for providing the armed forces with the equipment they need lies with the Ministry of Defence's Procurement Executive. About 45 per cent of the defence budget will be spent on equipment in 1986–87, making the Ministry British industry's largest customer. The Procurement Executive works with the Service users and industry to obtain the best long-term value over a project's life, from concept formulation (drawing on the research programme) through development and production to in-Service support. Where possible, work is placed with industry under firm-price contracts won through competition.

Research and Development

Research is undertaken by the Ministry's research establishments, which have a very wide technological capability. The Ministry also sponsors a substantial amount of research by industry and the universities. Around £400 million is expected to be spent on defence research and £1,900 million on development in 1986–87. Nearly all design and development of defence equipment is carried out by industry. The Ministry is also increasingly seeking to involve industry in the planning of the research programme and to promote civil applications. As part of the Government's policy of improving the strength of Britain's science base, the Ministry, together with the research councils, is funding a series of joint ventures with academic institutions in areas of strategic research.

Strategic Defence Initiative

Britain is participating in the United States' Strategic Defence Initiative (SDI), a research programme, projected to last some years, that was set up in 1983 to determine the feasibility of establishing an effective defence against ballistic missile attack. In March 1985 the United States invited its NATO and certain other allies to participate in the programme. Following detailed discussions about the nature and scope of the research which might be undertaken by British firms and institutions, Britain and the United States signed in December 1985 a Memorandum of Understanding to promote British participation, agreeing on a programme of information exchange, areas where British expertise might contribute to SDI research, consultative and review mechanisms, and safeguards protecting the ownership of British intellectual property rights and technology transfer. An SDI Participation Office has been established in the Ministry of Defence, with representatives from other government departments, and it works in close concert with British firms and institutions. This participation in the SDI programme is intended to enhance Britain's research capability in areas of high technology relevant to both defence and civil programmes, as well as providing direct economic benefits.

Alliance Co-operation

The need for a more efficient use of resources is well recognised by NATO members, and Britain plays a full part in the Conference of National Armaments Directors and in the Independent European Programme Group, both of which have as a principal aim the encouragement of greater armaments co-operation within the Alliance. Nevertheless, the importance of maintaining a sound national industrial base for defence procurement is recognised, and there is close consultation between government and industry in the National Defence Industries Council and other specialised bodies.

Successful European collaborative projects have included the Jaguar and Tornado aircraft, the FH70 howitzer, a number of helicopters, and the Martel missile. At present Britain is working with the Federal Republic of Germany and Italy on a self-propelled gun (SP70), with Italy on the EH101 helicopter, and with France and the Federal Republic of Germany on a new generation of anti-tank guided weapons. In addition, Britain signed an initial agreement in 1985 with the Federal Republic of Germany, Italy and Spain to design, develop and produce a supersonic fighter aircraft ready for service by 1995. Britain and the Federal Republic will each have a 33 per cent share of the work, Italy 21 per cent and Spain 13 per cent.

Britain also favours increased transatlantic co-operation and is working with the United States on an advanced Harrier aircraft and, together with other European countries, on the Multiple Launch Rocket System and the development of advanced air-to-air missiles.

Production

Equipment is manufactured in private firms and publicly owned industries. In January 1985 the Royal Ordnance Factories, formerly part of the Ministry of Defence, became an independent commercial organisation, Royal Ordnance plc.

The Government is planning to introduce private capital into the company at the earliest opportunity. The purpose of the change is to promote more extensive and effective competition in the supply of defence equipment in order to obtain greater value for money, more efficient use of resources and better innovation. The same principles are behind the Government's intention, announced in July 1985, to introduce from 1987 commercial management to two of the Royal Dockyards, at Devonport and Rosyth, which carry out most of the refitting and repair of Royal Navy ships.

Defence Sales   Sales of British defence equipment enable allies and friendly governments to take advantage of Britain's extensive research and development programmes to improve their own defence. The Defence Export Services Organisation of the Ministry of Defence provides a wide range of assistance to industry in promoting equipment and negotiating contracts with overseas customers. This includes collecting market information, demonstrating equipment, providing expert military advice, training and support, staging exhibitions and negotiating with overseas governments. Government and private companies employ International Military Services Ltd to obtain and carry out export contracts for British defence equipment and associated services. Britain is one of the West's top three defence exporters. It is estimated that in 1986–87 defence exports will constitute about 3 per cent of visible exports and sustain some 120,000 jobs.

Civil Defence

Civil defence arrangements are based on the extended and adapted use of the peacetime resources of government departments, local authorities, emergency services and nationalised industries, supplemented by the efforts of voluntary organisations and individual volunteers. Civil defence regulations introduced in 1983 require local authorities to make and keep up to date plans for a range of essential functions in the event of war; to arrange training and exercises for civil defence staff and volunteers; and to provide suitable emergency centres for direction of civil defence in wartime.

Following a review of existing arrangements by the Home Office in 1980, expenditure on civil defence has been growing steadily and reached £80 million in 1985–86. This is being used to improve the quality and readiness of central and local government planning; increase training opportunities arranged by the Home Office on staff college lines at the Civil Defence College, Easingwold; help local authorities to plan for better community involvement in civil defence; and improve the emergency system for decentralised government control and communications. Improvements are also being made in the communications, equipment and administrative facilities of the United Kingdom Warning and Monitoring Organisation. This includes the civilian Royal Observer Corps, which is organised to provide public warning of an attack, of the location and strength of nuclear explosions, and of the distribution and level of radioactive fall-out.

5 Justice and the Law

The Law

Although the United Kingdom is a unitary state, England and Wales, Scotland and Northern Ireland all have their own legal systems and law courts. There is substantial similarity on many points, but considerable differences remain in law, organisation and practice. In Northern Ireland procedure closely resembles that of England and Wales but there are often differences in enacted law. However, a large volume of modern legislation applies throughout the United Kingdom and there is a common distinction between criminal law, concerned with wrongful acts harmful to the community, and civil law, concerned with individuals' rights, duties and obligations towards one another.

The main sources of law are legislation, common law and European Community law. Legislation consists of Acts of Parliament, Orders (rules and regulations made by ministers under the authority of an Act of Parliament) and by-laws made by local government or other authorities exercising powers conferred by Parliament. Common law, the ancient law of the land deduced from custom and interpreted in court cases by the judges, has never been precisely defined or codified but forms the basis of the law except when superseded by legislation. European Community law is confined mainly to economic and social matters; in certain circumstances it takes precedence over domestic law. It is normally applied by the domestic courts, but the most authoritative rulings are given by the European Court of Justice.

Certain changes to United Kingdom law have been enacted as a result of rulings of the European Court of Human Rights in particular cases where the domestic law was in breach of the European Convention for the Protection of Human Rights and Fundamental Freedoms, to which the United Kingdom is a party.

Criminal Justice

There are four distinct stages in British criminal justice: making laws which define prohibited acts and provide for the treatment of offenders; preventing crime and enforcing the law—largely matters for the police; determining in the courts the guilt or innocence of people accused of crimes, and sentencing the guilty; and dealing with convicted offenders.

Action being taken by the Government in pursuit of its general strategy for the criminal justice system is aimed at maintaining and encouraging public confidence in the system, achieving greater efficiency in the police service and in courts' procedures, and retaining a proper balance between the rights of the citizen and the needs of the community as a whole.

With continuing concern in Britain, as in many other countries, over rising crime rates, public expenditure on the law and order programme reflects the special priority given by the Government to these services. Recent increases have been made to cover, in particular, greater police manpower, the probation service and extra spending on prison building. More than two-thirds of total expenditure is initially incurred by local authorities (with the help of central government grants), mainly on the police service.

A number of measures to strengthen the criminal justice system are being taken. The Drug Trafficking Offences Act 1986 contains powers to trace, freeze and confiscate the proceeds of drug trafficking in England and Wales and forms an important element in the Government's strategy to combat drug misuse. Legislation is before Parliament to update the framework of public order law by revising and codifying the common law public order offences in England and Wales, enabling the police to impose conditions on marches and assemblies likely to result in serious disorder or damage, serious disruption, or the intimidation of individuals, and by tightening the offence of incitement to racial hatred. Further government proposals have been announced to strengthen and modernise the powers of courts to deal with criminal offenders. These proposals, which complement a wide range of measures already introduced to prevent, deter, detect and punish crime, include increased maximum sentences for certain offences, further measures to confiscate criminal assets, measures to facilitate the prosecution of fraud, changes in the jury system, improved arrangements for compensating victims of crime and, in the interests of combating international crime, reform of the existing law on extradition.

The Criminal Law

The criminal law, like the law generally, is interpreted by the courts but changes in the law are matters for Parliament. In practice most legislation affecting criminal law is government-sponsored, but there is usually consultation between government departments and the legal profession, the police, the probation service (in Scotland, the social work agencies), and voluntary bodies.

Crime Statistics

Chief constables in England and Wales must supply statistics relating to offences, offenders, criminal proceedings and the state of crime in their areas. Crime statistics are published annually by the Home Office and further information about crime trends (as well as about police matters) appears in the annual reports of Her Majesty's Chief Inspector of Constabulary and (for London) the Commissioner of Police of the Metropolis. Similar arrangements operate in Scotland and Northern Ireland.

Differences in the legal systems, police recording practices and statistical classifications in the countries of the United Kingdom make it impracticable to analyse in detail trends in crime for the country as a whole. Nevertheless, it is clear that, as in Western Europe generally, there has been a substantial increase in crime since the early 1950s. However, official statistics cover only crime recorded by the police and may thus be affected by changes in the proportion of crimes which are undiscovered or unreported. The level of police manning and deployment of the force may also affect recording.

Table 4: Notifiable Offences Recorded by the Police, per 100,000 Population (England and Wales) 1985

Offence group	1985
Homicide	1
Violence against the person (excluding homicide)	243
Sexual offences	43
Burglary	1,751
Robbery	55
Theft and handling stolen goods	3,786
Fraud and forgery	271
Criminal damage[a]	710
Other offences	24

Source: Home Office.
[a] Excluding 'other criminal damage' valued at £20 and under.

Table 4 shows the rate of notifiable offences recorded by the police in 1985 in England and Wales. These figures show a 3 per cent increase over the previous year. However, 95 per cent of recorded crime is against property and during 1985 a 3 per cent reduction in the number of burglaries was recorded, a factor which suggests that the Government's crime prevention campaign is proving effective.

The number of notifiable offences recorded by the police in England and Wales in 1985 was 3·4 million[1]; 35 per cent were cleared up. The Scottish police recorded 461,970 crimes, of which 34 per cent were cleared up.

Criminological Research

A wide range of research into criminal and social policies is carried out by the Home Office and the Scottish Home and Health Department. Research is also carried out in university departments, much of it financed by the Government. The principal university criminological research establishment is the Institute of Criminology at Cambridge.

Criminal Injuries Compensation

The Criminal Injuries Compensation Scheme provides compensation to victims of violent crimes (including violence within the family), to people hurt while trying to arrest offenders and prevent offences and to those bereaved as a result of violence. Compensation is assessed on the basis of common law damages and usually takes the form of a lump-sum payment. In 1984–85, 19,771 awards were made and the total compensation was over £35 million. Proposals have been announced to place the scheme on a statutory basis, thus giving eligible applicants a definite right to receive compensation.

In Northern Ireland there is separate, statutory provision in certain circumstances for compensation from public funds for criminal injuries, and for malicious damage to property including the resulting losses of profits.

There has been a rapid growth in the number of locally run victim support schemes which offer practical help to the victims of crime on a voluntary basis. The Government provides financial assistance, both to local schemes and to their national association.

Measures to Combat Terrorism

Legislation to protect the public against terrorism has given the authorities certain exceptional powers for dealing with and preventing terrorist activities. It is embodied in two Acts of Parliament which take account of the need to achieve a proper balance between the safety of the public and the rights of the individual. While acknowledging that the special powers make inroads into civil liberties the Government believes that they should continue in force as long as a substantial terrorist threat remains. Nobody can be imprisoned for political beliefs; all prisoners, except those awaiting trial, have been found guilty in court of criminal offences.

The Northern Ireland (Emergency Provisions) Act 1978 (first introduced in 1973), which is in force in Northern Ireland, provides the security forces with special powers to search, question and arrest suspected terrorists; allows the Secretary of State for Northern Ireland to proscribe terrorist organisations and provides for certain serious offences to be tried by a judge sitting alone without a jury, to obviate the dangers of intimidation of jurors. The Prevention of Terrorism (Temporary Provisions) Act 1984 (first introduced in 1974), which is applicable throughout the United Kingdom, provides for the exclusion from Great Britain, Northern Ireland or the United Kingdom of people connected with terrorism related to Northern Ireland affairs and for the proscription of terrorist organisations in Great Britain. It also gives the police powers to arrest people suspected of being involved in terrorism (whether international or relating to

---

[1]Excluding 'other criminal damage' valued at £20 and under.

Northern Ireland) without warrant and hold them for 48 hours and, with the approval of the Secretary of State, for up to a further five days. Both Acts have been subject to independent review. The Emergency Provisions Act is renewable every six months and the Prevention of Terrorism Act annually; the latter has a total life of five years.

The security forces in Northern Ireland are subject to the law and can be prosecuted for criminal offences. Procedures for handling complaints against the police involve two independent elements: the Director of Public Prosecutions if allegations of criminal conduct are made; and the Police Complaints Board for Northern Ireland when complaints relate only to disciplinary offences.

The Criminal Jurisdiction Act 1975 makes it possible to try in Northern Ireland a person accused of certain offences committed in the Irish Republic. It also enables evidence to be obtained in Northern Ireland for the trial of offences in the Irish Republic. Reciprocal legislation is in force in the Irish Republic. One of the aims of the Anglo-Irish Agreement signed in November 1985 between the United Kingdom and the Irish Republic is to improve security co-operation in combating terrorism. The accession of the Irish Government to the European Convention on the Suppression of Terrorism early in 1986 is expected to increase the prospects of securing extradition from the Republic of people accused or convicted of terrorist crimes in Britain.

THE POLICE SERVICE

British police action in enforcing the law rests mainly upon common consent, for there is only a small number of officers in relation to the population (roughly one officer to every 400 or so people). Officers do not normally carry firearms (their only weapon is a truncheon) and there are strict limitations on police powers.

The powers of the police in England and Wales have been modernised and clarified by the Police and Criminal Evidence Act 1984, which at the same time has enhanced safeguards for the citizen. The Act does not generally extend to Scotland, where separate legislation applies.

The interception of communications on behalf of the police is regulated by the Interception of Communications Act 1985, which establishes a statutory framework governing the interception of messages in the public telecommunications and postal services and sets out the grounds on which certain Secretaries of State are empowered to authorise interception. So far as the police are concerned, these are the prevention and detection of serious crime, and, in some instances, the protection of national security. The other ground for interception is the safeguarding of the economic well-being of the United Kingdom. Interception outside the procedures established by the Act is a criminal offence.

Forces

Each of Britain's 52 police forces is responsible for law enforcement in its area, but there is constant co-operation among them. In order to improve their effectiveness, forces pay particular attention to ensuring that manpower and other resources are used as efficiently as possible.

Outside London most counties (regions in Scotland) have their own police forces, though in the interests of efficiency several have combined forces. The policing of London is in the hands of the Metropolitan Police Force, with headquarters at New Scotland Yard, and the City of London force. The strength of the regular police force in Great Britain at the end of 1985 was over 132,200 (including over 11,900 policewomen); in Northern Ireland the strength of the regular Royal Ulster Constabulary was almost 12,750, including over 4,460 full- and part-time members of the Royal Ulster Constabulary Reserve. The strength of the Metropolitan Police Force was over 26,700. It is recognised that the composition of the police force should reflect the make-up of a multiracial society and efforts are being made to encourage more members of the ethnic minorities to join the forces.

Police Authorities and Chief Constables

Each regular police force is maintained by a police authority. In England and Wales, these are committees of local councillors and magistrates, and in Scotland, they are the regional and islands councils. The police authority for the Metropolitan Police Force is the Home Secretary. In Northern Ireland the police authority is appointed by the Secretary of State.

The police authority's primary duty is to provide an efficient police force for its area. Its functions, some subject to ministerial approval, include appointing the chief constable, deputy chief constable and assistant chief constables; fixing the maximum permitted strength of the force; and providing buildings and equipment. In the Metropolitan Police area the commissioner of police and his immediate subordinates are appointed on the recommendation of the Home Secretary. The police authorities are financed by central and local government.

Chief constables are responsible for the direction and control of police forces and for the appointment, promotion and discipline of all ranks below assistant chief constable. They are generally answerable to the police authorities on matters of efficiency, and must submit a report every year.

Central Authorities

The Home Secretary and the Secretaries of State for Scotland and Northern Ireland are concerned with the organisation, administration and operation of the police service. They approve the appointment of chief, deputy and assistant chief constables, and may require a police authority to retire a chief constable in the interests of efficiency, call for a report from a chief constable on matters relating to local policing or institute a local inquiry. They can make regulations covering such matters as police ranks; qualifications for appointment, promotion and retirement; discipline; hours of duty, leave, pay and allowances; and uniform. Some of these regulations are first negotiable within the Police Negotiating Board for the United Kingdom, which has an independent chairman and representatives of the police authorities, police staff associations and the home departments. Matters of a non-negotiable kind and general questions are discussed by the Police Advisory Boards.

All police forces (except the Metropolitan Police, for which the Home Secretary is directly responsible) are subject to inspection by inspectors of constabulary reporting to the Home Secretary, the Secretary of State for Scotland or the Secretary of State for Northern Ireland. Inspectors maintain close touch with the forces they inspect and have advisory functions.

Status and Duties

A British police officer is not employed by or under the direction of the police authority or of the Government, and may be sued or prosecuted for any wrongful act committed in carrying out duties. Statutory procedures, normally including an independent element, govern the way in which complaints are handled. The establishment in 1984 of a new Police Complaints Authority, with powers to supervise the investigation of any serious complaint against a police officer, has substantially reformed the complaints system in England and Wales. In Scotland, complaints against police officers involving allegations of any form of criminal conduct are investigated by independent public prosecutors. Relations between the police and the community have been the subject of public discussion for a number of years. The part played by the police in recent industrial disputes, such as the 1984–85 coal industry dispute, and disturbances in 1985 in a number of English cities, have again focused attention on the role of the police and policing methods. It is recognised that the action of the police in enforcing the law rests mainly on their ability to secure the consent and support of the public. Police authorities in England and Wales and, for London, the Metropolitan Police Commissioner, are required by law to make arrangements for obtaining the views of local people on the policing of their area and for obtaining their co-operation in joint efforts to discourage and prevent crime, and consultative committees now operate in most police areas. Furthermore, the number of neighbourhood watch schemes in operation in England and Wales reached over 14,500 in 1986 and continues to increase.

Police work ranges from the protection of people and property, road or street patrolling (the trend is increasingly away from the car patrol and back to 'community' policing on foot) and traffic control to crime prevention, criminal investigation and arresting offenders. In urban areas, particularly, police officers have to deal with social problems and may bring in other social agencies and expert help. The main departments in all forces are the uniform department, criminal investigation department, traffic department and specialised departments, which in some forces include river or marine police, mounted police, and dog handlers.

In order to release as many uniformed police officers as possible for operational duties, police authorities employ nearly 39,200 civilians (including part-time employees) in England and Wales and over 2,300 in Scotland. The number of civilian support staff has been growing as forces secure economies by replacing police officers with civilians where posts do not require police powers and training. Traffic wardens (of whom there are over 4,700 in England and Wales and about 520 in Scotland) carry out specified duties concerned with traffic and parking. Wardens are under the control of the chief constable.

Each force has an attachment of volunteer special constables who perform police duties in their spare time, without pay, acting mainly as auxiliaries to the regular force. In Northern Ireland there is a part-time and full-time paid reserve.

Members of the police service may not belong to a trade union nor may they withdraw their labour in furtherance of a trade dispute. All ranks, however, have their own staff associations to represent their interests.

Common Services

A number of common services are provided by central government departments and by arrangements between forces. The most important are: training services; a Forensic Science Service in England and Wales (the Metropolitan Police maintains its own laboratory); telecommunications services which provide police radio equipment; and central and provincial criminal records available to all forces. Regional crime squad teams of detectives from several forces investigate major crimes involving inquiries in more than one police area. The Scottish Crime Squad assists forces in crime investigation and prevention.

Certain special services such as liaison with the International Criminal Police Organisation (Interpol) are provided for other British forces by the Metropolitan Police. The National Drugs Intelligence Unit, run from the Metropolitan Police headquarters, assists police forces and the Customs service throughout Britain. The services of the Fraud Squad, run jointly by the Metropolitan Police and City of London Police to investigate company frauds, are available in England and Wales.

In all areas of police work the use of scientific aids is widespread. A national police computer helps to rationalise records and speed up the dissemination of information.

Powers of Arrest

In England and Wales arrests may be made with and without a warrant issued by a magistrate. The police may arrest a person without a warrant under the arrest scheme established by the Police and Criminal Evidence Act 1984, which provides a general conditional power to arrest a person reasonably suspected of any offence. However, a person can only be arrested under the scheme if it is necessary in order to ensure that he (or she) can be brought before a court (for example, because of failure to give a satisfactory address for service of a summons or in order to prevent injury to persons or property). Furthermore, the Act categorises certain offences as 'arrestable' or 'serious arrestable' and provides a full power of arrest without warrant in respect of them for the protection of the public.

Detention, Treatment and Questioning

A code of practice on detention, treatment and questioning is one of four codes which the Home Secretary has issued under the 1984 Act. Failure to comply with the provisions of these codes can render a police officer liable to disciplinary proceedings.

An arrested person has a statutory right to consult a solicitor and to ask the police to notify a named person likely to take an interest in his or her welfare about the arrest. Where a person has been arrested in connection with a serious arrestable offence, but has not yet been charged, the police may delay the exercise of these rights in the interests of the investigation if certain criteria are met. The police must in most circumstances caution a person whom there are grounds to suspect of an offence before any questions are put for the purpose of obtaining evidence. Questions relating to an offence may normally not be put to a person after he or she has been charged with that offence or informed that he or she may be prosecuted for it.

The detention scheme in the Police and Criminal Evidence Act provides for a person to be detained only if, and for as long as, necessary for a purpose specified by law up to a maximum of 96 hours before charge. A person can only be detained beyond 36 hours if a warrant is obtained from a magistrates' court.

Reviews must be made of a person's detention (whether before or after charge) at regular intervals to check whether the criteria for detention are still satisfied. If they are not, the person must be released immediately.

As a practical means of developing public confidence in the treatment of people detained by the police, the Government is encouraging the establishment of schemes whereby lay visitors make random checks on the interrogation and detention of suspects in police stations.

Charging

As soon as there is sufficient evidence to charge a person, the police must decide on an appropriate method of dealing with him or her. As an alternative to charging immediately, they could for example decide to defer charging, to deal with the matter by summons or to take no further action and release the person with or without bail. Where immediate charge is appropriate the person may continue to be held in custody if the name or address furnished is considered suspect, if there are grounds for believing that detention is necessary for his or her own protection, to prevent harm to people or property, or if there is a risk that the person would otherwise fail to appear in court or could interfere with the administration of justice. When no such considerations apply, the person must be released with or without bail depending on the circumstances of the case. Where a person is detained after charge, there is provision in the Act for him or her to be brought before a magistrates' court quickly. This will usually be no later than the following day.

Grant of Bail by the Court

It is for the court to decide, under the provisions of the Bail Act 1976, whether an accused person in criminal proceedings should be released on bail. A court may only withhold bail in certain specified circumstances, for instance, if the court has substantial grounds for believing that the accused person would abscond, commit an offence, interfere with witnesses, or otherwise obstruct the course of justice if released on bail. A court may also impose conditions before granting bail. If bail is refused, the defendant may apply to a High Court judge or to the Crown Court for bail, and application can be made to the Crown Court for conditions imposed by a magistrates' court to be varied. The majority of people remanded by magistrates are given bail.

A person who thinks that the grounds for detention are unlawful[1] may apply to the High Court for a writ of habeas corpus against the person who detained him or her, requiring the person to appear before the court to justify the detention. An application for this writ is normally made by the person detained or by someone acting on his or her behalf. Similar procedures apply in Northern Ireland. The Prosecution of Offences Act 1985 established an independent Crown Prosecution Service for England and Wales which in 1986 took over responsibility for all criminal proceedings instituted by the police. Its measures include the provision of statutory time limits on the period from arrest to commencement of trial in criminal proceedings in England and Wales. Field trials to establish the appropriate time limits are in progress.

In Scotland, the police may detain and question a suspected person for a period of up to six hours. Thereafter the person must either be released or charged. An arrest must be accompanied by a criminal charge. Once a person has been charged there is little scope for questioning and only voluntary statements will normally be allowed in evidence at the trial. The court will reject statements unless satisfied that they have been fairly obtained. Anyone arrested must be brought before a court with the least possible delay (generally not later than the first day after being taken into custody), or—in less serious cases—liberated by the police, often on a written undertaking to attend court on a specified date. Where a prosecution on indictment is intended (that is, where an accusation of a more serious offence is to be made), the accused is brought before the sheriff to be committed, either for further examination or until liberated in due course of law. A judicial examination may take place. Eight days may elapse between commitment for further examination and commitment until liberated in due course of law. The latter—which is also described as 'full committal'—is commitment for trial. No evidence needs to be presented to the sheriff for such commitment. Anyone accused of a crime, except murder or treason, is entitled to apply for release on bail. Money bail has been virtually abolished and the courts, or the Lord Advocate, may release an accused person on conditions.

Breach of any of the conditions without reasonable excuse is a separate offence. There is a right of appeal to the High Court by the accused person against the refusal of bail, or by the prosecutor against the granting of bail, or by either party against the conditions imposed. The writ of habeas corpus does not apply in Scotland but if a person is to be prosecuted on indictment and has been kept in custody pending trial, the trial must begin within 110 days of the date of full committal. The trial of a person charged with a summary offence and held in custody must begin within 40 days.

CRIMINAL COURTS

The initial decision to prosecute normally rests, in England and Wales, with the police and thereafter the conduct of proceedings rests with the Crown Prosecution Service. In Scotland, public prosecutors decide whether or not to begin proceedings. In Northern Ireland there is a Director of Public Prosecutions. In England and Wales (and exceptionally in Scotland) a private person may institute criminal proceedings. Police may issue cautions and in Scotland the public prosecutor may warn, instead of prosecuting.

England and Wales

The new Crown Prosecution Service in England and Wales is headed by the Director of Public Prosecutions under the superintendence of the Attorney General. The Director appoints chief Crown prosecutors—for the most part

---

[1] Detention is lawful in pursuance of criminal justice, for contempt of court or of either House of Parliament and when expressly authorised by Parliament. It is also sometimes lawful in the case of the mentally disordered.

covering a police force area—who deal with the vast majority of cases in consultation with the police, who investigate, and the courts, who hear the cases. The Service is responsible for providing advocates to present cases in magistrates' courts and briefs barristers to appear on its behalf in the Crown Court. While the decision to prosecute is delegated, as far as possible, to the local level, certain categories of cases are referrable to the Director of Public Prosecutions; including large and complex fraud, obscene publications and exhibitions, and allegations affecting police officers.

While much of the prosecution work at the Central Criminal Court in London is conducted by a team of Treasury Counsel appointed by the Attorney General, experienced barristers are also nominated from time to time to lead a member of the Treasury team.

Scotland

In Scotland the Lord Advocate is responsible for the prosecution of all suspects but delegates most of the work to the Solicitor General (see p 128), to 12 advocates depute and to procurators fiscal. The permanent adviser to the Lord Advocate on prosecution matters is the Crown Agent, who is head of the procurator fiscal service and is assisted by a staff of civil servants with legal qualifications known as the Crown Office. Prosecutions in the High Court of Justiciary are prepared by procurators fiscal and the Crown Office and prosecuted by the Lord Advocate, Solicitor General and advocates depute, while crimes tried before the sheriff and district courts are prepared and prosecuted by the procurators fiscal, who are lawyers and full-time civil servants operating from offices within the various sheriff court districts. The police investigate offences and report to the procurator fiscal, who decides whether to prosecute, subject to the directions of the Crown Office.

Northern Ireland

The Director of Public Prosecutions for Northern Ireland, who is responsible to the Attorney General, prosecutes all offences tried on indictment, and may do so in summary cases of a serious nature. Other summary offences are prosecuted by the police.

Courts in England and Wales

Magistrates' courts dispose of the bulk of criminal cases in England and Wales, and conduct preliminary investigations into more serious offences, which go to the Crown Court for trial. The Crown Court, situated in a number of towns and cities, takes all criminal work above the level of magistrates' courts and trials are held before a jury.

Magistrates' courts hear and determine cases for which jury trial is not required. There are about 700 magistrates' courts in England and Wales and 27,750 magistrates ('justices of the peace', JPs). These are made up of about 60 full-time, legally qualified stipendiary magistrates, and some 27,690 unpaid lay magistrates. Magistrates are appointed by the Lord Chancellor except in Lancashire, Greater Manchester and Merseyside, where appointments are made by the Chancellor of the Duchy of Lancaster. Stipendiary magistrates may sit alone and usually preside in courts in urban areas where the workload is heavy. Otherwise a court normally consists of three lay magistrates who are advised on points of law and procedure by a legally qualified clerk who is also in charge of the court's administrative arrangements. When the clerk to the justices is not in court, the magistrates are advised by a qualified assistant.

Magistrates' courts try people charged with summary offences (less serious offences that can only be disposed of by magistrates) and people charged with 'either way' offences where summary trial seems to the court appropriate and the defendant agrees. Courts also conduct committal proceedings in the case of people charged with indictable offences and with either way offences not tried by them.

Magistrates must as a rule sit in open court to which the public and press are admitted. They cannot impose a sentence of more than six months' imprisonment nor a fine exceeding £2,000. If an offence carries a higher maximum penalty, they may commit the defendant for sentence at the Crown Court if they consider their own power inadequate.

Cases involving people under 17 are heard in juvenile courts. These are specially constituted magistrates' courts which either sit apart from other courts or are held at a different time. Only limited categories of people may be present and press reports must not identify any juvenile appearing either as a defendant or a witness. Where a young person under 17 is charged jointly with someone of 17 or over, the case is heard in the ordinary magistrates' court. If the young person is found guilty, the court may transfer the case to a juvenile court for sentence unless satisfied that it is undesirable to do so, in which case it has the power to impose a limited category of non-custodial sentence itself.

The Crown Court deals with trials of the more serious cases, the sentencing of offenders committed for sentence by magistrates' courts, and appeals from magistrates' courts. It sits at about 90 centres and is presided over by High Court judges, full-time 'circuit judges' and part-time recorders. All contested trials take place before a jury. Magistrates sit with a circuit judge or recorder to deal with appeals and committals for sentence.

The Crown Court may impose on a convicted offender a fine either limited by the statutory maximum, or where there is no statutory maximum, of unlimited amount, and, within the permitted statutory maximum, any other custodial or non-custodial penalty.

Appeals

A person convicted by a magistrates' court may appeal to the Crown Court against the sentence imposed if he has pleaded guilty; or against the conviction or sentence imposed if he has not pleaded guilty. Where the appeal is on a point of law, either the prosecutor or the defendant may appeal from the magistrates' court to the High Court (see p 124). Appeals from the Crown Court, either against conviction or against sentence, are made to the Court of Appeal (Criminal Division). A further appeal from the Court of Appeal to the House of Lords can be brought if the court certifies that a point of law of general public importance is involved and it appears to the court or the Lords that the point is one that ought to be considered by the House. A prosecutor or defendant may appeal to the Lords from a decision of the High Court in a criminal case.

The Attorney General may seek the opinion of the Court of Appeal on a point of law which has arisen in a case where a person tried on indictment is acquitted; the court has power to refer the point to the House of Lords if necessary. The acquittal in the original case is not affected, nor is the identity of the acquitted person revealed without his or her consent.

Scotland

In Scotland the High Court of Justiciary tries such crimes as murder, treason and rape; the sheriff court is concerned with less serious offences and the district court with minor offences. Criminal cases are heard either under solemn procedure, when proceedings are taken on indictment and the judge sits with a jury of 15 members, or under summary procedure, when the judge sits without a jury. All cases in the High Court and the more serious ones in sheriff courts are tried by a judge and jury. Summary procedure is used in the less serious cases in the sheriff courts, and in all cases in the district courts. District courts are the administrative responsibility of the district and the islands local government authorities. The judges are lay justices of the peace; the local authorities may appoint up to one-quarter of their elected members to be ex-officio justices. In Glasgow there are four stipendiary magistrates who are full-time salaried lawyers. Children under 16 who have committed an offence or are for other reasons specified in statute considered to need compulsory care may be brought before a children's hearing comprising three members of the local community (see p 122).

Scotland's six sheriffdoms are further divided into sheriff court districts, each of which has one or more sheriffs, who are the judges of the court.

The High Court of Justiciary, Scotland's supreme criminal court, is both a trial and an appeal court. Any of the following judges is entitled to try cases in the High Court: the Lord Justice General (the head of the court), the Lord Justice Clerk (the judge next in seniority) or one of the Lord Commissioners of Justiciary. The main seat of the courts is in Edinburgh, although the High Court on circuit also tries cases in other towns.

All appeals are dealt with by the High Court in Edinburgh. In both solemn and summary procedure, an appeal may be brought against conviction, or sentence, or both. The Court may authorise a retrial if it sets aside a conviction. There is no further appeal to the House of Lords. In summary proceedings the prosecutor may appeal on a point of law against acquittal or sentence. The Lord Advocate may seek the opinion of the High Court on a point of law which has arisen in a case where a person tried on indictment is acquitted. The acquittal in the original case is not affected.

Northern Ireland

The structure of Northern Ireland courts is broadly similar to that in England and Wales. The day-to-day work of dealing summarily with minor cases is carried out by magistrates' courts presided over by a full-time, legally qualified resident magistrate. Young offenders under 17 and young people under 17 who need care, protection and control are dealt with by juvenile courts consisting of the resident magistrate and two lay members (at least one of whom must be a woman) specially qualified to deal with juveniles. Appeals from magistrates' courts are heard by the county court.

The Crown Court deals with criminal trials on indictment. It is served by High Court and county court judges. Proceedings are heard before a single judge, and all contested cases, other than those involving offences specified under emergency legislation, take place before a jury. Appeals from the Crown Court against conviction or sentence are heard by the Northern Ireland Court of Appeal. Procedures for a further appeal to the House of Lords are similar to those in England and Wales.

Trial

Criminal trials in the United Kingdom take the form of a contest between the prosecution and the defence. Since the law presumes the innocence of an accused person until guilt has been proved, the prosecution is not granted any advantage, apparent or real, over the defence. A defendant (in Scotland, called an accused) has the right to employ a legal adviser and may be granted legal aid from public funds. If remanded in custody, the person may be visited by a legal adviser to ensure a properly prepared defence. In England, Wales and Northern Ireland during the preparation of the case, the prosecution usually tells the defence of relevant documents which it is not proposed to put in evidence and discloses them if asked to do so. The prosecution should also inform the defence of witnesses whose evidence may help the accused and whom the prosecution does not propose to call. The defence or prosecution may suggest that the defendant's mental state renders him or her unfit to be tried. If the jury (or in Scotland, the judge) decides that this is so, the defendant is admitted to a specified hospital.

Criminal trials are normally in open court and rules of evidence (concerned with the proof of facts) are rigorously applied. If evidence is improperly admitted, a conviction can be quashed on appeal. During the trial the defendant has the right to hear and cross-examine witnesses for the prosecution, normally through a lawyer; to call his or her own witnesses who, if they will not attend voluntarily, may be legally compelled to attend; and to address the court in person or through a lawyer, the defence having the right to the last speech at the trial. The defendant cannot be questioned without consenting to be sworn as a witness in his or her own defence. When he or she does testify, cross-examination about character or other conduct may be made only in exceptional circumstances; generally the prosecution may not introduce such evidence.

The Jury

In jury trials the judge decides questions of law, sums up the evidence for the jury and instructs it on the relevant law, and discharges the accused or passes sentence. Only the jury decides whether the defendant is guilty or not guilty. In England and Wales, if the jury cannot reach a unanimous verdict, the judge may direct it to bring in a majority verdict provided that, in the normal jury of 12 people, there are not more than two dissentients. In Scotland, where the jury consists of 15 people, the verdict may be reached by a simple majority. However, as a general rule, no person may be convicted without corroborated evidence. If the jury returns a verdict of 'not guilty' (or in Scotland 'not proven', which is an alternative verdict of acquittal), the prosecution has no right of appeal and the defendant cannot be tried again for the same offence. If 'guilty' the defendant has a right of appeal to the appropriate court. A jury is completely independent of the judiciary. Once members are sworn in, they are protected from all interference. Both the prosecution and the defence can object to particular jurors. People between the ages of 18 and 65 whose names appear on the electoral register, with certain exceptions, are liable for jury service and their names are chosen at random. (Proposals to increase the upper age limit from 65 to 70 have been announced.) Ineligible persons include the judiciary, priests, people who have within the previous ten years been members of the legal profession, the Lord Chancellor's Department, or the police, prison and probation services, and certain sufferers from mental illness. Disqualified persons also include those sentenced to two or more years' imprisonment and those who have, within the previous ten years, served any part of a sentence of imprisonment, youth custody or detention, or been subject to a community service order, or, within the previous five years, been placed on probation.

Coroners' Courts

Coroners investigate violent and unnatural deaths or sudden deaths where the cause is unknown. Deaths may be reported to the local coroner (who is either medically or legally qualified, or both) by doctors, the police, the registrar, various public authorities or members of the public. If the death is sudden and the cause unknown, the coroner need not hold an inquest if, after a post-mortem examination has been made, he or she is satisfied that the death was due to natural causes. Where there is reason to believe that the deceased died a violent or unnatural death or died in prison or in other specified circumstances the coroner must hold an inquest and it is the duty of the coroner's court to establish how, when and where the deceased died. A coroner may sit alone, or in certain circumstances, with a jury. In Scotland the office of coroner does not exist. The local procurator fiscal inquires privately into all sudden and suspicious deaths and may report the findings to the Crown Office. In a minority of cases a fatal accident inquiry may be held before the sheriff. For certain categories (such as deaths in custody) a fatal accident inquiry is mandatory. In addition, the Lord Advocate has discretion to instruct an inquiry in the public interest in cases where the circumstances give rise to public concern.

TREATMENT OF OFFENDERS
Sentencing

In England, Wales and Northern Ireland a person may be sentenced to custodial treatment only if the court is satisfied that no other sentence will suffice. Unless that person has previously received a custodial sentence of the same kind, he or she must also have been legally represented. In England and Wales, extended sentences longer than the normal maximum term may be imposed on persistent offenders. In the case of murder there is a mandatory penalty of life imprisonment. This is the maximum penalty for a number of serious offences such as robbery, rape, arson and manslaughter. The death penalty has been repealed for almost all offences (including murder and the other common serious crimes) and it is no longer used.

In Scotland similar safeguards exist in relation to the imposition of custodial sentences. Unless the sentence is limited by statute, the maximum penalty is determined by the status of the court trying the accused. In trials on indictment, the High Court may impose a sentence of imprisonment for any term up to life, and the sheriff court any term up to two years but may send any person to the High Court for sentence if the court considers its powers are insufficient. In summary cases, the sheriff may normally impose up to three months' imprisonment or six months' for some repeated offences, although his powers are extended by statute in some exceptional cases. In the district court the maximum term of imprisonment is 60 days.

The commonest sentence in courts throughout the United Kingdom is a fine, which is imposed in more than 80 per cent of cases. There is no limit to the size of fine which may be imposed on indictment, but in summary procedure the maximum in England, Wales and Northern Ireland is £2,000. In Scotland it is £2,000 in the sheriff court and £1,000 in the district court.

Non-custodial Treatment

The Government's policy is to maintain and develop an effective range of non-custodial sentences including fines, probation and absolute discharge. In England, Wales and Northern Ireland the court may impose conditional discharge when it considers there is no need to impose punishment; and 'binding over' where the offender pledges money, with or without sureties, to keep the peace and be of good behaviour.

Offenders aged 16 or over (17 in Northern Ireland) convicted of imprisonable offences may, with their consent, be given community service orders. The court may order between 40 and 240 hours' unpaid service (the maximum is 120 hours where the offender is under 17) to be completed within 12 months. (This does not apply in Northern Ireland.) Examples of work done include decorating the houses of old or disabled people and building adventure playgrounds. The number of community service orders increased by 72 per cent between 1980 and 1984, in England and Wales. In Scotland the number of community service orders made by the courts increased from 492 in 1980 to 2,533 in 1984.

Experimental schemes have been started to enable offenders to make direct reparation to their victims, either by paying financial compensation or by undertaking some service for them.

The sentence imposed on an offender in England, Wales and Northern Ireland may also, with his or her consent, be deferred for up to six months to enable a court to take into account conduct after some expected change in circumstances. In Scotland sentence may also be deferred with or without the offender's consent. There is no limit to the length of deferment.

The courts in England, Wales and Northern Ireland may order an offender to pay compensation for personal injury, loss or damage resulting from an offence. The Government favours the courts making full use of their compensation powers. Proposals have been announced for further improving and strengthening these powers, and seeking to ensure that the courts have detailed information about the victim's losses for consideration when sentencing the offender. In Scotland there is also a system of compensation by offenders.

In England, Wales and Northern Ireland a judge is free to pass a suspended sentence of not more than two years. The sentence is not served unless the offender is convicted of a further offence punishable with imprisonment; in that event the suspended sentence normally takes effect and another sentence may be imposed for the new offence. An offender receiving a suspended sentence of more than six months may be placed under the supervision of a probation officer for all or part of the period. Courts in England and Wales have the power, when passing a sentence of between three months' and two years' imprisonment, to order that part should be served and the rest held in suspense.

In certain circumstances courts may order forfeiture of property involved in the commission of crime (see p 106). An offender convicted of a serious crime may be disqualified from driving if a motor vehicle was used in its commission.

In most circumstances, after a rehabilitation period of from six months to ten years depending on the nature of the sentence imposed, a person convicted of a criminal offence need not disclose it, and the offence will not be held against him or her. This does not apply to those with a prison sentence of more than 2½ years.

Probation

At present in the United Kingdom the number of offenders subject to supervision in the community considerably exceeds the number in custody. The purpose of probation is to protect society by the rehabilitation of the offender, who continues to live a normal life in the community while subject to the supervision of a probation officer. Before placing an offender on probation, which may last from six months (12 months in Scotland) to three years, the court must explain the order in ordinary language, ensuring that the offender consents to the requirements of the order and understands that a failure to comply with them will make him or her liable to a penalty or to be dealt with for the original offence. In England and Wales such an order can be made only for offenders aged 17 years or more. In Scotland the minimum age is 16 years and in Northern Ireland 14 years. About 15 per cent of orders contain a variety of additional requirements concerning place of residence, attendance at day centres or treatment for mental illness. The probation service also administers supervision orders, the community service scheme and parole. In addition, social work services are provided in custodial establishments.

In England and Wales the cost of the probation service is shared between central and local government and it is administered locally by probation committees of magistrates and members co-opted from the local community. In Scotland it is administered by local authority social work departments and in Northern Ireland by a probation board, whose membership is representative of the community and which is funded by central government.

Probation committees provide and maintain day centres and hostels together with schemes and programmes designed to meet the needs of a broad range of offenders, and, if possible, drawing the community into partnership in responding to offending. In Scotland and Northern Ireland these responsibilities are undertaken respectively by local authority social work departments and the probation board.

In England, Wales and Northern Ireland, the services of probation officers are available to every court, of both criminal and civil jurisdiction. In Scotland, officers of the local authority social work department are similarly available.

Prisons

The Government aims to provide a humane, efficient and effective prison service. The daily average inmate population in 1985 in England and Wales was nearly 46,300 and is projected to rise to between 53,000 and 59,000 by 1994. In Scotland the average population in custody has remained fairly steady for the last decade at around 4,900. In 1985, however, it rose to 5,270. In Northern Ireland the daily average inmate population in 1985 was 2,043 and is expected to fall slightly in 1987–88.

Prisons to which offenders may be committed directly by a court are known as 'local prisons'; all are closed. Other prisons, open or closed, receive prisoners on transfer from local prisons. (Open prisons do not have physical barriers to prevent escape.) In England, Scotland and Wales sentenced prisoners are classified into groups for security purposes. There are separate prisons for women. There are no open prisons in Northern Ireland, where the majority of offenders are serving sentences for terrorist offences. The Government has announced measures to improve procedures for the security classification of prisoners.

People awaiting trial are entitled to privileges not granted to convicted prisoners and, as far as practicable, are separated from convicted prisoners. Those under 21 awaiting trial are, where possible, separated from older prisoners.

Many of the prisons in England and Wales were built in the nineteenth century, and are now in need of major repairs. Others are housed in converted premises which are expensive to maintain. The Government's aim is to match the number of places available to the size of the prison population by the end of the decade thereby reducing overcrowding to a minimum. In order to achieve this and to improve the standards of existing prison establishments, a major programme of building and refurbishment is now in progress. This includes the construction of 16 new prisons, three of which are already complete and in use. In Northern Ireland two new prisons—one for men and one for women—opened in 1986.

Remission of Sentence

Most prisoners in Great Britain are eligible for remission of one-third of their sentence provided it does not reduce the sentence to less than five days. In Northern Ireland the Secretary of State reviews life sentence cases in such a way as to reflect fully their gravity and to take account of the special circumstances of Northern Ireland. Remission may be forfeited for serious misconduct. There is no remission for prisoners serving sentences under civil law and those serving sentences of unspecified length (for example, the criminally insane, whose release depends upon improvement in their mental condition).

Parole and Life Licence

In England and Wales prisoners serving determinate sentences of more than 10·5 months become eligible for consideration for release on parole licence when they have served one-third of the sentence, or six months, whichever expires the later. (In Scotland they qualify after 12 months.) However, for those serving sentences of over five years for violence or drug trafficking, parole is granted only in exceptional circumstances, or otherwise for a few months at the end of the sentence. The parole licence remains in force until the date on which the prisoner would otherwise have been released from prison. It prescribes the conditions, including the maintenance of contact with a supervising officer, with which the offender must comply. In 1985 about 5·6 per cent of prisoners granted parole in England and Wales, and about 6·6 per cent in Scotland, were recalled to prison.

The release of prisoners serving life sentences is at the discretion of the Home Secretary or in Scotland the Secretary of State for Scotland, subject to a favourable recommendation by the Parole Board and after consultation with the judiciary. The Secretaries of State are not, however, bound to accept a recommendation by the Parole Board for release, nor are they bound by the views of the judiciary. At the discretion of the Home Secretary, people serving life sentences for the murder of police and prison officers, terrorist murders, murder by firearms in the course of robbery and the sexual or sadistic murder of children are normally detained for at least 20 years. At the end of 1985, there were about 2,025 life sentence prisoners detained in prisons in England and Wales of whom about 105 had been detained for over 15 years. Life sentence prisoners are released on licence for the rest of their lives subject to recall. Similar arrangements exist in Northern Ireland except that the recommendations are made to the Secretary of State by an internal review body.

In Northern Ireland prisoners serving a sentence of more than five days are eligible for remission of half of their sentence. A prisoner serving a sentence of more than 12 months who is released from prison with remission is liable to be ordered to serve the remaining balance of this sentence if convicted of fresh imprisonable offences during this period.

Repatriation

Selected prisoners who are nationals of countries which have ratified the Council of Europe Convention on the Transfer of Sentenced Persons may apply to be returned to their own country to serve the rest of their sentence there.

Prison Industries, Physical Education and Education

Prison industries aim to give inmates work experience which will assist them when released and to secure a return which will reduce the cost of the prison system. The main industries are clothing and textile manufacture, engineering, woodwork, laundering, electro-mechanical production, farming and horticulture. Most production caters for internal needs and for other public services but some of it is for the commercial market. A few prisoners are employed outside prison. Small payments are made for work; in some prisons, incentive schemes provide an opportunity for higher earnings on the basis of output and skill.

Education is financed by the prison service and staffed by local education authorities. In every establishment the education officer is assisted by a team of teachers. Education is compulsory, full-time, for young offenders below school-leaving age and, in England and Wales, part-time for those between 16 and 21. For older offenders it is voluntary. Some prisoners study for public examinations (including those of the Open University). Within the resources available there is a full adult education curriculum. Library facilities are available in all establishments. Vocational training is provided directly by the prison service. Physical education is voluntary for adult offenders but compulsory for young offenders. Some 50 per cent of prisons now have purpose-built physical education facilities while all but two of the remainder use gymnasia converted from other buildings.

Education in Northern Ireland prisons is traditionally an evening activity, but governors may and do permit prisoners who need help in basic education and those preparing for public examinations to spend part of their working week on educational pursuits. Recently, the distance-learning mode of study has been introduced in a wide range of subjects, lessening the need for evening classes. Prison education is provided by full-time and part-time staff. A wide range of educational and vocational training facilities, from remedial education to Open University level, is available.

Medical and Psychological Services

The prison medical service has a general responsibility for the physical and mental health of all those in custody. Each establishment has accommodation for sick people and patients can also be transferred to National Health Service hospitals. Psychiatric care is available.

The work of psychologists includes evaluating treatment programmes, studying management practices, contributing to the management and treatment programmes of individuals and groups, taking part in advisory and training work with staff and making assessments for treatment or allocation purposes.

Privileges and Discipline

Prisoners are entitled to write and receive letters and to be visited by relatives and friends, and those in open establishments may make telephone calls, as may remand prisoners in certain circumstances. Privileges include a personal radio, books, periodicals and newspapers, and the opportunity to make purchases from the canteen with money earned in prison. Depending on facilities prisoners may be granted the further privileges of dining and recreation in association, and watching television.

Breaches of discipline are dealt with by the prison governor, or by the boards of visitors (visiting committees in Scotland), who have power to order forfeiture of remission and forfeiture of privileges. Boards of visitors (and visiting committees) consist of lay people, two of whom must be magistrates.

Welfare

The welfare of prisoners is the concern of all prison staff. Much of this work is the responsibility of probation officers (in Scotland social workers) stationed in prisons who help prisoners in their relations with individuals and agencies outside and play a leading part in helping prisoners to make constructive resettlement plans before their release. Prisoners may also receive visits from specially appointed prison visitors whose work is voluntary.

Chaplains give spiritual help and advice to inmates and are increasingly involved in management decisions affecting their needs and quality of life.

Discharge and After-care

All prisons in England and Wales make pre-release preparations. Prisoners serving four years or more are considered for outside employment before release. For those selected, work is found outside the prison for about the last six months of sentence; during the period prisoners may live in a separate part of the prison or in a hostel outside. Normal wages are paid so that they can resume support for their families. (In Scotland pre-release arrangements differ from these in some respects.) Periods of home leave may be granted to those serving medium- or longer-term sentences to help them maintain family ties and to assist them with their resettlement. In Northern Ireland arrangements exist for prisoners serving fixed sentences to have short periods of leave near the end of their sentences and at Christmas.

The aim of after-care, run by the probation service (in Scotland, the local authority social services departments), is to assist offenders on return to society. Compulsory supervision is given to most offenders under 21 when released, adult offenders released on parole, and those released on licence from a life sentence. A voluntary system is offered to others. Assistance is also provided by voluntary societies, some of which are affiliated to the National Association for the Care and Resettlement of Offenders. There is also a Scottish Association for the Care and Resettlement of Offenders. Hostels and accommodation may be provided, often with government financial help. The Northern Ireland Association for the Care and Resettlement of Offenders, also a voluntary group, is mainly concerned with assisting petty criminals and alcoholics towards rehabilitation and social awareness.

Children in Trouble
England and Wales

In England and Wales no child under ten years can be found guilty of an offence. A child aged ten but under 17 who is alleged to have committed an offence may be brought before a court in either criminal or care proceedings. The court in criminal proceedings is usually, and in care proceedings is always, a juvenile court. Before an order may be made in care proceedings, it must be shown not only that the child has committed the offence, but also that he or she is in need of care or control which he or she is unlikely to receive unless the order is made; this further condition must also be satisfied where a court makes a care order in criminal proceedings. A number of orders are common to both care and criminal proceedings: in either the court may make a care order or a supervision order or, if the child's parents consent, an order requiring them to agree to exercise proper care and control over the child; it may also make an order under the mental health legislation.

Under a care order a local authority becomes responsible for deciding where the child should be accommodated. It may allow him (or her) to remain at home under supervision or place him or her with foster parents or in a voluntary or community home. For children too severely disturbed or disruptive to be treated in local authority homes, there are two special Youth Treatment Centres run by the Department of Health and Social Security. The authority must review each care order every six months and consider whether an application should be made to the court to end it; the order normally expires when the child reaches 18 or 19. When a child who is already under a care order as a result of an offence commits a further offence (for which an adult could be punished by imprisonment) a court may attach a charge and control condition to the order. This suspends for up to six months the local authority's discretion to place the child in his or her own home, but does not oblige the authority to place the child in a community home. The local authority may, for example, place the child with foster parents.

Under a supervision order (which may remain in force for not more than three years) a child normally lives at home under the supervision of a social worker or a probation officer, though the court may require him or her to live with a specified person. The court has power to require that the child comply with directions given by his or her supervisor or, in criminal proceedings, with requirements made by the court itself. By either of these means, the supervision order can be used to provide for a programme of 'intermediate treatment', consisting of participation, under a supervisor, in a variety of constructive and remedial activities through a short residential course or, more usually, attendance at a day or evening centre.

In criminal proceedings, the courts may order payment of compensation, or impose a fine or grant a conditional or absolute discharge. Payment of fines, compensation or costs incurred by juvenile offenders is normally the responsibility of their parents or guardians. Offenders, both boys and girls, may be ordered to spend a total of up to 24 hours of their Saturday leisure time (up to three hours on any one occasion) at an attendance centre. The centres, which provide physical education and instruction in practical subjects, are for those found guilty of offences for which older people could be sent to prison. Offenders aged 16 may be ordered to perform up to 120 hours of community service. Boys aged 14 to 16, for whom a non-custodial penalty would not be appropriate, may be sent to a junior detention centre for a term of three weeks to four months. The regime is similar to that in senior detention centres (see p 123). Youth custody, usually for periods in excess of four months, is available for boys and girls aged 15 or 16. The maximum sentence is 12 months. In the case of a very serious crime, detention in a place approved by the Home Secretary may be ordered, and must be ordered in the case of homicide.

Scotland

In Scotland the age of criminal responsibility is eight years but prosecution of children under the age of 16 years in court is rare and can take place only as instructed by the Lord Advocate; court proceedings normally take place only where the offence is of a serious nature, or where a child is prosecuted together with an adult. Instead, children under 16 (or in certain circumstances those aged between 16 and 18 if subject to a supervision requirement) who have committed an offence or are considered to be in need of care and protection may be brought before a children's hearing. The hearing, which consists of three lay people drawn from a panel for each region or islands area, determines in an informal setting whether compulsory measures of care are required and, if so, the form they should take. An official 'reporter' decides whether a child should come before a hearing. If the grounds for referral are not accepted by the child or parents, or if for any reason the child is not capable of understanding the explanation of the grounds, the case goes to the sheriff for proof. If he finds the grounds established, the sheriff remits the case to the reporter to arrange a hearing. The sheriff also decides appeals against any decision of a children's hearing.

Northern Ireland

The age of criminal responsibility in Northern Ireland is ten. Children under the age of 17 charged with committing a criminal offence may be brought before a juvenile court. If the child is found guilty of an offence punishable by imprisonment when committed by an adult, he or she may be sent to a training school, placed in the care of a 'fit person', possibly the area health and social services board, or put under supervision. Alternatively the court can order a period at an attendance centre or a remand home, or impose a fine or compensation. A conditional or absolute discharge is also possible. Whatever other order it makes, a juvenile court can also make an order requiring parents to ensure the child's good behaviour. Children brought before the courts in need of care and protection may be placed in care locally.

Young Adult Offenders

Offenders aged 17 to 20 years (16 to 21 years in Scotland) form a separate category from juvenile and adult offenders. In England and Wales, the penalties for young adults are fines and compensation, attendance centre orders and probation orders; offenders may also be sentenced to up to 240 hours of community service. As in the case of juvenile offenders, a custodial sentence may be imposed only when no other measure would be appropriate. The custodial sentences for offenders of this age are the detention centre order (for young men sentenced to a term of four months or less) and the youth custody sentence (for both sexes). For the most serious offences young adults may be sentenced to custody for life. Detention centres, which receive offenders directly from the courts, operate a consistent regime which is geared to the short sentences involved. This inculcates a high standard of discipline and effort; in senior centres it includes a full working week; younger offenders receive at least 15 hours of education a week. Both junior and senior centres provide one hour of physical training each day. The youth custody centre regime is designed for offenders who are usually serving a minimum sentence of over four months, and for those allocated from a local prison. The aim is to provide flexible but coherent programmes of activities which are as constructive as possible and can include an element of vocational training. Some young offenders sentenced to youth custody are held in local prisons and remand centres in special accommodation where as full a regime as possible is provided. Young offenders are eligible for parole on the same terms as adults and all are supervised after release.

In Scotland young offenders sentenced to detention serve their sentences either in a detention centre (in the case of males only) or a young offenders' institution, depending on the length of the sentence. Remission of part of the sentence for good conduct, release on parole, and supervision after release are available. In Northern Ireland, offenders aged between 17 and 21 who are sentenced to three years or less may be sent to a young offenders' centre.

Civil Justice

The Civil Law

The main sub-divisions of the civil law of England, Wales and Northern Ireland are: family law, the law of property, the law of contract and the law of torts (covering injuries suffered by one person at the hands of another irrespective of any contract between them and including concepts such as negligence, defamation and trespass). Other branches of the civil law include constitutional and administrative (particularly concerned with the use of executive power), industrial, maritime and ecclesiastical law. Scottish civil law has its own, often analogous, branches.

An inquiry into the system of civil justice in England and Wales was set up in early 1985. Its aim is to improve the machinery of civil justice through reforms in jurisdiction, procedure and court administration, and in particular to reduce delay, cost and complexity.

CIVIL COURTS
England and
Wales

The limited civil jurisdiction of magistrates' courts extends to matrimonial proceedings for custody and maintenance orders, adoption orders and affiliation and guardianship orders. The courts also have jurisdiction regarding nuisances under the public health legislation and the recovery of rates. Committees of magistrates license public houses, betting shops and clubs.

The jurisdiction of the 300 or so county courts covers actions founded upon contract and tort (with minor exceptions); trust and mortgage cases; and actions for the recovery of land. Cases involving claims exceeding set limits may be tried in the county court by consent of the parties, or in certain circumstances on transfer from the High Court.

Other matters dealt with by the county courts include hire purchase, the Rent Acts, landlord and tenant, and adoption cases. Divorce cases are determined in those courts designated as divorce county courts and outside London bankruptcies are dealt with in certain county courts. The courts also deal with complaints of race and sex discrimination. Where small claims are concerned (especially those involving consumers), there are special arbitration facilities and simplified procedures.

All judges of the Supreme Court (comprising the Court of Appeal, the Crown Court and the High Court) and all circuit judges and recorders have power to sit in the county courts, but each court has one or more circuit judges assigned to it by the Lord Chancellor, and the regular sittings of the court are mostly taken by them. The judge normally sits alone, although on request the court may, exceptionally, order a trial with a jury.

The High Court of Justice is divided into the Chancery Division, the Queen's Bench Division and the Family Division. Its jurisdiction is both original and appellate and covers all civil and some criminal cases. In general, particular types of work are assigned to a particular division. The Family Division, for instance, is concerned with all jurisdiction affecting the family, including that relating to adoption and guardianship. The Chancery Division deals with the interpretation of wills and the administration of estates. Maritime and commercial law is the responsibility of admiralty and commercial courts of the Queen's Bench Division. A consultative paper examining the issues involved in setting up a unified jurisdiction in family and domestic matters—a single 'family court'—was published in mid-1986.

Each of the 80 or so judges of the High Court is attached to one division on appointment but may be transferred to any other division while in office. The Lord Chancellor is president of the Chancery Division, administered by the vice-president, the Vice-Chancellor. The Queen's Bench Division is presided over by the Lord Chief Justice of England, who ranks next to the Lord Chancellor in the legal hierarchy, and the Family Division is headed by the President. Outside London (where the High Court sits at the Royal Courts of Justice) sittings are held at 25 Crown Court centres. For the hearing of cases at first instance, High Court judges sit alone. Appeals in civil matters from lower courts are heard by courts of two (or sometimes three) judges, or by single judges of the appropriate division, nominated by the Lord Chancellor.

Appeals

Appeals in matrimonial, adoption and guardianship proceedings heard by magistrates' courts go to a divisional court of the Family Division of the High

Court. Affiliation appeals are heard by the Crown Court, as are appeals from decisions of the licensing committees of magistrates. Appeals from the High Court and county courts are heard in the Court of Appeal (Civil Division) and may go on to the House of Lords, the final court of appeal in civil cases.

The ex-officio members of the Court of Appeal are the Lord Chancellor, the Lord Chief Justice, the President of the Family Division and the Master of the Rolls; the ordinary members are 23 Lords Justices of Appeal.

The judges in the House of Lords are the nine Lords of Appeal in Ordinary, who must have a quorum of three, but usually sit as a group of five, and sometimes even of seven. Lay peers do not attend the hearing of appeals (which normally take place in a committee room and not in the legislative chamber), but peers who hold or have held high judicial office may also sit. The president of the House in its judicial capacity is the Lord Chancellor.

Scotland

The main civil courts are the sheriff courts and the Court of Session. The civil jurisdiction of the sheriff court extends to most kinds of action and is normally unlimited by the value of the case. Much of the work is done by the sheriff, against whose decisions an appeal may be made to the sheriff-principal or directly to the Court of Session.

The Court of Session sits only in Edinburgh, and in general has jurisdiction to deal with all kinds of action. The main exception is an action exclusive to the sheriff court, where the value claimed is less than a set amount. It is divided into two parts: the Outer House, a court of first instance, and the Inner House, mainly an appeal court. The Inner House is divided into two divisions of equal status, each consisting of four judges—the first division being presided over by the Lord President and the second division by the Lord Justice Clerk. Appeals to the Inner House may be made from the Outer House and from the sheriff court. From the Inner House an appeal may go to the House of Lords. The judges of the Court of Session are the same as those of the High Court of Justiciary. The Lord President of the Court of Session holds the office of Lord Justice General in the High Court of Justiciary (see p 115).

The Scottish Land Court is a special court which deals exclusively with matters concerning agriculture. Its chairman has the status and tenure of a judge of the Court of Session and its other members are lay specialists in agriculture.

Northern Ireland

Minor civil cases in Northern Ireland are dealt with in county courts, though magistrates' courts also deal with certain classes of civil case. The superior civil law court is the High Court of Justice from which an appeal may be made to the Court of Appeal. These two courts, together with the Crown Court, comprise the Supreme Court of Judicature of Northern Ireland and their practice and procedure are similar to those in England. The House of Lords is the final civil appeal court.

Civil Proceedings

In England and Wales civil proceedings are instituted by the aggrieved person; no preliminary inquiry on the authenticity of the grievance is required. Actions in the High Court are usually begun by a writ of summons served on the defendant by the plaintiff, stating the nature of the claim. A defendant intending to contest the claim informs the court. Documents setting out the precise question in dispute (the pleadings) are then delivered to the court. County court proceedings are initiated by a summons served on the defendant by the court; subsequent procedure is simpler than in the High Court.

A decree of divorce must be pronounced in open court, but a procedure for most undefended cases dispenses with the need to give evidence in court and permits written evidence to be considered by the registrar.

Civil proceedings, as a private matter, can usually be abandoned or ended by compromise at any time. Actions brought to court are usually tried without a jury, except in defamation, false imprisonment, or malicious prosecution cases, when either party may, except in certain special circumstances, insist on trial by jury, or a fraud case, when the defendant may claim this right. The jury decides questions of fact and damages awarded to the injured party; majority verdicts may be accepted.

An action in a magistrates' court is begun by a complaint on which the court may serve the defendant with a summons. This contains details of the complaint and the date on which it will be heard. Parties and witnesses give their evidence at the court hearing. Domestic proceedings are normally heard by not more than three lay justices including, where practicable, a woman; members of the public are not allowed to be present. The court may order provision for custody, access and supervision of children, as well as maintenance payments for spouses and children.

Judgments in civil cases are enforceable through the authority of the court. Most are for sums of money and may be enforced, in cases of default, by seizure of the debtor's goods or by attachment of earnings (a court order requiring an employer to make periodic payments to the court by deduction from the debtor's wages). Other judgments can take the form of an injunction restraining someone from performing an illegal act. Refusal to obey judgment may result in imprisonment for contempt of court. Arrest under an order of committal may be effected only on a warrant.

The general rule is that the costs of the action (lawyers' charges, court fees and other payments) are within the discretion of the court. Normally, the court orders them to be paid by the party losing the action, but in the case of family law maintenance proceedings a magistrates' court can order either party to pay the whole or part of the other's costs.

In Scotland proceedings in the Court of Session or ordinary actions in the sheriff court are initiated by serving the defender with a summons (an initial writ in the sheriff court). In Court of Session actions the next step is the publication of the action in the court lists. A defender who intends to contest the action must inform the court; if he or she does not appear, the court grants a decree in absence in favour of the pursuer. In ordinary actions in the sheriff court the defender is simply required to give notice of intention to defend within a certain number of days after service of the initial writ, and this is followed by a formal appearance in court by the parties to the dispute or their solicitors.

In summary causes (involving small sums) in the sheriff court the procedure is less formal. The statement of claim is incorporated in the summons. The procedure is designed to enable most actions to be carried through without the parties involved having to appear in court. Normally they (or their representatives) need appear only when an action is defended.

Proceedings in Northern Ireland are similar to those in England and Wales. County court proceedings are commenced by a civil bill served on the defendant; there are no pleadings in the county court. Judgments of civil courts are enforceable through a centralised procedure administered by the Enforcement of Judgments Office.

Restrictive Practices Court The Restrictive Practices Court is a specialised United Kingdom court which deals with monopolies and restrictive trade practices. It comprises five judges and up to ten other people with expertise in industry, commerce or public life.

Administrative Tribunals Administrative tribunals consist of people or bodies exercising judicial functions outside the ordinary hierarchy of the courts. As a rule, they are set up under statutory powers which also govern their constitution, functions and procedure. Their composition and procedures vary greatly. Compared with the courts, they tend to be less expensive, less formal and more accessible; they also have expert knowledge of their particular subjects. The expansion of the tribunal system is comparatively recent, most tribunals having been set up since 1945. Independently of the executive, tribunals decide the rights and obligations of private citizens towards one another or towards a government department or other public authority. A number of important tribunals (notably the rent and industrial tribunals) decide disputes between private citizens. Some (such as those concerned with social security) resolve claims by private citizens against public authorities. A further group (including tax tribunals) decide disputed claims by public authorities against private citizens, and still others decide issues in dispute which do not directly affect financial rights or liabilities, such as entitlements to licences or the right to enter the United Kingdom. Tribunals usually consist of an uneven number of people so that a majority decision can be reached; some consist of one person sitting alone. Members are normally appointed by the minister concerned with the subject but other authorities have the power of appointment in appropriate cases. The Lord Chancellor (or the Lord President of the Court of Session in Scotland) makes most appointments where a lawyer chairman or member is required.

Appeals on a point of law from all the more important tribunals may be made in England and Wales to the High Court, in Scotland to the Court of Session and in Northern Ireland to the Court of Appeal. In some cases an appeal may be made to a specially constituted appeal tribunal, to a government minister or to an independent referee. The Employment Appeal Tribunal, which hears appeals on questions of law from decisions of industrial tribunals, has High Court and Court of Session status in Great Britain. The Council on Tribunals (an independent body, established in 1958) exercises general supervision over many tribunals, advising on draft legislation and rules of procedure, monitoring their activities and reporting on particular matters; those peculiar to Scotland are dealt with by the Scottish Committee of the Council. The Council has a similar responsibility with regard to public inquiries.

Administration of the Law

GOVERNMENT RESPONSI-BILITIES
The United Kingdom judiciary is entirely independent of the Government and is not subject to ministerial direction or control. There is no minister of justice. Responsibility for the administration of justice rests with the Lord Chancellor, the Home Secretary and the Secretaries of State for Scotland and Northern Ireland. Also concerned is the Prime Minister, who recommends the highest judicial appointments to the Crown.

England and Wales
The Lord Chancellor is the head of the judiciary (and sometimes sits as a judge in the House of Lords); he is concerned with court procedure and is responsible for the administration of all courts other than magistrates' and coroners' courts, and for a number of administrative tribunals. He also appoints magistrates, and has general responsibility for the legal aid and advice schemes. He is also responsible for the administration of civil law reform.

The Home Secretary is concerned with the criminal law (including law reform), the police service, prisons, and the probation and after-care service; and has general supervision over magistrates' courts, together with some specific responsibilities (such as approving the appointment of justices' clerks). Prison policy and the administration of custodial centres are functions of the Home Office Prison Department, and the Home Secretary appoints to each prison establishment a Board of Visitors representing the local community who need to satisfy themselves as to the state of prison premises, administration and treatment of inmates. They are required to report to the Home Secretary any abuse or matter of concern which comes to their attention. Boards have disciplinary powers in relation to serious breaches of discipline and hear applications or complaints from inmates. The Home Secretary is advised by a special Parole Board on the release of prisoners on licence.

Responsibility for the treatment of offenders under 17 is shared between the Home Office and the Department of Health and Social Security. The Home Secretary is also responsible for advising the Queen on the exercise of the royal prerogative of mercy to pardon a person convicted of a crime or to cancel all or part of a penalty imposed by a court.

The Secretary of State for the Environment is responsible for providing accommodation for all the superior courts in England and Wales, except the Central Criminal Court, which is the responsibility of the City of London.

The Attorney General and the Solicitor General (the Law Officers of the Crown for England and Wales) are the Government's principal advisers on English law, and represent the Crown in appropriate domestic and international cases. They are senior barristers, elected members of the House of Commons and hold ministerial posts. The Attorney General is also Attorney General for Northern Ireland. As well as exercising various civil law functions, the Attorney General has final responsibility for enforcing the criminal law; the Director of Public Prosecutions is subject to the Attorney General's superintendence. The Attorney General is concerned with instituting and prosecuting certain types of criminal proceedings, but must exercise an independent discretion, and must not be influenced by government colleagues. The Solicitor General is, in effect, the deputy of the Attorney General.

Scotland

The Secretary of State for Scotland recommends the appointment of all judges other than the most senior ones, appoints the staff of the High Court of Justiciary and the Court of Session and is responsible for the composition, staffing and organisation of the sheriff courts. District courts are staffed and administered by the district and islands local authorities. The Secretary of State is also responsible for the criminal law of Scotland, crime prevention, and the police and the penal system, and is advised on parole matters by the Parole Board for Scotland. The Secretary of State is also responsible for legal aid in Scotland and for the legal advice and assistance schemes.

The Lord Advocate and the Solicitor General for Scotland are the chief legal advisers to the Government on Scottish questions and the principal representatives of the Crown for the purposes of litigation in Scotland. Both are government ministers. The Lord Advocate is closely concerned with questions of legal policy and administration and is also responsible for the Scottish parliamentary draftsmen. He has overall responsibility for the prosecution of crime in Scotland and although he holds a ministerial post he must exercise an independent discretion in carrying out this responsibility.

Northern Ireland

In Northern Ireland the judiciary is appointed by the Queen on the advice of the Lord Chancellor. The administration of all courts is the responsibility of the Lord Chancellor, while the Northern Ireland Office, under the Secretary of State, deals with the police and the penal system. The Lord Chancellor has general responsibility for the legal aid and advice scheme in Northern Ireland.

THE PERSONNEL OF THE LAW

The courts of the United Kingdom are the Queen's Courts since the Crown is the historic source of all judicial power. The Queen, acting on the advice of ministers, is responsible for all appointments to the judiciary.

Judges

Full-time judges do not engage in politics, except for the Lord Chancellor, who is head of the judiciary, speaker of the House of Lords and a Cabinet minister. With the exception of lay magistrates, judges are normally appointed from practising barristers, advocates (in Scotland) or solicitors (see below). The judiciary is not a career service as in many other countries. Lay magistrates in England and Wales need no legal qualifications but on appointment undergo basic training to give them sufficient knowledge of the law, including the rules of evidence, and to enable them to understand the nature and purpose of sentencing. The Scottish district court justices of the peace likewise need no legal qualifications. In Northern Ireland lay magistrates serving on juvenile courts undertake training courses; resident magistrates are drawn from practising solicitors or barristers. In certain circumstances (for instance, in cases of misconduct or proven incapacity) judges of the inferior courts may be removed from their positions but, in order to safeguard the independence of the judiciary from the executive, superior judges in England and Wales and Northern Ireland (other than the Lord Chancellor who changes with the Government) are subject to removal only by the Queen on an address presented by both Houses of Parliament; in Scotland there is no statutory provision for removing judges of the Court of Session or High Court of Justiciary from office and special legislation would probably be needed to secure a dismissal.

The Legal Profession

The legal profession is divided into two branches: barristers (advocates in Scotland) and solicitors. Barristers are known collectively as the 'Bar', and collectively and individually as 'counsel'. Solicitors undertake legal business for lay clients, while barristers advise on legal problems submitted through solicitors and present cases in the higher courts; certain functions are common to both. Although people are free to conduct their own cases, most people prefer to be legally represented in the more serious cases.

The professional organisations for barristers are: the Senate of the Inns of Court and the Bar (in England and Wales),[1] the Faculty of Advocates (in Scotland) and the General Council of the Bar of Northern Ireland and the Executive Council of the Inn of Court of Northern Ireland. For solicitors they are: the Law Society, the Law Society of Scotland and the Law Society of Northern Ireland.

Legislation was introduced in 1985 to provide greater protection for the public against inadequate professional work by solicitors in England and Wales.

LEGAL AID, ADVICE AND ASSISTANCE

A person in need of legal advice or legal representation in court may qualify for help with the costs out of public funds, either free or with a contribution according to his or her means, under the legal aid and advice and assistance schemes.

People whose income and savings are within certain limits are entitled to help from a solicitor on any legal matter as it affects the applicant's particular circumstances. Such help includes advice on the relevant law, writing letters on the client's behalf, drafting wills and taking the opinion of a barrister or advocate. In England and Wales it may be extended to cover representation in civil proceedings in the magistrates' court, Mental Review Tribunal hearings and certain disciplinary proceedings before prisons' Boards of Visitors.

The scheme provides for initial work to be done up to a cost of £50 (£90 where the client is the petitioner for a divorce or judicial separation in England and Wales); thereafter the approval of the Law Society is required before further costs can be incurred.

---

[1] In England and Wales every barrister and every student wishing to become a barrister must be a member of one of the four Inns of Court in London (Lincoln's Inn, Inner Temple, Middle Temple and Gray's Inn).

Law Centres   In a number of urban areas law centres provide free advice to people of limited means. Most law centres (voluntary organisations financed from various sources, including the local authority) have at least two full-time salaried lawyers and many employ community workers. Much of their time is devoted to tenant–landlord disputes and other housing problems. Free legal advice is also available in Citizens Advice Bureaux, consumer and housing advice centres and in specialist advice centres run by various voluntary organisations.

Aid in Civil Proceedings   Legal aid, which covers representation before the court, is available for most civil proceedings to those who satisfy the financial eligibility conditions.

An applicant for legal aid must show not only that he (or she) has grounds for taking or defending proceedings but also that it is reasonable in all the circumstances of his case that he should receive, or continue to receive, legal aid. If legal aid is granted the case is conducted in the normal way except that no money passes between the client and the solicitor; all payments are usually made through the legal aid fund.

In certain circumstances the successful unassisted opponent of a legally aided party may recover his costs in the case from the legal aid fund. Also, where the assisted person successfully recovers or preserves money or property in the proceedings the legal aid fund may have a first charge on that money or property to recover the sums it has expended on the assisted person's behalf.

The civil legal aid schemes are administered by the Law Society, the Law Society of Northern Ireland and (at present) the Law Society of Scotland while ministerial responsibility for the schemes rests with the Lord Chancellor and, in the case of Scotland, the Secretary of State for Scotland.

Aid in Criminal Proceedings   In criminal proceedings in England and Wales a legal aid order may be made by the court concerned if it appears to be in the interests of justice and if a defendant qualifies for financial help. An order must be made (subject to means) when a person is committed for trial on a murder charge or where the prosecutor appeals or applies for leave to appeal from the Court of Appeal (Criminal Division) to the House of Lords. No person who is unrepresented can be given a custodial sentence for the first time unless given the opportunity to apply for legal aid.

The criminal legal aid scheme in England and Wales is administered by the courts, under the overall responsibility of the Lord Chancellor. Committees of the Law Society provide a right of recourse against the refusal of legal aid in some cases by a magistrates' court.

Under a national scheme the Law Society makes arrangements for duty solicitors to be available at magistrates' courts to provide initial advice and representation to unrepresented defendants, and also for duty solicitors to be available, on a 24-hour basis, to give advice and assistance to suspects at police stations. The services of a duty solicitor are free.

The arrangements for aid in criminal proceedings in Scotland and Northern Ireland are broadly similar, and in Scotland there is a duty solicitor scheme for accused people in custody in sheriff, and district, court cases and the 'interests of justice' test applies only in summary cases. In Northern Ireland a duty solicitor scheme has been introduced at the principal magistrates' court in Belfast. Legal aid for criminal cases in Scotland and Northern Ireland is free; the assisted person is not required to make any contributions towards the cost of his or her legal representation.

A government scrutiny of the operation and administration of the legal aid scheme in England and Wales was published in June 1986 and contained recommendations for a major restructuring of the system to provide a more efficient and effective service. Following the Legal Aid (Scotland) Act 1986, a new non-departmental public body, the Scottish Legal Aid Board, will assume responsibility for the administration of most legal aid functions in Scotland on 1 April 1987. Legal aid in solemn criminal cases (see p 114) will continue to be awarded by the courts.

LAW REFORM   While changes in the law are matters for Parliament, the duty of keeping the law under review lies with the Law Reform Committee, the Criminal Law Revision Committee and the Law Commission in England and Wales, and with the Scottish Law Commission in Scotland. The Law Reform Committee and the Criminal Law Revision Committee comprise judges and practising and academic lawyers, appointed respectively by the Lord Chancellor and the Home Secretary, to examine aspects of the civil and criminal law in England and Wales.

The Law Commission, a permanent body reporting to the Lord Chancellor and consisting of a High Court judge and four other members who are required to be practising and academic lawyers, scrutinises the law with a view to its systematic development and reform, and its simplification and modernisation. The Scottish Law Commission is similar, and reports to the Lord Advocate. Law reform in Northern Ireland is a matter for the Law Commission and the Office of Law Reform.

6   Social Welfare

The British social welfare system comprises the National Health Service, the personal social services and social security. The National Health Service provides a comprehensive range of medical services which are available to all residents, irrespective of means. Local authority personal social services and voluntary organisations provide help and advice to elderly people, disabled people and children in need of care. The social security system is designed to secure a basic standard of living for people in financial need by providing income during periods of inability to earn, help for families and assistance with costs arising from disablement.

Central government is directly responsible for the National Health Service, administered by health authorities and boards acting as its agents, and for the social security system. It has an indirect responsibility for the personal social services administered by local authorities. Joint finance and planning between health and local authorities aims to prevent overlapping of services and to encourage the development of community services.

Planned spending on social welfare in 1986–87 is: health £18,700 million and personal social services £3,203 million (together representing 16 per cent of general government expenditure); and social security nearly £43,000 million (31 per cent).

Expenditure on the health service has increased in real terms by some 12 per cent since 1980, and current spending is planned to grow further over the next two years. More patients are now being treated than ever before. Spending on social security is rising because of increased numbers of beneficiaries, especially retirement pensioners and the unemployed, and the value of retirement and most other long-term benefits has been increased in real terms since 1980. Major reforms to the social security system are being introduced under the Social Security Act 1986; these are designed to provide a clearer, simpler system which will be more capable of meeting genuine need (see p 152). Spending on the personal social services is determined by local authorities, and while constraints are placed by central government on the total expenditure of individual local authorities, gross current expenditure on personal social services has increased by 10 per cent in real terms since 1980–81, thus reflecting the priority given to this sector.

National Health Service

The National Health Service (NHS) is based upon the principle that there should be a comprehensive range of publicly provided services designed to help the individual to stay healthy and to provide effective and appropriate treatment and care where necessary. All taxpayers, employers and employees contribute to its cost so that those members of the community who do not require health care help to pay for those who do. Some forms of treatment, such as hospital care, are provided free of charge; others (see p 135) may be charged for.

Growth in real spending on the health service is being used to meet the needs of increasing numbers of elderly people (over 45 per cent of health authority expenditure on hospital and community services is spent on care of the elderly);

to take full advantage of advances in medical technology and to remedy shortfalls in such areas as renal services; to provide more appropriate types of care, often in the community rather than in hospital, for priority groups like the elderly, mentally ill and mentally handicapped people; to combat the growing health problems arising from alcohol and drug misuse; and to remedy disparities in provision between the regions of Britain.

The Government emphasises the importance of preventive health services, and the responsibility of individuals for their own health. While great progress has been made in eliminating infectious diseases such as poliomyelitis and tuberculosis, there has been less success in controlling the major causes of death—heart disease, cancer and stroke—which accounted for some two-thirds of all deaths in England in 1984. Because of the close link between such diseases and individual life-styles or social habits, emphasis is placed on helping people to adopt healthier ways of living through education and other policies.

The Government stresses the need for a partnership between the public and private health sectors and for improving efficiency in order to secure the best value for money and the maximum patient care. In order to secure more effective management of resources in the National Health Service, general managers drawn from inside and outside the Service have been appointed at all levels. Further measures have included improving the accountability of health authorities for the way in which they plan and manage their resources, increasing the proportion of total staff who provide direct patient care, such as doctors and nurses, and the introduction of a range of programmes to provide existing services at lower cost. Considerable savings have been made in many areas through a policy of competitive tendering for hospital ancillary services such as cleaning, catering and laundry. Economies are also made in prescribing by restricting the use of expensive branded products in favour of cheaper but equally effective generic equivalents.

ADMINIS-TRATION

The health ministers (the Secretary of State for Social Services in England and the Secretaries of State for Scotland, Wales and Northern Ireland) are responsible for all aspects of the health services in their respective countries. The health departments (the Department of Health and Social Security in England, the Scottish Home and Health Department, the Welsh Office and the Department of Health and Social Services in Northern Ireland) are responsible for national strategic planning. District health authorities in England and Wales and health boards in Scotland are responsible for planning and operational control of all health services in their areas. In England, because of its greater size and population, a tier of regional authorities is responsible for regional planning, resource allocation, major capital building work and certain specialised hospital services best administered on a regional basis. The authorities and boards co-operate closely with local authorities responsible for social work, environmental health, education and other services. Family practitioner committees (health boards in Scotland), accountable to the Secretary of State, arrange for the provision of services by doctors, dentists, pharmacists and opticians. Community health councils represent local opinion on the health services provided. (In Scotland this function is exercised by local health councils.)

In Northern Ireland health and social services boards are responsible for all health and personal social services in their areas. The representation of public opinion on these services is provided for by district committees.

Health Service Commissioners

There are three Health Service Commissioner posts (for England, Scotland and Wales) for dealing with complaints from members of the public about the health service. All three posts are held by the Parliamentary Commissioner for

Administration (Ombudsman). The jurisdiction of the Health Service Commissioner covers the failure of a health authority or family practitioner committee to carry out its statutory duties, a failure in a service provided, or maladministration causing injustice or hardship, but not actions taken solely in the exercise of clinical judgment or the actions of family doctors, for which separate complaints procedures exist. The Commissioner reports annually to ministers who lay the reports before Parliament, and may make other reports when necessary. In Northern Ireland the Commissioner for Complaints has a similar role.

Finance

About 86 per cent of the cost of the health service is paid for through general taxation; the rest is met from the National Health Service contribution paid with the National Insurance contribution and from the charges towards the cost of certain items such as drugs prescribed by a family doctor, and dental treatment. Health authorities may raise funds from voluntary sources. Certain hospitals increase their revenue by taking private patients who pay the full cost of their accommodation and treatment.

The charges for medical prescriptions do not apply to children under 16 years, expectant mothers and women who have had a baby in the last 12 months, women aged 60 and over and men aged 65 and over, patients suffering from certain medical conditions, war and armed forces disablement pensioners (for treatment of their disability), and families with very low incomes. Some 70 per cent of prescription items are supplied free of charge. No charges for dental treatment are made for dental examinations and denture repairs. Some groups of patients receive entirely free dental treatment, for example, women who are pregnant or who have had a baby in the last year, anyone under the age of 18, or 19 if in full-time education, and people receiving supplementary benefit or family income supplement (see p 157). Patients with low incomes may have their charges remitted. Some groups also receive grants towards the cost of spectacles.

Hospital medical staffs are salaried and can be employed full time or part time. Hospital doctors can accept private patients. Family practitioners (doctors, dentists, opticians and pharmacists) are self-employed contractors. Doctors (also known as general practitioners) are paid by a system of fees and allowances designed to reflect responsibilities, workload and practice expenses. Dentists providing treatment in their own surgeries are paid on a prescribed scale of fees. Pharmacists dispensing on their own premises are reimbursed for the cost of the items supplied together with professional fees. Ophthalmic medical practitioners and ophthalmic opticians taking part in the general ophthalmic service receive approved fees for each sight test made; opticians who dispense spectacles are paid a fee based on the number and type of pairs supplied.

PRIMARY HEALTH CARE

Primary health care is offered by doctors, dentists, opticians and pharmacists working within the Service as independent practitioners, and by health visitors, district nurses and midwives employed by the health authorities. A wide range of other services is also available, including the school health service and the chiropody service. The remedial professions of physiotherapy, occupational therapy and speech therapy are making an increasingly important contribution to primary care.

There have been substantial increases in primary care staff in recent years: for example, the number of doctors and dentists in England increased by 14 per cent and 20 per cent respectively between 1978 and 1984, and the average number of patients per doctor fell by 10 per cent, from 2,312 to 2,089.

Special funds have been earmarked by the Government for improving the quality of primary health care in inner city areas.

Family Practitioner Services

The family practitioner services are those given to patients by doctors, dentists, opticians and pharmacists of their own choice. Family doctors provide the first diagnosis in the case of illness and either prescribe a suitable course of treatment or refer a patient to the more specialised services and hospital consultants. Only ophthalmic medical practitioners and ophthalmic opticians may test sight; patients requiring treatment for a defect in sight or an eye disease are dealt with through the Hospital Eye Service. In order to provide the public with a wider and cheaper choice of spectacles, the monopoly on the supply of spectacles held by registered ophthalmic and dispensing opticians was ended in 1985 and unregistered opticians may now sell spectacles to adults under carefully prescribed conditions. The supply of NHS spectacles to children, those on low incomes and people requiring complex lenses was replaced during 1986 by a voucher system. Under this, people previously eligible for NHS spectacles are provided with vouchers which may be exchanged for low-priced spectacles on sale through the private market, or put towards the cost of higher-priced frames.

Some wide-ranging suggestions on possible extensions of the pharmacist's role have been the subject of a recent inquiry.

Health Visitors, District Nurses and Midwives

Health visitors are responsible for the preventive care and health education of all families, particularly those with young children. They work closely with general practitioners, district nurses and other professions. District nurses give skilled nursing care to people at home or elsewhere outside hospital; they also play an important role in preventive care and health education. Although almost all babies are born in hospital, some antenatal care and most postnatal care is given in the community by midwives and general practitioners, who also care for women who have their babies at home. All midwives are responsible for educating and supporting women and their families during the childbearing period.

Group Practices and Health Centres

About four-fifths of family doctors in Britain work in partnerships or group practices, often as members of health-care teams which also include health visitors and district nurses and sometimes midwives, social workers and other professional staff. About a quarter in Great Britain and over a half in Northern Ireland work in modern and well-equipped health centres, where medical and nursing services are provided. Health centres may also have facilities for health education, family planning, speech therapy, chiropody, assessment of hearing, physiotherapy and remedial exercises. Dental, pharmaceutical and ophthalmic services, hospital out-patient and supporting social work services may also be provided.

HOSPITALS AND SPECIALIST SERVICES

A full range of hospital services is provided by district general hospitals, including treatment and diagnostic facilities for in-patients, day-patients and out-patients, maternity departments, infectious disease units, psychiatric and geriatric facilities, rehabilitation facilities, convalescent homes and all forms of specialised treatment. There are also specialist hospitals or units for children, mentally ill, mentally handicapped and elderly people, and for the treatment of specific diseases; examples include the world-famous Hospital for Sick Children, Great Ormond Street, and the Brompton Heart and Chest Hospital in London. Hospitals designated as teaching hospitals combine treatment facilities with training medical and other students and research work.

Many of the hospitals in the National Health Service were built in the nineteenth century; some trace their origins to much earlier charitable foundations, such as the famous St Bartholomew's and St Thomas' hospitals in London. Much has been done to improve and extend existing buildings and

CONFERENCE AND EXHIBITION CENTRES

Above: The Greater Manchester Exhibition and Event Centre, opened officially in March 1986, has been created from the old Central Station as part of a scheme to revitalise 26 acres (some 10·5 hectares) of the city centre.

Below: The Queen Elizabeth II Conference Centre in London was formally opened by the Queen in June 1986. Centrally situated in Westminster near the Houses of Parliament, the Centre offers some of the world's finest conference facilities.

OVERSEAS TRADE

Barclays Bank's foreign exchange dealing room, London. In 1985 net overseas earnings by British banks amounted to £2,071 million.

Lloyd's Register of Shipping (LR), the world's oldest and largest ship classification society, is also involved in specialised engineering inspections and quality control worldwide. In 1985 it had overseas earnings of £29 million. Here, an LR surveyor in South America inspects a pressure vessel for the chemical industry.

A GEC Rolls-Royce offshore generating set under construction — part of a £10 million order for generating units for Brazilian offshore production platforms.

Below: The RD 150, a 50-tonne payload dumptruck, has economic fuel consumption and high productivity. A £60 million joint venture agreement with China involves (over a seven-year period) shipping the 30-tonne version in kit form for assembly in China and the creation of a training centre to help the transfer of skills.

OVERSEAS AID

This windpump in Turkhana Province, Kenya – designed and developed by Britain's Intermediate Technology Development Group – supplies water for some 2,000 people and their livestock.

Below: British aid funds of £112 million have helped in the construction of the Victoria Dam and Hydro-electric Project. Built by British contractors and consultants, the scheme forms part of the Mahaweli Development Programme, designed to increase Sri Lanka's power-generating capacity by about one-third and to irrigate and resettle some 45,000 hectares (over 110,000 acres) of land.

many new hospitals have been or are being opened. Major hospital schemes completed in England over the last five years have provided 27 accident and emergency departments, 122 X-ray rooms, 189 operating theatres, over 11,500 beds and 25 out-patient departments; over 150 other schemes, costing more than £1,000 million, are being planned or constructed.

Recent policy in England and Wales has been to provide smaller hospitals for local areas in preference to large district hospitals which may be remote from local communities. The latest development in hospital design is the 'nucleus' hospital of some 300 beds which makes more intensive use of space and facilities; it can be used either as the first stage of a new hospital or as an extension of an existing one. The world's first low-energy nucleus hospital, which is expected to use less than half the energy of an ordinary nucleus hospital, is under construction on the Isle of Wight.

National Health Service hospitals provide nearly half a million beds and have over 480,000 medical, nursing and midwifery staff. The hospital service is now treating more patients per year than ever before: between 1978 and 1984 the number of in-patient cases treated rose by 808,000 (15 per cent); the number of day case attendances by 341,000 (61 per cent) and there were 3·1 million (9 per cent) more out-patient attendances. Newer forms of treatment and diagnosis, such as kidney dialysis, hip replacements, laser treatment for certain eye conditions, and body scanning are being made more widely available. Community services such as the psychiatric nursing service, day hospitals, and local authority day centres have expanded so that more patients remain in the community and others are discharged sooner from hospital.

Private Medical Treatment

It is the Government's policy to encourage the private sector to meet a larger share of the nation's health needs in the belief that this will benefit the National Health Service by relieving pressure on it. Some health authorities share expensive facilities and equipment with private hospitals, and NHS patients are sometimes treated (at public expense) in the private sector to reduce waiting lists. The scale of private practice in relation to the NHS is, however, small. Some 6 per cent of acute hospital beds are in private hospitals and nursing homes and about 1,150 beds in health service hospitals in England are occupied by private patients. It is estimated that about half of those receiving acute treatment in private hospitals or hospital pay-beds are covered by provident schemes which make provision for private health care in return for annual subscriptions. In 1986 there were some 5 million subscribers to such schemes of whom the majority were involved in group schemes, some arranged by firms on behalf of employees. Subscriptions often cover more than one person (for example, members of a family). Private practice is also undertaken by family doctors and dentists. Many overseas patients come to Britain for treatment in private hospitals and clinics, and Harley Street in London is an internationally recognised centre for medical consultancy.

There is growing interest in alternative therapies such as homeopathy, osteopathy and acupuncture, which are mainly practised outside the National Health Service.

Organ Transplants

Over the past 25 years there have been significant developments in transplant surgery in Britain. Since 1972 the United Kingdom Transplant Service has provided a centralised kidney matching and distribution service. At the end of 1984 about 5,500 people were living with functioning kidney transplants and during 1985 some 1,300 more kidney transplants were performed. In 1983 a similar service was initiated for corneas, about 1,500 being transplanted each year. Heart transplant operations have been conducted at Papworth Hospital in Cambridgeshire since 1979 and at Harefield Hospital, West London, since 1980.

A third heart transplant centre has been established at the Freeman Hospital in Newcastle upon Tyne. By March 1986, 414 transplants had been performed; one-year survival is currently about 70 per cent and the three-year survival rate is 55 per cent. A programme of combined heart and lung transplants began at Harefield in December 1983, 58 having been performed by the end of March 1986. Other organs and tissues which are now successfully being transplanted include the liver, the pancreas and bone marrow. A voluntary organ donor card system enables people to indicate their willingness to become organ donors in the event of their death. Several million people now participate in the scheme.

Blood Transfusion

The blood transfusion service collects over 2 million donations of blood and over 44,000 donations of plasma each year from voluntary unpaid donors. Regional transfusion centres recruit donors and organise donor sessions in towns and villages, factories and offices, and within the armed forces. Donors must be between the ages of 18 and 65. The centres are also responsible for blood grouping and testing, maintaining blood banks, providing a consultancy service to hospitals, teaching in medical schools, and instructing doctors, nurses and technicians. Central laboratories manufacture blood products and undertake research. While the use of whole blood for transfusions remains an important part of the Service's work, there is increasing emphasis on the most efficient and effective use of blood and in particular its separation into components such as plasma for specific uses. A new laboratory is being built at Elstree, Hertfordshire, with the aim of achieving self-sufficiency in blood products in England and Wales.

Ambulance Services

Where necessary on medical grounds free transport by ambulance is provided by the health authorities. The ambulance service performs emergency work, dealing with sudden illness, urgent maternity cases, and accidents of all kinds; and non-urgent work, providing transport for people needing out-patient treatment at hospitals, clinics and day hospitals. In some areas the service for non-urgent cases is augmented by voluntary organisations using their own vehicles or by volunteers using their own cars. In Scotland an air ambulance service is available in the islands and in the remoter parts of the mainland.

Rehabilitation

Rehabilitation, an important part of which is patient care, begins at the onset of illness or injury and continues throughout with the aim of helping people to adjust to changes in life-style and to live as normally as possible. It is especially important for elderly, young, disabled, mentally ill and mentally handicapped people who need such help to resume life in the community. Rehabilitation activities are carried out in hospitals, centres in the community and in people's own homes through co-ordinated work by a range of professional workers including doctors, nurses, physiotherapists, occupational therapists, speech therapists, hearing therapists, clinical psychologists, dietitians and social workers. These staff may also work closely with the disablement resettlement service of the Manpower Services Commission (the Department of Economic Development in Northern Ireland), housing, education and social services departments of local authorities and with the voluntary sector.

Medical services may include the provision, free of charge, of artificial limbs and eyes, hearing aids, surgical supports, wheelchairs, and other appliances. Following assessment, very severely physically handicapped patients may be provided with environmental control equipment which enables them to operate devices such as alarm bells, radio and television, a telephone, and heating appliances. Nursing aids can be provided on loan for use in the home.

Local authorities may provide a range of facilities to assist patients in the transition from hospital to their own homes, including the provision of aids and adaptations, domiciliary care from home helps and professional help from occupational therapists and social workers. Voluntary organisations also provide valuable help in complementing the work of the statutory agencies and in widening the range of available services.

Hospices

A number of hospices provide care for the dying (including children) either directly in residential homes or through nursing and other assistance in the patient's own home. Control of symptoms and psychological support for patients and their families form the central features of the modern hospice movement, which originated in Britain and is now world-wide. Some hospices are administered entirely by the National Health Service; the remainder, some of which receive support from public funds, are run by independent charities. The Government is encouraging a greater co-operation between the voluntary sector and health authorities in this field.

Parents and Children

Special preventive services are provided under the health service to safeguard the health of expectant mothers and mothers with young children. Services include free dental treatment, dried milk and vitamins; vaccination and immunisation against certain diseases (see p 143); and health education, which is available to parents before and after childbirth through talks, discussion groups and demonstrations. Pregnant women are given antenatal care by their family doctor and hospital clinics, and working women have the right to visit the clinics during working hours. Some 98 per cent of women have their babies in hospital, returning home shortly afterwards to be attended by the family doctor, a midwife and a health visitor. The Government attaches great importance to improving the quality of maternity services, and to making them more sensitive to the needs and wishes of mothers and their families; it is advised by the Maternity Services Advisory Committee. The perinatal mortality rate (the number of stillbirths and deaths in the first week of life) has fallen in recent years and in 1985 stood at 9·8 per thousand births in England and Wales, compared with 15·4 per thousand in 1978.

A network of child health clinics in general practice premises or in the community provides facilities for surveillance by doctors, dentists and health visitors of the physical and mental health and development of pre-school children. Information on preventive services is given and welfare foods are distributed. About 95 per cent of babies under one year are taken to the clinics. The school health service offers health care and advice for schoolchildren, including medical surveillance and dental inspection and treatment where necessary.

Child guidance and child psychiatric services provide help and advice for children with psychological or emotional problems.

In recent years special efforts have been made to improve co-operation between the community-based child health services and local authority social services for children, particularly to prevent child abuse and to benefit the health and welfare of children in care.

Human Fertilisation and Embryology

The birth of the world's first 'test-tube baby' in Britain in 1978, using the technique of *in vitro* fertilisation, opened up new horizons for the alleviation of infertility and for the science of embryology, but also gave rise to unease at the apparently uncontrolled advances of science and the new possibilities of manipulating the early stages of human development. In view of this public concern, a committee of inquiry was established in 1982 under Baroness Warnock to examine the social, ethical and legal implications of developments in this field. Reporting in 1984, the committee concluded that certain specialised forms of infertility treatment, including artificial insemination by donor and *in vitro* fertilisation, were ethically acceptable, but that surrogate motherhood (the practice whereby one woman bears a child for another) organised by agencies should be prohibited; that research on human embryos was acceptable, but only up to the fourteenth day after fertilisation; and that a licensing authority should be established to regulate infertility services and research. Following the first birth to be arranged by a commercial surrogacy agency in Britain in January 1985, legislation to ban commercial surrogacy agencies, and advertising of or for surrogacy services, was passed later that year. The Government is considering its response to the wider recommendations of the committee and has made clear its intention to introduce comprehensive legislation as soon as possible.

Family Planning

Free family planning facilities are available through family planning clinics, hospitals and a domiciliary service. Most family doctors provide a similar service for women only.

Abortion

The Abortion Act 1967 allows the termination of pregnancy by a registered doctor if two registered doctors consider that its continuance would involve a greater risk to the life of the pregnant woman (or of injury to her physical or mental health or that of any existing children in the family) than if the pregnancy were ended. Termination may also be allowed if two doctors consider that there is a substantial risk that if the child were born it would suffer from such physical or mental abnormalities as to be seriously handicapped. Abortions are carried out in National Health Service hospitals or in private premises approved for the purpose by the Secretary of State. Over half of the 141,100 legal abortions to women resident in England and Wales in 1985 were performed in private hospitals and clinics. The Act does not apply in Northern Ireland.

Drug Misuse

The growing misuse of dangerous drugs such as heroin and cocaine has emerged as a serious social and health problem and the Government has made the fight against such misuse a major priority. Its strategy comprises action to reduce the supply of illicit drugs from abroad and to tighten controls on drugs produced and supplied in Britain; to provide even more effective law enforcement by the police and customs services; to increase the deterrent effects of the law; to support effective programmes to treat and rehabilitate misusers; and to discourage young people from experimenting with drugs. As part of its prevention policy, the Government initiated a £2·3 million publicity campaign in 1985 to dissuade young people from drug-taking and to advise parents, teachers and other professional staff on how to recognise and combat the problem. Additional funds of £2 million have been allocated to develop the campaign in 1986–87. Over £17 million has been provided for local treatment and rehabilitation projects for up to three years and an additional £5 million a year to regional health authorities in England from 1986–87 has been made available for the expansion of services for drug misusers. The Government has set up a drugs advisory service to advise district health authorities on the development of facilities in their areas, and has made funds available since April 1986 for local education authorities in England and Wales to appoint staff to promote and co-ordinate preventive work in their areas. Separate programmes and campaigns are in progress in Scotland.

The Government is advised on a wide range of matters relating to drug misuse and connected social problems by the Advisory Council on the Misuse of Drugs. The Council reported in 1982 on treatment and rehabilitation services, and in 1984 reviewed prevention policy and security arrangements for the storage and transit of controlled drugs.

Treatment for drug dependence is mainly provided on an out-patient basis.

Many hospitals provide specialist treatment for drug misusers, mainly in psychiatric units, or have special drug treatment units. Some addicts have a period of in-patient treatment when necessary. An increasing number of family doctors also treat addicts but only certain specialist doctors are licensed to prescribe heroin, cocaine and dipipanone (diconal). All doctors have a duty to notify the authorities of any patient they consider to be addicted to certain controlled drugs, and guidelines on good medical practice in the treatment of drug misuse have been issued to all doctors in Great Britain. The Home Secretary has statutory powers for dealing with doctors found to have prescribed irresponsibly.

A number of non-statutory agencies work with and complement the health service provision; advice and rehabilitation services including residential facilities, for example, are mainly provided by voluntary organisations. Support in the community is provided by the probation service and local social services departments.

Research on various aspects of drug misuse is funded by several government departments.

Solvent Misuse

Action is also being taken by the Government to curb the incidence of solvent abuse (the inhaling of vapour from glue, lighter fuel and other solvents) by young people. In 1983 voluntary guidelines were drawn up in co-operation with retailers to curb the sale of solvents, and legislation passed in Scotland added solvent misuse to the list of grounds on which a child may be considered to need compulsory care. In 1985 legislation was passed which made it an offence in England and Wales to supply such substances to children under 18 knowing or having reason to believe they are to be used to cause intoxication. (Such sales have been prosecuted successfully under common law in Scotland.) Information and guidance material have been distributed to parents, teachers and other professional workers to help them to educate young people on the dangers of the habit and to dissuade them from experimenting.

Smoking

Cigarette smoking is the greatest preventable cause of illness and death in Britain. It accounts for no fewer than 100,000 premature deaths each year and costs the NHS an estimated £370 million a year for the treatment of diseases attributable to smoking (for example, heart disease, lung cancer and bronchitis). Concerned at these harmful effects, the Government is following an active health education policy based on advice and education, supported by voluntary agreements with the tobacco industry aimed at reducing the level of smoking.

National public and media campaigns organised by the government-funded Health Education Council and the Scottish Health Education Group form the main thrust of official efforts to discourage smoking. In 1986 the Government launched a £1 million media campaign directed at young people in two test areas in England. The Government also supports the work of the voluntary organisation Action on Smoking and Health (ASH), and seeks to encourage restrictions on smoking in trains, buses, theatres and other public places. Health authorities have been encouraged to promote non-smoking as the normal practice on health service premises and to give help and advice to people who want to give up smoking.

Voluntary agreements between the Government and the tobacco industry regulate the advertising and promotion of tobacco products, tobacco product modification and sports sponsorship by the industry. A new voluntary agreement on tobacco advertising came into effect in April 1986. This provides for the use of six different health warnings about the dangers of smoking. It also contains measures to protect particularly vulnerable groups such as children, young people and young women in early childbearing years; and provide a mechanism for monitoring implementation of the agreement. Cigarette advertising is banned on television and radio by law and in cinemas by the voluntary agreement.

Cigarette consumption in Britain has fallen by over 20 per cent since 1978, reflecting a significant reduction in the proportion of people who smoke.

**Healthier
Eating**

There has been a growing public awareness in recent years of the importance to good health of a correct diet. Further evidence of this connection was provided in 1984 in a report on diet and cardiovascular disease produced by the government Committee on Medical Aspects of Food Policy. This advised that a reduction in the amount of certain fats in the diet could help to reduce the incidence or to delay the onset of cardiovascular disease. In order to help people to reduce their fat intake, the Government plans to introduce statutory requirements for the labelling of food to indicate fat content; full nutritional labelling which would include information on energy, protein and carbohydrate content is being encouraged on a voluntary basis. Certain supermarket chains have already introduced voluntary labelling schemes. In addition, the Health Education Council and the British Nutrition Foundation have produced practical dietary advice based on the committee's report.

Alcoholism

The far-reaching effects of alcohol misuse in terms of illness, family disruption, inefficiency at work, loss of earnings, accidents and crime are widely acknowledged. The Government considers that the reduction of such misuse requires a range of action by central and local government, voluntary and community bodies, the health professions, business and trade unions. Of great importance is the need for individuals to recognise and accept responsibility for their own health, while attempts to influence the minority who misuse alcohol must, to be realistic, respect the freedom of the majority who use alcohol responsibly.

The Government believes that emphasis should be placed on policies to prevent alcohol misuse and, in conjunction with the Health Education Council and other agencies, it continues to seek better information about the causes of problem drinking, to encourage healthier life-styles and to provide earlier identification and help for the problem drinker.

Treatment and rehabilitation include in-patient and out-patient services in general and mental hospitals and specialised alcoholism treatment units. Primary care teams (general practitioners, nurses and social workers) and voluntary organisations providing hostels, day centres and counselling services also play an important role. There is close co-operation between statutory and voluntary organisations and a new voluntary agency, Alcohol Concern, was established with government help in 1983 by merging a number of smaller bodies (funding for 1985–86 amounted to £450,000); the organisation is playing a prominent role in prevention of misuse, training for professional and voluntary workers and improving the network of local voluntary agencies and their collaboration with statutory bodies. The Scottish Council on Alcohol undertakes similar activities in Scotland. Research and surveys on various aspects of alcohol misuse are funded by several government departments.

**Health
Education**

Health education in England, Wales and Northern Ireland is promoted mainly by the government-financed Health Education Council. The Council mounts campaigns, produces health education material and engages in a range of research and evaluation work. It co-operates closely with the health authorities, professional organisations, voluntary bodies and industry. Its activities strongly support government action on smoking and problem drinking, and other topics covered include preparation for parenthood, diet and exercise, dental health, prevention of coronary heart disease and AIDS (see below). The Government's funding of the Council increased to £10·1 million in 1985–86. Health education in Scotland is promoted by the Scottish Health Education Group.

Almost all health authorities now have their own health education service which works closely with health professionals, health visitors, community groups, local employers and others to determine the most suitable local programmes. Increased resources in the health service are being directed towards health education and preventive measures.

Infectious Diseases

District health authorities (health boards in Scotland) carry out programmes of immunisation against diphtheria, measles, rubella (women and girls only), poliomyelitis, tetanus, tuberculosis and whooping cough.

Immunisation is voluntary. Parents are encouraged to protect their children since the benefits of immunisation far outweigh the small risk of adverse reactions. The proportion of children being vaccinated has been increasing since the end of 1978 following an earlier decline. A three-year campaign to increase the take-up of rubella immunisation among girls aged 10 to 14 and women who were not immune was launched in 1983. A series of measures is being taken to limit the spread of the disease AIDS (Acquired Immune Deficiency Syndrome). These include steps to improve the safety of blood and blood products through the screening of blood donations and the heat treatment of blood and blood products; the launch in early 1986 of a £2·5 million national publicity campaign to improve understanding of the disease and the ways in which its spread can be controlled; and the provision of an additional £2·5 million for the three London regional health authorities expected to carry the heaviest burden of the disease to provide treatment and counselling services. Research into the disease is continuing.

The Public Health Laboratory Service provides a network of bacteriological and virological laboratories throughout England and Wales which conduct research and assist in the diagnosis, prevention and control of communicable diseases. Its largest establishment is the recently rebuilt Central Public Health Laboratory at Colindale, in north-west London, which includes the National Collection of Type Cultures, the Food Hygiene Laboratory, and reference laboratories specialising in the identification of infective micro-organisms. Two surveillance centres, one in England and one in Scotland, investigate and monitor human communicable diseases. Microbiological work in Scotland and Northern Ireland is conducted mainly in hospital laboratories.

Cervical Screening

The cervical screening programme aims to reduce deaths from cancer of the cervix by ensuring that women at risk are screened regularly to identify the early signs of the disease. The Government has announced that all health authorities are to have computerised call and recall systems and adequate laboratory support for cervical cancer screening by 1988.

ENVIRON-MENTAL HEALTH

Environmental health officers employed by local authorities are responsible for the control of air pollution and noise, food hygiene and safety, occupational health and safety aspects of a variety of premises including offices and shops, the investigation of unfit housing, and in some instances for refuse collection and home safety. Doctors who specialise in community medicine and are employed by the health authorities advise local authorities on the medical aspects of environmental health, infectious diseases and food poisoning. They may also co-operate with the authorities responsible for water supply and sewerage. Environmental health officers at ports and airports carry out duties concerned with shipping, inspection of imported foods and disease control. In Northern Ireland district councils are responsible for noise control, collection and disposal of refuse, clean air, and food composition, labelling and hygiene.

Safety of Food   It is illegal to sell food unfit for human consumption or to apply any treatment, process or additive to food which makes it injurious to health. Premises where food or drink is prepared, handled, stored or sold must conform to certain hygiene standards. Environmental health officers may take for analysis or for bacteriological or other examination samples of any food on sale or in the distribution chain. Special regulations control the safety of particular foods such as milk, meat, ice-cream and shellfish. The Department of Health and Social Security, the Ministry of Agriculture, Fisheries and Food, the Scottish Office, the Welsh Office and the Department of Health and Social Services in Northern Ireland are the central departments responsible for giving advice and making regulations.

SAFETY OF MEDICINES   Under the Medicines Act 1968 the health and agriculture ministers are responsible for licensing the manufacture, marketing and importation of medicines for human and veterinary use. The Medicines Commission advises the ministers on policy regarding medicinal products. The Committees on Safety of Medicines, on Dental and Surgical Materials and on the Review of Medicines advise on the safety, quality and efficacy of medicinal products. The Committee on Safety of Medicines also monitors adverse drug reactions. The Act also controls the advertising, labelling, packaging, distribution, sale and supply of medicinal products.

RESEARCH   In 1985–86 the health departments spent about £25 million on research and development, in addition to expenditure by the Medical Research Council (the main government agency for the support of biomedical research). Priority areas include primary care, mental health and handicap, physical handicap and rehabilitation, care of the elderly and children, and dental and nursing research. The programme is administered in England and Wales by the Chief Scientist of the Department of Health and Social Security (in Scotland by the Chief Scientist of the Scottish Home and Health Department) who is supported by independent advisers covering a wide range of scientific disciplines. The Department is involved in international research and development, and all the health departments participate in the European Community's medical and public health research programme.

THE HEALTH PROFESSIONS   Only people whose names are on the medical or dentists' registers may practise as doctors or dentists in the National Health Service. University medical and dental schools are responsible for teaching; the National Health Service provides hospital clinical facilities for training. Full registration as a doctor requires five or six years' training in medical school and hospital, with an additional year's experience in a hospital; for a dentist, four or more years' training at a dental school is required. The regulating body for the medical profession is the General Medical Council and for dentists, the General Dental Council. The main professional associations are the British Medical Association and the British Dental Association.

The minimum period of training required to qualify for registration as a first level nurse in general, mental or mental handicapped nursing (and sick children's nursing in Scotland) is normally three years. Registration as a second level nurse (enrolled nurse) takes two years (in Scotland 18 months). Midwifery training for registered general nurses takes 18 months, and for other student midwives in England three years. Health visitors are registered general nurses with midwifery or approved obstetric experience who have successfully completed a one-year course in health visiting. District nurses are registered general nurses who have successfully completed a six-month course followed by a period of supervised practice in district nursing. The examining bodies for all nurses, midwives and health visitors are the National Boards for Nursing, Midwifery and Health Visiting established in England, Scotland, Wales and Northern Ireland. The regulation and registration of these professions is the responsibility of the United Kingdom Central Council for Nursing, Midwifery and Health Visiting.

Pharmacists in general practice and in hospital must be registered with the Pharmaceutical Society of Great Britain or the Pharmaceutical Society of Northern Ireland. A three-year degree course approved by the Pharmaceutical Society followed by a year's approved training is necessary before registration. The majority of medicines can be sold or dispensed only by, or under the supervision of, a registered pharmacist.

The General Optical Council regulates the professions of ophthalmic optician and dispensing optician; only registered ophthalmic opticians (or registered medical practitioners) may test sight. Training of ophthalmic opticians takes four years including a year of practical experience under supervision. Dispensing opticians take a two-year full-time course with a year's practical experience or a part-time day-release course while employed with an optician.

State registration may be obtained by chiropodists, dietitians, medical laboratory scientific officers, occupational therapists, orthoptists, physiotherapists and radiographers. The governing bodies are seven boards, corresponding to the professions, under the general supervision of the Council for Professions Supplementary to Medicine. Training lasts one to four years and only those who are state registered may be employed in the National Health Service and some other public services.

Dental therapists (who have undergone a two-year training course) and dental hygienists (who have undergone a training course of about a year) may carry out some simple dental work under the direction of a registered dentist.

ARRANGE-
MENTS
WITH OTHER
COUNTRIES

The member states of the European Community have special health arrangements under which Community nationals resident in a member state are entitled to receive any immediately necessary treatment, either free or at a reduced cost, during visits to other Community countries. There are also arrangements to cover people who go to work or live in other Community countries. In addition, there are reciprocal arrangements with some other countries under which immediately necessary medical treatment is available to visitors. Visitors are generally expected to pay if the purpose of their visit is to seek medical treatment. Visitors to or from countries with whom reciprocal arrangements have not been made are obliged to pay for any medical treatment they receive.

Personal Social Services

Responsibility for personal social services rests with the social services authorities (local authority social services departments in England and Wales, social work departments in Scotland and health and social services boards in Northern Ireland). Their services are directed towards elderly people, children and young people, families, people with mental illness or with physical or mental handicap, young offenders and other disadvantaged individuals and their carers. The major services include residential care, day care, community care and various forms of social work. Close co-operation is maintained between local authority social services departments and health authorities (and other agencies), and funding for joint schemes is being increased. In Scotland local authorities also undertake duties similar to those of the separate probation and prison after-care service in England and Wales.

Much of the care given to the elderly and disabled people is provided in the community itself, by their families, self-help groups and through voluntary agencies. The statutory sector offers the skilled care needed in particular services. The importance of the contribution made by the voluntary organisations is recognised especially when economies are being made in public expenditure and the demand on the statutory services is heavy.

The demand for personal social services is expected to rise over the next few years, owing to the number of elderly people and the changing pattern of care for mentally ill and mentally handicapped people and the chronically sick. The Government's policy, embodied in a 'Care in the Community' programme, is to speed up the transfer from hospital to care in the community of patients who do not specifically need hospital care. It believes that groups such as the elderly, the disabled, and mentally ill or handicapped people can lead more normal lives in the community, given appropriate support and facilities.

The Elderly

Services for elderly people are provided by statutory and voluntary bodies to help them to live at home whenever possible. (Only about 5 per cent of the elderly over 65 live in institutional accommodation.) These services may include advice and help given by social workers, domestic help, delivery of cooked meals, sitters-in, night attendants and laundry services as well as day centres, luncheon clubs and recreational workshops. Appropriate adaptations to the home can overcome problems of restricted mobility, and there is a wide range of environmental aids to help people with impaired hearing or vision. Mobile alarm call systems have been developed to help elderly housebound people obtain assistance in an emergency and in some areas 'good neighbour' and friendly visiting services are arranged by the local authority or a voluntary organisation. Many local authorities provide free or subsidised travel to elderly people within their areas. Social services authorities also provide residential care for the elderly and infirm and have powers to register homes run by voluntary organisations or privately.

Local authorities, as part of their responsibility for public housing, provide accommodation specially designed for elderly people; some of these developments have resident wardens. Housing associations and private builders also build this type of accommodation.

Disabled People

Local social services authorities provide a wide range of personal social services for disabled people to assist with social rehabilitation and adjustment to disability. They are also required to establish the number of disabled people in their area and to publicise services, which may include counselling on personal and social problems arising from disability; occupational, educational, social and recreational facilities, either at day centres or elsewhere; adaptations to homes (such as ramps for wheelchairs, and ground-floor toilets); aids to daily living; the delivery of cooked meals; and domestic or care attendant help. In cases of special need, assistance may be given with the installation of a telephone or a television set. For severely disabled people residential accommodation or respite care may be provided by local authorities and voluntary organisations, and specially designed housing may be available for those able to look after themselves. Some authorities provide free or subsidised travel for disabled people on public transport, and they are encouraged to provide special access facilities to public buildings.

Mentally Ill and Mentally Handicapped People

Social services authorities make arrangements for the provision of preventive care for mentally ill people and after-care for both mentally ill and mentally handicapped people in the community. Services include training centres for the mentally handicapped and day centres for the mentally ill, as well as social centres and a variety of residential care for mentally ill and mentally handicapped people of all ages. Social workers help patients and their families to deal with social and family problems arising from mental illness or mental handicap and in certain circumstances can make an application for a mentally disordered person's compulsory admission to and detention in hospital. The rights of compulsorily detained patients were extended by legislation in 1983, and a Mental Health Act Commission was set up to provide better safeguards. Corresponding legislation was introduced for Scotland in 1984, although the Mental Welfare Commission for Scotland was first established in 1962.

Two recent priorities have been to transfer mentally handicapped children from long-stay hospitals to community care, and, through a number of special projects, to improve care for elderly mentally ill people.

An important role in provision of services is played by the many voluntary organisations concerned with mental illness and mental handicap.

Help to Families

The Government believes in the central importance of the family to the well-being of society and that stable adult relationships are necessary to support and enhance family life. Social services authorities, through their own social workers, give practical help and advice to families facing special problems. This help includes services for children at risk of injury or neglect who require accommodation, and support for family carers who look after elderly and other family members in order to give them a respite. They also help lone parents, including unmarried mothers, and counsel divorced or separated women. There are now many refuges run by local authorities or voluntary organisations for women, often with young children, whose home conditions have become intolerable. The refuges provide short-term accommodation and support while attempts are made to alleviate the women's problems. Many authorities also contribute to the cost of social work with families (such as marriage guidance) carried out by voluntary organisations.

An initiative launched by the Government in 1983 seeks to increase voluntary sector provision in England for disadvantaged families with children under five. In the same year the Family Policy Studies Centre was established with official funding to review the impact of public policies on the family and to bring together research findings.

Child Care

Day care facilities for children under five are provided by local authorities, by voluntary agencies and privately. In allocating places in the day nurseries and other facilities they themselves provide, local authorities give priority to children with special social or health needs for day care. They also register, and provide support and advice services for, childminders, private day nurseries and playgroups operating in their areas.

The authorities are empowered to offer advice, guidance and assistance to families in difficulties to promote the welfare of children. The aim is to intervene at an early stage to reduce the need to receive children into care or bring them before a court.

The recognition, prevention and management of cases of child abuse are the joint concern of many authorities, agencies and professions, and local review committees provide a forum for discussion and co-ordination and draw up policies and procedures for handling these cases.

Authorities must receive into their care any child under the age of 17 who has no parent or guardian, who has been abandoned, or whose parents are unable to provide for him or her, if they are satisfied that such intervention is in the best interests of the child. The child remains in care until the age of 18 unless discharged to the care of parents, other relatives or friends. The local authority may find it necessary to assume the rights and duties of one or both parents. The parents must be notified and if they object the matter is decided in a court of law. When taking a decision concerning a child in care, the authorities have to give first consideration to the need to safeguard and promote the welfare of the child. Where children are in care, every effort is made to work with their families in order, where appropriate, to enable the children to return home.

Children in England and Wales may be brought before a juvenile court if they are neglected or ill-treated, exposed to moral danger, are beyond the control of parents, not attending school or (if ten years or over) have committed an offence other than homicide. At the same time it must be shown that the children need care or control which they are unlikely to receive unless a care order or other relevant order is made by the court. Local authorities are responsible for undertaking inquiries through social workers and consultation with parents, schools and the police. Children may be committed to the care of a local authority under a care order if the court considers this appropriate. As an alternative the court may order supervision by a social worker or a probation officer for up to three years.

Increasing use is being made of intermediate treatment, especially for young offenders. This is a community-based service which provides supervised activities, groupwork and individual counselling; a short, residential period may sometimes be included. A requirement to attend a programme of intermediate treatment may be added to a supervision order by the court.

The law relating to children in care in England and Wales is currently under review with the aim of rationalisation and amendment.

In Northern Ireland the court may send children to a training school, commit them to the care of a fit person (which includes a health and social services board), or make a supervision order. The law relating to children is being reviewed and the intention in future is to make a distinction between young offenders and children in need of care and protection. Strong emphasis is placed on preventive work.

In Scotland children in trouble or in need may be brought before a children's hearing, which can impose a supervision requirement on a child if it thinks that compulsory measures of care are appropriate. Under these requirements most children are allowed to remain at home under the supervision of a social worker but some may live with foster parents or in a residential establishment while under supervision. Supervision requirements are reviewed at intervals of not more than one year until terminated by a children's hearing or by the Secretary of State.

When appropriate, children in care are boarded out with foster parents, who receive an allowance to cover the cost of maintenance. If a foster home is not considered appropriate or cannot be found, the child may be placed in a children's home, voluntary home or other suitable residential accommodation. Community homes for children in care in England and Wales comprise local authority and some voluntary children's homes, and include community homes with education on the premises which provide long-term care usually for the more difficult children. In Scotland local authorities are responsible for placing children in their care in foster homes, in local authority or voluntary homes, or in residential schools. In Northern Ireland there are residential homes for children in the care of the health and social services boards; training schools and remand homes are administered separately. Regulations concerning community homes, registered voluntary homes and the boarding out of children in care are made by central government.

Adoption

It is generally accepted that adoption is an appropriate way to find a new family for a very wide range of children of all age groups, including those with physical and mental handicaps. About 2,000 of the 9,000 children adopted each year were previously in the care of a local authority. Since 1982 it has been possible for agencies to offer prospective adoptive parents an allowance if this would help to find a family for a child. Adoption is strictly regulated by legislation, and adoption societies must be approved by the respective social services minister. Local authorities can also provide an adoption service. The Registrars-General keep confidential registers of adopted children. Adopted people may be given details of their original birth record on reaching the age of 18, and counselling is provided to help them understand the circumstances of their adoption. In Northern Ireland the law on adoption is being reviewed to bring it broadly into line with the rest of the United Kingdom.

Custodianship Custodianship orders were introduced in 1985. A person who has cared for a child for some time (for example, a foster parent, step-parent or relative) can apply to a court for an order giving him or her the legal custody of the child. On the making of such an order the custodian will have the parental rights and duties of a natural parent and will be able to make decisions about a child's day-to-day care and upbringing, in the same way as a parent. Unlike an adoption order, a custodianship order may be revoked. In Northern Ireland the law is being reviewed to introduce custodianship provisions similar to those in the rest of the United Kingdom.

Social Workers The effective operation of the social services largely depends on the appointment of professionally qualified social workers trained in the methods of social work. Training courses in social work are provided by universities, polytechnics (in Scotland, central institutions) and colleges of further education; their length depends upon educational qualifications and previous experience and can extend from one to four years. The Central Council for Education and Training in Social Work recognises social work courses and offers advice to people considering entry to the profession.

Professional social workers (including those working in the National Health Service) are mainly employed by the social services departments of local authorities. Others work in the probation service, the education welfare service, or in voluntary organisations.

A review of training for staff in residential homes, the changing role of residential care and the range of services provided is in progress.

Voluntary Social Services

There is a long tradition in Britain of voluntary service to the community, and the partnership between the voluntary and statutory sectors is encouraged by the Government. It has been estimated that nearly a third of all adults take part in some form of voluntary work during the course of a year. Local and health authorities plan and carry out their duties taking account of the work of voluntary organisations, and include them in the planning process. Voluntary provision enables these authorities to continue the trend towards local community care rather than institutional care for the elderly, the mentally ill and mentally handicapped people.

An Opportunities for Volunteering Scheme, started by the Government in 1982, together with an Unemployed Voluntary Action Fund in Scotland and a Community Volunteering Scheme in Northern Ireland, have provided support for over 1,000 schemes by voluntary agencies to enable unemployed volunteers to help disadvantaged groups in the community. Voluntary organisations also participate in several other government schemes, including the Community Programme, the Voluntary Projects Programme and the Youth Training Scheme.

Voluntary organisations derive their income from several sources including voluntary contributions, central and local government grants, earnings from commercial activities and investments. Some 450 bodies receive direct grants from government health and social services departments; in 1984–85 these amounted to some £30 million out of a total government funding of £224·4 million to voluntary organisations. Tax changes in recent budgets have helped the voluntary movement to secure a larger flow of funds from industry.

Many voluntary organisations are charities, and in England and Wales the Charity Commission, a government agency, gives free advice to trustees of charities, initiating schemes to modernise their purposes or facilitate their administration where necessary. The Commission also maintains a register of charities, gives consent to land transactions by charities and holds investments for them. Voluntary organisations may qualify for charitable status if they are established for such purposes as the relief of poverty, the advancement of education or religion or the promotion of certain other purposes of public benefit including good community relations, the prevention of racial discrimination, protection of health and the promotion of equal opportunity. The Charities Aid Foundation, an independent body, aids the flow of funds to charity from individuals, companies and grant-making trusts.

Co-ordination of government interests in the voluntary sector throughout Britain is the responsibility of the Home Office Voluntary Services Unit.

Voluntary Organisations

There are thousands of voluntary organisations concerned with health and social welfare, ranging from national bodies to small individual local groups. 'Self-help' groups have been the most rapidly expanding part of the voluntary sector in the last decade—examples include bodies which provide playgroups for pre-school children, or help their members to cope with a particular disability. Many organisations belong to larger associations or are represented on local or national co-ordinating councils or committees. Some are chiefly concerned with giving personal service, others with the formation of public opinion and exchange of information. Some carry out both functions. They may be staffed by both professional and voluntary workers. While a majority of voluntary organisations are concerned with social welfare in the ways described, there is a growing interest among voluntary groups in cultural and environmental issues and in participating in schemes to promote employment.

The main co-ordinating body in England, which aims to provide central links between voluntary organisations and official bodies, is the National Council for Voluntary Organisations, which acts as a resource representative and development agency for the voluntary sector. It works to extend the involvement of voluntary organisations in dealing with a broad range of social issues, to protect the interests and independence of voluntary agencies, and to provide them with a range of advice, information and other services. The Scottish Council for Community and Voluntary Organisations, the Wales Council for Voluntary Action and the Northern Ireland Council for Voluntary Action perform similar functions.

The Volunteer Centre is a national voluntary organisation and centre for information and research on voluntary work. There are many full-time and part-time local volunteer bureaux which direct volunteers to opportunities for voluntary service in both the voluntary and statutory sectors.

Specialist voluntary organisations concerned with personal and family problems include the family casework agencies like the Family Welfare Association, Family Service Units and the National Society for the Prevention of Cruelty to Children; marriage guidance centres affiliated to the National Marriage Guidance Council; the National Council of Voluntary Child Care Organisations; the National Council for One Parent Families; Child Poverty Action Group and the Claimants' Union, both of which provide expert advice on social security benefits; and the Samaritans, which helps the lonely, the depressed and the suicidal.

Community service of many kinds is given by young people; this is often channelled through national and local organisations such as Community Service Volunteers, Scouts and Girl Guides, and the 'Time for God' scheme run by a group of churches.

Voluntary service to the sick and disabled is given by—among others—the British Red Cross Society, St John Ambulance, the Women's Royal Voluntary Service and the Leagues of Hospital Friends. Societies which help people with particular disabilities and difficulties include the Royal National Institute for the Blind, the Royal National Institute for the Deaf, the Royal Association for Disability and Rehabilitation, the Disabled Living Foundation, the Disablement Income Group, MIND (National Association for Mental Health), MENCAP (Royal Society for Mentally Handicapped Children and Adults), the Spastics Society, Alcoholics Anonymous, Age Concern, Help the Aged and their equivalents in Wales, Scotland and Northern Ireland.

National organisations whose work is specifically religious in inspiration include the Salvation Army, the Church Army, Toc H, the Committee on Social Service of the Church of Scotland, the Church of England Children's Society, the Church of England Council for Social Aid, the Young Men's Christian Association, the Young Women's Christian Association, the Catholic Marriage Advisory Council and the Jewish Welfare Board.

A wide range of voluntary personal service is given by the Women's Royal Voluntary Service, which brings 'meals on wheels' to housebound invalids and old people, provides flats and residential clubs for the elderly, helps with family problems, and assists in hospitals and clinics and in emergencies.

Over 1,000 Citizens Advice Bureaux give explanation and advice to people who are in doubt about their rights or who do not know about the state or voluntary services available. Some areas have law centres and housing advisory centres.

Social Security

The general aim of the social security programme is to provide an efficient and responsive system of financial help for people who are elderly, sick, disabled, unemployed, widowed or bringing up children. Certain benefits provide an income for people who have no earnings because they are retired, unemployed or sick. Others provide income for widows; assistance with extra expenses arising from disablement; compensation for injury or disease caused at work or while in the armed forces; and help with the cost of bringing up children. Alongside these benefits there are certain means-tested benefits for people who have insufficient means of support.

Social security benefits fall into two broad categories—contributory and non-contributory. Contributory benefits are paid from the National Insurance Fund, which consists of contributions from employed people and their employers, self-employed people and the Government. Non-contributory benefits are financed from general taxation revenue. Some are income-related—for example, supplementary benefit and housing benefit—but others, for example, child benefit, are not, and entitlement depends solely on meeting the qualifying conditions. Appeals relating to claims for the various benefits are decided by independent tribunals.

Expenditure on social security has nearly doubled in real terms since 1970. Part of the increase has been due to the rising numbers of the elderly, and part to the growth in unemployment; much, however, has been due to real improvement in the level of benefits, the creation of new benefits and increased family support.

The Department of Health and Social Security administers the services in Great Britain; in Northern Ireland they are administered by the Department of

Health and Social Services. Pensions and welfare services for war pensioners and their dependants are the responsibility of the Department of Health and Social Security throughout the United Kingdom. Advice on social security is given to the Government by the Social Security Advisory Committee.

Over the 40 years since the basic structure of the present social security system was established there have been many piecemeal changes and developments, and the system has become very complex. As spending on the system accounts for nearly one-third of all public expenditure, and pressures for improvements and increased expenditure are bound to continue, the Government considered that a re-examination of the system was required, and in 1984 initiated a series of reviews. Following the reviews and publication in 1985 of a consultative paper and a White Paper, *Reform of Social Security: Programme for Action*, government proposals for a wide-ranging reform of the structure of the system became law under the Social Security Act 1986. The main reforms, to be introduced by April 1988, include the modification of the State Earnings-related Pension Scheme, which is additional to the basic state pension, and new arrangements to encourage personal and occupational pension schemes; the introduction of a new range of income-related benefits to replace family income supplement, supplementary benefit and housing benefit; and the creation of a social fund to provide extra help for low-income families at times of special need such as bereavement and maternity.

As part of its plans to improve the management of the social security system and the quality of its service to the public, the Department of Health and Social Security is embarking on the biggest computerisation programme in Europe, which aims to link all of its local and central offices and the local offices of the unemployment benefit service into a single network.

CONTRI-
BUTIONS

At present, entitlement to National Insurance benefits such as retirement pension, sickness and invalidity benefit, unemployment benefit, widow's benefit, maternity allowance, death grant and child's special allowance is dependent upon the payment of contributions. Industrial injuries benefits are non-contributory, but are also payable from the National Insurance Fund. There are four classes of contributions. Class 1 contributions, which are related to earnings, are paid by employees and employers. The contribution is lower if the employer operates a 'contracted-out' occupational pension scheme (see below). Self-employed people pay a flat rate Class 2 contribution and a Class 4 contribution which is assessed as a percentage of profits or gains within certain limits; they are not eligible for unemployment and industrial injuries benefits. Voluntary Class 3 contributions are made by people wanting to safeguard rights to some benefits.

Employees who continue working after pensionable age (60 for women and 65 for men) do not pay contributions but the employer continues to be liable. People earning less than the lower earnings limit are not liable for contributions; neither are their employers. Self-employed people with earnings below a set annual amount may apply for exemption and those over pensionable age are excused payment of contributions.

BENEFITS

For most benefits there are two contribution conditions. First, before benefit can be paid at all, a certain number of contributions has to be paid; secondly, the full rate of benefit cannot be paid unless contributions have been made or credited up to a specific level over a specified period. Benefits are increased annually, the uprating being linked to increases in retail prices. The main benefits (payable weekly) are summarised below. The rates shown in Tables 5–9 are those effective until April 1987.

Retirement Pension

A state retirement pension is payable on retirement to women at the age of 60 and to men at the age of 65. (Legislation before Parliament would equalise the retirement age for men and women in the same occupation. This, however, would not affect the payment of state retirement pensions at different ages for men and women.) At present, the state pension scheme consists of a basic pension together with an additional earnings-related pension. Pensioners are permitted to earn up to £75 a week before the amount of their pension is reduced; those still at work who have put off or cancelled their retirement during the five years after minimum pension age may earn extra pension. A non-contributory retirement pension is payable to people over the age of 80 who meet certain residence conditions, and who have not qualified for a contributory pension. People whose pensions do not give them sufficient resources to live on may be entitled to supplementary pension, which is calculated on the same basis as supplementary benefit (see p 156).

Rights to basic pension are safeguarded for mothers who are away from work looking after children or for people giving up work to care for severely disabled relatives. Women contributors receive the same pension as men with the same earnings.

Employers are free to 'contract-out' their employees from the state scheme for the additional earnings-related pension and to provide their own occupational pension in its place, provided that the latter is at least as good as the state additional pension. The State remains responsible for the basic pension. There are at present around 90,000 occupational schemes, with some 11 million members—about half the working population. As part of a programme to reform the occupational pensions system, the Government has introduced measures to protect against inflation the pension rights of people who change jobs before pension age; to give workers the right on leaving a scheme to a fair transfer value; and (from November 1986) to require pension funds and other pension schemes to provide access to more information about their schemes. The Social Security Act 1986 gives all employees the right to choose a personal pension rather than staying fully in the State Earnings-related Pension Scheme or in an employer's scheme. Such pensions would qualify for contracting out of the State Earnings-related Pension Scheme and would enable people to choose from a wide range of schemes available from banks, building societies and trusts.

Mothers and Children

At present, a non-contributory maternity grant of £25 is payable for each living child born and for a stillborn child if the pregnancy lasts for at least 28 weeks. Contributory maternity allowance is a weekly benefit normally paid for 18 weeks, starting 11 weeks before the baby is expected to women who have recently paid full National Insurance contributions. A working mother is entitled to paid maternity leave if she has been working for the same firm for at least two years (five years in the case of part-time workers). The payment is calculated at 90 per cent of weekly earnings, less the standard maternity allowance, and is paid for the first six weeks of absence. From April 1987 maternity grant will be replaced by a payment from the social fund, while maternity allowance and maternity pay will be replaced by a statutory maternity scheme administered by employers.

Non-contributory child benefit is the main social security benefit for children. Tax free and normally paid to the mother, it is payable for children up to the age of 16 and for those up to the age of 19 if they continue in full-time non-advanced education. A sum in addition to child benefit, called one-parent benefit, is payable to certain people, whether parents or not, bringing up one or more children on their own. At present a weekly contributory child's special allowance is payable to a mother on the death of a former husband if the marriage was dissolved or annulled and he was contributing to the support of the children. A non-contributory guardian's allowance for an orphaned child is payable to a person who is entitled to child benefit for that child. In certain circumstances it can be paid on the death of only one parent.

Widows

At present, a widow's allowance may be payable for the first 26 weeks of widowhood, and an additional sum is often payable for each child. After this a widowed mother with a young family receives a widowed mother's allowance with an addition for each child. Widow's pension is payable to a widow who is 40 years or over when her husband dies or when her entitlement to widowed mother's allowance ends. Payment continues until the widow remarries or begins drawing retirement pension. Widows also benefit under the industrial injuries scheme. Under the Social Security Act 1986 all widows will receive a tax-free lump sum payment of £1,000 on bereavement, together with widowed mother's allowance or widow's pension, and the age at which widow's pension is payable will be raised by five years.

A man whose wife dies when both are over pension age inherits his wife's pension rights just as a widow inherits her husband's rights.

Sick and Disabled People

There is a large variety of benefits for people unable to work because of sickness or disablement. Statutory sick pay with additions for a wife or other adult dependants is payable by an employer for the first 28 weeks of an employee's illness. Employees not covered for statutory sick pay can claim sickness benefit instead, as can self-employed people.

An invalidity pension with additions for a wife and children is payable when statutory sick pay or sickness benefit ends if the beneficiary is still incapable of work. An invalidity allowance may be paid with the pension to those people who become sick more than five years before minimum retirement age. An additional earnings-related pension may also be payable. A severe disablement allowance may be payable to people of working age, including housewives, who are unable to work and do not qualify for the National Insurance invalidity pension.

Various benefits are payable for disablement caused by an accident at work or a prescribed disease. Disablement benefit is usually paid after a qualifying period of 15 weeks if, as a result of an industrial accident or a prescribed disease, there is a loss of physical or mental faculty. (During the qualifying period sick pay or sickness benefit may be payable.) The amount depends on the extent of the disablement as assessed by an adjudicating medical authority but for disablement of less than 20 per cent a gratuity is normally paid. In certain circumstances disablement benefits may be supplemented by unemployability supplement; constant attendance allowance; an additional allowance payable in certain cases of exceptionally severe disablement; a special hardship allowance for a person who is unfit to return to his or her regular job or to do work of an equivalent standard; and hospital treatment allowance, which raises the disablement pension or gratuity to the 100 per cent assessment rate during hospital in-patient treatment for the industrial injury or disease. Increases of disablement benefit for dependants may be payable with unemployability supplement.

A non-contributory, tax-free attendance allowance may be payable to severely disabled people at either a higher or a lower rate depending upon the amount of care and attention they require. An invalid care allowance may be payable to men and women aged between 16 and pension age who cannot go to work because they are caring for a severely disabled person receiving an attendance allowance.

Physically disabled people unable or virtually unable to walk may be entitled to a tax-free mobility allowance to help to pay their transport costs. People aged between 5 and 66 may claim and payment can continue up to the age of 75.

An independent organisation called Motability assists disabled drivers and passengers wanting to use their mobility allowance to obtain a vehicle.

Unemployment Benefit

Unemployment benefit is payable for up to a year in any one spell of unemployment. Periods covered by unemployment or sickness benefit, maternity allowance or some training allowances, which are eight weeks or less apart, are linked to form one period of interruption of employment. Generally anyone claiming unemployment benefit has to be available for employment, but unemployed people wishing to do voluntary work in the community can do so in certain circumstances without loss of entitlement to benefit.

Death Grant

At present, a death grant is payable on the death of a contributor or a contributor's near relative. It is normally £30 for an adult and a smaller sum for a child. From April 1987 the death grant will be replaced by a grant from the social fund.

Table 5: Benefit Rates

£

Category	Weekly rate
Retirement and widow's pensions and widowed mother's allowance	
Single person	38·70
Wife or other adult dependant	23·25
Child	8·05
Non-contributory retirement pension for people over 80	23·25
Maternity allowance	29·45
Child benefit	7·10
One-parent benefit (for the first or only child)	4·60
Guardian's allowance, child's special allowance	8·05
Widow's allowance (first 26 weeks of widowhood)	54·20
Unemployment benefit	
For beneficiary under pension age	
Single person	30·80
Wife or other adult dependant	19·00
For beneficiary over pension age	
Single person	38·70
Wife or other adult dependant	23·25
Child	8·05
Statutory sick pay (depending on level of earnings)	31·60 to 46·75
Sickness benefit	
For beneficiary under pension age	
Single person	29·45
Wife or other adult dependant	18·20
For beneficiary over pension age	
Single person	37·05
Wife or other adult dependant	22·25
Child	8·05
Invalidity pension	
Single person	38·70
Spouse or other adult dependant	23·25
Child	8·05
Invalidity allowance payable with retirement or invalidity pension	2·60 to 8·15

Table 5: Benefit Rates *(continued)*

£

Category	Weekly rate
Disablement benefit (100 per cent assessment)	63·20
Unemployability supplement	
Single person	38·70
Wife or other adult dependant	25·28
Special hardship allowance (maximum)	25·28
Constant attendance allowance (normal maximum)	25·30
Exceptionally severe disablement allowance	25·30
Industrial death benefit	
Widow's pension (first 26 weeks of widowhood)	54·20
Widow's pension (higher rate)	39·25
Widow's pension (lower rate)	11·61
Increase for each child	8·05
Attendance allowance	
Higher rate	30·95
Lower rate	20·65
Severe disablement allowance	23·25
Invalid care allowance	23·25
Wife or other adult dependant	13·90
Child	8·05
Mobility allowance	21·65

SUPPLEMEN-TARY BENEFIT

Supplementary benefit is payable to people aged 16 and over who are not in full-time work or at school and whose financial resources fall below a certain level. The amounts shown in Table 6 are the weekly levels laid down for the requirements of married couples, single householders and others. The benefit payable amounts to the difference between a person's existing resources and these levels. The long-term rates apply to people aged 60 or over and to those

Table 6: Supplementary Benefit

£

Category	Weekly rate
Ordinary rate	
Couple	48·40
Single householder	29·80
Non-householder 18 and over	23·85
Non-householder 16–17	18·40
Any other person aged 11–15	15·30
Child under 11 years	10·20
Long-term rate	
Couple	60·65
Single householder	37·90
Non-householder 18 and over	30·35
Non-householder 16–17	23·25

people aged less than 60 who have received supplementary benefit or long-term incapacity benefit continuously for one year, provided that the award is not subject to the condition of being available for employment. Families receiving supplementary benefit (as with family income supplement) are entitled to a number of other benefits including housing benefit (see below), help with the cost of spectacles, free school meals, milk and vitamins for expectant and nursing mothers and for children under school age, and exemption from National Health Service prescription charges and charges for dental treatment. Lump sum payments may also be made for special needs such as clothing, furniture and domestic appliances. The Social Security Act 1986 replaces supplementary benefit by income support which will consist of a basic allowance plus premiums for families, lone parents, pensioners and disabled people.

FAMILY INCOME SUPPLEMENT

Family income supplement is a cash benefit for families with low incomes where one of the parents is in full-time work and where there is at least one dependent child. It is payable when the gross weekly income of a family falls below a prescribed amount, which varies according to the number and ages of children in the family but is the same for single- and two-parent families. 'Full-time' work means, for the purpose of the benefit, work of at least 30 hours a week by either parent in two-parent families or 24 hours a week for one-parent families. The weekly rate of the supplement is half the difference between the family's gross income and the prescribed amount, up to a maximum figure depending on the number and age of children in the family. The maximum payable for a family with two children under 11, for example, would be £27·85. The Social Security Act 1986 replaces family income supplement by a more generous family credit paid to mothers.

Table 7: Family Income Supplement

£

	Weekly rate
Prescribed amount, family with one child (income below which supplement is payable)	
Child aged	
under 11	98·60
11–15	99·60
16 and over	100·60
Increase for each additional child	
Child aged	
under 11	11·65
11–15	12·65
16 and over	13·65

HOUSING BENEFIT

People with low incomes, whether in work or not, who have difficulty in paying their full rent and rates (local property taxes) may qualify for housing benefit, which is administered by local authorities (in Northern Ireland, by the Department of the Environment for owner-occupiers and by the Housing Executive for tenants). Council (public sector) tenants may apply for a rent rebate, and private tenants for a rent allowance. Both tenants and owner-occupiers may apply for rate rebates. The amount of benefit depends on four considerations: income; the amount of rent and rates paid; the size of the family; and the presence of other people in the household. Benefit is worked out

Table 8: Housing Benefit Needs Allowances   £

	Weekly rate
Single person	48·10
Couple/single parent	70·85
Single handicapped person	53·65
Couple (one handicapped) or single handicapped parent	76·40
Couple (both handicapped)	79·00
Dependent child addition	14·60
Pensioner addition	0·85

by comparing a 'needs allowance', which is intended to cover basic weekly living expenses (the amounts are shown in Table 8), against income. Where income equals the needs allowance, entitlement will be equal to 60 per cent of the eligible rent and rates. This amount is progressively increased or decreased if income is less than or greater than the needs allowance. Deductions from benefit are usually made if a non-dependant lives in the same household. People receiving supplementary benefit are entitled to a 100 per cent rebate or allowance of their eligible rent and rates subject to certain deductions. The Social Security Act 1986 radically simplifies the present scheme.

Table 9: War Pensions   £

Category	Weekly rate
Disablement benefits	
Pension for a private at 100 per cent rate	63·20
Unemployability allowances	
Personal allowance	41·10
Wife or other adult dependant	23·25
Addition for each child	8·05
Comforts allowance	5·45 to 10·90
Allowance for lowered standard of occupation (maximum)	25·28
Constant attendance allowance	
(depending on attention needed)	12·65 to 50·60
Age allowance (depending on degree of disability)	4·40 to 13·70
Exceptionally severe disablement allowance	25·30
Severe disablement occupational allowance	12·65
Clothing allowance (per year)	55·00 to 86·00
Death benefits	
Widow's pension (private's widow)	50·30
Childless widow under 40	11·61
Rent allowance (maximum)	19·15
Age allowance for elderly widows	
Aged 65–69	5·40
Aged 70–79	10·80
Aged 80 and over	13·55

WAR
PENSIONS
AND
RELATED
SERVICES

Pensions are payable to people disabled as a result of service in the armed forces or by certain injuries received in the merchant navy or civil defence during war-time, or to civilians injured by enemy action. The amount varies according to the degree of disablement and rank; an allowance is paid for dependants.

There is a range of supplementary allowances, the main ones being for unemployability, the need for constant attendance, the provision of extra comforts, and as compensation for a lower standard of occupation. An age allowance is payable to disabled pensioners aged 65 or over and whose assessment is 40 per cent or more. Pensions are also paid to war widows and orphans.

The Department of Health and Social Security maintains a welfare service for war pensioners, war widows and war orphans. It works closely with the many voluntary and ex-Service organisations who give financial aid and personal help to disabled ex-Service men and women and their families.

TAXATION

Social security benefits, other than child, maternity, sickness, invalidity and disablement benefit, are regarded as taxable income. Various income tax reliefs and exemptions are allowed on account of age or liability for the support of dependants. The following benefits are not taxable: supplementary benefit (except that paid to the unemployed), family income supplement, attendance allowances, mobility allowance, war disability pensions including supplementary allowances, and war widow's pension and allowances.

OTHER
BENEFITS

Other benefits for which unemployed people and those on low incomes may be eligible include exemption from health service charges (see p 135), grants towards the cost of spectacles, free school meals and free legal aid. Reduced charges are often made to the unemployed, for example, for adult education and exhibitions, and pensioners usually enjoy concessionary transport fares.

ARRANGE-
MENTS
WITH OTHER
COUNTRIES

As part of the European Community's efforts to promote the free movement of labour, there are regulations providing for equality of treatment and the protection of social security rights for employed and self-employed people working in another member state. The regulations also cover retirement pensioners and other beneficiaries who have been employed, or self-employed, as well as dependants. Benefits affected include child benefit and those for sickness and maternity, unemployment, retirement, invalidity, accidents at work and occupational diseases.

Britain also has reciprocal social security agreements with a number of other countries. Their scope and the benefits they cover vary, but the majority cover most National Insurance benefits and benefits for families.

7 Education

British education aims to develop fully the abilities of individuals, both young and old, for their own benefit and that of society as a whole. Compulsory schooling takes place between the ages of 5 and 16, although provision is made for children under 5, and many pupils remain at school beyond the minimum leaving age. Post-school education (mainly at universities, polytechnics and colleges of further and higher education) is organised flexibly to provide a wide range of opportunities for academic and vocational education and continuing study throughout life. For many years the education service has been characterised by change, and much of the post-1945 period has also been marked by growth: large increases in the number of pupils, the expansion of higher educational opportunities, and increased expenditure. Although the process of change continues, recent years have seen increasing reassessment and consolidation with a view to making the best use of resources in the light of difficult economic circumstances and a substantial drop in the birth rate.

Policies

The overriding objectives of the Government's education policies are to raise standards, ensure that education is attuned to the needs of industry and commerce, and achieve better value for money throughout the education system. In schools, standards of achievement are being raised by securing a broader and more balanced curriculum for all pupils, reforming the public examination system and improving the quality of teaching through better teacher selection, training and deployment. Parental preference as to school and the need for increased parental involvement in school organisation are receiving close consideration while gifted children from less well-off homes are being given the opportunity to attend certain independent schools.

Special attention is paid both to the provision of better pre-vocational education and training in schools and colleges for the 14- to 18-year-old age-group, and to the 40 per cent of lower-attaining pupils in the final years of compulsory education. It is recognised that co-operation between the education system and industry can help young people to acquire the skills necessary to maintain Britain's position as a leading industrial and trading nation. Many organisations already work to improve such links, and further contacts are being encouraged. An important objective has been to extend the knowledge and use of microcomputers in schools.

In February 1986, the Government published a wide-ranging Education Bill designed to raise educational standards in schools in England and Wales. The new legislation was foreshadowed in a White Paper, *Better Schools*, published in 1985. The main aims of the Bill are to reform the composition of school governing bodies and reallocate functions between school governors, local education authorities and head teachers; provide for the appraisal of the performance of teachers; and make in-service training of teachers more effective. In response to the report of an inquiry into the education of ethnic minority groups the Government has described its policies for encouraging children from the ethnic minorities to achieve their full potential.

A forecast decline of about one-third in the number of 18- to 21-year-olds by the mid-1990s and the need to restrict government funding are among the major factors which led the Government to review the future of higher education. A White Paper incorporating proposals for the higher education sector will be published before the end of 1986. A continuing aim is to encourage institutions to improve their management and planning, and become more flexible and responsive to the economic and social needs of the country. In line with the concern to maintain British expertise in science, engineering and technology, a shift in provision from the arts and social sciences towards these subjects and towards directly vocational courses is occurring, while higher education institutions and industry are being encouraged to collaborate more closely for their mutual benefit. A number of science parks have been set up by higher education institutions in conjunction with industrial scientists and technologists to encourage the use of advanced technology. The Government considers that access to higher education courses should be available to all those who can benefit from them and who have the necessary intellectual competence, motivation and maturity.

The already strong vocational element in many courses in the non-advanced sector of further education (which comprises courses whose level is at or below General Certificate of Education Advanced level or its equivalent) is also being increased. The role played by further education institutions in providing training and continuing education is of great importance, especially at a time of increasing technological change and high unemployment.

Administration
One of the distinctive features of the education service is the large degree to which responsibility for provision is decentralised. Overall responsibility for all aspects of education in England, and for the Government's relations with and support for universities throughout Britain, rests with the Secretary of State for Education and Science. The Secretaries of State for Wales, Scotland and Northern Ireland have responsibility in their respective countries for non-university education, and are consulted about education in universities.

The main concerns of the education departments (the Department of Education and Science in England, the Welsh Office, the Scottish Education Department, and the Department of Education for Northern Ireland) are formulating national education policies, allocating resources and influencing the other partners in the education service (the local education authorities, governing bodies of educational institutions, the teaching profession, the churches and voluntary organisations). The departments are also responsible for the supply and training of all teachers.

The provision of maintained, that is, publicly financed, school education and most post-school education outside universities is the responsibility of local education authorities. They employ teachers and other staff, provide and maintain buildings, supply equipment and materials and, in England and Wales, provide grants to students proceeding to further and higher education. Universities are self-governing institutions receiving most of their income from central government grants. In Scotland the central institutions, which provide most vocational higher education to degree level, and colleges of education, which provide teacher training, are administered by independent governing bodies. In Northern Ireland colleges of education are controlled by the Department of Education or by voluntary agencies.

Finance
Planned spending on education in 1986–87 is some £17,500 million, about 10 per cent of public expenditure. More than four-fifths of this expenditure is incurred by local authorities, which plan their spending according to local needs and circumstances.

Reductions in spending by authorities on schools partially reflect the declining number of schoolchildren, the removal of surplus school places, and savings in the provision of school meals and milk. Additional provision is being made to meet the cost of a large increase in the number of young people staying on at school after 16.

Local education authorities are directly responsible for the funding of most non-advanced further education courses. In order, however, to make training and vocational education more relevant to employment needs, responsibility for a quarter of the budget spent in England and Wales on work-related courses has been placed with the Manpower Services Commission.

An education support grant scheme introduced in England and Wales in 1985 enables the Government to support local authority expenditure on educational activities of national priority, such as improving the school curriculum, methods of assessment, records of achievement and school management. In 1986–87 it is intended to provide £28 million out of total expenditure of £40 million on 16 projects.

Support for the universities and certain other higher education institutions, and grants to students, account for most of the direct expenditure by central government. About 80 per cent of universities' income comes from public funds, the major part being recurrent grant paid by the Government to the University Grants Committee, which allocates the funds to individual universities and certain other institutions. The Committee also advises the Government on the future development of the universities. The independent University of Buckingham receives no assistance from public funds although its students can apply for mandatory grants.

Funds for advanced courses in polytechnics and other colleges of further education maintained by local authorities are allocated centrally. The National Advisory Body for Public Sector Higher Education advises the Government on how these resources should be allocated in England; the Wales Advisory Body has a similar function. There is no equivalent organisation in Scotland but the Scottish Tertiary Education Advisory Council has general advisory functions.

Many universities, polytechnics and other higher education institutions undertake training, research or consultancy for commercial firms, and the Government is encouraging them to secure a larger flow of funds from these sources. A number have endowments or receive grants or gifts from foundations and benefactors. Local education authorities, through their further education institutions, are empowered to sell goods and services arising as by-products of educational activities.

SCHOOLS

Parents are required by law to see that their children receive efficient full-time education, at school or elsewhere, between the ages of 5 and 16.

Some 9·7 million children attend Britain's 36,500 schools. Most receive free education financed from public funds, but a small proportion (roughly 6 per cent) attend schools wholly independent of direct public financial support.

Boys and girls are taught together in most primary schools, and 86 per cent of pupils in maintained secondary schools in England and Wales and 63 per cent in Northern Ireland attend mixed schools. In Scotland nearly all secondary schools are mixed. Most independent schools for younger children are co-educational; the majority providing secondary education are single-sex, although the number of mixed schools is growing.

No fees are charged to parents of children at maintained schools, and books and equipment are free, although in Northern Ireland a small proportion of grammar school pupils is admitted on a fee-paying basis.

Management

Schools supported from public funds are of two main kinds in England and Wales: county schools and voluntary schools. County schools are provided and maintained by local education authorities wholly out of public funds. Voluntary schools, mostly established by religious denominations, are also wholly maintained from public funds but the governors of some types of voluntary school contribute to capital costs. About a third of the 26,500 primary and secondary schools supported by public funds in England and Wales are voluntary schools, most of them Anglican or Roman Catholic. Each publicly maintained school has a governing body, which includes governors appointed by the local education authority and teacher and parent representatives. The Government considers that the powers and duties at present exercised by governing bodies give them too restricted a role in school management in relation to that of the education authority or the head teacher. As part of its strategy to improve standards, it proposes to change the composition of such bodies and to extend their powers. The Education Bill provides for equal numbers of parent and local authority governors, so that no single interest predominates. In future, governing bodies would have responsibility for the main policies of their schools, and for the preparation of a statement of their schools' curricular aims and objectives. They would also have ultimate responsibility for school discipline and a larger say in the appointment and dismissal of staff.

In Scotland most of the schools supported from public funds are provided by education authorities and are known as public schools (in England this term is used for a type of independent school, see p 165). There is a statutory requirement to establish school councils whose membership includes teachers, parents, people interested in religious education, and in certain cases representatives of further education and of the community at large.

In Northern Ireland there are three main categories of grant-aided school: controlled schools, owned and managed by the area education and library boards and having all their expenditure met from public funds; voluntary schools, mainly under Roman Catholic management and also maintained largely by public funds; and voluntary grammar schools, which may be under either Roman Catholic or non-denominational management and receive grants from the Department of Education. Since the end of 1985 all grant-aided schools have included elected parents and teachers on their boards of governors. It is government policy to encourage integrated education, providing for both Protestant and Roman Catholic pupils, where there is a local desire for it; a small number of integrated schools have been opened with assistance from charitable trusts.

In England, Wales and Scotland parents have a statutory right to express a preference for a particular school for their children, and have an effective channel of appeal at local level. Schools also have to publish basic information about themselves and their public examination results.

Nursery and Primary Schools

Although there is no statutory requirement to provide education for the under-fives, successive governments have expanded nursery education. Current expenditure plans allow for the maintenance of existing levels of provision or a small increase, mainly by converting surplus primary school accommodation to nursery use. In England 43 per cent (and in Scotland 36 per cent) of three- and four-year-olds receive education in nursery schools or classes or in infants' classes in primary schools. In addition, many children (at least 40 per cent of three- and four-year-olds) attend informal pre-school playgroups organised by parents and voluntary bodies such as the Pre-School Playgroups Association.

Compulsory education begins at five when children in England and Wales go to infant schools or departments; at seven many go on to junior schools or departments. The usual age for transfer from primary to secondary schools is 11 in England, Wales and Northern Ireland, but a number of local authorities in England have established 'first' schools for pupils aged 5 to 8, 9 or 10 and 'middle' schools covering various age-ranges between 8 and 14. In Scotland the primary schools take children from 5 to 12.

Secondary Schools

The publicly maintained system of education aims to give all children an education suited to their particular abilities. About 90 per cent of the maintained secondary school population in England and Wales attend comprehensive schools, which take pupils without reference to ability or aptitude and provide a wide range of secondary education for all or most of the children of a district. The schools can be organised in a number of ways, including those that take the full secondary school age-range from 11 to 18; middle schools whose pupils move on to senior comprehensive schools at 12, 13 or 14, leaving at 16 or 18; and schools with an age-range of 11 or 12 to 16 combined with a sixth-form or a tertiary college for pupils over 16. Tertiary colleges provide a full range of vocational courses for students over 16, as well as academic courses. Most other children receive secondary education in 'grammar' or 'secondary modern' schools to which they are allocated after selection procedures at the age of 11.

Scottish secondary education is almost completely non-selective; the majority of schools are six-year comprehensives. Because of local circumstances there are some comprehensive schools at which courses may last only four years or less; pupils may transfer at the end of their second or fourth years to a six-year comprehensive.

In Northern Ireland secondary education is organised largely along selective lines, based on a system of testing. There are, however, certain areas where secondary schools operate on a non-selective basis.

Independent Schools

Independent schools are outside the publicly maintained sector, but they must register with the appropriate education department and are open to inspection. They can be required to remedy serious shortcomings in their premises, accommodation or instruction and to exclude anyone regarded as unsuitable to teach in or to be the proprietor of a school.

There are about 2,500 independent schools educating 550,000 pupils of all ages. They charge fees, varying from about £100 a term for day pupils at nursery age to £2,000 a term for senior boarding pupils. Many offer bursaries to help pupils from less well-off families. Such pupils may also be helped by local education authorities—particularly if the authorities' own schools cannot meet the needs of individual children—or by the Government's assisted places scheme, under which assistance is given in relation to parental income (over 230 schools participate in the scheme). The Government also gives income-related help with fees to pupils at certain specialist music and ballet schools.

There is great variety of provision within the independent sector, ranging from small kindergarten to large boarding schools and from new and in some cases experimental schools to ancient foundations. A number of independent schools have also been established by religious and ethnic minorities. The 550 boys', girls' and mixed preparatory schools are so called because they prepare children for the Common Entrance Examination to senior schools. The normal age range is from seven-plus to 11, 12 or 13, but many of the schools now have pre-preparatory departments for younger children.

Independent schools for older pupils—from 11, 12 or 13 to 18 or 19—include about 500 which are sometimes referred to as 'public schools'. Today the term is becoming less frequently used but refers to the mainly boys' schools (which are increasingly admitting girls) belonging to the Headmasters' Conference and/or the Governing Bodies Association and to schools in membership of the Governing Bodies of Girls' Schools Association. They should not be confused with the state-supported public schools in Scotland.

Special Educational Needs

Special educational needs embrace learning difficulties arising from emotional or behavioural disorders as well as physical or mental handicap. Local education authorities in England and Wales must ensure that children with special needs are educated in ordinary schools provided that the parents' wishes have been taken into account and that this is compatible with meeting the needs of the child, with the provision of efficient education for the other children in the school, and with the best use of resources. In Scotland, school placing is a matter for agreement between education authorities and individual parents. With the exception of mentally handicapped children, children with special educational needs in Northern Ireland are provided for in the same way as in England and Wales, although it is intended to introduce similar arrangements for mentally handicapped children also.

There are almost 2,000 special schools (both day and boarding), including those run by voluntary organisations, which cater for a wide variety of handicap.

Teachers

Teachers in publicly maintained schools are appointed by local education authorities or school governing bodies. There are about 545,000 teachers in maintained and independent schools, and the overall pupil–teacher ratio in primary and secondary schools is about 18·5 to 1. Teachers in these schools must hold qualifications approved by the appropriate education department (see p 174).

The Curriculum

The content of the secular curriculum in maintained schools in England and Wales is the responsibility of the local education authority and of the schools' governors. In practice, responsibility is largely devolved on head teachers and their staff. Under provisions contained in the Education Bill, head teachers would be responsible for determining and organising the curriculum within their schools, taking into consideration the policy of their local education authority and that of their governing body. The Government is in favour of a broad and balanced education which is relevant to the needs of the modern world, and of widening educational opportunities as much as possible. It considers that secondary pupils up to the age of 16 should follow a broad curriculum including English, mathematics and science with elements of physics, chemistry and biology; some study of the humanities including history; religious and physical education; and both practical and aesthetic activities. Most pupils should also study a foreign language. One aim of the Government's policy is to seek to ensure that girls do not limit their career prospects, as some now do, by dropping the study of the physical sciences, design and technology, and certain other subjects too early in their school education. A programme of development projects has been introduced to provide a more effective education with a practical slant for lower-attaining pupils who do not benefit fully from existing courses. A large number of school–industry links schemes have been initiated in recent years in order to improve liaison between schools and the world of work.

In Wales, the Welsh language is taught and is used as either the main or secondary medium of teaching in some schools. The content and management of the curriculum in Scotland is the responsibility of education authorities and individual head teachers though guidance is issued by the Scottish Education Department. Provision is made for teaching in Gaelic in Gaelic-speaking areas. A new curriculum structure for 14- to 16-year-olds has been established which includes the compulsory study of English, mathematics and science. In 1984, as part of a development programme for 16- to 18-year-olds, a flexible system of vocational courses based on modules or short units of study was introduced in schools and colleges in disciplines ranging from business and administration to engineering and industrial production. Though designed primarily to improve the preparation of young people for working life, the courses are also intended to meet the needs of many adults entering training or returning to education. The courses lead to the award of a new National Certificate.

In Northern Ireland major programmes of curriculum review and development are in progress in both primary and secondary schools. The objective in the secondary sector is to improve the quality and relevance of education for all pupils in the 11-to-16 age-range, with more emphasis on economic and political awareness, technological understanding, personal development and the encouragement of study skills. At the same time teaching methods are being reconsidered.

Over the last 20 years much has been done by the educational authorities to meet difficulties encountered by the ethnic minorities. English language teaching has received priority, but attention has been increasingly directed at the question of mother-tongue teaching. Emphasis has been placed on the need for schools to take account of the ethnic and cultural backgrounds of pupils. Measures are being taken not only to improve the achievement of ethnic minority pupils but also to prepare all children, not just those of ethnic minority origin, for living in a multi-ethnic society.

In England and Wales curriculum development is promoted by the School Curriculum Development Committee, in Scotland by the Consultative Committee on the Curriculum and in Northern Ireland by the Council for Educational Development. At some 500 teachers' centres in England and Wales, teachers meet for curriculum development work, discussion and in-service training.

Technical and Vocational Education Initiative

A growing recognition of the need to equip pupils of all abilities with the skills needed by modern commerce and industry led the Government to launch the Technical and Vocational Education Initiative in England and Wales in 1983 and in Scotland in 1984. The scheme, consisting of a series of pilot projects devised and managed by local education authorities, is funded and administered by the Manpower Services Commission. Projects provide general, technical and vocational education for some 40,000 young people aged 14 to 18 leading to nationally recognised qualifications. The pilot scheme is to be extended into a national scheme in 1987.

Computers

Great importance is attached to the acquisition and use of computers by schools, in view of the growing importance to the economy and society of information technology. As a result of the Government's Micros in Schools and Micros in Primaries schemes, every secondary and almost all primary schools in Britain now have at least one microcomputer and the average in secondary schools is now 13 (making a total of about 100,000 machines). A six-year Microelectronics Education Programme (MEP) in England, Wales and Northern Ireland which began in 1980, and the separate Scottish Microelectronics Development Programme (SMDP), aimed to give young people a better understanding of the new technology and its applications. With the ending of the MEP in March 1986 a new Microelectronics Education Support Unit has been set up to assist the work of local education authorities. Priority is being given to curriculum development (especially in subjects such as science, mathematics, crafts, design and technology) including the production and supply of more and better computer software; in-service teacher training; and the provision of information.

For three years from 1985 special funds are being made available to promote the use of educational software in schools. Britain has developed a world lead in several aspects of computer education and the large number of countries which have bought British educational software, signed licensing agreements or purchased consultancy services from the MEP and its successor or SMDP include India, Australia, Mexico, Israel, the United States, Tunisia, Canada, the Netherlands and Belgium.

British School Technology

British School Technology, an independent education centre to promote the teaching of technology in secondary schools and colleges, has been developed with funding of £2·5 million over three years (beginning in 1984) from the Department of Trade and Industry and the Manpower Services Commission. The centre provides help to local education authorities wanting to introduce courses into their schools, assists in training teachers, co-operates with examination boards to assess new courses, and assists new firms planning to produce equipment for British schools and for export.

Religious Education in Schools

In England and Wales all children in county or voluntary schools receive religious education by law and take part in a daily corporate act of worship unless their parents choose otherwise. In county schools, and sometimes in voluntary schools, non-denominational religious instruction is given in accordance with a locally agreed syllabus which may include the study of comparative religions. Syllabuses have been revised in many areas to take account of the faiths of the local population. In all kinds of voluntary schools there is the opportunity for denominational instruction. In Scotland religious instruction must be given, the content being determined by education authorities and schools in accordance with the wishes of the local community. Certain schools provide for Roman Catholic children but in all schools there are safeguards for the individual conscience. In controlled schools in Northern Ireland clergy have a right of access which may be used for denominational instruction; in voluntary schools corporate worship and religious education are controlled by the management authorities.

Examinations

At present the principal examinations taken by secondary school pupils in England, Wales and Northern Ireland at the age of 16 and over are those leading to the General Certificate of Education (GCE) at Ordinary (O) level and to the Certificate of Secondary Education (CSE). Both are normally taken after five years of secondary education. The GCE Advanced (A) level is normally taken after a further two years' study. The highest grade (grade 1) in the CSE is accepted as equivalent to the standard of a higher grade pass (grades A to C) at GCE O-level, and these are the qualifying grades for entry to further education and training. The A-level examination is the standard for entrance to university and other higher education, and to many forms of professional training. Entries for GCE examinations are also accepted from private candidates and those attending further education establishments. Pupils take on average five or more O-levels and two or three A-levels. The numbers achieving success in these examinations have increased considerably in recent years, and fewer than one in ten pupils left school without a single graded result in 1984. In 1984 nearly 27 per cent of school leavers achieved five or more higher grades at O-level or CSE (grade 1), while 17 per cent achieved at least one A-level.

In order to improve examination courses and raise standards of performance, the Government decided to replace GCE O-level and CSE examinations by a single qualification, the General Certificate of Secondary Education (GCSE); two-year courses leading to the new qualification were introduced in England, Wales and Northern Ireland in the autumn of 1986. GCSE syllabuses and assessment procedures will comply with nationally agreed guidelines, known as national criteria. The main objective of this and other policies is to bring 80 to 90 per cent of all pupils at least to the level achieved by pupils of average ability in individual subjects (CSE grade 4), and to do this over a broad range of skills and competence in a number of subjects. The Government will introduce from 1989 another new examination, the Advanced Supplementary (AS) level, to be taken alongside existing A-levels. The AS level, the first courses for which will begin in 1987, will provide an opportunity for sixth-form pupils to study a wider range of subjects than at present; students specialising in the arts and humanities, for example, would be able to continue the study of mathematics and technological subjects at the new level.

The Certificate of Pre-Vocational Education, a new qualification awarded for the first time in 1986, is intended for those at school or college who wish to continue in full-time education for a year after the age of 16 to prepare either for work or for vocational courses. It is being devised by the Business & Technician Education Council and the City and Guilds of London Institute (see p 174).

The Secondary Examinations Council has been established to co-ordinate and supervise systems of examination and assessment in England and Wales designed principally for pupils in secondary education.

The public examination system in Scotland is different from that in other parts of Britain. Scottish pupils take the Scottish Certificate of Education (SCE) at Ordinary grade at the end of their fourth year of secondary education (equivalent to the fifth year in England and Wales). Pupils in the fifth and sixth years sit the SCE Higher grade, and passes at this grade are the basis for entry to university, college of education or professional training. For those who have completed their main studies at the Higher grade but wish to continue their studies in particular subjects there is the Certificate of Sixth Year Studies.

Reforms of the examination system are already under way in Scotland. New Standard grade courses and examinations were introduced in 1984 and will eventually replace the Ordinary grade. Standard grade courses will cater for the whole ability range with syllabuses at three levels—Foundation, General and Credit—and all pupils will be assessed in examinations against nationally determined standards of performance. The Higher and post-Higher examinations are also being revised to ensure compatibility with the new Standard grade.

Under the Government's plan for the reform of non-advanced further education in Scotland, the National Certificate was introduced in 1984–85 for students over 16 who had successfully completed a programme of vocational courses based on study units known as modules (see p 166).

Records of Achievement

The Government has decided that all pupils in England and Wales should, by the end of the decade, be issued with a written record of their school achievements and performance when they leave school; this would reflect achievements across the whole educational programme of the school going beyond examination results.

Educational Standards

Her Majesty's Inspectors report to ministers on the quality of education provided in all schools (and in most further education establishments outside the universities) and advise local education authorities, schools and the Government; their reports on individual establishments are published (except in Northern Ireland). Local education authorities also employ inspectors or advisers to guide them on maintained schools.

The Assessment of Performance Unit of the Department of Education and Science promotes the development of methods of assessment and monitors the achievement of schoolchildren. Programmes of monitoring have been undertaken in English language and mathematics at the ages of 11 and 15, in science at the ages of 11, 13 and 15, and in the first foreign language at the age of 13. A survey of performance at the age of 15 in design and technology is to be undertaken in 1988.

Educational Aids

Teachers and pupils use a range of aids to assist the processes of teaching and learning. Most schools have audio-visual equipment such as slide projectors and overhead projectors, and educational broadcasting is of major importance. Each year more than 600 hours of school radio and 1,000 hours of television are transmitted by the BBC and the independent broadcasting companies. Teachers' notes, pupils' pamphlets and computer software accompany many broadcast series. Virtually all primary and secondary schools are now equipped with microcomputers which are used for computer-assisted learning (see p 167).

The autonomous Council for Educational Technology for the United Kingdom is the central organisation for promoting the application of audio-visual, technological and other aids to education and training.

Careers Education and Guidance

Increasing importance is being attached by schools (and by further education establishments) to careers education to increase young people's awareness of further education and careers opportunities and generally help them to prepare for post-school life. The work of careers officers at local level is supported by careers information material produced by the Government's Careers and Occupational Information Centre. The Government is sponsoring the development of a computer-assisted careers guidance system for students in universities, polytechnics and colleges.

Health and Welfare of Schoolchildren

Physical education, including organised games, is part of the core curriculum of all maintained schools, and playing fields must be available for pupils over the age of eight. Most secondary schools have a gymnasium.

The government health departments are responsible for the medical inspection of schoolchildren and for advice on, and treatment of, specific medical and dental problems associated with children of school age. The Government believes that the education service has a key role to play in preventing and dealing with juvenile drug misuse, and it is encouraging teachers to help to tackle this problem.

Local education authorities are free to decide what milk, meals or other refreshment to provide at their schools, and what charges to make. (In Northern Ireland, school meals must be provided.) Provision has to be made free of charge, however, for pupils from families receiving certain social security benefits. Under certain conditions the authorities must provide free school transport, and they have discretionary powers to assist with the cost of travel to school.

POST-SCHOOL EDUCATION

Post-school education for young people above school-leaving age is provided at a range of levels. More than a third of young people receive some form of post-school education, compared with a fifth in 1965, while some 14 per cent of young people in the 18-year-old age-group entered full-time higher education courses (that is, first degree, postgraduate and other advanced courses of a standard higher than GCE A-level) in 1985. The number of degrees awarded per age-group is comparable with that of other developed countries and the proportion of people in all further and higher education also compares well, taking into account the large proportion of part-time students and the large group of students receiving professional training in firms rather than in educational institutions.

Post-school education is provided at universities, polytechnics, the Scottish central institutions and other publicly maintained or assisted colleges; the latter have a variety of titles including colleges of higher or further education, colleges of technology, colleges of art, agricultural colleges and adult education centres. There are also many independent specialist establishments, such as secretarial and correspondence colleges and colleges for teaching English as a foreign language. A number of voluntary and public bodies provide cultural and general education, sometimes with assistance from local education authorities and central government, and many education and training schemes are run by public or private organisations, or firms.

The Government is seeking to improve awareness of the opportunities for further education and training through the development of national information services, such as the Educational Counselling and Credit Transfer Information Service funded by the Department of Education and Science.

Higher education, in the form of degree and other post-A-level advanced courses, is provided by universities, polytechnics, the Scottish central institutions and institutions of further and higher education, some concerned wholly with teacher training. Reduced public expenditure on higher education has necessitated some restructuring of courses and departments in universities and other colleges. However, a decline in the intake of new students by universities in the years 1981–83 has now been reversed, and expansion elsewhere meant that in 1984–85 there were 51,000 more full-time home students in higher education than in 1980–81. One of the Government's main objectives in higher education is to bring about a change in the balance of provision in favour of scientific, technological and directly vocational courses.

In order to maintain British expertise in information technology and related fields, a three-year initiative was launched in 1982 to expand higher education and research in electronics, engineering and computer science by providing 5,000 extra student places, and additional staff and research fellowships in universities, polytechnics and Scottish central institutions. Under a separate scheme, some 950 researchers and lecturers have been appointed, mostly in the natural sciences and technology. The Engineering and Technology Programme announced in 1985 will, when fully operational, provide a further 5,000 student places in engineering, information technology and related scientific disciplines.

The term 'further education' is generally used to define all post-school education other than higher education, and comprises non-advanced courses (of A-level standard or below). Non-advanced and some advanced courses are provided by 740 colleges of further education, almost all of them controlled by local education authorities. Non-advanced courses are also provided by adult education centres.

Much of the provision outside the universities is broadly vocational in purpose; it extends from lower-level technical and commercial courses to advanced courses for those aiming at higher-level posts in commerce, industry and administration, or taking up a variety of professions (for example, town planning or estate management). The system is flexible and permits the student to acquire whatever qualifications his or her capabilities and time allow.

A large proportion of students on non-advanced courses attend part time, either by day release or block release from employment or during the evenings. A particular feature of the further education system is its strong ties with commerce and industry: some two-thirds of spending in the non-advanced sector, for example, is devoted to work-related studies. Co-operation with the business world is encouraged by the Government and its agencies, and employers are often involved in designing courses. A series of College–Employer Links Projects, launched in 1984, help colleges to meet the education and training needs of local firms by identifying the particular skills and qualifications required by employers and developing ways of providing them. Further education colleges provide much of the education element in industrial training programmes like the Youth Training Scheme and the Training Opportunities Scheme, both sponsored by the Manpower Services Commission. The former scheme offers the opportunity of two years' planned work experience and training to 16-year-old school-leavers and one year's to 17-year-old school-leavers; the latter provides people aged 19 and over with the opportunity to acquire new skills.

Students

Some 972,000 students were taking full-time courses in 1984–85, including sandwich courses (where substantial periods of full-time study alternate with periods of supervised experience on a relevant job), at universities and major establishments of further education in Britain. Of these about 292,000 were at universities while another 274,000 were following advanced courses outside universities, at colleges of further and higher education, polytechnics and Scottish central institutions. More than 406,000 take non-advanced courses, most of them studying for recognised vocational or educational qualifications.

There were also about 3·2 million part-time students, over 542,000 of whom are released by their employers for further education during working hours. Many of the remainder take part in adult education classes.

Over 90 per cent of full-time students on advanced courses are helped by grants from public funds, which are mandatory for those students taking first degree and other comparable courses who qualify under national rules. (Grants for other courses may be given at the discretion of a local education authority.) Grants cover tuition fees and maintenance, but parents contribute to maintenance costs according to their income. They are awarded by local education authorities in England and Wales up to first degree level; equivalent schemes are administered in Scotland by the Scottish Education Department, and in Northern Ireland mainly by the education and library boards. For postgraduate study and research, grants are offered by the education departments and the research councils. Some scholarships are available from endowments and from particular industries or companies.

Universities

There are 46 universities in Britain, including the Open University, compared with 17 in 1945. They are governed by royal charters or in some cases by Act of Parliament, and enjoy complete academic freedom, appointing their own staff and deciding which students to admit, what and how to teach, and which degrees to award. The English universities are: Aston (Birmingham), Bath, Birmingham, Bradford, Bristol, Brunel (London), Cambridge, City (London), Durham, East Anglia, Essex, Exeter, Hull, Keele, Kent at Canterbury, Lancaster, Leeds, Leicester, Liverpool, London, Loughborough, Manchester, Newcastle upon Tyne, Nottingham, Oxford, Reading, Salford, Sheffield, Southampton, Surrey, Sussex, Warwick, York and the independent University of Buckingham. The Royal College of Art, the Cranfield Institute of Technology, the London Graduate School of Business Studies and the Manchester Business School also have university status. The federated University of Wales comprises seven constituent institutions. The Scottish universities are: Aberdeen, Dundee, Edinburgh, Glasgow, Heriot-Watt (Edinburgh), St Andrews, Stirling and Strathclyde (Glasgow). In Northern Ireland there are the Queen's University of Belfast and the University of Ulster.

The universities of Oxford and Cambridge date from the twelfth and thirteenth centuries, and the Scottish universities of St Andrews, Glasgow, Aberdeen and Edinburgh from the fifteenth and sixteenth centuries. All the other universities were founded in the nineteenth and twentieth centuries.

Admission to universities is by examination or selection. Of the 292,000 full-time university students in 1984–85 (excluding those at the Open University and the University of Buckingham), about 47,500 were postgraduate. About half lived in colleges, halls of residence and other accommodation owned by universities.

There are some 30,000 full-time university teachers paid wholly from university funds. The ratio of staff to students is about one to ten, one of the most favourable in the world.

Except at the Open University, first degree courses are mainly full time and usually last three or four years, though medical and veterinary courses usually require five or six years. Degree titles vary according to the practice of each university; in England, Wales and Northern Ireland the most common titles for a first degree are Bachelor of Arts (BA) or Bachelor of Science (BSc) and for a second degree Master of Arts (MA), Master of Science (MSc), and Doctor of Philosophy (PhD); in Scotland Master is used for a first degree in arts subjects. Uniformity of standards between universities is promoted by the practice of employing external examiners for all university examinations, and the general pattern of teaching is fairly similar throughout Britain.

Research is an important feature of university work; many staff combine research with their teaching duties and about half of postgraduate students are engaged on research projects.

The Open University

The Open University is a non-residential university which provides part-time degree and other courses, using mainly a combination of correspondence courses, television and radio broadcasts, and summer schools, together with a network of study centres for contact with part-time tutors and counsellors and with fellow students. No formal academic qualifications are required to register for these courses, but the standards of the University's degrees are the same as those of other universities. Its first degree, for which courses began in 1971, is the BA (Open), a general degree awarded on a system of credits for each course completed. The University also has a programme of higher degrees, BPhil, MPhil and PhD, available through research, and MA and MSc through taught courses. In 1983, courses started for English-speakers in Belgium, and the University has advised many other countries on the setting-up of similar institutions. A Continuing Education Programme, including short courses of community education, in-service training for teachers and other staff, and up-dating courses for managers, scientists and technologists, is the fastest-growing aspect of the University's work. In 1986 some 140,000 students were following Open University courses, more than half at degree level.

Polytechnics and Other Institutions

A major contribution to post-school education in England and Wales is made by the 30 polytechnics which have been established since 1967. They provide courses in a wide range of subjects at all levels, though the trend is towards a concentration on advanced work. Courses may lead to first and higher degrees, certain graduate-equivalent qualifications, the examinations of the main professional bodies, and to qualifications such as those of the Business & Technician Education Council (see p 174). One-year 'access' courses provide a foundation and an appropriate test before enrolment on a course of higher education for prospective students who lack the standard entry qualifications. Polytechnics have close links with commerce and industry, and many polytechnic students have jobs and attend on a part-time basis. Similar provision is made in Scotland in the 16 central institutions and a number of further education colleges, and in Northern Ireland by the University of Ulster.

Institutes and colleges of higher education, formed by the integration of teacher training with the rest of higher education, also account for a significant proportion of higher education students, and other further education colleges run some, usually specialised, higher education courses.

Initial plans were announced in 1984 for the establishment of Britain's first independent institute of information technology, to be funded mainly by sponsorship from British electronics manufacturers and users. The institute would be located in Milton Keynes, to the north-west of London.

Council for National Academic Awards

An increasing proportion of students on advanced courses in Great Britain outside the universities are taking courses leading to the qualifications of the Council for National Academic Awards (CNAA). The Council awards degrees and other academic qualifications comparable in standard with those granted by the universities. The courses range from science and technology to the arts, social studies, business studies and law, but the proportion of technological, business or other broadly vocational courses is much higher than in universities.

Other Examining Bodies

The Business & Technician Education Council (BTEC) plans and administers a unified national system of courses at technician or equivalent level for students in industry, commerce and public administration in England, Wales and Northern Ireland. Courses leading to BTEC awards are available at polytechnics, colleges of further and higher education, and in some schools. The Scottish equivalent of the Council is the Scottish Vocational Education Council, which is also the awarding body for the non-advanced National Certificate in Scotland.

A National Council for Vocational Qualifications will be established in autumn 1986; it will devise a new system of qualifications within a framework to be called the National Vocational Qualification, which is to be put into operation by 1991.

Qualifications in a wide range of craft skills are offered by the City and Guilds of London Institute, and a variety of qualifications in commercial and office practice are awarded by the Royal Society of Arts.

Teacher Training

All entrants to teaching in England and Wales must have taken a recognised course of teacher training. Courses are offered by institutes of higher education, most universities, many polytechnics and by certain other colleges. Non-graduates usually qualify by way of three- or four-year courses leading to the Bachelor of Education (BEd) degree; graduates take a one-year Postgraduate Certificate of Education.

In Scotland all teachers in education authority schools must be registered with the General Teaching Council for Scotland. It is government policy that all entrants to the teaching profession in Scotland should be graduates. New primary teachers qualify either through a four-year BEd course or a one-year postgraduate course of teacher training at a college of education. Teachers of academic subjects at secondary schools must hold a degree containing two passes in the subject which they wish to teach. In certain non-academic subjects, a relevant specialist diploma has been acceptable in place of a degree, but this provision is being phased out.

In Northern Ireland teacher training is provided by the two universities and the two colleges of education. The principal courses are BEd (three- or four-year honours), BA and BSc with education (three, four or five years) and the one-year Certificate of Education for graduates.

The number of teachers to be trained to teach in primary schools is being greatly increased in order to meet the anticipated rise in the number of primary schoolchildren over the next few years. There will also be more admissions to undergraduate courses of initial training for teachers of certain subjects in secondary schools, including those subjects (like mathematics and physics) where there have been long-standing shortages. Admissions to postgraduate training courses for secondary teachers, the route by which about three-quarters of all newly trained secondary teachers qualify, are due to remain at the present level until 1990.

The Government is taking steps to improve the quality of teaching by revising selection, training and placement procedures for new teachers, and by providing more in-service training opportunities. Management training courses for head teachers are also being provided. The Government believes that more systematic planning is required by schools and local education authorities to match in-service training to both the career needs of teachers and to the curricular needs of schools; the Education Bill contains provisions to make such training more effective in England and Wales.

Since 1983–84 a system of in-service training grants has operated to stimulate training in selected priority areas. In 1986–87 three new subjects will be included in England and Wales: training to assist school teachers to respond to ethnic diversity; microelectronics in schools; and management training for teachers in further education. In addition, a special programme will be initiated to support the introduction of the General Certificate of Secondary Education. In Scotland the main priorities for 1986–87 are training in technological education and in combating drug misuse.

Measures taken to strengthen initial teacher training in England and Wales have included the establishment of a Council for the Accreditation of Teacher Education to review all existing courses and to issue new criteria against which courses can be assessed. The Education Bill gives the Government powers to require local education authorities to appraise the performance of teachers. In Scotland, following recommendations of working parties on teacher training, postgraduate courses are being revised. All new pre-service and major in-service courses provided by colleges of education must be approved both by the Scottish Education Department and a validating body.

Adult and Continuing Education

It is becoming increasingly recognised that education is a process which continues throughout adult life. The scope of adult and continuing education has widened in recent years and now includes, in addition to the development of the individual through cultural, physical and craft pursuits, such subjects as basic education (for example, in literacy and numeracy); education for disadvantaged groups and those with special needs such as ethnic minorities or the disabled; consumer education; health education; and pre-retirement education. Continuing education also includes training for those in employment to enable them to keep pace with technological change. The Government has taken a number of recent initiatives to improve opportunities for both adult and continuing education. In 1982 it launched a Professional, Industrial and Commercial Updating Programme (PICKUP), designed to help colleges, polytechnics and universities to meet the need to up-date and broaden the skills of those in mid-career in industry, commerce and the professions. A programme to encourage the expansion of educational opportunities for the adult unemployed, called REPLAN, was launched in 1984. A new 'college of the air', bringing together broadcasters, educationists and sponsors, will provide, from 1987 onwards, vocational education and training courses below degree level.

Apart from provision for mature students at universities, courses are provided by further education colleges, adult education centres, residential colleges, extra-mural departments of universities, the Open University and various other bodies including a number of voluntary organisations. Most of the provision is made by the local education authorities in a wide variety of establishments, including schools used for adult evening classes and 'community schools' which provide educational, social and cultural opportunities for the wider community. Most courses are part time. Local authorities also maintain or aid many of the short-term residential colleges or centres which provide courses lasting between a weekend and a fortnight. Long-term residential colleges, grant-aided by central government departments, provide courses of one or two years and aim to provide a liberal education without academic entry tests. Most students admitted are entitled to full maintenance grants.

University extra-mural departments and the Workers' Educational Association, the largest recognised voluntary body, provide extended part-time courses of liberal studies; they also run short courses for special (including vocational) interests. Various kinds of education and training are provided by a wide range of other organisations, including the National Federation of Women's Institutes, the Young Men's Christian Association and the Pre-Retirement Association.

The National Institute of Adult Continuing Education is a centre of information, research, development work and publication for adult and continuing education, as well as a channel of co-operation and consultation for the many interested organisations in England and Wales. The Institute also administers with government funding the Unit for the Development of Adult Continuing Education which undertakes research and development work; the Adult Literacy and Basic Skills Unit, covering proficiency in literacy, numeracy and communications skills; and a large part of the REPLAN programme. The Institute's counterpart in Scotland is the Scottish Institute of Adult and Continuing Education.

In Scotland the Scottish Community Education Council advises the Government and promotes all community education matters including adult literacy and basic education and the youth service.

In Northern Ireland the Council for Continuing Education advises the Department of Education on adult and continuing education matters.

Teaching Methods

The general pattern of teaching and learning on full-time courses of higher education remains a mixture of lectures, prescribed or suggested reading, seminars and tutorials, exercises and tests, and, where appropriate, practical work or work experience. Educational aids are widely used.

Radio and television programmes, both specifically educational and general, are important media for continuing education and are often linked to a range of supplementary publications, courses and activities. The BBC, the independent television companies and Channel 4 provide programmes which range from basic education and progressive vocational training to domestic, social and craft skills. The BBC also works with the Open University (see p 173), producing and broadcasting radio and television programmes as part of the University's courses.

EDUCATIONAL RESEARCH

Research into the theory and practice of education and the organisation of educational services is supported financially by central and local government, the Economic and Social Research Council, philanthropic organisations, universities and other higher education institutions, teachers' associations and certain independent bodies.

The major research institute outside the universities is the autonomous National Foundation for Educational Research in England and Wales, with income mainly from funds received from research projects and from corporate members, including local education authorities, teachers' organisations and universities; it also receives a small government grant. The Scottish Council for Research in Education and the Northern Ireland Council for Educational Research have similar functions.

EDUCATIONAL LINKS OVERSEAS

Schoolchildren, students, teachers and others concerned with education come to Britain from overseas to study, and British people work and train overseas. Many opportunities for such movement are the result of international co-operation at government level within the European Community and within the Commonwealth, and of educational schemes, courses and professional contacts organised in Britain by officially funded and voluntary organisations. The British aid programme encourages links between educational institutions in Britain and developing countries.

British membership of the European Community is creating closer ties with other member countries. Both in schools and in the colleges and universities there has been an expansion of interest in European studies and languages, and exchanges of teachers, schoolchildren and students take place. Britain has adhered to the Statute of the European Schools (nine of which have been established throughout the Community including one at Culham, Oxfordshire) to provide education for children of people employed in Community institutions.

Overseas Students in Britain

Students come to Britain from countries throughout the world to study at universities or other educational institutions or for professional training. British universities, polytechnics and other further education establishments have built up their reputation overseas by offering tuition of the highest standards, maintaining low student-to-staff ratios, and providing courses and qualifications to meet present-day and possible future needs. First degree courses tend to be shorter and more intensive than in many other countries (three years is the normal length in England, Wales and Northern Ireland; three or four years in Scotland).

In the academic year 1984–85 there were about 35,000 overseas students at universities and 21,000 at polytechnics and other establishments of further and higher education. In addition, many thousands of people from abroad were training for such occupations as nursing, law, banking and accountancy, and service and other industries. About half of all overseas students were from the Commonwealth and Britain's dependencies. Many come to Britain for advanced training: some 30 per cent of students enrolled for full-time postgraduate study or research in Britain in 1984–85 came from overseas.

Most overseas students pay their own fees and expenses or hold awards from their own governments. Those following courses of higher or further education are charged fees which cover the full cost of their courses. Nationals of other member countries of the European Community are generally charged the lower level of fees that applies to British students.

The Government continues, however, to make considerable provision for students and trainees from developing countries under its overseas aid programme. Some 12,150 were financed in 1985 under regional programmes of technical co-operation, by awards under the Commonwealth Scholarship and Fellowship Plan, and under British Council schemes. Expenditure on overseas students (including some studying overseas) totalled £62 million. The Government increased its financial support for overseas students by £46 million over the three years 1983–84 to 1985–86, using the money to finance a number of new measures including provision for some five to six thousand additional scholarships and awards each year. Under a new Overseas Development Administration Shared Scholarship Scheme, launched in 1986–87, 750 awards over five years are available mainly at postgraduate level for students from the developing countries of the Commonwealth, with costs being shared between the Government and the educational institutions.

Outside the aid programme, the Overseas Research Students Awards Scheme, funded by the Department of Education and Science, provides assistance for overseas research students of high ability to attend British universities while the Foreign and Commonwealth Office Scholarships and Awards Scheme, which operates in some 90 countries, is designed to benefit individuals likely to hold positions of responsibility in their future careers.

Many public and private scholarships and fellowships are available to students from overseas (and to British students who want to study overseas). Among the best known are the British Council Scholarships, the Commonwealth Scholarship and Fellowship Plan, the Fulbright Scholarship Scheme, the Marshall

Scholarships, the Rhodes Scholarships, and the Churchill Scholarships for men and women in all walks of life. Most British universities and colleges offer scholarships for which graduates of any nationality are eligible.

A number of British colleges of further education have entered into arrangements with British universities to provide courses for overseas students before they enter university.

English as a Foreign Language

The continuing increase in interest in English as a foreign language is reflected in the growth of the number of private language schools in Britain and the larger proportion of these recognised by the British Council. At the same time the British Council has expanded the volume of its own teaching of English overseas by opening several new centres and extending existing ones, and runs a programme for teaching English related to specific jobs and skills. Publications and other material relating to English language teaching have also increased in number and are now a large component in many publishers' lists, constituting a major export.

The BBC's English by Radio and English by Television services provide a world-wide facility for the individual learner at home.

Educational Exchanges

The promotion of cultural and educational relations with other countries is a major concern of the British Council, which plays an important part in the management of the aid programme to education. It recruits teachers for work overseas, organises short visits overseas by British experts, and encourages cultural exchange visits. It also runs schemes to promote academic interchange between universities and higher education institutions in Britain and other countries, and exchange schemes in other scientific, educational and cultural areas. Co-operation between universities in Britain and developing countries is promoted by means of recruiting staff for overseas universities, the secondment of staff from British universities, interdepartmental faculty link schemes, local staff development, short-term teaching and advisory visits, and general consultancy services.

The Central Bureau, a charitable foundation financed by the Government, aims to enrich British education through international contact and exchange. It is responsible, with the League for the Exchange of Commonwealth Teachers, for teacher exchanges with various West European and Commonwealth countries and the United States. It develops links and exchanges between schools, further education establishments and local authorities, and organises study visits for teachers, education administrators and young workers. It also administers the Language Assistant Scheme in Britain and provides an information service on aspects of educational exchange. In 1985 the Central Bureau and the British Council set up, at the Government's request, the Youth Exchange Council which develops, implements and evaluates policy on youth exchanges between Britain and other countries.

The Association of Commonwealth Universities promotes co-operation between member universities in 29 Commonwealth countries. It organises meetings, provides information and academic appointments services, administers the Commonwealth Scholarship and Fellowship Plan in Britain, and generally promotes the movement of academic and administrative staff and of students from one country to another.

The Commonwealth Education Liaison Committee supplements normal direct dealings on education between the countries of the Commonwealth. The United Kingdom Council for Overseas Student Affairs is an independent body serving overseas students, and organisations and individuals concerned in student affairs.

The Youth Service

The youth service forms part of the education system and is concerned with promoting the personal development and social education of young people by providing opportunities for them to participate in a wide range of leisure-time activities. Young people take part in the youth service on a voluntary basis. Extending the range of experiences open to young people and giving them opportunities to participate in the running of their organisations are seen as key elements in the provision.

The youth service is a partnership between central government, local authorities and voluntary youth organisations; at local level the youth service is provided by voluntary organisations and local education authorities. Government education departments formulate broad policy objectives and encourage their achievement through financial assistance and advice. The need to achieve better planning, management and co-ordination of the youth service in England, which was emphasised in an official review published in 1982, has been endorsed by the Government. In 1985 the Government established the National Advisory Council for the Youth Service for England and Wales to advise ministers and others on the scale and direction of youth service activity. In Wales the Youth Work Partnership was set up in 1985 to promote the co-ordination and development of services there.

National voluntary youth organisations promote the major share of youth activities through local groups which raise most of their day-to-day expenses by their own efforts. Many receive financial and other assistance from local education authorities, which also provide facilities in many areas. The voluntary organisations vary greatly in character and include the uniformed and church organisations. Many local authorities and voluntary youth organisations have responded to new needs in society by making provision, for example, for the young unemployed, young people from the ethnic minorities, young people in inner cities or rural areas and those in trouble or especially vulnerable. Other areas of concern are homelessness, work with girls, and provision for handicapped young people. Among the largest of the voluntary youth organisations are the Scout and Girl Guides Associations (with about 530,000 and 736,000 members), the National Association of Youth Clubs (about 700,000), the National Association of Boys' Clubs (some 174,000), the Young Men's Christian Association (750,000) and clubs run by the churches. The Young Farmers' Clubs are distinguished as a movement in which decisions are taken by the members themselves. There are also organisations like the Outward Bound Trust providing opportunities for adventurous outdoor pursuits. The three pre-service organisations (the Sea Cadet Corps, Army Cadet Force and Air Training Corps), with a membership of some 100,000, undertake activities related to the work of the armed forces. Many authorities have youth committees on which official and voluntary bodies are represented, and employ youth officers to co-ordinate youth work and to arrange in-service training. There are also youth councils which are representative bodies of young people from local youth organisations. At national level many voluntary organisations belong to the National Council for Voluntary Youth Services, a representative and consultative body which aims to develop the partnership between voluntary and statutory bodies in England. Similar councils exist in Wales, Scotland and Northern Ireland. The British Youth Council is a national forum for young people, youth organisations and youth councils, including the youth wings of the major political parties, and represents young people at an international level. The youth service in England and Wales can draw on information, advice, training and research services provided by the National Youth Bureau, which is funded primarily by central government and issues a range of publications.

Youth Workers

In England and Wales a basic two-year training course at certain universities and higher education colleges leads to the status of qualified youth and community worker. A number of Bachelor of Education degree courses include a youth and community option and there are courses for graduates who wish to become youth workers. In Scotland one-, two- and three-year courses are provided at certain colleges of education and in Northern Ireland courses are provided by the University of Ulster. All school teachers who qualify before the end of 1988 are recognised as qualified youth workers.

Full-time youth workers are supported by some 500,000 part-time workers, many of them unpaid, both qualified and unqualified. Short courses and conferences on youth and community work are held. There are also in-service courses for serving youth workers and officers. Both initial and in-service courses are validated by the Council for Education and Training in Youth and Community Work.

Other Organisations Concerned with Young People

A substantial sum of money is awarded by the many grant-giving foundations and trusts each year for activities involving young people. The Royal Jubilee Trusts, formed in 1978 from King George's Jubilee Trust (started in 1935 at the time of the Silver Jubilee of King George V) and The Queen's Silver Jubilee Trust, which arose from the 1977 Queen's Silver Jubilee Appeal, support work involving young people aged 8 to 25 (King George's Jubilee Trust) and young people up to the age of 25 involved in voluntary community service work (The Queen's Silver Jubilee Trust). King George's Jubilee Trust has distributed nearly £6 million since 1935 and The Queen's Silver Jubilee Trust over £10 million since 1978. In addition, The Prince's Trust, which was set up in 1976 to help disadvantaged young people aged 14 to 25, has disbursed some £2 million to individuals and small *ad hoc* groups.

The Duke of Edinburgh's Award Scheme, which operates through bodies such as local authorities, schools, youth organisations and industrial firms, enables young people from Britain and other Commonwealth countries to take part, with the voluntary assistance of adults, in a variety of challenging activities in four areas: community service, expeditions, the development of personal interests and social and practical skills, and physical recreation.

Voluntary Service by Young People

Thousands of young people voluntarily take part in community service designed to assist those in need, including the elderly and the disabled, and many others work on environmental projects. Organisations providing opportunities for community service, such as Community Service Volunteers, International Voluntary Service and the British Trust for Conservation Volunteers, receive grants from the Government. Many schools also organise community service activities as part of the curriculum and voluntary work in the community is sponsored by a number of churches.

8 The Environment

By comprehensive land-use planning and development control Britain has had considerable success in resolving the conflicting demands of industry, commerce, housing, transport, agriculture and recreation and in reducing environmental pollution. The underlying approach is to promote efficiency, economy and amenity in the use and development of land, respecting both the needs of development and the interests of conservation. There is no 'national plan' for urban and land development, but there is a statutory system of land-use planning applying to virtually every kind of development, and there are laws dealing specifically with environmental health and the control of pollution. In general, all development requires local 'planning permission', and applications for permission are dealt with in the light of development plans which set out strategies for each area on such matters as housing, transport, industry and open land. However, many minor developments are subject to a general permission under which they do not need a specific planning application; the opportunity is being taken to expand this general permission wherever possible. Throughout Britain voluntary organisations take an active interest in planning, conservation and the control of pollution.

Planning

The system of land-use planning in Great Britain involves a centralised structure under the Secretaries of State for the Environment, Wales and Scotland and compulsory planning duties for local planning authorities. The Department of the Environment brings together the major responsibilities in England for land-use planning, housing and construction, countryside policy and environmental protection. The Welsh Office and the Scottish Development Department have broadly equivalent responsibilities. Large-scale planning in England and Wales excluding London is primarily the responsibility of the county councils and the metropolitan district councils, while district councils and, in London, the councils of the London boroughs and the City of London are responsible for most local plans and development control, the main housing functions and many environmental health matters. In Scotland planning functions are undertaken by regional and district councils whose responsibilities are divided on a basis broadly similar to that in England and Wales. In the more rural regions and the islands, all planning responsibilities are carried out by the regional and islands councils respectively. In Northern Ireland the Department of the Environment for Northern Ireland is responsible for planning matters through six divisional planning offices which work closely with the district councils. The councils have local environmental health responsibilities.

General problems of industrial development are dealt with jointly by a number of government departments, but each development proposal normally requires the local planning authority's consent.

Development Plans

The development plan system in England and Wales involves 'structure' and 'local' plans. Structure plans are prepared by county planning authorities and require ministerial approval. They set out broad policies for the development and other use of land including measures for the improvement of the physical environment and traffic management. Local plans provide detailed guidance, either generally for development expected to start within about ten years, or, more specifically, in 'action area' plans, where implementation is to be given short-term priority, and in 'subject' plans which concentrate on special issues such as mineral working. The plans are normally prepared by district planning authorities, although sometimes by county planning authorities, and must conform generally to the approved structure plan. In exceptional cases, with ministerial approval, the adoption of a local plan may precede the approval of a structure plan. Local plans are adopted by the planning authorities without being subject to ministerial approval unless called in by the Secretary of State. All plans are kept under review and may be altered from time to time. In Greater London and the other six metropolitan areas in England structure and local plans will in future be gradually replaced by new unitary development plans. This follows abolition of the county planning authorities in those areas on 1 April 1986. Unitary development plans will be prepared and normally adopted by London borough and metropolitan district planning authorities. They will contain both general policies and detailed proposals for land use and development control. Like local plans, unitary development plans can be called in by the Secretary of State in exceptional circumstances.

Scotland has a broadly similar system which can also include the production of a regional report by regional and islands authorities, outlining their priorities and policies. Under Northern Ireland's single-tier system, plans are prepared by the Department of the Environment for Northern Ireland.

Public Participation

Members of the public and interested organisations are given an opportunity to express their views on the planning of their areas during the formative stages of the structure and local plans. The local planning authorities must ensure adequate publicity for matters proposed for inclusion in the plans; representations may be made about them to the authorities. These opportunities for public participation are additional to provisions for objecting to prepared plans. In the case of structure plans the Secretary of State normally holds an examination in public of matters on which he or she requires more information in order to reach a decision. In the case of local plans objectors have a right to be heard at a public local inquiry held by the planning authorities. There will be similar provisions for participation in the preparation of unitary development plans and for making objections to them. Usually the planning authorities will hold a public local inquiry to hear objectors to unitary development plans. The Secretary of State has the option, however, of holding an examination in public into the general policies only of unitary development plans.

Where specific proposals for development differ substantially from the intentions of a development plan, they must be publicised locally. Other schemes affecting a large number of people are usually advertised by the local planning authority, and applications seeking permission for certain types of development must also be advertised. (In Scotland there is a system of neighbour notification of planning applications, under which the applicant must notify the proprietors of land and buildings adjoining the site of a proposed development at the same time as the application is submitted to the local planning authority.) The applicant has a right of appeal to the Secretary of State if planning permission is refused or is granted subject to conditions. Most appeals are transferred for decision to inspectors (in Scotland reporters) appointed by the Secretary of State.

Similar provision is made in Northern Ireland for public participation in the planning process and for the hearing of representations at public inquiries. For planning applications which do not give rise to public inquiries there is a right of appeal to an independent Planning Appeals Commission.

Major Schemes

The Secretaries of State can direct that a planning application be referred to them for decision. This power is exercised sparingly and usually only in respect of proposals of national or regional importance, for example, proposals for a major new airport or coalfield. The applicant and the local planning authority have the right to be heard by a person appointed by the Secretary of State and a public inquiry is normally held for this purpose. In the case of development schemes of exceptional importance the departments concerned have set up procedures to aid the progress of the inquiry by helping the parties to resolve peripheral matters beforehand. Where highway development is proposed, the government minister concerned can hold such inquiries as he or she considers appropriate; these generally relate to the compulsory acquisition of land.

New Towns

The 32 new towns designated since 1946 (see map, p 184) represent one of the most significant achievements in recent British planning. Twenty-one of them are in England, two in Wales, five in Scotland and four in Northern Ireland. Most of them had an existing town or village as a nucleus. The new towns programme has taken account of a number of policy objectives, notably the dispersal of industry and population from congested cities to the surrounding regions, and the stimulation of the regional economy in areas suffering from the decline of old industries or in need of industrial diversification. The new town development corporations' priorities now are to maximise private investment in housing and employment and to achieve a balanced community able to generate its own growth. The new towns have a total population of over 2 million and by the time their growth is complete are expected to house 2·5 million people. Several have become regional centres for shopping and office accommodation.

In England the new towns programme is nearing completion, with fourteen having been substantially completed and their development corporations (which supervised the planning and development of the towns) dissolved. Target dissolution dates for the seven remaining development corporations have now been set in the late 1980s and early 1990s. When a development corporation is wound up, its remaining assets are transferred to the Commission for the New Towns, which manages the assets and arranges for their disposal, mainly to the private sector. The New Towns and Urban Development Corporations Act 1985 provides for the eventual dissolution of the Commission. The dissolution of the five Scottish development corporations will not begin before the 1990s. In Wales responsibility for Newtown rests with the Development Board for Rural Wales (known as 'Mid-Wales Development') while the corporation responsible for Cwmbran is to be dissolved in 1988. In Northern Ireland development of the new towns has been incorporated in a new District Towns Strategy which is the responsibility of the Department of the Environment for Northern Ireland.

Inner City Policies

Revitalising the inner areas of many towns and cities is one of the most important tasks in modern planning. Past policies have produced many successes including the replacement of most of the slums and the improvement of much old housing, but other problems remain. They include high unemployment, decay and dereliction, and population structures with relatively large proportions of the disadvantaged and the elderly. It is the Government's policy to work out, in co-operation with local authorities, a package of measures for the most badly affected areas that is most likely to improve conditions and encourage, as far as possible, local voluntary action, notably by means of 'partnerships' (see p 185), and the co-operation of the private sector in regenerating local economies. Various special measures, aimed at increasing

New Towns

Orkney Islands

Shetland Islands

0 20 40 60 80 100 120 km

0   20   40   60   80 miles

Scotland

Glenrothes ▲

Cumbernauld ▲ ▲ Livingston

▲ East Kilbride

▲ Irvine

▲ Londonderry

Ballymena ▲

Northern Ireland ▲ Antrim

▲ Craigavon

Washington ▲

Peterlee ▲
Aycliffe ▲

Central Lancashire
▲ New Town

▲ Skelmersdale

▲ Warrington

Runcorn

England

▲ Telford Corby ▲ ▲ Peterborough

Newtown ▲ ▲ Redditch ▲ Northampton

Milton ▲ Stevenage
Keynes ▲
Welwyn Garden City ⌐ ▲ ▲ Harlow
Hemel Hempstead Hatfield ▲ ▲ Basildon

Wales

Cwmbran ▲ Bracknell ▲

Crawley ▲

employment opportunities and the involvement of residents in the rejuvenation of their areas, have been introduced.

Urban
Programme

The inner city areas have been given greater resources and priority by central government for a number of years. The 'Urban Programme' has been increased from a 1977–78 level in England and Wales of under £30 million to £317 million in 1986–87. The programme complements the main social, environmental and economic programmes of local authorities, often by providing extra facilities which would otherwise not be available, such as day nurseries, centres for the elderly and language classes for ethnic minorities, and covers industrial, commercial, environmental and recreational provision as well. The Urban Programme in its present form is to be simplified from 1987–88 as part of a gradual attempt to improve its effectiveness. Proposals were announced in the autumn of 1986 with a view to further concentrating resources on areas with special problems and needs, and to achieving a more tangible impact with available funds. The Urban Programme represents only a part of the central assistance to urban, and other, local authorities. The main contributions are through the annual rate support grant, housing subsidy and other programmes.

In certain places, special schemes are in operation. A co-ordinated 'partnership' approach is in operation in seven English areas (Birmingham, Liverpool, Manchester/Salford, Newcastle upon Tyne/Gateshead and the inner London boroughs of Hackney, Islington and Lambeth) in which central and local government work together to tackle urban problems where they are at their most severe. Each partnership has a three-year action programme rolled forward annually, which is based on the needs of the area and its particular priorities. Partnerships receive allocations of urban programme resources ranging from £10 million to £25 million a year. In 1985 the Government announced the establishment of five 'city action teams' (one for the inner London boroughs and one for each of the other partnership areas) to secure improved co-operation between government departments in developing and implementing their policies and programmes for these areas.

In February 1986 a new initiative was announced, involving the creation of 'task forces' to intensify and bring together the efforts of government departments, local government, the private sector and the local community in eight inner city areas: two in London, and one in Leeds, Middlesbrough, Leicester, Manchester, Bristol and Birmingham. Funds in addition to those available under existing programmes would be provided and the initiative would be co-ordinated by the Secretary of State for Employment.

To meet the particular problems and opportunities of the London docklands and the Merseyside dock area following large-scale dock closures, the Government has set up urban development corporations modelled on the new town development corporations, and these are receiving some £67 million in 1986–87. Elsewhere in England 23 'programme authorities' have been identified where the problems are on a slightly smaller scale but still merit special attention. These authorities prepare their own Inner Area Programmes and, like the partnerships, receive special allocations of Urban Programme resources. In August 1986 proposals were announced to create a further 22 programme authorities. They are being invited to submit co-ordinated Inner Area Programmes for the first time in 1987–88.

Urban Development Grant aims to promote the economic and physical regeneration of deprived urban areas by encouraging private sector investment. Grant is available for capital investment projects which would not otherwise go ahead and would contribute to meeting the special social needs of inner urban areas. Since the scheme was launched in 1982, some 191 projects have been approved, representing a total capital investment of over £480 million. Under the Housing and Planning Bill the Government will be able to pay Urban Regeneration Grants to promote the regeneration of specific run-down urban areas by private enterprise.

National garden festivals, based on the European idea of garden shows, are being introduced with the aim of rejuvenating inner urban areas and reclaiming derelict sites. The first festival in Liverpool in 1984, which had international status and attracted nearly 3·4 million visitors, was followed by a second in Stoke-on-Trent in 1986, and further festivals will be held in Glasgow in 1988, Gateshead in 1990 and in Wales in 1992.

In Scotland, where the Urban Programme amounts to £35 million in 1986–87, a major urban renewal exercise in Glasgow to regenerate the city's east end (the Glasgow Eastern Area Renewal Project) has been organised on somewhat similar lines to the partnership areas in England, and a further eight Scottish districts have been designated under the Inner Urban Areas Act. In addition, the Scottish Development Agency operates the Local Enterprise Grants for Urban Projects Scheme (equivalent to the Urban Development Grant). In Northern Ireland, inner city problems on a substantial scale are largely confined to Belfast, where a major housing programme is supplemented by Urban Development Grants, an environmental improvement scheme and a comprehensive development programme to regenerate the commercial parts of the inner city. In 1986–87 these programmes have a combined allocation of £8 million.

In Wales, where the Urban Programme is administered by the Welsh Office, the Secretary of State for Wales has launched a new community-based initiative for the south Wales valleys aimed at bringing about a substantial improvement in the environments of the town centres and surrounding areas. Ideas on how the valley communities can be revitalised and improved have been sought from within the communities. The Welsh Office will use existing mechanisms of assistance and make additional resources available to bring about change.

Enterprise Zones

Since 1981 the Government has set up 25 'enterprise zones' (see map, opposite). The aim of this experimental policy is to see how far industrial and commercial activity can be stimulated by the removal of certain tax burdens and by relaxing or speeding up the application of a number of administrative controls. The zones, which vary widely but all contain land suitable for development, range in size from about 50 to 450 hectares (about 120 to over 1,100 acres). Benefits in the zones include exemption from rates (the local property tax); 100 per cent allowances for corporation and income tax purposes for capital expenditure on industrial and commercial buildings; a much simplified planning system in which most forms of development are automatically permitted; and a reduction in government requests for statistical information.

Simplified Planning Zones

The Housing and Planning Bill, introduced in early 1986, would provide for the establishment of 'simplified planning zones', which would be somewhat akin to enterprise zones and where a reduction in bureaucratic control through a mixture of deregulation and incentives would encourage businesses, especially small firms, to locate there.

Housing

The pattern of housing tenure has changed considerably in recent years, with a substantial increase in owner-occupation and a decline in privately rented accommodation. Between the end of 1971 and 1985 the proportion of owner-occupied dwellings in Great Britain rose from 51 to 62 per cent of the housing stock, while the proportion accounted for by dwellings rented from a local authority or new town authority fell from 31 to 27 per cent, and the

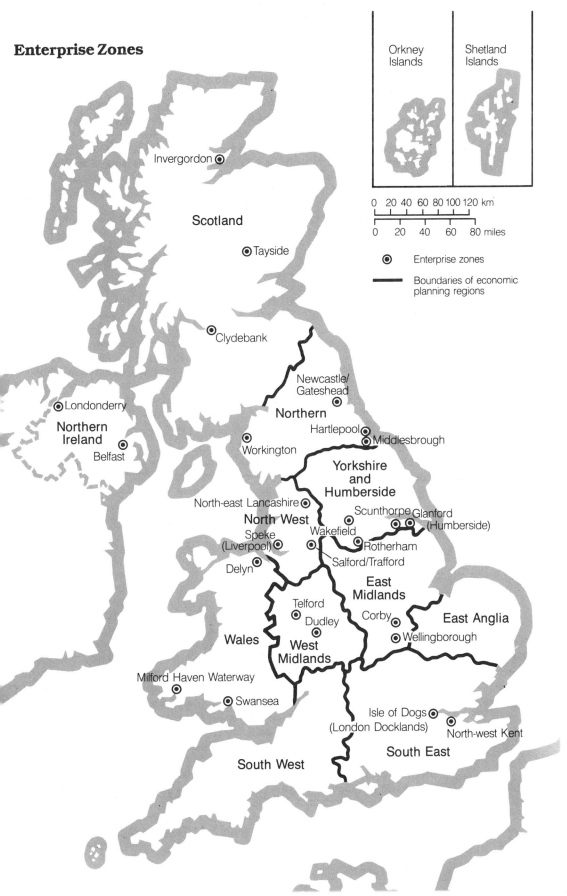

Enterprise Zones

Orkney Islands

Shetland Islands

0 20 40 60 80 100 120 km

0   20   40   60   80 miles

◉ Enterprise zones

── Boundaries of economic
    planning regions

Invergordon ◉

Scotland

◉ Tayside

◉ Clydebank

◉ Londonderry

Northern
Ireland

◉
Belfast

Newcastle/
Gateshead
◉

Northern

Hartlepool
◉ ◉ Middlesbrough

◉
Workington

Yorkshire
and
Humberside

North-east Lancashire ◉

North West

Scunthorpe Glanford
◉ ◉◉ (Humberside)

Speke
(Liverpool) ◉

Wakefield
◉
◉ Rotherham

Salford/Trafford

◉
Delyn

East
Midlands

Wales

Telford
◉
◉ Dudley

West
Midlands

Corby
◉

Wellingborough
◉

East Anglia

Milford Haven Waterway
◉

◉ Swansea

Isle of Dogs ◉
(London Docklands)

◉
North-west Kent

South West

South East

proportion of other types of tenure fell from 19 to 11 per cent. The fall in the last category reflected the decline in privately rented dwellings, while the number of housing association dwellings increased substantially during this period. There are variations, however, in the distribution of tenure between different parts of the country; in Scotland almost half of the dwellings are rented from public authorities while in Wales about two-thirds of dwellings are owner-occupied. The encouragement of a further extension of home ownership is a major aim of the Government's housing policy, while the emphasis of public sector housing policy has shifted from new building to modernisation, improvement and making better use of existing dwellings.

There are some 22 million dwellings, houses being much more common than flats (the ratio is roughly four to one), and around 50 per cent of families live in a post-1945 home. Throughout this century pressure on housing accommodation has been increased more by the rapid rise in the number of separate households than by the increase in population. While the number of people has increased by about two-fifths, the number of households has more than doubled. The 1981 Census showed the total number of households in Great Britain as 19·5 million. Improvements in living standards were continuing: only 1·3 per cent were not in self-contained accommodation, 4·3 per cent lived at an average density of more than one person per room and 3·2 per cent were lacking or sharing use of a bath.

New house construction is undertaken by both public and private sectors but over the past few years the private sector has built many more dwellings than the public sector. In addition, over 6 per cent of the new building in 1985 was carried out by voluntary housing associations and societies. Public authorities provide dwellings mainly for renting while private interests build mainly for sale to owner-occupiers.

Administration

As with environmental planning, responsibility for formulating housing policy and supervising the housing programme is borne by the Secretary of State for the Environment in England and by the Secretaries of State for Wales, Scotland and Northern Ireland. Although the policies are broadly similar throughout Britain, provisions may differ slightly in Northern Ireland and Scotland from those in England and Wales.

The construction or structural alteration of housing is subject to building regulations laid down by the Government. Building in the private sector is regulated by an independent organisation, the National House-Building Council, which sets standards and enforces them by inspection and certification. Almost all new private houses are covered by the Council's insurance scheme which provides ten-year guarantees against major structural defects. A two-year guarantee is also given against faulty workmanship. Most lenders will only make a loan for purchase of a new house if it is covered by the Council's certificate.

Local authorities are responsible for the payment of house renovation grants and the implementation of housing renewal programmes. Many have housing advisory centres to provide information on aspects of housing.

Home Ownership

The number of people owning their own homes has more than trebled in the last 35 years, and the number of owner-occupied dwellings amounted to over 12 million in 1985, compared with 4 million in 1951. Most public sector tenants have the right to buy the homes they occupy at discounts which vary according to the length of their occupancy. Local authorities have been asked to encourage low-cost home ownership by selling land to builders to construct homes for 'first-time' buyers, or to individuals or groups to build their own 'first-time' homes in partnership with private builders; by improving homes for sale; by selling dilapidated homes for improvement by the purchaser ('homesteading'); by offering shared ownership (part owning, part renting); and by using local authority guarantee powers to facilitate lending by building societies.

In Northern Ireland the concept of shared ownership has been developed in the public sector by the Northern Ireland Housing Executive and in the private sector by the Northern Ireland Co-ownership Housing Association. The Executive has offered most of its homes for sale to the tenants and over 30,000 have been sold.

Mortgage Loans   Most people buy their homes with a mortgage loan (for which the properties are regarded as securities) from such sources as building societies, banks, insurance companies, industrial and provident societies, and local authorities. Some companies also make loans for house purchase to their own employees.

Building societies are by far the largest sources of such loans, their share of the market being about 79 per cent in 1985. For first-time buyers they usually advance about 90 per cent of their valuation of a property with the help of an appropriate insurance guarantee but it is possible to borrow up to 100 per cent. Loans are normally repayable over periods of 20 or 25 years (up to 30 or 35 years in certain circumstances) by equal monthly instalments to cover capital and interest. Ordinary mortgage loans from building societies are usually available to purchasers on average income or above. People with insufficient income to obtain a mortgage for outright purchase may be able to participate in a scheme in which a housing association buys the home and sells a share in it to them, allowing them to rent the remainder and to purchase it later if they wish.

Owner-occupiers are entitled to tax relief on interest payments arising on up to £30,000 of their mortgage loans (on their main home only). Under the Homeloan Scheme first-time home buyers who have saved for two years and are buying a home in the lower price range may qualify for an extra loan of £600 interest-free for up to five years, and a tax-free bonus of up to £110.

Public Sector   Most of the public housing in Great Britain is provided by 460 local housing
Housing   authorities. The authorities are: in England and Wales (outside London), the district councils; in London, the London borough councils and the Common Council of the City of London; and in Scotland, the district and islands councils. Other public housing authorities are the new town authorities, the Scottish Special Housing Association, which supplements building by local authorities in Scotland, and the Development Board for Rural Wales. The Northern Ireland Housing Executive is responsible for the provision and management of public housing in Northern Ireland.

Subsidies may be made available to the authorities to assist them with housing costs, and guidance is given on design and layout. Public housing authorities own about 6 million houses and flats. The number of homes owned by each authority varies widely, from 148 homes in the Isles of Scilly to 129,000 in Birmingham. Most authorities own between 2,500 and 15,000 dwellings.

Local authorities meet the capital costs of new house construction and of modernisation of their existing stock by raising loans on the open market, by borrowing from the Public Works Loan Board (an independent statutory body set up to make loans to local authorities) or from the capital receipts generated by the sale of local authority houses and housing land. Current expenditure, including maintenance and management costs and loan interest and repayment, is met from rents, which may be supplemented by subsidies from the Government and, where required to balance housing revenue accounts, from the rates. Local authorities are required to charge their tenants reasonable rents (which keep a balance between the interests of tenants and ratepayers).

Sheltered housing (usually accommodation with an alarm system and resident warden) is provided for those elderly people who need this degree of support, but increasing emphasis is being placed on schemes to help elderly people to continue to live in their own homes and on schemes to adapt existing housing to meet the housing needs of physically handicapped people. Local authorities have a statutory duty to ensure that accommodation (not necessarily owned by the authority) is available for homeless people who have dependent children or are vulnerable on grounds such as age or disability.

The Housing Act 1980 established a charter for public sector tenants in England and Wales, giving them statutory rights which include security of tenure, provision for a resident member of the tenant's family to succeed to the tenancy on the death of the tenant, rights of subletting and taking in lodgers, and, at the landlord's discretion, reimbursement for improvements made by the tenant. With a few exceptions, public sector tenants of at least two years' standing can buy their house or flat at a discount which depends on the length of occupation. Similar provisions are made for Scotland and Northern Ireland under separate legislation. By the end of 1985 some 631,000 tenants in Great Britain had bought their homes under these provisions. The Housing and Building Control Act 1984 further extended the rights of public sector tenants by giving them the right to repair and the right to exchange their homes.

A National Mobility Scheme, sponsored by the Department of the Environment, the Scottish Development Department, the Welsh Office and the Department of the Environment for Northern Ireland, has been introduced to assist tenants who need to move to another area for employment or social reasons. Tenants who wish to move by exchanging homes are able to make use of a computer-based national information scheme.

Privately Rented Housing

There has been a steady decline in the number of rented dwellings available from private landlords (including tied accommodation), from over 50 per cent of the housing stock in 1951 to less than 10 per cent in 1984 (about 2 million dwellings). Major factors have been the increased demand for owner-occupation, the greater availability of public rented housing and the operation of rent restriction. Privately rented dwellings are predominantly found in older housing. Many landlords are individuals owning a small amount of property, but some rented housing is provided by larger property owners, including property companies.

Most private lettings are subject to the system of protection provided by the Rent Act 1977 (and similar legislation in Scotland) and associated legislation. Where the letting is a fully protected 'regulated tenancy', the tenant or the landlord may apply for a 'fair rent' to be fixed by independent rent officers and there is a wide degree of security of tenure. More limited provisions apply where there is a resident landlord, when a 'reasonable rent' may be fixed by a rent tribunal (in Scotland by a rent assessment committee). The Housing Act 1980 (and similar legislation for Scotland and Northern Ireland) introduced an additional system of 'shorthold' lettings, giving tenants security of tenure for an agreed period of between one and five years, after which the landlord is guaranteed repossession. In London and in Scotland a fair rent must be registered for a shorthold; elsewhere it is optional. The 1980 Act also introduced for England and Wales the system of 'assured' tenancies, which allows approved bodies to let newly built property at freely negotiated rents outside the Rent Acts. Tenants and most other residential occupiers may not be evicted without a court order. Harassment of residential occupiers is a criminal offence. Occupiers may, depending on their personal circumstances, be eligible for housing benefit to assist them in paying their rent and rates.

In Northern Ireland only pre-1956 properties subject to rent restriction come under statutory control, and rent levels are linked to those of the Northern Ireland Housing Executive. Rent increases are permitted only for properties which meet a prescribed standard. There is an uncontrolled rent sector, comprising mostly furnished accommodation.

Housing Associations

Housing associations extend the choice of housing by providing accommodation available for rent or sale through new building or the rehabilitation of older property. The associations normally cater for people who would otherwise look to a local authority for a home, and also provide particularly for the special needs of elderly, disabled and single people.

The associations, which are non-profit-making, have grown under government encouragement and now own some 500,000 homes. Individual associations range in size from a group of 'almshouses' for fewer than ten old people to associations with more than 10,000 homes. In Great Britain housing schemes carried out by associations qualify for government grant if the association is one of over 2,600 registered with the Housing Corporation, a statutory body. Rented homes owned by housing associations come within the fair rent arrangements, and most housing association tenants have rights under the tenants' charter in the Housing Act 1985—in Scotland the Tenants' Rights, Etc (Scotland) Act 1980—including, in some cases, the right to buy or the possibility of a discount on the purchase of an alternative home. Housing associations also provide accommodation on a shared ownership basis, allowing the occupier to part-rent and part-own a home, and they can purchase improved older properties for outright sale. Both activities are eligible for government grants.

In Northern Ireland assistance is available to associations registered with the Department of the Environment for Northern Ireland. Rent levels are linked to those of the Northern Ireland Housing Executive. Tenants have rights under a tenants' charter, but not the right to buy, although housing associations may sell their dwellings voluntarily.

Improving Older Houses

In urban areas of Britain slum clearance and redevelopment used to be major features of housing policy. Large-scale clearance is now virtually at an end, although there are still pockets of unfit housing for which demolition is considered the best solution. Greater emphasis has been placed on the retention of existing communities accompanied by the modernisation and conversion of sub-standard homes. Although housing conditions have improved considerably, problems remain in some areas where there are high concentrations of dwellings lacking basic amenities or requiring substantial repairs.

More recently there has been concern about the problems associated with high-density local authority estates in inner city areas, some of which have not been popular with tenants, and about serious structural defects found in some local authority dwellings. Authorities are tackling these problems in a variety of ways including refurbishment and sale to the private sector.

The Government's Urban Housing Renewal Unit, set up in 1985, is working with local authorities to deal with the problems of their run-down council estates. Measures which are being developed include local housing management along the lines of the Department of the Environment's Priority Estates Project (see below); the injection of private sector skills and resources; capital investment in the refurbishment of the housing stock; community refurbishment schemes to enable previously unemployed people to work on environmental improvements; and the development of tenant management and ownership co-operatives.

The Priority Estates Project was set up in 1979 to promote locally based housing management, under which housing officers on the estates are responsible for providing a co-ordinated range of services. Important elements include local budgetary control of key management functions such as repairs, lettings, rent collection, caretaking and grounds maintenance, and effective consultation with tenants and their involvement in initiatives to improve the estate. There are more than 80 estate management initiatives in 53 local authorities involving about 80,000 dwellings. These authorities manage about a third of the English council housing stock. In 1983 the Welsh Office set up similar arrangements in Wales.

Over 800,000 home improvement grants were paid to householders in Great Britain between 1980 and 1986. There are four types of grant: improvement grants, for carrying out improvements to a good standard; intermediate grants, for the provision of standard amenities (such as a bath and an inside lavatory) and associated repairs; grants for substantial and structural repairs to pre-1919 houses (pre-1957 in Northern Ireland and pre-1964 in Scotland, where a grant can cover all forms of repair work); and special grants for providing standard amenities and repairs (not available in Scotland) and means of escape from fire in houses which are in multiple occupation. In addition, since 1978 grants for loft insulation have been paid in respect of some 2 million homes.

Declaring 'general improvement areas' and 'housing action areas' enables local authorities in England and Wales to tackle the improvement of whole areas of older housing systematically. General improvement areas (of which there are more than 1,600) contain fundamentally sound houses and a stable population. Housing action areas (of which there are about 260 in England and Wales) are characterised by relatively poor housing and bad environmental conditions combined with social stress. Local authorities have special powers to bring about an improvement in living conditions for the benefit of residents. In both types of area government financial aid for environmental improvement (such as landscaping and work to improve the external appearance of buildings) is available to local authorities. In these areas home improvement grants may range up to 75 per cent of the eligible expense limit, and in certain cases of hardship up to 90 per cent. 'Enveloping', introduced in 1982, involves the renovation of the external fabric of whole terraces or streets of mainly privately owned property in housing action areas which has deteriorated beyond routine maintenance. It is carried out by local authorities at public expense, and the encouragement it gives to residents is reflected in the increased take-up of grants for improvements to the interiors after enveloping.

An 'improvement-for-sale' scheme has also been introduced; the Government helps to meet any loss a local authority may make in buying, improving and selling run-down or neglected housing.

In Scotland housing action area powers are available for the improvement of areas in which at least half the houses fail to meet a statutory tolerable standard. Since 1975 some 1,400 housing action areas, covering houses requiring improvement or demolition, have been declared by local authorities. Outside such areas in Scotland local authorities have powers to require the improvement of houses below the statutory tolerable standard, or lacking certain basic amenities, by improvement orders. In housing action areas or where an improvement order has been made, grants of 75 per cent (up to 90 per cent in cases of hardship) of the eligible expense limit may be made. Government financial aid is also given towards the costs incurred by local authorities in improving the environment of predominantly residential areas.

Northern Ireland has a major problem of derelict and unfit housing, especially in Belfast, the situation having been made worse by civil disturbance. Concerted measures are being taken in housing action areas, and there is a continuing programme of rehabilitation in Belfast. Housing receives priority in Northern Ireland's social and environmental programme.

Conservation

Britain is one of the leading countries in the conservation movement. A wide range of groups, including many voluntary organisations, are active in it. The Council for Environmental Conservation is a national coalition of non-governmental organisations which focuses attention on major issues.

Historic Buildings, Ancient Monuments and Conservation Areas

Lists of buildings of special architectural or historical interest are compiled, as required by the planning Acts, by the Secretary of State for the Environment and the Secretaries of State for Scotland and Wales; some 380,000 buildings are listed in England, over 33,000 in Scotland and 10,600 in Wales. It is against the law to demolish, extend or alter the character of any listed building without special consent from the local planning authority or the appropriate Secretary of State; where consent is given to demolish a building, the Royal Commission on Historical Monuments (for England) and similar bodies for Scotland and Wales have an opportunity to make a photographic and written record of the building. Emergency 'building preservation notices' can be served by the local planning authority to protect buildings not yet listed.

Maintaining royal parks (which are open to the public) and palaces is the responsibility of the Secretaries of State for the Environment, Scotland and Wales. The Historic Buildings and Monuments Commission for England (known as English Heritage) is charged with protecting and conserving England's architectural and archaeological heritage; it manages some 400 ancient monuments on behalf of the Secretary of State for the Environment and gives grants for the repair of ancient monuments, historic buildings and buildings in conservation areas in England. In Scotland and Wales similar functions are performed by the Historic Buildings and Monuments Directorate of the Scottish Development Department and by Cadw (Welsh Historic Monuments) with advice from an ancient monuments board and a historic buildings council for each country. Local authorities can make grants and loans for any building of architectural or historic interest. The National Heritage Memorial Fund provides assistance towards the cost of acquiring, maintaining or preserving land, buildings, works of art and other items of outstanding interest which are also of importance to the national heritage. In 1985–86 the Fund gave assistance, for example, towards the National Trust's acquisition of a stretch of important coastline on the Menai Straits, north Wales. The Government gave the Fund an additional £25 million in 1985 to enable it to secure the preservation of Kedleston Hall (Derbyshire), Nostell Priory (West Yorkshire) and Weston Park (Shropshire), and a further £10·5 million in 1986 in order to top up its reserves.

Local planning authorities have designated for special protection over 5,000 'conservation areas' of particular architectural or historic interest. Grants and loans are available for works which make a significant contribution towards the preservation or enhancement of such an area.

In Northern Ireland the Department of the Environment for Northern Ireland has 160 historic monuments in its care, and some 640 monuments are scheduled for protection. The Department is also responsible for listing buildings of special architectural or historic interest and for the designation of conservation areas; there are some 7,000 listed buildings and 50 conservation areas. It may also provide grants and loans to help with the repair and maintenance of listed buildings and to preserve or enhance conservation areas. It has the advice of a Historic Buildings Council and a Historic Monuments Council.

Among the voluntary organisations which campaign for the preservation of buildings are the Society for the Protection of Ancient Buildings and the Ancient Monuments Society; the Georgian Group; the Architectural Heritage Society of Scotland; the Ulster Architectural Heritage Society; the Victorian Society; and the Council for British Archaeology. The National Trust (for Places of Historic Interest or Natural Beauty), an independent charity with more than 1·3 million members, owns and protects some 200 historic buildings in addition to 246,900 hectares (more than 610,000 acres) of land and 750 km (466 miles) of coastline in England, Northern Ireland and Wales. Scotland has its own National Trust.

Architectural Standards

Besides helping to conserve the finest buildings inherited from the past, the Government encourages high standards in new building. The Secretary of State for the Environment, in collaboration with the independent Royal Institute of British Architects (RIBA) and the National House-Building Council, makes awards for good design in housing, with categories for renovation as well as new building. Scotland and Wales have similar but separate awards schemes. The Government has also encouraged the use of architectural competitions, and has set an example in the award of some of its own contracts. Royal Fine Art Commissions for England and Wales and for Scotland advise government departments, planning authorities and other public bodies on questions of public amenity or artistic importance.

The RIBA, the principal professional body for architects, exercises control over standards in architectural education and encourages the maintenance of high architectural standards in the profession. The Royal Incorporation of Architects in Scotland is allied to it, as is the Royal Society of Ulster Architects. The Civic Trust, with associate trusts in Scotland, Wales and north-east and north-west England, encourages high standards in urban design and the protection and improvement of the environment.

Tree Preservation

The local planning authorities have power to protect trees and woodlands in the interest of amenity by means of tree preservation orders. When granting planning permission for development, a local planning authority must, where appropriate, impose conditions to secure the preservation or planting of trees. Landowners generally must replace trees which die or are removed or destroyed in contravention of a preservation order.

Green Belts

In order to restrict the further sprawl of large built-up areas, to prevent neighbouring towns merging into one another, or to preserve the special character of a town and the amenities of the countryside, 'green belts' (areas where it is intended that the land should be left open and free from further building development and where people can seek recreation) have been established on the fringes of certain urban areas. Much of London's green belt, for example, is agricultural land or woodland, some of which is used for recreation. Some 1·9 million hectares (4·7 million acres) of land have been designated as green belt in Great Britain.

The Coast

The maritime local planning authorities are responsible for planning land use at the coast providing, for example, recreational facilities and amenities for holidaymakers and local residents; at the same time they attempt to safeguard and enhance the coast's natural attractions and preserve areas of scientific interest. The protection of the coastline against erosion is administered centrally by the Ministry of Agriculture, Fisheries and Food, the Welsh Office and the Scottish Office.

A comprehensive study of the coastline of England and Wales, undertaken by the Countryside Commission (see p 195) in 1966–70, recommended that certain stretches of undeveloped coast of particular scenic beauty should be treated as heritage coast. Jointly with local authorities, the Commission has defined 37 of these coasts so far, protecting nearly 1,200 km (750 miles).

In 1965 the National Trust launched its Enterprise Neptune campaign to raise funds for the nation to acquire stretches of coastline of great natural beauty and recreational value. More than £7 million has been raised so far and as a result the Trust has under its protection 724 km (450 miles) of coastline in England and Wales. Under a campaign launched in 1985 the Trust is raising funds to acquire a similar length considered at risk. Some 128 km (80 miles) of coast in Scotland are protected by conservation agreements with the National Trust for

Scotland. In Northern Ireland 66 km (41 miles) of coast and coastal path have been acquired by the National Trust.

In exceptional cases economic arguments override conservation; development associated with North Sea oil and gas is occurring on remote and unspoiled coastal areas in Scotland, for instance, but planning guidelines drawn up by the Scottish Development Department aim to ensure that oil-related activities are sited so as to make the best use of existing labour and infrastructure and to minimise the effect on the coastline. Provision has also been made for funds to be set aside for the restoration of sites once there is no further need for them.

Countryside Commissions

Two Countryside Commissions (one for England and Wales, the other for Scotland) are responsible for encouraging and promoting measures to conserve and enhance the natural beauty and amenity of the countryside and for encouraging the development of facilities for open-air recreation in the countryside. These include the provision by local authorities (sometimes in association with other bodies) and private individuals of country parks and picnic sites often within easy reach of towns; the provision or improvement of recreational paths; the encouragement of amenity tree-planting schemes; and the increased use of reservoirs, canals and other waterways for bathing, sailing and other activities. Some 200 country parks and 240 picnic sites have been recognised in England and Wales by the Countryside Commission. In Scotland 33 country parks are recognised and a large number of local authority and private sector schemes for the provision of a variety of countryside facilities have been approved for grant aid. The Commissions undertake research projects and experimental schemes, working in consultation with local authorities and such bodies as the Nature Conservancy Council (see p 196) and the Sports Councils. The Commissions give financial assistance to public, private and voluntary bodies and individuals carrying out countryside recreation and amenity projects, and landscape conservation projects.

National Parks, Areas of Outstanding Natural Beauty and National Scenic Areas

The Countryside Commission (for England and Wales) is empowered to designate, for confirmation by the appropriate minister, national parks and 'areas of outstanding natural beauty'; to define heritage coasts in conjunction with local authorities (see p 194); and to make proposals for the creation of long-distance footpaths and bridleways. Ten national parks have been established, covering 13,600 sq km (5,250 sq miles), or 9 per cent of the area of England and Wales. Some 36 areas of outstanding natural beauty have been designated and confirmed, covering 17,000 sq km (6,600 sq miles).

The land in these designated areas generally remains privately owned, but agreements or orders to secure additional public access may be made by local authorities. Steps are taken to preserve and enhance the landscape's natural beauty by high standards of development control, and by positive measures, for which grants are available, such as tree planting and the removal of eyesores. In the national parks other measures for the benefit of the public include the provision of car parks, camping and caravan areas, and information centres. All national parks and some other designated areas have warden services. Most local authority expenditure on national parks is met by government grants.

In Northern Ireland the Ulster Countryside Committee advises the Department of the Environment on the preservation of amenities and the designation of areas of outstanding natural beauty. Eight areas of outstanding natural beauty have been designated, covering 259,500 hectares (641,000 acres), and seven areas are being managed as country parks and one as a regional park.

In Scotland there are no national parks as such, but there are 40 'national scenic areas', covering more than 1 million hectares (2·5 million acres), or 13 per cent of the country, where certain kinds of development are subject to consultation with the Countryside Commission for Scotland, and in the event of a disagreement, with the Secretary of State for Scotland. More than 98 per cent of the land in Scotland is designated countryside within which the Commission may provide grants for a wide range of countryside projects.

There are seven forest parks in Great Britain, covering some 243,000 hectares (600,000 acres) and administered by the Forestry Commission, and nine in Northern Ireland administered by the Forest Service of the Department of Agriculture. Camping and other recreational facilities are provided.

Many voluntary organisations are concerned to preserve the amenities of the countryside; they include the Councils for the Protection of Rural England and of Rural Wales, the Association for the Protection of Rural Scotland and the Ulster Society for the Preservation of the Countryside.

Local Footpaths and Open Country

County councils in England and Wales are required to prepare and keep under review definitive maps showing public rights of way; they are also responsible for keeping rights of way free from obstruction, and signposted. If a path is not shown on the map, a private citizen may claim that it is a public right of way if it has been regarded as such and used without hindrance for at least 20 years. Public footpaths are maintained by local authorities, which also supervise landowners' duties to repair stiles and gates. Local authorities in Great Britain can create paths, close existing paths no longer needed for public use and divert paths to meet the needs of either the public or landowners. Local planning authorities can also convert minor roads into footpaths or bridleways to improve the amenities of their area. There are 14 approved long-distance footpaths and bridleways in England and Wales covering some 2,700 km (1,685 miles) and three approved long-distance routes in Scotland covering some 580 km (360 miles). Voluntary organisations concerned with footpaths include the Open Spaces Society, the Scottish Rights of Way Society and the Ramblers Association.

There is no automatic right of public access to open country, although many landowners permit more or less free access. Local planning authorities can secure access by means of agreements with landowners; if agreements cannot be obtained, authorities may acquire land or make orders for public access. Similar powers cover Scotland and Northern Ireland.

Common land, a large proportion of which is open to the public, totals an estimated 600,000 hectares (1·5 million acres) in England and Wales. (There is no common land in Scotland or Northern Ireland.) This land is usually privately owned, but people other than the owner may have various rights on or over it, for example, of pasture for farm animals. Commons are protected by law and cannot be built on or enclosed without the consent of the Secretaries of State for the Environment or Wales.

Nature Conservation

The official body responsible for nature conservation in Great Britain is the Nature Conservancy Council, which has the functions of establishing, maintaining and managing nature reserves, advising the Government, providing general information and advice, and commissioning or supporting research. There are 214 national nature reserves covering some 155,420 hectares (384,040 acres). Some 5,000 sites of special scientific interest have been notified for their flora, fauna or geological or physiographical features.

The Forestry Commission has 340 sites of special scientific interest on its land (covering 70,000 hectares [173,000 acres]) on which nature conservation is a primary objective of management. Local authorities have declared about 130 local nature reserves. Voluntary nature conservation trusts and the Royal Society for the Protection of Birds play an important part in protecting wildlife, having established between them some 1,770 reserves. The trusts are affiliated to a parent organisation, the Royal Society for Nature Conservation. The Royal Society for the Protection of Birds, with over 413,000 members and 80,000 young ornithologists, is the largest voluntary wildlife conservation body in Europe.

In Northern Ireland the Committee for Nature Conservation advises the Department of the Environment for Northern Ireland on nature conservation matters including the establishment and management of terrestrial and marine nature reserves and the declaration of areas of special scientific interest.

The Wildlife and Countryside Act 1981 extended the list of protected species, restricted the introduction into the countryside of animals or plants not normally found in the wild and afforded greater protection for areas of special scientific interest and other important habitats. In Northern Ireland two orders, which became operative in 1985, have brought legislation into line with the rest of Britain on species and habitat protection.

Other conservation measures promoted by the Government have included a ban (in conjunction with other European Community countries) on the import of whale products and certain seal pup products, a system of licensing zoos to ensure that captive animals are kept in suitable conditions, and stricter controls for the protection of wild birds. It is proposed to designate certain areas, of importance for their landscape, historic and habitat value, 'environmentally sensitive areas' as a result of a change in European Community regulations allowing governments to make special payments to farmers to continue their traditional farming methods for the sake of preserving the countryside and its wildlife.

Land Reclamation and Use

Derelict land is often concentrated in places associated with nineteenth-century industrial development, but the restructuring of particular industries over the past decade or so is continuing to add significantly to this problem in certain areas. Dereliction can take various forms and can include mineral waste tips, old mineral workings, former industrial sites such as steelworks, disused railways and docks, and contaminated sites.

In England, central government grants are available under the Derelict Land Act 1982 to local authorities and to other public bodies, to the private sector and to nationalised industries for the reclamation of derelict land in order to bring it into beneficial use or to improve its appearance. The expenditure provision for the derelict land reclamation programme in 1986–87 is £78·4 million. The main priority is given to reclamation schemes in urban, particularly inner city, areas that lead to development by the private sector for industry, commerce and especially housing. Between 1 April 1979 and 31 March 1985 some 8,377 hectares (20,700 acres) of derelict land were reclaimed in England with the aid of some £400 million of derelict land grant.

In Scotland and Wales responsibility for derelict land reclamation rests with the respective development agencies, which may acquire and reclaim land, employ local authorities as their agents (in Scotland) or make grants to local authorities for the purpose (in Wales). In Northern Ireland grants may be paid to landowners who restore or improve derelict sites.

To prevent new dereliction, planning controls require that when permission is given for mineral working various measures must be taken to minimise the disturbance caused by the work and to secure whatever restoration is practicable, either progressively or when working ceases. The use of land for disposal of waste materials is also subject to conditions restricting the height of waste tips or requiring treatment of waste on completion of workings.

In Wales, land use is additionally encouraged by the Land Authority for Wales, a statutory body with powers to make land available for development in circumstances where the private sector would find this difficult or impossible.

Land Registers   In England the Government has instituted, and made available for inspection, registers of under-used land held by local authorities, nationalised industries and other public bodies; some 60,000 hectares (148,000 acres) have been registered. Of this, some 15,000 hectares (38,000 acres) have been deregistered mainly because the land has been sold to the private sector or brought into use. There is power to direct a public body to dispose of registered land; some 25 such directions had been issued by January 1986. Registers are also published for certain areas of Wales.

Environmental Improvement Scheme   In July 1986 the Government launched a special initiative to encourage a wide range of local environmental improvement work to be undertaken both by volunteers and by the Manpower Services Commission Community Programme teams. The initiative, which is being co-ordinated by a new organisation called UK 2000 bringing together representatives of the participating organisations and a number of independent members, aims to improve the natural and built environment and people's enjoyment of it, and will also create new jobs and provide work and training for the participants. Voluntary organisations will promote programmes of work and will assist in the setting up of local projects such as creating parks, footpaths and other areas of greenery in cities, conserving the industrial heritage and the natural environment, tackling litter problems and providing tourist information and facilities.

Control of Pollution

Government measures to control environmental pollution are long established, and are complementary to the planning system and the various measures to conserve amenities and the country's heritage.

The Control of Pollution Act 1974, which applies to England, Scotland and Wales, sets out a wide range of powers and duties for local and water authorities, including control over wastes, air and water pollution and noise, and contains important provisions on the release of information to the public on environmental conditions. In particular, it introduced a new system for the comprehensive planning of waste disposal operations so as to ensure that disposal is carried out to satisfactory standards and that where practicable waste materials are recovered and recycled. The Act also increased the penalties for a large number of pollution offences. The provisions relating to noise and air pollution are fully in force, as are a substantial number of those relating to waste on land. Similar legislation applies in Northern Ireland.

Administration   Executive responsibility for pollution control rests in general with local and water authorities, although certain registered industrial processes are controlled by the Industrial Air Pollution Inspectorate (of the Health and Safety Executive). Local authorities are responsible for matters such as collection and disposal of domestic wastes; control of air pollution from domestic and certain non-registered industrial premises; and noise abatement measures. Sewerage and sewage treatment and disposal are the responsibilities of regional water authorities in England and Wales, of local authorities in Scotland and of the Department of the Environment in Northern Ireland. The regional water authorities in England, the Welsh Water Authority, the river purification boards and islands councils in Scotland and the Department of the Environment for Northern Ireland are responsible for control of water pollution.

An independent standing Royal Commission on Environmental Pollution advises the Government on national and international matters concerning the pollution of the environment, on the adequacy of research and on the future possibilities of danger to the environment. It has so far produced 11 reports covering a wide range of topics.

Central government is principally concerned with formulating policy, exercising general budgetary control, promoting the necessary legislation, and advising pollution control authorities on its implementation. The Secretary of State for the Environment has general responsibility for co-ordinating the work of the Government on environmental protection and in this is assisted by a Central Directorate of Environmental Protection within the Department. In Scotland, Wales and Northern Ireland the respective Secretaries of State are responsible for pollution control co-ordination in their countries. They are assisted by the Scottish Development Department, the Water and Environmental Protection Division of the Welsh Office, and the Department of the Environment for Northern Ireland respectively. From 1 April 1987 the Industrial Air Pollution Inspectorate, the Radiochemical Inspectorate and, in the Department of the Environment and the Welsh Office, the Hazardous Waste Inspectorate (see below), will be amalgamated in a single unified inspectorate for England and Wales to be known as Her Majesty's Inspectorate of Pollution.

The Land

The main risks of land pollution lie in the indiscriminate dumping of waste materials on land, careless disposal of pesticides and chemicals and the deposition of materials from the atmosphere and from flood-water. The Control of Pollution Act places a duty on waste disposal authorities to ensure that there are adequate arrangements to dispose of controlled wastes. It requires them to draw up and revise periodically a waste disposal plan and establishes a licensing system for most waste disposal sites, treatment plants and storage facilities receiving controlled wastes. In addition, it provides for a more intensive control system for certain especially hazardous or difficult wastes. Hazardous waste inspectorates have been set up in the Department of the Environment, the Welsh Office and the Scottish Development Department to advise local authorities on how to improve their control of waste management and to work towards environmentally acceptable standards for dealing with hazardous wastes.

It is a criminal offence to leave litter in any public place in the open air or to dump rubbish except in designated places. To help to counteract the problem of litter, also an aspect of the UK 2000 scheme (see p 198), financial support is given to the Keep Britain Tidy Group, which provides a comprehensive litter abatement programme in collaboration with local authorities.

Recycling and Materials Reclamation

The Government encourages the reclamation and recycling of waste materials wherever this is practicable and economic in order to reduce imports and waste disposal costs and to help to conserve natural resources. Industry already makes considerable use of reclaimed waste material such as metals, paper and textiles. Local authorities collect about 200,000 tonnes of waste paper and about 100,000 tonnes of ferrous scrap annually. In an increasing number of areas there are 'bottle banks' and 'can banks' where the public can deposit used glass and metal containers respectively. Voluntary organisations also arrange collections of waste material. Waste disposal authorities have powers under the Control of Pollution Act to take full account of opportunities for waste reclamation and have a duty when drawing up their waste disposal plans to include information on disposal methods to be used, including reclamation.

Water Pollution

There has been a steady and significant improvement in water quality: the level of pollution in the tidal Thames, for example, has been reduced to a quarter of the 1950s' level and over 100 different kinds of fish have been identified there since 1964. A major scheme has been launched to clean up the Mersey, the largest British estuary still suffering from severe pollution. Discharges of polluting matter into rivers and estuaries have been controlled for many years and recently powers have been extended to provide full control over discharges into underground and coastal waters. Information on all aspects of water pollution is publicly available on registers maintained by the individual water authorities. More than 95 per cent of the population is provided with main drainage, and public authority sewage treatment works serve over four-fifths of the population—a very high proportion by international standards.

Marine Pollution

Control of marine pollution from ships is based largely on international conventions drawn up under the auspices of the International Maritime Organisation, a United Nations agency with headquarters in London, and implemented for British ships by domestic legislation. The Merchant Shipping (Prevention of Oil Pollution) Regulations 1983 and the Prevention of Oil Pollution Act 1986 make it an offence for ships of any nationality to discharge oil or oily mixtures into British territorial waters and for British registered ships to make similar discharges anywhere into the sea, except in accordance with the regulations.

To deal with spillages of oil or chemicals at sea, which may cause coastal pollution or threaten wildlife, the Department of Transport has a Marine Pollution Control Unit which can call also upon the resources of the Marine Survey and Coastguard services. The main treatment method is to spray dispersant from aircraft or surface vessels, and emergency cargo transfer equipment is available to remove oil from a damaged tanker. Local authorities have the primary role in dealing with oil and chemical pollution of beaches and inshore waters, and receive government advice and support. In a major incident the Marine Pollution Control Unit would co-ordinate and lead the onshore response.

The development of the offshore oil industry has brought an increased risk of oil pollution in the North Sea. Offshore operators must ensure that oil does not escape into the sea and are required to have contingency plans for dealing with oil spilled accidentally. Discharges containing oil are controlled under the Prevention of Oil Pollution Act 1971. Discharges of chemicals are controlled and monitored by a non-statutory Chemical Notification Scheme, administered by the Department of Energy in consultation with fisheries departments.

The Food and Environment Protection Act 1985 (which superseded the Dumping at Sea Act 1974) tightened the controls over dumping at sea, the most significant change being the introduction of specific controls on marine incineration. Under the Act a licence has to be obtained for the permanent deposit of any substance or article into tidal waters and the sea. Dumping at sea is permitted on the basis of the scientific criteria set out in the annexes to the Oslo Convention (International Convention for the Prevention of Marine Pollution by Dumping from Ships and Aircraft 1972) and the London Convention on the Prevention of Marine Pollution by Dumping Wastes and Other Matter 1972.

Clean Air

Responsibility for clean air rests primarily with local authorities. Under the provisions of the Clean Air Acts 1956 and 1968 they may declare 'smoke control areas' within which the emission of smoke from chimneys constitutes an offence. About two-thirds of the premises in conurbations are now covered by smoke control orders. Emissions from most industrial premises are also subject to the control of local authorities under the Clean Air Acts and the Public Health Acts. The emission of dark smoke from any trade or industrial premises or from the chimney of any building is in general prohibited, and new furnaces must be capable as far as practicable of smokeless operation. The height of the chimney serving a new furnace must generally be approved by the local authority, and approved grit and dust arrestment plant has to be installed. Regulations prescribe specific limits to the quantities of grit and dust which may be emitted from certain furnaces. Industrial premises that have the greatest potential for giving rise to noxious or offensive emissions are, in England and Wales, under the control of the Industrial Air Pollution Inspectorate of the Health and Safety Executive. In Scotland this function is discharged by the Industrial Pollution Inspectorate. The Inspectorates require the best practicable means to be used to prevent emissions or render them harmless. Similar legislation and controls apply in Northern Ireland.

Strict controls are in force on emissions from motor vehicles, and Britain has played a constructive role in European Community discussions on tighter limits. The maximum permitted lead content of petrol in Britain was reduced to 0·15 grammes per litre on 31 December 1985. The European Community has adopted a directive which requires the introduction of unleaded petrol throughout the Community by October 1989. The first unleaded petrol in Britain went on sale at selected service stations in June 1986.

Considerable progress has been made towards the achievement of cleaner air and a better environment, especially in the last 30 years or so. Total emissions of smoke in the air have fallen by about 85 per cent since 1960. The domestic smoke control programme has been particularly important in achieving this result. London no longer has the dense smoke-laden 'smogs' of the 1950s and in central London winter sunshine has increased by about 50 per cent since 1958. Similar improvement has been achieved in other cities including Glasgow and Sheffield. National sulphur dioxide emissions have fallen by nearly 40 per cent since 1970. The Government intends to achieve further reductions of 30 per cent from the 1980 levels of emissions of both sulphur dioxide and nitrogen oxides by the end of the 1990s.

Britain has become increasingly involved in international air pollution issues such as acid rain, and with the possible implications of growing concentrations of carbon dioxide in the atmosphere. While the causes of acid rain are becoming more clearly understood, there are still uncertainties about the likely effectiveness of remedial strategies. To help resolve these uncertainties, Britain is supporting a programme of research, substantially expanded in 1986, on air pollutants, their effects and the technology for their control, and is also participating in international research programmes and monitoring schemes.

Noise

The Control of Pollution Act 1974 (and similar legislation in Northern Ireland) requires local authorities to inspect their areas for noise nuisance and gives them the power to deal with it. It also enables them to designate 'noise abatement zones' within which registered levels of noise from classified premises may not be increased without their permission. The Act contains specific provisions to control noise from construction and demolition sites. It also contains provisions enabling individuals to take action against noise amounting to a nuisance.

Transport is one of the main offenders in noise pollution, and control measures are aimed at reducing noise at source, through requirements limiting the noise that aircraft and motor vehicles may make, and at protecting people from its effects. The Road Vehicles (Construction and Use) Regulations 1986 set out the permissible noise levels for various classes of vehicles when new and when in use. More stringent limits will begin to take effect for new vehicles in 1988.

Under the Land Compensation Act 1973 and similar legislation in Scotland, compensation is payable for loss in property values caused by physical factors including noise arising from the use of new or improved public works such as roads and airports. Regulations made under the Acts also enable highway authorities to carry out or make grants for insulation of homes subject to specified levels of increased noise caused by new or improved roads. Noise insulation may also be provided where construction work for new roads is likely to seriously affect nearby homes.

Noise emission levels of almost all aircraft on the United Kingdom Register of Civil Aircraft are regulated in accordance with standards agreed by the International Civil Aviation Organisation. All subsonic jets on the United Kingdom Register now have to meet the noise certification criteria, while jets on overseas registers entering Britain must meet these criteria by 1 January 1988. Various operational restrictions have been introduced to reduce noise disturbance further, and people living in the worst affected areas round a number of airports may be eligible for noise insulation grants.

Radioactivity

Radiation resulting from industrial and other processes represents only a small fraction of that to which the population is exposed from the natural environment. Nevertheless, that fraction is subject to stringent control because of possible effects on health or longer-term genetic effects. Under the Radioactive Substances Act 1960 users of radioactive materials other than those subject to licence under the Nuclear Installations Act 1965 must be registered by the appropriate department, and authorisation is also required for the disposal of radioactive waste. The Health and Safety Executive, through its Nuclear Installations Inspectorate, is the authority concerned with the granting of nuclear site licences for commercial nuclear installations. No installation may be constructed or operated without a licence granted by the Executive. The National Radiological Protection Board established under the Radiological Protection Act 1970 provides an authoritative point of reference on radiological protection.

Radioactive Waste Disposal

Radioactive wastes vary widely in nature and level of activity, and the practices followed reflect this variation. Some wastes are dispersed safely in the environment. The Nuclear Industry Radioactive Waste Executive is responsible for developing and operating disposal facilities for solid wastes with a low or intermediate level of activity; four possible sites had been identified by early 1986 and exploratory geological investigations are being carried out to confirm their suitability for development as disposal facilities only for low-level radioactive wastes. A study by independent consultants, commissioned by the Department of the Environment, into the best practicable environmental options for the management of radioactive waste, was completed in early 1986. It examined all the main options for the disposal and storage of low-level and intermediate-level wastes in the light of a range of assumptions about future growth in nuclear power and the level of reprocessing, and demonstrated that for every type of such waste, several storage and disposal options are practical and safe. Research is also being carried out, in collaboration with other countries, into disposal of high-level wastes, but these will first be stored in vitrified form for at least 50 years.

9 Religion

Everyone in Britain has the right of religious freedom (in teaching, worship and observance) without interference from the community or the State. Churches and religious societies may own property, conduct schools, and propagate their beliefs in speech and writing. There is no religious or denominational bar to the holding of public office.

There are two established churches, that is, churches legally recognised as official churches of the State: in England the (Anglican) Church of England, and in Scotland the (Presbyterian) Church of Scotland. Clergy of the established churches work in services administered by the State, such as the armed forces, national hospitals and prisons, and are paid a salary by the State. Clergy of other denominations are also appointed. Voluntary schools provided by religious denominations may be wholly or partly maintained from public funds. The churches' involvement in broader social issues and the practical help they give to groups of many kinds—from young people to the bereaved and homeless—was highlighted in the Church of England report *Faith in the City: A Call for Action by Church and Nation*, published in 1985, which made recommendations for alleviating the problems of the inner cities and other areas of social deprivation.

There is no precise or uniform information about the number of church adherents since no inquiries are normally made about religious beliefs in censuses or other official returns, and each church adopts its own criteria in counting its members. Membership figures in this chapter are therefore approximate.

About one-sixth of the adult population in Britain are members of a Christian church and there are considerable regional variations in church membership: England has the lowest membership with 13 per cent, Wales has 23 per cent, Scotland 37 per cent, and Northern Ireland the highest with 80 per cent.

There has been a decline in recent years in both the number of full-time ministers and the recorded adult membership of the larger Christian denominations. This has been accompanied by a significant growth among small break-away, independent, or Pentecostal churches and new religious movements.

The Church of England

The Church of England's relationship with the State is one of mutual obligation—privileges accorded to the Church balanced by certain duties which it must fulfil. The Sovereign must always be a member of the Church, and promises to uphold it; Church of England archbishops, bishops and deans are appointed by the Sovereign on the advice of the Prime Minister; all clergy take an oath of allegiance to the Crown. The Church can regulate its own worship. The two archbishops (of Canterbury and York), the bishops of London, Durham and Winchester, and 21 other bishops (according to their seniority as diocesan bishops) sit in the House of Lords. Clergy of the Church (together with those of the Church of Scotland, the Church of Ireland and the Roman Catholic Church) are not allowed to sit in the House of Commons.

The Church has two provinces: Canterbury, comprising 30 dioceses (including the Diocese of Europe), and York, with 14 dioceses. The Archbishop of Canterbury is 'Primate of All England', and the Archbishop of York 'Primate of England'. The dioceses are divided into 13,400 parishes. In 1984 it was estimated that, in the two provinces (excluding the Diocese of Europe), some

235,000 people were baptised into the Church; of these 198,000 were under one year old (33 per cent of live births). In the same year there were 79,600 confirmations. Attendances at services on a normal Sunday are around 1·2 million. Many people who rarely, if ever, attend services, nevertheless regard themselves as belonging to the Church of England (amounting perhaps to some 60 per cent of the population).

The central governing body, the General Synod, has both spiritual authority and legislative and administrative powers; and bishops, clergy and lay members are involved in decisions. Certain important issues must be referred for the approval of the dioceses before being decided by the Synod. Lay members are associated with church government in the parishes through the ancient office of churchwarden and the modern parochial church councils.

The General Synod is the centre of an administrative system dealing with such matters as education, mission, inter-church relations, social questions, recruitment and training for the ministry, church work at home and overseas and the care of church buildings, particularly those of historical and architectural interest. It is also concerned with church schools (which are maintained from public funds) and colleges of education, theological colleges, and centres for training women in pastoral work. At present, men only are admitted to the priesthood, but in 1984 the General Synod voted in favour of legislation being prepared to enable women to be ordained priests; final decisions on the matter, however, are not expected to be taken for some years.

The Church has its own courts whose jurisdiction today extends only to church property and matters of ecclesiastical discipline.

Church finance is administered locally by the parishes and the dioceses, with contributions to a central fund for the maintenance of central services, including capital expenditure on training and theological colleges and grants for training candidates for ordination. The State makes no direct financial contribution to church expenses. The Church's endowment income is mainly administered by the Church Commissioners, the body largely responsible for the payment of clergy stipends and pensions.

The Anglican Communion

The Anglican Communion comprises 28 autonomous provinces in Britain and overseas and three regional councils overseas with a total membership of about 70 million. In the British Isles, there are four provinces: the Church of England (established), the Church in Wales, the Scottish Episcopal Church in Scotland, and the Church of Ireland.

Every ten years the Lambeth Conference meets for unofficial consultation among all Anglican bishops (the next Conference will be held in Canterbury in 1988). Presided over by the Archbishop of Canterbury, the Conference has no executive authority, but enjoys great prestige, and its findings on doctrine, discipline, relations with other communions, and attitudes to political and social questions are widely studied. The Anglican Consultative Council (an assembly of laymen and clergy as well as bishops) meets every two or three years and is designed to provide consultations within the Anglican Communion and to serve as an instrument of common action. The Council will meet in Singapore in 1987.

The Church of Scotland

The Church of Scotland has a presbyterian form of government, that is, government by elders, all (including ministers) of equal rank. Its status as the national church derives from the Treaty of Union 1707, and the Church of Scotland Act 1921 which confirmed its complete freedom in all spiritual matters. It appoints its own officers, and its decisions on questions of doctrine and discipline are not subject to parliamentary discussion or modification.

Both men and women are admitted to the ministry and each of 1,758 churches is governed locally by the Kirk Session, consisting of the minister and the elected elders of the Church; above the Kirk Session is the Court of the Presbytery, then the Court of the Synod, and finally the General Assembly, consisting of elected ministers and elders, which meets annually under the presidency of an elected moderator who serves for one year. The Sovereign is represented at the General Assembly by the Lord High Commissioner. The adult communicant membership of the Church of Scotland is over 870,500.

The Free Churches

The expression 'Free Churches' is commonly used to describe those Protestant churches in Britain which, unlike the Church of England and the Church of Scotland, are not established. In the course of history they have developed their own convictions in church order and worship. All the major Free Churches—Methodist, Baptist, United Reformed and Salvation Army—admit both men and women to the ministry.

The Methodist Church, the largest of the Free Churches with nearly 500,000 adult full members, originated in the eighteenth century following the evangelical revival under John Wesley, and is based on a 1932 union of most of the separate Methodist Churches. The Methodist Churches which did not join the union include the Independent Methodists (4,100 members) and the Wesleyan Reform Union (with some 3,300 members). The Methodist Church in Ireland has over 21,000 members in Northern Ireland.

The Baptists are nearly all grouped in associations of churches, most of which belong to the Baptist Union of Great Britain and Ireland (formed in 1813), with a total membership of about 168,300. In addition, there are separate Baptist Unions for Scotland, Wales and Ireland and other Baptist Churches.

The United Reformed Church, with some 136,000 members, was formed in 1972 when the Congregational Church in England and Wales (the oldest community of dissenters in Britain) and the Presbyterian Church of England merged—the first transdenominational union of churches in Britain since the Reformation in the sixteenth century. In 1981 there was a further union with the Re-formed Association of the Churches of Christ.

Among the other Free Churches are the Presbyterian Church in Ireland (with some 132,800 regular communicants in Ireland); the Presbyterian (or Calvinistic Methodist) Church of Wales, which arose from the revivalist movement led in 1735 by Howell Harris; the Union of Welsh Independents; the Free Church of Scotland; the United Free Church of Scotland; the Free Presbyterian Church of Scotland; the Reformed Presbyterian Church of Scotland; the Reformed Presbyterian Church of Ireland; and the Non-Subscribing Presbyterian Church of Ireland.

Other Protestant denominations include: the Unitarian and Free Christian Churches; the Churches of Christ (known also in the United States as Disciples of Christ), which have been an organised community in Britain since the early nineteenth century; the British Province of the Moravian Church, which is an international missionary church; the Free Church of England (or Reformed Episcopal Church), which was formed in 1844 as a direct result of the Oxford Movement; and the Congregational Federation, formed from Congregational Churches which did not enter the United Reformed Church. There are also the Pentecostalists, who are increasing in numbers. Their two main bodies operating in Britain are the Assemblies of God and the Elim Pentecostal Church, many of whose members are of West Indian origin. There are also a growing number of black-led churches.

The Religious Society of Friends (Quakers), with about 17,500 adult members in Britain and 450 places of worship, came into being in the middle of the seventeenth century under the leadership of George Fox. Silent worship is central to its life as a religious organisation and Friends work for peace and the relief of suffering in many parts of the world.

The Salvation Army, founded in Britain in 1865, has since spread to 88 other countries. Within Britain there are 55,000 active members operating from nearly 1,000 centres of worship. The Salvation Army's distinctive ministry of Christian evangelism and practical care is also expressed through the work of 170 social service centres, ranging from hostels for the homeless to homes for the elderly, for abused children and for teenagers on probation, and recreational centres for Service personnel.

A recent development in Christian worship has been the house church movement, which began in the early 1970s and now has an estimated membership of over 180,000. Each house church has an average of 100 members, the majority of whom are former members of various Protestant denominations; groups of between 15 and 20 members hold services and prayer meetings in private houses, with the position of chairman being taken in rotation. House churches receive money from their members to enable them to support their leaders and carry out missionary and social work.

There are also a number of other religious organisations in Britain all of which were founded in the United States in the last century. These include the Jehovah's Witnesses, the Church of Jesus Christ of Latter-Day Saints (the Mormon Church), the Christian Scientists and the Spiritualists.

The Roman Catholic Church

The Roman Catholic hierarchy in England and Wales, which became temporarily extinct during the sixteenth century, was restored in 1850; the Scottish hierarchy became extinct in the early seventeenth century and was restored in 1878. There are now seven Roman Catholic provinces in Great Britain, each under an archbishop, 29 episcopal dioceses (21 in England and Wales, eight in Scotland), and over 3,000 parishes. In Northern Ireland, there are six dioceses, some with territory partly in the Irish Republic. It is estimated that there are some 5·7 million adherents to the Roman Catholic faith in Britain. Men only are admitted to the priesthood. In 1982 Pope John Paul II paid a pastoral visit to Britain, the first by a reigning pontiff.

The Roman Catholic Church attaches great importance to the education of its children and requires its members to try to bring up their children in the Catholic faith. A number of schools for Catholic children are staffed by members of the religious orders (to the extent of one teacher in 20). These orders also undertake other social work such as nursing, child care, and the conduct of homes for old people. The great majority of Catholic schools are maintained out of public funds and new schools may be established with government grants.

Jewry

Jews first settled in England at the time of the Norman Conquest, but the present community in Britain dates from 1656, having been founded by those of Spanish and Portuguese origin (known as Sephardim). Later and more numerous settlers were of German and eastern European origin, known as Ashkenazim. The present community, numbering about 385,000, is the second largest in Europe.

The community is, broadly speaking, divided into two groups. About 80 per cent of the majority Ashkenazi Jews are Orthodox and most acknowledge the jurisdiction of the Chief Rabbi, with the Sephardi Orthodox element following their own spiritual head (the Haham). The Reform movement which was founded in 1840 and the Liberal and Progressive movement which followed in 1901 account for the remaining 20 per cent.

Jewish congregations in Britain number about 350. Jewish denominational schools (some of them supported by public funds) are attended by about one in three Jewish children. There are a number of charitable and welfare agencies caring for the aged and handicapped.

The officially recognised representative body is the Board of Deputies of British Jews.

Other Religious Communities

Christian communities of foreign origin, including the Orthodox, Lutheran and Reformed Churches of various European countries, together with the Armenian Church, have established their own centres of worship, particularly in London. Britain has a long tradition of religious tolerance, a feature which has been much in evidence during the past 30 years with the acceptance of a wide variety of religious beliefs and traditions brought in by substantial numbers of immigrants of different nationalities. There are now large and growing communities of Muslims, Hindus and Sikhs, and arrangements have been made in places of work to allow the members of non-Christian religions to follow their religious observances.

Britain's Muslim population is estimated at around 1·5 million, the largest number of whom originate from Pakistan and Bangladesh, with sizeable groups from India, Cyprus, the Arab world, Malaysia and parts of Africa. There is also a growing community of British-born Muslims, mainly the children of immigrant parents, but including an increasing number of converts to Islam. The Islamic Cultural Centre (and London Central Mosque) on the edge of Regent's Park is the most important Muslim institution in the Western world, and there are over 1,000 mosques and prayer centres throughout Britain.

There are an estimated 175,000 members of the Sikh religion and over 140,000 followers of Hinduism in Britain. Both groups originate from India and each has 150 or more temples throughout the country. The Hindu Centre in London provides religious and social services as well as meeting the cultural needs of the Indian community.

There are well over 100 Buddhist groups and centres and at least seven monasteries and a number of temples. All schools of Buddhism are represented. The Buddhist Society, with its headquarters in London, publicises the principles of Buddhism and encourages their study and practice; it adheres to no one school of Buddhism.

Co-operation among the Churches

The British Council of Churches, with representatives or observers from all the main Christian churches in the British Isles, facilitates common action and seeks to further Christian unity. It works through five divisions: Christian Aid (which has a separate constitution); Conference for World Mission; Ecumenical Affairs; Community Affairs; and International Affairs.

The Free Church Federal Council (which has a concordat with the British Council of Churches) comprises most of the Free Churches of England and Wales. It promotes unity and joint action among the Free Churches and is a channel for communication with central and local government.

Inter-church conversations about the doctrinal and practical issues involved in the search for unity now take place through international as well as national bodies. The Roman Catholic and Orthodox Churches are represented on some of these as well as the Anglican and some of the Free Churches.

The Anglican and the main Free Churches also participate in the World Council of Churches (of which the British Council of Churches is an associated national council). This links together some 300 churches in over 100 countries for co-operation and the study of common problems. The Council of Christians and Jews works for better understanding among members of the two religions and deals with problems in the social field. The British Council of Churches has also established a Committee for Relations with People of Other Faiths.

The Sharing of Church Buildings Act 1969 enables agreements to be made by two or more churches for the sharing of church buildings.

10 National Economy

In 1986 the British economy entered its sixth year of sustained growth from the low point of the recession in May 1981. This represented the longest upswing since 1945. Inflation has fallen, investment, exports and productivity have risen substantially and the current account of the balance of payments has remained in surplus. However, unemployment has continued to rise throughout the period although, since early 1983, the rate of increase has fallen and the number of people in work has risen.

ECONOMIC BACKGROUND

Britain has an open economy, in which international trade is a vital part of economic performance. In 1985 exports of goods and services accounted for about one-third of its gross domestic product (GDP), one of the highest shares in the major economies. The proportion has increased over the last two decades from about 20 per cent in the early 1960s. Similar rises have occurred in most other developed countries, reflecting the growing importance of international trade in an increasingly interdependent world economy.

The economy is primarily based on private enterprise, and government policy is aimed at encouraging the private sector, which accounts for three-quarters of GDP and a similar proportion of total employment.

The traditional economic strength of Britain, as a pioneer in the industrial revolution, has been manufacturing. However, the period since 1945 has seen a marked rise in living standards and, as in other major developed countries, the increase that has taken place in real disposable income has led to a faster growth of demand for services than for manufactures. An adjustment to the relative size of the manufacturing sector has also resulted from the growth of North Sea oil output. Services now account for nearly three-fifths of GDP and of employment, compared with just under half in 1950, while manufacturing accounts for about a quarter, compared with just over one-third in 1950.

Some 2·5 per cent of Britain's employed labour force is engaged in agriculture—a lower proportion than in any other major industrialised country. However, because of a high level of productivity, Britain is able to produce nearly two-thirds of its own food.

Britain's energy position has been transformed in the last decade. With the discovery and exploitation of oil and natural gas from the Continental Shelf under the North Sea, the country has become self-sufficient in energy in net terms. Together, the oil and gas sectors accounted for 5 to 6 per cent of GDP in 1985. Coal—traditionally the most important source of energy—still accounts for over a third of Britain's needs.

One of the world's largest exporters of visible goods, Britain accounts for about 5 per cent of the total. It is among the major exporters of aerospace products, electrical equipment, most types of machinery, chemicals and oil. It is also one of the world's largest importers of agricultural products, raw materials and semi-manufactures.

The broad historical pattern of Britain's overseas trade has been a deficit on visible trade offset by a surplus on transactions in invisibles. The significant contribution made by invisibles to the current account is partly a reflection of

Britain's position as a major financial centre. The banks, insurance under-writers and brokers, and other financial institutions of the City of London provide world-wide financial services, and the City contains perhaps the most comprehensive and advanced capital market in the world.

Economic Growth

The marked rise in living standards experienced since 1945 has been accompanied by the emergence of new industries and the renewal and improvement of much of the country's infrastructure. At the same time, in spite of short periods of rapid economic expansion, the rate of growth has been low in comparison with the rates in most other industrialised countries, averaging 2 to 3 per cent annually up to 1973 but only about 1 per cent from then until the recession of the early 1980s. Since then, however, the underlying rate of growth has been some 3 per cent a year. In 1985 Britain had the highest rate of growth among member countries of the European Community.

Inflation and Competitiveness

From the late 1960s until about 1980 high levels of inflation reduced Britain's competitiveness. Huge rises in the price of oil in 1973–74 and 1979 and substantial increases in the money supply and public spending were followed by upsurges in inflation; retail prices rose by 24 per cent in 1975 and by 18 per cent in 1980. Earnings also grew rapidly; in 1980 the underlying rate of increase was about 21 per cent. From 1981 inflation declined and, in the years 1983–85, remained at an annual rate of 5 to 6 per cent, falling to 2·4 per cent by July 1986. Over the same period earnings rose at an underlying rate of 7 to 8 per cent a year.

In the late 1970s competitiveness suffered from a much more rapid increase in unit labour costs than in most other industrialised countries, as well as a marked appreciation in sterling, which rose by 18 per cent between 1978 and 1980. Partly as a result of weakness in the world oil market, sterling then depreciated; between 1980 and 1984 the value fell by 18 per cent but the average level in 1985 was the same as in 1984. With a further decline in oil prices in late 1985 and early 1986, the fall in sterling was resumed; it depreciated by 4 per cent between the end of 1985 and the middle of 1986. Sterling depreciation, together with greater moderation in pay settlements and a substantial rise in productivity since the end of 1980 (see p 211), led to a considerable improvement in competitiveness; between early 1981 and late 1985 Britain's unit labour costs, adjusted for movements in the exchange rate, fell by one-quarter.

Industrial Production

In the decade to 1973 output of the manufacturing industries grew at a faster rate than the economy as a whole. After the oil price rises of 1973–74, however, and with increasing competition from overseas—from both developed and newly industrialising countries—manufacturing output fell sharply so that in 1975 it was 8 per cent lower than two years previously. Output then increased from this trough but, following another oil price rise and stagnation in the world economy, fell back in the period 1979 to 1981. It has since risen every year and is now growing at an underlying annual rate of about 3 per cent although it remains below the level of the mid-1970s. However, output of the production industries as a whole (manufacturing, energy and water) was at its highest ever in 1985. In that year energy output was more than twice the level of ten years earlier.

Investment

Fixed investment grew by about 5 per cent a year during the 1960s but between 1970 and 1983 it held steady apart from cyclical variations. Fixed investment was higher in 1984 and 1985, however, influenced by rising company profits and an acceleration in anticipation of the reductions in capital allowances announced in the 1984 Budget. Although, with a falling oil price, profits of oil companies declined in 1985, profits (net of stock appreciation) of non-oil industrial and commercial companies were 30 per cent higher than in 1984. A further influence may have been increased capacity utilisation as Britain recovered from recession since 1981. Over the period 1975 to 1985 there was an increase in the private sector's share of total investment (excluding transactions in existing dwellings and land) from 58 to 79 per cent. Over the same period the share of investment undertaken by the services sector increased from 40 to 49 per cent while that of manufacturing fell from 16 to 13 per cent.

Employment and Productivity

Britain has an employed labour force of some 24 million. The number of jobs in the economy is increasing; between early 1983 and late 1985 employment rose by over 700,000 while self-employment is at its highest level since 1921. There has also been a large growth in the working population; demographic factors have meant that the number of people reaching working age has exceeded that reaching retirement age, and there has also been a rise in the number of women seeking work. As a result, no corresponding fall in unemployment has occurred. As in other industrialised countries, this has proved an intractable problem since the early 1970s. From a level of 300,000 to 400,000 in the mid-1960s, unemployment rose to over 1 million in the late 1970s (representing around 5 to 6 per cent of all employees) and then increased again very sharply after 1979 to reach 3 million by the end of 1982. The rate of increase has since slowed; by July 1986 unemployment was 3·2 million, equal to 11·7 per cent of the working population.

Although unemployment remains high, other labour market indicators have improved. Overtime in manufacturing has risen and short-time working has fallen. The parallel to rising unemployment has been increasing productivity. Shedding of surplus labour has led to gains in efficiency; between 1980 and 1985 output per head rose by 14 per cent in the economy as a whole and by 27 per cent in manufacturing alone.

Overseas Sector

Britain's overseas trade performance fluctuated during the 1970s. In general, imports of food, energy, raw materials and manufactured goods were greater than visible exports, which were largely manufactured goods. This deficit on visible trade was wholly or partly offset by a surplus on invisibles, which cover earnings from services, together with interest, profits and dividends, and transfers.

In the years 1980 to 1982 Britain ran surpluses on visible trade. Since then, however, with the economy recovering from recession, imports—especially of manufactures—have risen more sharply than exports and the deficit on visible trade has reappeared. After a long period of deterioration in the balance of trade in manufactures there was a deficit in 1983—the first since 1945. The deficit continued in the following two years. Substantial net earnings on invisible trade, however, have kept the current account in surplus.

Membership of the European Community from 1973 has had a major impact on Britain's pattern of trade, increasing the proportion with other member countries and reducing the share of Commonwealth trade. Between 1972 and 1985 the proportion of Britain's exports of goods going to other member countries of the Community rose from 30 to 46 per cent while that going to other Commonwealth countries fell from 19 to 11 per cent. Imports followed a similar trend. Trade with the newly industrialising countries, including Singapore, Korea, Taiwan and Malaysia, has risen substantially.

The strength of overseas earnings from invisibles has been maintained by the continued adaptation to new conditions, particularly following the abolition of exchange controls in 1979, and growth in world markets of insurance, banking, tourism, construction, consultancy and other services. In 1985 exports of services were valued at about one-third of exports of goods; the growth of overseas assets has resulted in high net receipts of investment income.

The substantial cumulative surplus on current account from 1980 onwards implies a corresponding increase in Britain's net external assets, which are estimated to have risen from £12,500 million at the end of 1979 to about £90,000 million at the end of 1985. Following the abolition of exchange controls in 1979, investment outflows, particularly portfolio investment, increased sharply. There has been an acceleration in the growth of portfolio investment since 1984, partly a reflection of investment by banks as they moved into lending in readily marketable forms (such as floating rate notes) and away from traditional loans. British banks' sterling lending abroad has also been at a high level since the abolition of exchange controls.

Oil

The development of North Sea oil and gas production has had a significant effect on the economy; in 1986 Britain was the world's fifth largest oil producer. The benefits to the balance of payments began to appear in the second half of the 1970s; in 1980 Britain had its first surplus on oil trade. By 1985 the surplus amounted to £8,200 million. In 1974 oil accounted for some 4 per cent of Britain's visible exports and 19 per cent of visible imports; by 1985 the proportions were 21 per cent and 10 per cent respectively. Exports, mainly to other European Community countries, are equivalent to more than half of domestic production. They are partly offset in balance of payments terms by imports of other grades of crude oil from the Middle East and elsewhere.

North Sea oil helped to alleviate the fall in real national income which Britain, along with other industrialised countries, suffered following the oil price rises of the 1970s. It has helped to ease the task of controlling public sector borrowing, contributing to the Government's counter-inflation strategy. Even after production runs down, the stock of external assets (see above) that has been built up largely because of North Sea oil will provide a steady flow of income.

The price of oil fell sharply in early 1983 and, after almost three years of virtual stability, again in late 1985 and early 1986. Although a fall in the oil price may lead to some loss of revenues from oil exports and oil taxation, consumers and non-oil industry can be expected to benefit.

Sterling

As a reflection of Britain's position as a net oil exporter, sterling has been strong during periods of high world demand for oil. Sterling appreciated markedly in 1979 and 1980, with rising oil prices, but, as the oil market weakened, sterling fell back. The sterling index shows the value of the currency as a weighted average (1975 = 100) of its exchange rate against other currencies. In July 1986 the index was 75·9 compared with an average of 96·1 in 1980.

ECONOMIC STRATEGY

In the decades after 1945 British governments sought to influence the rate of growth and the level of employment by macroeconomic policy measures (for example, by variations in government expenditure, taxes or controls on consumer credit). At the same time they attempted to keep inflation down and to achieve approximate equilibrium in the balance of payments. However, each time the economy expanded, inflation tended to accelerate and a strong rise in imports typically gave rise to a balance of payments problem. The effects would finally lead to the imposition of restraints on home demand. The cyclical pattern of stimulus followed by restraint became known as 'stop-go'.

From the late 1960s until about 1980, fluctuations in wage and price levels had an adverse effect on competitiveness, profitability and business confidence. This was associated with an increase in unemployment over the period. At various times governments attempted to control pay rises and (less frequently) price rises by means of voluntary or statutory controls, but such policies were largely unsuccessful.

The Government elected in 1979 has adopted economic policies which in many ways represent a break with those of earlier governments. Monetary and fiscal policies are set to bring about lower inflation while providing for continued growth in output. Microeconomic policies are designed to enhance the prospects for output and employment by improving incentives, removing unnecessary controls, ensuring that markets work properly and generally increasing the adaptability of the economy. The Government believes that the pursuit of these policies will ensure that the increase since 1983 in the number of jobs in the economy will be maintained.

Monetary Policy

Controlling the growth of the money supply is central to the aim of a sustained fall in the rate of inflation. Among the money supply measures, targets are set for increases in the M0 narrow liquidity measure and the sterling M3 broad liquidity measure.[1] The target ranges for these are 2 to 6 per cent and 11 to 15 per cent respectively in 1986–87.

Increased competition in financial markets, however, resulting from deregulation, has led to a change in the pattern of financial transactions. The growth of interest-bearing sight deposits has meant that people are more willing to use these deposits as a form of investment while building societies are tending to hold an increased proportion of their reserves as bank deposits. These developments mean that sterling M3 is less reliable than previously as a guide to potential spending. The monetary indicators, therefore, form only part of the Government's overall judgment on monetary conditions. Other variables, particularly short-term interest rates and the exchange rate, are also taken into account.

Supply Side Policies

While designing macroeconomic policy with the intent of reducing inflation, the Government has sought to improve the supply response, and hence the efficiency, of the economy through microeconomic policies. Action has been taken to expose more of the economy to market forces. Direct controls (for example, on pay, prices, foreign exchange, dividend payments and commercial credit) have been abolished, competition in domestic markets strengthened, labour market reforms introduced and a substantial programme of transferring activities from the public to the private sector is under way. In addition, regulatory burdens on business are being reduced.

In the labour market the Government has sought to improve work incentives by reducing personal income tax rates and raising tax thresholds and also by encouraging the extension of share ownership among employees. Wide-ranging reforms of personal taxation have been proposed in a Green Paper. To improve employment prospects, the Government has also abolished the National Insurance surcharge (a tax on employed labour) and established a graduated structure of National Insurance contribution rates which has reduced the cost to employers of hiring lower-paid workers. The Government has also taken steps to achieve a better-balanced legal framework for industrial relations and is working to improve vocational training. Obstacles to the mobility of labour have been reduced. For example, the rights of those leaving occupational pension schemes early have been improved, thus bringing down the costs of changing jobs. Among the objectives of a proposed reform of the social security system is an improvement in incentives to work and save. The Government has

---

[1] M0 is notes and coin in circulation with the public and banks' holdings of cash and their operational balances at the Bank of England. Sterling M3 comprises notes and coin in circulation with the public and private sector sterling sight and time deposits in Britain.

introduced legislation to limit the scope of wages councils. However, in spite of these measures and although unemployment has remained at a high level, wages have continued to rise in excess of the inflation rate. This has taken place despite the Government's emphasis on the link between pay and jobs: it has repeatedly warned that, if employment is to rise faster, wages must rise more slowly.

To improve the working of capital markets, the Government has abolished controls on foreign exchange transactions, company dividends, hire purchase and bank lending. Competition among financial institutions is being encouraged within a new statutory framework of investor protection. The Government is also taking steps to reduce the distorting effects of the tax system on investment and savings decisions by, among other things, reducing corporation tax and the system of capital allowances. Planning restrictions on industrial investment have been eased, while industrial subsidies (both generally and in the context of regional policy) have been made more selective and more closely related to job creation. Particular efforts have been made to improve the flow of investment funds to small firms and to assist innovation in industry.

Fiscal Policy

Monetary policy has been complemented by a firm fiscal policy whose aim has been a progressive reduction in public borrowing as a proportion of GDP. In the early years of the financial strategy the public sector borrowing requirement amounted to around 3 per cent of GDP but by 1985–86 this had fallen to 2·25 per cent—the lowest since 1971–72. Further reductions are envisaged.

Economic Management

The Treasury has prime responsibility for the formulation and conduct of economic policy, which also involves the Departments of Trade and Industry, Employment, Energy, the Environment and Transport and the Ministry of Agriculture, Fisheries and Food. Other bodies are concerned with specific aspects of economic policy. These include the Bank of England (the central bank), the National Economic Development Council (in which the Government meets representatives of industry under the chairmanship of the Prime Minister), the Office of Fair Trading and the Monopolies and Mergers Commission.

On matters of major public policy such as the broad economic strategy, and on the economic problems it faces, the Government makes known its purposes and keeps in touch with developments throughout the economy by means of informal and continuous links with the chief industrial, financial, labour and other interests. Final responsibility for the broad lines of economic policy rests with the Cabinet.

NATIONAL INCOME AND EXPENDITURE

The value of all goods and services produced in the economy is measured by GDP. This can be expressed either in terms of market prices (the prices people pay for the goods and services they buy) or at factor cost (the cost of the goods and services before adding taxes and subtracting subsidies). It can also be expressed in current prices or in constant prices (that is, removing the effects of inflation in order to measure the underlying growth in the economy). In 1985, GDP at current factor cost totalled £304,400 million.

Gross domestic product is conventionally estimated in three different ways as the sum totals of expenditures, incomes or outputs in a given year. Each method yields the same total in principle, but in practice there are slight differences. Over the longer term the average of the three is the best indicator of growth in the economy. The output measure is usually considered the most reliable measure of short-term movements. In 1985 the index of the average estimate of GDP at constant factor cost was 110·5 (1980 = 100), compared with 92·0 in 1975, an increase of some 20 per cent.

Expenditure   Table 10 gives figures for the expenditure-based measure of GDP, at both current market prices and current factor cost, and shows how two other main aggregates used in the national accounts, gross national product and national income, are derived.

Table 10: Gross Domestic Product, Gross National Product and National Income

£ million

	1975	1985
Total final expenditure	135,157	450,170
less imports of goods and services	29,004	98,603
Gross domestic product at market prices	106,153	351,567
plus net property income from abroad	890	3,400
Gross national product at market prices	107,043	354,967
less factor cost adjustment (taxes less subsidies)	10,350	49,102
Gross domestic product at factor cost	95,803	302,465
Gross national product at factor cost	96,693	305,865
less capital consumption	11,633	41,846
National income (net national product)	85,060	264,019

Source: *United Kingdom National Accounts 1986 Edition.*

Table 11 shows the categories of total final expenditure in 1985. Consumption accounted for 61 per cent of domestic expenditure. Between 1975 and 1985 the proportion of final expenditure devoted to exports averaged 21·8 per cent.

Table 11: Total Final Expenditure 1985 at Market Prices

	£ million	per cent
Consumers' expenditure	213,208	47·4
General government final consumption	74,012	16·4
Gross domestic fixed capital formation	60,118	13·4
Value of physical increase in stocks and work in progress	528	0·1
Total domestic expenditure	347,866	77·3
Exports of goods and services	102,304	22·7
Total final expenditure	450,170	100·0

Source: *United Kingdom National Accounts 1986 Edition.*

Personal Incomes and Expenditure   Personal incomes at current prices before tax rose rapidly and fairly steadily from £97,335 million in 1975 to £309,908 million in 1985. Personal disposable income (that is, personal incomes after deductions—mainly taxation and National Insurance contributions) was £239,781 million in 1985, 2·8 per cent higher in real terms than in 1984. Consumers' expenditure amounted to 70 per cent of pre-tax personal income in 1985 compared with 67 per cent in 1975.

Table 12 shows the pattern of consumers' expenditure in 1985. Housing, food, alcoholic drink, clothing and footwear, and fuel and power together accounted for 48 per cent of the total. Consumers' expenditure increased by 3·5 per cent in real terms between 1984 and 1985. The changes in the pattern between 1975 and 1985 in Britain were paralleled in other industrialised countries, with declining proportions spent on food, and on clothing and footwear. Over the longer term, as incomes rise (real personal disposable income in Britain having more than doubled since 1945), people tend to spend increasing proportions on consumer durables and services—personal, financial and leisure services in particular.

Saving as a percentage of personal disposable income has fluctuated over the last decade and was lower in 1985 (11·1 per cent) than in 1975 (12·7 per cent). (Movements in the personal savings ratio may reflect people's wish to compensate for the rise or fall in the real value of assets fixed in money terms in response to changes in price levels.)

Sources of Income

The proportion of total personal income accounted for by income from employment was 64 per cent in 1985; average gross weekly earnings in April 1985 in Great Britain were £187·90 for full-time male workers and £123·90 for full-time female workers. The three other main sources of personal income were self-employment (10 per cent), income from rent, dividends and interest (10 per cent) and current grants from general government (15 per cent).

Current Government Expenditure

Current expenditure on goods and services by central government and local authorities amounted to £74,012 million in 1985; it rose by 10 per cent in real terms over the period 1975 to 1985. The main cause of this was the growth over the period in the social services, especially education and the National Health Service.

In addition to their expenditure on goods and services, public authorities transfer large sums to other sectors, mainly the personal sector, by way of National Insurance and other social security benefits, grants, and interest and subsidies. Central government also makes grants to local authorities to finance about half of their current expenditure.

Gross Domestic Product by Industry

Table 13 shows GDP by industry in 1975 and 1985. Over a period of time agriculture and manufacturing have come to account for smaller proportions of national income, while energy and services have grown relatively. Services now account for about 60 per cent of GDP.

Table 12: Consumers' Expenditure in 1975 and 1985

	1975	1985	
	per cent	per cent	£ million
Food (household expenditure)	18·3	14·0	29,950
Alcoholic drink	7·4	7·4	15,783
Tobacco	4·2	3·3	7,006
Clothing and footwear	8·0	7·0	14,894
Housing	13·4	14·9	31,711
Fuel and power	4·4	5·0	10,657
Household goods and services	7·7	6·6	14,067
Transport and communication	14·4	16·8	35,806
Recreation, entertainment and education	9·2	9·2	19,593
Other goods and services	11·8	14·3	30,437
Other items[a]	1·3	1·5	3,304
Total	100·0	100·0	213,208

Source: *United Kingdom National Accounts 1986 Edition.*
[a] Household expenditure overseas plus final expenditure by private non-profit-making bodies minus expenditure by foreign tourists in Britain.

Table 13: Gross Domestic Product by Industry[a]

	1975		1985	
	£ million	per cent	£ million	per cent
Agriculture, forestry and fishing	2,507	2·6	5,485	1·8
Energy and water supply	5,041	5·3	34,335	11·2
Manufacturing	27,638	29·2	76,800	25·1
Construction	6,299	6·6	18,651	6·1
Distribution, hotels and catering; repairs	11,927	12·6	40,384	13·2
Transport	5,263	5·6	12,913	4·2
Communication	2,509	2·6	8,044	2·6
Banking, finance, insurance, business services and leasing	10,010	10·6	42,473	13·9
Ownership of dwellings	5,589	5·9	17,775	5·8
Public administration, defence and social security	7,321	7·7	21,599	7·1
Education and health services	9,012	9·5	26,187	8·6
Other services	5,000	5·3	17,978	5·9
Total	98,116	103·6	322,624	105·5
Adjustment for financial services	−3,374	−3·6	−16,883	−5·5
Gross domestic product at factor cost (income-based)	94,742	100·0	305,741	100·0

Source: *United Kingdom National Accounts 1986 Edition.*
[a] Before provision for depreciation but after deducting stock appreciation.

11 Framework of Industry

Among the most prominent trends in industrial activity in Britain during the 1970s and 1980s have been the growth of the offshore oil and gas industries together with related products and services; the rapid development of electronic and microelectronic technologies and their application to a wide range of other sectors; and a continuous rise in the service industries' share of total employment. Industrial output in Britain has twice been affected by recession since 1973, partly as a result of fluctuations in oil prices. Output declined for two years after 1973, and then recovered steadily until 1979. It fell again in 1980 and 1981, increased in 1982 and has risen strongly since then. A marked increase in productivity has been a major factor in easing the process of economic recovery. In early 1986 total output was 14 per cent higher than at the low point of the recession in early 1981. Gains in productivity, however, meant that this increased output was produced with fewer workers. Consequently, employment, though increasing, was still lower than in 1981. Table 14 shows gross domestic product (GDP) by sector and the percentage of total GDP and of total employment in each sector in 1985.

Table 14: Gross Domestic Product[a] by Industry in 1985

Standard Industrial Classification Revised 1980		£ million	% of total	% Employment
0	Agriculture, forestry and fishing	5,485	1·8	1·6
1	Energy and water supply	34,335	11·2	2·9
2–4	Manufacturing	76,800	25·1	25·8
5	Construction	18,651	6·1	4·5
6–9	Services	187,353	61·3	65·2
	Adjustment for financial services	−16,883	−5·5	—
Gross domestic product at factor cost (income-based)		305,741	100·0	100·0

Sources: *United Kingdom National Accounts 1986 Edition* and *Monthly Digest of Statistics.*
[a] Before depreciation but after providing for stock appreciation.

The Government is pursuing policies designed to help British industry become more competitive and responsive to market forces, both at home and abroad (see p 227), and also to encourage development in advanced industries such as microelectronics and biotechnology. These objectives are also borne in mind by the Government when participating in the formulation of European Community industrial policies.

This chapter describes some of the general features of industrial organisation in Britain, such as the forms of enterprise, methods of financing and industrial association. It looks at factors affecting productivity and competitiveness, including investment, technological advance, research and development, and management and workforce training, as well as means of improving standards of design and quality assurance. It also outlines the framework of incentives for general industrial development provided by the Government, and by Community institutions, and the regulatory framework within which industry operates.

INDUSTRIAL ORGANISATION

The forms of industrial organisation and the patterns of ownership and control are varied. The main categories of organisation are: unincorporated businesses (sole traders and partnerships) of which there are at least 1 million; incorporated companies; and public sector enterprises, which are owned by the Government (see p 228). Incorporation means that companies are entered on an official register of companies (see p 238); at the end of 1985 there were over 1 million companies on the registers, though a proportion of these were not actively trading. About 6,000 of these companies were public limited companies. There are about 16 major public sector enterprises with an employed labour force of 1·3 million. The Government is pursuing a programme of 'privatisation' whereby some of these enterprises are transformed into incorporated companies and their shares sold to the public (see p 229). Employees in such companies are being given a preferential right to buy shares in their new companies and employee share ownership in general has been facilitated by changes in legislation, thus enabling employees to have a financial interest in the profitability of their companies. Although not numerous, co-operative enterprises (which are also incorporated companies) increased in number from 300 in 1979 to 1,400 in mid-1986, and since 1980 there has been a rise in the number of 'buy-outs' in which the staff, or management, of a company raises the finance to purchase it.

In some sectors a small number of large companies and their subsidiaries are responsible for a large proportion of total production. However, it is rare for a few shareholders to have a controlling interest since shares in these companies are usually distributed among many holders or held by insurance companies or pension funds representing a cross-section of the community.

Private enterprises account for about 75 per cent of GDP in Britain and for the greater part of activity in the agricultural, manufacturing, construction, distributive, financial and miscellaneous service sectors. There is substantial public ownership in the energy, transport and communications sectors. Unincorporated businesses, corporate enterprises and public sector enterprises contribute about 20, 55 and 8 per cent of GDP respectively (the remainder being accounted for by central and local government).

About 100 companies registered in Britain each had net assets of over £500 million in 1985. In terms of annual sales three of the top ten industrial groups in Europe were British, with British Petroleum second, Shell Transport and Trading third, and BAT Industries seventh. Alongside the larger organisations the many hundreds of thousands of small firms play an essential part in the economy.

Industrial Financing

Over half of companies' funds for further investment and other purposes are internally generated, with banks providing the chief external source of finance. The main forms of short-term finance available in the private sector are bank overdrafts, trade credit, bill financing (essentially a more formal kind of trade credit) and factoring (making cash available to a company in exchange for its debts). Types of medium- and long-term finance include bank loans, the mortgaging of property and the issue of securities and shares to the public through The Stock Exchange. The leasing of equipment may also be regarded as a form of finance. Other sources of finance for industry include the Government (see p 229), the European Community and specialist financial institutions.

Capital gearing (the ratio of debt to equity) has historically been low relative to most other countries, reflecting the highly developed stock market in Britain. In 1982 the ratio had fallen to 46 : 100 from 54 : 100 in 1977; for large companies it had fallen faster, to 40 : 100 in 1984.

The 1980s have been particularly notable for the growth of venture capital schemes run by financial institutions in both the public and private sectors to provide 'start-up' and development finance for small and new firms. The organisation of an Unlisted Securities Market and over-the-counter markets has enabled fast-developing young companies to raise capital through share issues, even if they are not eligible for a full Stock Exchange listing.

Industrial Association

There are several types of voluntary association representing private enterprises and covering, with varying degrees of completeness, most of British industry. The central body representing British business and industry is the Confederation of British Industry (CBI). The CBI represents about 250,000 businesses, directly or indirectly (through employers' organisations and trade associations), as well as the majority of public sector enterprises. For its members, it acts as an advisory and consultative body, providing them with information and statistics, ascertaining their collective views and representing them nationally to the Government and public as well as internationally. CBI representatives sit on such bodies as the National Economic Development Council, the Manpower Services Commission and the Health and Safety Commission.

Chambers of commerce are open to producers and traders of all kinds and are organised on a geographical basis. They exist to provide export assistance as well as advisory and information services and training courses. There are 85 local chambers of commerce, representing 55,000 firms, affiliated to regional associations and the Association of British Chambers of Commerce. Additional central organisations serve Scotland, Wales and Northern Ireland.

Trade associations consist of companies producing or retailing a particular product or group of products, and about 650 major associations are listed by the Department of Employment. They exist to provide common services, regulate trading practices and represent their members to government departments. Employers' organisations are usually concerned with the negotiation of wages and conditions of work in a particular industrial sector, although sometimes one institution may undertake the function of both a trade association and an employers' organisation.

Other voluntary associations include industrial development associations for particular regions or areas and the Scottish Council (Development and Industry) in Scotland.

PRODUCTIVITY AND COMPETITIVE-NESS

Although output per head in Britain has generally been low by international standards, it has risen sharply since 1981. The rise for manufacturing has been greater than for the economy as a whole. The index for the whole economy in 1985 was 113·8 (1980 = 100). Table 15 shows the output and employment indices for 1984 and 1985. There was a fall in employment in production industries between these years, but this was more than offset by a rise in employment in service industries, which led to an overall increase. Output and output per head in both production and service industries rose between 1984 and 1985. The Government believes that the increased competitiveness resulting from these productivity gains will lead to a sustained rise in living standards and a rise in employment.

Among the factors affecting productivity are capital investment, innovations and improvements in products and processes, and the performance and training of management and labour. The following sections outline trends and developments in these areas.

Table 15: Industrial Output and Employment (Indices: 1980 = 100)

	Output		Employment[a]	
	Index 1984	Index 1985	Index 1984	Index 1985
Agriculture, forestry and fishing	121·3	117·1	94·2	93·6
Production industries	103·2	108·1	80·6	80·2
of which: Energy and water supply	110·1	120·1	87·3	84·6
Manufacturing	100·7	103·8	79·9	79·7
Construction	98·6	99·8	79·0	77·5
Services	109·3	113·4	100·3	102·3
of which: Distribution, hotels, catering and repairs	108·2	112·0	100·5	103·6
Communications	115·4	123·2	98·2	98·9
Financial and business services	133·0	145·0	111·2	116·1
Whole economy	106·7	110·7	92·5	93·4

Sources: *United Kingdom National Accounts 1986 Edition* and *Monthly Digest of Statistics.*
[a]Excluding self-employment.

Investment

Total fixed capital expenditure increased by 2 per cent between 1984 and 1985 in real terms. In the recession of 1979–81, investment fell by almost 14 per cent, but began to recover in 1982. The fall occurred mainly in manufacturing investment, which fell substantially between 1979 and 1983, recovering significantly in 1984 and 1985. Investment in distribution, financial services and transport fell slightly between 1979 and 1981, but otherwise has shown a consistent rising trend. Investment in major sectors of the economy in 1985 (at 1980 prices) is shown in Table 16. The figures for manufacturing industry do not include expenditure on leased assets since these are attributed to the service industries on the basis of ownership. Manufacturing industry is, however, the major user of leased assets. The practice of leasing has grown rapidly since the early 1970s but is likely to decline owing to changes made in the tax treatment of capital investment in the 1984 Budget (see p 227).

Technological Advance

Britain was a pioneer in both computing and telecommunications and has an important computer industry. It is among the world's leading nations in the production and use of micro- and minicomputers as well as in the provision of computing services and systems. Extensive use of electronics and automated controls is to be found across the whole range of industry. The use of computerised control is widespread in steel mills, coal mines, oil refineries and chemical plants. The use of robots is increasing rapidly, especially in the motor industry: Britain was the world's sixth largest user of industrial robots at the end of 1985 according to the British Robot Association. Greater use of robotics and of other new technologies such as fibre optics and optoelectronics is encouraged by various Department of Trade and Industry schemes.

The use of personal computers in offices is now common, and advanced data transmission systems and databases are being developed. New technology is also being used in the area of personal banking and sales as electronic funds transfer at point of sale (EFT-POS) equipment begins to be installed in addition to the automated teller machines which are now widespread.

Table 16: Gross Fixed Capital Formation (Investment) by Sector

	£ million 1985 (at 1980 prices)	Index 1985 (1980 = 100)
Agriculture, forestry and fishing	787	77·3
Oil and gas extraction	2,351	98·0
Other energy and water supply	2,977	90·5
Manufacturing	5,852	90·3
Construction	568	121·6
Distribution, hotels, catering and repairs	4,109	126·9
Transport and communications	3,848	99·2
Finance and business services		
Leased assets	3,808	176·5
Other assets	4,891	138·4
Other services	6,335	127·6
Dwellings	8,475	97·7
Transfer costs of land and buildings	2,309	137·9
Whole economy	46,310	110·9

Source: *United Kingdom National Accounts 1986 Edition.*

British industry has a record of success in biotechnology. The pharmaceuticals sector is among the world leaders in the production of antibiotics by fermentation and there has also been steady improvement of fermentation techniques in the production of food and beverages. Biotechnology has gained a new impetus from research achievements in genetic engineering and cell fusion. The Department of Trade and Industry and other government bodies are encouraging the exploitation of new developments. A Biotechnology Unit at the Laboratory of the Government Chemist is the focus for government co-operation with industry.

The British Technology Group (BTG) promotes the industrial application of developments of all kinds made in public sector research institutions and universities (see p 230). Some of the major technical achievements which it has exploited or supported are cephalosporin antibiotics, pyrethroid insecticides, glass-reinforced cement, carbon fibre and advanced integrated circuits.

Research and Development

Industrial expenditure on research and development in 1983 was £4,163 million, of which £3,637 million was spent by private sector companies and £526 million by public sector companies and by some 40 research associations formed by groups of companies in a particular sector. The main areas of expenditure were electronics (£1,463 million), chemicals and allied products (£735 million), aerospace (£720 million), mechanical engineering (£290 million), and motor vehicles (£240 million).

Estimated outturn figures for government-funded research and development in 1984–85 include: Ministry of Defence, £2,106 million; Department of Trade and Industry, £365 million; Science and Engineering Research Council, £269 million; Department of Energy and United Kingdom Atomic Energy Authority, £232 million; Ministry of Agriculture, Fisheries and Food, £126 million; Agricultural and Food Research Council, £46 million; and Department of Transport, £35 million.

The Government has sponsored a major programme in advanced information technology, known as the Alvey programme, which comprises research projects involving collaboration between industry, academic institutions and other research organisations. The programme runs over the years 1983–88 with a total budget of £350 million, over half of which is being provided by the Government. The four main areas of research are software engineering, man–machine interfaces, very large-scale integrated circuits and intelligent knowledge-based systems. By the end of 1985, most of the funds were committed to over 230 projects with, typically, two or three firms and one or two universities taking part in each project. Over 60 firms, 40 universities, six polytechnics and six research establishments are now involved in the programme. The European Community's research programme into the development and application of information technologies, the European Strategic Programme of Research into Information Technology (ESPRIT), has a budget of 1,500 million ECUs[1] (£1,030 million) for the five years 1984–89, of which 50 per cent will be provided by the Community. British companies are participating in a large proportion of the projects.

The BRITE programme (Basic Research in Industrial Technology) is a Community project designed to encourage collaborative research into applications of advanced technology in some of the more traditional industries and has substantial British participation. It has a budget of 125 million ECUs (£85 million) over the four years 1985–88.

Many British companies are participating in projects in the Eureka programme, which aims to encourage European co-operation in the development and production of high technology products with global sales potential, and which has the support of 18 European governments and the European Commission.

Management Education

Management education is provided by all the polytechnics and many colleges of further education, while Regional Management Centres have been established in England and Wales by associations of some of these colleges, with some similar organisations in Scotland. Universities make an important contribution, especially through the full-time postgraduate programmes at business schools such as those of London, Manchester, City, Durham and Strathclyde universities. Training courses for managers are offered by several independent colleges, including the Management College, Henley-on-Thames, Ashridge College, Berkhamsted, and the Cranfield School of Management, Bedford. The British Institute of Management, which has a representative role for the management and administrative professions, has a particular interest in management training, while there are also a number of professional bodies concerned with standards and training in specialised branches of management.

Engineering Council

The Engineering Council was established under Royal Charter in 1981. Its objectives are to advance education in, and to promote the science and practice of, engineering (including relevant technology) for the public benefit and thereby promote industry and commerce in Britain. The Council maintains a register of 300,000 professional engineers (which includes chartered engineers), technician engineers and engineering technicians. In co-operation with the various professional institutions and other organisations concerned with training in engineering, it has set standards for education, training and experience, and accredited courses by which people qualify for registration.

Technical and Vocational Training

A well-trained workforce is essential for economic growth, and recent technological advances have created a need for an even greater quantity, range and quality of technical and vocational training, both for young people and for

---

[1] ECU = European Currency Unit, based on a 'basket' of national currencies including sterling, the value of which is recalculated daily.

adults. The main responsibility for training rests with employers and indi-viduals. The Business & Technician Education Council (BTEC), a privately funded body, deals with the education and training of technicians and their equivalents in the professions and commerce, by designing syllabuses and validating courses offered at colleges of further education and elsewhere in England and Wales; its Scottish equivalent is the Scottish Vocational Education Council. The BTEC is working with the Engineering Council and the Engineer-ing Industry Training Board to co-ordinate their systems of assessing and certifying the skills of those receiving technician education and training, and with the City and Guilds of London Institute to develop the pre-vocational courses of the two organisations into a more coherent and comprehensive system.

The Government is increasing its responsibility for some aspects of training. It is estimated to have spent some £450 million on this in 1979–80, rising to nearly £1,500 million in 1985–86. The Manpower Services Commission (MSC), which consists of representatives of employers, unions and local authority and educational interests, is the main agency through which the Government institutes action and monitors progress in training. Its main scheme is the Youth Training Scheme, which offers a course of planned work experience integrated with off-the-job training for unemployed 16- or 17-year-old school-leavers. The scheme provides two years of training for 16-year-olds and one year for 17-year-olds, leading to a recognised qualification. The Technical and Vocational Education Initiative aims at providing four-year courses with a strong technical and vocational element in schools and colleges for 14- to 18-year-olds. About 85 per cent of education authorities were participating by 1986–87.

The aim of the Government's adult training strategy is to encourage employers and others to give adult training a high priority and to secure an adequate supply of people with up-to-date skills. The MSC's adult training schemes are grouped into two main programmes—the Wider Opportunities Training Pro-gramme, a broad-based series of schemes aimed at enhancing unemployed people's employability, and a Job-Related Programme which aims to enhance the skills of both employed and unemployed people, including the Job Training Scheme, which trains unemployed people in skills for which there is a known local labour demand. Greater emphasis is to be placed in 1986–87 on assistance to small firms and potential entrepreneurs. The MSC is also encouraging the use of open learning methods (using video and tapes) on all training courses, and hopes to establish a broadcasting College of the Air in 1987 to provide vocational courses below degree level. In 1985–86 the MSC's adult training schemes helped over 200,000 people (of whom half were unemployed) and are expected to help over 250,000 people in 1986–87.

The Open University, which provides degree courses using distance learning techniques, notably television broadcasts, has set up the Open University Business School, which offers part-time courses leading to a diploma in management. The School, which is strongly supported by the British Institute of Management, has been used by almost 2,000 companies and organisations since it opened in 1983. Managers continue to work while studying, which is of particular use to those small companies which cannot afford to release staff on a full-time basis.

Design

Good design is seen as crucial for maintaining and improving the quality and competitiveness of goods and services; the Department of Trade and Industry gives priority to its campaign to encourage greater awareness in industry and commerce (among both producers and customers) of the value of good design. It organises conferences to underline the importance of design and has taken steps to include design education in the school system and widen awareness of design in business schools. Advice and assistance on design matters are available from the government-sponsored Design Council, while the Computer-Aided Design Centre also provides assistance to individual firms. The Design Council has centres in London, Cardiff and Glasgow, and its operations include giving advice on design problems; the organisation of product displays at overseas trade fairs, conferences and seminars on design; providing help for design education; and the production of a range of publications. A funded consultancy scheme, operated by the Design Council on behalf of the Government, offers firms employing up to 500 people a maximum of 15 working days' consultancy at subsidised rates. The Council provides annual awards for consumer and contract goods, engineering products and components, computer software, medical equipment, and motor vehicles and accessories. The Society of Industrial Artists and Designers is the representative professional body in Great Britain of industrial designers.

Standards for Products and Processes

The Government is working for recognition of the importance of standards, believing that they can serve to improve the quality and thereby the international competitiveness of products. In 1983 the Government launched a long-term National Quality Campaign, supported by a number of non-government bodies including the British Standards Institution (BSI—see below). The campaign has included the setting up in 1984 of a National Quality Information Centre run by the Institute of Quality Assurance, and assistance to industry in training and consultancy work associated with quality assurance. The National Accreditation Council for Certification Bodies, set up to assess certification bodies applying for government accreditation, was established in 1985.

The British Standards Institution (BSI) prepares and publishes standards which specify dimensions, performance and safety criteria, testing methods and codes of practice for a large range of products and processes in most fields of production. It is a voluntary body, working by consensus, and funded by sales of standards, subscriptions and government grant. The board of the BSI includes representatives of all sectors of industry (both employers and workers), professional institutions, consumers and the larger government departments. The BSI, with government support, co-operates with other countries in achieving international agreements on standards. A new, faster, approach to harmonising product standards within the European Community, intended to help break down internal trade barriers and based on the simple requirement of safety, was agreed in May 1985.

Measurement Standards

The National Physical Laboratory (NPL), a research establishment of the Department of Trade and Industry, is responsible for providing the measurement standards and calibration facilities necessary to ensure that measurements in Britain are made on a common basis and to the required accuracy. It maintains links with national standards laboratories all over the world to ensure international compatibility in measurements essential for overseas trade and technological co-operation. Based within the NPL, the National Measurement Accreditation Service (NAMAS) provides a focal point for the voluntary accreditation of calibration and testing facilities in Britain. It forms a link between the national standards maintained by the NPL and accredited measurement laboratories, including those servicing manufacturers and other producers, contractors, regulating bodies, quality assessment and product certification schemes, the Government, the health service and consumer bodies. NAMAS accredited laboratories offer calibration of scientific instruments and provide official certificates for electrical, mechanical, flow, optical, pressure, thermal and time measurements.

The National Weights and Measures Laboratory, also part of the Department of Trade and Industry, is responsible for administering the Weights and Measures Act 1985, which is largely concerned with standards and measuring equipment for use in trade. In 1984 the Government appointed a committee to review the metrological control of weighing and measuring equipment for commercial use taking account of the impact of modern technology and trading conditions; the Government has accepted many of its recommendations, including the introduction of a 'self-verification' scheme for approved manufacturers.

GOVERNMENT AND INDUSTRY

The Department of Trade and Industry is the department chiefly responsible for relations between the Government and industry. It is responsible for oversight of several nationalised industries, for industrial science, technology and research, for industrial policy and assistance, for overseas trade and export promotion, for competition policy and consumer affairs, for company legislation and for the Patent Office. In support of these activities it collects comprehensive statistics through the Business Statistics Office.

The aim of the Government's industrial policy is to increase the national production of wealth and promote and enhance the vitality and competitiveness of British trade and industry, within a proper regulatory framework. The heart of the policy is the control of inflation as the basis for sustained economic growth and the creation of a social and economic climate conducive to enterprise and initiative. To this end the Government is reducing the extent of state ownership, and industrial investment agencies in the public sector have been encouraged to secure private sector participation in their projects. Competition policy has been strengthened and other measures have been introduced to promote efficiency and competitiveness, including campaigns to enhance standards and quality assurance, to lay greater emphasis on training and skills, to increase links between industry and education and to remove unnecessary controls on companies. The Government is also encouraging the development of small businesses by reducing their administrative burdens, adjusting taxation and other policies.

Successive governments have aimed to provide an environment favourable to industrial expansion. In the case of industrial plant and machinery there is an annual allowance against profits for tax purposes of 25 per cent (on a reducing balance basis) beginning in the year in which expenditure occurs. There is an allowance for investment in industrial property of 4 per cent a year (on a straight-line basis). Special arrangements exist for short life (usually high technology) assets. There is a 100 per cent allowance for scientific research. Progressive reductions in the main rate of corporation tax were brought into effect as a result of the 1984 Budget.

The Department of Trade and Industry's schemes of assistance to industry and commerce were regrouped in April 1985 under four headings: support for innovation; support for national and regional investment; business and technical advisory services; and support for exports. Assistance provided by the Department in 1985–86 amounted to about £818 million (compared with some £895 million in the previous year). Various other agencies in the public sector provide aid, either for defined activities (such as tourism) or for specific geographical areas. The latter include inner urban areas, for which the Government has schemes of social and economic regeneration; enterprise zones—areas in which, as an experiment, economic activity is relieved of certain tax burdens and administrative controls; and freeports (also experimental) in which traders are freed from certain customs requirements. This national industrial assistance is supplemented by assistance from European Community funds (see p 234). Direct investment from overseas is encouraged, overseas firms generally being offered the same facilities and incentives as British-based companies.

Inward
Investment

The Department of Trade and Industry's Invest in Britain Bureau provides foreign companies with advice and assistance on all aspects of locating and relocating businesses in Britain, and on expanding existing facilities. Britain has for many years been the leading country for United States manufacturing investment in Europe and has attracted over one-third of all Japanese investment in the European Community since 1951.

Industrial
Awards

Recognition of outstanding industrial performance is conferred annually by the Queen's Awards for Export and Technology, the Export Awards for Smaller Manufacturers (for firms employing fewer than 200 people) and the MacRobert Award, the major award for engineering in Britain (made by the Fellowship of Engineering for successful technological innovation). The Queen's Awards are made to firms in all sectors of industry (including services) on the advice of a committee composed of businessmen, trade union representatives and civil servants.

Nationalised
Industries

The major nationalised industries are: the electricity supply industry (including the Central Electricity Generating Board and 12 area electricity boards in England and Wales); the British Gas Corporation; British Coal; the British Steel Corporation; British Rail; and the Post Office. In total the industries account for around 7·7 per cent of GDP and employ about 6 per cent of all employees.

The managing boards and staffs of the nationalised industries are not civil servants although they are responsible to ministers who appoint the chairman and members of each board. Ministers are responsible for agreeing with the industries their general strategies and have the power to give general directions as to how the industry should be run, but do not interfere in day-to-day management. The Government's policy is to encourage the nationalised industries to behave as far as possible as commercial enterprises, and this is carried out through the financial framework, set by the Government, within which the industries are expected to operate. This is designed also to integrate the industries' medium-term commercial aims with the requirements of government policy on the management of the economy. The main elements of the framework are: clear government objectives for the industries; regular corporate plans and performance reviews; systematic monitoring; agreed principles relating to investment appraisal and pricing; external financing limits; and financial targets and performance aims.

To ensure that nationalised industry investment earns an adequate economic return, there is a 'required rate of return' which investment programmes are expected to achieve. The current rate is 5 per cent in real terms before tax. Financial targets are set for individual nationalised industries to give them a framework similar to those of private sector companies which need to earn profits. They are supported by a series of performance aims, covering costs and standards of service, which are considered particularly important for industries with some monopoly power where financial targets would not automatically impose pressures for operating efficiency. External financing limits, which control the amount of finance (grants and borrowing) that a nationalised industry can raise from external sources in any financial year, are an important short-term operating control. They are set in the light of a nationalised industry's financial target and its expected performance and investment requirements. Nationalised industries are planning to finance a greater proportion of investment from internally generated funds.

External scrutiny of nationalised industry efficiency is conducted by the Monopolies and Mergers Commission (see p 235), which carries out up to six investigations each year at the instigation of ministers, and these investigations are complemented on occasion by studies undertaken by management consultants. Nationalised industry matters are also considered by parliamentary committees such as the Treasury and Civil Service Committee and the Public Accounts Committee.

Privatisation

The Government believes that reform of the nationalised industries is essential to economic recovery, and that the best way to improve performance in the long term is to expose the industries to market forces, through privatisation and the promotion of competition. Privatisation also provides a major opportunity for the Government to pursue its policy of widening share ownership, encouraging both employees and the general public to take a direct stake in British industry. Businesses which have been privatised include British Aerospace, British Telecom, Cable and Wireless, the National Freight Consortium, Jaguar, Amersham International, Enterprise Oil, Britoil, Associated British Ports and British Shipbuilders' warship-building yards. Many other state enterprises have also been sold and, altogether, 400,000 jobs have been transferred to the private sector. Planned privatisations include British Airways, British Gas, the National Bus Company, Rolls-Royce, the British Airports Authority and a number of water supply authorities. To stimulate efficiency, the Government has relaxed the statutory monopolies of a number of nationalised industries.

Support for Innovation

Expenditure on research and development supported by the Department of Trade and Industry is aimed at improving the capability of firms to exploit technological opportunities and encouraging firms to undertake innovative projects which promise high returns. A growing proportion of expenditure is going towards work carried out in industry, especially in areas such as micro-electronics, fibre optics and computer software; other work is done at research associations and in government research establishments. The Department's research establishments are the National Physical Laboratory (responsible not only for measurement standards, but also for research and development in related fields of national importance, including the properties of industrially important materials, and information technology), the National Engineering Laboratory (research and development in mechanical engineering, including manufacturing systems and robotics, materials applications, fluid power, pumps, fans and heat exchangers, and structural analysis and testing), the Warren Spring Laboratory (control engineering, materials handling, metal extraction, mineral processing, waste materials processing and environmental technology), and the Laboratory of the Government Chemist (analytical services mainly to central and local government, public institutions and international organisations).

'Support for Innovation' is the Department of Trade and Industry's general facility for providing selective financial support for research and development projects leading to new products and processes and for longer-term applied research projects. In 1985–86 the Department spent £440 million on scientific and technological assistance. The Department is advised by a Technology Requirements Board and a number of advisory committees of senior industrialists and academics on the overall allocation of its resources to particular technologies and industrial sectors.

The Advisory Council for Applied Research and Development, whose membership includes academics, industrialists and trade unionists engaged in all aspects of research and development in a wide variety of industrial sectors, is a source of independent advice to ministers collectively on applied research and development in both the public and private sectors, on the linkage between this research and scientific research supported by government departments, on the development and application of technology, and on the role of Britain in international collaboration in such activities. The Council has published a number of reports on aspects of new technology. It is served by a secretariat in the Cabinet Office.

British Technology Group

The objective of the British Technology Group (BTG) is to promote the development of new technology into commercial products, particularly where the technology originates from public sector sources, such as universities, polytechnics, research councils and government research establishments. It offers to take responsibility for protecting and licensing inventions from these sources, provides funds for development, seeks licensees and negotiates licence agreements with industry. As part of its technology transfer role it can also offer project finance to companies that want to develop new products and processes based on new technology. Through its joint venture finance the BTG can provide up to 50 per cent of the funds required and expects to recover its investment by means of a percentage levy on sales of the resulting product or process. This finance is available to companies of all sizes. The BTG is not a grant-giving body. It seeks to make a return on its investments and approaches every transaction on a commercial basis.

The BTG currently has a portfolio of 1,750 British patents and patent applications, over 600 licensees in Britain and overseas, 360 development projects at universities and other public sector institutions, and 230 projects with industrial companies.

In cases where a particular technology requires the setting up of a new company, the BTG can perform a catalytic role in launching start-up companies.

Support for Investment

In 1985–86, the industry departments in Great Britain spent £76 million on national selective assistance, £359 million on regional development grant and £110 million on regional selective assistance.

National Selective Assistance

The Department provides investment support for major projects which are judged to have exceptional national benefits and which would not proceed without assistance. The Department also operates schemes of selective assistance to support investment in microelectronics, fibre optics and optoelectronics and advanced manufacturing technology.

Guarantees are provided for the repayment of loans and interest incurred in the purchase of new ships and mobile offshore installations built in Britain.

Regional Development

Economic imbalance between different parts of the country is due partly to the steady decline over the years, in certain regions, of older industries, such as coal, steel, shipbuilding and textiles, and partly to the tendency of many newer and expanding industries to develop elsewhere. Thus the traditional industrial areas, mainly in Scotland, Wales, Northern Ireland and the north of England, have experienced, for many years, higher unemployment rates than regions such as the South East, and have suffered from net outward migration and industrial dereliction. In order to help to restore the economies of the areas of greatest need the Government has provided incentives to encourage industrial development in designated 'assisted areas'. Following a review of policy in Great Britain (Northern Ireland is treated separately), the Government has reaffirmed its commitment to maintain an effective regional industrial policy to ease the process of change in areas which have been dependent on declining industries and encourage the setting up of new businesses there. A new structure of

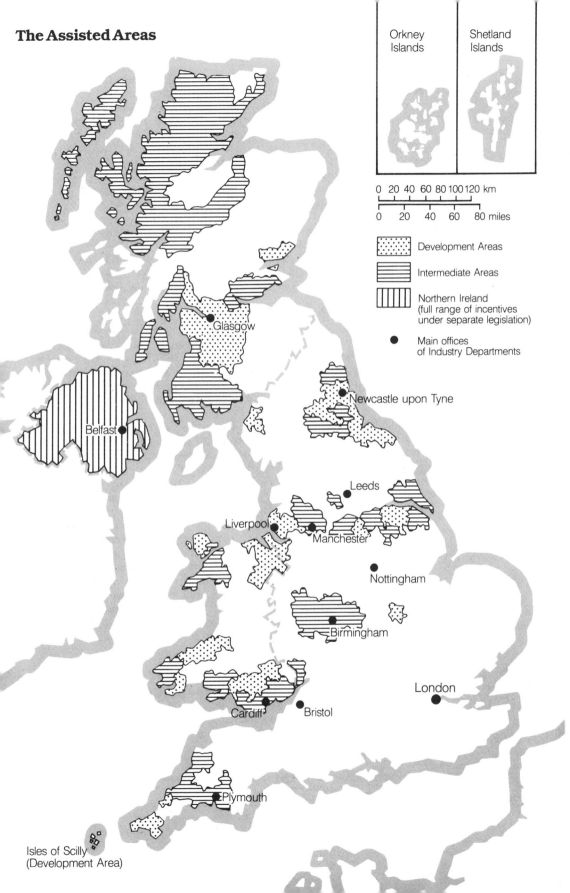

The Assisted Areas

Orkney Islands

Shetland Islands

```
0   20 40  60 80 100 120 km
0    20    40    60    80 miles
```

Development Areas

Intermediate Areas

Northern Ireland
(full range of incentives
under separate legislation)

● Main offices
of Industry Departments

Glasgow

Newcastle upon Tyne

Belfast

Leeds

Liverpool

Manchester

Nottingham

Birmingham

London

Cardiff

Bristol

Plymouth

Isles of Scilly
(Development Area)

regional industrial incentives, more directly linked to job creation, and a revised designation of the assisted areas, were introduced in 1984.

There are two categories of assisted areas: 'development areas' and 'intermediate areas', with the former being adjudged to have the greatest need for assistance (see map, p 231). Regional development grants are payable for investment in qualifying activities in the development areas, either as a proportion of capital expenditure limited by a cost-per-job ceiling or as an amount for each new job created, whichever is the more advantageous to the investor. Small firms are not, in general, subject to a cost-per-job ceiling. All manufacturing industries and some service industries are eligible for regional development grants. In addition, regional selective assistance may be payable to manufacturing and certain service sector projects that create or safeguard employment throughout the assisted areas.

The Government provides factories and workshops where the private sector is unwilling to invest in them. Special grants are available towards the improvement of the infrastructure in the assisted areas and towards the clearance of derelict land.

The Department of Trade and Industry takes the lead in the formulation of regional industrial policy and administers the regional development grant and regional selective assistance schemes in England. The Welsh and Scottish Offices administer these schemes in their respective countries. Factories in the assisted areas are provided, often in association with the private sector, by the government-funded English Industrial Estates Corporation (known as English Estates), and by the Scottish and Welsh Development Agencies.

Northern Ireland

The Industrial Development Board, formed in 1982 under the aegis of the Northern Ireland Department of Economic Development, offers a range of incentives similar to those available in the assisted areas (in some cases at higher rates). Incentives automatically available to manufacturing industry include grants of up to 20 per cent of the cost of new fixed assets, training grants, grants for key workers moving to Northern Ireland and exemption from local authority rates (local property taxes) for manufacturing premises. Manufacturing and service industry projects which create jobs may be eligible for grants of up to 50 per cent of the cost of new fixed assets, interest relief grants, favourable rental terms for factories, and grants to assist with setting-up costs and research and development costs. The Board can also provide equity and loan capital for new and expanding businesses, assist the development of new high-technology products and processes, and promote joint ventures with overseas companies. Other incentives include corporation tax relief of up to 80 per cent for certain new projects; 30 per cent grants for approved energy conservation projects; grants to attract and retain good management; and an advisory service on production methods.

Development Agencies

Government regional policies have been aimed at encouraging new industries in order to offset the decline in traditional activities. Accordingly the Scottish and Welsh Development Agencies promote industrial development in their respective countries. They encourage investment by overseas companies, provide equity and loan capital for industrial projects (which they are expected to do with a maximum of private sector participation), provide government factories, and have powers to assist small firms and undertake land reclamation.

Rural Industries

The Development Commission is responsible for promoting the economic and social development of rural England. It provides small factories and workshops which are built and managed by English Estates, and administers a grant scheme for the conversion of redundant buildings to industrial or commercial premises. The Commission's main agency, the Council for Small Industries in Rural Areas, provides technical management and financial advice, training facilities and loans to small businesses from 32 county offices. The Commission also supports voluntary bodies in rural areas to encourage community activity and self help and provides finance for small-scale rural housing and transport schemes. Though its responsibility extends over the whole of rural England, the Commission's resources are concentrated in the areas of greatest need, which are designated as rural development areas.

In Scotland and Wales similar services are provided generally through the development agencies, but separate bodies cater for two particular rural areas. In Scotland the Highlands and Islands Development Board provides loans and grants for viable projects in manufacturing, agriculture, fisheries and services, makes available training grants and advice, and builds factories. The Development Board for Rural Wales (usually referred to as 'Mid-Wales Development') provides factories, key worker housing and advice for small businesses. It has a general responsibility to promote the economic and social well-being of mid-Wales and a particular responsibility for the new town of Newtown, Powys.

Business and Technical Advisory Services

Business and technical advisory services include consultancy grants for firms employing up to 500 people which wish to improve the quality or design of their products, their manufacturing organisation and techniques or to resolve technical problems. Grants are also available to all manufacturing firms and in some cases to service companies, towards the cost of feasibility studies by consultants into the exploitation of biotechnology, microelectronics applications, advanced manufacturing systems (computer-aided design and manufacture, robotics, flexible manufacturing systems or computer-aided production management) and the use of integrated circuits.

Small Firms

The Department of Employment is responsible for the formation of policy towards the small business sector. Together with the Small Business Division of the Scottish Development Agency and the Business Development Unit of the Welsh Development Agency, the Department provides advice and guidance on a wide range of business problems affecting small firms (in manufacturing, generally defined as those firms employing less than 200 people) and those seeking to set up businesses. In Northern Ireland the Local Enterprise Development Unit, established to promote the development of small industries, provides grants, loans, help with obtaining premises and management advice to new and expanding companies. Local enterprise agencies, independent of the Government, also provide counselling and other services for small businesses.

The Government has been particularly concerned since the late 1970s to encourage small firms; between 1980 and 1984 there were about 140,000 more business starts than closures. It has introduced a framework of measures aimed at reducing burdens and providing incentives for enterprise and risk-taking. These have included a loan guarantee scheme, under which the Government guarantees repayment of 70 per cent of medium-term loans made by participating financial institutions; a business expansion scheme, under which tax reliefs are available to private individuals investing in small businesses; and the enterprise allowance scheme, which enables longer-term unemployed people to claim an allowance while establishing a new business. A range of other tax concessions has also been made for small firms. The development of new sources of venture capital has been promoted and a number of private sector initiatives have been made by the clearing banks and by groups of large firms and financial institutions. Priority is being given to the provision of relevant and accessible training for those setting up or running small businesses, together with appropriate advisory services. Local Enterprise Agencies, partnerships between firms and organisations in both the public and private sectors, which exist to provide advice and training for small businesses and also provide small business workshops, are being encouraged.

Support for Exports

The Department of Trade and Industry's programme of export support is directed by the British Overseas Trade Board, whose members are mainly business people with practical knowledge of exporting. Liaison is maintained with the extensive network of Foreign and Commonwealth Office commercial staff overseas. Services provided include advice on individual export markets and opportunities, assistance for exhibitors at overseas trade fairs and specialist advice on tariffs, regulations, technical requirements and product approval procedures.

Tourism

Direct government support for the tourism industry is provided by five statutory bodies. The British Tourist Authority (BTA) is responsible for the overseas promotion of tourism to Great Britain. The English, Scottish and Wales Tourist Boards, which promote tourism in their respective countries, encourage the development and improvement of tourist accommodation and amenities, and administer grants or loans for projects to provide or improve tourist amenities, and interest relief grants. The Scottish Tourist Board, unlike its English and Welsh counterparts, is also empowered to carry out its own overseas promotional activities in consultation with the BTA; these activities are intended to supplement, rather than replace, the overseas promotional work undertaken by the BTA. The Northern Ireland Tourist Board (NITB) has a promotional role similar to that of the other boards; the BTA carries out overseas promotional activities on behalf of the NITB on an agency basis.

The BTA offers a trophy annually for the most outstanding tourist development for overseas visitors; in 1985 the trophy was won by the Wigan Pier heritage and leisure centre.

European Community Regional Policy and Aid

The European Community seeks to increase the degree of convergence between the economies of member states and to ensure a more balanced distribution of economic activities within the Community. The principal responsibility for helping depressed areas remains with national authorities but the Community may complement schemes through aid from a number of sources.

European Regional Development Fund

The European Regional Development Fund was established in 1975. Its purpose is to contribute to the correction of the main regional imbalances within the Community by participating in the development and structural adjustment of regions whose development is lagging behind and in the conversion of declining industrial regions. The Fund's resources are allocated between member states on the basis of quota ranges; Britain has the third largest quota range. By December 1985 about £1,924 million had been allocated to Britain, mainly for the assisted areas (see p 230) and Northern Ireland, since 1975. In addition, about £132 million has been allocated to Britain for specific programmes running over several years to improve the environment and encourage the development of employment in certain steel, shipbuilding and textile closure areas and in the border regions of Northern Ireland.

European Investment Bank

The European Investment Bank (EIB) is a self-governing institution set up by the Treaty of Rome with member states of the European Community subscribing to its capital. The Bank's aims are to help to stimulate development in less-favoured regions, to modernise or convert industries, to help to create new activities and to offset structural difficulties affecting certain sectors. The EIB also serves projects of common interest to several member states or the

Community as a whole. It has loaned about £4,200 million since 1973 for projects in Britain, mostly for public works such as the Sullom Voe oil terminal, and manufacturing projects in the assisted areas.

European Coal and Steel Community

The European Coal and Steel Community (ECSC) provides loans and grants to encourage rational distribution of production and a high level of productivity in the coal and steel industries while safeguarding employment and avoiding unfair competition. Areas eligible for aid are coal industry projects, conversion schemes, construction of housing for workers, allowances for redeployed workers and research, including research of a social or medical nature. Exchange risk cover may be provided by the Government on certain ECSC loans for projects qualifying for regional selective assistance. The British borrower takes on only a sterling liability.

COMPETITION POLICY AND CONSUMER PROTECTION

A major feature of the Government's economic policy is the stimulation of competition and the control of practices which are restrictive or anti-competitive. Linked to this policy is the encouragement of fair trading, with the particular aim of helping consumers and safeguarding their rights. The Parliamentary Under-Secretary of State for Corporate and Consumer Affairs, who is answerable to the Secretary of State for Trade and Industry, has special responsibilities for competition policy and consumer affairs (although certain matters, such as safety of foodstuffs and road vehicles, are the concern of other departments). The Office of Fair Trading, a government agency headed by the Director General of Fair Trading, has various executive responsibilities relating to competition policy and consumer protection.

Competition Policy

Competition policy is supported by machinery for scrutinising and regulating monopolies, mergers, anti-competitive practices and restrictive trade practices, and by powers to regulate any structural changes or anti-competitive practices which operate against the public interest. The Director General of Fair Trading administers the Fair Trading Act 1973, which deals with monopolies and mergers, the Restrictive Trade Practices Act 1976, which deals with restrictive trading agreements, the Resale Prices Act 1976, which deals with minimum resale price maintenance, and the Competition Act 1980, which deals with anti-competitive practices.

The Government is working to increase competition in professional services, through relaxation of unjustifiable restrictive practices including restrictions on fee sales and on advertising. Measures are being taken to improve competition in conveyancing. The opticians' monopoly on the dispensing of spectacles was ended in 1984, and certain professional groups (for example, accountants, solicitors and veterinary surgeons) have eased restrictions on advertising by their members. Building societies are to be allowed to offer a greater range of services than they are able to do at present, which will bring more competition to the fields of financial services and estate agency. Financial services generally are to be subject to a greater degree of regulation in the interests of investor protection, and there will be special provision for consideration of the implications for competition policy by the Director General.

Monopolies and Mergers

The Government believes that most mergers have a 'market rationale' and in most cases does not wish to intervene. However, it recognises the need to control companies with excessive market shares.

The Secretary of State for Trade and Industry and the Director General of Fair Trading can refer monopolies for investigation by the Monopolies and Mergers

Commission, an independent body whose members are drawn from a variety of backgrounds, including lawyers, economists, industrialists and trade unionists. The legislation defines a monopoly as a situation where at least a quarter of a particular kind of goods or service is supplied by or to a single person, or by two or more people acting in a way which prevents, restricts, or distorts competition. Local monopolies can also be referred to the Commission, and the Secretary of State can refer public sector industries. If the Commission finds that a monopoly operates against the public interest, the Secretary of State for Trade and Industry has powers to take action to remedy or prevent the harm which the Commission considers may exist. Alternatively the Director General may be asked to negotiate undertakings to remedy the adverse effects identified by the Commission.

Proposals for a merger (defined as occurring when two or more enterprises are brought under common ownership or control) may be referred to the Commission by the Secretary of State for Trade and Industry, taking account of advice from the Director General, if the merger would result in or intensify a monopoly or if the total value of gross assets to be taken over would exceed £30 million. If the Commission finds that a merger or proposed merger may be expected to operate against the public interest, the Secretary of State can prevent it from taking place or obtain undertakings to remedy the adverse effects identified; or, if it has already taken place, he can require it to be reversed. There are special provisions for newspaper mergers.

In 1984, following a review of its mergers policy, the Government said that it would continue to make reference decisions primarily on competition grounds; and, in evaluating the competitive situation, it would have regard to the international context—to the extent of competition in the domestic market from overseas sources and to the competitive position of British firms in overseas markets.

Anti-competitive Practices

Subject to limited exemptions, the Director General can investigate any business practice (whether in the public or private sectors) which may restrict, distort or prevent competition in the production, supply or acquisition of goods or services in Britain. If the Director General concludes that a practice is anti-competitive he may either accept an undertaking from the business responsible for the practice or, in default of such an undertaking, refer the matter to the Commission to establish whether it operates against the public interest. On an adverse finding by the Commission, the Secretary of State has powers to take remedial action.

The Public Sector

The Competition Act empowers the Secretary of State to refer to the Monopolies and Mergers Commission any questions on the efficiency and costs of, the service provided by, or the possible abuse of a monopoly situation by, various bodies in the public sector. It is the Government's intention that at least one major examination of each industry should take place every four years.

Restrictive Trade Practices

Under the Restrictive Trade Practices Act 1976 restrictive trading agreements have to be registered with the Director General of Fair Trading. Broadly, an agreement is registrable if two or more parties to it, engaged in business in Britain in the supply of goods or services, accept some limitation on their freedom to make their own decisions about matters such as prices or conditions of sale. Failure to register an agreement means that the restrictions are void and the parties are liable to legal proceedings. Having placed an agreement on the register, the Director General has the duty of referring it to the Restrictive Practices Court and the Court must declare the restrictions in it contrary to the public interest unless the parties can satisfy the Court by reference to criteria laid down in the Act that this is not the case. Restrictions declared contrary to the public interest are void and the Court can order the parties not to give effect to them or make any similar agreement. In practice, however, many agreements do not need to be referred to the Court because, for example, the parties choose to give up the restrictions rather than go to court, or the Secretary of State accepts the Director General's advice that the restrictions are not significant enough to warrant reference to the Court.

European Community

The objective of the European Community's competition policy is to ensure that there is free and fair competition in trade between member states and that the government trade barriers dismantled by the Treaty of Rome are not replaced by private barriers which fragment the common market. The competition rules are set out in the Treaty of Rome. These are directly applicable in the law of member states. In most areas of economic activity their enforcement is the responsibility of the European Commission, which has powers to investigate and terminate alleged infringements and to impose fines.

The Treaty prohibits agreements or concerted practices which are likely to affect trade between member states and have as their object, or effect, the prevention, restriction or distortion of competition within the common market. Agreements meeting specified criteria may be exempted from this prohibition and, subject to particular conditions and safeguards, certain categories of agreement are exempted completely: these include agreements in respect of exclusive distribution and purchasing, patent licensing, research and development, and motor vehicle distribution and servicing. The Treaty also prohibits any abuse of a dominant position within the common market or a substantial part of it to the extent that it affects trade between member states.

Consumer Protection

In addition to laws designed to benefit customers by providing effective competition, there is a body of legislation whose purpose is to ensure that consumers are adequately protected.

The Fair Trading Act 1973 provides machinery (headed by the Director General of Fair Trading) for the continuous review of consumer affairs, for action to deal with trading practices which unfairly affect consumers' interests and with persistent offenders under existing law, and for the negotiation of self-regulatory codes of practice to raise trading standards. The Director General is also responsible for the operation of legislation which regulates consumer credit and hire business and estate agency work.

The consumer's interests with regard to the purity of foods, the description and performance of goods and services and pricing information are safeguarded by the Food Act 1984, the Medicines Act 1968, the Trade Descriptions Acts 1968 and 1972, the Prices Act 1974, the Unfair Contract Terms Act 1977, the Sale of Goods Act 1979 and the Supply of Goods and Services Act 1982. The marking and accuracy of quantities are regulated by the Weights and Measures Act 1985. The Consumer Protection Acts 1961 and 1971 and the Consumer Safety Act 1978 empower the Government to control the supply of most goods in the interests of safety. A White Paper proposing major changes in the law to prevent unsafe products being marketed was published in 1984 and legislative proposals to implement some of these measures received royal assent in July 1986. The Government intends to introduce legislation implementing the remaining proposals and to clarify the laws prohibiting misleading price indications.

Legislative proposals to offer greater protection to investors by establishing a new regulatory framework for the financial services sector have been put before Parliament.

Consumer Advice and Information

Advice and information on consumer matters is provided to the general public at local level by the trading standards or consumer protection departments of local authorities and in some areas by specialist Consumer Advice Centres. Citizens Advice Bureaux also provide advice to the public on consumer matters.

The independent, non-statutory National Consumer Council (and associated councils for Scotland and Wales), which receives government finance, ensures that the consumer's view is made known to those in government and industry whose decisions affect the consumer's interest. In Northern Ireland the General Consumer Council for Northern Ireland (which became fully operational in April 1985) has wide-ranging responsibilities in the field of consumer protection and consumer affairs in general.

Consumer councils for the energy, rail and other nationalised industries and the privatised gas industry investigate questions of concern to the consumer, while some trade associations in industry and commerce have established codes of practice. In addition, several private organisations work to further consumer interests. The largest is the Consumers' Association, funded by the subscriptions of its membership of over 820,000. The Association conducts an extensive programme of comparative testing of goods and investigation of services; its views and test reports are published in its monthly magazines and other publications. The Association provides a legal advice service on subscription. Local consumer groups, many belonging to a national federation, also promote consumers' interests and provide information and advice.

The European Community's consumer programme covers a number of important topics, such as health and safety, protection of the consumer's economic interests when purchasing goods and services, promotion of consumer education and strengthening the representation of consumers. A directive on liability for defective products was adopted in 1985 and must be implemented in Britain by 1988. The views of British consumer organisations are represented by the Consumers in the European Community Group (UK).

COMPANY LAW

The formation and conduct of companies is regulated by the Companies Act 1985. 'Incorporation' involves registering with the Registrar of Companies in Cardiff, Edinburgh or Belfast, depending on whether a company's registered office is in England or Wales, Scotland or Northern Ireland. The Act also deals with capital structure, the rights and duties of directors and members, and the preparation and filing of accounts. Most corporate businesses are 'limited liability' companies. Each company is a legal entity distinct from its members, who are not as such liable for its debts. The liability of members of a limited company is limited to contributing an amount related to their shareholding. In unincorporated businesses, such as sole proprietorships or partnerships, by contrast, individuals are personally liable for any business debts (except where a member of a partnership is a limited liability company).

Companies may be either public or private. A company must satisfy three conditions before it can be a public limited company (plc): it must be limited by shares and have a share capital; it must state in its memorandum of association that it is to be a public limited company; and it must meet specified minimum capital requirements. All other registered companies are, by definition, private companies and, as such, prohibited from offering their shares to the public.

The consolidation of the Companies Acts 1948–83 has been completed and came into force in July 1985; it restates existing law in a clearer and more convenient form, and makes application and interpretation easier for those concerned with the regulation of company affairs. The consolidation resulted in the Companies Act 1985 and three smaller Acts: the Business Names Act 1985, which regulates the names under which people may carry on business in Great Britain; the Company Securities (Insider Dealing) Act 1985, which restates the law on insider dealing; and the Companies Consolidation (Consequential Provisions) Act 1985, which deals with the technical aspects of the consolidation.

The Insolvency Act 1985 affects both corporate and individual insolvency proceedings. It introduced for England, Wales and Scotland a licensing procedure to ensure the professional competence, integrity and independence of people who act as trustees of bankrupt individuals, or as liquidators, receivers or administrators of bankrupt companies. The bankruptcy legislation has been modernised and simplified. It applies only to England and Wales and will come into force in December 1986; the position of Scotland is covered by separate legislation which came into force in April 1986. The Act also amended and supplemented the legislation relating to the winding-up of limited companies and the appointment of receivers in England, Wales and Scotland. A new framework for dealing with directors of limited companies who are demonstrably unfit to act as such came into operation in April 1986: they can be disqualified from office and, in some cases, held personally liable for a company's debts. The Act also introduced procedures to enable individual and corporate debtors to reach agreements with their creditors without the necessity for formal bankruptcy or insolvency proceedings. These procedures, applying to England, Wales and Scotland, will come into effect in December 1986.

INDUSTRIAL AND INTELLECTUAL PROPERTY

There is a substantial body of legislation designed to secure the rights of the originators of inventions, new industrial designs and trade marks. These matters are administered by the Patent Office, which includes the Design Registry and the Trade Marks Registry. The Patent Office is a division of the Department of Trade and Industry. Protection is also available under the European Patent Convention and the Patent Co-operation Treaty, and benefits may be claimed in other countries by virtue of the International Convention for the Protection of Industrial Property. The Government has reviewed the law on copyright and related matters, with particular attention to the problems raised by private tape recordings of sound and video copyright works, the application of copyright to industrial designs, and the use of photocopying. In April 1986 it published a White Paper setting out legislative and other proposals covering the whole field of copyright and other aspects of intellectual property, including the future operation of the Patent Office. Legislation to extend copyright protection to owners of computer software was passed in July 1985. The penalties for trading in pirate sound and film recordings (including video) were greatly increased in 1983.

The Government is concerned to encourage innovation by providing a more adequate legal and administrative system for the protection of the ownership of ideas by means of patents, registered designs, trade marks and copyright, and to improve awareness of the value of these intellectual property rights and of their accessibility and usage, particularly by individuals and small businesses. Proposals to facilitate the computerisation of the Patent Office's registers and to extend the law on trade marks to include services have been put before Parliament.

12 Manufacturing and Service Industries

The manufacturing and service industries, together with construction, account for about 88 per cent of gross domestic product (GDP), the remainder being accounted for by energy production and agriculture. Since 1950, GDP has more than doubled in real terms and both manufacturing and services have contributed to this growth. As in other developed economies, rising living standards have led to a faster growth of demand for services than for manufactures, so that the proportion of GDP accounted for by services has increased steadily. About 26 per cent of the employed labour force was engaged in manufacturing in 1985 (compared with about 40 per cent in 1950) and around 67 per cent of visible exports consisted of manufactured or semi-manufactured goods. In the same year, 65 per cent of the employed labour force was engaged in service industries, and international trade in services produced a surplus on current account of £5,800 million. Among the traded services covered in this chapter, business services and tourism show the greatest growth. Financial services, which have also shown significant growth, are not included in this chapter, nor are large non-traded service sectors such as education, health, and public administration and defence.

Manufacturing

Manufacturing output as a whole fell after 1973, following the rise in international oil prices, but grew again gradually between 1975 and 1979. Following further rises in energy costs, manufacturing output declined signifi-cantly between 1979 and 1981 in almost all of the industrialised market economies. Additional factors depressing output in Britain were high domestic interest rates and, for exporters, a rise in the exchange value of sterling which raised the prices of British goods in overseas markets and lowered the price of foreign goods in Britain. Output remained low in 1982, but rose by 2·9 per cent in 1983, by 3·9 per cent in 1984 and by 3·0 per cent in 1985.

The figures in Table 17 show the relative size of the sectors of manufacturing and their growth rates.

The recovery has been most notable in the chemicals and electrical and instrument engineering sectors, which are also the sectors which have shown the highest growth over the last decade. Extensive reorganisation, re-equipment and modernisation in long-established industries such as steel manufacture, vehicle-building and shipbuilding have greatly increased productivity. Utilisa-tion of advanced technology, especially microelectronics, is steadily increasing in all sectors. A major stimulus has been provided by the various needs of the offshore oil and gas industries.

Since manufacturing industry lies mainly in the private sector, investment in manufacturing tends to be determined by market considerations and to reflect expectations of profitability. There are discernible cycles in the level of investment: 1983 saw the beginning of an upturn in the latest trough. Total direct investment in 1985 was £7,950 million at current prices, comprising £6,394 million on plant and machinery, £994 million on new building and £562 million on vehicles. In addition, assets worth an estimated £1,599 million were purchased by financial companies to lease to manufacturers.

Most manufacturing is carried out by private enterprise. Though the greater parts of the iron and steel and shipbuilding industries are in public ownership, the Government is reducing the extent of state ownership of industry. Table 18 shows the size distribution of manufacturing establishments. About 55 per cent of the largest establishments were in engineering and metals and vehicle manufacturing. Within the private sector, the 100 largest companies accounted for 34 per cent of manufacturing employment in 1983. (A company may consist of one or more establishments.)

The largest manufacturing companies (by £ million turnover in the latest financial year) are BAT Industries (14,426), Imperial Chemical Industries (9,909), Unilever (5,859), General Electric Company (4,800), Imperial Group (4,593), Ford Motor Company (3,752), BL (3,402), Gallaher (2,839) and Associated British Foods (2,776).

Table 17: Manufacturing—Net Output, Index of Production and Investment

	Net output (£ million) 1984	Index of production (1980 = 100)		Gross domestic fixed capital formation (£ million) 1985
		1984	1985	
Metal manufacturing	2,416	108·2	113·2	397
Other minerals and mineral products	3,758	95·0	94·4	500
Chemicals and man-made fibres	7,548	113·5	118·3	1,321
Mechanical engineering	8,508	87·4	92·8	} 1,020
Other metal goods	3,735	101·0	99·0	
Electrical and instrument engineering	9,966	123·0	130·7	912
Motor vehicles and parts	3,670	81·1	86·3	} 924
Other transport equipment	3,553	91·5	94·7	
Food, drink and tobacco	9,582	102·0	101·2	1,356
Textiles	2,110	93·7	98·3	} 1,352
Clothing, footwear and leather	2,426	101·5	105·5	
Paper, printing and publishing	6,873	96·4	98·6	} 1,161
All other manufacturing	5,400	99·3	99·2	
Total	69,545	100·7	103·8	7,950

Source: *United Kingdom National Accounts 1986 Edition.*

The statistics in the following sections, relating to the main sectors of manufacturing industry, are supplied by the Statistical Division of the Department of Trade and Industry. Unless otherwise stated, export and sales figures include parts and export figures include re-exports.

Table 18: Manufacturing: Size Distribution of Establishments

Number of employees	Number of establishments	% of total establishments	% of total employment
Under 20	76,739	74·9	11·0
20 to 499	24,069	23·5	42·2
500 to 1,499	1,276	1·2	20·0
1,500 or more	361	0·4	26·8

Source: *Report on the Census of Production 1983.*

MINERAL PRODUCTS

1985	Labour[a] ('000s)	Sales[b] (£ million)	Exports (£ million)	Imports (£ million)
Metal manufacturing	206	8,163	3,896	4,973
of which: iron and steel products	145	5,019	2,178	2,540
non-ferrous metals	61	3,144	1,718	2,433
Non-metallic mineral products	192	7,755	2,337	2,436
of which: building materials and				
abrasives	95	1,364	69	91
glass and glassware	47	2,474	309	434
refractory and ceramic goods	51	2,186	410	191

[a] Employees in employment (Great Britain) at June 1985.
[b] Sales of principal products.

Iron and Steel Products

Most of the early developments in iron and steel production originated in Britain, and Britain is the world's tenth largest steel-producing nation (by volume). The British Steel Corporation (BSC), formed as a public corporation in 1967, has accounted in recent years for 82 to 85 per cent of Britain's crude steel production by volume and is the world's fourth largest steel company. BSC invested heavily in modernising its production capacity in the 1960s and 1970s. The basic oxygen process is now used for bulk steel production with the electric arc process for more specialised tasks; the traditional open-hearth process disappeared in 1980. Because of a world-wide over-supply of steel, BSC has had to accelerate the closure of its older steelworks and reduce capacity at other works. Rationalisation of the industry has involved some transfers of assets between BSC and the private sector and the closure in both sectors of plants which cannot be made profitable. Productivity doubled between 1981 and 1985 and is now among the best in the world.

British producers' deliveries of finished steel were 12·9 million tonnes in 1985, of which 69 per cent was used by home industry, the remainder being directly exported. The private sector is particularly strong in the manufacture of more specialised steels and of finished products for the engineering industry. The industry is concentrated in Wales, northern England and Scotland. As a member of the European Coal and Steel Community, Britain co-operates with the other members in efforts to rationalise the structure and improve the profitability of the steel industry throughout the Community. Britain welcomed the ending of all direct government subsidy to the steel industries of member countries at the beginning of 1986, but remains concerned about the effects of continuing indirect subsidy, particularly on energy, transport and labour costs, in some countries.

Non-ferrous Metals

Britain has one of the largest non-ferrous metal processing and fabricating industries in Europe. Output in 1985 included: aluminium (293,000 tonnes of primary metal and 102,000 tonnes of secondary metal); refined copper (64,000 tonnes of primary metal and 62,000 tonnes of secondary metal); refined lead (148,000 tonnes of primary metal and 160,000 tonnes of secondary metal); and zinc (74,000 tonnes of slab metal). Primary metal production relies mainly on imported ores, concentrates and partially refined metal.

Britain is also a major producer of specialised alloys for high technology requirements in the aerospace, electronic, petrochemical, and nuclear and other fuel industries. Titanium and titanium alloys are produced and used in aircraft production, power generation and North Sea oil production.

Nearly half of the industry is situated in the midlands. Europe's largest nickel refinery and only titanium granule plant are situated in Wales, near Swansea, West Glamorgan, and in Deeside respectively. There is a zinc smelter of some 100,000 tonnes capacity at Avonmouth. Two large-scale aluminium smelters in Lynemouth, Northumberland, and Anglesey, Gwynedd, provide 75 per cent of Britain's requirements for primary aluminium. A wide range of semi-manufactures is produced in copper, lead, zinc and aluminium and their alloys, and, particularly in aluminium and copper, firms are engaged in smelting, casting and fabrication by rolling, extrusion and drawing; advanced techniques of powder metallurgy and pressure die-casting are also employed, which help to conserve energy and materials. In recent years considerable progress has been made in the development of 'superplastic' alloys, which are more ductile and elastic than conventional alloys. Aluminium lithium, a new alloy which is up to 20 per cent lighter than traditional materials, is currently being developed by a British company with plans to use it in aircraft construction.

Exports of aluminium and aluminium alloys reached £400 million in 1985 while exports in the same year of copper, brass and other copper alloys reached £353 million. Exports of silver, platinum and other precious metals totalled over £439 million in 1985. The major export markets for the whole industry are the United States and the rest of the European Community.

Building Materials

The manufacture of most building materials is now based on highly mechanised systems. Five major companies supply about 72 per cent of total brick deliveries. The cement industry is chiefly concerned with the manufacture of Portland cement for the home market. This was invented by Joseph Aspdin and patented in 1824. Three firms dominate the industry, the largest being Blue Circle Industries.

Glass-reinforced cement composites were invented in Britain in the mid-1970s and are manufactured under licence in over 40 other countries.

Ceramic and Refractory Goods

The pottery industry, centred largely in Staffordshire, supplies almost all home needs for domestic and industrial pottery. It uses largely indigenous clay from Cornwall and Devon. (Britain is the world's largest exporter of china clay, which was the country's largest mineral export until the discovery of North Sea oil.) There has been considerable re-equipment in the industry; kilns fired by gas or electricity have replaced all the coal-fired kilns, and new decorating techniques and automatic and semi-automatic machinery, such as automatic glazing machines, have been introduced. More recently there has been investment in new technology such as fast-firing and once-firing kilns. Domestic pottery, including china, earthenware and stoneware, accounts for 60 per cent of the industry's output; the other main divisions are glazed tiles, sanitary ware and electrical ware, and such specialised industrial products as acid-proof stoneware, porous ceramics and laboratory porcelain. Production of tableware is concentrated in two major groups, Wedgwood and Royal Doulton. Britain is the world's principal manufacturer of fine bone china, much of which is exported; famous makes include Wedgwood, Spode, Royal Worcester, Royal Doulton, Minton, Aynsley, Coalport and Royal Crown Derby.

Research is being conducted into ceramics for use in housebuilding and diesel and jet engines. Important industrial ceramics invented in Britain include silicon carbides developed by the United Kingdom Atomic Energy Authority and sialons developed at the University of Newcastle upon Tyne.

Refractory goods include heat-resisting materials such as magnesite, silica and high-alumina bricks, crucibles, kiln linings and radiants for gas and electric fires.

Glass

Britain's glass industry is one of the biggest in the world and all types of glass product are made. Glass containers form the largest part of the industry; another major section is devoted to the manufacture of flat glass in its various forms, chiefly by the float glass process developed in Britain by Pilkington Brothers and licensed to glassmakers throughout the world. Pilkingtons have also developed an energy-saving window glass which reflects room heat without impairing visibility. There is also a craft sector producing high-quality handmade lead crystal glass.

CHEMICALS AND MAN-MADE FIBRES

1985	Labour[a] ('000s)	Sales[b] (£ million)	Exports (£ million)	Imports (£ million)
Chemicals	326	20,077	9,414	7,048
of which: basic industrial chemicals	118	8,896	4,772	4,181
paints, varnishes and printing inks	32	1,390	272	141
pharmaceuticals	81	3,422	1,483	660
soap and toilet preparations	37	2,154	492	265
Man-made fibres	15	588	435	384

[a] Employees in employment (Great Britain) at June 1985.
[b] Sales of principal products.

Chemicals

The chemicals industry is one of the most successful industries in Britain as well as being its fifth largest industrial sector, accounting for about 10 per cent of manufacturing net output. It produces a complete range of products including basic industrial chemicals (inorganic chemicals, basic organic chemicals, plastics, fertilisers and other products), pharmaceuticals, soap, toiletries and explosives. The industry is also the third largest in Europe and the fifth largest in the Western world. Western Europe is the major export market, and organic chemicals, plastics and pharmaceuticals account for more than 50 per cent of chemical exports by value. The areas of highest growth between 1985 and 1986 were formulated pesticides, synthetic resins and plastics, dyestuffs and pigments, organic chemicals and inorganic chemicals.

The largest British chemicals group, Imperial Chemical Industries, is the fifth largest chemicals company in the world, accounting for around 25 per cent of production in Britain. Exports account for 50 per cent of its production. The industry is represented by the Chemical Industries Association.

Basic Industrial Chemicals

A high proportion of inorganic chemicals production consists of relatively simple bulk chemicals, such as sulphuric acid and metallic and non-metallic oxides, serving as basic materials for industry. The most important products in the organic chemicals range (by weight) are ethylene (1,447,000 tonnes produced in 1985), propylene (973,000 tonnes) and benzene (835,000 tonnes).

Outside the inorganic and organic sectors is a wide range of general chemicals formulated for specific uses.

Plastics

Many of the basic discoveries in plastics, including polyethylene, were made in Britain. Over 30 per cent of production is exported. Expansion in recent years has mainly been in thermoplastic materials, of which the most important are polyethylene (used in coverings and packaging—notably for foodstuffs), polyvinyl chloride (known as PVC and used for a wide range of industrial purposes and consumer goods), polystyrene (used for toys, light mouldings and many consumer goods) and polypropylene (which can be fabricated as mouldings, films and fibres). A new group of plastics materials reinforced with carbon fibres is also in commercial production; they have up to three times the strength but are only 20 per cent of the weight of steel, and are being increasingly used in aircraft and vehicle manufacture. Styrene-butadiene and polybutadiene rubbers used for tyres, high-styrene rubbers for shoe soles and flooring, and nitrile rubbers for use where oil resistance is required are also in large-scale production, together with neoprene rubber.

British companies also produce large quantities of coextruded oriented polypropylene which is used in packaging food and other consumer products and which is increasingly replacing cellulose films on grounds of versatility and cost. ICI is among the world's top three producers of polyethylene terephthalate, a new form of polyester used to produce plastic bottles.

Paint

The industry produces a wide range of decorative and industrial paints and varnishes. Specialised products include new ranges of synthetic resins and pigments, powder coatings, non-drip and quick-drying paints and paints needing only one top coat. Two significant recent innovations have been solid emulsion paint and a temporary water-based finish for vehicle bodies and road markings, which can be removed easily by chemical treatment. The industry has set a timetable for eliminating lead as a drier in paints and is conducting research to find effective replacements.

Agricultural Chemicals and Fertilisers

Notable recent British discoveries and developments include pyrethroid insecticides, ICI's diquat and paraquat herbicides, and systemic fungicides and aphicides. The development of chemical fertilisers also owes much to the pioneer work of British scientists. Manufacture of chemical fertilisers, particularly ammonium nitrate, is dominated by a few large firms producing almost entirely for the domestic market. A substantial proportion of world research and development in agrochemicals is conducted in Britain.

Pharmaceuticals

British scientists have played a major part in the development of essential drugs and medicinal products, and about 12 per cent of the world's research in pharmaceuticals takes place in Britain. Britain is the world's fourth largest exporter of pharmaceutical products. Among the more recent major developments pioneered in Britain have been: the introduction of new semi-synthetic penicillins; the development of salbutamol, sodium cromoglycate and inhaled beclomethasone dipropionate, which have revolutionised the treatment of asthma; ibuprofen, an important advance in the treatment of arthritis; cimetidine and ranitidine, which have profoundly affected the treatment of peptic ulceration; humulin, a synthetic human insulin; and beta-blockers, used in the treatment of heart disease. Britain is among the world leaders in the production of antibiotics by fermentation.

The British company, Celltech, exploiting research done by the Medical

Research Council, is a leader in the commercial production of monoclonal antibodies, which are used as raw materials for other products and in the purification of alpha-interferon and blood-typing products. The company is also working on a range of other products such as calcitonin, which may be useful in treating osteoporosis (brittle bones) and macrophage activating factor, which enhances the activity of the body's immune system. A range of immuno-radiometric assays for specific biochemicals is also under development in Britain.

Britain is foremost among the world's developers of molecular graphics, a computer-aided technique for studying the structure of complicated organic molecules on a visual display unit, eliminating the need for many physical tests of drugs.

Cosmetics,
Toiletry and
Perfumery

The industry is made up of British and many international companies which often have manufacturing facilities in Britain. There are large companies in the sector, sometimes with interests in the pharmaceutical, soap or detergent industries, and also a number of small independent companies. Exports of the industry's products in 1985 were £340 million, compared with imports of less than £200 million. The home market amounted to about £1,150 million at manufacturers' prices.

Other Chemical
Products

Many specialised chemical products are manufactured, including dyestuffs, formulated adhesives and sealants, chemically treated oils and fats, essential oils and flavouring materials, explosives, industrial gases, products for the treatment of leather and textiles, adhesive film, cloth and foil, and surfactants (surface-active agents) for many purposes. There is also major production of soaps and detergents. Work is progressing on the use of epoxy and anaerobic adhesives and cyanoacrylates in engineering as replacements for spot-welding and riveting, especially in the motor industry.

Man-made
Fibres

Britain played a major role in the early development of man-made fibres and continues to be an important producer of these fibres, mainly through a small number of large companies. The main types of fibre are still those first developed—regenerated cellulosic fibres such as viscose and the major synthetic fibres such as nylon polyamide, polyester (a British invention) and acrylics. Extensive research continues to produce a wide variety of innovative products with characteristics designed to meet market needs, such as anti-static and flame-retardant fibres. Polyolefins (polypropylene and polyethylene) find signifi-cant use in carpets, carpet backing and other household and industrial textiles. More specialist products include the aramids (with very high thermal stability and strength), elastanes (giving very high stretch and recovery), melded fabrics (produced without the need for knitting or weaving) and carbon fibres (originally developed for the aerospace industry but now finding numerous wider applications).

Mechanical
Engineering

The mechanical engineering sector comprises industries manufacturing all types of non-electrical machinery, machine tools, industrial engines, mechani-cal handling equipment, construction equipment and industrial plant. Since much of the production of the industry is of capital equipment, it suffered particularly during the recession which began in 1979. Output dropped substantially between 1979 and 1981 and remained at about the same level until 1984 when there was a recovery of output in some sectors of the industry. This recovery strengthened in 1985 when growth of output in mechanical engineer-ing as a whole was 6 per cent, with rises of 22 per cent in printing machinery, 20 per cent in machine tools, 18 per cent in fork-lift and other industrial trucks,

MECHANICAL ENGINEERING AND METAL GOODS

1985	Labour[a] ('000s)	Sales[b] (£ million)	Exports (£ million)	Imports (£ million)
Mechanical engineering	775	18,785	8,295	6,159
of which: industrial plant and steelwork	74	3,095	584	262
agricultural machinery and tractors	35	1,285	847	625
machine tools	79	1,539	600	617
textile machinery	11	291	220	167
process machinery	44	987	654	492
mining, construction and mechanical handling equipment	82	3,065	1,592	930
Other metal goods	382	8,514	1,218	1,380
Instrument engineering	112	2,358	1,494	1,754

[a] Employees in employment (Great Britain) at June 1985.
[b] Sales of principal products.

13 per cent in steelwork and chemical industry machinery, 11 per cent in construction equipment and 10 per cent in mining machinery. Over 40 per cent of the industry's sales are exported, and exports in 1985 amounted to 11 per cent of all visible exports.

Industrial Plant and Steelwork and Process Machinery

The industry manufactures almost every type of industrial (including process) plant and steelwork. Of particular importance are fabricated products such as pressure vessels, heat exchangers and storage tanks for chemical and oil-refining (process) plant, steam-raising boilers (including those of high capacity for power stations), nuclear reactors, water and sewage treatment plant and fabricated steelwork for bridges, buildings and industrial installations. The industrial plant industry comprises both equipment manufacturers and contractors responsible for the design, engineering, construction and commissioning of complete plants for process industries. Equipment for the chemicals and related industries, such as processing, bottling and packaging machines as well as mixing equipment and furnaces, ovens and kilns, is also produced.

Agricultural Machinery and Tractors

Britain is the Western world's largest producer of agricultural tractors, which make up two-thirds of the country's total output of agricultural equipment. There was a substantial downturn in the world tractor market between 1976 and 1983 which resulted in a fall in production of over 50 per cent in Britain over this period. Output grew by 30 per cent in 1984, but fell by 14·5 per cent in 1985 to 87,857 units. The industry also produces a wide range of other general and specialised agricultural equipment such as fruit, vegetable and root harvesters. Britain's total output of agricultural machinery and tractors in 1985 was £900 million, of which 65 per cent was exported, with a trade surplus of £174 million.

The major domestic exhibitions for the industry's products are the Royal Smithfield Show and the Royal International Agricultural Show. The former is held in London in December, the latter in July at the National Agricultural Centre, near Coventry, which also provides regular demonstrations of technical developments in agriculture. Much of the new machinery is designed for use in a variety of conditions to meet the needs of overseas farmers, and since 1984 the

Royal International Agricultural Show has had a specialised tropical machinery centre, where demonstrations of such machinery are given.

Machine Tools   Britain produces a very wide range of machine tools. Almost all are purchased by the engineering, vehicles and metal goods industries. As these sectors were among those most affected by the recession in world manufacturing, production of machine tools contracted between 1980 and 1983. However, new orders increased substantially in 1984 and 1985.

The most commonly used metal-cutting machine tools are milling, grinding and turning machines. The manufacture of computerised numerically controlled machine tools and the adoption of flexible manufacturing systems are becoming increasingly important. The latter development has contributed to the doubling of the number of robots installed in Britain since 1983. The United States was again the largest export market for the industry in 1985 (£68·4 million). The next were the Federal Republic of Germany (£25·4 million), Canada (£14·7 million) and France (£13·3 million). The Machine Tool Trades Association represents most of the industry and is responsible for an international exhibition held in Britain every four years, the next in 1988.

Textile   British inventions have remained the foundation of many textile processes in
Machinery   use internationally and progress has been made in applying automated techniques (including the use of microelectronics) in the industry. In 1985, some 66 per cent of the industry's total sales were to export markets. Recent innovations in Britain include computerised colour matching and weave simulation, friction spinning, high-speed computer-controlled knitting machines, and electronic jacquard attachments for weaving looms.

Construction,   Almost the whole range of plant required by the construction industry is
Mining,   produced, including excavating, earth-moving and road-making equipment,
Mechanical   pile-drivers, and quarry crushing and screening plant. Overseas sales of mining
Handling   machinery and equipment are substantial, while exports of construction
and Other   equipment amounted to £584 million in 1985 (80 per cent of output). The
Equipment   privately owned company J. C. Bamford is the world's second largest manufacturer of backhoe loaders. It exports 60 per cent of its output and has remained profitable in a market in which world demand fell by over 30 per cent between 1980 and 1984.

The British mining equipment industry is very strong, especially in the production of shearing equipment, hydraulic roof supports, conveying equipment, flameproof transformers, switchgear and subsurface transport control systems. About 85 per cent of British coal is mined using the longwall method, which was developed in Britain. British manufacturers are the leaders in the production of equipment for this type of mining. Exports of coal-mining equipment in 1985 were £213 million.

Mechanical handling equipment is used not only for construction and related activities but throughout industry generally. It extends from individual units and accessories to complete operating systems, the main products being cranes and transporters, lifts, escalators, conveyors, elevators, hoists, powered industrial trucks and air bridges. Electronically controlled and completely automatic handling systems are also produced.

Britain is also an important producer of other machinery such as industrial engines, pumps, valves and compressors, and pneumatic and hydraulic equipment.

Metal Products   The castings industry plays an important role in meeting the needs of manufacturers for essential components for products sold both in Britain and abroad. Its main customers are the vehicle, mechanical engineering, and building and construction industries. The larger mechanised foundries are dominant, but many smaller craft foundries meet needs for specialised and low-volume castings. Output (by volume) has been falling and the industry has been progressively changing. While some foundries have been closing, many others have been investing in new melting equipment, moulding equipment and processes, and process and quality control equipment, both to meet demands for castings of higher quality and strength and to improve working and environmental conditions. A process patented in 1985 by a new British company enables the production of perfect aluminium-casting dies in a single semi-skilled operation, rather than the complex skilled operation necessary at present, and promises to reduce greatly the cost of such dies.

Instrument Engineering

This industry produces a wide range of goods which need an exceptional degree of precision in their manufacture. Non-electrical measuring equipment forms an important part of output. Other sectors of the industry include photographic, cinematographic and reprographic equipment; watches, clocks and time recorders; and medical and surgical instruments and appliances. Important advances have been made in the application of recent developments in mechanical and electronic engineering to production and quality control.

ELECTRICAL AND ELECTRONIC ENGINEERING

1985	Labour[a] ('000s)	Sales[b] (£ million)	Exports (£ million)	Imports (£ million)
Data-processing equipment	⎱ 74	3,223	3,314	3,920
Office equipment	⎰	166	229	293
Communications equipment and other electronic capital equipment	339	5,551	2,256	1,873
of which: communications equipment[c]	199	4,095	1,234	984
electrical instruments and control systems	n.a.	1,285	852	740
medical electronic equipment[c]	n.a.	171	170	149
Electronic components	n.a.	2,235	1,568	2,148
Consumer electrical and electronic goods and other electrical equipment	n.a.	3,268	1,067	2,011

[a] Employees in employment (Great Britain) at June 1985.
[b] Sales of principal products.
[c] The probable contribution of small firms is not included in the sales figures.
n.a. = not available.

This group of industries suffered much less than other manufacturing industries as a result of the world-wide recession of the early 1980s. Output fell slightly from 1980 to 1981, but began to recover in 1982 and has grown steadily since then. The outstanding sector has been the electronic data-processing equipment sector, whose output nearly doubled between 1983 and 1985. Britain produces a wide range of both capital and consumer electrical and electronic goods. Advances in microelectronics have meant that the borderlines between office machinery, data-processing equipment, telecommunications equipment and consumer electronic equipment are becoming ever harder to define. Britain is in the forefront of these developments, having originated many of the breakthroughs in the area.

Computers

The computer sector, which has grown strongly over the past five years, produces an extensive range of computer systems, central processors and peripheral equipment, from large computers for large-scale data-processing and scientific work to mini- and microcomputers for use in control and automation systems and for home, educational and office use. The number of innovative companies in the sector, both in hardware and software, is very large. There are about 300 such companies of all sizes in 'Silicon Glen' in Scotland and a similar number of mainly small firms in the Cambridge area.

Companies are constantly developing applications for new technology in the office. In 1984, a major British computer manufacturer, ICL, introduced a product known as the 'One-per-desk' which combines a personal computer, business software and an advanced push-button telephone in one unit. The company claims a world lead in this type of product. Major new mainframe computers, the Series 39 range, were introduced in 1985.

Office Machinery and Revenue Control Equipment

The office machinery industry produces a wide range of equipment including microfilm readers/printers, duplicators and rapid high-volume photocopiers.

British companies are strongly involved in the development of electronic revenue control equipment, including electronic funds transfer and point of sale equipment. The first large-scale trial of cashless shopping in Britain began in Northampton in October 1985, using equipment manufactured by ICL. The scheme involves over 100 retailers. Recent export orders include one for integrated store systems for a group of 139 retail stores across the United States. The stores will have point of sale terminals, information displays, printers and mini-computers and will be linked by a national network, giving management instant access to information on the whole business. British-made computerised ticketing equipment is being installed throughout British Rail's network; this is the world's largest order to date for revenue control equipment.

Communications Equipment and Other Electronic Capital Equipment

The dependence of the telecommunications industry on electronic techniques is increasing as new switching systems are introduced. The main products are switching and transmission equipment, telephones and terminals for telex, facsimile and teletex. British Telecom (BT) is the main customer for network equipment and carries out research and development work in co-operation with suppliers. Mercury Communication has been licensed to compete with BT in the provision of network services, while the market for terminals and telephones has been fully liberalised. Innovative work is being particularly stimulated by the expansion of cable television and the growth in value added network services.

In 1984, two cellular radio networks began operation. These provide sophisticated telephone services on portable telephones, and have been very successful. A large number of British companies are engaged in producing equipment for use with these networks.

One important sector of the industry produces transmission equipment and cables for telecommunications networks and other purposes: its products include submarine cables and cables insulated by a wide variety of materials. The feasibility of using optical fibres (hair-thin strands of glass) in communications was first demonstrated in Britain in 1966: they have a much higher capacity and better durability and efficiency than copper cables. Britain now has an advanced production capacity in this field. Well over half of the world's underseas communications cables have been made and laid by one British company, STC. Hitherto these have been copper cables, but the company is currently participating in laying the first optical fibre cable between Britain and the United States.

Another expanding sector of the industry is that which covers the manufacture of radio communications equipment, radar, radio and sonar navigational aids for ships and aircraft, thermal imaging systems, alarms and signalling equipment, public broadcasting equipment and other capital goods. British equipment is used extensively overseas, for defence, aviation, shipping, health and educational purposes.

Electrical Instruments and Control Systems

This sector produces a range of electrical and electronic measurement and test equipment as well as analytical instruments. Production of process control equipment is a large and expanding area along with the manufacture of numerical control and indication equipment for use in machine tools.

Electronic Medical Equipment

British companies are among the leaders in several types of advanced electronic medical equipment. Pioneering work has been undertaken in magnetic resonance imaging (MRI), a technique in which the patient is placed in a strong magnetic field and scanned with radiofrequency (RF) energy. The body interacts with this energy and the information generated is processed by computer to construct images of internal organs and tissues. For certain types of examination, MRI is becoming the preferred technique.

British companies also produce other advanced electronic medical equipment including ultrasound scanners, electromyography systems and patient monitoring systems for intensive and coronary care and other uses.

Electronic Components

The components sector manufactures a wide range of both active and passive electronic components. The comprehensive indigenous industry is supplemented by subsidiaries of a number of large overseas companies. The sector serves domestic requirements and is also very active in international trade. The manufacture of integrated circuits is an area of particularly rapid change. Britain has strength in the manufacture of advanced components, especially in semi-custom devices such as gate arrays. In 1985 the Inmos company launched the first of its 'transputer' family of innovative, high-speed, 16- and 32-bit microprocessors—'computers on a chip'—with support devices and development systems.

Basic Electrical Equipment

The main products of this very important sector are power equipment (generators, turbines, motors, converters, transformers and rectifiers) and switchgear, starting and control gear. Electrical equipment for motor vehicles and aircraft as well as other electrical equipment for industrial use are also produced.

Electrical and Electronic Consumer Goods

All types of electrical and electronic consumer goods are produced in Britain. The 'white goods sector' produces domestic appliances such as heating and cooking equipment, washing machines and driers, refrigeration appliances, vacuum cleaners, irons and electric kettles. This sector is dominated by a few large firms.

The major electronic goods produced are radio and television sets, music centres and high-fidelity audio and video equipment. In the audio field, British manufacturers have a reputation for high-quality goods but are less strong in the mass market. Equipment is also manufactured for reception of Britain's 'Prestel' and teletext services.

MOTOR VEHICLES AND OTHER TRANSPORT EQUIPMENT

1985	Labour[a] ('000s)	Sales[b] (£ million)	Exports (£ million)	Imports (£ million)
Motor vehicles (including bodies, trailers, caravans and engines)	153	7,385	1,995	5,190
Motor vehicle parts	128	3,420	2,071	1,773
Other transport equipment	280	6,627	4,170	3,033
of which: shipbuilding and repairing	88	1,236	208	57
railway equipment	31	188	70	18
aerospace equipment	152	5,026	3,820	2,804

[a] Employees in employment (Great Britain) at June 1985.
[b] Sales of principal products.

Motor Vehicles and Cycles

The motor vehicle industry manufactures cars and commercial vehicles, caravans and trailers, and parts and components. Output of cars and commercial vehicles is dominated by three groups which account for 93 per cent of car production and some 96 per cent of commercial vehicle output: Rover, in which there is a majority public shareholding, Ford and Vauxhall. The remainder is in the hands of smaller, specialist producers of cars, heavy commercial vehicles, buses and coaches. The Rover board of management is working in agreement with the Government for the return of the company, as a whole or in parts, to the private sector. Jaguar, a luxury car manufacturer and formerly part of the Rover group, was privatised in 1984 and has had great success in recent years. Major makers of components include Lucas and GKN.

In recent years the home market has been increasingly supplied by imports, mainly from other European countries and Japan, but British manufacturers are responding strongly to the competition, and the industry remains one of the major export sectors. The Japanese manufacturer Nissan opened a car assembly plant in Britain in 1986, while Rover's volume car division has reached agreement with Honda of Japan on the production of an executive car to be built in both Japan and Britain and on other joint projects. The principal trade associations for the industry are the Society of Motor Manufacturers and Traders and, on the retail side, the Motor Agents Association. Motor industry shows are held annually at the National Exhibition Centre, Birmingham, and in London in alternate years.

The motor-cycle industry has contracted over the last two decades and the domestic market is largely supplied by imports. On the other hand, the market for pedal cycles is mainly supplied by British firms, the largest of which is TI Raleigh.

Railway Equipment

British Rail is the dominant customer for railway equipment in the British market, the other major user being London Regional Transport. In the past British Rail met its rolling stock requirements from its wholly owned subsidiary, British Rail Engineering Ltd (BREL). However, since early 1985 all British Rail's orders have had to be put out to open tender, and BREL now competes alongside the large private sector, which supplies a full range of equipment, including diesel engines, transmission systems, electric traction and control gear, signalling, heating and ventilating systems, and track equipment. The private sector also sells to overseas railway and rapid-transit authorities, and BREL has begun to export as well. The private sector undertakes electrification and other major project work abroad and, like British Rail, provides overseas consultancy services.

Aerospace

Britain's aerospace industry is one of the largest and most comprehensive in the Western world. The products of the industry include civil and military aircraft, helicopters, aero-engines, guided weapons, hovercraft and space satellites, supported by a comprehensive range of aircraft and airfield equipment and systems.

The main British airframe manufacturer is British Aerospace (BAe), which is privately owned. In May 1985 the Government disposed of its residual ordinary shareholding in the company, but retained a special share which ensures that, without government consent, no change can be made to those of BAe's articles of association which restrict foreign ownership of shares and require the directors to be British nationals.

The major publicly owned companies are Rolls-Royce and Short Brothers (although the Government plans to return Rolls-Royce to the private sector in the first half of 1987). Rolls-Royce is responsible for almost the entire output of aero-engines in Britain; it is one of the world's three leading aero-engine manufacturers and over 10,000 of the world's civil and military aircraft are powered by Rolls-Royce engines.

Production of BAe includes such civil aircraft as the BAe748 feederliner and the BAe125 business jet, the BAe146 family of passenger airliners and the Jetstream 31 executive commuter aircraft. The company is in the process of developing an advanced turboprop airliner, which is due to enter into service in 1987. It is a highly fuel-efficient aircraft aimed at the regional airline market and will replace the long-established BAe748. BAe is a full partner in the European consortium Airbus Industrie; it manufactures the wings for the A300 Airbus and designs and manufactures the wings for the A310 derivatives and for the 150-seat A320 Airbus, which is scheduled to enter into service in spring 1988. Military aircraft include the unique Harrier vertical/short take-off and landing aircraft, the Hawk advanced trainer, the Anglo-French Jaguar tactical fighter/ operational trainer and the Tornado multi-role combat aircraft, a collaborative venture involving Britain, the Federal Republic of Germany and Italy. The same three countries are also planning to build a fighter aircraft for service in 1995, with British Aerospace as the main British airframe contractor.

BAe is also a major producer of guided weapons including the Rapier ground-to-air missile. Collaborative guided weapon projects between Britain and its NATO partners are becoming increasingly important.

Short Brothers, which is based in Belfast, produces the Skyvan transporter, the SD330 and 360 commuter airliners, airframe components and missiles. In March 1985 the company was awarded a contract to supply a new basic trainer aircraft, the Tucano, to the Royal Air Force. In addition to performing a wide range of aerospace equipment work, Westland Helicopters manufactures the Sea King and Lynx military helicopters and in 1982 introduced the W30 helicopter for civil offshore and commuter uses. The development of the E101 multi-role helicopter is being undertaken by Westland in collaboration with the Italian company Giovanni Agusta.

Rolls-Royce aero-engines in production include the collaboratively produced RB199 for the Tornado, the RB211 civil engine family, the Pegasus vectored-thrust engine for the Harrier and the Gem helicopter engine. The company is a significant participant in the V2500 project (an engine being developed by the International Aero Engine Company, a five-nation consortium, to power 150-passenger airliners) and is developing a new helicopter engine, the RTM322, in partnership with Turbomeca of France. Rolls-Royce has an agreement with General Electric of the United States on mutual participation in the high technology developments of their respective commercial engines. Industrial versions of Rolls-Royce aero-engines are being produced for use in oil and gas transmission and as stand-by power generators, while marine versions are used to power a new generation of warships.

Aviation equipment manufacturers provide a wide range of systems essential to engines and aircraft, including engine and flight controls, electrical generation, mechanical and hydraulic power systems, cabin furnishings, flight decks and information displays. They also supply radar and air traffic control equipment, ground power supplies and flight simulators, to airports and airlines throughout the world.

The aerospace industry carries out an extensive programme of research and development on airframes, aero-engines and equipment, including avionics, while considerable research is also undertaken by universities and government research establishments. As a result of research carried out in Britain and elsewhere, the industry is now able to make extensive use of lightweight carbon fibre composites (as alternatives to traditional metals) and of advanced digital cockpit controls and computer-controlled electronic signalling. It is also expecting to use aluminium lithium to replace more conventional metals.

Aerospace production and exports, which are fairly evenly divided between aircraft, engines and equipment (including avionics), have made considerable progress over the past few years and now stand at record levels.

The main trade association for the industry is the Society of British Aerospace Companies, which organises a major international air show at Farnborough, Hampshire, every two years (the next is in 1988).

Space
Technology

Britain was one of the first countries to develop space science and technology and remains one of the few countries that has both built and launched its own satellites. While retaining an involvement in space transportation systems, particularly through Ferranti's production of the inertial guidance system for the European rocket, Ariane, the space industry's major strength is now in the manufacture of satellites. BAe has been prime contractor for all the telecommunications satellite projects of the European Space Agency (ESA), including the series of five European Communications Satellites for EUTELSAT (the European telecommunications satellite authority) and the large multi-mission satellite, Olympus, to be launched in 1987, equipped with experimental direct-broadcasting-by-satellite channels, an advanced on-board switched multi-beam business services payload by Marconi Defence Systems (MDS) and an experimental payload to explore new frequencies for commercial services. Internationally, BAe has a major role—larger than that of any company outside the United States—in the latest series of INTELSAT-6 global telecommunications satellites now being built for the International Telecommunications Satellite Organisation, and it is leading the team which will supply between three and nine satellites for the second generation system of the International Maritime Satellite Organisation, commencing in 1988. BAe has also developed and built some 17 space pallets (payload and instrument carriers) for the United States Space Shuttle; the pallets can fly either as part of Europe's Spacelab or independently.

MDS has primed many telecommunications satellite payloads, including those for the maritime communications satellites; it is also a world-wide supplier of satellite sub-systems. Currently the company is leading the payload development for Europe's advanced remote sensing satellite, ERS-1, investigating oceans and coastal regions, as well as that for Britain's own Skynet-IV defence communications satellites. On the latter project MDS is in a joint partnership with BAe.

The space industry continues to contribute to the ESA's scientific satellites through BAe's prime contractorship for the Giotto satellite which investigated Halley's Comet in 1986. British firms will be leading the development of the man-tended platforms which will form part of the ESA's Columbus programme, expected to be operational from 1994. Britain's space industry capabilities also extend to the design and manufacture of all types of satellite ground stations to meet the requirements of British Telecom and for business and data communications and television transmission.

British Aerospace and Rolls-Royce are working on the development of a new spacecraft able to take off like an aircraft and powered, both in its flight through the atmosphere and in space, by a single engine. It is known as 'HOTOL' (horizontal take-off and landing). Savings in weight would be achieved by designing the engine so that it could 'breathe in' air from the atmosphere to add to its fuel mix.

Shipbuilding and Marine Engineering

Britain has a long-established tradition of shipbuilding and remains active in the construction, conversion and repair of merchant vessels, warships and offshore structures. In 1985 British shipbuilding companies accounted for about 1 per cent of total world completions; over 55 per cent of output was for overseas registration. Most of the major British shipyards have been reorganised in recent years, with the construction, in several cases, of covered-berth ship facilities which are among the most advanced and efficient in the world.

The public sector, which comprises British Shipbuilders and the Belfast company of Harland & Wolff, accounted for some 94 per cent of British merchant shipbuilding in 1985 and for all slow-speed marine diesel engines. Because of world-wide over-capacity in the general shipbuilding sector, British Shipbuilders is now moving into more specialist areas including ferries and offshore support vessels of various kinds. Production has been modernised through computer-aided design and manufacture and the development of the modular approach to shipbuilding, which involves the building up of vessels from major sub-assemblies that are supplied already fitted with pipework and electrical and other systems.

The building of warships and other associated craft—both for the Royal Navy and for export—is now the major area of shipbuilding in Britain. In line with government policy, British Shipbuilders' warship building yards, along with general marine engineering work and ship repairing activities, have been transferred to the private sector. The Royal Dockyards at Rosyth and Devonport, which refit ships of the Royal Navy, are to be leased to commercial management by April 1987.

The private sector plays an important role in the construction and repair of tugs, purpose-built coasting and short-sea cargo vessels, smaller product tankers, fishing boats, and other small craft which are required to meet the needs of the armed forces, harbour and pilotage authorities, and the leisure market.

The private sector also provides the offshore oil and gas industry with consultancy services (including advice on exploiting hydrocarbons under difficult conditions) and has modern and well-equipped construction facilities able to build all types of fixed platforms and semi-submersible units for drilling, production and emergency/maintenance support, drillships, jack-up rigs, modules and offshore loading systems. The world's first manned submersible made largely of glass-reinforced plastics was built by a British company, and a wide range of submersible and other operational equipment is marketed. Conventional yards within British Shipbuilders can also supply both traditional and specialised support vessels.

**FOOD, DRINK
AND TOBACCO**

1985	Labour[a] ('000s)	Sales[b] (£ million)	Exports (£ million)	Imports (£ million)
Food manufacturing	**481**	**26,013**	**2,254**	**6,002**
of which: organic oils and fats	} 113	1,148	87	730
meat and fish products		4,362	692	2,073
milk and milk products	42	3,841	288	624
fruit and vegetable processing	34	1,101	101	650
production of bread, biscuits and flour confectionery	136	3,606	139	71
sugar, ice-cream, cocoa, chocolate and sugar confectionery	70	3,570	398	721
animal feedstuffs and other foods	86	8,371	550	1,134
Drinks	**101**	**5,226**	**1,344**	**1,092**
of which: brewing and malting	} 55	2,120	101	116
wines, cider and perry		281	46	576
distilling and compounding	21	1,501	1,145	163
Tobacco	**20**	**1,484**	**456**	**114**

[a] Employees in employment (Great Britain) at June 1985.
[b] Sales of principal products in 1984.

Britain has one of the world's largest and most sophisticated food processing industries, and processed foods have accounted for a growing proportion of total domestic demand for food in recent decades, though the rate of growth has slowed since the early 1970s. Convenience foods, particularly certain frozen foods, yoghurts and instant snacks, have formed the fastest-growing sector. The market is also growing in foods for consumers concerned about the effects of their diet on their health and weight. The Government is legislating to require the fat content of processed foods to be marked on labelling. A high rate of innovation applies to processed foods, largely owing to the need to increase sales in a food market which is not growing in size, given a nearly static population. While Britain is a net importer of foodstuffs, the level of imports declined between 1970 and 1980, though it has since risen somewhat. The most marked reductions in imports have been in dairy, meat, fish, fruit and vegetable products, and oils and fats. Exports, mainly within the European Community, have grown steadily. Basic research is being conducted into yeasts and new sources of protein. Ranks Hovis McDougall and ICI have agreed on a joint biotechnology venture to produce on a large scale myco-protein, a natural micro-fungus which converts carbohydrates to high-grade protein; the product will be used to make, among other things, meat, poultry and fish substitutes.

Food from Britain is a body with a wide remit to improve the marketing of British food and agricultural produce both domestically and overseas. In 1985 it launched a quality assurance scheme based on a 'foodmark' guarantee of quality.

Bacon Curing, Meat and Fish Products

The industry uses about one-quarter of Britain's pigmeat in the production of cured bacon and ham, and one-third is processed into sausages, pies, canned hams, pâtés and similar products. Other meat products include canned and preserved meat, meat extracts and pastes and meat used to prepare other foodstuffs. A wide range of fish, including shellfish, is processed by freezing, canning, smoking or coating in batter or breadcrumbs. Products include fish portions, complete fish meals, smoked fish and spreads.

Dairy Products

Production of milk was some 15,411 million litres in 1985, of which just under half was for sale as liquid milk. Nine out of ten households in Britain receive pasteurised milk in bottles through a daily door-step delivery system employing about 41,000 roundsmen (not included in the employment figure in the table) driving electric vehicles. There are 773 establishments buying and heat-treating milk for liquid sales. Domestic milk consumption per head (1·9 litres—3·3 pints—per week in 1985) is among the highest in the world.

The main milk products are butter (204,000 tonnes produced in 1985), cheese (253,000 tonnes), cream (46,000 tonnes), full-cream condensed milk (169,000 tonnes), full-cream milk powder (48,000 tonnes) and skimmed milk powder (235,000 tonnes). The dairy industry accounted for 64 per cent of new butter supplies to the British market in 1985, 67 per cent of new cheese supplies, and nearly all of other milk products. Production of butter and cheese has increased significantly in recent years: butter exports in 1985 were 33,000 tonnes and cheese exports 29,000 tonnes, compared with 16,000 tonnes and 10,700 tonnes respectively in 1976. The other main exports are skimmed milk powder (158,000 tonnes in 1985) and whole milk powder (42,000 tonnes). The industry's interests are represented by the Dairy Trade Federation.

Fruit, Vegetable and Other Products

Fruit and vegetable products include canned, frozen, crystallised and dried fruit and vegetables, prepared nuts, pectin, jam, marmalade, pickles and sauces. Other products of the food processing industry include sugar, sugar preparations and honey, egg-based products, oils and fats, coffee, cocoa, tea and spices, and cereal preparations. The oils and fats industry comprises a small number of seed-crushing companies (producing about 417,000 tonnes of crude oil a year) and several refiners, with a combined output of about a million tonnes of refined oils and fats. These products are used for a number of purposes including food manufacturing, animal feedingstuffs, soap and paints.

Bakery Products

About 60 per cent of bread in Britain is manufactured in large mechanised bakeries, most of which use a process (the 'Chorleywood' process) developed by the industry's principal research organisation, the Flour Milling and Baking Research Association, and now widely used in other countries. Two groups are predominant: Associated British Foods and Ranks Hovis McDougall. There is a growing consumer interest, however, in locally baked varieties, production of which is usually allied to the production of cakes and other flour confectionery. In recent years demand for wholemeal bread has grown considerably. Biscuits and related products are a major sector of the industry and have gained a world-wide reputation. Another sector is grain milling and the production of various specialised flours and meal.

Confectionery

The cocoa, chocolate and sugar confectionery industry is composed of a small number of very large manufacturers and many medium-sized and small companies. The three main manufacturers are Rowntree Mackintosh, Cadbury Schweppes and Mars. Britain has a large share of world trade in chocolate and sugar confectionery.

Beverages

Of prime importance among the alcoholic beverages produced in Britain, and in the food and drink industry as a whole, is Scotch whisky. There are about 100 distilleries in Scotland and the well-known brands of blended Scotch whisky are made from the products of a number of different distilleries. Guinness plc, owners of Arthur Bell and Sons and the Distillers Company, accounts for about '0 per cent of Scotch whisky output. Over 80 per cent of all Scotch whisky produced is exported. The principal overseas markets are the United States (which takes nearly 30 per cent of whisky exports from Britain), the rest of the European Community and Japan. Production of gin in Britain rose steadily from the early 1950s until 1980; some of the larger manufacturers own distilleries overseas. Production of vodka in Britain also increased in the 1970s.

In the brewing and malting industry there are six major brewery groups whose products are sold nationally, and about 60 smaller enterprises who mainly supply locally or regionally. In addition, there are about 100 small independent brewers, many producing traditional cask-conditioned ales, for which there has been a growing demand in the last decade. Firms have introduced new production methods, including continuous brewing processes, and automated batch production plants are well established. The main raw materials used are malt, hops and some sugar. British malt, which is made almost entirely from home-grown barley, is used by brewers throughout the world. Lager has increased steadily in popularity since the late 1960s and accounts for nearly 40 per cent of beer sales.

Cider, perry and wine producers form the smallest sector of the drinks industry and are located mostly in southern and south-western England. Cider sales rose sharply in the early 1980s, but have now stabilised at 1983 levels.

The soft drinks industry has expanded markedly in the last decade. There are some very large companies among about 20 producing brands which are marketed on a national scale, while other companies supply regional markets. There is some specialisation among firms in the production of various types, such as carbonated drinks, cola-based drinks, squashes and cordials, 'mixers', fruit juices and health drinks.

Tobacco

The British tobacco industry manufactures about 80 per cent of cigarettes and tobacco goods sold in Britain. Over 90 per cent of output is provided by three major manufacturers (the Imperial Group, Gallaher and Carreras Rothmans). The industry specialises in the production of high-quality cigarettes made from flue-cured tobacco and achieves significant exports, mainly of cigarettes—countries in Europe, the Middle East and Africa are important markets. Britain's most important source of raw tobacco is Brazil, followed by the United States, Zimbabwe, India and Canada. By voluntary agreement with the Government, cigarette manufacturers restrict their advertising, print health warnings on packets and are reducing the tar yield of cigarettes.

TEXTILES, FOOTWEAR, CLOTHING, LEATHER AND FUR GOODS

1985	Labour[a] ('000s)	Sales[b] (£ million)	Exports (£ million)	Imports (£ million)
Textile industry	228	5,749	1,859	3,192
of which: woollen and worsted industry	41	1,429	576	420
cotton and silk industry	38	1,073	413	1,522
hosiery and other knitwear	81	1,624	440	593
carpets, rugs and matting	16	853	176	296
Footwear	48	997	164	687
Clothing, hats and gloves	188	3,677	781	1,547
Made-up textiles	25	734	108	197
Fur goods	4	51	113	62
Leather and leather goods	23	677	260	406

[a] Employees in employment (Great Britain) at June 1985.
[b] Sales of principal products.

Despite its contraction over a number of years, this is still a large group of related industries, employing 500,000 people and making substantial exports. Its main products are yarn, woven and knitted fabrics, apparel, household textiles and carpets based mainly on wool, cotton and man-made fibres. The textiles industry is made up of a few large multi-process companies such as Courtaulds and Coats Viyella, and a large number of small and medium-sized firms.

The textiles and clothing industries in Britain, as in other developed countries, have been affected by low-cost imports from developing countries. Trade in textiles and clothing is regulated by the Multi-Fibre Arrangement (MFA) of the General Agreement on Tariffs and Trade. The MFA allows a measure of restraint on imports of textiles and clothing from low-cost countries into industrialised countries; negotiations on a fourth MFA began in 1986. The use of computers and robots and other automated techniques in production processes is helping the textiles, footwear and clothing industries to compete against low-cost countries.

Wool

In 1985 exports of tops (combed wool and hair), yarns, fabrics and other wool textile products exceeded imports by about 37 per cent. The industry is one of the largest in the world and includes the world's biggest wool textile company, Illingworth, Morris. There are two main branches, woollen and worsted. An increasing amount of man-made fibre is now blended with wool. West Yorkshire is the main producing area but Scotland and the west of England are also famous as specialised producers of high-quality yarn and cloth. Large quantities of raw wool are scoured and cleaned in Britain in preparation for spinning. British mills also process the bulk of rare fibres, such as cashmere and mohair, entering world trade. The largest markets for woollen and worsted fabrics are the rest of the European Community, Japan and the United States.

Cotton

During the nineteenth century cotton was Britain's chief consumer goods industry and cotton piece goods its largest export. Low-cost competition has cut progressively into British markets and made necessary reorganisation, modernisation and the introduction of new techniques. Production includes yarns and fabrics of cotton, spun man-made fibres and mixtures of these.

Linen

The linen industry is centred in Northern Ireland, where the lighter types of fabrics for apparel, furnishings and household textiles are produced. The heavyweight canvas for sailcloth, tents, awnings and tarpaulins is mainly produced in Scotland.

Hosiery and Knitwear

The hosiery and knitwear industry comprises about 900 companies situated mainly in the East Midlands and Scotland, of which most are small to medium in size. The industry produces fabrics, outerwear, underwear, tights, socks, stockings, gloves and accessories.

Carpets

Some 60 per cent of the value of carpet and rug output (70 per cent in volume terms) is made up of tufted carpets, in the production of which the pile, usually with a high man-made fibre content, is inserted into a pre-woven backing. Woven carpets, mainly Axminster, account for most of the remainder of sales. There is a higher wool content in woven types, although in these, too, more use is being made of man-made fibres. The high quality and variety of design make Britain one of the world's leading producers of woven carpets.

Jute

Jute products are manufactured in the Dundee area. Jute yarn and man-made polypropylene yarn are used in the manufacturing of carpets, cordage and ropes and woven into fabrics for a wide range of applications in the packaging, upholstery, building and motor-car industries. New uses for jute, for example as a plastics reinforcement and for decorative wall coverings, have also been developed.

Clothing

The British clothing industry is one of the largest in Europe; it is highly labour intensive with about 5,800 companies (predominantly small ones), accounting for 3 to 4 per cent of Britain's total employment in the manufacturing sector. It supplies about two-thirds of domestic demand, while exports have risen since the mid-1970s. A wide range of clothing is imported from European and Asian countries.

Footwear and Leather

The footwear manufacturing industry is made up predominantly of small companies. Though necessarily largely labour intensive, the industry includes some of the most technologically up-to-date factories in the world and supplies more than 40 per cent of all the shoes sold in Britain. Imports have risen in recent years, but latterly at a very slow rate. Leather tanning and the manufacture of leather goods are also long-established industries; all types of leather (particularly for footwear, clothing and gloves) and leather goods are produced, and about one-third of leather production is exported.

OTHER MANUFAC-TURING

1985	Labour[a] ('000s)	Sales[b] (£ million)	Exports (£ million)	Imports (£ million)
Timber and wooden furniture	200	5,104	397	2,124
Paper and paper products	143	6,791	834	2,996
Printing and publishing	343	7,685	786	543
Processing of rubber and plastics	167	6,538	1,534	1,897
Toys and sports goods	23	431	226	408
Other manufacturing	50	1,005	825	892

[a] Employees in employment (Great Britain) at June 1985.
[b] Sales of principal products.

Furniture and Timber

The furniture industry comprises about 3,000 companies, mostly small to medium-sized with only a few of any significant size. A wide range of products is manufactured, the greater part of production being accounted for by domestic furniture and the remainder by office, contract, school and other furniture.

Domestic production of softwood timber has been steadily increasing but the timber-using industries are mainly dependent on imported supplies. A large proportion of timber sales goes to the construction industry.

Paper and Board Manufacture and Conversion

There were about 110 paper and board mills in 1985, operated by 80 companies; total production was 3·7 million tonnes. The largest British groups are Wiggins Teape, the Dickinson Robinson Group, Reed International and the Bowater Corporation. Overseas paper and board groups with manufacturing investments in Britain include Georgia Pacific, Kimberly Clark and Consolidated Bathurst. The main types of paper and board produced are printing and writing papers and board, corrugated case materials, packaging paper and board, and tissue. There has been a significant trend towards waste-based packaging grades in order to reduce the industry's reliance on imported woodpulp supplies. The use of recycled waste paper is increasing and research is helping to extend it. Waste paper provides over half of the industry's fibre needs. Domestically produced wood pulp represents only a small percentage of raw material supplies.

The packaging and converting industries manufacture a variety of products, including cardboard boxes, cartons, fibreboard packaging and business stationery products.

Printing and Publishing

The printing and publishing industries produce a wide range of items, including newspapers, periodicals, books, business stationery and greetings cards. Mergers have led to the formation of large groups in the newspaper, magazine and book publishing sectors, but general printing, engraving, bookbinding and a large part of publishing remain essentially industries of small firms. The book publishing industry is a major exporter. Production processes include high-speed printing, electronic engraving, advanced processes of photographic reproduction and computer typesetting. Security printers (of, for example, banknotes and postage stamps) have a high reputation and are important exporters, the major company being De La Rue. The most important overseas markets for printed matter are the United States, Australia and the Irish Republic.

Rubber

Tyres and tubes represent about 41 per cent of sales of rubber manufactures, the most important other goods being vehicle components and accessories, conveyor belting, cables, industrial, hydraulic and marine hoses, latex foam products and rubber footwear, gloves and clothing. Rubber is also used for inflatable life-rafts, containers for fuel and other industrial liquids, and seals for storage tanks and other products where there are problems of air exclusion and vapour suppression. Tyre manufacturers include subsidiaries of United States and other overseas companies. The industry's consumption of rubber includes natural, synthetic and recycled rubber.

Plastics Production

In addition to plastics components and accessories supplied to many different industries, the plastics processing industry manufactures a wide range of building materials, such as pipes, sheeting for roofs, sanitary ware, tanks and other products. It also supplies packaging products, including bottles, containers and bags; domestic and industrial hollow-ware; many kinds of household goods; and vinyl and other floorcoverings. Extensive research is being conducted into the use of plastics in engineering products, particularly those associated with transport.

Toys, Games and Sports Equipment

There are about 500 manufacturers of a wide range of toys and games, but few of significant size. About 40 per cent of total production is exported, the major markets being France, the Federal Republic of Germany and the United States. British diecast toys and plastic toys (including model construction kits) are well established in overseas markets.

There are about 350 manufacturers of sports equipment, many of which are small companies with a high reputation for craftsmanship. British fishing tackle and golf and tennis equipment have a world-wide reputation. The main export markets are France, the rest of the European Community and the United States.

Other Products

Jewellery, gold and silverware and the refining of precious metals is an industry in which British craftsmen are world famous. The Royal Mint makes coins for some 67 overseas countries. Other miscellaneous manufacturing includes musical instruments, film processing and small stationery goods.

Construction

The construction industry accounts for 6 per cent of gross domestic product. The total value of output in Great Britain in 1985 was £27,870 million, of which new work accounted for £14,924 million (53 per cent) and repairs and maintenance the remainder. In housing, new work was valued at £4,764 million and repairs and maintenance at £6,820 million. About 1 million people are employed in the industry (including apprentices), accounting for nearly 5 per cent of total employment. There are also about 469,000 self-employed.

The industry includes firms engaged on the construction, alteration, repair, and maintenance of buildings, highways, bridges, tunnels, airfields, drainage and sewerage systems, docks, harbours and canals, sea defence works, offshore structures, electrical wiring, heating and other installation work, and structural work connected with power stations and telecommunications. Efficiency and productivity within the industry are benefiting from new computerised techniques such as the use of electronic load safety measures for cranes, distance measuring equipment, computerised stock ordering and job costing, and computer-aided design.

Government sponsorship of the construction industry is the responsibility of the Department of the Environment. Building regulations prescribe minimum standards of construction in England and Wales. Made by the Secretary of State for the Environment and administered and enforced by local authorities, the regulations apply to new building, the installation or replacement of fittings, and alterations and extensions to existing buildings. There are broadly similar controls under separate legislation in Scotland and Northern Ireland. As an alternative to local authority building control and in order to simplify procedures, an optional system of private certification of compliance with building regulations is provided for in the Housing and Building Control Act 1984 and was introduced in 1985. The British Board of Agrément, sponsored by the Department, assesses and issues reports and certificates relating to products and systems for use in the construction industry.

Structure

Construction work is carried out both by private contractors and by public authorities which employ their own labour. In 1985 about 89 per cent of the work was done by private firms. Although there were about 95,000 firms employing two or more people, 95 per cent of them employed fewer than 25. Some large firms are vertically integrated, owning quarries and workshops, mechanised plant and standard builders' equipment; some undertake responsibility for projects from initial design to finished building. All but the smallest projects are generally carried out under professional direction, either by architects or, in the case of the more complicated civil engineering projects, by consulting engineers. The latter, acting on behalf of a client, may advise on the feasibility of projects, draw up plans and supervise the construction work.

The Property Services Agency (PSA), which is an integral part of the Department of the Environment, is responsible for the construction programmes undertaken directly by the Government, including work for the armed forces both in Britain and overseas.

Housing

During 1985 a total of 194,300 dwellings were started in Great Britain. Starts in the public sector were 33,000 and those for private owners 161,200. Some 187,000 dwellings were completed, 38,200 in the public sector and 148,800 in the private sector.

Civil Engineering Projects

Among important construction projects in hand or recently completed in Britain were the Heysham and Torness nuclear power stations, the Thames Barrier, which forms part of London's flood defences, new air terminals at Heathrow and

Gatwick, the new Lloyd's insurance building, the Queen Elizabeth II Conference Centre in London, the new British Library, the Docklands Light Railway, and the M25 motorway.

Research and Advisory Services

The national research and advisory body on all aspects of construction and building is the Building Research Establishment, which is part of the Department of the Environment. It has four laboratories, including a fire research station.

Research is also carried out by the major construction and materials firms, universities, colleges of technology and research associations. The research associations also provide advisory services.

The Building Centre Group consists of six building centres throughout Britain, most of which provide exhibition and information services on materials, products, techniques and building services.

Overseas Construction

In 1984–85 the value of new contracts obtained overseas by British construction companies amounted to £2,400 million, compared with £2,300 million in the previous year. Work worth a further £2,400 million was carried out overseas in the year, a slightly higher figure than in the previous year. The value of work outstanding at the end of the year remained unchanged at £3,200 million. There was a movement away from traditional markets, such as Africa and the Middle East, towards the Americas and east Asia. Major contracts obtained in 1984–85 included a new arrivals terminal at Dubai airport, a major share of an Anglo-German project for the installation of a microwave communications system serving the whole of Malaysia, a share of the early phases of the Singapore mass rapid transit railway, further work on the Cairo wastewater project and a share of the construction of two tunnels under the Anacostia river in Washington, D.C., for the latest addition to the Washington metro system.

The interests of the various sectors of the construction industry overseas are promoted by the Export Group for the Constructional Industries, the Association of Consulting Engineers, the British Consultants Bureau (whose members include architects, surveyors and management consultants), the Buildings Materials Export Group, and the Federation of Manufacturers of Construction Equipment and Cranes.

Service Industries

Growth has been faster in the service sector in Britain than in the rest of the economy in recent decades. In 1985 services contributed about 58 per cent of gross domestic product compared with 45 per cent in 1960 and accounted for 65 per cent of employees in employment compared with 48 per cent in 1960. Overseas trade in services, particularly financial services, has also grown, and in 1985 overseas earnings from services amounted to nearly half the value of exports of manufactures.

Between 1976 and 1985 total service employment rose by over 1 million, compared with a fall in employment in all other sectors. Much of this, however, was accounted for by growth in part-time (principally female) employment. Since the late 1970s employment has grown more rapidly in the private sector than in the public sector, a reversal of the pattern of the 1960s and the early 1970s, partially reflecting the Government's policy of restricting employment in public sector services.

The fastest-growing sectors within services in the 1970s, measured by employment, were financial and business services, professional and scientific services (mainly health and education) and miscellaneous services (mainly leisure and personal services). In the 1980s the financial services have continued to grow strongly. Among trends in the miscellaneous sector is a growth in franchising, an operation in which a company owning the rights to a particular form of trading sells them to franchisees, usually by means of an initial payment with continuing royalties. Hotel, catering and cleaning businesses are the main services in which franchising has developed.

Among the reasons for the growth in services is the fact that real personal disposable income has more than doubled since 1945. As real incomes rise people tend to spend a greater proportion of income on personal, financial and leisure services. While, to some extent, consumers have exchanged services (such as public transport, laundries and cinemas) for goods (motor cars, washing-machines and television sets), this has generated demand for fresh services in the distribution, maintenance and repair of these goods. Increased consumer expenditure on the running costs of motor cars is a significant factor in the rise in consumer expenditure on services. Demand for British air travel, hotel and catering services has resulted from the increase in real incomes in other countries.

Other factors include a greater readiness to use banking services and the spread of home ownership, which has increased demand for legal and estate agency services. Demographic changes, such as the increase in the elderly as a component of the population, help to explain the growth of medical services. Shorter working hours tend to raise the demand for leisure services.

Changes in technology have also played a part in the growth of services. Examples range from the computer services industry to the provision of cash and credit by means of cards and the growth of information systems such as viewdata and teletext. It is thought that there are now about 1 million people employed in the 'tradeable information sector', which encompasses activities such as the supply of financial and business information, printing and publishing, on-line computerised technical services, consultancy, and aspects of education and training services and of the entertainment industry.

DISTRIBUTION

There were over 4 million people engaged in the distributive and allied trades in Great Britain in mid-1985, together with a large number of owners of businesses. There were 932,000 people in wholesaling, just over 2 million in retailing, 1 million in hotels and catering, and 206,000 in the repair of vehicles and consumer goods. The distributive and allied trades accounted for about 13 per cent of national income in 1985.

WHOLESALE TRADES

In 1984 there were some 108,400 businesses engaged in wholesaling and dealing, with a turnover (including sales to other wholesalers and dealers) of some £159,000 million. The main areas in which wholesalers are dominant are groceries and provisions, petroleum products, and ores and metals. A number of large retailers carry out the functions of the wholesaler by having their own warehouses and buying and distributive organisations.

The wholesale grocery trade had a turnover of some £6,080 million in 1984. The trade is divided between 'cash and carry' and the traditional delivered trade in a ratio of 2 to 1. The cash and carry sector, with some 560 depots, grew in importance during the 1960s and 1970s by offering discounts to customers who purchased in bulk and limiting expenditure on premises, credit and delivery facilities. Grocery wholesaling has greatly diminished in recent years; over two-thirds of groceries are now delivered direct from manufacturers to the large multiple food retailers, by-passing the traditional wholesalers.

Landmark, Nurdin and Peacock, the Dee Corporation and Booker predominate in the wholesale grocery trade. London's wholesale markets play a significant part in the distribution of foodstuffs. New Covent Garden is the main market for fruit and vegetables, Smithfield for meat and Billingsgate for fish.

The co-operative movement in Britain has its own wholesale organisation, the Co-operative Wholesale Society (CWS), to serve the needs of retail societies; its turnover was £2,345 million in 1985–86. Retail societies are encouraged to buy from the CWS, which supplies about two-thirds of their requirements.

In the grocery trade there are a number of voluntary groups which have been formed by wholesalers with small independent retailers, whereby the retailers are encouraged by discounts and other incentives to buy as much as possible from the wholesaler. This has helped to preserve many smaller retail outlets for the wholesaler, including the traditional 'corner shops' and village stores, of value to local communities, and has given small retailers the advantages of bulk buying and co-ordinated distribution.

RETAIL TRADES

Turnover of the retail trades has been growing slowly in real terms in recent years, despite the recession. In 1985 retail sales were 12 per cent higher than in 1984, representing, however, only a 5 per cent increase in volume. In 1984 there were an estimated 231,000 businesses in the retail trade in Great Britain each with a turnover of more than £18,700 (see Table 19). Their turnover was about £82,000 million and they invested £2,100 million. As the large multiple retailers (those with ten or more outlets) have grown in size and diversified their product ranges, there has been a decline in the number of retail businesses and outlets. The decline has been particularly evident among small independent businesses and retail co-operative societies. Shops selling durable household goods have experienced the fastest growth in turnover in recent years, while mixed retail businesses have recorded the slowest growth.

The largest multiple retailers in the packaged grocery market are the retail co-operatives, Sainsbury, Tesco, Asda, Dee Corporation, Argyll Stores, Fine Fare, Safeway Food Stores and Kwik Save Discount Group. Retail co-operative societies are voluntary organisations controlled by their members, membership being open to anyone paying a small deposit on a minimum share; at the end of 1985 the 103 retail societies had over 8 million members and more than 5,300 retail outlets. Turnover in 1985 amounted to in excess of £4,800 million. Retail co-operatives and the Co-operative Wholesale Society (see above) are members of the Co-operative Union as are a number of other co-operative bodies such as the Co-operative Bank. In 1985–86 Sainsbury had about 266 stores and sales were valued at £3,575 million. Tesco had some 365 outlets and the company's sales amounted to £3,335 million.

The leading mixed retail businesses are Marks and Spencer (with sales of £3,658 million in 1985–86), Boots, F. W. Woolworth, the John Lewis Partnership, House of Fraser, W. H. Smith & Son, Debenhams and British Home Stores.

There are a number of discount stores operating on the principle of selling most or all of their goods at a reduced price. Electrical goods, furniture, carpets and do-it-yourself supplies are some of the main items sold by discount stores.

About 20 million people regularly shop by post. In 1985 sales by general mail order firms totalled some £2,952 million, representing 3·4 per cent of retail sales and 6·6 per cent of retail sales excluding food shops. The volume of mail order sales increased rapidly in the 1970s but fell off somewhat after 1980. Leading items sold by mail order are clothing, footwear, furniture, household textiles, and radio, television and electrical goods. The two main mail order firms are Great Universal Stores and Littlewoods.

Trends

One of the most significant trends in retailing in recent years has been the increase in the proportion of turnover accounted for by large multiple retailers; they have 58 per cent of retail turnover. Other important trends have been the increase in very large self-service stores selling a wide variety of products, diversification by food multiples into selling a wider range of goods, the development of specially designed shopping precincts, the growth of shops selling computers, software and video-cassettes, and an increasing emphasis on price competition.

Table 19: Retail Trade in Great Britain 1984[a]

	Number of businesses	Number of outlets	Number of people engaged ('000s)	Turnover[b] (£ million)
Single-outlet retailers	201,633	201,633	813	24,268
Small multiple retailers	28,207	73,670	349	10,604
Large multiple retailers (ten or more retail outlets)	949	67,850	1,164	47,469
of which: Co-operative societies	114	5,813	108	4,349
Food retailers	77,486	106,843	850	31,360
Drink, confectionery and tobacco retailers	41,992	57,344	260	8,686
Clothing, footwear and leather goods retailers	28,684	56,020	285	7,476
Household goods retailers	39,379	57,144	282	12,000
Other non-food retailers	35,350	47,998	214	6,869
Mixed retail businesses	5,301	10,900	391	14,787
Hire and repair businesses	2,597	6,904	42	1,163
Total retail trade	230,789	343,153	2,326	82,342

Source: *British business.*
[a] Figures cover businesses above the threshold of value added tax (£18,700 at that time).
[b] Includes value added tax.
Note: Differences between totals and the sums of their component parts are due to rounding.

Supermarkets, Superstores and Hypermarkets

There are supermarkets in most towns and cities in Britain. The main multiple grocery companies have been steadily increasing the size of their main supermarkets. The trend to greater size has led to a growing number of superstores and hypermarkets, self-service stores offering a wider range of food and non-food merchandise and which have at least 2,500 sq m (26,900 sq ft) and 5,000 sq m (53,800 sq ft) respectively of selling space. They are designed primarily for shoppers with cars, and substantial free car-parking space is usually provided. In Britain the first such store was opened in the mid-1960s and by January 1985 there were some 302 superstores and 44 hypermarkets, while planning permission for a further 61 superstores and six hypermarkets had been granted. Government policy on planning and large retail development was reaffirmed in 1985 when local planning authorities were urged to take account of the trend for new stores to be located outside existing shopping centres and of the benefits to the public of a wide range of shopping facilities. Although commercial competition is not a planning consideration, it was emphasised that authorities will, exceptionally, need to take into account the effect of the trend on the vitality and viability of established town centres. Since 1980 there has been an increase in 'mini-superstores' in the range 1,000 to 2,500 sq m (10,760 to 26,900 sq ft).

*Shopping
Centres*

Britain has a variety of new purpose-built shopping centres. The largest are the Manchester Arndale and the centre in Milton Keynes, which, both covering more than 93,000 sq m (1 million sq ft), are among the largest in Europe. Other large centres are at Town Square, Basildon, the Eldon Square Development in Newcastle upon Tyne, Brent Cross in London, the Mander Centre in Wolverhampton and the Luton Arndale.

Diversification

Many of the large multiple groups have diversified over the last few years to offer a much bigger range of goods and services than previously. This has been especially noticeable for the large food retailers, which often sell non-food products, such as beer, wines and spirits, clothing and household appliances, as well as packaged groceries. Another trend is that many superstores and large supermarkets offer fresh as well as packaged food, often with special counters or areas for fresh meat, fish, vegetables and bread baked on the premises. Some large retailers have in recent years begun to provide financial and estate agency services.

Promotions

Retailers are placing greater emphasis both on price competition and quality as a means of promoting sales. With the growth of payments by credit card, certain of the large retailers have issued their own credit cards for regular customers in an attempt to increase sales, particularly of high-value goods.

*Use of
Technology*

Laser-scanning electronic check-outs are already having a major impact on retailing in Britain. A low-power laser beam at the point of sale scans a bar code on the package of each item and the price is automatically retrieved from a central computer. The customer is given a receipt showing the price and identity of each item purchased, while the store's stock records are altered automatically. Substantial savings are expected from improved stock control and a reduction of individual price marking in stores. Key Markets introduced the first operational laser-scanning electronic check-out in Britain at Spalding (Lincolnshire) in 1979. Computerised shopping services are being introduced in the home which enable people to order goods from retailers. Some large multiple retailers are using electronic order and invoice systems in dealing with their suppliers, following a legal change permitting tax invoices in forms other than paper. Small independent retailers, also, are using electronic ordering, pricing and delivery systems. High-speed labelling techniques, including the use of electronic printers which can overprint labels, the use of pressure-sensitive glues and printing in foil instead of ink, are being adopted in order to save time and labour costs.

A single nationwide 'electronic funds transfer at the point of sale' (EFT-POS) system is to be established for the retail market in co-operation with the English and Scottish clearing banks. The system will use magnetically striped cards and terminals installed in retail premises to transfer funds directly from cardholders' accounts to the accounts of retailers. Various pilot projects are already in operation.

**Vehicle and
Petrol Retailing**

In June 1985 some 270,000 people were employed in Great Britain in the retail distribution of motor vehicles and parts and in petrol stations. In spite of the continuing increase in the number of road vehicles, the number of petrol stations is declining and at the end of 1985 there were some 21,140 (4 per cent fewer than in 1984), of which 32 per cent were owned by oil companies. There were about 10,568 outlets selling diesel fuel. Self-service stations are becoming increasingly important and in 1985 they accounted for 39 per cent of petrol stations. Some 176,000 people were employed in the repair of motor vehicles in mid-1985.

Hotels and Catering

The hotel and catering trades employed 1 million people in Great Britain in mid-1985: 262,000 in hotels and other residential establishments; 192,000 in restaurants, cafés and snack bars; 258,000 in public houses and bars; 155,000 in clubs; and 120,000 in canteens. A large number of self-employed people are also engaged in hotels and catering. There were 12,900 hotel businesses in Great Britain in 1984, with a turnover of £3,370 million. Many licensed hotels as well as most of the numerous guest houses are small, with fewer than 20 rooms. Of the major hotel business groups the biggest is Trusthouse Forte Ltd, which runs 800 hotels including 200 in Britain, and has catering and leisure interests. The total turnover of holiday camps and camping and caravan sites was about £456 million in 1984. Among the largest firms running holiday centres (including holiday camps with full board, self-catering centres and caravan parks) are Butlins, Pontins, Ladbroke Holidays, Warners and Haven Leisure. There were over 41,900 businesses in Great Britain in 1984 with a total turnover of more than £3,770 million, which were engaged in the sale of food for consumption both on and off the premises. These include restaurants, snack bars, cafés, fish and chip shops and other establishments selling 'take-away' food. Britain has a very wide range of restaurants of which a substantial number specialise in the dishes of other countries such as Chinese, Italian, Indian and Greek foods. 'Fast-food' catering, in which establishments sell hot food such as hamburgers or chicken to be eaten either on the premises or elsewhere, is becoming increasingly significant. There are about 60,800 'pubs' (public houses, which mainly sell beer, wines and spirits for consumption on the premises) in Great Britain, with a total turnover of £6,760 million in 1984.

BUSINESS SERVICES

Business services include advertising, market research, management consultancy, exhibition and conference facilities, computer services and auction houses. Most of these sectors have grown rapidly in recent years.

Advertising

Advertising expenditure rose by 3 per cent in 1985 to £4,441 million, according to the Advertising Association. Advertising in the press accounted for 63 per cent of the total, television for 31 per cent, posters for 3·7 per cent, commercial radio for 1·8 per cent and cinema for 0·4 per cent. Advertising has been growing fastest in the free distribution press and directories. Advertising campaigns are planned mainly by advertising agencies, of which there are several hundred in Britain; in some cases they also provide marketing, consumer research and other services.

Computing Services

Britain is acknowledged as a world leader in the provision of software and computing services, and software developed in Britain has contributed to developments in the applications of computers in numerous countries. The industry comprises software houses, which provide professional services such as consultancy, the writing of programs to meet the computing needs of their clients, and, increasingly, packaged software designed for a wider market; computer bureaux, where the main emphasis is on processing customers' data; and systems houses, which specialise in the provision of complete systems (hardware and software).

The computing services industry is one of the fastest-growing sectors of the British economy: annual growth has been running at between 15 and 20 per cent a year since the mid-1970s and turnover now stands at over £2,000 million. The industry employs around 62,000 people, excluding people working on 'in-house' computer activities, who number several hundred thousand. About 200 computing service companies are members of the Computing Services Association, the leading trade association. Many of the companies are subsidiaries of firms engaged in activities such as banking, insurance, manufacturing and distribution.

Management Consultancy

There are thought to be some 6,000 management consultants in Britain, of whom 3,000 are practising members of the Institute of Management Consultants. Among the largest management consultancy companies are the 29 members of the Management Consultants Association, whose turnover amounted to £168 million in 1985. Revenue earned within Britain comprised £142 million, an increase of 40 per cent on the previous year, while overseas revenue amounted to £26 million. The Association reports a growing demand for services supporting the application of information technology, particularly micro-processing, to all aspects of business.

Market Research

The 31 members of the Association of Market Survey Organisations (AMSO) accounted for about 70 per cent of total turnover by market research companies in 1985. The turnover of AMSO members increased to £136 million in 1985 from £117 million in 1984. The largest company, the AGB group, had a turnover of £28·7 million. Research on behalf of food and soft drinks companies accounted for 21 per cent of revenue. Research on behalf of financial institutions and groups with international interests has increased.

Exhibition and Conference Centres

With the steady increase in new and renovated facilities, some 80 towns and cities are well equipped to hold conferences and exhibitions. Among the most modern facilities are the National Exhibition Centre at Birmingham, the Wembley Conference Centre, the Queen Elizabeth II Conference Centre and the Barbican Centre for Arts and Conferences in London, the Brighton Centre in Sussex, the Harrogate Centre in North Yorkshire, the Bournemouth International Centre in Dorset, St David's Hall in Cardiff, the Scottish Exhibition and Conference Centre in Glasgow, the G-MEX Centre in Manchester and the Royal Centre in Nottingham. Other large facilities are the Earls Court, Olympia and Wembley Arena sites in London. Britain is one of the world's three leading countries for international conferences (the others being the United States and France); the Union of International Associations, based in Brussels, estimated that about 9 per cent of the world's main international conferences were held in Britain in 1985. Britain is actively promoted overseas as an international conference and exhibition venue.

Auction Houses

Britain's chief auction houses are active in the international auction markets for works of art, trading on the acknowledged expertise of British valuers and dealers. The two largest houses, Sotheby's and Christie's, are established world-wide and had turnovers of £473 million and £365 million in 1985–86 respectively.

Other Business Services

Other business services include land and estate companies, estate agents, and typewriting, duplicating, document copying, translating and employment agencies.

MISCELLANEOUS SERVICES

Some 99,000 people were employed in film, theatre, literary, musical, broadcasting and related services in Great Britain in mid-1985, 292,000 in sanitary services, 132,000 in research and development services and 262,000 in services connected with sport, recreation, gambling and betting. Other services provided included hairdressing and beauty parlours (86,000 employees), laundries, dyers and dry cleaners (65,000), photographic studios, religious organisations, tourist offices, learned societies, employers' and trade union organisations, and funeral services.

Film and Television

Major trends in the film and television industry in recent years include the development of the specialised film and television services sector and the extension of video and cable television services. Technical developments, such as the use of magnetic video tape instead of film, and the exploitation of computer-generated graphics, have been responsible for changes both in the production and exhibition of film and television material. They have also played a part in the growth of the specialised sector, in which relatively small studios, mostly based in London, provide a wide range of film and television services, including the making of advertising films, 'special effects' sequences for feature and other films, documentary and educational programmes, and cartoon films. In addition, new audio-visual technology is being adopted in industrial, commercial, medical and scientific contexts for information, observation and training purposes.

The Department of Trade and Industry conducts an annual inquiry into the value of overseas transactions relating to the production and exhibition of cinema and television material. For many years the inquiry has shown a surplus of receipts over expenditure. In 1984 receipts by film and television companies were £318 million, while expenditure was £195 million, a surplus of £123 million. Film companies' receipts totalled £229 million and television companies' receipts £91 million, the North American market accounting for about three-fifths of revenue in both cases. Some 323 film companies and 18 television broadcasting companies were covered in the 1985 inquiry.

Legislation was passed in 1985 to reduce statutory intervention in the film industry and to increase the flow of both public and private funds for domestic film production.

TRAVEL AND TOURISM

The travel business is another growth sector and some 2,685 travel agencies, with about 6,115 offices (over 90 per cent of the total), belong to the Association of British Travel Agents (ABTA). In general travel agents are small businesses but many ABTA members have more than one office. There are a few large firms (of which the biggest is Thomas Cook with over 280 branches). Computerised information and booking systems are being introduced in travel agencies. There are also 525 tour operator members of ABTA; some 225 companies are both retail agents and tour operators. The leading tour operators are British Airways (through its subsidiaries, Sovereign and Enterprise), Cosmos, Horizon, Intasun, Rank Travel and Thomson. ABTA operates financial protection schemes to safeguard its members' customers, maintains codes of conduct drawn up with the Office of Fair Trading, and offers a free conciliation service to help to resolve complaints against members and an independent arbitration scheme for tour operators' customers.

Tourism is one of Britain's most important industries and is recognised as a major and growing source of employment. Spending by British residents and overseas visitors on tourism in Britain during 1985 amounted to around £12,000 million (excluding fares paid on travel to and from Britain). It is estimated that upwards of 1 million jobs in Britain were supported directly or indirectly by tourism spending in 1985 and that new jobs are being created at a rate of more than 50,000 a year.

In 1985 a record 14·5 million overseas visitors to Britain (6 per cent more than in the previous year) spent £5,451 million, 18 per cent more than in 1984. British residents made 21·8 million trips abroad and spent £4,877 million, giving a surplus on the travel account of £574 million. About 55 per cent of overseas visitors to Britain came from Western Europe, 26 per cent from North America and about 19 per cent from elsewhere in the world. There was a 1 per cent decrease in visits abroad by British residents in 1985; the majority of visits (88 per cent) were to Western Europe.

Official support for the promotion of tourism to and within Britain is provided by the British Tourist Authority and the tourist boards for England, Scotland, Wales and Northern Ireland. Funding for the tourist boards has been increased for 1986–87 and the boards have been asked by the Government to encourage tourism in regions of the country where unemployment is high and where there is potential for development. Voluntary registration schemes exist for tourist accommodation throughout Britain and facilities offered by registered establishments are listed in the boards' accommodation guides. Information on tourist facilities and accommodation is available from official information centres throughout Britain (most of which are administered by local authorities) and on videotex information services in Britain and overseas.

13 Energy and Natural Resources

Energy and non-fuel minerals make an important contribution to the British economy. The approximate value of minerals produced in 1984 was £25,839 million, of which crude oil accounted for 79 per cent, coal 8 per cent and natural gas 5 per cent.

All minerals in Great Britain are privately owned, with the exception of gold, silver, oil and natural gas (which are owned by the Crown), and coal and some minerals associated with coal. In Northern Ireland gold and silver are owned by the Crown, while rights to petroleum and other minerals are vested in the Government. On the United Kingdom Continental Shelf the right to exploit all minerals except coal is vested in the Crown. The exclusive right to extract coal, or license others to do so, both on land and under the sea, is vested in the National Coal Board. Normally, ownership of minerals belongs to the owner of the land surface but in some areas, particularly where mining has taken place, these rights have become separated. Mining and quarrying, apart from coalmining, are usually carried out by privately owned companies.

Water resources are normally sufficient for domestic and industrial requirements; supplies are obtained from surface sources such as mountain lakes and from underground sources by such means as wells and boreholes.

Energy

Britain has the largest energy resources of any country in the European Community and is a major world producer of oil, natural gas and coal. The other main primary sources are nuclear power and some water power; secondary sources are electricity, coke and very small quantities of town gas. Since 1980 Britain has been self-sufficient in energy in net terms as a result of the continued growth in offshore oil production, and self-sufficiency should be maintained for a number of years. Coal is the country's richest natural resource and estimated proven recoverable reserves are 4,600 million tonnes; total coal resources are many times higher. A major capital investment programme in the coal industry is in progress. Nuclear power provided about 20 per cent of electricity generated by the public supply system in 1985.

Privately owned companies predominate in offshore oil and gas production and oil refining, while publicly owned bodies are responsible for most coal production and electricity generation and distribution. In Great Britain the Secretary of State for Energy is responsible for these industries, except for electricity in Scotland which is the responsibility of the Secretary of State for Scotland. The Secretary of State for Northern Ireland is responsible for all energy matters in the Province.

Energy Policy The Government's energy policy is designed to ensure the secure, adequate and economic provision of energy to meet Britain's requirements. The Government seeks to ensure that all economic forms of energy are produced, supplied and used as efficiently as possible, having regard also to the international application of the technologies involved. Oil and gas resources continue to be developed profitably. The Government attaches importance to the development of a competitive coal industry and to the safe and economic development of nuclear power. Particular attention is paid to achieving the most cost-effective use of energy through the adoption of energy efficiency measures.

Britain is actively engaged in international collaboration on energy questions, notably through its membership of the European Community and of the International Energy Agency (IEA, a body with 21 member countries attached to the Organisation for Economic Co-operation and Development). Since its establishment in 1974, the IEA has agreed a wide range of co-operative measures to reduce member nations' dependence on imported oil, and it continues to support the adoption of realistic energy pricing policies by all member countries, both to discourage wasteful use of energy and to stimulate new methods of utilising and saving it.

ENERGY CONSUMPTION

Inland primary energy consumption amounted to 326·9 million tonnes of coal equivalent in 1985 (see Table 20), 4·7 per cent more than in 1984, but still below the level of the 1970s, reflecting energy conservation and lower levels of industrial production. Consumption of coal and of oil in 1985 was affected by unusual patterns of deliveries and changes in stocks resulting from the dispute in the coalmining industry in 1984 and early 1985. Energy consumption by final users in 1985 amounted to 56,333 million therms[1] on a 'heat supplied' basis, of which domestic users consumed about 30 per cent, industrial users 29 per cent, transport 27 per cent and public services 6 per cent.

Table 20: Inland Energy Consumption (in terms of primary sources)

million tonnes coal equivalent

	1975	1980	1983	1984	1985
Oil	136·5	121·4	106·1	135·2	115·0
Coal	120·0	120·8	111·5	79·0	105·3
Natural gas	55·4	71·1	74·8	76·5	82·3
Nuclear energy	10·9	13·4	18·1	19·5	22·1
Hydro-electric power	2·0	2·0	2·4	2·1	2·1
Total	324·8	328·7	312·9	312·2	326·9

Source: Department of Energy.
Note: Differences between totals and the sums of their component parts are due to rounding.

ENERGY EFFICIENCY

The aim of obtaining the best value for money from energy consumed is an integral part of the Government's strategy to increase the efficiency with which energy is supplied and used throughout the economy. Studies have indicated that some 20 per cent of Britain's energy consumption is wasted, equivalent to expenditure of some £7,000 million a year. In 1983 the Government set up the Energy Efficiency Office within the Department of Energy with the objectives of emphasising to consumers the value of using energy more efficiently and of making Britain the most energy-efficient country in the Western world. As part of the Office's plan to ensure that energy users took up the schemes and services available, 1986 was designated Energy Efficiency Year. Over 1,000 events were

[1] 1 therm = 105,506 kilojoules.

held in Britain, many of them sponsored by the fuel supply industries, the energy efficiency industries and other sectors with energy interests.

Energy ministers are engaged on a programme of meetings with senior managers in industry, commerce and local authorities to promote the benefits of improved energy efficiency and to increase awareness of the technology and guidance available. By June 1986 some 20,000 senior managers had attended these meetings. The Government's programme on energy efficiency in industry and commerce also includes financial assistance towards the cost of energy efficiency surveys and the establishment of monitoring and targeting systems in specific sectors, as well as grants for demonstration projects to stimulate the use of new technologies or new applications of existing technology. Regional energy efficiency officers provide help to companies and support for firms' energy managers, of whom there are over 8,500. Research and development programmes include feasibility studies on combined heat and power or district heating schemes.

In the domestic sector a show giving information and advice on energy efficiency in the home has visited some 200 locations, including shopping centres and home exhibitions throughout Britain. Grants are available to householders for loft and hot water-tank insulation, and there are also grants towards the establishment of community insulation projects to help low-income families to install insulation. Home energy audits are being developed so that householders can assess how efficiently they use energy.

The Government sets certain compulsory standards including minimum insulation standards for new buildings and a maximum heated temperature of 19°C (66°F) for non-domestic buildings.

OFFSHORE OIL AND GAS

Britain's energy position has been transformed by the discovery of substantial oil and gas reserves offshore in the United Kingdom Continental Shelf (UKCS). The total area covered by production licences is some 107,040 sq km (43,317 sq miles) out of a total designated area of about 651,650 sq km (251,600 sq miles), over which Britain has exercised its rights to explore and exploit the seabed and subsoil. Expenditure on offshore and onshore exploration and development amounted to some £2,800 million in 1985. By the end of 1985, 2,864 wells had been or were being drilled in the UKCS (1,300 development wells, 1,036 exploration wells and 528 appraisal wells).

Offshore Supplies

The Offshore Supplies Office of the Department of Energy is responsible for ensuring that British industry has a full and fair opportunity in the supply of goods and services to the UKCS; for supporting British firms' research and development projects for new products and techniques for use in oil and gas exploration; and for promoting Britain's offshore interests overseas. Britain's offshore supplies industry is the second largest in the world (after that of the United States). In 1985 goods and services valued at £3,420 million were ordered for UKCS developments, the British share of orders received being £2,720 million (80 per cent).

OIL

Before the 1970s Britain was almost wholly dependent for its oil supplies on imports, the only indigenous supplies coming from a small number of land-based oilfields. However, the first notable discovery of oil in the UKCS was made in 1969 and the first oil was brought ashore in 1975. Output of crude oil from the UKCS in mid-1986 was about 2·2 million barrels (290,000 tonnes) a day, making Britain the world's fifth largest producer.

North Sea Fields

There were 30 offshore fields producing crude oil in mid-1986. The largest fields are Brent and Forties, while six more fields are under development; other

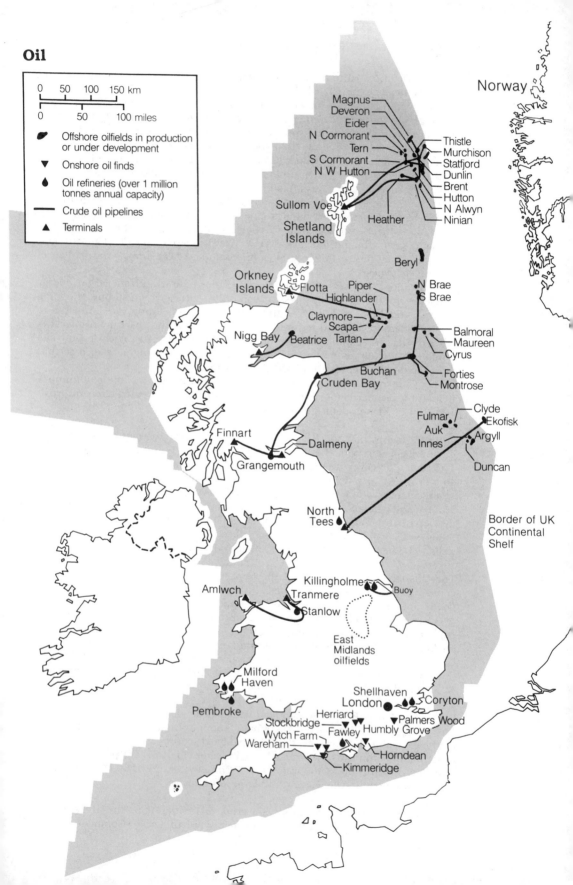

Oil

Scale:
0 50 100 150 km
0 50 100 miles

Offshore oilfields in production or under development
Onshore oil finds
Oil refineries (over 1 million tonnes annual capacity)
Crude oil pipelines
Terminals

Norway

Magnus
Deveron
Eider
N Cormorant
Tern
S Cormorant
N W Hutton
Thistle
Murchison
Statfjord
Dunlin
Brent
Hutton
N Alwyn
Ninian
Heather
Sullom Voe
Shetland Islands

Beryl

Orkney Islands
Flotta
Piper
Highlander
N Brae
S Brae
Claymore
Scapa
Tartan
Nigg Bay
Beatrice
Balmoral
Maureen
Cyrus
Buchan
Cruden Bay
Forties
Montrose
Clyde
Ekofisk
Fulmar
Auk
Innes
Argyll
Duncan
Finnart
Dalmeny
Grangemouth
North Tees
Border of UK Continental Shelf

Amlwch
Tranmere
Stanlow
Killingholme
Buoy
East Midlands oilfields

Milford Haven
Pembroke
Shellhaven
London
Coryton
Herriard
Palmers Wood
Stockbridge
Fawley
Humbly Grove
Wytch Farm
Wareham
Horndean
Kimmeridge

⌐⌐ ⌐⌐ant finds may prove to have commercial potential after further appraisal. Production ⌐ ⌐ most large fields is controlled from production platforms of either steel or concrete which have been built to withstand severe weather including gusts of wind of up to 260 km/h (160 mph) and waves of 30 m (100 ft).

Britain's primary oil production, including condensates and petroleum gases, amounted to about 127·5 million tonnes in 1985 (see Table 21), 1·3 per cent more than in 1984. Output is around its maximum, and production is forecast to decline slowly in the rest of the 1980s. Britain should remain a significant producer well into the 1990s and, on a smaller scale, into the twenty-first century. The Government's oil policy is intended to encourage exploration and development with the objective of maximising economic oil production for the foreseeable future. Remaining proven reserves of oil in the UKCS amount to about 750 million tonnes while the total remaining reserves of the UKCS could be as high as 4,120 million tonnes.

Structure of the Oil Industry

There are several large oil companies operating in Britain or engaged in work in the UKCS. In total there are about 280 companies with interests in the North Sea. The two leading British oil companies are British Petroleum (BP), in which the Government has a 32 per cent stake, and Shell Transport and Trading, which are the two largest industrial companies in Britain in terms of turnover. In late 1985 a small Oil and Pipelines Agency took over the residual functions of the British National Oil Corporation, which has been abolished. The Agency markets the crude oil received by the Government as petroleum royalty taken in kind, manages the Government's pipeline and storage system, and holds the Government's rights under participation agreements with the oil companies.

Land-based Fields

Onshore production of crude oil is much less significant than offshore production. In 1985 it amounted to 380,000 tonnes, about 67 per cent of which came from Britain's largest onshore field at Wytch Farm (Dorset), which started production in 1979. Eleven other onshore fields are in operation, notably Beckingham/Gainsborough and Welton in Lincolnshire, and Humbly Grove in Hampshire.

Refineries

At the beginning of 1986 the distillation capacity of Britain's 14 oil refineries stood at 92·8 million tonnes a year. Excess capacity is being eliminated, while existing refineries are being adapted to the changing pattern of demand by the construction of new upgrading facilities ('catalytic crackers') which are leading to a higher output of motor spirit and naphtha at the expense of fuel oil.

Consumption and Trade

Deliveries of petroleum products for inland consumption (excluding refinery consumption) in 1985 totalled 70·1 million tonnes, including 20·4 million tonnes of motor spirit, 17·4 million tonnes of gas and diesel oil (including derv fuel used in road vehicles), 16·3 million tonnes of fuel oil and 6·9 million tonnes of kerosene.

Exports of crude oil have grown rapidly and in 1985 amounted to 79·6 million tonnes. Virtually all exports went to Britain's partners in the European Community and the IEA, the largest markets being the Netherlands, France and the United States. Some 19 million tonnes of petroleum products were also exported. The volume of imports of crude oil has fallen considerably to about 24 per cent of the level of the peak year of 1973. Heavy crude oil continues to be imported to enable the full range of petroleum products to be made efficiently, as not all of these can be made from the light crude oil produced in the UKCS. The main sources of crude oil imports in 1985 were Norway (which supplied about 44 per cent by value), Nigeria (12 per cent), and Turkey and Saudi Arabia (which each supplied 8 per cent).

Table 21: Oil Statistics

million tonnes

	1975	1980	1983	1984	1985
Oil production[a]					
land	0·1	0·2	0·3	0·3	0·4
offshore	1·5	80·3	114·6	125·6	127·1
Refinery output	86·6	79·2	70·9	73·2	72·9
Deliveries of petroleum products for inland consumption	91·2	71·2	64·5	81·4	70·1
Exports (including re-exports):					
crude petroleum	1·1	38·5	68·3	75·9	79·6
refined petroleum products and process oils	17·3	16·1	15·9	16·4	18·9
Imports:					
crude petroleum	100·8	44·8	22·8	25·0	26·9
refined petroleum products and process oils	23·1	14·1	17·3	28·5	25·0

Sources: Department of Energy and HM Customs and Excise.
[a] Crude oil plus condensates and petroleum gases derived at onshore treatment plants.

Oil Pipelines

Oil pipelines brought ashore about 80 per cent of offshore oil in 1985. Some 1,620 km (1,010 miles) of major submarine pipeline have been built to bring ashore oil from a number of North Sea oilfields (see map, p 276). Major crude oil onshore pipelines in operation from harbours, land terminals or offshore moorings to refineries include those connecting Finnart to Grangemouth, Tranmere to Stanlow, Amlwch to Stanlow, and Cruden Bay to Grangemouth. Onshore pipelines also carry refined products to major marketing areas; for example, a 423-km (263-mile) pipeline runs from Milford Haven to the midlands and Manchester.

Research

The leading oil companies have extensive research and development programmes in support of oil exploration and production and on new and improved fuels. All aspects of production are covered, including the design of production facilities and enhanced oil recovery techniques. Research centres are at Sunbury-on-Thames (BP), Ellesmere Port in Cheshire and Sittingbourne in Kent (Shell), and Abingdon in Oxfordshire (Esso). The main government research and development effort in offshore technology is undertaken by the Department of Energy with the advice of the Offshore Energy Technology Board. In 1986–87 the Department expects to spend some £24 million in support of offshore technology.

GAS

Public supply of manufactured gas in Britain began in the early nineteenth century in central London. For many years gas was produced from coal but during the 1960s, when growing supplies of oil were being imported, there was a switch to producing town gas from oil-based feedstocks. However, in the late 1960s, following the first commercial natural gas discovery in the UKCS in 1965 and the start of offshore gas production in 1967, supplies of offshore natural gas grew rapidly and natural gas has now replaced town gas in the public supply system in Great Britain. Originally used almost exclusively for lighting, gas is now used for domestic cooking and heating and for industrial and commercial purposes.

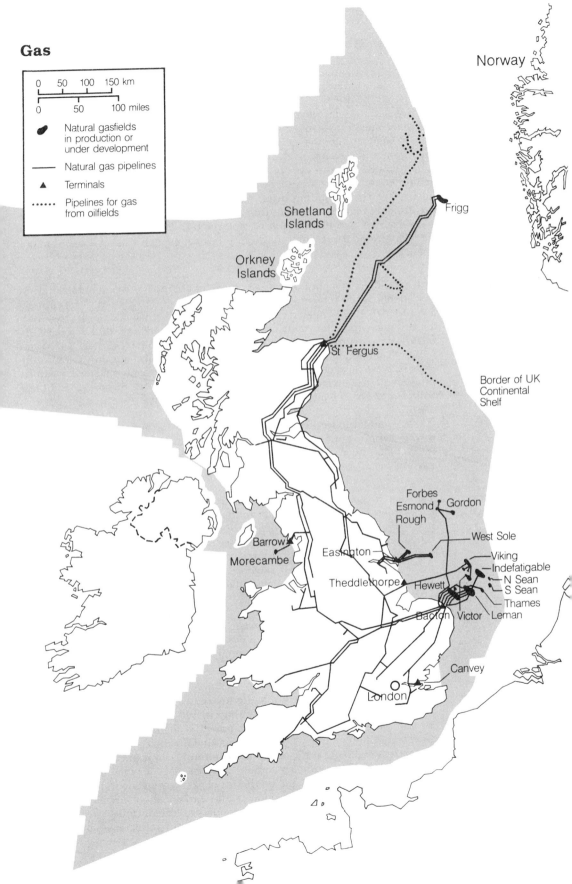

Gas

0 50 100 150 km
0 50 100 miles

- Natural gasfields in production or under development
- Natural gas pipelines
- ▲ Terminals
- ..... Pipelines for gas from oilfields

Norway

Shetland Islands

Orkney Islands

Frigg

St Fergus

Border of UK Continental Shelf

Forbes
Esmond Gordon
Rough

West Sole

Barrow
Morecambe

Easington

Viking
Indefatigable
N Sean
S Sean
Thames
Leman

Theddlethorpe

Hewett

Bacton Victor

Canvey

London

Structure

The gas industry in Great Britain has been under state ownership and control since 1949. However, in 1985 the Government announced its intention to transfer all the assets of the British Gas Corporation to the private sector, and the Gas Act 1986 provides for the privatisation of the Corporation and for the sale of the successor company's shares. In August 1986 the Corporation's assets were transferred to the new company, British Gas plc. The Government's intention is that shares in the company will be offered for sale later in 1986.

In 1985–86 the turnover of the Corporation and its subsidiary companies amounted to £7,687 million, of which gas supply accounted for £7,109 million. Its current cost operating profit was £688 million. British Gas has a large investment programme, amounting to £2,500 million (at 1985 prices) in the five years from 1985 to 1990, a large part of which is accounted for by investment in the Rough and Morecambe fields (see below). British Gas has some 90,000 employees.

Production

In 1985 indigenous natural gas accounted for about 74 per cent of total natural gas supplies, the remainder coming from Norway. Production of natural gas amounted to 42,947 million cubic metres (mcm), of which 3,220 mcm were used for drilling, production and pumping operations offshore, and some 39,393 mcm were used mainly by the public supply gas industry. Production comes mainly from seven major gasfields: Leman, Frigg (UK), Indefatigable, Viking, Hewett, West Sole and Victor. British Gas has undertaken a major investment programme to develop the Morecambe field in the Irish Sea as an additional source in the peak winter months, and the first supplies were brought ashore in 1985.

Total remaining recoverable gas reserves, including possible gas from existing discoveries and potential future discoveries, are in the range of 868,000 mcm to 2·85 million mcm. Indigenous offshore natural gas reserves are likely to meet most of the demand from the British market well into the 1990s.

Transmission and Storage

The British Gas national high-pressure pipeline system of some 5,600 km (3,500 miles) provides for the distribution of natural gas. It is supplied by feeder mains from four North Sea shore terminals, and from a new terminal in Barrow-in-Furness (Cumbria), which began operating in 1985. The whole of the high-pressure transmission system is regularly inspected; British Gas has developed the world's most advanced computerised inspection vehicle for high-pressure pipelines that detects flaws as it travels through them.

Various methods of storage of natural gas to meet peak load conditions are used including salt cavities and storage facilities for liquefied natural gas. British Gas has also developed the partially depleted Rough field as a major gas store. This, the first such use of an offshore field, involves the injection into the Rough reservoir in the summer months of gas drawn from the national transmission system for recovery during periods of peak winter demand.

Consumption

Sales of gas by the public supply industry in Britain totalled 18,390 million therms in 1985, 6·3 per cent more than in 1984. About half of all gas sold by British Gas to its 16·8 million consumers is for industrial and commercial purposes, the remainder being for household use. Gas is used extensively in industries requiring the control of temperatures to a fine degree of accuracy such as the pottery industry and certain processes for making iron and steel products. In 1985, 5,783 million therms of gas were sold to industry in Britain, 247 million therms to fuel producers and 2,678 million therms to commercial and other non-domestic users. The domestic load includes gas for cookers, space heaters, water heaters and refrigerators, but an increasingly large part of domestic demand is for gas for central heating. In 1985, 9,682 million therms were sold to domestic users.

Research

British Gas conducts research at five research stations into all aspects of gas supply and use. Total expenditure on research and development and on technical services and testing amounted to about £75·8 million in 1985–86. Work on processes for the manufacture of substitute natural gas from coal is one of its main research projects. A demonstration coal gasification plant ('slagging gasifier') has been built at the Westfield Development Centre in Fife. Other research is concerned with the design, efficient operation and maintenance of the transmission and distribution systems, with the efficient use of gas in its various industrial and domestic applications, and with research supporting the exploration programme.

COAL

Coalmining in Britain can be traced back to the thirteenth century. It played a crucial part in the industrial revolution of the eighteenth and nineteenth centuries and in its peak year, 1913, the industry produced 292 million tonnes of coal, exported 74·2 million tonnes and employed over a million workers. In 1947 the coal mines passed into public ownership by means of the Coal Industry Nationalisation Act 1946, which set up the National Coal Board (NCB) as a statutory corporation to manage the industry.

The National Coal Board

The NCB (which trades under the name British Coal) has, with limited exceptions, exclusive rights over the extraction of coal in Great Britain, but is empowered to license private operators to work small mines and opencast sites. It also has powers to work other minerals, where discoveries are made in the course of searching for, or working, coal; and to engage in certain petrochemicals activities beneficial to the future of the coal industry. Retail sales remain largely in private hands, although the NCB makes bulk sales to large industrial consumers.

At the end of March 1986 there were 133 NCB collieries in operation. The main coal-bearing regions are shown on the map on p 282.

Production

Output recovered in 1985–86 from the low levels resulting from a lengthy industrial dispute in 1984–85. The total output of 104·5 million tonnes comprised 88·2 million tonnes of deep-mined coal, 14·1 million tonnes from opencast mines and 2·2 million tonnes from other sources (including recovered slurry).

Development

Britain's coal industry is one of the largest in Western Europe, and one of the world's most technologically advanced. The NCB has a substantial capital investment programme, which amounted to £660 million in 1985–86. Considerable progress has been made in techniques for mining coal. Developments are concentrated on the increasing use of heavy-duty equipment, such as powered roof supports, power loaders and armoured flexible conveyors, capable of sustained high performance with minimum maintenance, and on the introduction of computerised automatic monitoring and remote control of machines.

Although many good seams of coal have now been worked out because of the early development of the industry, total coal resources in Britain are estimated at 190,000 million tonnes, of which about 45,000 million tonnes are considered to be recoverable using established technology and 4,600 million tonnes are judged to be 'proved recoverable'. Production at the new mining complex at Selby in North Yorkshire (one of the world's most advanced deep mines) is planned to build up to 10 million tonnes a year. Investment of £400 million

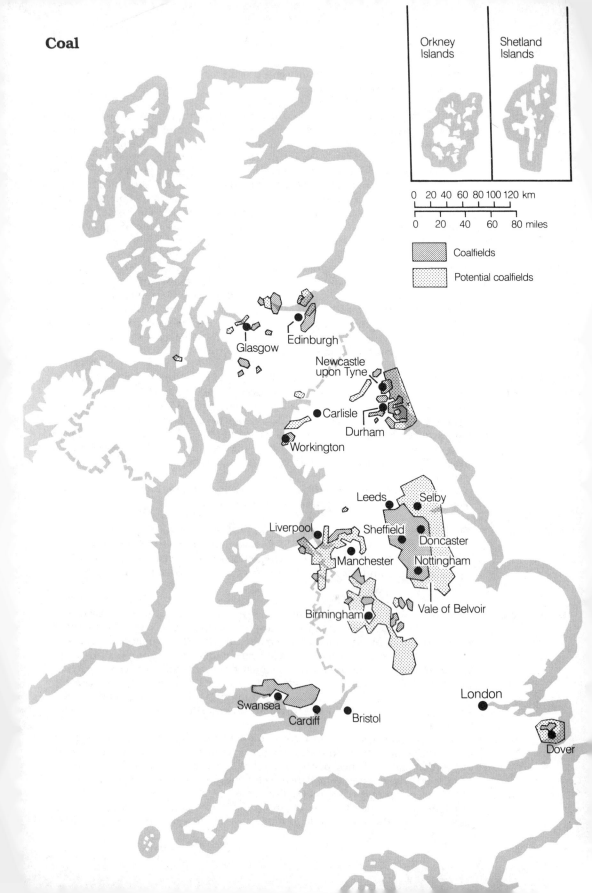

Coal

Orkney Islands

Shetland Islands

0 20 40 60 80 100 120 km

0 20 40 60 80 miles

Coalfields

Potential coalfields

Glasgow

Edinburgh

Newcastle upon Tyne

● Carlisle

Durham

Workington

Leeds

Selby

Liverpool

Sheffield

Doncaster

Manchester

Nottingham

Vale of Belvoir

Birmingham

Swansea

Cardiff

Bristol

London

Dover

has been allocated to develop a new mine at Asfordby in the Vale of Belvoir (Leicestershire).

The first coal to be discovered on a significant scale in Northern Ireland is a substantial deposit of lignite (brown coal) on the eastern shore of Lough Neagh, where reserves are estimated at 420 million tonnes. Further deposits have been discovered and are being appraised to determine their size and the feasibility of mining.

Consumption

In 1985–86 inland consumption of coal was 118·4 million tonnes of which 73 per cent was by power stations, 10 per cent by coke ovens and 10 per cent by domestic users. With a substantial proportion of coal being used by power stations for electricity generation, NCB sales of coal to them totalled 87·4 million tonnes in 1985–86. Exports of coal in 1985–86 were 3·3 million tonnes, while imports amounted to 12·1 million tonnes.

Research

In 1985–86 the NCB spent £57 million on research. It has two main research establishments: the Mining Research and Development Establishment at Stanhope Bretby (Staffordshire), for work on mining methods and equipment, particularly improving the performance and reliability of equipment and developing systems for remote and automatic control; and the Coal Research Establishment at Stoke Orchard (near Cheltenham), concerned with the utilisation of coal, including a major research and development programme on fluidised bed combustion for industrial steam-raising and heating. This project has led to successful commercial exploitation, and development work continues. Agreements to exchange technical information have been signed by the NCB with several countries. Britain is responsible through an NCB subsidiary for the management of a service which provides information on and analyses of coal topics under the auspices of the International Energy Agency.

ELECTRICITY

The first public supply of electricity in the world was in 1881, at Godalming (Surrey). In 1948 all municipal and private undertakings in Great Britain were acquired under the Electricity Act 1947 and vested in the British Electricity Authority and 14 regional boards, except in the north of Scotland where they became the responsibility of the North of Scotland Hydro-Electric Board (NSHEB), which had been set up in 1943. Two subsequent Acts (1954 and 1957) effected a measure of decentralisation and established the present structure of public corporations. Electricity from the public supply system is available to all premises in Britain except for some very remote rural households. The public supply industry employed about 150,000 people and invested some £1,700 million in 1985–86. The main transmission system (national grid) in Great Britain is one of the largest fully interconnected power networks in the Western world.

The Energy Act 1983 allows private generation to compete with the public supply industry. It entitles private generators of electricity to sell their electricity to the boards on terms reflecting costs fairly incurred by the boards, and allows them to use the public transmission and distribution system.

Structure

The Electricity Council is the central co-ordinating body of the supply industry in England and Wales. It has a general responsibility for promoting the development and maintenance of an efficient, co-ordinated and economical system of electricity supply. Electricity is generated and transmitted by the Central Electricity Generating Board (CEGB), which is responsible for the operation and maintenance of power stations and the national grid. Twelve area electricity boards are responsible for distribution and for the retail sale of

Electricity

Orkney Islands

Shetland Islands

| 0 | 20 | 40 | 60 | 80 | 100 | 120 km |

| 0 | 20 | 40 | 60 | 80 miles |

■ Conventional power stations (1,000 MW and over)

● Nuclear power stations

○ Under construction

♦ Power-producing reactors of the UKAEA or BNFL

★ Hydro-electric power stations (over 45-MW capacity)

▲ Pumped storage schemes

····· Boundary of the SSEB and NSHEB

Dounreay

Fasnakyle

▲ Foyers

Peterhead ■

Rannoch   Errochty

Cruachan ▲   ★ Clunie

Lochay

Sloy

Longannet

Torness

Inverkip   Cockenzie

Hunterston B   Hunterston A

Chapelcross   Blyth B ■

Hartlepool ●

Calder Hall

Heysham I   ○ Heysham II

Ferrybridge C ■   Drax

Eggborough   Thorpe Marsh

Wylfa   Fiddler's   West Burton

Ferry   Cottam

Dinorwig ▲   Ince   High Marnham

▲ Ffestiniog

● Trawsfynydd   Ratcliffe-on-Soar

★ Rheidol

Sizewell A ●

Tilbury

Pembroke ■   Berkeley   W. Thurrock   ● Bradwell

Aberthaw B   Oldbury   Didcot   ■ Grain

Littlebrook   Kingsnorth

Hinkley Pt. A   Hinkley Pt. B   Fawley

Dungeness B

Winfrith ♦   Dungeness A

electricity. In 1985–86 the income of the electricity supply industry in England and Wales was £10,742 million.

In Scotland two boards, the NSHEB and the South of Scotland Electricity Board (SSEB), generate, distribute and sell electricity. The boundary separating their areas runs from Dumbarton on the Firth of Clyde to Newburgh on the Firth of Tay (see map, p 284). In 1985–86 the turnover of the SSEB and the NSHEB was £887 million and £311 million respectively.

In Northern Ireland generation, transmission and distribution are carried out by the publicly owned Northern Ireland Electricity Service.

Consumption
Sales of electricity in 1985 amounted to 240,387 gigawatt hours (GWh). Domestic users took 37 per cent of the total, industry 36 per cent and commercial and other users the remainder. About one-fifth of domestic sales is for space heating, one-sixth for water heating and one-tenth for cooking. Electricity is used in industry mainly for motive power, melting, heating and lighting. It is supplied to 24·3 million consumers of whom 21·5 million are in England and Wales, 1·7 million are supplied by the SSEB, 578,000 by the NSHEB and 566,000 are in Northern Ireland.

Generation
Generation by the public supply electricity industry in Britain amounted to 279,972 GWh in 1985. Conventional steam power stations provided over 77·2 per cent of the total, nuclear stations 20·1 per cent and gas turbine, hydro-electric and diesel plant 2·6 per cent. Public supply power stations consumed 115 million tonnes of coal equivalent in 1985, of which coal accounted for 65 per cent and oil 16 per cent. The output capacity of the 172 generating stations of the electricity boards at the end of 1985 totalled 63,794 megawatts (MW) including 52,021 MW run by the CEGB, 6,230 MW by the SSEB, 3,213 MW by the NSHEB and 2,290 MW by the Northern Ireland Electricity Service. An analysis of electricity generation by and output capacity of the public supply system is given in Table 22.

Table 22: Generation by and Capacity of Public Supply Power Stations

| | Electricity generated (GWh) | | | Per cent | Output capacity[a] |
	1975	1980	1985	1985	(MW)
Nuclear plant	26,518	33,462	56,354	20·1	6,399
Other steam plant	219,692	227,973	216,255	77·2	49,826
Gas turbines and oil engines	699	451	1,084	0·4	3,486
Pumped-storage plant	1,153	1,188	2,831	1·0	2,788
Other hydro-electric plant	3,201	3,309	3,447	1·2	1,295
Total	251,263	266,383	279,972	100·0	63,794
Electricity supplied (net)[b]	233,236	247,667	258,242		

Source: Department of Energy.
[a] At 31 December 1985.
[b] Electricity generated less electricity used at power stations (including electricity used for pumping at pumped-storage stations).

Generation of electricity outside the public supply system is relatively small (17,583 GWh in 1985). The major sources outside the fuel industries are the chemicals, engineering, paper, and iron and steel industries and the nuclear power plants of the United Kingdom Atomic Energy Authority (UKAEA) and British Nuclear Fuels plc. In 1985 these nuclear plants supplied 4,073 GWh of electricity to the public supply system.

The most recent large-scale power stations are based on units of 500 MW and 660 MW. Station capacities have increased and there are 15 stations each with a capacity of 2,000 MW or more including Kingsnorth (Kent), Europe's largest mixed-fuel station burning either coal or oil. The Drax coal-fired station (North Yorkshire), which has an output capacity of 4,000 MW, is the largest coal-fired station in Western Europe. The larger units have a higher thermal efficiency (the ratio of the net electrical energy output to the heat energy input) than earlier units and their introduction, coupled with the closure of less efficient plant, has resulted in a gradual rise in overall thermal efficiency, leading to substantial savings in fuel consumption. Average thermal efficiency of conventional steam stations in England and Wales rose from 20·91 per cent in 1947–48 to 34·65 per cent in 1985–86.

The pumped-storage station at Dinorwig (Gwynedd), the largest of its type in Europe, has an average generated output of 1,680 MW. (In pumped-storage schemes electricity generated in off-peak periods is used to pump water to high-level reservoirs from which it descends to drive turbines, rapidly providing a large supply of electricity at peak periods or to meet sudden increases in demand.)

The CEGB, together with Electricité de France, has constructed a 2,000-MW cross-Channel cable link, increasing the capacity for the transmission of electricity between the two countries. The first stage of the link began operating in January 1986, and the entire network will be operational by November 1986.

The Government is keen to encourage combined heat and power (CHP) schemes. As part of a programme to study the potential for CHP/district heating in particular locations in Britain, the Government has given financial assistance to consortia from Belfast, Edinburgh and Leicester for the preparation of a prospectus for a combined CHP/district heating scheme. It is expected that all of these studies will be completed by the end of 1987.

Nuclear Power

Britain has been developing nuclear power for several decades and in 1956 the world's first large-scale nuclear power station, at Calder Hall (Cumbria), began to supply electricity to the national grid. The Government believes that nuclear power has a vital role in helping to meet Britain's long-term energy requirements. There are 14 nuclear power stations in operation controlled by the electricity authorities. Four other stations also feed electricity to the national grid: the two original Magnox stations (both with a net capacity of about 200 MW) operated by British Nuclear Fuels plc at Calder Hall and Chapelcross (Dumfries and Galloway); and two experimental or prototype stations run by the UKAEA—at Winfrith (Dorset) and a prototype fast reactor at Dounreay (Highland).

Nuclear Power Programme

Under the first commercial programme, nine Magnox stations with a total gross capacity of about 4,000 MW were commissioned between 1962 and 1971, the largest being Wylfa (Gwynedd), which has a capacity of 840 MW. The second series of orders was based on the Advanced Gas-cooled Reactor (AGR). Hinkley Point B (Somerset) and Hunterston B (Strathclyde) began operating in 1976, while three more AGRs began operating in 1985: Dungeness B (Kent), Hartlepool (Cleveland) and Heysham (Lancashire). All the AGRs are 1,320-MW units except Dungeness B (1,200 MW). Construction is in progress on two further 1,320-MW AGRs—a second station at Heysham and a station at Torness (Lothian)—and these should be completed by 1988. The CEGB has also applied for the consent of the Secretary of State for Energy to build a 1,200-MW pressurised water reactor at Sizewell (Suffolk). This application is subject to the results of a public inquiry (completed in 1985) and to the necessary consents and safety clearances being obtained.

British Nuclear Fuels

British Nuclear Fuels plc provides nuclear fuel services covering the whole fuel cycle: uranium conversion, uranium enrichment (through its shareholding in Urenco Ltd), fuel element fabrication, transport and reprocessing of spent fuel, and the manufacture of specialised fuel element components. All of its shares are held by the Government. The company is organised into four divisions, covering uranium enrichment, based at Capenhurst (Cheshire); fuel manufacture at Springfields (Lancashire); reprocessing (operations) at Sellafield (Cumbria) where valuable unused uranium and plutonium are recovered from the spent fuel; and reprocessing (engineering) at the headquarters at Risley (Cheshire). There is a large-scale investment programme in progress involving expenditure of some £3,700 million over the next ten years. The major part of this expenditure relates to the Sellafield site and comprises the refurbishment of facilities for treating spent fuel from Magnox power stations, the construction of a thermal oxide reprocessing plant (THORP) which will take spent fuel from Britain's AGRs and overseas reactors, and the construction of facilities to process and package radioactive waste. The remainder of the programme involves the construction of further centrifuge enrichment plant at Capenhurst, and refurbishment and construction of new plant at Springfields.

Nuclear Research

The UKAEA carries out research and development to ensure that nuclear power is economic, safe and environmentally acceptable. Its work is undertaken by research establishments at Harwell (Oxfordshire), Risley, Winfrith, Springfields, Windscale (Cumbria), Dounreay and Culham (Oxfordshire). In addition, safety research is carried out at the Safety and Reliability Directorate at Culcheth (Cheshire). Work connected with the development of the fast reactor and its fuel cycle takes place principally at Dounreay and represents a major programme for the UKAEA.

Since April 1986 the UKAEA has operated as a trading fund, which allows it to function on a commercial basis. Under the new arrangements the UKAEA's research and development work for the Department of Energy is on a customer–contractor basis. The UKAEA also carries out work for a number of other customers including the electricity generating boards, British Nuclear Fuels plc, other government departments and industry.

Co-operation on nuclear energy between Britain and other countries takes place within a framework of intergovernmental agreements—such as that signed in 1984 with Belgium, France, the Federal Republic of Germany and Italy setting out collaboration on the development of the fast reactor—membership of bodies such as the International Atomic Energy Agency, and through direct links on research between the UKAEA and equivalent organisations overseas.

Britain takes part in the co-operative research programmes of the European Atomic Energy Community (Euratom), including one on establishing the feasibility of achieving controlled thermonuclear fusion. A major component of this programme is the Joint European Torus (JET) project at Culham, which started operating in 1983.

Nuclear Safety

The Government and the nuclear industry give high priority to safety and the industry has an excellent safety record. Responsibility for safety at nuclear sites rests with the operators who must protect their workers and the public by complying with the Health and Safety at Work etc. Act 1974, with conditions of their nuclear site licences under the Nuclear Installations Act 1965 and by keeping discharges within the limits and conditions set by authorisations granted under the Radioactive Substances Act 1960. In England authorisations are granted jointly by the Secretary of State for the Environment and the Minister of Agriculture, Fisheries and Food, and in Scotland and Wales by their respective Secretaries of State. The terms of the authorisations are designed to ensure that those most exposed to the effects of discharges receive less than the maximum dose limit recommended by the International Commission on Radiological Protection. Within the limits, operators of nuclear facilities are required to keep discharges as low as reasonably achievable and failure to do so makes them liable to prosecution. Compliance with the legislation is overseen by the Nuclear Installations Inspectorate of the Health and Safety Executive, by the Radiochemical Inspectorate of the Department of the Environment and inspectors from the Ministry of Agriculture, Fisheries and Food in England and Wales, and by the Industrial Pollution Inspectorate in Scotland.

Britain is playing a major part in international discussions on nuclear safety. The International Atomic Energy Agency has drawn up an outline programme which would include the establishment of two international conventions: one on the reporting and exchange of information on nuclear accidents with possible transboundary effects, and one on co-ordinated emergency response and assistance in the event of such an accident.

Research on Electricity

The Electricity Council draws up a general programme of research, some of it direct research carried out by the Council and electricity boards and some of it in co-operation with selected industrial research associations and through research contracts placed with universities and other organisations. Some of the work is done in collaboration with the two Scottish electricity boards and the Northern Ireland Electricity Service which contribute towards its cost (£157 million in 1985–86). Collaboration on research between the supply industry and the plant manufacturers is co-ordinated by the Power Engineering Research Steering Committee. The research establishments run by the CEGB comprise the Central Electricity Research Laboratories at Leatherhead (Surrey), the Berkeley Nuclear Laboratories in Gloucestershire and the Marchwood Engineering Laboratories on Southampton Water. Research on distribution technology and electricity utilisation is undertaken at the Electricity Council Research Centre at Capenhurst (Cheshire) and by the area boards.

RENEWABLE SOURCES OF ENERGY

The Department of Energy is supporting research to develop the techniques for the exploitation of renewable sources of energy and to promote the commercial use of those technologies which are or are soon expected to become cost-effective. Renewable energy sources, however, are not expected to make a major contribution to energy supplies this century, although they may have a greater role in the twenty-first century. The Department of Energy's estimate is that some £13 million was spent in 1985–86 in support of its renewable energy programme; work is being concentrated on the most promising technologies, for example, wind energy, passive solar design, wastes as fuel, and geothermal hot dry rocks.

Wind power constitutes a resource of considerable national significance. The Department is supporting two major construction projects: a 60 m (200 ft) diameter horizontal-axis wind turbine generator of 3 MW on Orkney and a new medium-scale vertical-axis machine of 160 kW at Carmarthen Bay (Dyfed). In addition, the Department, a private sector company, the Central Electricity Generating Board and the European Community are collaborating on the construction of a 1-MW, 55 m (180 ft) diameter, wind turbine at the Board's site at Richborough (Kent). Four other medium-size horizontal-axis machines have recently been brought into operation. Three were built by private sector companies (two on Orkney and one at Ilfracombe, Devon) and the fourth was built by the Central Electricity Generating Board at Carmarthen Bay. The Department of Trade and Industry is supporting, through its National Engineering Laboratory at East Kilbride, the development of a test site for small-scale and medium scale wind turbines at Eaglesham, near Glasgow.

Under its geothermal hot dry rock programme, the Department is investigating the economic possibilities of extracting heat from rocks at great depth. Research is mainly carried out by the Camborne School of Mines in Cornwall, where a project is being conducted to establish the technology for creating a suitable deep underground heat exchange zone from which the heat could be withdrawn.

The Department and an industrial consortium have jointly funded a study of the technical and financial viability of a tidal energy barrage in the Severn estuary, which would be financed, built and operated by the private sector. Advanced investigations and site exploration are planned, and studies are also envisaged on a proposal for a similar energy barrage in the Mersey estuary.

The Department's work on passive solar design has shown that this could meet a significant proportion of the demand for space heating in buildings, and the adoption of effective passive design features is being encouraged.

Biofuels offer possibly the largest contribution from the renewable energy resources in the medium term. The main work of the Department's programme is on the demonstration of the various technologies involved.

Non-fuel Minerals

Although much of Britain's requirements of industrial raw materials is met by imports, non-fuel minerals produced in Britain make an important contribution to the economy. Output of non-fuel minerals in 1984 totalled 302 million tonnes, valued at £1,371 million. The total number of employees in the extraction industry was 37,000 in 1984. The locations of some of the more important minerals produced in Britain are shown on the maps on p 290.

Exploration

Exploring for and exploiting indigenous mineral resources to meet the needs of industry are being encouraged by the Government to enhance security of supplies. The British Geological Survey is carrying out a long-term programme for the Department of Trade and Industry aimed at identifying areas with the potential for economic extraction of minerals.

Production

The tonnage extracted of some of the main non-fuel minerals produced in Britain is given in Table 23. In terms of value, production of common sand and gravel was estimated at £388 million in 1984, limestone and dolomite £343 million, clays £219 million, igneous rock £139 million, sandstone £57 million, salt £56 million, tin £38 million, potash £35 million, gypsum and anhydrite £16 million, fluorspar £14 million and chalk £13 million. Britain is a major world producer of several important industrial minerals including china clay, ball clay, fuller's earth, celestite and gypsum, and also produces significant amounts of limestone, dolomite, chalk, fluorspar, potash, salt, industrial sands, fireclay, common clay and shale, barytes and talc, mostly for home consumption. Small amounts of diatomite, slate, calcspar, chert and flint, anhydrite and china stone are also produced. In 1984 the production of metal from non-ferrous ores totalled 15,800 tonnes, mainly lead mostly from northern England, and zinc and tin from Cornwall—the Cornish mines at that time satisfying about two-thirds of Britain's demand for primary tin. Small amounts of copper and silver were produced in association with tin and zinc. Planning permission has recently been granted for a large opencast tungsten mine at Hemerdon (near Plymouth).

Some Minerals Produced in Britain

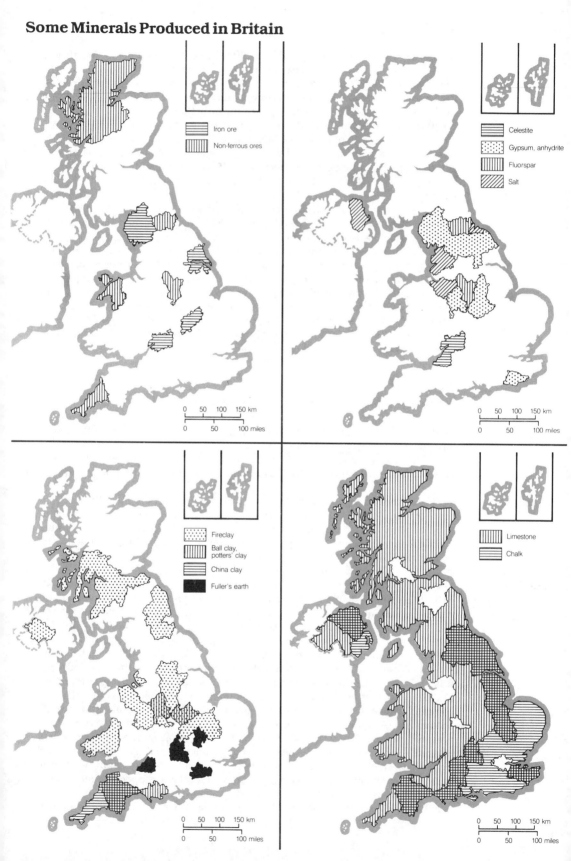

Iron ore
Non-ferrous ores

Celestite
Gypsum, anhydrite
Fluorspar
Salt

Fireclay
Ball clay, potters' clay
China clay
Fuller's earth

Limestone
Chalk

0 50 100 150 km
0 50 100 miles

The maps above are based on county or regional boundaries and not those for geological outcrops.

Production of sand, gravel and crushed rock (from limestone, igneous rock and sandstone) as aggregates for use in construction constitutes over half, by value, of Britain's output of non-fuel minerals. Britain is the world's second largest producer of marine-dredged sand and gravel (15·4 million tonnes in 1984).

Table 23: Production of Some of the Main Non-fuel Minerals

million tonnes

	1974	1979	1984
Common sand and gravel	120·3	111·5	106·0
Special sands	6·0	5·8	4·3
Igneous rock	43·1	36·2	36·8
Limestone and dolomite	102·5	92·2	93·5
Chalk	20·5	16·3	12·0[a]
Sandstone	14·7	13·5	15·1
Gypsum	3·5	3·5	3·1
Salt including salt in brine	8·4	7·8	7·1
Common clay and shale	30·9	21·6[a]	17·8[a]
China clay, ball clay and			
potters' clay	4·3	4·4	3·6
Fireclay	1·7	1·7	0·8[a]
Iron ore	3·6	4·3	0·4
Potash	—	—	0·5
Fluorspar	0·2	0·1	0·1

Source: *United Kingdom Mineral Statistics 1985.*
[a] Great Britain only.

Water

Britain's water resources are normally sufficient for domestic and industrial requirements. Supplies are obtained partly from surface sources such as mountain lakes, streams impounded in upland gathering grounds and river intakes (one-third comes from rivers), and partly from underground sources by means of wells, adits and boreholes. Water for public supply in Britain amounted to about 18,700 megalitres (Ml) a day in 1985 and average daily supply per head was nearly 330 litres. About 99 per cent of the population in Great Britain and over 96 per cent in Northern Ireland are connected to the public water supply system.

In general, householders pay for their domestic water supply, sewerage and sewage disposal services through charges based on the rateable value of their property, whereas industrial users are charged for their water supply according to actual metered consumption. Since 1983 optional metering for domestic users has been available throughout England and Wales, and legislation to permit the introduction of compulsory domestic water metering on a trial basis is planned.

England and Wales

In England and Wales the Secretaries of State for the Environment and for Wales are jointly responsible for policy in relation to the conservation, augmentation, distribution and proper use of water resources and provision of water supplies; the provision of sewerage and sewage disposal services; the restoration and maintenance of the wholesomeness of rivers and other inland waters; and the use of inland waters for navigation and recreation. The Minister of Agriculture, Fisheries and Food and the Secretary of State for Wales are responsible for policy relating to land drainage, flood protection, sea defence, and the protection and development of fisheries.

Water Authorities

Nine regional water authorities in England and the Welsh Water Authority in Wales are responsible for the management of water services; the development of water resources; water distribution and supply; the prevention of pollution; sewerage; sewage treatment; river management; land drainage; sea defence; recreation; and freshwater fisheries. Water authorities' estimated revenue for 1986–87 is some £2,680 million. Their management boards are appointed by ministers. However, legislation is planned to privatise the water authorities in England and Wales, with a view to removing government financial controls, improving services and involving the public and the workforce more closely in ownership of the industry.

District councils usually act as agents of water authorities for the design, construction, operation and maintenance of public sewers in their areas.

Statutory Water Companies

There are 30 statutory water supply companies, accounting for about one-quarter of total supplies, which are operating under the Water Act 1973. Special arrangements govern the relationship of these companies to the water authorities.

Supplies

Some 29,000 Ml a day were abstracted in England and Wales in 1984, of which public water supplies accounted for 16,400 Ml a day. The Central Electricity Generating Board took some 7,000 Ml a day primarily for cooling in connection with electricity generation, other industry about 4,000 Ml a day and the remainder was used in agriculture.

Water authorities have powers to restrict consumption when there are severe water shortages. Under the Drought Act 1976 they can limit or prohibit the use of water and, if necessary, restrict domestic water supplies.

Scotland

In Scotland responsibility for public water supply, sewerage and sewage disposal rests with the nine regional and three islands councils. In addition, the Central Scotland Water Development Board is primarily responsible for developing large water sources and supplying water in bulk to its five constituent member authorities, the regional councils in central Scotland.

Scotland has a relative abundance of unpolluted water from upland sources. About 803 million cubic metres of water were abstracted in Scotland in 1984 for public water supplies. The Secretary of State for Scotland is responsible for the promotion of the conservation of water resources and the provision by water authorities of adequate water supplies, and also has a duty to promote the cleanliness of rivers and other inland waters and the tidal waters of Scotland.

Northern Ireland

The Water Service of the Department of the Environment for Northern Ireland is responsible for water supply and sewerage throughout Northern Ireland. The Department is also responsible for the conservation, cleanliness and planned development of Northern Ireland's water resources. Northern Ireland has abundant potential supplies of water for both domestic and industrial use. An average of 691 Ml of water a day was supplied in 1985.

Development Projects

Investment is taking place to ensure that there is an adequate water supply to meet future demand. Recent projects have included the Kielder Reservoir in Northumberland, officially opened in 1985, one of the largest man-made reservoirs in Europe. The Thames Water Authority is constructing an 80-km (50-mile) distribution system to meet the growing demand for water in London. When completed in 1994, it will be the largest urban distribution system in the world. In 1985–86 capital expenditure on water supply, sewerage and sewage disposal amounted to some £810 million in England and Wales, £97 million in Scotland and £27 million in Northern Ireland.

Research   The central research organisation for the water industry in Britain is the Water Research Centre. Its membership includes water undertakings, consulting engineers, manufacturers and overseas organisations. It has three laboratories: at Stevenage (Hertfordshire), which deals with water and waste water treatment; at Medmenham (Buckinghamshire), which is concerned with environmental protection (including water quality and pollution); and at Swindon (Wiltshire), which is concerned with instrumentation, water mains and sewers. Other organisations conducting research include Hydraulics Research Limited, universities, the Meteorological Office and the Natural Environment Research Council.

14 Agriculture, Fisheries and Forestry

Agriculture

British agriculture is noted for its high level of efficiency and productivity. Employing less than 3 per cent of the working population, the industry produces nearly two-thirds of Britain's food requirements compared with just under a half in 1960, and four-fifths of that which can be grown in a temperate climate compared with nearly two-thirds in 1960. The food share of Britain's total imports has fallen from about a quarter in the 1960s to around 10 per cent in 1985. Gross output in 1985 was £11,883 million, about 4 per cent of gross domestic product. Britain is also a major exporter of agricultural produce and food products, agrochemicals and agricultural machinery.

The Government aims to foster an efficient and competitive agriculture industry through the provision and sponsorship of research, development and advisory services, the provision of financial support where appropriate, measures to control disease, pests and pollution, and improved marketing arrangements for food and food products. It also encourages the industry to adopt high standards on animal welfare. Legislation proposed in 1986 would give agriculture ministers a responsibility to achieve a balance between the interests of agriculture, the economic and social interests of rural areas, conservation and recreation.

Land Use

Just over three-quarters of the land area is used for agriculture, the rest being mountain, forest or put to urban and other uses. The area of agricultural land has been declining, although there has been a net reduction in the rate of loss in recent years. There are 12 million hectares (30 million acres) under crops and grass. In hill country, where the area of cultivated land is often small, some 6 million hectares (over 15 million acres) are also used for rough grazing. Soils vary from the thin poor ones of highland Britain to the rich fertile soils of low-lying areas such as the fenlands of eastern England. The cool temperate climate and the even distribution of rainfall ensure a long growing season; streams rarely dry up and grassland is green throughout the year.

Farming

The average area (including rough grazing) of full-time businesses of 250 standard man-days[1] or more is 125 hectares (300 acres). In 1985 there were some 240,000 farm holdings in Britain and it is estimated that some 90 per cent of total output came from full-time businesses capable of providing full-time employment for at least one person and that these represent just under half the total number of holdings. Large businesses of 1,000 standard man-days or more, although accounting for only 12 per cent of holdings, provided about half

---

[1] A standard man-day represents 8 hours' productive work by an adult worker under average conditions.

the total output. In Wales and Northern Ireland, output from smaller farms is more significant than in the rest of Britain.

In England, Scotland and Wales, 70 per cent of holdings are wholly or mainly owner-occupied. Virtually all the farms in Northern Ireland are owner-occupied.

The number of people engaged in agriculture is just over 690,000. The labour force continues to decline slightly, and the level of mechanisation to increase. Labour productivity rose by 69 per cent between 1975 and 1985. Investment has increased the level of capital per person employed in the industry which is now about the same as in manufacturing industry compared with 80 per cent in 1960. Total farming income in 1985 was an estimated £1,154 million.

There are about 365,000 tractors and some 55,000 combine harvesters in use. A wide variety of other machines for harvesting and preservation of grass are also employed. Horticultural crops such as blackcurrants and brussels sprouts are frequently harvested by machine, and milking machines are used on the vast majority of dairy farms. The majority of farms have a direct electricity supply, the remainder having their own generators.

Although dairy herd monitoring and account analysis have been computerised for many years, the recent introduction of the microcomputer has produced major changes in farm business management. Budgeting and the monitoring of cash-flow and performance are now frequently computerised, while computer models of typical farms allow a wide range of crops and livestock to be considered, along with demands for labour, land, capital and buildings. The Government provides a topical information service to farmers and growers through the Prestel viewdata service.

PRODUCTION

Home production of the principal foods is shown as a percentage by weight of total supplies (that is, output plus imports minus exports) in Table 24.

Table 24: British Production as a Percentage of Total Supplies

Food product	1974–76 average	1985 estimate
Meat	82	90
Eggs	98	97
Milk for human consumption (as liquid)	100	100
Cheese	63	67
Butter	13	64
Sugar (as refined)	26	55
Wheat	61	103
Potatoes for human consumption	88	89

Source: Ministry of Agriculture, Fisheries and Food.

Livestock

About three-fifths of full-time farms are devoted mainly to dairying or beef cattle and sheep. The majority of sheep and cattle are reared in the hill and moorland areas of Scotland, Wales, Northern Ireland and northern and south-western England. Beef fattening occurs partly in better grassland areas, as does dairying, and partly on arable farms. British livestock breeders have developed many of the cattle, sheep and pig breeds with world-wide reputations, for example, the Hereford and Aberdeen Angus beef breeds, the Jersey, Guernsey and Ayrshire dairy breeds, Large White pigs and a number of sheep breeds. Because of developments in artificial insemination and embryo transfer, Britain is able to export semen and embryos from high-quality donor animals.

Table 25 shows the number of livestock and output of livestock products.

CRAFTS

A Cambridge harpsichord maker, working on the keyboard of a new instrument. His company makes harpsichords and clavichords, using traditional methods to re-create the authentic sound of the original instrument.

Watercolour paper being dried. A small British company uses a modern application of the ancient 'tub sizing and loft drying' technique to produce this high-quality neutral paper with good stability, compatible with all water-based colours.

AGRICULTURE

Some 38,000 hectares (over 95,000 acres) of land, mostly in southern England, are used for growing orchard fruits. 'Greensleeves' (left) and 'Malling Jupiter' (below) are two new varieties of high-yielding dessert apples bred by the Institute of Horticultural Research at East Malling (Kent).

Below: A 'whole-crop' harvester for developing countries — the result of research at the National Institute of Agricultural Engineering — which in addition to harvesting the grain breaks down the straw to form animal feed.

Two aspects of the Royal International Agricultural Show, held annually at Stoneleigh (Warwickshire). Above: Crop demonstration plots. Right: Preparing Romney sheep for the Show.

This incubator for orphaned or weak piglets was developed at the Ministry of Agriculture, Fisheries and Food's Experimental Husbandry Farm.

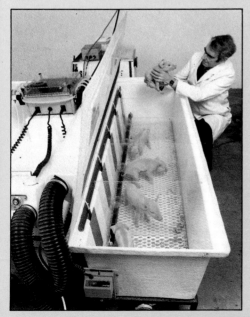

ENVIRONMENTAL PROTECTION

This portable water-testing kit permits rapid assessment of water quality, and is used in disaster-stricken areas throughout the world by relief and aid agencies.

A device to measure acid rain used by the Macaulay Institute of Soil Research, Scotland, as part of Britain's programme of research on air pollutants.

Cattle and
Sheep

Most dairy cattle in England and Wales and a significant proportion in Scotland and Northern Ireland are bred by artificial insemination. The average size of dairy herds in Britain was 58 in 1985 while the average yield of milk per dairy cow has increased from 3,406 litres (748 gallons) in 1965 to 4,748 litres (1,044 gallons) in 1985, a rise of 42 per cent. Average household consumption of liquid milk per head in 1985 was 1·9 litres (3·3 pints) per week.

About two-thirds of home-fed beef production derives from the national dairy herd, in which the Friesian breed is predominant. The remainder is derived from suckler herds producing high-quality beef calves in the hills and uplands, where the traditional British beef breeds, such as Hereford and Aberdeen Angus, continue to be important. Imported breeds which have established themselves include the Charolais, Limousin, Simmental and Belgian Blue.

Britain has a long tradition of sheep production with more than 40 breeds and many crosses between them. Research has provided vaccine and serum protection against nearly all the epidemic diseases. Although lamb production is the main source of income for sheep farmers, wool is also important.

Grass supplies 60 to 80 per cent of the feed for cattle and sheep; grass production has been enhanced by the increased use of fertilisers, irrigation and methods of grazing control, and improved herbage conservation for winter feed. Rough grazings are used for extensively grazed sheep and cattle, producing young animals for fattening elsewhere.

Table 25: Livestock and Livestock Products

	1974–76 average	1983	1984	1985
Cattle and calves ('000 head)	14,708	13,290	13,213	12,855
Sheep and lambs ('000 head)	28,430	34,069	34,802	35,569
Pigs ('000 head)	8,028	8,174	7,689	7,862
Poultry ('000 head)	140,133	127,618	127,456	128,931
Milk (million litres)	13,490	16,590	15,592	15,411
Eggs (million dozen)	1,141	1,049	1,022	1,023
Beef and veal ('000 tonnes)	1,125	1,044	1,136	1,115
Mutton and lamb ('000 tonnes)	255	298	298	305
Pork ('000 tonnes)	617	776	709	737
Bacon and ham ('000 tonnes)	226	212	212	208
Poultry meat ('000 tonnes)	666	804	845	874

Source: Ministry of Agriculture, Fisheries and Food.

Pigs and
Poultry

Pig production occurs in most areas but is particularly important in eastern and northern England. There is an increasing concentration into specialist units and larger herds. Artificial insemination is available throughout Britain.

Output of poultry meat and eggs has continued to benefit from better husbandry and genetic improvements. Since 1975 poultry meat production has increased by almost a third and reached about 874,000 tonnes in 1985. Production of broilers from holdings of over 100,000 birds accounts for just over a half of total production. In 1985, egg production was over 1,000 million dozen. About two-thirds of laying birds are in flocks of 20,000 or more. Britain remains broadly self-sufficient in poultry meat and eggs.

Animal Welfare

It is an offence to cause unnecessary pain or distress to livestock on commercial farms. Regulations control such operations as castration and tail docking, and require owners of intensive units to arrange for the daily inspection of their stock and the equipment on which it depends. There are advisory codes and recommendations for the welfare of all major species of farm animals and compliance with them is monitored by the State Veterinary Service. The welfare of farm animals is also protected by regulations.

The Farm Animal Welfare Council, an independent body set up by the Government, keeps under review the welfare of farm animals on agricultural land, at markets, in transit and at the place of slaughter.

Crops

The farms devoted primarily to arable crops are found mainly in eastern and central southern England and eastern Scotland. Large-scale potato and vegetable production is undertaken in the fens (in Cambridgeshire and south Lincolnshire), the alluvial areas around the rivers Thames and Humber and the peaty lands in south Lancashire. Early potatoes are an important crop in south-west Wales, Kent and south-west England. High-grade seed potatoes are grown in Scotland and Northern Ireland.

Table 26 gives figures on the area, harvest and yield of the main crops.

Table 26: Main Crops

	1974–76 average	1983	1984	1985 forecast
Wheat				
Area ('000 hectares)	1,680	1,695	1,939	1,900
Harvest ('000 tonnes)	5,280	10,802	14,950	11,951
Yield (tonnes per hectare)	4·39	6·37	7·70	6·29
Barley				
Area ('000 hectares)	2,251	2,143	1,978	1,969
Harvest ('000 tonnes)	8,441	9,980	11,057	9,668
Yield (tonnes per hectare)	3·75	4·65	5·59	4·91
Oats				
Area ('000 hectares)	240	108	106	136
Harvest ('000 tonnes)	835	466	518	578
Yield (tonnes per hectare)	3·48	4·32	4·89	4·24
Potatoes				
Area ('000 hectares)	214	196	200	192
Harvest ('000 tonnes)	5,377	5,857	7,398	6,892
Yield (tonnes per hectare)	25·10	29·90	37·00	35·80
Oilseed				
Area ('000 hectares)	37	222	269	296
Harvest ('000 tonnes)	75	562	923	891
Yield (tonnes per hectare)	2·03	2·53	3·43	3·01
Sugar Beet				
Area ('000 hectares)	200	199	199	206
Harvest ('000 tonnes)	5,454	7,494	9,134	8,240
Yield (tonnes per hectare)	27·27	38·30	45·90	40·00

Cereals

About a quarter of the wheat crop is normally used for flour milling, and about one-third for animal feed. Between 15 and 20 per cent of the barley crop is used for malting and distilling and about half for animal feed. Exports of wheat and barley have increased substantially, accounting in recent years for about a quarter of total production. There has been a rapid increase in the oilseed rape crop; the seed is crushed to obtain vegetable oil and the solid matter left is used for animal feed.

Sugar

Sugar from home-grown sugar beet provides about 50 per cent of requirements, most of the remainder being refined from raw sugar imported from developing countries under the Lomé Convention.

Horticulture

In 1985 the land utilised for horticulture was about 226,000 hectares (559,000 acres), of which vegetables grown in the open (excluding potatoes) accounted for 157,450 hectares (389,070 acres), orchards for 38,400 hectares (95,100 acres), small fruit for 15,940 hectares (39,400 acres), bulbs and flowers grown in the open for 5,180 hectares (12,800 acres) and hardy nursery stock for 7,090 hectares (17,520 acres). Crops grown in glasshouses accounted for 2,230 hectares (5,510 acres).

Field vegetables account for just over 40 per cent of the value of horticultural output and are widely grown throughout the country. Most horticultural enterprises are increasing output per unit area with the help of improved planting material, new techniques and the widespread use of machinery. Some field vegetables, for example, are raised in blocks of compressed peat or loose-filled cells, a technique which reduces root damage and allows plants to establish themselves more reliably and evenly.

Glasshouses are used for growing tomatoes, cucumbers, lettuce, flowers, pot plants and nursery stock. Widespread use is being made of automatic control of heating and ventilation, and semi-automatic control of watering. Energy-efficient glasshouses use thermal screens and other methods, while low-cost plastic tunnels extend the season for certain crops previously grown in the open.

Under the European Community's Common Agricultural Policy (see p 300), a wide range of horticultural produce is subject to common quality standards.

EXPORTS

The Government is keen to encourage the growth of exports related to agriculture and their value is increasing in real terms; they amounted to £5,759 million in 1985, of which exports of food and drink accounted for £4,728 million, with the main markets being Western Europe, North America and the Middle East. Exports include speciality products such as fresh salmon, Scotch whisky, biscuits, jams and conserves, as well as beef and lamb carcasses and cheese. Food from Britain, a national marketing organisation responsible for improving the marketing of British produce in the domestic and overseas markets, was set up in 1983. The British Food Export Council represents its export arm for fresh and processed food and drink, and identifies suppliers for customers, organises programmes of visits and meetings for overseas customers, and, with the British Overseas Trade Board, co-ordinates British pavilions at the world's major agricultural exhibitions. The British Agricultural Export Council provides a similar service for the agricultural and horticultural supply industries; products and services offered by its members include all types of machinery, seeds, fertilisers, chemicals, feedingstuffs, livestock and semen, veterinary preparations and equipment, and consultancy. In 1985, Britain exported over 90,000 wheeled agricultural and forestry tractors, maintaining its position as the world's largest exporter.

One of the world's largest agricultural events, the annual Royal International Agricultural Show, held at Stoneleigh in Warwickshire, provides an opportunity for overseas visitors to see what British agriculture has to offer. A typical attendance for the four open days is 200,000 including 16,000 from overseas.

Virtually every British agricultural machinery manufacturer is represented at the show, which is also the most important pedigree livestock event in the country. The show's specialised sections cover livestock improvement, farm mechanisation including working demonstrations of agricultural equipment, electronics, arable cropping, horticulture, forestry, new technology and research, tropical agricultural applications and a food hall. Other major agricultural displays include the annual Royal Smithfield Show, held in London, which exhibits agricultural machinery, livestock and carcasses, and the annual Royal Highland Show, held in June at Ingliston near Edinburgh. There are also several important regional shows.

MARKETING

Agricultural products are marketed by private traders, producers' co-operatives and marketing boards, the latter being producers' organisations (each including a minority of independent members appointed by agriculture ministers) with certain statutory powers to regulate the marketing of milk, wool and potatoes. For the most part the boards buy from producers or control contracts between first buyers; the Potato Marketing Board, however, maintains only a broad control over marketing conditions leaving producers free to deal individually with buyers. For home-grown cereals, meat and livestock, apples and pears, there are marketing organisations representing producer, distributor and independent interests.

Food from Britain is responsible for improving the marketing of food and agricultural products, both in the domestic market and abroad. It has introduced a 'foodmark' symbol under which producers are able to guarantee the quality of fresh and lightly processed foods to the consumer.

Co-operatives

Substantial investment—£80 million in new fixed assets in 1975–85—is being made by agricultural and horticultural co-operatives concerned with marketing and storing products. A number of central co-operative grain stores have been established, and new vegetable groups have been formed to meet the demand from retailers for a continuous supply of fresh, quality produce; fruit marketing co-operatives are also expanding. Food from Britain provides a full range of advisory services for co-operatives and the Government assists their development with grants.

ROLE OF THE GOVERNMENT

Four government departments have joint responsibility—the Ministry of Agriculture, Fisheries and Food, the Department of Agriculture and Fisheries for Scotland, the Welsh Office and the Department of Agriculture for Northern Ireland.

Common Agricultural Policy

The stated aims of the European Community's Common Agricultural Policy, which accounts for about two-thirds of the Community's budget, are to increase agricultural productivity and thereby to ensure that the agricultural community has a fair standard of living, to stabilise the agricultural market, to guarantee regular supplies of food and to provide these supplies at a reasonable price.

Decisions on the level of price support are taken annually by the Council of Ministers on the basis of proposals presented by the European Commission. For many commodities these measures consist of a minimum intervention price at which agencies of the member states will purchase production, thereby putting a floor in the market, and levies made on imports to maintain internal support prices. Schemes may be introduced for subsidised disposal of stocks to consumers within the Community where this can be done without disrupting internal markets. The export of surpluses is facilitated by the provision of export refunds to enable Community exporters to sell on world markets at the going price. There is also provision for certain direct payments, including beef and sheepmeat premiums, to producers.

The support prices, as well as rates of levy, export refunds and other aids, are set in European Currency Units and are converted into the currencies of the member states at fixed rates of exchange (commonly called 'green rates') which do not vary automatically in line with changes in market exchange rates. The green rates can thus be out of line with the market rate of exchange between each currency and the European Currency Unit, giving rise to different real support price levels in the different member states. Monetary compensatory amounts, based on the percentage difference between the green and market rates of each currency, are applied to prevent distortions in trade. They operate as import subsidies and export levies for countries whose currencies' market rates are below the green rates, and as import levies and export subsidies in the opposite case.

In order to reduce the costs of the agricultural policy, the British Government has sought to obtain improvements in its operations, in particular by bringing support prices more into line with the realities of the market and by containing the costs of the policy. In recent years tougher prices have been agreed, but the Government considers that measures to rationalise the policy further are necessary.

The Community's agricultural expenditure is channelled through the European Agricultural Guidance and Guarantee Fund. The Fund's guarantee section finances market support arrangements, while the guidance section provides funds for structural reform, for example, farm modernisation and investment, and payments to assist certain farmers to change to alternative enterprises.

Price Guarantees, Grants and Subsidies

Expenditures in Britain in 1985–86 on price guarantees, grants and subsidies and on Common Agricultural Policy market regulations were estimated to be £320 million and £1,890 million respectively. About £1,310 million was reimbursed from the Community budget.

Potatoes and wool are not covered by the Common Agricultural Policy; price guarantees for potatoes are operated through the Potato Marketing Board and the Department of Agriculture for Northern Ireland, and a price stabilisation fund for wool is administered by the British Wool Marketing Board.

Producers also receive support through certain capital and production grants, some based on Community decisions. Grants are available to assist farmers and horticulturists with farm improvement plans, and there is special financial help for hill and upland farmers in the form of headage payments on cattle and sheep (known as compensatory allowances). Community assistance may also be made to help to improve facilities for the marketing and processing of agricultural products and to provide a premium payment to specialised beef producers, while launching aid is available to production and marketing groups in the horticultural sector.

Smallholdings and Crofts

Local authorities provide some 6,570 statutory smallholdings in England and 964 in Wales. They make loans of up to 75 per cent of required working capital to their tenants. Land settlement in Scotland has always been carried out by the Government, which, while now seeking to dispose of holdings to sitting tenants, still owns and maintains about 121,000 hectares (299,000 acres) of land settlement estates, comprising some 1,610 crofts and holdings.

Within the crofting areas of Scotland (in Strathclyde, Highland, Western Isles, Orkney Islands and Shetland Islands) much of the land is held by tenants known as crofters. Crofting is administered by the Crofters Commission, and benefits from government grants for land improvements and some other agricultural work.

Tenancy Legislation

The agricultural holdings legislation protects the interests and rights of landlords and tenants. Rent is a matter for negotiation between landlord and tenant and may be varied by agreement or, failing agreement, by arbitration. Most agricultural tenants have the right to contest a notice to quit, which is then ineffective unless the landlord obtains consent to its operation from an independent body (in England and Wales the Agricultural Land Tribunal and in Scotland the Scottish Land Court). On termination of tenancy, the tenant is entitled to compensation in accordance with a special code. There are provisions for succession of a close relative on the death of a tenant but this does not apply in England and Wales to new tenancies coming into effect on or after 12 July 1984.

Practically all farms in Northern Ireland are owner-occupied, but, under a system known as 'conacre', farmers not wishing to farm all their land let it annually to others. About one-fifth of agricultural land is so let, and is used mainly for grazing.

Agriculture and Protection of the Countryside

Agriculture ministers have a general duty to have regard to the desirability of conserving the natural beauty and amenity of the countryside, and a specific duty to further conservation in exercising certain of their functions relating to capital grants for farms in areas designated as national parks or sites of special scientific interest or in the Norfolk Broads. Under proposed legislation agriculture ministers will have a new duty to try to achieve a reasonable balance between the interrelated needs of the countryside: agriculture, social and economic needs, conservation and recreation. In England and Wales the Agricultural Development and Advisory Service (see below) advises farmers on, and actively promotes, aspects of conservation such as wildlife habitats, landscape features and farm buildings, and encourages the industry to adopt high standards of pollution control. In addition, research programmes include studies on the ecological impact of pesticides and on biological methods of pest control and other aspects of environmental protection. A countrywide survey of environmental data on farms was initiated in April 1985, and in February 1986 an initiative was launched to improve the rural environment and provide opportunities for long-term unemployed people in the rural areas of England, with a parallel one planned for Wales. Representatives of farming and conservation interests have developed a network of farming and wildlife advisory groups to provide a forum for integrating agriculture and conservation.

Safety at Work

The Agricultural Inspectorate of the Health and Safety Executive is responsible for enforcing regulations relating to the health and safety of workers in agriculture. These cover such matters as the guarding of field and stationary machinery, workplaces, the fitting of safety cabs to tractors, and the use of chemicals.

Professional, Scientific and Technical Services

In England and Wales the Government's Agricultural Development and Advisory Service (ADAS) provides a wide range of professional, scientific, technical and veterinary services for agriculture and its ancillary industries. Some of the services are free but others are charged for. Similar services are provided in Scotland by the Department of Agriculture and Fisheries and three regional agricultural colleges and a section of the State Veterinary Service, which, in England and Wales, is a constituent part of ADAS. In Northern Ireland these services are available from the Department of Agriculture's advisory service and specialist divisions, together with agricultural colleges.

ADAS provides information and advice to farmers and growers on such matters as dairy husbandry, livestock, horticulture, farm management, mechanisation and agronomy. It identifies problems requiring further investigation and carries out the necessary research and development. It also advises the Government on the scientific, technical and business implications of policy proposals and assists in implementing policies concerning animal and plant health, disease and pest eradication, land drainage and other capital grant schemes, and safeguarding agricultural land in relation to other land uses. The Service runs 19 experimental husbandry farms and horticulture stations, six agricultural science laboratories with three sub-centres, one veterinary laboratory and 19 veterinary investigation centres.

The Minister of Agriculture, Fisheries and Food has endorsed the conclusions of a 1984 review which recommended that ADAS should concentrate more of its research and development activities on development, be committed to the use of computer-based information technology as a means of providing information and advice to the industry, and give more emphasis to conservation and animal welfare work; and that the industry should contribute more to the cost of the advisory and other services from which it benefits.

CONTROL OF DISEASES AND PESTS
Animals

England, Scotland and Wales are free from many serious animal diseases. If they were to occur, diseases such as foot-and-mouth disease and swine vesicular disease would be combated by a slaughter policy applied to all infected animals and those exposed to infection, and by control over animal movements during the outbreaks. Rigorous measures are being taken to eradicate sheep scab and warble fly. The incidence of bovine tuberculosis is very low; cattle (except for certain categories) are tested at regular intervals, and reactors to the test are slaughtered, compensation being paid to the owners. Because of compulsory measures to eradicate brucellosis, begun on an area basis in 1972, England and Wales were declared free of the disease for all practical purposes in 1981, following a similar declaration for Scotland in 1980. In September 1984 vaccination replaced slaughter as the means of controlling Newcastle disease in poultry.

Strict controls are exercised on the import of animals, meat and meat products, live poultry and other captive birds, and poultry meat, so as to prevent the introduction of animal or poultry diseases. Special measures apply to prevent the introduction of rabies, and most animals are subject to import licence and six months' quarantine; exceptions to this rule include such farm animals as pigs, cattle, sheep and goats. There are severe penalties for breaking the law. There have been no cases of rabies outside quarantine in Britain since 1970.

Northern Ireland has been kept free from the major animal diseases, including rabies, foot-and-mouth disease and swine vesicular disease, and in 1982 the incidence of brucellosis was reduced to the point where the country was officially declared brucellosis-free.

Professional advice and action on the control of animal disease and the welfare of farm livestock is the responsibility of the government veterinary services, which have laboratory facilities and investigation centres performing specialist research work and advising private practitioners responsible for treating animals on the farm.

Plants

The agricultural departments are responsible for limiting the spread of plant pests and diseases and for preventing the introduction of new ones. They also issue the health certificates required by other countries to accompany plant material exported from Britain. Certification schemes are operated to encourage the development of healthy, vigorous and true-to-type planting stocks.

Pesticides

The Food and Environment Protection Act 1985 has given the Government powers to control the supply and use of pesticides in Britain, these replacing the previous non-statutory arrangement under the Pesticide Safety Precautions Scheme. The Act provides for the creation of a statutory scheme for the approval of pesticides on the basis of their safety, efficacy and, where necessary, humaneness in use. It also provides for controls on the import, sale, supply, storage, distribution, advertisement and use of pesticides, and for the release of information to the public about pesticides. Some measures came into force in 1985; others followed in 1986.

Veterinary Medicinal Products

The manufacture, sale and supply of veterinary medicinal products is prohibited except under licence. Licences are issued by the agriculture ministers, who are advised on safety, quality and efficacy by the Veterinary Products Committee comprising independent experts.

AGRICULTURAL AND FOOD RESEARCH

The Agricultural and Food Research Council (AFRC), the Government and private industry are responsible for the research effort. There is a network of institutes financed by the Council and seven Scottish agricultural research institutes supported by the Department of Agriculture and Fisheries and advised by the Council. Known as the Agricultural and Food Research Service, this network currently conducts work valued at about £130 million annually.

The Council, an autonomous body, receives funds from the science budget, through the Department of Education and Science, and income from work commissioned by the Ministry of Agriculture, Fisheries and Food. Some funds are also received from industry and other outside bodies. The Council supervises research carried out at a number of sites throughout Britain. Following a review in 1985 the Council is drawing its existing research stations together administratively into eight institutes to minimise duplication of work and provide a more efficient management structure. The new institutes are for research into animal disease, animal physiology and genetics, grassland and animal production, arable crops, horticulture, plant sciences, food, and agricultural engineering. Broadly similar areas are covered by the seven Scottish research institutes controlled by the Department of Agriculture and Fisheries but the research is directed particularly to the needs of northern Britain. The AFRC advises on research at these institutes. Research in Northern Ireland is carried out by the Department of Agriculture in association with the Queen's University of Belfast and is mainly directed towards local problems; three agricultural colleges also cover applied research in agricultural science and food technology.

The Council also has a number of units and groups associated with universities, and through its research grant schemes, supports projects in universities, polytechnics and colleges.

Genetic manipulation is a high priority in the Council programme and, apart from contributing to a basic understanding of plant processes at the molecular level, is applied in a variety of scientific areas, from animal vaccine production to the development of new plant varieties. Other research within the Council's institutes has led to the development of embryo cleavage and transplantation in commercial animal husbandry, so that animals with desirable characteristics can be multiplied much more rapidly than by conventional means. Some of the techniques can also be applied to transport embryos between countries, thereby avoiding the risk of carrying disease which may occur when live adult farm animals are moved. An international vaccine bank for emergency control of foot-and-mouth disease is held at one of the Council's institutes.

The Government is planning a programme of collaborative research between industry and public sector research bodies to investigate the uses of biotechnology in the genetic engineering of plants.

Some 80 per cent of the British wheat acreage and about half the potato acreage are planted with varieties bred by the publicly financed research programme. Investigations into some naturally occurring insecticides have led to the development of a completely new class of insecticides, the pyrethroids, which are used world-wide. A combination of research in plant breeding, physiology, disease control and improved storage methods has established a viable dry bulb onion production industry.

EDUCATION
AND
TRAINING

University and other degree and postgraduate courses provide training in the scientific and technological aspects of agriculture and horticulture, the emphasis being on science and economics. There are also degree and postgraduate courses in veterinary medicine. Science-based sandwich courses, leading to a Business & Technician Education Council (BTEC) Higher National Diploma and available at agricultural colleges, are designed for students wishing to enter farming or horticulture with a good knowledge of the managerial and technological aspects of the industry. The three-year BTEC National Diploma, also organised on a sandwich basis, is a general course in agriculture with some colleges offering special subjects such as arable farming, livestock production, dairy farming and farm mechanisation. Both diploma courses, validated by the BTEC, normally require 12 months' previous practical experience. In addition, there are one-year full-time National Certificate courses providing a basic education in agriculture or horticulture, and a one- or two-year part-time practical course in the basic principles of agriculture, horticulture or forestry followed by more specialised study. In Scotland new and restructured courses have replaced the Higher and Ordinary National Diplomas.

In Great Britain the Agricultural Training Board runs the Agricultural and Horticultural Training Scheme, which can lead to the issue of craft certificates or to a full apprenticeship. The scheme is flexible to allow mature workers to participate as well as young people entering agriculture and horticulture through youth training schemes. In Northern Ireland agricultural training courses are the responsibility of the Department of Agriculture.

Fisheries

Britain is one of Europe's most important fishing nations. The fishing industry provides about 66 per cent of British fish supplies, and is an important source of employment and income in a number of ports. In 1985 there were 16,150 fishermen in regular employment and nearly 5,800 occasionally employed. The Government aims to encourage the development of a viable, efficient and market-orientated fisheries industry within the framework of the European Community's Common Fisheries Policy. The main concerns of government fisheries policy are conservation and exploitation of sea fish stocks, financial support for fleet modernisation and other measures, the improvement of the industry's technical and economic performance, the development of a viable fish farming industry, and protection of the aquatic environment.

Fish Caught

In 1985 demersal fish (caught on or near the bottom of the sea) accounted for about 53 per cent by weight of total British landings, pelagic fish (caught near the surface) for 37 per cent and shellfish for 10 per cent. Landings of all types of fish (excluding salmon and trout) by British fishing vessels totalled 760,000 tonnes. Cod and haddock each represented about 27 per cent of the total value of demersal and pelagic fish landed, while whiting (7 per cent), mackerel (7 per cent) and plaice (5 per cent) were the other most important sources of earnings to the industry.

The British fish farming industry is a substantial and expanding business mainly concerned with the production of salmon and trout although shellfish and eel farming are growing. Estimated production in 1985 was 12,000 tonnes of trout and 7,000 tonnes of salmon.

Imports of fresh, frozen, cured and canned fish and shellfish in 1985 totalled 385,000 tonnes, those of fish meal 236,000 tonnes and those of fish oils 265,000 tonnes. Exports and re-exports of fish and fish products amounted to 304,000 tonnes. Following a British initiative, member states of the European Community banned from January 1982 the import of primary whale products in order to help to conserve whale populations.

The Fishing Fleet

Some 64 per cent of the British catch is taken by the 7,367 vessels of the inshore fleet employing a variety of catching methods. The deep-sea fleet, comprising 217 larger vessels, has been reduced in number as fishing opportunities and the profitability of operations in distant waters have declined.

Administration

The fisheries departments are responsible for the administration of legislation concerning the fishing industry and for fisheries research. The safety and welfare of crews of fishing vessels and other matters common to shipping generally are provided for under legislation administered by the Department of Transport.

The Sea Fish Industry Authority provides financial aid for the purchase of new fishing vessels, vessel improvements, the provision and improvement of processing plants, cold stores and ice plants and towards the formation of fishermen's co-operatives. Other functions include research and development, training, dissemination of information, publicity and promotion.

Fishery Limits

Community countries, and certain non-Community countries having fishery agreements with the Community, may fish up to Britain's 12-mile limit. Designated countries may also fish in specified areas of Britain's 6-to-12-mile zone. No foreign vessels may fish within Britain's 6-mile limit.

Common Fisheries Policy

With the extension of fishery limits to 200 miles in the mid-1970s, new arrangements became necessary to control Community fishing in the greatly extended area. Britain has a particularly strong interest in such control, since a sizeable proportion of the total catch within the 200-mile limits of member states is taken in British waters, while the loss of fishing opportunities in distant waters (such as Iceland) has reduced the British industry's total catch more than that of other Community states.

In January 1983 member states reached an agreement on a common fisheries policy providing for new arrangements on access to coastal waters applicable for a period of at least 20 years. Its other features include a revised marketing regime, regulations covering technical conservation measures such as mesh sizes for nets, the allocation of catch quotas among member states within each year's total allowable catch, effective enforcement of the rules and financial aid to promote the adaptation and development of the Community fishing fleet and the fish farming industry.

Fishery relations between the European Community and other countries are governed by long-term framework agreements. Reciprocal agreements are in force with Norway, the Faroe Islands and Sweden. Non-reciprocal agreements are in force with Canada, the United States, Senegal, Guinea-Bissau, Guinea, Equatorial Guinea, São Tomé and Príncipe and the Seychelles. Quotas have also been established in international waters in the north-west Atlantic.

Fisheries Research

The Ministry of Agriculture, Fisheries and Food has a research directorate comprising laboratories dealing with marine and freshwater fisheries, shellfish, marine pollution, fish farming and diseases. Work on the utilisation of fish is undertaken by a research station at Torry, Aberdeen. There are also two seagoing research vessels. In Scotland the Department of Agriculture and Fisheries maintains laboratories on marine and freshwater fisheries research as well as three seagoing vessels. The two research programmes are co-ordinated. Department of Agriculture laboratories in Northern Ireland monitor marine and freshwater fisheries.

Freshwater Fisheries

The most valuable freshwater fish are salmon and sea-trout. Sea fishing for salmon is prohibited in waters outside a limit of six miles from the coasts of the British Isles. In Scotland, salmon fishing is a private right. In England and Wales, water authority licences are required for coastal and estuary netting.

Forestry

Woodland covers an estimated 2·1 million hectares (5·2 million acres) in Great Britain: about 7·3 per cent of England, 12·6 per cent of Scotland and 11·6 per cent of Wales. The Government supports the continued expansion of forestry in order to reduce dependence on imports of timber and to provide employment in forestry and related industries.

The area of productive forest in Great Britain is 2 million hectares (4·9 million acres), 44 per cent of which is managed by the Forestry Commission and the rest by private owners. The rate of new planting in 1985 was 5,200 hectares (12,800 acres) by the Commission and some 16,000 hectares (40,000 acres) by private woodland owners mainly in Scotland. Most planting is of conifers in upland areas though the planting of broadleaved trees is encouraged on suitable sites. An increasing proportion of new planting is being done by private owners.

Total employment in state and private forests in Great Britain was estimated at about 17,000 in 1985, with a further 8,000 people engaged in processing home-grown timber.

British woodlands meet only 10 per cent of the nation's consumption of wood and wood products. At present only just over half of the Commission's woodlands are in production. Home timber production, however, is expected to double over the next 20 years.

The Forestry Commission and Forestry Policy

The Forestry Commission is the national forestry authority in Great Britain. The Commissioners give advice on forestry matters and are responsible to the Minister of Agriculture, Fisheries and Food and the Secretaries of State for Scotland and Wales. In pursuing timber production, forestry policy also takes into account amenity, environmental and employment criteria, and the Commission's activities include wildlife conservation, the landscaping of plantations and the provision of facilities for recreation. The Commission has also encouraged the setting up of new timber-using industries.

The Government has asked the Commission to sell some of its land and plantations in order to rationalise its holdings with a view to improving the Commission's efficiency and the commercial effectiveness of the forestry enterprise. Holdings have been reduced by 83,000 hectares (205,000 acres) as a result of sales. The Commission is financed partly by the Government and partly by receipts from sales of timber and other produce and from rents.

Private Forestry

A substantial number of private woods are in ownerships of under 100 hectares (250 acres) in extent. The Government encourages private forestry through appropriate tax reliefs. There is also a forestry grant scheme under which the Commission aids planting by private owners. A special scheme encourages the planting of broadleaved trees by the payment of higher levels of grant.

Forestry Education and Research

Degree courses in forestry and associated studies are provided at three universities and there are supervisory, craft and managerial level courses. The Forestry Training Council, set up by the Forestry Commission, assists the development of systematic training and the co-ordination of training in the state and private sectors. The Furniture and Timber Industry Training Board is concerned with training for private sector employees in the home timber trade.

Forestry research is carried out by the Commission at two research stations. Aid is also given for research work in universities and other institutions, including the Commonwealth Forestry Institute in Oxford.

Forestry in Northern Ireland

The Department of Agriculture may acquire land for afforestation and give financial and technical assistance for private planting. Financial provision is made annually by Parliament.

The state forest area has grown steadily since 1945. By 1985, 73,000 hectares (180,000 acres) of plantable land had been acquired, of which 56,000 hectares (138,000 acres) were planted. There were about 13,500 hectares (33,000 acres) of privately owned forest. Some 400 people work in state forests.

15 Transport and Communications

Major improvements in the movement of passengers and freight have resulted from the construction of a network of motorways, the extension of fast inter-city rail services (such as those operated by high-speed trains), the modernisation of many ports, the use by airlines of more efficient and quieter aircraft, and expansion schemes at many airports. The Channel Tunnel, on which construction work could begin in 1987, is expected to have a significant impact on travel between Britain and the continent of Europe. Communications are benefiting from developments in microelectronics, computer and satellite technology, and advances in materials, for example, the application of optical fibres in telecommunications.

Transport policy rests on the fundamental aims of promoting economic growth and higher national prosperity, and ensuring a reasonable level of personal mobility, while improving safety (particularly on the roads), minimising damage to the environment and using energy economically. Britain is taking an active part in the development of a common transport policy by the European Community, this being seen as essential for the application of the Treaty of Rome's competition rules and the development of the Community's internal market. While major sectors of transport and communications operations are publicly owned, the Government is arranging for the introduction of private capital into a number of them as part of its policy of reducing state involvement as much as possible. This is also part of the Government's wider aim of increasing competition, so ensuring value for money, in transport services, both within Britain and internationally. Measures to increase competition are being taken in a number of sectors such as the bus industry and airline services.

Inland Transport

Passenger and freight traffic is carried mainly by road. At the end of 1985 there were 21·2 million vehicles licensed for use on the roads of Great Britain, of which 18·2 million were private cars and light goods vehicles, 0·6 million other goods vehicles, 1·1 million motor cycles, scooters and mopeds, and 120,000 public road passenger vehicles (including taxis). Private ownership of cars has been growing rapidly for many years and the car is the most popular form of transport, with car and taxi travel accounting for some 82 per cent of passenger mileage within Great Britain. Buses and coaches account for about 8 per cent of passenger mileage, rail for 7 per cent and air 0·6 per cent. Road haulage has a dominant position in the movement of inland freight, accounting for about 86 per cent of tonnage carried and for over three-fifths of tonne-km. Railways, inland waterways, coastal shipping and pipelines are important in carrying certain types of freight, particularly bulk goods.

ROADS   Motor vehicle traffic in Great Britain is continuing to grow, having risen by 3 per cent in 1985 to some 284,400 million vehicle-km. Improvements are continually being made in the network of trunk roads (which form a basic network linking major centres of population, industrial areas and ports) to accommodate the growth in traffic. A number of motorways (roads specially designed for long-distance traffic) have been built, while other improvements, such as the construction of bypasses, have helped to make travelling easier and faster, particularly over long distances and between cities, and have relieved many towns and villages of heavy through traffic. Although motorways account for less than 1 per cent of road mileage, they carry nearly 13 per cent of traffic including 16 per cent of heavy goods vehicle traffic. Motorways have attracted a greater volume of traffic (particularly heavy lorries) than originally expected, necessitating the structural renewal of a number of the older sections.

In 1985 the road network totalled some 372,016 km (231,160 miles), of which 2,850 km (1,771 miles) were trunk motorways (see Table 27).

Table 27: Road Length (as at April 1985)

km

	Public roads	Trunk roads (including motorways)	Trunk motorways[a]
England	265,476	10,125	2,405
Scotland	50,373	3,127	212
Wales	32,495	1,777	120
Northern Ireland	23,672	594	113
Britain	372,016	15,623	2,850

Sources: Department of Transport, Northern Ireland Department of the Environment, Scottish Development Department and Welsh Office.
[a] In addition, there were 77 km (48 miles) of local authority motorway in England and 24 km (15 miles) in Scotland. In April 1986 some 60 km (37 miles) of trunk motorway were under construction in England and 14 km (9 miles) in Scotland.

The main aims of the Government's programme to improve trunk roads are to meet the needs of industry, to keep heavy lorry traffic away from towns and villages, and to improve road safety. In England particular attention is being given to improving access to ports on the east and south coasts, and to ensuring good road access to the planned Channel Tunnel terminal (see p 319). Much of the London area has benefited from the M25 London orbital route, the final stage of which will be completed later in 1986. A further crossing of the Thames is planned at Dartford (Kent) to handle the expected increase in traffic on the M25 between the north and south banks of the river. In Wales the priorities are improvements to the coast road in north Wales (including the construction under the Conwy estuary of a £177 million tunnel, the first immersed tube road tunnel to be built in Britain) and the upgrading of roads which are important for industrial redevelopment. Although most of the motorway and dual carriageway network in central Scotland has been completed, an extension to the southern end of the M74 is under construction. Other priorities are the improvement of strategic routes such as those to the north and north-east (which are important for North Sea oil-related activities), some of the west-coast routes, and the construction of more bypasses. In Northern Ireland the emphasis is on building new links to the motorway network, constructing more bypasses, and improving roads in the Belfast area and other urban areas. Priority for new roads in urban areas of Great Britain is being given to those designed to meet the needs of industry and commerce, serve new industrial or housing estates, provide links to the national trunk road network or to complement traffic management schemes.

Administration

Responsibility for trunk road motorways and other trunk roads in Great Britain rests in England with the Secretary of State for Transport, in Scotland with the Secretary of State for Scotland and in Wales with the Secretary of State for Wales. The costs of construction, improvement and maintenance are paid for by central government. The highway authorities for non-trunk roads in England are the county councils, the metropolitan district councils, the London borough councils and the Common Council of the City of London. In Wales the authorities are the county councils, and in Scotland the regional or islands councils. In Northern Ireland the Northern Ireland Department of the Environment is responsible for the construction, improvement and maintenance of public roads.

Research into all aspects of road construction, traffic engineering and safety, and into problems associated with transport is carried out by the Transport and Road Research Laboratory, the research arm of the Department of Transport.

Road Safety

Britain and the other members of the European Community have promoted road safety throughout 1986, which the Community designated as European Road Safety Year. Many conferences and other events were held, and member states concentrated on a number of major publicity themes, which in Britain concerned publicity on children and young people, cyclists and motor cyclists, and drinking and driving. Although Great Britain has one of the highest densities of road traffic in the world, it has a good record on road safety, experiencing one of the lowest road accident death rates in the Community. In 1985, 5,200 people were killed on the roads, about 71,000 seriously injured and 241,400 slightly injured. A comprehensive framework of legislation summarised in the *Highway Code* (which sets out the standard of conduct for road users) has contributed to the long-term decline in casualty rates. Other factors have been better road design and construction, segregating vehicles from pedestrians, and the publicity campaigns conducted nationally by government departments and the Royal Society for the Prevention of Accidents and locally by local authorities to persuade people to take greater care on the roads. However, the main recent contributory factor has been the compulsory wearing of seat belts in the front seats of cars and light vans, which was introduced for a three-year period in 1983; in 1986 the regulations were made permanent. Since the implementation of compulsory wearing there has been a substantial net reduction in road casualties, estimated at a minimum of 200 deaths and 7,000 serious injuries a year. Regulations have been made requiring rear seat belts or child restraints to be fitted to new cars first registered from 1 April 1987.

Comprehensive regulations govern the design of vehicles, their use on the roads, and the maintenance and testing of their mechanical condition. Under a national 'type approval' scheme in Great Britain, all new cars must be of a type that has been certified as meeting the required standards, and there is a similar scheme for new goods vehicles. Private cars and light vans which are three or more years old must be tested annually at private garages authorised as test stations. (In Northern Ireland private cars six or more years old are tested at official vehicle inspection centres.) Heavy goods vehicles are subject to annual tests carried out at special testing stations.

Minimum ages are laid down for driving: 16 for riders of mopeds and disabled drivers of specially adapted vehicles; 17 for driving cars and other passenger vehicles with nine or fewer seats (including that of the driver), motor cycles and goods vehicles not over 3·5 tonnes gross laden weight; 18 for goods vehicles over 3·5 but not over 7·5 tonnes; and 21 for passenger vehicles with over nine seats and goods vehicles over 7·5 tonnes. All drivers of motor vehicles, except new residents holding certain non-British licences, are required to pass the driving test before being granted a full licence to drive. Learners must display 'L' plates on their vehicle and be accompanied while driving (with certain exceptions) by a qualified driver. There are national speed limits of 60 mph (97 km/h) on single carriageway roads and 70 mph (113 km/h) on dual carriageway roads (including motorways), unless a lower limit is indicated. In built-up areas there is a general limit of 30 mph (48 km/h).

Under the Transport Act 1981, breath testing has become the main means of determining a driver's alcohol level; the statutory limit of breath alcohol concentration for drivers is 35 microgrammes of alcohol in 100 millilitres of breath. Several measures have been introduced to improve the safety of motor cyclists, including the restriction of learner drivers to the less powerful machines, a two-part motor-cycle driving test and a limit on the duration of the motor-cycle provisional licence.

Traffic in Towns

Traffic management schemes are being operated in many urban areas to minimise congestion, create a better environment and improve road safety. They may include computerised traffic control systems, one-way systems, bus priority measures, parking controls and limited road construction. Many towns have shopping precincts which are specially designed for pedestrians and from which motor vehicles are excluded for all or part of the day. In most town centres parking is restricted and waiting limits apply. City centres often have controlled parking zones, where payment is required for on-street parking. An experiment in central London involving the use of wheel clamps to immobilise illegally parked vehicles began in 1983 and will continue until 1987 to enable its effects to be fully assessed.

Urban traffic control systems, with traffic signals controlled by a central computer, are in operation in 49 cities in Britain. Systems developed by the Department of Transport and British firms have achieved international repute and are the most commonly used in the world. The most modern of these systems, which continuously measures and responds to the flow of traffic, is already in operation or about to be installed in 25 locations including London, Coventry, Maidstone, Southampton, Cambridge and Worcester.

ROAD HAULAGE

Road haulage traffic amounted to 99,100 million tonne-km in 1985. There has been a move towards larger and more efficient vehicles carrying heavier loads—about 71 per cent of the traffic, in terms of tonne-km, is carried in vehicles of over 28 tonnes gross laden weight. Much of the traffic is moved over short distances, with 76 per cent of the tonnage being carried on hauls of 100 km (62 miles) or less, although the growth in road haulage has been concentrated on long-distance traffic. Public haulage (private road hauliers carrying other firms' goods) accounts for 64 per cent of freight carried in Great Britain in terms of tonne-km.

The environmental problems caused by lorries have become a matter of public concern. The Government has introduced a number of measures to bring economic benefits and increased protection to the environment and the public. Safeguards on the design of lorries include restrictions on their dimensions, while a number of measures have been taken to improve the enforcement of lorry weights and safety. More bypasses are being built to keep lorries away from residential areas. There is a programme of research and development, involving vehicle and engine manufacturers, to reduce the noise from heavy lorries to less than half the 1981 level and produce a quiet heavy vehicle for the 1990s. To encourage the use of railways and inland waterways for the carriage of freight, grants of up to 60 per cent are available towards the cost of construction or modernisation of privately owned facilities where there are significant environmental benefits by the removal of heavy goods vehicle traffic from the roads.

Structure of the Industry

Road haulage is predominantly an industry of small, privately owned businesses. Many of the 130,300 holders of an operator's licence in 1985 had only one vehicle and the average size of a vehicle fleet is only about four. The biggest operator in Great Britain is the National Freight Consortium set up by a consortium of managers and employees to acquire the National Freight Company from the Government.

Licensing and Other Controls

Those operating goods vehicles over 3·5 tonnes gross weight (with certain special exemptions) require an operator's licence, obtained on showing good repute and ability to maintain vehicles properly and control loading and drivers' hours. Licences are divided into restricted licences for firms carrying their own goods and standard licences, subdivided into 'national only' and 'international', for hauliers operating for hire or reward. (In Northern Ireland operators carrying their own goods do not require a licence.) Proof of professional competence is required to obtain a standard licence. Regulations lay down limits on the hours worked by drivers of goods vehicles, and there are also minimum rest periods. Tachographs (which automatically record speed and distance covered, driving time and stopping periods) must be fitted and used in most goods vehicles over 3·5 tonnes gross weight in Great Britain.

International Road Haulage

International road haulage has grown rapidly and about 23 million tonnes a year are carried in road vehicles to and from the continent of Europe and the Irish Republic. Some 870,400 road goods vehicles were conveyed by ferry to the Continent in 1985, of which nearly half were unaccompanied trailers. France is the destination for over a quarter of the traffic to mainland Europe. The average length of haul for British registered vehicles is some 860 km (534 miles) in each direction, compared with 73 km (45 miles) for internal road haulage. International road haulage is governed mainly by bilateral agreements which are in force with 26 other countries. In June 1986 the European Community member states agreed to the principle of full liberalisation of international road haulage within the Community, to be implemented by 1992.

PASSENGER SERVICES

There has been a long-term decline in the use of local bus services, mainly because of the growth in ownership of private cars. In 1985–86 buses or coaches carried some 5,640 million passengers on local services in Great Britain, 25 per cent fewer than in 1975. Bus operators have taken action to contain costs and to improve productivity by increasing the proportion of bus services operated by one-person vehicles and reducing or rationalising services, particularly in rural areas. Encouragement has also been given to the promotion of unconventional services in rural areas, such as community buses operated by voluntary drivers, postbuses (Post Office vehicles carrying mail and passengers) and social car-sharing schemes. However, the industry's decline has continued, and the Transport Act 1985 (see p 314) contains a number of measures to stimulate competition in local bus services and increase private sector participation in the industry.

These measures follow the reforms enacted in the Transport Act 1980, which removed restrictions on operating long-distance express coach services and excursions, allowing free competition between operators. This had a noticeable effect on long-distance express coach services, bringing about reductions in fares, the provision of more services and an increase of 40 per cent in the number of passengers carried.

Public Transport Operators

The largest single bus and coach operator in Britain is the National Bus Company, which operates in England and Wales through some 60 subsidiaries and has a network of long-distance coach services; it has a fleet of about 14,500 vehicles. The Scottish Transport Group operates the main bus services in Scotland outside the major cities and also runs ferries to the islands off the west coast of Scotland; it has 3,100 vehicles. In Northern Ireland almost all road passenger services are provided by subsidiaries of the Northern Ireland Transport Holding Company. Citybus Ltd operates services in the city of Belfast and Ulsterbus Ltd operates most of the services in the rest of Northern Ireland. These companies have some 330 and 1,050 vehicles respectively.

London Regional Transport (LRT) is a nationalised industry, established under the London Regional Transport Act 1984, with its board members appointed by the Secretary of State for Transport. Within LRT three separate wholly owned subsidiaries have been established: London Buses Ltd (operating some 5,000 buses), London Underground Ltd and LRT Bus Engineering Ltd. Financial support is provided by central government with a contribution from London's ratepayers. LRT is required to involve the private sector in the provision of services where this is more efficient, and has been set targets for reductions in operating costs and revenue support. Passenger transport executives are responsible for the day-to-day management and operation of local transport in Greater Manchester, Merseyside, South Yorkshire, Tyne and Wear, West Midlands and West Yorkshire in England and Strathclyde in Scotland. Under the Local Government Act 1985 the executives in England report to passenger transport authorities appointed by the district councils. The executives operate 9,000 vehicles, while some 5,300 vehicles are operated by other local authority undertakings.

There are some 5,700 privately owned undertakings (of which the majority have fewer than five vehicles) comprising about 30,800 vehicles; only a small proportion of these operators provide scheduled local bus services.

Double-deck buses are the main type of vehicle used for urban road passenger transport in Britain and there are some 25,600 in operation. In addition, there are 43,200 single-deck buses and coaches, and 79 trams (at Blackpool and Llandudno which have Britain's only remaining tramway systems).

Taxis

There are about 39,100 licensed taxis in Great Britain, mainly in urban areas; London has some 13,500. In London and a number of other cities taxis must be purpose-built to conform to very strict requirements and drivers must have passed a test of their knowledge of the area. Hire cars with drivers may be booked only through the operator and not hired on the street; in most areas outside London hire cars are licensed.

Transport Act 1985

Major changes in the control of the bus industry and in the operation of bus services are being implemented under the Transport Act 1985, which is intended to encourage competition in the industry, making it more responsive to passenger needs.

The Act provides for the privatisation of the National Bus Company, which is required to submit to the Secretary of State for Transport a programme for the transfer of its operations to the private sector for implementation by January 1989. The Government's intention is that each subsidiary should be sold individually, with a preference for a buy-out by its management and/or employees. Passenger transport executives and local authorities running municipal bus undertakings are required to form public transport companies, operating under the Companies Acts, to which their bus undertakings will be transferred. This is intended to lead to the establishment of a number of separate competing companies except in London.

Under the Act the system of road service licensing (under which a local bus operator needs a road service licence before starting operations) will be abolished in Great Britain (except in London) in October 1986. Transitional arrangements for the new system, under which operators have to register their services with the traffic commissioners (one for each of the nine traffic areas of Great Britain), have been established. Operators wishing to run commercial local services after October 1986 were required to register by the end of February 1986. Local authorities and passenger transport executives are looking at the list of 15,000 registered services with a view to identifying gaps and to examining additional services which they consider to be socially necessary and are prepared to subsidise. They are inviting applications for operating these services by open competitive tender to ensure that value for money is obtained. Registered services must be run for at least three months to the end of January 1987, but thereafter, when the new deregulated system is fully in operation, six weeks' notice will be required for new registration, variation or cancellation of services.

The Act also provides for new arrangements for the operation of taxis and hire cars, with the intention of increasing their role in public transport. Operators of licensed taxis are able to provide shared-ride services at separate fares. Restrictions by local authorities on granting taxi licences have been limited so that a licence can be refused only if a local authority is satisfied that there is no unfulfilled demand for taxis in its area. Taxi operators are also able to run regular local services and can tender in competition with bus operators for the services being subsidised by local authorities. In addition, they may apply for a 'restricted' bus operator's licence, allowing them to run one or two minibuses without having to obtain a full bus operator's licence.

Transport services in rural areas are expected to benefit in a number of ways, primarily through greater competition. In addition, two new grants have been introduced: a rural innovation grant, administered in England by the Development Commission and in Scotland and Wales by the appropriate Secretary of State; and a transitional grant, payable on a sliding scale for four years to bus operators.

RAILWAYS

Railways were pioneered in Britain, and the Stockton and Darlington Railway, opened in 1825, was the first passenger public railway in the world to be worked by steam power. Under the Transport Act 1947 the four large railway companies in Great Britain were brought under public ownership, and in 1962 the British Railways Board was set up to manage railway affairs and subsidiary activities. In Northern Ireland the Northern Ireland Railways Company Ltd, a subsidiary of the Northern Ireland Transport Holding Company, operates the railway service on some 320 km (200 miles) of track.

Operations

In 1985–86 the Board's turnover, including financial support and income from other activities but excluding internal transactions, was £3,145 million, of which £1,333 million was derived from rail passenger services and £499 million from rail freight services. British Rail received £896 million in grants towards its operations as compensation for the public service obligation to operate parts of the rail passenger system which would not otherwise cover their costs. Following a report, published in 1983, which reviewed the finances of British Rail and identified a number of opportunities for improved efficiency and reductions in costs, the Government has set the Board new objectives including a reduction in its public service obligation grant from the Government to £710 million in 1986–87.

At the end of March 1986 the Board employed some 173,800 people. Statistics of British Rail's operations are given in Table 28.

Passenger Services

The passenger network (see map, p 316) comprises a fast inter-city network, linking the main centres of Great Britain; local stopping services; and commuter

Main Railway Passenger Routes

Orkney Islands

Shetland Islands

0 20 40 60 80 100 120 km

0 20 40 60 80 miles

InterCity and principal routes

Other routes
(for Scotland and Wales)

Inverness

Aberdeen

Dundee

Perth

Stirling

Glasgow

Edinburgh

Berwick

Londonderry

Larne

Belfast

Carlisle

Newcastle upon Tyne

Middlesbrough

Darlington

Scarborough

Harrogate
Leeds
Bradford

York

Hull

Blackpool

Preston

Manchester

Doncaster

Grimsby

Liverpool

Retford

Holyhead

Sheffield

Stoke

Newark

Grantham

Crewe

Stafford

Derby

Nottingham

King's Lynn

Norwich

Shrewsbury

Wolverhampton

Leicester

Peterborough

Birmingham

Northampton

Worcester

Coventry

Ipswich

Hereford

Rugby

Cambridge

Fishguard

Cheltenham

Newport

Gloucester

Oxford

Colchester

Swansea

Swindon

LONDON

Cardiff

Reading

Margate

Bristol

Bath

Salisbury

Gatwick

Ashford

Dover

Taunton

Southampton

Folkestone

Exeter

Weymouth

Bournemouth

Worthing

Hastings

Eastbourne

Newton Abbot

Portsmouth

Brighton

Penzance

Plymouth

Table 28: Railway Operations

	1980	1983	1984–85	1985–86
Passenger journeys (million)	760	695	701	708
Passenger-km (million)	30,300	29,500	29,800	30,300
Freight train traffic (million tonnes)	153	145	68[a]	140
Trainload and wagonload traffic (million net tonne-km)	17,640	17,144	12,031[a]	16,047
Assets (at end of period):				
Locomotives	3,379	2,850	2,711	2,181
High Speed Train power units	142	197	197	197
Other coaching vehicles	21,074	16,969	16,439	16,170
Freight vehicles[b]	119,507	54,510	45,174	39,007
Stations	2,787	2,619	2,524	2,526
Route open for traffic (km)	17,645	16,964	16,803	16,729

Source: British Railways Board.
[a] Reflects a considerable decline in coal traffic as the result of a major industrial dispute in the coalmining industry.
[b] In addition, a number of privately owned wagons are operated on the railway network for customers of British Rail; some 14,500 were authorised for working on the network at the end of March 1986.

services in and around the large conurbations, especially London and south-east England. British Rail runs about 1,500 InterCity expresses each weekday, serving about 150 business and leisure centres. Journey times on inter-city routes have been reduced substantially as more track has been made suitable for high-speed operations and as a result of faster trains, notably the InterCity 125s, operated by High Speed Trains (HSTs), the world's fastest diesel trains, which travel at maximum sustained speeds of 125 mph (201 km/h). InterCity 125 trains (which provide nearly half of InterCity train mileage) operate on the London–Bristol–south Wales route, the London–Edinburgh–Aberdeen route, the London–Plymouth–Penzance route, the London–Sheffield route and the route linking south-west England or south Wales with Birmingham and north-west England or north-east England and Edinburgh.

Electrification is continuing; in May 1986 electric trains were introduced on a further 99 route km (62 miles). A number of electrification schemes, involving a total of 928 route km (577 miles), are in progress. The most significant is a £306 million scheme to electrify the east-coast main line between London and Edinburgh (including the line from Doncaster to Leeds). Initial work on the scheme, which will involve electrification of some 636 km (395 miles), began in 1985. The first main stage, involving electrification from Hitchin to Peterborough, is due to be completed by 1987, while the line to Leeds will be electrified by 1989, with completion of the scheme to Newcastle upon Tyne and Edinburgh in 1991. New rolling stock, including 31 'Electra' locomotives, which will have a maximum speed of 225 km/h (140 mph), has been ordered for the east-coast services. The west-coast main line, British Rail's busiest InterCity route, is already electrified. London, the West Midlands and the North West were linked by electric trains in the 1960s, electrification being extended to Glasgow in 1974.

British Rail has developed ways of reducing costs on its local passenger services including the installation of automatic level crossings and radio signalling. It has begun to replace the fleet of diesel multiple-unit trains by two new types of vehicle with greater reliability and low maintenance costs: a lightweight railbus (with a bus-type body) and a medium-weight diesel multiple-unit.

Freight
The most important freight commodities handled are coal and coke, iron and steel, building materials and petroleum. Over 90 per cent of rail-freight revenue is obtained from traffic in bulk commodities, most of it in trainloads.

Greater efficiency is being obtained with the introduction of new types of wagon with larger capacities and capable of higher speeds, and of new, more powerful locomotives, the latest of which can haul loads of 1,000 tonnes at speeds of up to 130 km/h (81 mph). A network of some 130 daily scheduled 'Speedlink' high-speed freight services has been established between the major industrial centres. Other developments, such as the concentration of freight traffic at fewer but better-equipped terminals and a computer-based total operations processing system, which monitors all consignments and freight train and wagon movements in Great Britain, have contributed to a significant increase in productivity and competitiveness.

Other Activities
British Rail has several other subsidiary activities. British Rail Engineering Ltd, whose income amounted to £471 million in 1985–86, constructs locomotives and rolling stock as well as undertaking heavy maintenance and overhauls for British Rail; it also manufactures rolling stock for overseas railways. The Railway Technical Centre at Derby is the largest of its type in the world. Transmark provides consultancy services overseas on railway and associated operations. Travellers-Fare is responsible for catering facilities at 163 stations, while InterCity catering provides restaurant and buffet facilities on most InterCity trains.

In order to concentrate its resources on running the main railway business, British Rail has privatised its hotels, shipping and hovercraft businesses since 1980 and sold over £350 million of surplus property. It has attracted a further £350 million of private sector funds for commercial development schemes in connection with railway and station improvements. British Rail has also adopted a policy of competitive tendering for its rolling stock needs, and has invited private sector firms to play a greater role in train and station catering.

Other Urban Railways
Some 762 million passenger journeys were made on London Regional Transport trains in 1985–86. London's 'Underground' trains operate on 408 km (254 miles) of railway, of which about 167 km (104 miles) are underground, and serve 273 stations. There are 3,875 railway cars. Substantial investment is in progress, particularly on station modernisation and ticketing facilities. The Docklands Light Railway, a £77 million project financed by London Regional Transport and the London Docklands Development Corporation, is under construction and the 12-km (7·5-mile) route (which will have 16 stations) is expected to be in operation in 1987.

Other public rail services in Great Britain are the Glasgow Underground and the Tyne and Wear Metro, a new 55-km (34-mile) light rapid transit system with over 40 stations, which is the largest provincial urban transport scheme in Britain in the twentieth century.

Private Railways
There are over 40 small privately owned passenger-carrying railways in Great Britain, mostly operated on a voluntary basis and providing limited services for tourists and railway enthusiasts. The main aim of most of these railways, such as the Bluebell Railway in East Sussex, is the preservation of steam traction.

Channel Tunnel
Britain and France have agreed to facilitate the construction of a fixed link across the Channel and have chosen the project submitted by the Channel Tunnel Group/France Manche (now known jointly as Eurotunnel) for twin single-track rail tunnels with a vehicle shuttle service for cars, coaches and goods vehicles. The project, estimated to cost some £2,600 million at 1985

prices, will be the largest civil engineering project in Europe to be undertaken by the private sector, which will provide all the finance. It is expected to bring substantial benefits to industry and to travellers through the quicker carriage of both passengers and freight. Members of the Channel Tunnel Group are Balfour Beatty Construction Ltd, Costain UK Ltd, George Wimpey International Ltd, Midland Bank plc, National Westminster Bank plc, Tarmac Construction Ltd and Taylor Woodrow Construction Ltd, while Granada Group plc and Mobil Oil Co Ltd are associate members.

The 49-km (30-mile) link will carry through rail services and a drive-on, drive-off vehicle shuttle service using specially designed shuttle trains. Journey time between the two terminals, Cheriton (near Folkestone) and Fréthun in France, will be some 30 minutes, with trains travelling at a maximum speed of 160 km/h (100 mph). Through passenger and freight services are planned, and British Rail envisages investment of nearly £400 million for these services in new passenger and freight rolling stock, track and signalling improvements, a new passenger terminal at Waterloo (London), freight facilities and a train maintenance depot. The terminal at Cheriton will cover 140 hectares (350 acres) and will contain a rail loop for the shuttle trains to run into the tracks beside the platforms. Road improvements in Kent are planned to ensure good access to the tunnel terminal. The Government is keeping the environmental aspects of the scheme under review to ensure that damage is kept to a minimum.

The Channel Link Treaty with France was signed in February 1986. It contains provisions to safeguard the governments' interests in matters such as safety and the environment, deals with matters of national jurisdiction, provides arrangements for arbitration in the event of disputes over interpretation of the Treaty between the governments and the concessionaires, sets out the private sector nature of the scheme, and provides for compensation to the promoter in the event of political interference or cancellation by the Government. The concession agreement between the promoters and the governments was signed in March 1986. However, this will not come into effect until after the enactment of the Channel Tunnel Bill (which would authorise construction and make the necessary financial and legal provisions) and the subsequent ratification of the Treaty. Subject to the passage of the Bill and the ratification, construction work could begin in 1987 with a view to services being inaugurated in 1993.

INLAND WATERWAYS

The inland waterways of Great Britain are popular for recreation, make a valuable contribution to the environment and play an important part in land drainage and water supply. They are also used to a limited extent for freight-carrying. An official survey of inland waterway freight traffic reported that in 1984, 64 million tonnes of freight were carried on inland waterways and estuaries, covering some 2,400 million tonne-km (1·3 per cent of freight traffic by tonne-km in Great Britain). About 44 per cent (in tonne-km) was carried in the South East, mainly on the River Thames. Of the 3,200 km (2,000 miles) of canal and river navigations controlled by the publicly owned British Waterways Board, some 550 km (340 miles) are maintained as commercial waterways. The Board also operates docks, warehouses and inland freight terminals, and has a barge fleet, although most of the traffic on its waterways is conveyed by independent carriers. In 1985–86 the Board's turnover amounted to £18·2 million and it received government grants of £43·5 million to maintain its waterways to statutory standards.

Ports

There are over 300 ports in Great Britain, but many are small harbours of only local significance and do not handle cargo regularly. Most port authorities operate with statutory powers and responsibilities under private Acts of Parliament. They are of three broad types: trusts, local authorities and statutory companies.

Major ports controlled by trusts include Clyde, Dover, Forth, London, Medway, Milford Haven, and Tees and Hartlepool. Local authorities control many small ports but also the much larger ports of Bristol, Portsmouth and the new oil ports in Orkney and Shetland.

Associated British Ports, established under the Transport Act 1981 as a statutory corporation, wholly owned by Associated British Ports Holdings PLC (a private sector company), owns and operates 19 ports including Southampton, Grimsby and Immingham, Hull, Newport, Cardiff and Swansea. Other port undertakings owned by statutory companies include Felixstowe, Liverpool and Manchester.

Port Traffic

In 1985 traffic through the ports of Great Britain amounted to 451 million tonnes comprising 148 million tonnes of exports, 142 million tonnes of imports and 161 million tonnes of domestic traffic (which included offshore traffic, landings of sea-dredged aggregates and material shipped for dumping at sea). About 62 per cent of the traffic was in fuels, mainly petroleum and petroleum products. Some 72 per cent of the 13·5 million tonnes of traffic (10·8 million tonnes of imports and 2·7 million tonnes of exports) which entered or left Northern Ireland by sea in 1985 represented traffic with the rest of Britain.

Britain's main ports, in terms of total tonnage handled, are given in Table 29. Offshore oil developments have had a substantial effect on port traffic by greatly increasing the flow through certain North Sea ports, such as Tees and Hartlepool and the Forth ports, creating new oil ports at Flotta in Orkney and Sullom Voe in Shetland, and reducing oil traffic at many traditional oil-importing terminals. Two other significant changes have affected traffic at British ports in the last 20 years. First, traditional major ports, such as London, Liverpool and Manchester, have lost general (non-bulk) cargo traffic to ports like Dover and Felixstowe which have developed specialised facilities to meet a world-wide switch from conventional handling methods to container and roll-on modes. While non-fuel traffic has been growing only slowly, container and roll-on traffic has more than trebled since 1970 to 58 million tonnes in 1985 and now accounts for about 40 per cent of non-fuel foreign and coastal traffic. The leading ports for container traffic are Felixstowe, London and Southampton and for roll-on traffic are Dover (Britain's leading seaport in terms of the value of trade handled), Felixstowe, Grimsby and Immingham, and Harwich. Secondly, ports on the south and east coasts have increasingly gained traffic at the expense of those on the west coast as the emphasis of Britain's trade has switched towards the continent of Europe.

Development

Modernisation of Britain's ports has been carried out primarily to accommodate the growth in container and roll-on traffic, to speed the handling of bulk commodities, and as a result of the changing nature and direction of Britain's trade. Many ports have modernised facilities and improved productivity by changing port layout, introducing new handling equipment and reducing manning levels. Most major new developments have been at east- and south-coast ports. For example, at Felixstowe a £42 million container terminal, completed in 1986, has raised the port's container-handling capacity by about 50 per cent. Extra capacity for ferry services is being provided at Dover, Portsmouth and Ramsgate, and a new freight ferry terminal at Dartford on the Thames is under construction.

Purpose-built terminals for oil from the British sector of the North Sea have been built at Hound Point on the Forth, on the Tees, at Flotta and at Sullom Voe

Table 29: Traffic through the Principal Ports of Great Britain[a]

million tonnes

	1965	1975	1980	1983	1984	1985
Sullom Voe	—	—	28·5	54·3	59·7	59·0
London	64·6	50·3	54·2	47·0	48·0	51·7
Milford Haven	24·8	44·9	39·3	30·7	32·1	32·5
Tees and Hartlepool	12·1	20·2	39·4	33·8	32·6	30·6
Forth	6·1	8·4	28·8	28·8	29·8	29·1
Grimsby/Immingham	8·3	22·0	22·2	29·0	26·8	29·1
Southampton	24·4	25·3	23·9	25·3	27·4	25·2
Orkney	—	0·4	15·4	16·1	16·1	16·1
Medway	22·3	21·7	17·2	8·6	11·5	10·9
Liverpool	31·7	23·4	12·3	11·3	10·8	10·4
Clyde	15·3	13·6	8·7	9·6	10·5	9·9
Manchester	15·8	14·5	12·7	11·4	10·7	9·5

Source: Department of Transport.
[a] Belfast and Larne are the main ports in Northern Ireland and handled 6 million tonnes and 3·6 million tonnes respectively in 1985.

(one of the largest oil terminals in the world). Three of the four jetties at Sullom Voe can handle oil tankers of up to 350,000 deadweight tonnes, and the fourth jetty handles the export of liquefied petroleum gases and can accommodate vessels with a capacity of up to 75,000 cubic metres. A £54 million terminal has been built at Braefoot Bay in the Firth of Forth to handle tankers carrying natural gas liquids brought by pipeline from the plant at Mossmorran (Fife). Supply bases for offshore vessels have been built at a number of ports, mostly on the east coast.

Shipping

Britain remains a leading maritime nation, but in common with the fleets of other developed countries, the British fleet has been adversely affected by the world recession in shipping and increasing international competition. It has declined substantially from a peak of 53·4 million deadweight tonnes[1] (33·7 million gross tonnes) in 1975 to 21·8 million deadweight tonnes (14·3 million gross tonnes) in 1985. A large tonnage of ships, particularly of tankers, has been scrapped or sold.

In July 1985, 19 million deadweight tonnes of trading vessels of 100 gross tonnes and over were both owned and registered in Britain: 622 vessels totalling 7·4 million tonnes being usually employed as dry bulk cargo, liner or cellular container ships; and a further 279 vessels of 11·6 million tonnes as oil, chemical or gas carriers. The merchant fleet figure of 21·8 million deadweight tonnes also includes non-trading vessels, such as fishing vessels, tugs and dredgers, and shipping registered in Britain but owned in other Commonwealth countries.

British cargo liner tonnage is dominated by a relatively small number of large private sector groups and container consortia. The representative body for the majority of shipowners is the General Council of British Shipping, although certain sectors have their own associations.

[1] Deadweight tonnage denotes the maximum load which a vessel can carry before submerging the load-line. Gross tonnage indicates the total capacity of the enclosed space on a ship.

Services

About 94 per cent of Britain's overseas trade by weight, about 80 per cent by value, is carried by sea, while the proportion of passengers travelling to or from Britain by sea is more than one-third, compared with about one-half in the early 1960s.

Cargo Services

In 1985 British seaborne trade amounted to 285 million tonnes (valued at £127,700 million) or 1 million million tonne-km (596,000 million tonne-miles). Ships registered in Britain carried 23 per cent by weight, 20 per cent in terms of tonne-mileage and 36 per cent by value. Tanker cargoes accounted for over half this trade by weight, but only 19 per cent by value, and foodstuffs and manufactured goods accounted for three-quarters by value.

Many of the deep-sea liner services from Britain are operated by container ships. There are many roll-on services, accommodating passengers and their cars and, in some cases, commercial vehicles, between Britain and the continent of Europe and several freight-only roll-on services to the Irish Republic, the continent of Europe, and to some more distant countries.

British shipping companies operating liner services have associated with each other and with the companies of other countries operating on the same routes in a series of 'conferences' designed to secure standardisation and stability of rates, and to maintain frequency and regularity of services. The essential principle of a conference is a common tariff of freight rates and other conditions of service to be applied by each member line. Conferences serve all the major trades to and from Britain. In 1985 Britain acceded to the United Nations Convention for Liner Conferences, a wide-ranging code of conduct governing relations among shipping companies that are members of conferences.

Passenger Services

Almost all of the 26·3 million passengers who arrived at or departed from British ports in 1985 travelled to or from the continent of Europe or the Irish Republic, services on other routes having largely been withdrawn as a result of the growth of air services. Remaining long-distance passenger ships are used for cruising and in 1985 some 71,000 passengers embarked on pleasure cruises from British ports.

Traffic from the southern and south-eastern ports accounts for a substantial proportion of traffic to the continent of Europe. The main British operators are Sealink UK Ltd (a subsidiary of British Ferries Ltd) and Townsend Thoresen. Sealink UK Ltd and its continental partners (Société Nationale des Chemins de Fer Français, and Stoomvaart Maatschappij Zeeland of the Netherlands) operate about 15 ships on continental routes.

Cross-Channel hovercraft services are provided by Hoverspeed Ltd, with routes between Dover and Boulogne, and Dover and Calais. A hovercraft crossing takes about one-third of the time taken by ships, and hovercraft carry about one-sixth of the traffic on the short-sea crossings to France. Hoverspeed operates five hovercraft including two British Hovercraft Corporation SR.N Super 4s which have been structurally enlarged so that each accommodates 418 passengers and 55 cars, making them the largest hovercraft in the world.

Passenger and freight ferry services are also operated to many of the offshore islands, such as the Isle of Wight, Orkney, Shetland and a number of other Scottish islands.

Role of the Government

The Department of Transport is the government department responsible for most matters connected with merchant shipping, including Britain's relations with other governments and international organisations on shipping matters. The general policy is one of minimum intervention by the Government and the encouragement of free and fair competition. Under the Merchant Shipping Acts the Department does, however, administer many regulations for marine safety and welfare, and for preventing and cleaning up pollution from ships. The Acts also contain certain reserve powers for protecting shipping and trading interests from measures adopted or proposed by overseas governments.

Safety at Sea

Britain's merchant fleet is one of the safest in the world with a lower record of ship losses than the world average.

The Coastguard Service, administered by the Department of Transport, is responsible for initiating and co-ordinating civil marine search and rescue action in the United Kingdom Search and Rescue Region. It can call upon the lifeboats of the Royal National Lifeboat Institution (a voluntary body which operates 257 lifeboats), Ministry of Defence aircraft (including helicopters from 11 airfields around the coast), a long-range civilian helicopter based at Sumburgh (Shetland), and any other ships or aircraft available to assist in search or rescue action. In 1985 the Coastguard Service took action in 5,475 incidents (including cliff rescues) in which over 9,700 people were assisted.

The lighthouse authorities (for England and Wales the Corporation of Trinity House, for Scotland the Northern Lighthouse Board and for Ireland the Commissioners of Irish Lights) control about 370 lighthouses, many minor lights and buoys, and a number of lightships, some of which are being replaced by unattended sea marks or by light towers. In Britain there are 50 pilotage authorities for the 93 pilotage districts and about 1,425 licensed pilots. Trinity House is the largest pilotage authority, licensing some 570 pilots in 40 districts in England and Wales. In some cases the harbour authority or local council is the pilotage authority. However, the Government is planning to introduce legislation under which the pilotage authorities would be abolished and their responsibilities transferred to harbour authorities.

Compliance with traffic separation schemes around the shores of Britain is mandatory for all vessels of countries party to the 1972 International Collision Regulations. The most important scheme affecting British waters is in the Dover Strait, the world's busiest seaway. Britain and France operate radar surveillance of the strait to keep watch on ships not conforming to the scheme and, through the Channel Navigation Information Service, broadcast navigational information to ships in the strait. The Service, which operates from Dover, has a radar-linked, automatic data-processing system for detecting and tracking vessels, making it one of the most advanced centres in the world.

Civil Aviation

Britain's substantial civil air transport industry is continuing to develop to meet the increasing demand for air travel, particularly international travel. The airlines are re-equipping their fleets with the most modern aircraft, while many airports are being substantially modernised and expanded.

Role of the Government

The Secretary of State for Transport is responsible for international matters (including negotiation of air service agreements with more than 100 other countries, the licensing and control of public transport operations into Britain by overseas operators and British participation in the activities of international aviation bodies), airports policy, amenity matters (such as aircraft noise), aviation security policy and investigation of accidents.

The Government's civil aviation policy aims to encourage a sound and competitive multi-airline industry in Britain, to promote competition in international and internal services, and to maintain high standards of safety. It has liberalised airline services within Britain, and in its negotiations with other countries on bilateral air service agreements it is proposing the adoption of more liberal measures. Negotiations with some other members of the European

Community have already resulted in greater competition, leading to increased traffic and lower fares.

Civil Aviation Authority

The Civil Aviation Authority (CAA) is an independent statutory body, responsible for the economic, technical and operational regulation of the industry. It is also responsible for the aerodrome navigation services at certain British airports and, jointly with the Ministry of Defence, for the provision by the National Air Traffic Services of air navigation services. Members of the CAA board are appointed by the Secretary of State for Transport.

Under the Civil Aviation Act 1982 its primary objectives are to ensure that British airlines provide air services to satisfy all substantial categories of public demand at the lowest charges consistent with a high standard of safety and an economic return for efficient operators, and to further the reasonable interests of air transport users. Other duties are to ensure that British airlines compete effectively on international routes, to secure the most effective use of airports in Britain and to have regard to the need to minimise the adverse effects of civil aviation on the environment.

Air Traffic

In 1985 a total of some 52·9 million passengers travelled by air (international terminal passengers) to or from Britain, 3·4 per cent more than in 1984. Total capacity offered on all services by British airlines amounted to 13,408 million available-tonne-km in 1985: 10,166 million tonne-km on scheduled services and 3,242 million tonne-km on non-scheduled services. British Airways accounts for some 76 per cent of scheduled services flown by British airlines.

In 1985 the value of Britain's overseas trade carried by air was some £28,700 million and the proportions carried by air amounted to approximately 18·7 per cent of the value of exports and 16·5 per cent of imports. Air freight is important for the carriage of goods with a high value-to-weight ratio, especially where speed of movement is essential. Precious stones, live animals, medicinal and pharmaceutical products, clothing, leather and skins, and scientific instruments are major categories where a relatively high proportion of exports is sent by air.

British Airways

British Airways is one of the world's leading airlines, and in terms of international passengers carried and of international passenger-km flown it is the largest in the world. During 1985–86 British Airways' turnover was £3,149 million (including £2,981 million from airline operations) and it recorded a net pre-tax profit of £183 million. British Airways ceased to be a statutory body in 1984 when it was re-established under the Civil Aviation Act 1980 as British Airways PLC, a public limited company under government ownership. The Government intends to sell its shareholding in the company to private investors as soon as practicable.

Airline Operations

British Airways' route network, covering some 520,900 km (323,700 miles) of unduplicated scheduled route, is among the largest in the world. The airline serves 145 destinations in 72 countries and in 1985 carried 18·4 million passengers. International scheduled services are operated to the rest of Europe, the Middle East, the Far East, Australasia, East and South Africa, North America, South America and the Caribbean. Within Britain it runs some 1,350 services a week to 14 towns and cities. Scheduled Concorde supersonic services are operated from London (Heathrow) to New York and to Miami via Washington, crossing the North Atlantic in about half the time taken by subsonic aircraft. Other activities carried out include engine overhaul work and investments in a number of hotel companies and air companies in Britain and other countries.

British Airways operated 159 aircraft in April 1986: 31 Boeing 747s, 47 Boeing 737s, 24 Boeing 757s, 19 Lockheed TriStars, 26 BAC One-Elevens, 5 HS 748s and 7 Concordes.

Independent Airlines

The independent airlines carry 7·8 million passengers a year on scheduled services and 14·2 million on charter flights. The main independent scheduled airline is British Caledonian Airways, which operates a fleet of 27 aircraft and carried 2·4 million scheduled service passengers in 1985. Its scheduled services are primarily to the continent of Europe; North, West and Central Africa; the United States; the Middle East; and Hong Kong. Other operators of scheduled passenger services include British Midland, Air UK, Dan Air Services and Virgin Atlantic. Britannia Airways, Dan Air Services, Monarch Airlines, Air Europe and Orion Airways are the leading independent airlines operating charter passenger services.

Helicopters

Helicopters are engaged on a variety of work, but are mainly employed on the large-scale operations connected with the development of Britain's offshore oil and gas resources. Light aircraft and helicopters are also involved in other activities, such as charter operations, search and rescue services, crop-spraying, and aerial survey and photography. The two main helicopter operators in Britain are Bristow Helicopters and British Airways Helicopters, with 62 and 31 helicopters respectively.

Safety

The CAA is responsible for air safety, both airworthiness and operational safety. Its Operations Division deals with the preparation and application of safety requirements concerning airline and private aviation operations, flight crew licensing and training, aerodromes, and fire and rescue services. The Airworthiness Division is responsible for the airworthiness standards of aircraft registered in Britain, the licensing of aircraft maintenance engineers and the approval of work schedules to which British transport aircraft are maintained.

Every company operating aircraft used for public transport must possess an Air Operator's Certificate, which is granted by the CAA when it is satisfied that the operator is competent to secure the safe operation of its aircraft. The CAA's flight operations inspectors (who are experienced airline pilots) check that satisfactory operating standards are maintained.

Each member of the flight crew of a British registered aircraft must hold the appropriate official licence issued by the CAA. Except for pilots with acceptable military or other qualifying experience, all applicants for a first professional pilot's licence must have undertaken a full-time course of ground and flying instruction which has been approved by the CAA.

Air Traffic Control and Navigation Services

Responsibility for civil and military air traffic control over Britain and the surrounding seas rests with the National Air Traffic Services (NATS). The Controller of the NATS reports to both the CAA and the Ministry of Defence. At some 19 civil aerodromes, including most of the major British airports, the NATS provides the navigation services necessary for the operation of aircraft taking off and landing, and integrates them into the flow of traffic within British airspace. To provide its services, the NATS uses radar, some 100 navigational beacons, landing aids, air/ground communications and an extensive telecommunications network.

Airports

Of the 135 licensed civil aerodromes in Britain, about one-fifth each handles more than 100,000 passengers a year. Ten handle over 1 million passengers a year and these are shown in Table 30. In 1985 Britain's civil airports handled a total of 71·8 million passengers (70·4 million terminal passengers and 1·4 million in transit), and 850,000 tonnes of freight. London's Heathrow airport is the world's busiest airport for international travel and is Britain's most important airport for passengers and air freight, handling 31·6 million passengers and 525,000 tonnes of freight in 1985. Gatwick is the world's fourth busiest international airport.

Table 30: Passenger Traffic at Britain's Main Airports

million passengers

	1975	1980	1983	1984	1985
London (Heathrow)	21·3	27·5	26·8	29·2	31·3
London (Gatwick)	5·3	9·7	12·5	14·0	14·9
Manchester	2·6	4·3	5·1	6·0	6·1
Glasgow	1·8	2·3	2·4	2·7	2·7
Aberdeen	0·6	1·4	1·7	1·8	1·7
Luton	1·9	2·1	1·7	1·8	1·6
Birmingham	1·1	1·6	1·6	1·7	1·6
Belfast (Aldergrove)	1·2	1·5	1·4	1·6	1·6
Edinburgh	0·8	1·2	1·3	1·5	1·6
Newcastle upon Tyne	0·6	0·9	1·0	1·1	1·0

Source: Civil Aviation Authority.
Note: Statistics relate to terminal passengers only and exclude those in transit.

Ownership and Control

Seven airports—Heathrow, Gatwick and Stansted in south-east England, and Glasgow, Edinburgh, Prestwick and Aberdeen in Scotland—are owned and managed by BAA plc, established under the Airports Act 1986 as the successor company to the statutory British Airports Authority. A separate subsidiary company will be established to operate each of the airports, which together handle about 75 per cent of air passengers and 85 per cent of air cargo traffic in Britain. All of the shares in BAA plc are at present held by the Secretary of State for Transport, but the Government's intention is to sell the shares during the first half of 1987.

Many of the other public airports are controlled by local authorities and the Act also provides for the larger airports to be formed into companies. Where any airport's turnover exceeds £1 million in at least two of the previous three years, the local authorities will be required to form a company operating under the Companies Act 1985 to run the airport's business and will be encouraged to introduce private capital into the new companies.

All airports used for public transport and training flights must be licensed by the CAA. Stringent requirements, such as the provision of adequate fire-fighting, medical and rescue services, suitable physical characteristics and visual aids, must be satisfied before a licence is granted. Strict aviation security measures are in force.

Development

The Government's policy is to promote a strong and competitive British airline industry by providing airport capacity where it is needed and by making effective use of existing resources, especially at Heathrow, Gatwick and Stansted. It is also encouraging the maximum use of regional airports.

A fourth major terminal at Heathrow was opened in April 1986, raising the airport's capacity from 30 million to 38 million passengers a year. Gatwick's current capacity is some 16 million passengers a year, but the second terminal, the first phase of which is due to open in 1988, will eventually raise this to

25 million passengers. Following a public inquiry, planning permission was granted in 1985 for the expansion of Stansted airport to an eventual capacity of 15 million passengers a year; in 1986 work began on the first phase, which would provide capacity of some 7 million to 8 million passengers a year.

Facilities have also been improved at regional airports, with major terminal or runway improvements undertaken at Manchester, Birmingham, Leeds/Bradford and Newcastle upon Tyne airports. The Government intends to assist in developing further opportunities for new routes and services, and will encourage the development of Manchester as a 'regional hub' airport.

Communications

The Government has introduced two major Acts to establish a new framework for telecommunications services, one of the most rapidly growing sectors of the economy. The British Telecommunications Act 1981 separated the Post Office into two corporations, one for postal and banking services and the other for telecommunications (British Telecommunications, known as British Telecom), and provided for a limited relaxation of the statutory monopoly in telecommunications. The Telecommunications Act 1984 strengthened the measures taken to promote competition in a number of ways including removing British Telecom's exclusive privilege of running public telecommunications systems and instituting new arrangements requiring those running telecommunications systems (including British Telecom), with certain limited exceptions, to be licensed by the Secretary of State for Trade and Industry or, under delegated authority, by the Director General of Telecommunications. There is provision for licences to contain certain conditions including obligations to provide services and requirements to connect with other systems. In British Telecom's case the obligations to provide services ensure the continued existence of a universal telecommunications service throughout the country and that certain essential services, such as public emergency services, public call box services, maritime emergency services and services in rural areas, are maintained. Mercury Communications Ltd is licensed as the second major public telecommunications network and provides a full range of services.

In 1982 a general licence for 'value added network services' was issued, permitting a wide variety of commercial services (other than the basic service of conveying or switching a message) to be run in competition with British Telecom over the public telecommunications networks. The licence was the first of its kind and has placed the British system among the most liberal in the world. Over 190 operators have registered under the general licence proposals for nearly 800 different services, such as viewdata, conference calls, electronic mail, and message storage and retrieval systems. Further liberalisation of the licensing arrangements for value added and data network services took effect in 1986.

Private sector firms are now able to supply, install and maintain most types of subscribers' apparatus attached to the telecommunications network. British Telecom's monopoly over the supply and maintenance of a customer's first telephone instrument connected to its network ceased at the end of 1984, and maintenance of newly installed call-routing apparatus will be fully open for competition by November 1986.

The Office of Telecommunications, a government department established under the Telecommunications Act 1984, is the independent regulatory body for the telecommunications industry. It is headed by the Director General of Telecommunications, whose functions are to ensure that licensees comply with the conditions of their licences; to promote effective competition in the telecommunications industry; to provide advice to the Secretary of State for

Trade and Industry and to users on telecommunications matters; and to investigate complaints about services. The Director General also has a duty to promote the interests of consumers in respect of prices, quality and variety in telecommunications services.

Under the 1984 Act British Telecom was reconstituted as a public limited company and a majority of the ordinary voting shares were sold to private investors in 1984. It has nearly 1·6 million registered shareholders and 88 per cent of its 230,000 employees are shareholders.

BRITISH TELECOM

British Telecom serves some 17 million residential and 4 million business telephone customers. It operates one of the world's largest public telecommunications networks, with almost 21·5 million telephone exchange lines, more than 104,000 telex connections, 76,500 public payphones and a wide range of specialised voice, data, text and visual services. Over 80 per cent of homes in Britain now have a telephone. The inland telephone and telex networks are fully automatic. International services are also highly developed, and international direct dialling is available from any telephone line in Britain to nearly 170 countries, representing 93 per cent of the world's telephones. Automatic telex service is available to nearly 200 countries.

In 1985–86 the company made a pre-tax profit of £1,810 million on a turnover of £8,387 million. Expenditure on capital equipment and other assets totalled £1,973 million, of which £422 million went on modernising exchanges with digital equipment. All capital spending came out of the company's earned income. About £160 million was spent on research and development.

Network Modernisation

British Telecom is investing substantial sums in the modernisation and expansion of its network to meet the increasing demand for basic telephone services and for more specialised services. By March 1986 the company had nearly 125,000 km (78,000 miles) of optical fibre cable laid in its trunk network in Britain, accounting for some 40 per cent of the network, a higher proportion than any other world operator. There were more than 180 digital exchanges in service. About half of its customers are served by modern local exchanges of various types. The combination of digital exchange switching and digital transmission techniques, using optical fibre cable and microwave radio links, is substantially improving the quality of telephone service for residential and business customers, compared with traditional analogue techniques, as well as making possible a wider range of services through the company's main network.

The new main digital exchanges can connect voice and data to customers simultaneously, and support advanced services including text, fast facsimile, picture videotext, graphics and slow-scan television. British Telecom was the world's first operator to offer a pilot service, to selected business customers, over an 'integrated services digital network'. This service began in the London area in 1985 and has since been extended to other main business centres in Britain.

A wide range of high-speed switched data transmission services has been available to business computer users since 1982.

General Services

British Telecom provides numerous facilities and services including a free facility for emergency calls to the police, fire, ambulance, coastguard, lifeboat and air–sea rescue services; a free directory inquiries service (which has been modernised and now uses computer-stored information retrieval techniques); and various other chargeable operator-connected services, such as transfer charge and alarm calls. The operator-handled Freefone service, enabling users to contact organisations at the called customer's cost, has been supplemented since mid-1985 by new automatic 'LinkLine' facilities, enabling callers to contact organisations anywhere in Britain, either free or at local call rates.

British Telecom provides a number of customer-dialled recorded telephone information services, now known as Guidelines, including Timeline (formerly known as the Speaking Clock). The company also provides value-added recorded services in various centres at higher call charges, and is required to make its network facilities available for similar premium services provided by other organisations operating under the general value added network services licence.

A public payphone service modernisation programme, costing some £160 million, is in progress and by March 1987 all public payphones will be equipped with push-button equipment. A number of cashless call developments are being carried out including the Phonecard service, using prepaid encoded cards, which was initially introduced in main railway stations, airports and other heavily used sites, but has been extended to many other parts of Britain. In the Bristol and Bath area, an AccountCall facility was introduced in March 1986, enabling public telephone users to insert a specially coded British Telecom card, instead of money, and have the cost of calls charged to a private or business telephone service account. There are some 300,000 rented payphones on premises to which the public has access and these are also being upgraded with modern push-button equipment.

Prestel, British Telecom's public viewdata service, the first of its kind when introduced in 1979 and enabling a wide variety of computer-stored information to be called up on a special television receiver via the telephone, increased the numbers of sets with its registered home and office users by 20 per cent during 1985–86 to nearly 70,000. Through its 'Gateway' links with other databases, a wide range of other services, such as home shopping and banking services and holiday booking and reservation facilities, has become available. Prestel has been open to access from anywhere in the world since 1981.

There has been rapid growth in British Telecom's mobile communications services including the jointly owned cellular radio network (see p 330). Its radiopaging service had 337,000 customers by March 1986.

Voicebank, which stores recorded telephone messages for callers on a central computer mailbox, extended its service from London to other main business centres in England and Scotland during 1985–86.

Telecom Gold, British Telecom's main electronic mail service, serves some 44,000 mailboxes.

International Services

British Telecom International is the company's division handling international networks and services. It is the second largest shareholder in the International Telecommunications Satellite Organisation (of which 110 countries are members) and in the International Maritime Satellite Organisation, with interests in a number of other consortia.

A digital international exchange is already in service in London and two more were ordered in 1985. Laying of the world's first international undersea optical fibre cable, between Britain and Belgium, was completed during 1986 and work will begin on laying the first transatlantic optical fibre cable (TAT8) in the autumn of 1987. An agreement was reached in mid-1986 to lay a further high-capacity transatlantic optical fibre cable (TAT9) in 1991. This will have twin branches to Britain and France from the main cable and will be the first to incorporate an undersea exchange.

By the end of March 1986 companies sending computer data world-wide from Britain were able to use international 'Packet SwitchStream' services to 66 networks in 47 countries.

High-speed international satellite links to and from Britain were expanded during 1985–86. The main business systems terminal at British Telecom International's 'Teleport' earth station in London became operational at the end of 1985 and 'SatStream' private circuit digital links, using small-dish satellite earth stations, were extended to cover North America and a number of countries in Western Europe. An 'International KiloStream' service, offering digital private circuits for voice, text and visual services at speeds up to 64,000 bits a second, is available to the United States, Australia and Japan.

Direct-dial maritime satellite services have been introduced for vessels world-wide, via the earth station at Goonhilly in Cornwall. Limited in-flight operator-controlled telephone call facilities have been introduced via Portishead Radio Station near Bristol, and trials of an automatic service via satellite for aircraft passengers will begin in 1988 on transatlantic routes, using specially equipped British Airways aircraft.

Digital transmission techniques have been introduced for services to the United States, Japan, Hong Kong and Australia via the Madley earth station near Hereford. The service to Japan includes the world's first wholly digital intercontinental public telephone service, giving faster connections and clearer speech.

British Telecom's overseas consultancy service, Telconsult, was engaged on 74 contracts in 30 countries during 1985–86.

MERCURY

Mercury Communications Ltd, a subsidiary of Cable and Wireless plc, operates under licence as the second telecommunications carrier in Britain, enabling the company to offer a wide range of services, both nationally and internationally. It is establishing a new telecommunications system involving an optical fibre trunk network centred on Birmingham, with cables laid alongside railway tracks between major towns and cities. A southern loop incorporates London and Bristol, and a northern loop Leeds and Manchester, and the network is being extended to Scotland, Wales and the south coast of England. International links are provided by two satellite communications centres: one in London's Docklands, serving North America; and the other in Oxfordshire, serving the Far East. Switched telephony services for large-scale customers began in May 1986, and the provision of services to small business users and to residential subscribers is planned later in 1986.

OTHER MAJOR TELECOMMUNICATIONS OPERATORS

Cable and Wireless plc provides or manages a wide range of telecommunications activities, mostly overseas in over 60 countries. The company used to be in the public sector, but in 1985 the Government sold its remaining 23 per cent shareholding.

Racal Vodafone Ltd (part of the Racal Electronics group) and Telecom Securicor Cellular Radio Ltd (a joint venture between British Telecom and Securicor) have been licensed by the Government to run competing national cellular radio systems, which started in 1985 and now cover wide areas of Britain.

BROADBAND CABLE SYSTEMS

By mid-1986 eight companies had been licensed to run local broadband cable systems. At present they mainly provide television programmes, but some will also provide interactive services including (in co-operation with British Telecom or Mercury) voice telephony services.

THE POST OFFICE

The Post Office, founded in 1635, pioneered postal services and was the first to issue adhesive postage stamps as proof of advance payment for mail. The Royal Mail provides deliveries to 23 million addresses and handles 43 million letters and parcels each working day (11,000 million items a year). Mail is collected from over 100,000 posting boxes, as well as from post offices and large postal users. The Post Office has a monopoly on the conveyance of letters, but under the British Telecommunications Act 1981 the Secretary of State for Trade and Industry has the power to suspend the monopoly in certain areas or for certain categories of mail and to license others to provide competing services. The Secretary of State has relaxed the monopoly on letters subject to a minimum fee of £1, and has issued general licences enabling mail to be transferred between document exchanges and allowing charitable organisations to carry Christmas and New Year cards.

All the 80 offices equipped with mechanical handling equipment are in operation and are gradually taking over the work of hundreds of sorting offices handling letters manually. Each address in Britain has a postcode and the British system is the most sophisticated in the world, allowing mechanised sorting down to part of a street on a postman's round and, in some cases, to an individual address. Some 34 large parcel centres, each serving a group of counties, have taken over the work of 1,200 offices which handled parcels manually.

As well as postal and National Girobank services, post offices handle a wide range of transactions. In much of its counter service the Post Office acts as agent for government departments and local authorities. The Post Office has adopted a scheme for introducing new technology into its counter services to reduce costs and raise productivity, while providing an improved range of services to customers. There are nearly 22,000 post offices, of which some 1,500 are operated directly by the Post Office and the remainder on an agency basis by sub-postmasters.

Specialist Services

The Post Office provides a range of specialist services. 'Datapost International', a door-to-door delivery service, has overnight links throughout Britain and international services to 82 countries including most of Europe and North America. 'Datapost Sameday' provides a rapid delivery within or between some 84 main cities and towns in Britain. 'Intelpost', the world's first international public facsimile transmission service sending letters and other documents electronically, provides high-speed mail links between more than 100 post offices in Britain as well as to and from the United States and 26 other countries. The Philatelic Bureau in Edinburgh handles about one-third of the Post Office's philatelic business, much of it involving sales to overseas collectors or dealers. The British Postal Consultancy Service offers advice and assistance on all aspects of postal business to overseas postal administrations, and nearly 40 countries have used its services since 1965.

16 Employment

As a major industrial country, Britain has a labour force with high levels of technical and commercial skill. However, in common with other industrialised countries, it has suffered in recent years from high levels of unemployment. The long-term solution to this lies in economic growth, which in turn depends upon low inflation, financial stability and efficient, competitive industries. Improving the operation of the labour market should help to create the most suitable economic climate in which business can flourish and create more jobs. The Government is helping to achieve this in a number of ways, including increasing the flexibility of the labour market, removing burdens on employers and making training more relevant to the economy's needs.

TRENDS IN EMPLOYMENT

The total workforce in June 1985 was 27·6 million, of whom 21·5 million (11·9 million men and 9·5 million women) were classed as employees in employment (see Table 31). Britain has one of the highest proportions of people of working age in jobs or seeking work among all the major industrialised countries, and the workforce (which rose by about 1 million between March 1983 and the end of 1985) is continuing to grow as the population of working age increases and as more women look for work. Recent trends have included the continuing growth in the proportion of the workforce accounted for by women, as more married women have sought work, especially in part-time employment; and a substantial increase in self-employment. Between 1979 and 1985 the number of self-employed people rose by 36 per cent to 2·6 million, representing 9·5 per cent of the working population (the highest proportion since 1951).

There have been substantial changes in the nature and location of employment, with a marked shift, as in other industrialised countries, from manufacturing to service industries. Between 1955 and 1985 the proportion of employees in employment engaged in service industries rose from 45 per cent to 65 per cent as higher living standards and technological developments stimulated the growth of many service industries. During the period 1977 to 1985 the number of employees in service industries rose by over 1 million (8 per cent) to 14 million (see Table 32). Employment in most service industries, with some exceptions, such as public administration, education, transport, postal services and communications, has grown considerably. The largest rise in this period was in the banking, finance and insurance sector (by 30 per cent to nearly 2 million), while other sectors with significant increases included hotels and catering (21 per cent), medical and other health services (16 per cent) and wholesale distribution and repairs (14 per cent). Manufacturing industry accounted for 40 per cent of employees in employment in 1955, but by 1985 the proportion had fallen to 26 per cent. Between 1977 and 1985 employment in manufacturing fell by 25 per cent to 5·5 million. Nearly all manufacturing industries have experienced a decline in employment as markets for manufactured goods have changed and as new technology has brought greater efficiency and, in some cases, reduced the demand for labour.

UNEMPLOY-MENT

As in nearly all the major industrialised nations, unemployment in Britain has continued to rise (see Table 31), although the increase in the mid-1980s has been much smaller than in the first years of the decade. In July 1986 some 3·3 million people, 11·9 per cent of the working population (11·7 per cent on a seasonally adjusted basis), were unemployed. While unemployment has increased in all regions, the higher rates are in areas which had the greatest dependence on traditional manufacturing industries.

The Government's employment strategy is to maintain an economic, financial and industrial climate in which businesses can operate successfully and create jobs. It is taking action to improve the labour market by encouraging better training, removing regulatory barriers which hinder recruitment by firms, and providing an extensive range of employment and training measures for those most affected by unemployment (particularly the long-term unemployed and the young) to help them into productive work.

Table 31: Manpower in Britain 1975–85

thousands

Year (June)	Employees in employ- ment[a]	Self- employed	Unem- ployed[b]	Armed forces	Working population[c]
1975	22,710	1,993	845	336	25,877
1976	22,543	1,949	1,185	336	26,094
1977	22,619	1,904	1,251	327	26,209
1978	22,777	1,904	1,235	318	26,342
1979	23,157	1,925	1,132	314	26,631
1980	22,972	2,033	1,359	323	26,841
1981	21,870	2,137	2,275	334	26,737
1982	21,400	2,189	2,606	324	26,682
1983	21,059	2,240	2,887	322	26,605
1984	21,242	2,515	2,983	326	27,113
1985	21,467	2,623	3,114	326	27,594

Sources: Department of Employment and Northern Ireland Department of Economic Development.
[a] Part-time workers are counted as full units.
[b] Excluding adult students. Figures are adjusted for discontinuities and seasonal factors and are on the basis of calculation in use from March 1986, excluding school-leavers.
[c] Not seasonally adjusted and including school-leavers.

Help for the Unemployed

In 1985–86 over £2,250 million was spent on the Government's employment and training measures and up to 700,000 people were being directly helped each month. Several special schemes, as well as the Youth Training Scheme and adult training measures (see p 337), are in operation.

The Enterprise Allowance Scheme, introduced for an experimental period in 1982 and extended to the whole of Great Britain in 1983, helps unemployed people wishing to start their own business but who would be deterred by the prospect of losing unemployment or supplementary benefit once they began. Entrants, who must have at least £1,000 to invest in the business, receive an allowance of £40 a week for a year while they start the business. Some 152,000 people have benefited from the scheme. Provision for the scheme has been increased, to £153 million in 1986–87, and the number of places available is to rise to 100,000 a year from 1987–88 onwards.

The Community Programme provides up to a year's employment for long-term unemployed adults on projects which are of benefit to local communities and are run by sponsoring bodies, primarily local authorities or voluntary organisations, but with funds provided by the Government. Expenditure on the programme totalled some £693 million in 1985–86 and by March 1986 the programme had some 200,000 participants engaged on about 10,300 projects. Additional resources are being devoted to the programme and the target for the number of filled places has been increased to 255,000 by November 1986. In

Northern Ireland similar assistance for the long-term unemployed is provided through the Action for Community Employment scheme and Enterprise Ulster, which together provided an average of some 5,000 jobs throughout 1985–86 at a cost of some £25 million.

The Job Release Scheme enables older workers (disabled men aged 60 to 63, men aged 64 and women aged 59) to retire early with an allowance provided that their employer replaces them with an unemployed person. Since its establishment in 1977 some 300,000 workers have taken early retirement under the scheme.

A number of pilot initiatives to help the long-term unemployed began in nine areas in January 1986. These led to the establishment of a Restart Programme, under which everyone in Great Britain who has been unemployed for a year or more will be invited to an in-depth interview at a local jobcentre by March 1987. The interviews are designed to see whether the participants can be placed in a suitable job, enter the Enterprise Allowance Scheme, take up a place on the Community Programme, enter a suitable training course, work on voluntary projects or participate in a Jobclub (see p 336). A one-week Restart Course has been established to assist the long-term unemployed with job-hunting techniques. To help those accepting low-paid jobs, a Jobstart allowance of £20 a

Table 32: Employees in Employment

Industry or service (1980 Standard Industrial Classification)	Thousands (as at June)				Per cent (1985)
	1977	1981	1984	1985	
Primary sector	1,106	1,061	974	952	4·4
Agriculture, forestry and fishing	388	352	340	338	1·6
Energy and water supply	718	709	634	613	2·9
Manufacturing[a]	7,328	6,220	5,542	5,533	25·8
Construction	1,215	1,138	989	970	4·5
Services	12,969	13,450	13,738	14,012	65·3
Wholesale distribution and repairs	1,058	1,127	1,179	1,209	5·6
Retail distribution	2,087	2,090	2,143	2,203	10·3
Hotels and catering	877	949	1,015	1,058	4·9
Transport	1,030	985	882	872	4·0
Postal services and communications	419	438	429	432	2·0
Banking, finance and insurance	1,519	1,740	1,887	1,972	9·2
Public administration	1,989	1,904	1,869	1,880	8·8
Education	1,602	1,602	1,590	1,600	7·5
Health	1,184	1,289	1,349	1,368	6·4
Other services	1,204	1,327	1,393	1,418	6·6
Total	22,617	21,870	21,242	21,467	100·0

Sources: Department of Employment and Northern Ireland Department of Economic Development.

[a] In June 1985 employment in the main sectors of manufacturing industry included 848,000 in office machinery, electrical engineering and instruments; 792,000 in mechanical engineering; 626,000 in food, drink and tobacco; 546,000 in textiles, leather, footwear and clothing; 498,000 in paper products, printing and publishing; 452,000 in timber, wooden furniture, rubber and plastics; 348,000 in chemicals and man-made fibres; and 288,000 in motor vehicles and parts.

Note: Differences between totals and the sums of their component parts are due to rounding; for 1977 the difference also reflects the inclusion in the total of some employees whose industrial classification could not be ascertained.

week is payable to people unemployed for over one year who take a full-time job with gross earnings of less than £80 a week.

Other schemes include the Voluntary Projects Programme (with a similar Community Volunteering Scheme in Northern Ireland), which allows unemployed people to take voluntary work without losing entitlement to state benefits; the Community Industry Scheme, which provides temporary job opportunities for personally and socially disadvantaged young unemployed people aged 17 to 19; the New Workers Scheme, introduced in April 1986 to complement the extended Youth Training Scheme by giving employers a financial incentive to recruit those aged 18 to 20 at wages reflecting their relative inexperience; and the Job Splitting Scheme, which is designed to increase opportunities for part-time work.

EMPLOYMENT SERVICES

In Great Britain responsibility for employment policy and for the payment of unemployment benefit rests with the Department of Employment, while advice on manpower policy issues is provided by the Manpower Services Commission (MSC), a body on which employers, trade unions, local authorities and educational interests are represented. The MSC is separate from the Government but accountable to the Secretaries of State for Employment, Scotland and Wales. Most of its activities are financed from public funds. It is advised by a network of area manpower boards on which employers, employees and other local interests are represented.

The main public employment services (other than the careers service) are provided in Great Britain by the MSC, which offers a comprehensive service for employers needing staff and for people, whether or not already in employment, seeking jobs. It operates through a network of about 1,000 local 'jobcentres' which handle all except professional, scientific, technical and managerial occupations, for which the MSC's Professional and Executive Recruitment is responsible. Self-service facilities for job-seekers are being increased, with a number of new small jobcentres being located in libraries and local authority establishments. New technology is being utilised to provide job-seekers with direct access through computer terminals to information on training and employment.

Self-help centres, known as 'Jobclubs', for the long-term unemployed were set up on an experimental basis in 1985 and the MSC is to increase the number of centres from 37 in April 1986 to 300 by the end of 1986 and to 450 by the end of April 1987. They are located mainly at jobcentres and provide free facilities (such as the use of telephones and typewriters), together with intensive coaching and expert advice on job-seeking techniques.

Registration for employment is voluntary for all unemployed people, whether or not they wish to claim benefits. In the year to March 1986, 2·5 million vacancies were notified and 1·9 million people were placed in employment (including job-seekers who were placed in a job more than once during the year).

In Northern Ireland, the Northern Ireland Department of Economic Development, through its network of 28 'jobmarkets', provides a guidance and placement service for all age groups, offering a range of services for employers and employees. A computerised vacancy information system is planned to be introduced in jobmarkets by 1988.

Services for Disabled People

The public employment service provides a resettlement service to disabled people. Specially trained Disablement Resettlement Officers advise on rehabilitation and training courses and on the comprehensive range of special schemes and facilities available. In 1985–86 the MSC found jobs for some 78,000 disabled people. The Disabled Persons (Employment) Act 1944 requires employers who employ 20 or more people to include 3 per cent registered disabled people within their workforce. As part of its 'Fit for Work' campaign to improve the employment prospects of disabled people, the MSC runs a scheme of annual awards for firms which excel in carrying out constructive policies on the employment of disabled people.

The MSC runs a network of 27 Employment Rehabilitation Centres, which provide facilities for those who have been ill or injured or are handicapped to return to working fitness (some 15,000 a year). It also provides financial assistance to voluntary and other bodies providing employment rehabilitation courses.

Sheltered employment is provided for the severely disabled in Great Britain by Remploy Ltd and in Northern Ireland by Ulster Sheltered Employment Ltd, both non-profit-making companies, and by local authorities and voluntary organisations.

Professional and Executive Recruitment

Professional and Executive Recruitment is a specialist branch of the MSC which, on a fee-paying basis, helps employers looking for professional, managerial, scientific or technical staff and assists people seeking employment at this level. It operates nationally, through a network of offices, and offers a comprehensive recruitment service based on a weekly jobs newspaper which is issued to all enrolled job-seekers, for whom the service is free. In Northern Ireland the Professional and Executive Personnel Service is part of the general employment service offered by jobmarkets.

Careers Service

Under the Employment and Training Act 1973 local education authorities must provide a careers service to include vocational guidance for people attending all educational institutions (except universities, which have their own careers service) and an employment service for those leaving them. Authorities may also provide an employment service for other people, mainly young people in their early post-school years. The employment service provided by the MSC is also available to young people.

The careers services in Wales and Scotland are the responsibility of the respective Secretary of State. In Northern Ireland it is an integral part of the Department of Economic Development.

The MSC Careers and Occupational Information Centre publishes material to help people looking for jobs to make an informed choice, and distributes careers literature to some 15,000 schools, careers offices and other centres.

TRAINING SERVICES

Over half of the occupational training in Britain is carried out and funded by employers. Statutory industrial training boards operate in seven industries to ensure adequate training by raising a levy from employers and disbursing grants for approved training. The majority of boards may exempt employers whose training is satisfactory from payment of most of the levy. In other industries, non-statutory training bodies, membership of which is voluntary, take responsibility for the development and encouragement of training.

The Government funds training through the MSC. In recent years the MSC has evolved a comprehensive strategy to help to improve the supply of trained manpower needed by the economy, to provide opportunities for people to acquire new skills, and to improve the effectiveness of training generally. In 1981 the Government announced a new initiative on training based on three important objectives for the 1980s and beyond: better arrangements for skill training to agreed standards; improving the vocational education and training of all young people; and opening up more opportunities for adults to train.

Development of Youth Training

The Youth Training Scheme, introduced in Great Britain in 1983, was expanded from April 1986 so that it now offers two years of training for 16-year-old school-leavers (including at least 20 weeks off-the-job training) and one year for

17-year-old school-leavers, with a minimum of seven weeks off-the-job training. The scheme is primarily employer-based and is open to both employed and unemployed young people. All trainees will have the opportunity to obtain a vocational qualification or credit towards such a qualification, and a certificate giving their qualifications and experience. Broadly based training is provided in the first year, with more specific training thereafter. Over 1 million young people participated in the original one-year scheme and about 60 per cent of those leaving went into jobs. In 1986–87 about 360,000 people are expected to enter the two-year programme and by 1988–89, when it is fully in operation, about 500,000 people are likely to be in training at any one time, up to 200,000 more than under the original programme. Government funding is planned to rise from £800 million in 1985–86 to £925 million in 1986–87 and to over £1,100 million in 1988–89.

In Northern Ireland the Youth Training Programme, launched in 1982 and administered jointly by the Northern Ireland Department of Economic Development and the Department of Education, is intended to meet the vocational education and training needs of young people in the two years following the minimum school-leaving age of 16. In their first year the young people receive off-the-job training, work experience and further education, and in the second year they are able to develop their vocational skills within employment (with at least eight weeks off-the-job training and/or further education) or within full-time training. In 1986–87 some 17,800 young people are expected to enter the programme.

The Technical and Vocational Education Initiative, administered by the MSC in Great Britain in co-operation with local education authorities, is intended to stimulate the provision of technical and vocational education for 14- to 18-year-olds. Projects provide an integrated course of full-time education leading to nationally recognised qualifications. Some 85 per cent of education authorities are operating or have applied to run such schemes, and by mid-1986, 74 projects were in operation, covering some 39,500 students. The results of these pilot projects have been encouraging, and the Government has announced the extension of the initiative to give all those aged between 14 and 18 the opportunity to experience the wider curriculum available.

Vocational Qualifications

Following the report of a review group, a major reform of the system of vocational qualifications is being implemented. A new national framework of such qualifications, to be called the National Vocational Qualification, will be fully operational in England, Wales and Northern Ireland by 1991. A National Council for Vocational Qualifications has been set up and will be responsible for developing and monitoring the framework and accrediting qualifications of bodies offering awards within it.

Adult Training

In line with the new initiative on training, in 1984 the MSC launched its adult training strategy, under which its adult training programmes have been restructured to provide help for a substantially greater number of people, and training has been more closely directed towards the skills needed by employers. The number participating in the adult training programmes rose from some 100,000 in 1983–84 to 220,000 in 1985–86.

The MSC's largest programme is the Job Training Scheme, which complements the training given in industry and commerce by providing people aged 18 and over with the opportunity to acquire new skills and improve existing skills. Training is carried out in a nationwide network of skillcentres under the control of the MSC's Skills Training Agency and at many colleges and other training providers. About 500 different courses are available in a wide range of occupations. Greater emphasis is being given to training for those running or hoping to start small businesses. The MSC's Training for Enterprise Scheme offers courses in business management skills to those interested in becoming self-employed or running a small business.

The MSC also provides support for employers' training efforts to help improve the skills of the workforce and to encourage more and better training. A programme of local grants to employers provides help for training employers' workforces or new recruits, and the National Priority Skills Scheme is run through industrial training organisations to help to tackle key skill needs. The adult training strategy aims to develop a better and more responsive training system, by using its own training programmes to demonstrate to employers and individuals the benefits of good training and by encouraging training providers to be responsive to labour market needs and modern training methods.

Training for the unemployed in basic work-related skills is being expanded under the Wider Opportunities Programme. The MSC is paying particular attention to improving the way training is carried out. Increased use of open learning methods and materials is being supported through the Open Tech Programme, with the aim of making training at technical and supervisory levels available to all adults who can benefit from it in a form which can be adapted to meet their own study circumstances. By April 1986, 250,000 people had participated in the Open Tech Programme and by April 1987 the number involved is expected to have increased to 500,000. A pilot training loans scheme, designed to encourage adults to undertake vocational training of their choice, was launched for a three-year period in April 1986.

The Skills Training Agency provides training services to employers in a wide range of trades designed to equip selected employees with new or improved skills of direct and immediate benefit to their companies. This training, specially tailored to the employer's needs, is carried out either at the local skillcentre or, using the Agency's Mobile Training Service, in the company's own premises. The Agency also provides training for overseas clients, either training students in Britain or sending instructors abroad.

CONDITIONS OF EMPLOYMENT The Employment Protection (Consolidation) Act 1978 provides a number of safeguards for employees. For example, most employees are entitled to receive from their employers written information on their terms and conditions of employment, disciplinary rules and the procedure available to employees wishing to raise complaints; minimum periods of notice when employment is to be terminated are also laid down for both employers and employees. Employees with a minimum period of service of two years are entitled to lump-sum redundancy payments if their jobs cease to exist (for example, because of technological improvements or a fall in demand) and their employers cannot offer suitable alternative work, the cost being partly met from a fund subscribed to by both sides of industry. Protection against unfair dismissal is provided by machinery under which an employee who has been in continuous employment, normally for two years or more, may complain against an employer of unfair dismissal, and, if successful, obtain reinstatement, re-engagement or compensation. Legal support is given to the right to trade union organisation (with certain exceptions) by making it unfair to dismiss a person because of membership or participation in the activities of an independent trade union; rights of employees are also protected in regard to penalisation short of dismissal because of trade union membership or activities. Other rights for employees include limited payment when work is not available for reasons other than as a result of a strike, lock-out or other industrial action, and maternity rights for female employees.

Legislation forbids any employment of children under 14 years of age, and employment in any industrial undertaking of children who have not reached the statutory minimum school-leaving age (16).

Immigrant Workers

In general, people coming to Britain for employment need a work permit issued by the Department of Employment. Among other conditions, work permits are issued only for work requiring a recognised professional qualification, or a high degree of skill or experience, where the Department is satisfied that the worker is necessary and there is no suitable worker in Britain or in other European Community countries to fill the post. In general, the age limits for permits in most categories are 23 to 54 years. People coming for certain kinds of specialist employment (for example, ministers of religion and representatives of the overseas media) and the self-employed do not require work permits but may require entry clearances issued by a British Consulate or High Commission.

Permits are also issued under the Training and Work Experience Scheme for nationals of countries outside the European Community who are undertaking limited periods of training or work experience leading to the acquisition of a particular occupational skill or qualification and to young people from outside the European Community to undertake short periods of employment to broaden their work experience and, if appropriate, to improve their knowledge of English.

European Community workers entering another member state have the same rights as nationals of that state as regards facilities of the national employment services, pay and working conditions, trade union rights, vocational training facilities, access to housing and property, and social security and industrial injury benefits.

Discrimination

The Race Relations Act 1976 makes it unlawful to discriminate on grounds of colour, race, nationality (including citizenship) or ethnic or national origin, in employment, training and related matters. The Department of Employment operates a Race Relations Employment Advisory Service with advisers based in the main areas where there are large ethnic minority communities. Its general aim is to promote equal opportunity in employment and its advisers offer help and guidance to employers and unions on a wide range of issues which arise in the employment of a multiracial workforce. The Commission for Racial Equality's code of practice gives practical guidance to employers and others on the best arrangements for implementing policies to eliminate racial discrimination and to enhance equality of opportunity.

Equal Opportunities

The Sex Discrimination Act 1975 makes it unlawful to discriminate on the grounds of sex or marital status in employment, training and related matters. The Equal Pay Act 1970, as amended in 1984, requires that a woman doing the same or broadly similar work as a man, or work which has an equal value, should receive equal pay and conditions of employment. The Sex Discrimination Bill includes provisions which would result in British legislation conforming more fully to a European Community directive on equal treatment. The Bill would also make unlawful the dismissal of a woman on the grounds of age when a man in similar circumstances was allowed to continue in employment.

Earnings

Pay rates for manual occupations, and increasingly for non-manual occupations, are normally set by collective bargaining (see p 345). Basic rates of pay vary widely, and in private industry rates paid locally often exceed the rates specified in national agreements. Higher rates are usually paid for overtime and shift work, and weekly earnings may be further increased by incentive bonus schemes.

According to the latest available information from the Department of Employment's New Earnings Survey, the average weekly earnings (including overtime payments) in April 1985 of full-time employees on adult rates were £171 (£192·40 for men and £126·40 for women). Earnings were higher for non-manual employees (£184·60) than for manual employees (£153). Some 49 per cent of manual employees and 19 per cent of non-manual employees received overtime payments. Women's earnings are markedly lower than those of men, partly because on average they work shorter hours, with less overtime paid at premium rates, and partly because they tend to be concentrated in the less well-paid jobs.

Remuneration in commercial, technical and professional careers is normally by annual salary paid monthly, often on a scale carrying annual increments. Most of the senior posts in business, the professions and the Civil Service command salaries in the range of £15,000 to £30,000 a year gross before tax. The posts with salaries in the range of £30,000 to £100,000 a year include those of Cabinet ministers, top-ranking judicial appointments, the highest positions in government departments and the largest municipal authorities, editors of daily newspapers, leading members of professions and the higher managerial posts in industry, commerce and banking. A number of company directors have salaries exceeding £100,000 a year and some other people, such as leading pop musicians and other star entertainers, may receive similar amounts through fees, royalties or fixed contracts.

Hours of Work The basic working week in Great Britain is in the range 37·5 to 40 hours for manual work and 35 to 38 for non-manual work; a five-day week is usually worked. Actual hours worked differ from basic hours; in 1985 for full-time employees they were 41·9 for men compared with 37·3 for women. Men and women in non-manual occupations generally work less overtime than manual workers.

Legislation limits the permissible hours of work for young people. Hours of work of adult men and of women in non-industrial jobs are not restricted by statute, but the maximum hours of women employed in industrial undertakings are controlled and, in addition, they are not allowed to work at night or perform shiftwork. However, the Sex Discrimination Bill would provide for the removal of these restrictions.

Holidays with Pay Apart from industries where conditions are controlled by wages councils (see p 347), there are no general statutory entitlements to holidays, and holiday entitlements are normally determined by collective agreements. These generally provide for at least four weeks' paid holiday a year, and over 80 per cent of manual workers covered by national collective agreements have entitlements of more than four weeks, with some 20 per cent having five weeks or more. Non-manual workers tend to have longer holidays than manual workers. Holiday entitlements may also be dependent upon length of service.

Additional Benefits Additional benefits exist in varying degrees. About half of employees in employment are covered by pension schemes provided by their employers. Many employees are also covered by occupational sick pay schemes which are additional or complementary to the state schemes, and by schemes to provide private medical treatment. A smaller number are covered by schemes for redundancy payments above the statutory minimum. Such benefits are more usual among clerical and professional employees receiving a standard salary than among manual workers. Employees may have use of a company car and some firms provide profit-sharing and share-saving schemes. The Government has encouraged employee share ownership by extending tax reliefs to profit-sharing and share option schemes. The number of schemes open to all employees in a company has increased from less than 30 in 1979 to over 1,000 in 1986 involving over 1·25 million workers. The provision of low-priced meals at the place of employment is usual in large undertakings and quite common in smaller ones. Many offices and shops which are unable to provide canteen facilities for their staff have adopted luncheon voucher schemes. Among the other executive fringe benefits sometimes available are life assurance, free medical insurance, telephone allowances and low-interest loans.

TRADE UNIONS

Trade unions have members in virtually every occupation and represent nearly half the working population. As well as negotiating pay and other terms and conditions of employment with employers, they provide certain benefits and services—for example, educational facilities, legal advice and benefit payments during industrial disputes—which vary from union to union. Trade unions vary widely in the composition of their membership, and may be organised either by occupation (for example, they may recruit clerks or fitters wherever employed) or by industry, while some are based on a combination of both.

During the 1970s trade unionism increased, particularly among clerical, supervisory, technical and administrative workers, but in the 1980s there has been a decline, greater than the fall in employment, reflecting the relatively greater decline in certain industries (especially in manufacturing) with a high level of union membership. At the end of 1984 the total membership of British trade unions was about 11·1 million, of whom 79 per cent were in the 22 largest unions with over 100,000 members. The number of unions has also fallen as there has been an increase in mergers, and a number of small unions and of long-established craft unions have been absorbed by larger unions. At the end of 1985 there were 409 trade unions on the list maintained by the Certification Officer under the Employment Protection Act 1975. To be eligible for entry on the list a trade union must show that it consists wholly or mainly of workers and that its principal purposes include the regulation of relations between workers and employers, or between workers and employers' associations. Certain rights and privileges are reserved for independent trade unions.

Among the largest unions are the Transport and General Workers Union (1·5 million members), the Amalgamated Engineering Union (1 million) and the General, Municipal, Boilermakers and Allied Trades Union (847,000); of the non-manual workers' unions, the largest are the National and Local Government Officers' Association (766,000 members) and the National Union of Public Employees (673,000).

The central organisation of most unions consists of a national executive council, usually elected by a secret ballot of the individual members of the union and responsible to the annual conference of delegates from local branches. Between conferences, councils are the highest authority of unions, and carry out policy decisions made by the conference delegates. Most unions also have regional and district organisations. At the level of the individual member there are local branches, covering one or more workplaces. The organising of members in individual places of work, and the negotiation of local pay agreements with management at the workplace, may be done by full-time district officials of the union, or, in many cases, by workplace representatives, often called 'shop stewards', who are chosen by their fellow members in the place of work to represent them. Where two or more unions have members in the same workplace, representatives' or shop stewards' committees may be formed to discuss matters of common concern.

A number of trade unions are affiliated to the Labour Party and some sponsor Members of Parliament. Any trade union wishing to use money for political purposes must set up a separate fund, subject to special rules, one of which must allow any member who objects to contributing to the fund to opt out. Some 5·9 million members contribute to a political fund and at the end of 1985, 50 unions maintained such a fund.

Trades Union Congress

In Britain the national centre of the trade union movement is the Trades Union Congress (TUC), which was founded in 1868. The TUC's objects are to promote the interests of its affiliated organisations and to improve the economic and social conditions of working people. Its affiliated membership comprises 91 trade unions which together represent 9·9 million people, or some 90 per cent of all trade unionists in Britain, and it exercises power through influence rather than through sanctions. The TUC deals with all general questions which concern trade unions, both nationally and internationally, and provides a forum in which affiliated unions can collectively determine policy. It is consulted by the Secretary of State for Employment before the appointment of employee representatives on the Manpower Services Commission, the Advisory, Conciliation and Arbitration Service and certain other official bodies with an interest in employment matters. There are eight TUC regional councils for England, and a Wales Trades Union Council.

The annual Congress convenes in September to discuss matters of concern to trade unionists. A General Council represents it between Congresses and is responsible for carrying out Congress decisions, watching economic and social developments, providing educational and advisory services to unions, and presenting to the Government the trade union viewpoint on economic, social and industrial issues. The TUC is also empowered to mediate in inter-union disputes in certain circumstances, and uses its authority to try to resolve such difficulties.

The TUC, as well as many individual unions, conducts extensive educational services for members, mainly concerned with industrial subjects, trade unionism, and the principles and practice of industrial relations.

The TUC plays an active part in international trade union activity, through its affiliation to the International Confederation of Free Trade Unions and the European Trade Union Confederation. It also nominates the British workers' delegation to the annual International Labour Conference.

Scotland and Northern Ireland

Trade unions in Scotland also have their own national central body, the Scottish Trades Union Congress, which in many respects is similar in constitution and function to the TUC. Trade unions in Northern Ireland are represented by the Northern Ireland Committee of the Irish Congress of Trade Unions (ICTU), although the majority of trade unionists in Northern Ireland belong to unions based in Great Britain. Over 75 per cent of Northern Ireland trade unionists are members of organisations affiliated to the ICTU, while the majority belong to unions which are also affiliated to the TUC. The Northern Ireland Committee of the ICTU has no political affiliations and enjoys a high degree of autonomy.

Legal Framework

The beginnings of the present law on industrial relations were established a century ago, when trade union members were freed from liability to charges of criminal conspiracy; at the same time trade unions were granted certain immunities, including immunity from liability to damages for the economic effects of strike action. Peaceful picketing during strikes was also made legal. At the beginning of the present century unions were given a wide degree of immunity from legal action under the civil law, and the immunities of those organising industrial action were also strengthened.

The Employment Acts 1980 and 1982 were designed to obtain a better balance between rights and responsibilities in industrial relations. The 1980 Act enabled the Government to make funds available to encourage the wider use of secret union ballots and to produce codes of practice to promote good industrial relations. It limited lawful picketing to the picket's own place of work and restricted the scope for secondary action such as blacking and sympathetic strikes. It provided greater protection for the individual working in a 'closed shop' (that is, under an agreement between the employer and one or more unions that union membership is a condition of employment) and removed legal protection from any new closed shop which had not been approved in a secret ballot by 80 per cent of the employees affected. As provided for in the Act, the Government has published codes of practice on the conduct of picketing and the closed shop. Illegal activities such as violence on picket lines are subject to the criminal law, which is enforced by the police, but unlawful picketing is a matter for employers to restrain by means of civil law.

The 1982 Act was designed to carry the process further. It increased the compensation for employees unfairly dismissed for non-membership or membership of a union and introduced compensation (from government funds) for certain employees dismissed because of non-membership of a union in a closed shop between 1974 and 1980, when they had no protection. The Act also removed legal protection from all closed shops (not only from new ones, as in the 1980 Act) where within two years of the legislation taking effect the closed shop had not been supported in a secret ballot held in the previous five years by 80 per cent of the employees affected or by 85 per cent of those voting in the ballot. Where legal protection is removed, any dismissal for non-membership of a union is unfair. Terms in commercial contracts specifying the use of union labour only were made unenforceable and discrimination on the basis of union membership in the awarding of contracts was made unlawful. Industrial action which seeks to persuade employers to discriminate in this way or to interfere with the supply of goods or services on grounds of union membership is unlawful. The Act also ended the position which gave trade unions almost complete immunity from all civil actions by bringing their position into line with that of their individual officials and members. This means that trade unions now have immunity only for action taken in furtherance or contemplation of a lawful trade dispute. There were also changes to the definition of a trade dispute upon which immunity for civil actions depends. Disputes between employer and employees (that is, most industrial action) continue to qualify as lawful trade disputes, but disputes which have become unlawful are those where there is no disagreement between an employer and his or her employees, or those which have little to do with the normal subject of a trade dispute (such as terms and conditions of work).

The Trade Union Act 1984 was introduced by the Government to increase democracy in trade unions. It requires that all voting members of the principal executive committee of a union should be elected by a secret and direct ballot of the members at least once every five years, and requires unions to compile and maintain a register of members' names and addresses. It also removes legal immunity from trade unions which call a strike or take other industrial action without first holding a secret ballot of members concerned and securing a majority vote for this action. In addition, the Act requires trade unions with political funds to ballot their members at regular intervals to decide whether the funds should be retained. Unless members had been balloted in the previous ten years, trade unions with political funds were required to hold a ballot in 1985–86 and all of the 38 unions involved voted to retain their funds. In general, the new legislation was opposed by the TUC and by most trade unions, and the TUC is looking at industrial relations legislation with a view to putting forward alternative proposals.

Northern Ireland has a broadly similar but separate system of industrial relations legislation.

EMPLOYERS' ORGANI- SATIONS

Many employers in Britain are members of employers' organisations, some of which are wholly concerned with labour matters although others are also concerned with commercial matters or trade associations. The primary aims of such organisations are to help to establish suitable terms and conditions of employment, including a sound wage structure and proper standards of safety, health and welfare; to promote good relations with employees and the efficient use of manpower; and to provide means of settling any disputes which may arise. Combined employers' organisations and trade associations may also represent members' points of view as manufacturers or traders to the Government on commercial matters.

Employers' organisations are usually organised on an industry basis rather than a product basis, for example, the Engineering Employers' Federation. A few are purely local in character or deal with a section of an industry or, for example, with small businesses; most are national and are concerned with the whole of an industry. In some of the main industries there are local or regional organisations combined into national federations, while in others, within which different firms are engaged in making different principal products, there is a complex structure with national and regional federations for parts of an industry as well as for the industry as a whole. Altogether there are some 340 employers' associations known to the Certification Officer. Those which are national organisations negotiate the national collective agreements for their industry with the trade unions concerned; most of these national organisations belong to the Confederation of British Industry.

Confederation of British Industry

The Confederation of British Industry (CBI) is the largest central employers' organisation in Britain, representing directly or indirectly some 250,000 businesses which together employ about half the working population. It aims primarily to ensure that Government, national and international institutions and the public understand the needs, intentions and problems of business. Membership ranges from the smallest to the largest companies, private sector and nationalised, and covers a broad spectrum which includes manufacturing, agriculture, construction, distribution, mining, finance, retailing and insurance. Most national employers' organisations, trade associations and some chambers of commerce are members. Policy is determined by a council of 400 members, and there is a permanent staff of 340, while there are 13 regional offices and an office in Brussels. The CBI is the British member of the Union of Industries of the European Community. The CBI nominates the employers' representatives on a number of bodies including the National Economic Development Council, the Manpower Services Commission, the Health and Safety Commission and the Advisory, Conciliation and Arbitration Service.

INDUSTRIAL RELATIONS

The structure of industrial relations in Britain has been established mainly on a voluntary basis. The system is based chiefly on the organisation of employees and employers into trade unions and employers' associations, and on freely conducted negotiations at all levels. The government-funded, but independent, Advisory, Conciliation and Arbitration Service (ACAS) provides its services where the usual methods of resolving disagreements have failed. Because of the publicity they receive, strikes are commonly thought to occur much more frequently in Britain than in other countries. International comparisons show, however, that Britain's record on industrial disputes is better than those of a number of other major industrialised countries. In 1985 some 6·4 million working days were lost in Britain through industrial stoppages, of which about two-thirds were accounted for by a major dispute in the coal industry, while the number of recorded disputes was the lowest for nearly 50 years.

Collective Bargaining and Joint Consultation

In most industries terms and conditions of employment and procedures for the conduct of industrial relations are settled by negotiation and agreement between employers or employers' associations and trade unions. Agreements may be industry-wide, as is generally the case in the public sector, but are often supplemented by local agreements in companies or factories (plant bargaining), and bargaining and consultation are increasingly being conducted at plant level.

In some industries, companies and factories, negotiations are conducted by meetings held when necessary, while in others, joint negotiating councils or committees have been established on a permanent basis. The scope of the various bodies (from national joint industrial councils for whole industries to works councils and committees in individual workplaces) varies widely, and can cover such additional matters as production plans, investment, training, education, welfare and safety. Normally these arrangements for collective bargaining suffice to settle all questions which are raised, but there is often provision for matters not so settled to be referred for settlement to independent conciliation or arbitration. The Employment Protection Act 1975 as amended by the Employment Act 1980 makes provision for information needed for collective bargaining purposes to be disclosed by employers to trade unions, subject to certain safeguards.

Advisory, Conciliation and Arbitration Service

The Advisory, Conciliation and Arbitration Service is an independent statutory body with the general duty of promoting the improvement of industrial relations, and in particular of encouraging collective bargaining and the development and (where necessary) reform of collective bargaining machinery. ACAS is controlled by a council consisting of a full-time chairman and nine part-time members experienced in industrial relations, of whom three are nominated after consultation with the CBI, three after consultation with the TUC, and three are independent. The Service conciliates in industrial disputes in both the public and private sectors. ACAS assistance is sought in some 1,500 disputes each year. In addition, there are some 160 further requests a year for ACAS to provide arbitration, which it may do either by appointing single arbitrators or boards of arbitration or by referring cases to the Central Arbitration Committee (see below). Although ACAS has prime responsibility for helping to resolve disputes, and has also set up major committees of inquiry, the Secretary of State for Employment retains powers to appoint a court of inquiry or committee of investigation into a dispute, but these are rarely used.

The Service gives advice on all aspects of industrial relations and employment policies to employers, managers, trade unions, employee representatives and individuals, and it handles nearly 280,000 inquiries a year. Specialist staff make nearly 10,000 advisory visits a year. ACAS also carries particular responsibility for attempting conciliation on complaints of infringement of individual employee rights (such as individual complaints of unfair dismissal, complaints under the Equal Pay Act 1970, including claims for equal pay for work of equal value, and complaints on employment matters under the Sex Discrimination Act 1975 and the Race Relations Act 1976). There are nearly 43,000 such cases each year. In 1985 the Work Research Unit, whose task is to promote, jointly through trade unions and employers, the improvement of work structures and the quality of working life, was incorporated within ACAS.

Central Arbitration Committee

The Central Arbitration Committee is an independent standing arbitration body. It provides boards of arbitration for the settlement of trade disputes referred to it with the consent of the parties concerned and adjudicates on claims, including those made under the disclosure of information provisions of the Employment Protection Act and under the Equal Pay Act.

Office of Manpower Economics

The Office of Manpower Economics is an independent non-statutory organisation responsible for servicing independent review bodies which advise on the pay of various public-sector groups. These are the Top Salaries Review Body, the Armed Forces' Pay Review Body, the Doctors' and Dentists' Review Body, and the Review Body for Nurses and other National Health Service professions. The Office also provides services for the Pharmacists' Review Panel, the Police

Negotiating Board and the Civil Service Arbitration Tribunal. It is responsible for research into pay and associated matters as requested by the Government.

Wages Councils

In a small number of industries and trades where the organisation of employers or employees or both is not strong enough to provide a basis for successful voluntary arrangements, there are statutory wage-regulating bodies, known as wages councils. These are composed of equal numbers of representatives of employers and employees in the respective sector, with three independent members. There are 26 wages councils covering about 2·75 million workers, primarily in service industries such as retailing, catering and hairdressing. The system has been criticised as an obstacle to the creation of jobs, and the Wages Act 1986 provides for changes in the powers and functions of wages councils with the intention of simplifying the requirements imposed by the councils. Wages orders will be restricted to workers aged 21 or over and the councils will be able to set only a single minimum hourly rate, a single overtime rate and a limit on deductions for accommodation provided. Before making an order, a council will be required to consider the effect on employment.

HEALTH AND SAFETY AT WORK

Employers have a duty at civil and criminal law to take reasonable care of their employees, and others affected by their work activities, and to provide a safe system of working, while employees have a duty of care towards each other and also to take care of their own safety. The principal legislation is the Health and Safety at Work etc. Act 1974. Its purpose is to secure the health, safety and welfare of people at work and to provide for the protection of the public whose health and safety might be affected by work activities. The Act places general duties on everyone concerned with work activities, including employers, the self-employed, employees, manufacturers and suppliers.

The 1974 Act is superimposed on earlier health and safety legislation, such as the Mines and Quarries Act 1954, the Factories Act 1961 and the Offices, Shops and Railway Premises Act 1963 and the various regulations made under them. The earlier legislation imposes specific obligations and standards on, for example, occupiers of particular types of premises or employers engaged in particular activities and covers such matters as the fencing of machinery, precautions against the exposure of people to toxic dusts and gases, precautions against fire, dangerous substances and special risks, the safe condition of premises, and cleanliness, lighting, temperature and ventilation.

Some of the earlier legislation was replaced immediately by the 1974 Act, but the remainder continues in force pending its progressive replacement by regulations and codes of practice. Regulations made under the Act govern the establishment of first-aid facilities, the control of work with lead and the control of major accident hazards in industry, each set being supported by either an approved code of practice or other guidance material, and there are others in the course of development.

A basic principle underlying the 1974 Act is that employers, in consultation with their employees, should have the responsibility of working out health and safety arrangements, within the broad obligations of the law, to suit their own workplaces. Employers with five or more employees must draw up a written policy for safety and health, and must inform their employees of the policy and of the arrangements for its implementation. In workplaces where negotiations take place with a trade union, the union may appoint safety representatives to be the employees' official channel for representation and consultation over safety matters.

The Health and Safety Commission

The Health and Safety Commission, established by the 1974 Act and account-able to Parliament through the Secretary of State for Employment, has responsibility for developing policies, including guidance, codes of practice, or proposals for regulations. In the case of proposals for changes in legislation, the Commission consults the people who will be affected by them and makes recommendations to the Secretary of State concerned. The Commission has an independent chairman, three members appointed after consultation with the CBI, three after consultation with the TUC, and two after consultation with local authority associations. The Commission has six subject advisory committees (on toxic substances, on dangerous substances, on dangerous pathogens, on genetic manipulation, on the safety of nuclear installations, and on medical matters), and 11 industry advisory committees, for agriculture, ceramics, construction, education, foundries, health services, oil, paper and board, printing, railways and rubber.

The Health and Safety Executive

The 1974 Act also set up the Health and Safety Executive, which includes government inspectorates covering a range of work activities: the Factory Inspectorate (which also deals with a large number of activities outside factories such as hospitals and educational establishments) and inspectorates for mines and quarries, agriculture, major sources of industrial air pollution, nuclear installations, and explosives. It also includes the Medical Division and the Research and Laboratory Services Division. The inspectors, who have powers of entry and enforcement, seek compliance with health and safety legislation in individual workplaces and give advice. The Medical Division, through the Employment Medical Advisory Service, provides a nationwide service of advice on the medical aspects of employment problems to employers, employees, trade unions, doctors and others.

The Research and Laboratory Services Division provides scientific and medical support and testing services, and carries out research both in its own laboratories and through universities and other institutions on a contract basis, often jointly funded by industry. Areas of study include explosion risks, fires, protective equipment, methods for monitoring airborne contaminants, occupational medicine and hygiene, and the safety of engineering systems.

In some premises, mostly offices, shops, warehouses, restaurants and hotels, health and safety legislation is enforced by inspectors appointed by local authorities, working under guidance from the Health and Safety Commission. Some other official bodies work under agency agreement with the Health and Safety Commission, for example, the Railway Inspectorate (concerned with worker safety on railways), the Industrial Pollution Inspectorate for Scotland (concerned with the control of emissions to the atmosphere) and the Department of Energy (concerned with health and safety in the oil industry).

Northern Ireland

In Northern Ireland, the Health and Safety Agency, roughly corresponding to the Health and Safety Commission, and an Employment Medical Advisory Service were set up by the Health and Safety at Work (NI) Order 1978. The Northern Ireland Department of Economic Development, through its Health and Safety Inspectorate, is responsible for ensuring compliance with health and safety legislation, which is broadly similar to that for Great Britain.

17 Public Finance

Public finance is concerned with taxation, expenditure and borrowing by central and local government and the financing of public corporations. Central government raises money from individuals and companies by direct and indirect taxation and from National Insurance contributions. It spends money on goods and services, such as health and defence, and in payments to people, such as social security and pensions. Local government receives substantial grants from central government and raises revenue mainly through rates (local property taxes). From these resources it provides services such as education, police and fire services, and refuse collection. The external finance of the nationalised industries and other public corporations also has to be financed by government—from taxation or borrowing. The diagram (see p 357) shows the relative importance of the various items of receipts (including borrowing) and expenditure for the public sector.

The government department responsible for broad control of public finance and expenditure is the Treasury. The Bank of England (the central bank) advises the Government on financial matters, executes monetary policy and acts as banker to the Government.

PLANNING PUBLIC FINANCE

The background to the present Government's planning of public finance is the medium-term financial strategy introduced in 1980. The Government's aim is to maintain a firm financial framework, with a progressive reduction in monetary growth and public borrowing as a proportion of national output, in order to secure a fall in inflation and create the conditions for sustainable growth. With commitments also to reduce taxation and curb the role of the state, the Government has therefore sought to reduce public expenditure as a proportion of national output as well. The objective is to hold public expenditure broadly level in real terms so that economic growth will lead to the reduction sought. Public expenditure as a proportion of gross domestic product fell from over 46 per cent in the early 1980s to 44·5 per cent in 1985–86. A continued steady decline is projected, to 41 per cent by 1988–89.

Table 33, showing projections for the public sector borrowing requirement, indicates the planning total for public expenditure rising from £139,100 million in 1986–87 to £153,000 million in 1989–90.

The Planning Cycle

Each year the Government conducts a review (the 'public expenditure survey') of its expenditure plans for the forthcoming three years and publishes the resulting totals, together with any changes in National Insurance, in the Autumn Statement around November. Details of these plans and of the aims of government expenditure and the output obtained are given in the annual public expenditure White Paper which appears early in the following year, before the Budget.

The Government's updating of the medium-term financial strategy and consequent plans for financing expenditure over the following year, including any tax changes, are set out in the *Financial Statement and Budget Report*, published with the Budget around the end of the financial year (31 March). Details are announced subsequently in the Finance Bill, which is presented to Parliament shortly after the Budget and becomes law during the summer.

Table 33: Projections of the Public Sector Borrowing Requirement

£ thousand million

	1986–87	1987–88	1988–89	1989–90
General government expenditure	163	170	175	180
Public expenditure planning total	139	144	149	153
General government receipts	156	164	174	182
of which: taxes	118	124	132	139
National Insurance	26	28	29	31
Fiscal adjustments[a]	—	2	6	9
Market and overseas borrowing of public corporations	—	−1	—	—
Public sector borrowing requirement	7	7	7	7
Per cent of gross domestic product	1·75	1·75	1·5	1·5

Source: *Financial Statement and Budget Report 1986–87.*
[a] These imply lower taxes or higher expenditure than assumed in the figures for general government expenditure and receipts.
Differences between totals and the sums of their component parts are due to rounding.

PUBLIC EXPENDITURE

Planned public expenditure for 1986–87 has been set at just over £139,000 million. Of this, £103,000 million is allocated to central government, £35,000 million to local authorities and £2,000 million to nationalised industries and other public corporations (excluding those to be privatised in 1986–87). The reserve (see below) accounts for £4,500 million. In line with international conventions, proceeds from privatisation, projected at £4,750 million, count as negative public expenditure.

Central government spending is largely voted by Parliament through the annual Supply Estimates (see p 352). The rest consists mainly of those social security payments which are made out of the National Insurance Fund. The largest departmental programmes are those on social security payments (31 per cent of planned departmental spending in 1986–87), defence, and health and personal social services (each 13 per cent). See Table 34.

About half of local authority spending is financed by grants from central government. The rest is met from rates and from borrowing. Education accounts for around one-third of local authority spending.

Of the total contribution of public corporations to the planning total, about half is attributable to the external finance (that is, grants from the Government and borrowing within Britain and from overseas) of the nationalised industries.

Of planned expenditure in 1986–87, cash payments to the personal sector—for example, pensions and other social security benefits—comprise over one-third; pay (other than that included in departmental running costs) and purchases of goods and services each about one-quarter; and departmental running costs a little under one-tenth. The economic breakdown of each department's spending varies. Planned capital spending in 1986–87 by central and local government is £14,200 million and that by nationalised industries and other public corporations £4,600 million.

Reserve

Planned expenditure includes an unallocated reserve to cover all additions to departmental spending during the year, whether arising from revisions to the estimated size of demand-led programmes, policy changes or new initiatives. For 1986–87 the reserve is £4,500 million. Larger amounts have initially been set for each of the next two years but some will normally be allocated to departments as spending plans are made firmer.

Table 34: Planned Expenditure by Central Government Departments and Local Authorities 1986–87

£ million

	Central government[a]	Local authorities[a]
Defence	18,525	—
Foreign and Commonwealth Office	1,959	—
European Community	650	—
Agriculture, Fisheries and Food	2,017	152
Trade and Industry	1,512	70
Energy	115	—
Employment	3,639	102
Transport	2,396	2,379
Environment—housing	1,338	1,480
Environment—other environmental services	599	3,105
Home Office	1,524	4,026
Education and Science	2,469	11,850
Arts and Libraries	321	412
Health and Social Security—health and personal social services	15,120	2,604
Health and Social Security—social security	39,724	3,207
Scotland	3,731	3,784
Wales	1,450	1,435
Northern Ireland	3,707	640
Chancellor's departments	1,995	—
Other departments	1,526	—
Totals	104,320[b]	35,246

Source: *The Government's Expenditure Plans 1986–87 to 1988–89* (the public expenditure White Paper).
[a] Including finance for public corporations.
[b] Difference between total and the sum of its component parts is due to rounding.
Note: Expenditures on certain services (such as education) are made under the programmes for Scotland, Wales and Northern Ireland in addition to other departmental programmes.

Cash Limits

Some 40 per cent of public expenditure is subject to control by cash limits (external financing limits in the case of nationalised industries). Another 40 per cent consists of demand-led services (for example, social security benefits) on which, once policy and rates of payment have been determined, expenditure in the short run depends on the number of eligible recipients. The remaining 20 per cent is current expenditure of local authorities, which central government does not directly control; however, the major part of the contribution by central government to such expenditure, the rate support grant, is subject to cash limits.

Once fixed, cash limits are not usually revised during the course of the year unless a decision is taken to alter the level of provision for the service concerned. There is, however, a limited facility for carrying forward underspending on the capital components of cash limits. If any overspending of cash limits occurs, a corresponding deduction is normally made from the limits for the following year.

The Estimates

The annual public expenditure survey conducted by the Treasury provides the basis for the Estimates which each government department submits to the Treasury in December, giving details of its cash requirements for the financial year beginning in the following April. After approval by the Treasury, these Supply Estimates are presented to Parliament in March, usually at the same time as the Budget (see p 353). Parliament approves them in July as part of the Annual Appropriation Act, expenditure between 1 April and this date being covered by Votes on Account approved before the start of the financial year. Supplementary Estimates may also be presented to Parliament during the course of the year. If any Supply Estimate is overspent, the Public Accounts Committee (see below) will investigate fully before Parliament is asked to approve any Excess Vote to balance the account. In each parliamentary session, up to three 'Estimates days' are available for debates on the Supply Estimates, following scrutiny by select committees of the House of Commons.

In 1986–87 the Supply Estimates totalled £99,000 million of which £75,000 million was direct spending by central government and £24,000 million transfers to other parts of the Government or the public sector. Some items of central government expenditure, for example, the salaries and pensions of judges, are paid directly out of the Consolidated Fund (see below) as standing services and are not subject to annual approval by Parliament.

Examination and Audit of Public Expenditure

Examination of public expenditure is carried out by select committees of the House of Commons, which study in detail the activities of particular government departments and require the attendance of ministers and officials for cross-examination. The audit of the Government's spending which follows up the control inherent in parliamentary approval of the Estimates is exercised through the functions of the Comptroller and Auditor General and the Public Accounts Committee.

Comptroller and Auditor General

The Comptroller and Auditor General, an officer of the House of Commons appointed by the Crown, has two distinct functions. As Comptroller General, he has the duty to ensure that all revenue and other public money payable to the Consolidated Fund and the National Loans Fund (see below) is duly paid and that all payments out of these funds are authorised by statute. As Auditor General, his duties are to certify the accounts of all government departments and those of a wide range of other public sector bodies; to examine revenue accounts and inventories; and to report the results of his examinations to Parliament. He also has wide statutory powers to carry out, and report to Parliament on, examinations of economy, efficiency and effectiveness in the use of resources by those bodies he audits or to which he has right of access.

Public Accounts Committee

The Public Accounts Committee considers the appropriation and other accounts of government departments and the Comptroller and Auditor General's reports on them and on the economy, efficiency and effectiveness of departments' use of their resources. The Committee takes evidence from the official heads of departments and relevant public sector bodies and submits to Parliament reports which carry considerable weight, and its recommendations are taken very seriously by the departments and organisations that it examines. The Government's formal reply to the reports is presented to Parliament by the Treasury in the form of Treasury minutes and the reports and minutes are usually debated annually in the House of Commons.

Central Government Financial Funds

The Government's sterling expenditure is largely met out of the Consolidated Fund, an account at the Bank of England into which tax receipts and other revenues are paid. This is also known as the Exchequer. Any excess of expenditure over receipts is met by the National Loans Fund, which is another official sterling account at the Bank of England and is the repository for funds borrowed by the Government. The National Insurance Fund, into which contributions are paid by all employers and employed people, is used mainly to pay for social security benefits; a small proportion of the Fund is used to help finance the National Health Service.

THE BUDGET

The Budget—usually in March or April—sets out the Government's proposals for changes in taxation and is the main occasion for an annual review of economic policy. The proposals are announced to the House of Commons by the Chancellor of the Exchequer in the Budget statement and are published in the *Financial Statement and Budget Report*. This report also contains a review of recent developments in the economy, together with an economic forecast—one of the two which the Government is required to publish each year (the other being contained in the Autumn Statement)—and sets out the fiscal and monetary framework within which economic policy operates. This is the medium-term financial strategy (see p 349).

The Budget statement is followed by the moving of a set of Ways and Means (or Budget) resolutions in which the proposals are embodied. When passed by the House of Commons, these resolutions give temporary effect, under the Provisional Collection of Taxes Act 1968, to certain of the tax proposals; they are the foundation of the Finance Bill, in which the proposals are set out for detailed consideration by Parliament, becoming law as the Finance Act, usually in the following July. The effect of the Provisional Collection of Taxes Act is thus to enable the Government to collect certain taxes provisionally, at the levels provided by the Budget proposals, pending enactment of the Finance Bill.

The bulk of the tax proposals are concerned with changes in the rates or coverage of taxes, the introduction of new taxes or the abolition of existing ones and changes in the administrative machinery. These changes are made not only with regard to the revenue required but also with regard to their effect on the way the economy performs.

For two taxes—income tax and corporation tax—annual Ways and Means resolutions followed by Finance Act clauses are required to maintain their existence, since they are annual rather than permanent taxes. Thus, a Budget and a Finance Act are necessary at or about the beginning of each financial year. Tax changes can be made at other times of the year, however, either by specific legislation or by the use of the regulator, which permits limited changes between Budgets in value added tax (by up to 25 per cent) and the main excise duties (by up to 10 per cent).

The 1986 Budget provided for a cut in the basic rate of income tax—from 30 per cent to 29 per cent—to improve incentives. It introduced the Personal Equity Plan to encourage wider share ownership. It also aimed to reduce unemployment, both through increasing flexibility in the labour market and by means of a programme of direct help.

**TAX
REVENUE**

The three principal sources of tax revenue are: taxes on income, which include income tax and corporation tax; taxes on capital, which include capital transfer tax and capital gains tax; and indirect taxes, which include customs and excise duties, value added tax (VAT), rates (which are set and collected by local authorities to help meet their expenditure), stamp duties and licence duties (for example, on motor vehicles).

Table 35 shows the provisional revenue of central government from taxation and other sources in 1985–86 and the forecasts for 1986–87.

Taxes on individual incomes are progressive in that larger incomes bear a proportionately higher rate of tax. Thresholds and rate bands for income tax, capital transfer tax and capital gains tax are raised automatically each year in line with the rise in retail prices over the previous calendar year unless the Government proposes otherwise and Parliament approves. The Inland Revenue assesses and collects the taxes on income and capital and the stamp duties. The Customs and Excise collects the most important taxes on expenditure (the customs and excise duties and VAT).

Taxes on Income

Income Tax

Income tax is imposed for the year of assessment beginning on 6 April. For 1986–87 the basic rate of 29 per cent applies to the first £17,200 of taxable income. A rate of 40 per cent applies to the £17,201–£20,200 band, 45 per cent to the £20,201–£25,400 band, 50 per cent to the £25,401–£33,300 band and 55 per cent to the £33,301–£41,200 band, ending with a maximum rate of 60 per cent on taxable income over £41,200. These rates apply to both earned and investment incomes.

A number of personal allowances and reliefs reduce the amount of a person's taxable income compared with gross income. The main allowances are £2,335 for the income of a single person or the earned income of a wife and £3,655 for the income of a married man. Among the most important of the reliefs is that for mortgage interest payments on borrowing for house purchase. Relief at the basic rate is usually given 'at source' (that is, passed directly by the tax authorities to the building society or bank making the loan rather than to the individual taxpayer). Another relief is that under the business expansion scheme, whereby certain investors in trading companies without a Stock Exchange quotation (usually small companies) are able to obtain relief on up to £40,000 invested in any one year.

Assuming only the basic personal allowances, a single person with an income of £10,000 a year in 1986–87 pays £2,223 in income tax while a married man with the same income pays £1,840. The amount of tax payable by a single person varies from, for example, £773 on an annual income of £5,000 to £26,702 on one of £60,000.

The income of married couples is usually taxed as if it all belonged to the husband. A couple may, however, choose to have the wife's earnings charged separately for tax on condition that the husband receives the single instead of the married personal allowance. Any investment income is taxed jointly.

In March 1986 the Government published a Green Paper on the reform of personal taxation. This discussed the possibility of introducing a system of independent taxation with a uniform—transferable—personal allowance. Independent taxation would give married women the same opportunity for privacy in their tax affairs as their husbands. Transferable allowances would enable married couples to reduce their tax bill by transferring any 'unused' portion of one partner's allowance to the other partner.

Most wage and salary earners pay their income tax under a Pay-As-You-Earn (PAYE) system whereby tax is deducted (and accounted for to the Inland Revenue) by the employer, thus enabling them to keep as up to date as possible with their tax payments.

In general, income tax is charged on all income which originates in Britain (including, from April 1987, the earnings of overseas entertainers and sportsmen) and on all income arising abroad of people resident in Britain. Interest on certain British government securities belonging to people not ordinarily resident in Britain is exempt. Britain has entered into agreements with many countries providing for relief from double taxation; where such agreements are not in force unilateral relief is often allowed. British residents working abroad for the whole year benefit from 100 per cent tax relief.

Corporation Tax

Company taxation in Britain is at a significantly lower rate than in most other industrialised countries. Companies pay corporation tax on their profits

Table 35: Consolidated Fund Revenue 1985–86 and 1986–87

	1985–86 Latest estimate (£ million)	1986–87 Budget forecast (£ million)	Percentage of total
Inland Revenue			
Income tax	35,100	38,500	35·5
Corporation tax[a]	10,700	11,700	10·8
Petroleum revenue tax[b]	6,400	2,400	2·2
Capital gains tax	930	1,050	1·0
Development land tax[c]	60	35	—
Capital transfer tax (inheritance tax)[d]	890	910	0·8
Stamp duties	1,230	1,430	1·3
Total Inland Revenue	55,300	56,000	51·6
Customs and Excise			
Value added tax	19,300	20,700	19·1
Oil	6,500	7,300	6·7
Tobacco	4,300	4,700	4·3
Spirits, beer, wine, cider and perry	4,200	4,400	4·1
Betting and gaming	730	800	0·7
Car tax	880	980	0·9
Other excise duties	20	20	—
European Community own resources			
Customs duties, etc.	1,200	1,300	1·2
Agricultural levies	160	160	0·1
Total Customs and Excise	37,300	40,400	37·2
Vehicle excise duties[e]	2,400	2,500	2·3
National Insurance surcharge[f]	30	—	—
Gas levy	520	500	0·5
Broadcast receiving licences	990	1,000	0·9
Interest and dividends	910	840	0·8
Other[g]	8,400	7,400	6·8
Total Consolidated Fund revenue	105,800	108,600	100·0

Source: *Financial Statement and Budget Report 1986–87.*
[a] Including advance corporation tax:

Net of repayments	3,800	4,100	3·8

[b] Including advance payments.
[c] Abolished from March 1985.
[d] Including estate duty.
[e] Including driving licence receipts.
[f] Abolished from April 1985.
[g] Including the 10 per cent of own resources refunded by the European Community to meet the costs of collection, other receipts from the Community, privatisation proceeds and oil royalties.
Differences between totals and the sums of their component parts are due to rounding.

remaining after deduction of certain allowances. A company which distributes profits to its shareholders is required to make to the Inland Revenue an advance payment of corporation tax. In general, this payment is set against a company's liability to corporation tax on its income and the recipient of the distribution is entitled to a tax credit, which satisfies his or her liability to income tax at the basic rate.

The main rate of corporation tax is 35 per cent, with a reduced rate of 29 per cent for small companies (those with profits below £100,000 in a year). Marginal relief between the main rate and the small companies' rate is allowed for companies with profits between £100,000 and £500,000. There is a 4 per cent annual writing-down allowance for industrial buildings and a 25 per cent writing-down allowance for machinery and plant; short-life machinery and plant may be wholly written off over its life.

Petroleum Revenue Tax

Petroleum revenue tax (deductible in computing profits for corporation tax) is charged on profits from the production, as opposed to the refining or other forms of processing, of oil and gas under licence in Britain and on its Continental Shelf. The rate of tax is 75 per cent. Each licensee of an oilfield is charged on the profits from that field after deduction of certain allowances and reliefs which, among other things, encourage exploration, appraisal and future field development. The tax is computed at half-yearly intervals and the bulk of it is collected in monthly instalments.

Taxes on Capital
Inheritance Tax

Inheritance tax applies to transfers of personal wealth made up to seven years before the donor's death and to transfers relating to property held in most types of trust. It is chargeable on a cumulative basis over a seven-year period. The rates of tax are progressively higher on successive slices of the cumulative total of chargeable transfers. The first £71,000 is exempt; the rates on higher amounts rise from 30 per cent on the slice between £71,000 and £95,000 to 60 per cent on the excess over £317,000. There is, however, tapered relief for transfers made between three and seven years before the donor's death. This ranges from relief of 20 per cent for transfers made between three and four years of death to relief of 80 per cent for those made between six and seven years of death.

Capital Gains Tax

Capital gains realised on the disposal of assets are liable to capital gains tax or, in the case of companies, to corporation tax. The rate of tax is 30 per cent but individuals are exempt from tax in respect of total net gains of up to £6,300 in any one year and most trusts on gains of up to £3,150. The effects of inflation since April 1982 are allowed for when measuring gains. The tax on gifts and certain deemed disposals of assets may be deferred until the assets are sold. Certain assets, including the principal private residence, chattels worth less than £3,000 (and any chattels with a predictable life of less than 50 years except those on which the expenditure qualifies for a capital allowance), private motor cars, and National Savings Certificates and Bonds are normally exempt. Gains on government securities and corporate bonds are exempt from the tax, as are gains on shares owned under the Personal Equity Plan provided they have been held for at least one calendar year.

Taxes on Expenditure
Value Added Tax

Value added tax (VAT) is a broadly based tax, chargeable at 15 per cent. It is collected at each stage in the production and distribution of goods and services by taxable persons (generally those whose business has a turnover of more than £20,500 a year). The final tax is borne by the consumer. When a taxable person purchases taxable goods or services, the supplier charges VAT (the taxable person's input tax). When the taxable person supplies taxable goods or services to customers, then they in turn are charged VAT (the taxable person's output tax). The difference between the output tax and the input tax is paid to Customs and Excise.

Planned Receipts and Expenditure for the Public Sector 1986-87

Pence in every pound

Receipts			Expenditure
Income tax	24	11	Defence
		1	Foreign and Commonwealth Office
		1	Agriculture, Fisheries and Food
Corporation tax	7	1	Trade and Industry
		2	Employment
Capital taxes	2	3	Transport
		2	Environment – housing
Value added tax	13	2	Environment – other environmental services
		3	Home Office
Local authority rates	10	9	Education and Science
Duties on petrol, alcoholic drinks and tobacco	10	11	Health and Social Security – health and personal social services
Other expenditure taxes	6	26	Health and Social Security – social security
Petroleum revenue tax and oil royalties	2		
		5	Scotland
National Insurance and other contributions	16	2	Wales
		3	Northern Ireland
Interest and dividends	4	1	Chancellor's departments
		2	Other departments
Gross trading surpluses and rent	2	3	Reserve
Other items and adjustments	1	11	Gross debt interest
Public sector borrowing requirement	4	1	Adjustments (net of privatisation proceeds)
Total	100	100	**Total**

Cash totals £163,000 million

Sources: *Financial Statement and Budget Report 1986-87* and *The Government's Expenditure Plans 1986-87 to 1988-89.*
Difference between total receipts and the sum of component parts is due to rounding.

There are two methods by which certain goods and services are relieved from VAT: one is by charging VAT at a zero rate (a taxable person does not charge tax to a customer but reclaims any input tax paid to suppliers); the other is by exemption (a taxable person does not charge a customer any output tax and is not entitled to deduct or reclaim the input tax). Zero-rating applies to most food; books, newspapers and periodicals; fuel (except for petrol and other fuels for road use) and power; construction of new buildings; exports; certain international services; public transport fares; caravans and houseboats; young children's clothing and footwear; drugs and medicines supplied on prescription; specified aids for handicapped people; and certain supplies by or to charities. Exemption applies to land (including rents), insurance, postal services, betting, gaming (other than by gaming machines and lotteries), finance, education, health, burial and cremation, and supplies by trade unions and professional bodies to their members.

Excise Duties

Oils used for road fuel bear duty at the basic rate. Heavy oil not used for road fuel and light oil used for furnace fuel bear a lower duty and, except for lubricating oil, are zero-rated for VAT. Oil used as chemical feedstocks, or otherwise than as fuel, and most lubricating oils are relieved from duty. There are duties on spirits, beer, wine, made-wine, cider and perry, mainly related to alcoholic strength. The cigarette duty is based partly on a charge per 1,000 cigarettes and partly on a percentage of retail price. Duty on other tobacco products is based on the weight of the finished product. The principal betting duties are the general betting duty, which is charged at a rate of 8 per cent of the stake money, except for on-course betting, which is charged at 4 per cent; pool betting duty (which applies to football pools), charged at a rate of 42·5 per cent of the stake money (33·3 per cent for charity pools); and bingo duty, charged at 10 per cent. Revenue is also raised from licences on the operation of gaming machines and casinos.

The licence duty on a private motor car or light van is £100 a year; for motor cycles it is £10, £20 or £40 a year according to engine capacity. The licence duty on goods vehicles is charged on the basis of gross weight and, if over 12 tonnes, according to the number of axles; the duty is designed to ensure that such vehicles cover at least their road costs through the tax paid (licence duty and fuel duty). Taxis and buses are taxed according to seating capacity.

Car Tax

New cars, motor cycles, scooters, mopeds and some motor caravans, whether British made or imported, are chargeable with car tax at 10 per cent on the wholesale value. VAT is charged on the price including car tax.

Stamp Duty

Transfers or sales of property (other than of stocks and shares) above a value of £30,000 are subject to stamp duty of 1 per cent on the whole of the purchase price. Transfers or sales of stocks and shares are subject to stamp duty of 0·5 per cent regardless of the amount. Transfers by gift are subject to a fixed 50p duty. Transfers to charities are exempt.

Customs Duties

Customs duties are chargeable in accordance with the Common Customs Tariff of the European Community (no such duties are chargeable on goods which qualify as Community goods). Special customs import and export procedures are operated under the Common Agricultural Policy and Community levies are chargeable on a wide range of agricultural products from non-Community countries.

PUBLIC SECTOR BORROWING

A continuing reduction in the public sector borrowing requirement (PSBR) as a percentage of gross domestic product is an important part of the Government's medium-term financial strategy; the percentage is projected to fall steadily from

2 per cent in 1985–86 to 1·5 per cent in 1988–89 and 1989–90 (see Table 33). As part of the policy of controlling the rate of growth of the money stock, the Government seeks to finance the PSBR by sales of public sector debt to the public outside the banking system. The outturn for the PSBR in 1985–86 was £5,900 million compared with a forecast of £7,100 million at the time of the 1985 Budget. Sales of government stock (known as gilt-edged stock as there is no risk of default) to the non-bank private and overseas sectors amounted to £5,100 million in 1985–86 and sales of National Savings instruments £2,200 million. Gilt-edged stock is marketable and is traded on The Stock Exchange. Individuals may also make transactions through post offices in stocks included on the National Savings Stock Register. Pension funds and insurance companies have the largest holdings. The Government issues both conventional and indexed stock (on which principal and interest are linked to the movement in the retail prices index).

National Savings instruments are non-marketable and are designed to attract personal savings. Their importance relative to gilt-edged stock as a source of government funding has increased in recent years. The chief instruments are National Savings Certificates, Income Bonds, Indexed Income Bonds, Deposit Bonds, National Savings Investment and Ordinary Accounts, Premium Savings Bonds and Yearly Plan. In 1985–86 the main contributors to funding were Income Bonds (£890 million net) and fixed-interest Savings Certificates (£808 million net). The contribution made by net accrued interest from National Savings as a whole (that is, interest added less that paid out) amounted to £1,610 million in 1985–86.

The other principal debt instruments of central government are Treasury bills and certificates of tax deposit. Treasury bills are 91-day bills sold at a weekly auction to the discount houses, which guarantee to take up the whole of the offer; certificates of tax deposit are non-marketable and may be purchased by individuals or corporate bodies to be tendered in settlement of a range of taxes.

The bulk of public corporations' borrowing is met by central government through the National Loans Fund although their temporary borrowing needs are met largely from the market, often under Treasury guarantee. That part of local authority borrowing met by central government is supplied by authorisation of Parliament through the Public Works Loan Board from the National Loans Fund. (The Board remains an independent body even though it is merged for administrative purposes with the former National Debt Office, forming the National Investment and Loans Office.) The local authorities also borrow directly from the market, both short-term and long-term, through a range of instruments. Some public corporations and local authorities also borrow on occasion, under special statutory power and with Treasury consent, in foreign currencies.

The National Debt

Net central government borrowing each year represents an addition to the National Debt. At the end of March 1986 the National Debt amounted to some £171,000 million of which about £4,000 million was in currencies other than sterling. Of the £168,000 million sterling debt, £130,000 million consisted of gilt-edged stock; of this, 34 per cent had a maturity of up to five years, 39 per cent a maturity of over five years and up to 15 years and 27 per cent a maturity of over 15 years or undated. The remaining sterling debt was made up mainly of national savings (£24,000 million), certificates of tax deposits, Treasury bills, and Ways and Means advances (very short-term internal government borrowing).

18 Banking and Financial Institutions

Britain's position as a major financial centre reflects the wide range of specialised financial services provided. The City of London has the greatest concentration of banks in the world (responsible for about a quarter of total international bank lending), the world's biggest insurance market (with about one-fifth of the international market) and a Stock Exchange with a larger listing of securities than any other exchange, and remains the principal international centre for transactions in a large number of commodities. Its tradition of informal dealing and its position between the time zones of the United States and the Far East enable it to complete large-scale transactions with economy and speed.

The financial services sector accounts for 5 to 6 per cent of the total output of the British economy and for 4 to 5 per cent of employment. The net overseas earnings of British financial institutions in 1985 were £7,584 million.

Development of Financial Services

The increase in the rate of international movements of capital in the 1960s and 1970s took the form mainly of increased bank lending and foreign exchange trading. London became the international centre of this activity, particularly in the eurocurrency markets (see p 371), and the number of overseas banks represented in London is larger than in any other financial centre. In the 1980s, with increasing international competition in financial services and with developments in technology, there has also taken place a rapid growth in the international markets for securities. London again has played an important role, especially in the market for eurobonds, in a variety of currencies (see p 371). The London Stock Exchange (see p 370) is reorganising itself, partly in order to adapt to this situation, and has changed its membership rules with the result that numerous financial institutions in London, both British and foreign-based, have formed new alliances with each other. A new trading system for The Stock Exchange is expected to come into operation in October 1986.

To help Britain's financial services industry to respond to the new competitive climate, while at the same time maintaining adequate safeguards for the investing public, the Government proposes to establish a new supervisory framework and associated institutional structure for much of the industry, under legislative proposals introduced in December 1985. Investment businesses (those effecting transactions in, managing or giving advice on securities of all kinds, financial and commodity futures, life assurance, options contracts and certain other instruments—but not wholesale moneymarket instruments) will require authorisation and will have to obey rules of conduct based on principles set out in the legislation. When this comes into force, powers will be given to the Secretary of State for Trade and Industry to authorise and regulate the carrying on of investment business. However, the majority of these powers will be transferable to a designated agency as long as it meets specified criteria. The agency, in turn, will be able to recognise self-regulatory organisations (SROs) provided that they offer investors protection at least equivalent to that provided by the agency. Both the agency and the SROs will be practitioner-based bodies: the Securities and Investment Board has already been established to fulfil the agency role. Membership of an SRO will be one of the ways for investment businesses to become authorised.

The Government also in late 1985 put forward proposals for improving the supervision of Britain's banking system and introduced legislation aimed at widening the range of activities that building societies are able to engage in.

In making these various proposals the Government has made provision for improved co-operation between supervisors in different financial sectors, while seeking to avoid any harm thereby to efficiency, competitiveness and flexibility within the sectors themselves. The Bank of England, H.M. Treasury and the Department of Trade and Industry have prime responsibility for supervision in different parts of the financial sector.

Changes within the financial services sector as a whole are expected to erode traditional distinctions between financial institutions, with single firms providing a broader range of services, both in domestic and international markets.

THE BANK OF ENGLAND

The Bank of England was established in 1694 by Act of Parliament and Royal Charter as a corporate body; the entire capital stock was acquired by the Government under the Bank of England Act 1946. The Bank's main functions are to execute monetary policy, to act as banker to the Government, to act as a note-issuing authority and to exercise prudential supervision over and provide central banking facilities for the banking system. It also manages the Exchange Equalisation Account on behalf of the Treasury. More generally the Bank has a responsibility for overseeing the soundness of the financial system as a whole.

The Government's economic policy is based on the medium-term financial strategy, which aims to achieve a continued fall in the rate of inflation by means of successive reductions in the rate of growth in the money supply, and thus of 'money GDP' (the average measure of gross domestic product at current market prices), over a medium-term period. On behalf of the Government the Bank conducts operations in the financial markets (see p 370) designed to influence the trend rate of monetary growth and of interest rates.

As banker to the Government, the Bank of England is responsible for arranging government borrowing and for managing the National Debt.

The Bank of England has the sole right in England and Wales of issuing banknotes. The note issue is fiduciary, that is to say, it is no longer backed by gold but by government and other securities. The Scottish and Northern Ireland banks have limited rights to issue notes; these issues, apart from an amount specified by legislation for each bank, must be fully covered by holdings of Bank of England notes. Responsibility for the provision of coin for circulation lies with the Royal Mint, a government department.

The Bank is able to influence money market conditions through its dealings with the discount houses (see p 366), which developed in the nineteenth century as bill brokers for industrialists. The discount houses hold mainly Treasury, local authority and commercial bills and negotiable certificates of deposit financed by short-term loans from the banks. If on any given day there is a shortage of cash in the banking system as a result, for example, of large tax payments or heavy sales of government securities, the Bank relieves the shortage either by buying bills from the discount houses or by lending directly to them. This permits the banks to replenish their cash balances at the Bank by recalling some of their short-term loans to the discount houses. The Bank conducts its operations in such a way as to keep short-term interest rates within an unpublished band.

Under the Banking Act 1979 deposit-taking businesses require authorisation from the Bank of England unless they are specifically exempted from the authorisation provisions of the Act and are subject to the Bank of England's supervision.

On behalf of the Treasury, the Bank manages the Exchange Equalisation Account (EEA), which holds Britain's official reserves of gold, foreign exchange, SDRs (which are claims on the International Monetary Fund) and European Currency Units (ECUs). Using the resources of the EEA, the Bank may intervene in the foreign exchange markets to check undue fluctuations in the exchange value of sterling.

DEPOSIT-TAKING INSTITUTIONS

Deposit-taking institutions may be broadly divided into the 'monetary sector', which includes the banks and is supervised by the Bank of England, and those institutions outside the monetary sector, of which the most important are the building societies and the National Savings Bank. Within the monetary sector a further distinction is drawn by the Bank of England, under the Banking Act 1979, between recognised banks and licensed deposit-taking institutions. The latter include smaller banking institutions providing a range of services too narrow to qualify them for recognised status, and the majority of the finance houses (see p 369). In June 1986 there were 296 recognised banks, the main types being the members of the Association for Payment Clearing Services, merchant banks, discount houses and foreign banks. The monetary sector also includes Girobank (see p 365), certain banks in the Channel Islands and the Isle of Man, the Trustee Savings Banks (see p 365) and the Banking Department of the Bank of England. (The Government proposes to abolish the distinction between recognised banks and licensed deposit-takers and to make them all subject to the same Bank of England authorisation and supervisory arrangements.)

Another useful distinction is that between 'retail' banking and 'wholesale' banking. Retail banking is mainly concerned with the cash withdrawal and transmission of deposited funds—the main reason why people keep bank accounts. Competition between the banks and the building societies in the provision of money transmission services increased during the 1970s and is expected to increase further. Wholesale business involves the taking of large deposits at high rates of interest, the deployment of funds in money market instruments (see p 371) and the making of large loans and investments. Nearly all the commercial banks in Britain engage in some wholesale activities and some, like the merchant and overseas banks, centre their business on them. Many of such wholesale dealings are conducted on the inter-bank market, that is, among the banks themselves.

The Banks

The major retail banks are those with a significant branch network, which offer a full range of financial services to both individuals and companies, including the provision of current and deposit accounts and various kinds of loan arrangements, together with a full range of money transmission facilities.

The dominant banks in England and Wales are the 'big four': Barclays, Lloyds, Midland and National Westminster. The major Scottish banks are Bank of Scotland, Clydesdale and Royal Bank of Scotland. Following its merger with Williams and Glyn's in 1985, the Royal Bank of Scotland is the only bank to have a significant network of branches throughout Great Britain. Other important retail banks are the Trustee Savings Bank, Co-operative Bank, Yorkshire Bank and Girobank. Northern Ireland is served by branch networks of four banks, two being subsidiaries of British banks and two subsidiaries of Irish banks.

With the growth of the financial services sector since the 1970s, and with a relaxation of restrictions on competition among financial institutions, the major banks have increasingly diversified the services they provide. They have lent more money for house purchases, and have established or acquired substantial interests in finance houses, leasing and factoring companies, merchant banks and unit trust companies. In view of proposed reforms in the securities industry, some banks have in the 1980s established links with traders in stocks and shares.

The banks provide loan facilities to companies and, since the 1970s, have provided more medium- and long-term loans than they did formerly. They have also become important providers of finance for small firms: they have supported the loan guarantee scheme under which 70 per cent of the value of loans to small companies is guaranteed by the Government, and some banks have set up special subsidiaries to provide equity finance for small companies.

The clearing banks also conduct extensive international operations which account for a substantial proportion of their assets and profits. In addition to maintaining overseas subsidiaries they are very active in the eurocurrency markets (see p 371).

Deposits and Assets

The sterling deposits of the London and Scottish banks amounted to some £126,000 million in February 1986, of which £48,000 million was sight deposits (that is, could be withdrawn on demand) and £78,000 million was time deposits. Foreign currency deposits were £75,500 million. Total deposits of the big four banks were: National Westminster £59,400 million, Barclays £44,300 million, Midland £35,500 million, and Lloyds £32,900 million. The total assets of the London and Scottish banks amounted to some £236,000 million (of which £147,000 million was in sterling). Sterling advances to British residents amounted to some £85,000 million, of which £32,000 million was for individuals. The banks' main liquid assets consist of balances at the Bank of England, money at call (mainly loans to discount houses), their holdings of Treasury and some other bills, and short-dated British government securities. They also hold a proportion of their assets as portfolio investments (mainly longer-dated British government securities) or trade investments.

Branches and Accounts

The 'big four' banks operate through some 10,440 branches and sub-branches. National Westminster has the largest number (3,170), followed by Barclays (2,870), Lloyds (2,230) and Midland (2,160). Nearly two-thirds of all adults in Britain have a current account and over one-third a deposit account.

Payment Systems and Services

In December 1985 the London-based inter-bank clearing systems were reorganised to place the administrative responsibilities under the control of three separate companies operating under a newly formed umbrella organisation, the Association for Payment Clearing Services. These responsibilities had previously been exercised by the Committee of London Clearing Bankers (which was replaced in September 1985 by a wider-based representative body, the Committee of London and Scottish Bankers). The three clearing companies cover bulk paper clearings (cheques and credit transfers); high-value clearings for same-day settlement (automated payments and 'town clearing'); and bulk electronic clearings (through Bankers Automated Clearing Services, comprising standing orders and direct debits). Membership of each of these clearing companies is open to any bank or financial institution that meets certain published criteria, which include meeting a minimum volume of transactions in that clearing and having settlement account facilities at the Bank of England.

In addition to the money transmission services handled by the three clearing companies, nearly all the major banks (and increasingly building societies) have substantial networks of automated teller machines or cash dispensers. These give customers access to cash and other services up to 24 hours a day.

All the major retail banks offer their customers cheque guarantee cards which entitle holders to reciprocal encashment facilities up to £50 a day. The same card will also guarantee transactions with retailers up to the same amount.

Credit cards associated with the major retail banks are becoming an increasingly popular means of payment. Access operates within the Mastercard world system and Barclaycard within VISA.

Uniform eurocheques supported by a uniform eurocheque card are now available from all major banks. These standard-format, high-security cheques may be used to obtain cash or make payments in Britain or overseas. The cheques are made out in the currency of the country in which they are being used, with a guarantee limit of approximately £100 per cheque, but without limit on the number of cheques that may be drawn in respect of a single transaction.

Girobank

Girobank, a wholly owned subsidiary of the Post Office, provides a wide range of banking and money transmission services for personal and corporate customers, operating through more than 20,000 post offices. It became a clearing bank in 1983 and in 1985 it became a recognised bank under the Banking Act 1979. Accounts and transactions are maintained by a central computer at Bootle, Merseyside, which is linked to a network of regional offices. In March 1986 Girobank had 1·9 million personal customers, with balances of some £535 million; business balances amounted to £484 million. There were about 420 million transactions in the year ended March 1986.

Trustee Savings Banks

The Trustee Savings Banks (TSBs), originally founded as small local banks in the nineteenth century, have operated for much of their history under the supervision of government agencies. The Trustee Savings Banks Act 1985 provides for the TSB Group to reorganise under the Companies Act as a public limited company and to issue shares.

TSBs provide a wide range of banking services including cheque accounts and credit services for businesses as well as individuals. The Group has its own credit card, Trustcard, which operates within the VISA system, and TSB Trust Company provides a wide range of savings, insurance, life assurance and unit trust facilities.

There are four individual banks in the Group with about 1,600 branches, 13 million accounts and total deposits of over £10,000 million.

Merchant Banks

Merchant banks have traditionally been primarily concerned with the accepting (or guaranteeing) of commercial bills and with the sponsoring of capital issues on behalf of their customers. Today they have a widely diversified and complex range of activities with important roles in international finance and the short-term capital markets, the provision of expert advice and financial services to British industrial companies, especially where mergers, takeovers and other forms of corporate reorganisation are involved, and in the management of investment holdings, including trusts, pensions and other funds. A number of merchant banks have become part of financial conglomerates offering an even wider range of financial services than hitherto.

Overseas Banks

Some 460 overseas banks and financial institutions were represented in Britain in 1986 through branches, subsidiaries, representative offices and consortia. A total of 399 were directly represented while 64 were represented only through a stake in a consortium. Of those directly represented, 64 were from the United States, 40 from Japan and 150 from Europe. They provide a comprehensive banking service in many parts of the world and engage in the financing of trade not only between Britain and other countries but also between third countries.

Citibank of the United States is expanding its activities in the retail banking market in Britain and has joined the high-value clearing system (see p 364).

British Overseas Banks

A number of banking institutions have their head offices in Britain but operate mainly abroad, often specialising in particular regions such as Latin America or East Asia through extensive branch networks. The major bank in this sector is Standard Chartered.

The Discount Houses

The discount houses represent an institution unique to the City of London. They act as intermediaries between the Bank of England and the rest of the banking sector, promote an orderly flow of short-term funds between the Government and the banks, and lend to the Government by guaranteeing to buy up the whole of the weekly offer of Treasury bills (which are 91-day instruments). In return for acting as intermediaries, the discount houses have privileged access to the Bank of England as 'lender of last resort'. Assets of the discount houses consist mainly of Treasury and commercial bills, government and local authority securities and negotiable certificates of deposit denominated in both sterling and United States dollars.

Building Societies

Building societies are mutual institutions which raise short-term deposits from individual savers, who are generally able to withdraw their money on demand or at short notice, and provide long-term loans at variable rates of interest on the security of property—usually private dwellings purchased for owner-occupation.

Building societies have grown very rapidly since 1918, reflecting a continued high growth of owner-occupation. They account for most lending for house purchase in Britain and in recent years they have overtaken the banks as the principal repository for the personal sector's liquid assets; over a half of all adults have building society accounts. The societies have expanded the range of services to investors, a variety of saving schemes have been established, and a growing number of societies provide cheque facilities and automated cash withdrawal systems.

Competition among the building societies and between building societies and other financial institutions has increased in the 1980s and a system of agreed rates of interest for loans by and deposits with the societies has fallen into disuse.

The three largest societies (the Halifax, Abbey National and Nationwide) account for 45 per cent of the total assets of the movement and the 15 largest for some 85 per cent. Mergers between building societies are a continuing trend. At the end of 1985 there were 167 registered building societies with total assets of £121,000 million; over £26,000 million was advanced in new mortgages in the course of the year.

The Government has introduced new legislation which would relax some of the present restrictions and allow the societies to diversify their financial and housing services. Among these are that up to 10 per cent of a society's commercial assets could be used for purposes other than loans on first mortgage of owner-occupied houses, with up to 5 per cent placed in new types of asset such as unsecured loans, housing and investments in subsidiaries and associates. Societies would also be allowed to offer a wider range of banking and money transmission services (including reciprocal encashment and paying arrangements with other financial institutions) as well as estate agency, insurance broking, share dealing, personal pensions and other facilities. There would also be changes to the arrangements for the prudential supervision of building societies, including the establishment of a new supervisory commission, and provisions allowing a society to convert into a company. The legislation is planned to come into effect early in 1987.

National Savings Bank

The National Savings Bank is run by the Department for National Savings and provides a system for depositing and withdrawing savings at 20,000 post offices around the country or by post. There are about 18·5 million accounts. Ordinary Accounts earn interest at 3 or 6 per cent a year (depending on the balance maintained); the first £70 of annual interest is tax free. Investment Accounts earn a higher variable rate of interest, which is taxable. At the end of June 1986 the sum of the two accounts totalled £7,400 million. The National Savings Bank does not offer lending facilities. As with other National Savings instruments, its deposits are employed to finance the Government's public sector borrowing requirement. The other instruments include tax-free savings certificates, which either pay fixed rates of interest or a (lower) fixed rate of interest combined with index-linking; and taxable Income Bonds, Indexed-Income Bonds and Deposit Bonds, where interest is paid without deduction of tax at source. At the end of June 1986 the total amount of money invested in National Savings was £32,000 million.

INVESTING INSTITUTIONS

The investing institutions are those which collect savings and invest them in the securities market and other long-term assets. The main investing institutions are the insurance companies, the pension funds, the unit trusts and investment trusts.

Insurance Companies

The British insurance industry provides a comprehensive and competitive service domestically and internationally. It has been estimated that British insurers handle some 20 per cent of general insurance business placed on the international market. The London market is the world's leading centre for insurance where, in addition to the British companies and Lloyd's, a large number of overseas companies are also represented. It is the world centre for the placement of international reinsurance and, partly as a consequence, many British companies have formed close relationships with overseas companies. Some British insurance companies confine their activities to domestic business but most large companies undertaking general business transact a substantial amount overseas through branches, agencies or affiliated local companies. Over a half of the non-life premium income of British insurance companies and Lloyd's is derived from overseas. Insurance companies carrying on business in Britain are supervised by the Department of Trade and Industry under the Insurance Companies Act 1982. About 840 companies are authorised to carry on one or more classes of insurance business in Britain, of which some 160 are from overseas. The total net assets of these companies were £134,135 million at the end of 1984.

Around 400 companies belong to the Association of British Insurers and these account for about 90 per cent of the world-wide business of the British insurance companies market.

Long-term insurance is handled by some 280 authorised insurance companies and is also available through certain friendly societies. Some 90 per cent of this business is transacted through the members of the Association of British Insurers. Lloyd's underwriters also write short-term life business.

Lloyd's

Lloyd's, established in the seventeenth century, is an incorporated society of private insurers in London. Although its activities were originally confined to the conduct of marine insurance business, a very considerable world-wide market for the transaction of other classes of insurance business in non-marine, aviation and motor markets has been built up. Long-term life and financial guarantee business is not covered. Lloyd's, which does not accept insurance itself, is regulated by a series of special Acts of Parliament, dating from 1871 to 1982.

Lloyd's is not a company but a market for insurance administered by the Council of Lloyd's, where business is carried out for individual underwriting members for their own account and risk and in competition with each other and with insurance companies. Insurance may only be placed through Lloyd's brokers who negotiate with Lloyd's underwriting agents on behalf of the insured. Only elected underwriting members of Lloyd's, for whom insurance is transacted with unlimited liability and who have met the most stringent financial regulations laid down by the Council, are permitted to accept insurance risks at Lloyd's; these and other safeguards give security to a Lloyd's policy.

In January 1986 there were some 28,940 underwriting members of Lloyd's grouped into about 370 syndicates managed at Lloyd's by underwriting agents who are responsible for accepting risks and for settling claims on behalf of the members of their syndicates.

Insurance Brokers

Insurance brokers, acting on behalf of the insured, are an essential part of the Lloyd's market and a valuable part of the company market. Many brokers specialise in reinsurance business, acting as intermediaries in the exchange of contracts between companies, both British and overseas, and often acting as London representatives of the latter. The Insurance Brokers (Registration) Act 1977 provides for the registration of insurance brokers with the Insurance Brokers Registration Council and makes Britain the first country to introduce self-regulation of insurance brokers. In November 1985, 17,500 individuals and 3,300 companies were registered with the Council. The British Insurance Brokers' Association, which sponsored the Act, has about 3,800 members.

European Community Directives

In accordance with the Treaty of Rome, insurance and reinsurance in the European Community are regulated by directives addressed to the governments of member states and intended to harmonise the legislation of the various member countries. Directives cover reinsurance, compulsory motor insurance, freedom of establishment for life and non-life insurers, Community co-insurance and insurance intermediaries. Britain strongly supports the removal of national regulations and exchange controls that restrict the creation of a full common market in services, particularly financial services, within the European Community.

Pension Funds

Virtually all occupational pension schemes are supervised in order to protect the interests of the members. Pension contributions are invested either directly in the securities and other investment markets or through intermediaries such as insurance companies. The market value of assets held by pension funds rose from £2,000 million in 1957 to about £157,270 million in 1985 when 17 per cent was in British government securities and 66 per cent in company securities. The pension funds have grown strongly since 1960 to become a dominant force in securities markets. Under government proposals to encourage the expansion of occupational schemes and personal pensions, it is envisaged that both types of provision for retirement will be subject to investor protection legislation (see p 361).

Investment and Unit Trusts

Investment and unit trusts enable investors in securities to spread their risks and obtain the benefit of skilled management. Investment trusts are companies which observe certain requirements of The Stock Exchange and the tax authorities and invest in securities for the benefit of their shareholders. At the end of 1985 their investments totalled over £17,170 million, of which nearly one-half was held overseas.

Unit trusts are constituted by trust deed between a management company and a trustee company which holds the assets. Normally, the managers sell units to the public and also repurchase them on demand. The sums held must be invested in securities. The costs of running the trust are met partly by an initial charge which forms part of the price of a unit and partly by a periodic service charge which is usually taken out of the trust's income. Authorisation by the Department of Trade and Industry is needed before units can be offered to the public; this is granted only if the trust deed meets the Department's requirements. Trusts are allowed to hold up to 25 per cent of their assets in shares traded on the Unlisted Securities Market (see p 371) and certain other secondary markets; within this total up to 5 per cent may be held in the form of other unlisted securities. Under the Government's proposals for the financial services industry (see p 361), authorised unit trusts will be able to invest in a wider range of assets in order to allow a greater variety of investment opportunities to be offered to the public. In April 1986 there were 2·8 million unit holdings with a total value of £26,000 million.

SPECIALISED INSTITUTIONS

The specialised institutions are agencies created to meet the needs of specific groups of borrowers—mostly industrial and commercial—which were not adequately covered by other institutions. They are to be found in both the public and the private sectors. Some of the latter were set up with official support but with financing from banks and other financial institutions. They may offer loan finance or equity capital.

The main private sector institutions are described below. Among public sector agencies are the British Technology Group, the Scottish and Welsh Development Agencies, the Industrial Development Board in Northern Ireland, the Co-operative Development Agency and the Export Credits Guarantee Department.

Finance Houses

Finance houses are major suppliers of hire-purchase finance for the personal sector and of short-term credit and leasing to the corporate sector. Some 80 per cent of all their business is accounted for by the 46 firms which constitute the Finance Houses Association (FHA). At the end of 1985 credit outstanding to the members of the FHA was over £20,600 million. Many of the finance houses are owned by banks, and most of them are licensed deposit-taking institutions.

Leasing Companies

Leasing companies buy and own plant or equipment required and chosen by businesses and lease it at an agreed rental. This form of finance grew quickly in importance in the 1970s, partly because the leasing companies were able to take advantage of investment incentives to the benefit of customers whose tax position would otherwise have made them unavailable. The restructuring of capital allowances in the 1984 Budget, however, is expected to reduce the advantage of some forms of leasing after an interim period. In 1985 the 73 members of the Equipment Leasing Association acquired assets in Britain valued at some £5,800 million, which represented about 20 per cent of total private sector investment in plant and machinery.

Factoring Companies

Factoring consists of making cash available to a company in exchange for the sums owing to it. Since the early 1960s factoring has developed as a major financial service, covering international activities as well as domestic trade. In 1985 member companies of the Association of British Factors handled business of £4,600 million (representing over 90 per cent of all factoring business in Britain) and 4,170 companies made use of the Association's services.

Finance Corporations

Finance corporations meet the need for medium- and long-term capital (including venture capital) when such funds are not easily or directly available from traditional sources such as The Stock Exchange or the banks.

Investors in Industry (known as *3i*) supports investment programmes over the whole range of industry. During the year ended 31 March 1986 the corporation invested £320 million. Within the last few years it has become increasingly prominent in financing management 'buy-outs', which involve the purchase of businesses by managing and other staff from their owners. The shares in Investors in Industry are owned by the Bank of England (15 per cent) and the individual London and Scottish clearing banks.

Other finance corporations include Equity Capital for Industry, the Agricultural Mortgage Corporation, the Commonwealth Development Finance Company and the Commonwealth Development Corporation (the last two being no longer confined to the Commonwealth in their activities).

A number of venture and development capital companies have been formed since the late 1970s which take equity stakes in small and medium-sized firms. Many of these companies are subsidiaries of the banks.

FINANCIAL MARKETS

The main organised financial markets are the securities markets, of which The Stock Exchange is the most important, and the money markets. Other important markets in the City of London are the foreign exchange market, the financial futures market, the Lloyd's insurance market (see p 367) and the gold bullion and commodity markets.

The Stock Exchange

The Stock Exchange has its main trading floor and central administration in London. There are also trading floors in Glasgow, Liverpool, Birmingham and Dublin.

Transactions on The Stock Exchange are undertaken on behalf of individuals and institutional investors (pension funds or insurance companies, for example) by brokers who effect purchases or sales with dealers in securities known as 'jobbers'. The broking and jobbing functions have been kept separate traditionally, in what is known as the 'single-capacity' system. This system is to be replaced by a new one in October 1986, however (see p 371).

The number and variety of securities (stocks and shares) officially listed on The Stock Exchange are greater than in any other market in the world and its turnover of company securities is roughly equivalent to that of all the other European exchanges combined. Some 6,900 securities are quoted on The Stock Exchange; at the end of March 1986 these had a market value of £1,247,580 million. About 5,000 securities of companies were quoted including a number of leading overseas securities. Company issues represent four-fifths of the securities at market valuation, the remainder being British, Irish Republic and other overseas government and corporation stocks as well as eurobonds (see p 371). Institutional investors, such as pension funds, now own a higher proportion of ordinary shares than individuals.

A market in traded options, in the shares of prominent British companies, enables investors not only to buy options to purchase or sell shares in future at pre-fixed prices but also to trade in the options themselves. In May 1984 trading began in a stock index option and in May 1985 a currency options market came into operation.

In recent years the largest market for new issues has been that for British government securities (known as 'gilt-edged' stocks), which have accounted for 75 to 80 per cent of transactions by value. New issues are made on the Government's behalf by the Bank of England.

New Trading and Regulatory Systems

The Stock Exchange has agreed to certain changes which will make it more competitive internationally. In particular, membership rules were relaxed in March 1986, permitting wider ownership of Stock Exchange member firms, and in October 1986 minimum scales of commission charged to the investing public by brokers are to be abolished, together with the single-capacity system. Dealers in securities will thus be able to deal both on behalf of clients and on their own behalf as principals. New arrangements are being implemented to prevent conflicts of interest from arising in this situation. A new automated system for share quotations will also come into operation by October 1986. The scale of the changes taking place has led to their being referred to colloquially as the 'Big Bang'.

The securities industry is subject to a combination of statutory regulation, under competition policy and company law, and non-statutory regulation by the Council of The Stock Exchange, the Council for the Securities Industry (CSI) and the City Panel on Takeovers and Mergers. Under the Government's proposed regulatory framework (see p 361), the Council of the Stock Exchange is expected to become a recognised self-regulatory organisation. The CSI was wound up in 1985 and will be replaced by a body with more extensive statutory powers—the Securities and Investments Board (see p 362). The Takeover Panel will continue to function as a non-statutory body.

Other Securities Markets

The Unlisted Securities Market, which deals generally in the securities of small companies unable or unwilling to obtain a full Stock Exchange listing, was opened in 1980, since when the number of companies with shares traded has risen from about a dozen to nearly 350. The Stock Exchange also proposes to set up a 'third tier' market for securities in small unlisted companies in October 1986. This will formalise trading in a number of securities, mainly those of small companies trying to raise risk capital, which is currently carried out directly with securities dealers in the 'over-the-counter' market. Limited trading in listed securities takes place through a telephone-based dealing system, ARIEL, owned mainly by the 'accepting' house merchant banks.

The Money Markets

The London money markets channel wholesale funds (mainly short-term) from lenders to borrowers. They consist of a series of integrated groups of financial institutions conducting negotiations primarily by telephone, telex and automated dealing systems, there being no physical market-place. The discount houses play an important role (see p 366). Money transactions are negotiated through money broking firms. The main financial instruments dealt in are bills, certificates of deposit (CDs) and short-term deposits. The bill markets and the markets on which the discount houses borrow from the rest of the banking system are often referred to as the 'traditional' markets. Newer markets, known as 'parallel' markets, emerged in the 1960s, and include the inter-bank market and the market in CDs. Since a large proportion of the latter are held by banks the CD market is effectively an extension of the inter-bank market.

Financial Futures

The London International Financial Futures Exchange trades on the floor of the Royal Exchange. Some 220 banks and other financial institutions are members of the market, which allows parties affected by movements in interest rates or exchange rates to reduce their vulnerability. Trading takes place in financial instruments of differing maturities and denominated in a number of currencies.

Eurobond and Eurocurrency Markets

The eurocurrency market enables banks to deal in deposits and loans denominated in a currency other than that of the country in which the bank is situated. Transactions can thus be carried out in eurodollars, eurodeutschmarks, euroyen and so on. While Paris is the main centre for the eurosterling market, London is the main world centre for other eurocurrency markets.

The eurobond market performs a similar service in transferring funds from lenders to borrowers but over a longer period by means of bonds issued in currencies other than that of the issuing country. Transactions in both markets tend to be in large denominations. The markets developed in the late 1950s following the restoration of convertibility between the major currencies, partly in order to avoid incurring the costs of exchange control and other regulations. The participants in the markets include multinational corporations, nationalised industries, and central and local governments as well as the international banking community.

The Foreign Exchange Market

The market consists of banks, other financial institutions and several firms of foreign exchange brokers which act as intermediaries between the banks. It provides those engaged in international trade and investment with foreign currencies for their transactions. The banks are in close contact with financial centres abroad and are able to quote buying and selling rates for both spot and forward delivery in a wide range of currencies and maturities. The forward market enables traders who, at a given date in the future, are due to receive or make a specific foreign currency payment, to contract in advance to sell or buy the foreign currency involved for sterling at a fixed exchange rate. A Bank of England survey in 1986 showed that average daily turnover on London's foreign exchange market is about £60,000 million, making it the largest such market in the world.

The London Gold Market

Anyone may deal in gold but, in practice, dealings are largely concentrated in the hands of the five members of the London gold market, who meet twice daily to establish a London fixing price for gold. This price provides a reference point for world-wide dealings. Although much interest centres upon the fixings, active dealing takes place throughout the day. London and Zurich are the main world centres for gold dealings.

Commodity, Shipping and Freight Markets

Britain remains the principal international centre for transactions in a large number of commodities, although most of the sales negotiated in London relate to consignments which never pass through the ports of Britain. The need for close links with sources of finance and with shipping and insurance services often determined the location of these markets in the City of London. There are also futures markets in cocoa, coffee, grains (wheat and barley), rubber, soya bean meal, sugar, pigmeat, non-ferrous metals (aluminium, copper, lead, nickel, silver and zinc), potatoes, gas oil (heating oil) and crude petroleum oil. The markets are collaborating in the development of new arrangements to safeguard participants.

In ship brokerage, London's Baltic Exchange is responsible for about a half of the world's tramp fixtures; some four-fifths of air-freight broking business is also conducted there. A freight futures market came into operation in 1985. Many of the commodities markets are also operated from the Baltic Exchange.

19 Overseas Trade

Although small in area and accounting for only about 1 per cent of the world's population, Britain is the fourth largest trading nation in the world—and, as a member of the European Community, part of the world's largest trading area, which accounts for about one-third of all trade.

Overseas trade has been of vital importance to the economy for hundreds of years, and especially since the mid-nineteenth century, when the rapid growth of industry, commerce and shipping was accompanied by Britain's development as an international trading centre. Exports of goods and services in 1985 were equivalent to about one-third of gross domestic product. Britain is a major supplier of machinery, vehicles, aerospace products, electrical and electronic equipment and chemicals, and a significant oil exporter. It relies upon imports for about one-third of total consumption of foodstuffs, and for many of the raw materials needed for its industries. Trade in invisibles is also of great significance to the economy: in 1985 overseas earnings from services were equivalent to about 30 per cent of those from total visible exports.

VISIBLE
TRADE

In 1985 Britain's exports of goods were valued at about £78,100 million and its imports of goods at about £80,100 million on a balance of payments basis (see Table 36). Between 1984 and 1985 the volume of exports rose by 5 per cent, while import volume grew by 3 per cent. The value of exports and imports increased by 11 and 7 per cent respectively during the same period.

Table 36: Exports and Imports 1982–85 (balance of payments basis)

	1982	1983	1984	1985
Value (£ million)				
Exports f.o.b.[a]	55,565	60,776	70,367	78,072
Imports f.o.b.[a]	53,234	61,612	74,758	80,140
Volume index (1980 = 100)				
Exports	101·9	103·8	112·5	118·6
Imports	101·5	109·7	121·9	125·7
Unit value index (1980 = 100)				
Exports	116·2	125·7	136·0	143·5
Imports	116·7	127·5	139·7	145·2
Terms of trade (1980 = 100)[b]	99·6	98·6	97·4	98·8

Source: *Monthly Review of External Trade Statistics.*
[a] f.o.b. = free on board, that is all costs accruing up to the time of placing the goods on board the exporting vessel having been paid by the seller.
[b] Export unit value index as a percentage of import unit value index.

Commodity
Composition

Britain has traditionally been an importer of food and raw materials and an exporter of manufactured goods. In recent years manufactured goods have accounted for a growing proportion of imports but a declining proportion of exports partly due to a rising oil surplus. However, the proportion of exports accounted for by manufactured goods increased slightly in 1984 and 1985. Manufactured goods were responsible for about two-thirds of exports in 1985 with machinery accounting for 23 per cent of the total (see Table 37). Chemicals accounted for 12 per cent. Sectors which have become relatively less important include passenger motor cars and textiles, the latter accounting for a little over 2 per cent of exports in 1985 compared with 5 per cent in 1970.

The growth in importance of North Sea oil exports is reflected in the rapid rise in the share of fuels in total exports, from 5 per cent in 1976 to 21 per cent in 1985.

Recent changes in Britain's import pattern are similar to those which have affected other major industrialised countries, although to a lesser degree. There has been a large rise in the share of finished manufactures, which accounted for 44 per cent of imports in 1985 compared with 23 per cent in 1970. Since 1962 imports of semi-manufactures have formed a larger part of the total import bill than basic materials, reflecting the tendency for producer countries to

Table 37: Commodity Composition of Trade 1985[a]

	Exports (f.o.b.)		Imports (c.i.f.)[b]	
	£ million	per cent	£ million	per cent
Non-manufactures	23,827	30·4	25,180	29·7
Food, beverages and tobacco	4,970	6·3	9,274	10·9
Basic materials	2,145	2·7	5,389	6·4
Fuels	16,712	21·3	10,517	12·4
Manufactured goods	52,514	67·0	58,288	68·7
Semi-manufactures	19,833	25·3	21,251	25·1
of which: Chemicals	9,411	12·0	6,903	8·1
Textiles	1,701	2·2	3,032	3·6
Iron and steel	1,857	2·4	1,716	2·0
Non-ferrous metals	1,380	1·8	1,904	2·2
Metal manufactures	1,620	2·1	1,508	1·8
Other	3,864	4·9	6,188	7·3
Finished manufactures	32,681	41·7	37,037	43·7
of which: Machinery	18,038	23·0	18,376	21·7
Road vehicles	3,911	5·0	6,802	8·0
Clothing and footwear	1,331	1·7	2,766	3·3
Scientific instruments and photographic apparatus	2,968	3·8	2,937	3·5
Other	6,433	8·2	6,156	7·3
Miscellaneous	1,991	2·5	1,322	1·6
Total	78,331	100·0	84,790	100·0

Source: *Monthly Review of External Trade Statistics.*
[a] On an overseas trade statistics basis. (This differs from a balance of payments basis because, for imports, it includes the cost of insurance and freight and, for both exports and imports, includes returned goods.)
[b] c.i.f. = cost, insurance and freight, that is including shipping, insurance and other expenses incurred in the delivery of goods as far as their place of importation in Britain. Some of these expenses represent earnings by companies resident in Britain and are more appropriate to the invisibles account.
Note: Differences between totals and the sums of their component parts are due to rounding.

undertake processing of primary products up to the semi-finished and, occasionally, the finished stage. The decline in the proportion of food imports (to some 9 per cent of total imports in 1985 compared with 40 per cent in the 1950s) reflects the increasing extent to which demand for food has been met by domestic agriculture as well as the smaller share of expenditure devoted to food.

Geographical Distribution of Trade

About four-fifths of Britain's exports and imports are with developed countries (see diagram below). In the last 30 years or so trade with Western Europe has become increasingly important, representing about 60 per cent of Britain's trade in 1985 compared with about 30 per cent in 1950. Trade with other Commonwealth countries has declined in importance.

European Community countries accounted for six of the top ten export markets and for six of the ten leading suppliers of goods to Britain in 1985 (see Table 38). From 1981 to 1985 the United States was Britain's largest single market while the Federal Republic of Germany was Britain's largest single supplier from 1982 to 1985; in 1985 each accounted for some 15 per cent of total exports or imports. There have been a number of changes in the trends of Britain's overseas trade in recent years. The increase in wealth of the oil-exporting countries during the 1970s led to a sharp increase in their imports from all sources; by the early 1980s they were taking some 12 per cent of Britain's exports. There was then a fall in the capacity of these countries to absorb imports so that, by 1985, their share of Britain's exports had fallen to 8 per cent. In 1973 the oil-exporting countries supplied 10 per cent of Britain's imports but, with Britain achieving self-sufficiency in oil, the proportion had fallen to 3 per cent by 1985. Japan now accounts for around 5 per cent of Britain's imports, about twice the proportion of ten years previously.

Geographical Distribution of Trade 1985

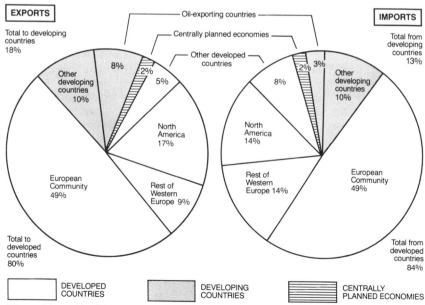

Differences between totals and the sums of their component parts are due to rounding.
Source: *Monthly Review of External Trade Statistics.*

Table 38: Britain's Main Markets and Suppliers 1985[a]

	Value (£ million)	Share (per cent)
Main markets		
United States	11,499	14·7
Federal Republic of Germany	8,947	11·4
France	7,752	9·9
Netherlands	7,345	9·4
Irish Republic	3,643	4·7
Italy	3,466	4·4
Belgium/Luxembourg	3,348	4·3
Sweden	3,007	3·8
Canada	1,692	2·2
Spain	1,553	2·0
Main suppliers		
Federal Republic of Germany	12,601	14·9
United States	9,920	11·7
France	6,632	7·8
Netherlands	6,551	7·7
Norway	4,367	5·2
Italy	4,294	5·1
Japan	4,117	4·9
Belgium/Luxembourg	4,017	4·7
Irish Republic	2,816	3·3
Sweden	2,466	2·9

Source: *Monthly Review of External Trade Statistics.*
[a] On an overseas trade statistics basis. Exports are f.o.b.; imports c.i.f.

INVISIBLE TRANSACTIONS

Transactions on invisible trade fall into three main groups: services (receipts and payments arising from services, as distinct from goods, supplied to and received from overseas residents); interest, profits and dividends (income arising from outward and inward investment and other capital transactions); and transfers between Britain and other countries.

Invisible trade is of fundamental importance to Britain's economy; overseas earnings from invisibles amounted to £80,608 million in 1985. Britain's earnings are usually exceeded only by those of the United States and France. Britain has nearly always earned a surplus on invisibles and there has not been a deficit since 1947; its surplus is normally second in size to that of the United States though some way behind it. In 1985 Britain's surplus was £5,713 million (see Table 39). The British Invisible Exports Council, which is financed almost entirely by contributions from the private sector, promotes measures to encourage invisible trade.

Earnings from services rose in value by 13 per cent in 1985 to £24,253 million; in volume terms this represented a rise of about 9 per cent. Debits, at £18,441 million, were about 5 per cent higher by value and 2 per cent greater in volume terms. The surplus on services increased to £5,812 million in 1985, with improvements in civil aviation, travel, financial services and other services more than offsetting deteriorations in the government and sea transport accounts.

The surplus on interest, profits and dividends is estimated to have been £3,400 million in 1985. Earnings on portfolio investment (investment in overseas securities) rose by about 45 per cent above the 1984 level to £5,459 million, reflecting the continuing growth in overseas investment following the abolition of exchange controls in 1979 and changes in the method of foreign currency lending by banks located in Britain.

The deficit on transfers in 1985 was £3,499 million, largely on government transactions (mainly contributions and subscriptions to the European Community and other international organisations and bilateral aid).

Table 39: Britain's Invisible Transactions 1985

£ million

	Credits	Debits	Balance
Services	**24,253**	**18,441**	**5,812**
Private sector and public corporations	23,763	16,666	7,097
of which: Sea transport	3,272	4,429	−1,157
Civil aviation	3,188	2,835	353
Travel	5,451	4,877	574
Financial and other services	11,852	4,525	7,327
General government	490	1,775	−1,285
Interest, profits and dividends	**53,032**	**49,632**	**3,400**
Private sector and public corporations	52,479	48,124	4,355
General government	554	1,507	−953
Transfers	**3,323**	**6,822**	**−3,499**
Private	1,511	1,648	−137
General government	1,812	5,174	−3,362
Total invisible transactions	**80,608**	**74,895**	**5,713**

Source: *United Kingdom Balance of Payments 1986 Edition.*
Note: Differences between totals and the sums of their component parts are due to rounding.

COMMERCIAL POLICY

Britain remains committed to the open multilateral trading system and to the further liberalisation of world trade. To this end it has taken a leading part in the activities of such organisations as the General Agreement on Tariffs and Trade (GATT), the International Monetary Fund, the Organisation for Economic Co-operation and Development (OECD) and the United Nations Conference on Trade and Development and has given full support to a new round of multilateral trade negotiations. Since joining the European Community in 1973, Britain has conducted its external commercial policy through the Community. Britain has consistently sought liberalisation of the Community's internal market and has been pressing for action to be taken on the harmonisation of technical standards, the reduction of frontier formalities and the establishment of a free market in services. The Community's common customs tariff is, at an average of 7 to 8 per cent, at a similarly low level to the tariffs of other major industrialised countries.

General Agreement on Tariffs and Trade

Tariff and non-tariff barriers to trade have been considerably reduced in the seven rounds of multilateral trade negotiations completed since 1947 under the auspices of the GATT, the most recent being the Tokyo Round (1973–79). Britain participates in these negotiations as a member of the European Community. In 1982 the GATT devised a programme to liberalise and expand trade. GATT members also agreed to make determined efforts to ensure that trade policies and measures were consistent with the principles and rules of the GATT, and to resist protectionist policies in formulating and implementing national trade policies. Britain has contributed to the implementation of the GATT programme, in particular to work on trade in services, which is of great importance to Britain's employment and overseas earnings. An eighth round of multilateral trade negotiations in the GATT is in prospect.

European Community Trade Agreements

There is duty-free trade between those member states which joined the European Community prior to 1 January 1986. Portugal and Spain joined on that date; duties on their trade with other Community countries are being phased out over a seven- to ten-year period. Britain applies the common customs tariff to all countries neither belonging to, nor having any special arrangement with, the Community.

The Community has reciprocal preferential trading agreements with the European Free Trade Association countries (Austria, Finland, Iceland, Norway, Sweden and Switzerland), Cyprus, Israel, Malta and Turkey, and non-reciprocal agreements with Algeria, Morocco, Tunisia, Egypt, Jordan, Lebanon, Syria, Yugoslavia, and, under the third Lomé Convention, a group of 66 African, Caribbean and Pacific developing countries. The Lomé Convention gives these countries free access (subject to certain safeguards) to the Community for industrial goods and most agricultural products.

Tariff preference is also given to developing countries (under the Generalised Scheme of Preferences), the Faroe Islands and the overseas dependencies and territories of member states.

CONTROLS ON TRADE

Britain maintains few restrictions on its international trade. Most goods may be imported freely and only a narrow range of goods is subject to any sort of export control.

Import Controls

In accordance with its international obligations under the GATT and to the European Community, Britain has progressively removed almost all quantitative import restrictions imposed on economic grounds. Only about 7 per cent of Britain's visible imports are subject to any form of non-tariff restraint and about 80 per cent of imports are admitted into Britain duty free. The few remaining quantitative restrictions mainly affect textile goods (in view of the rapid contraction of the domestic textile industry) and stem primarily from the Multi-Fibre Arrangement (MFA) under which there exists a series of agreements covering international trade in textiles, designed to balance the interests of both exporting and importing countries. The last MFA expired in July 1986. Negotiations on a renewal for a further four to five years are in progress. All quantitative restrictions have been removed from imports of goods of Community origin (except for restraints for a three- to four-year transition period on imports of certain categories of textile product from Portugal and Spain), but certain internationally recognised restrictions operated by the Department of Trade and Industry on a few goods such as firearms, ammunition and nuclear materials continue to apply. Other government departments operate certain restrictions on non-economic grounds (on goods such as meat and poultry, animals, birds, bees, fish and plants and some of their derivatives, controlled drugs, explosives, certain citizens' band radios and indecent or obscene articles) for reasons of health, safety, conservation or social policy.

Export Controls

The great majority of British exports are not subject to any government control or direction. However, there are controls governing exports of military equipment and industrial goods of strategic significance as well as nuclear products and certain metals, and metal scrap. There are also controls, for health certification purposes, on cattle, swine and certain meat exported to another member state of the European Community; endangered species of animals and plants and some of their derivatives, in accordance with international agreements; photographic material over 60 years old and valued at £400 or more per item and other articles over 50 years old (including works of art) valued at £16,000 or more (£4,000 or more in the case of British historical portraits); controlled drugs; British spirits (beverages) in casks of less than 40 litres; and Common Agricultural Policy products.

GOVERNMENT SERVICES

The Government assists exporters by creating conditions favourable to the export trade and by providing information and advice about opportunities for trade in other countries, services designed to help exporters and improve exporting practices, and credit insurance facilities.

British Overseas Trade Board

The British Overseas Trade Board (BOTB) directs Britain's official export promotion services, which include the provision of export intelligence, assistance to British exporters in appointing agents and researching potential markets overseas, help at trade fairs and other promotional events overseas, and support for firms participating in trade missions. It mainly comprises representatives of commerce and industry with personal involvement in exporting, but also includes representatives of the Department of Trade and Industry, the Export Credits Guarantee Department (ECGD), and the Foreign and Commonwealth Office; it operates under the general authority of the Secretary of State for Trade and Industry, who is the president.

Exporters wanting assistance and advice can consult the regional offices of the BOTB throughout Britain and, through these offices, the commercial posts of the British Diplomatic Service overseas. The Scottish Export Office (Industry Department for Scotland), the Welsh Office and the Industrial Development Board for Northern Ireland (Department of Economic Development) also act as BOTB regional offices.

Export Credit Insurance

The Export Credits Guarantee Department provides credit insurance for about one-third of the country's export trade and insures exporters of both goods and services against non-payment by overseas buyers. The main risks covered include insolvency or protracted default of the buyer, governmental action which stops the British exporter receiving payment, new import restrictions, and war or civil disturbance in the buyer's country. Cover may commence from the date of shipment or from the date of contract (at higher premiums).

This insurance may be supplemented by guarantees of repayment given direct to banks financing exports sold on credit of two years or more, whether in sterling or in foreign currencies. Alternatively, for contracts over £1 million, the ECGD will guarantee loans direct to overseas buyers enabling them to pay on cash terms, or 'lines of credit' similarly covering an agreed buying programme of an overseas country. The banks provide finance against these guarantees. The ECGD is also prepared to support the issue of performance bonds in the commercial market in respect of cash or near-cash contracts worth over £250,000.

Investment insurance is provided for new British investment overseas against expropriation, war damage and restrictions on remittances.

BALANCE OF PAYMENTS

The balance of payments statistics record transactions between residents of Britain and non-residents. The transactions are classified into three groups: current account (visibles and invisibles); investment and other capital transactions; and official financing. The balance on current account shows whether Britain has had a surplus of income over expenditure.

Traditionally Britain has had a deficit on visible trade and a surplus on trade in invisibles and this was again the case in 1985. However, in 1980, 1981 and 1982 visible trade was also in surplus. In 1985 Britain had a surplus on current account for the sixth consecutive year. The deficit on visible trade in 1985 was more than £2,000 million lower than in 1984, when performance was more seriously affected by a dispute in the coal industry. The surplus on invisibles in 1985 was only slightly higher than a year earlier but its composition was very different. The surplus on services rose sharply in 1985 with improvements in financial services and travel. The surplus on interest, profits and dividends fell as net payments on the foreign currency operations of British banks increased. The deficit on transfers rose with an increased deficit on transactions with European Community institutions.

A description of visible trade and invisible transactions is given on pp 373–7.

Table 40: Britain's Balance of Payments 1981–85

£ million

	1981	1982	1983	1984	1985
Current account					
Visible trade balance	−3,360	2,331	−835	−4,384	−2,111
Invisible transactions balance	2,799	1,606	3,969	5,596	5,713
Current balance	6,159	3,937	3,134	1,212	3,602
Financial account					
Transactions in assets and liabilities					
British external assets	−49,581	−31,023	−30,815	−31,256	−50,021
British external liabilities	43,071	28,506	26,142	24,920	42,725
Allocation of Special Drawing Rights	158	—	—	—	—
Balancing item	193	−1,420	1,539	5,124	3,694

Source: *United Kingdom Balance of Payments 1986 Edition.*

Capital Flows

Britain's exchange controls were abolished during 1979 and residents are free to acquire foreign currency for any purpose including direct and portfolio investment overseas. Controls on the lending of sterling abroad have also been removed and non-residents may freely acquire sterling for any purpose. Gold may be freely bought and sold. The abolition of exchange controls means that Britain meets its full obligations on capital movements under the OECD Code on Capital Movements and under European Community directives. The Government welcomes both outward and inward investment. Outward investment helps to develop markets for British exports, while providing earnings in the form of interest receipts, profits and dividends. Foreign investment in Britain creates employment; introduces new technology, products, management styles and attitudes; and provides an opportunity to increase exports or substitute imports. Inward investment is particularly encouraged by the Department of Trade and Industry's Invest in Britain Bureau.

In 1985 direct investment overseas by British residents was £7,307 million. British residents' portfolio investment overseas totalled £18,220 million, most of which was investment by banks located in Britain, reflecting a change in their method of foreign currency lending. The inflow of direct and portfolio investment into Britain amounted to £10,435 million. An analysis of transactions in Britain's external assets and liabilities is given in Table 41.

Table 41: Summary of Transactions in External Assets and Liabilities 1983–85[a]

£ million

	1983	1984	1985
Overseas direct investment in Britain	3,438	425	3,370
Overseas portfolio investment in Britain	1,888	1,419	7,065
British direct investment overseas	−5,301	−5,957	−7,307
British portfolio investment overseas	−6,520	−9,550	−18,220
Borrowing from overseas	21,392	23,124	32,263
Deposits and lending overseas	−19,123	−15,914	−22,006
Official reserves[b]	607	908	−1,758
Other external liabilities of general government	−576	−48	27
Other external assets of general government	−478	−743	−730
Total	−4,673	−6,336	−7,296

Source: *United Kingdom Balance of Payments 1986 Edition.*
[a] Assets: increase (−)/decrease (+); liabilities: increase (+)/decrease (−).
[b] Drawings on (+)/additions to (−).

External Assets and Liabilities

At the end of 1985 Britain's identified external assets exceeded identified external liabilities by £80,400 million; private sector net assets were estimated at £79,700 million and public sector net assets at £800 million.[1]

Direct private investment overseas by British residents (investment in branches, subsidiaries and associated companies) totalled £76,700 million at the end of 1985 and portfolio investment £100,600 million. At the end of 1981 (the latest year for which data are available) more than four-fifths of direct investment was in developed countries. One-third of the total was in the United States and just under one-fifth in the European Community. In terms of industries, manufacturing accounted for 37 per cent of direct investment holdings, distribution for 28 per cent, oil for 20 per cent and banking and insurance for the remaining 15 per cent.

Direct investment in Britain by overseas residents amounted to £40,600 million at the end of 1985 and portfolio investment to £32,100 million. At the end of 1981 investment from developed countries accounted for virtually all of overseas direct investment in Britain. Fifty-seven per cent originated in the United States and 23 per cent in the European Community. Slightly under 50 per cent was in manufacturing industry.

[1] The significance of any inventory of Britain's aggregate external assets and liabilities is limited because a variety of claims and obligations are included that are very dissimilar in kind, in degree of liquidity and in method of valuation.

20 Promotion of Science and Technology

Britain has for centuries encouraged research and innovation, and its record of achievement in relation to size of population is in many respects unsurpassed. This record has been maintained throughout the twentieth century. For example, fundamental contributions to modern molecular genetics were made by the working out of the structure of the molecule of deoxyribonucleic acid (DNA) by Professor Francis Crick, Professor Maurice Wilkins, and an American colleague, James Watson, at Cambridge University in 1952. More recent achievements include the research carried out by Mr Patrick Steptoe and Dr Robert Edwards which made possible the birth of the world's first test-tube baby in Britain in 1978, and work on brain and body scanners (based on computerised X-ray readings, nuclear magnetic resonance or ultrasonics) and on monoclonal antibodies (used to diagnose animal diseases and which have the potential to combat human virus diseases). Other notable contributions in recent years have been made by Professor Dennis Gabor on holography (the production of three-dimensional images using lasers), Professor Stephen Hawking on black holes (hypothetical regions of space) and Professor Frederick Sanger on molecular biology. Nobel prizes for science have been won by 68 British citizens, a number exceeded only by the United States, and Table 42 lists British citizens who have won Nobel prizes for science (excluding economic science) since 1970.

Total expenditure in Britain on research and development in 1983 was about £6,700 million, 2·6 per cent of the gross domestic product. About half was provided by industrial enterprises, with a significant contribution also being made by private endowments, trusts and charities. Nationalised and private sector industries finance their own research programmes, and many run their own laboratories. Expenditure on industrial research and development in 1983 was £4,163 million, of which £3,637 million was spent by private sector companies and £526 million by the public sector and by some 40 research associations formed by groups of companies in a particular sector. The main areas of expenditure were electronics (£1,463 million), chemicals and allied products (£735 million), aerospace (£720 million), mechanical engineering (£290 million) and motor vehicles (£240 million).

The Government finances about half of the total expenditure on research and development in Britain, of which roughly a quarter is carried out in government research establishments. Government finance for research and development also goes to industry and the universities. Considerable expenditure is directed towards applied research and the development of new or improved materials, products and processes. In many areas Britain participates in European and other international projects.

Table 42: Recent British Winners of Nobel Prizes for Science

	Year of award	Category	Subject
Sir Bernard Katz	1970	Physiology or Medicine (jointly)	The role of neural transmitter substances
Professor Dennis Gabor	1971	Physics	Invention of holography
Professor Rodney Porter	1972	Physiology or Medicine (jointly)	Discoveries concerning the chemical structure of antibodies
Professor Brian Josephson	1973	Physics	Work on superconductivity (abnormally high conductivity at low temperatures)
Professor Nikolaas Tinbergen	1973	Physiology or Medicine (jointly)	The organisation of individual and social behaviour patterns
Professor Sir Geoffrey Wilkinson	1973	Chemistry (jointly)	Work on organometallic compounds
Sir Martin Ryle and Professor Anthony Hewish	1974	Physics	Development of new types of radio telescopes
Sir Nevill Mott	1977	Physics (jointly)	Theoretical investigations of the electronic structure of magnetic systems
Dr Peter Mitchell	1978	Chemistry	Contributions to the understanding of biological energy transfer
Sir Godfrey Hounsfield	1979	Physiology or Medicine (jointly)	Computer-assisted assembly of X-ray information in three dimensions
Dr Frederick Sanger	1980	Chemistry (jointly)	Determination of base sequences in nucleic acids
Dr Aaron Klug	1982	Chemistry	Work on the structure of viruses and genetic material in cells
Sir John Vane	1982	Physiology or Medicine (jointly)	Clarification of the pathways of prostaglandin metabolism in the body
Dr César Milstein	1984	Physiology or Medicine (jointly)	Production of monoclonal antibodies

Government and Scientific Research

Responsibility for basic civil science in Britain rests with the Secretary of State for Education and Science, and responsibility for technology mainly with the Secretary of State for Trade and Industry, but in all cases the Prime Minister has overall responsibility. In general, applied research and development is undertaken in accordance with the 'customer–contractor principle' under which government departments, as customers, define their research requirements. The work is undertaken by contractors including government laboratories, research councils, universities, research associations and industry. Departments with major scientific or technological needs generally have a Chief Scientist's organisation, which helps to formulate requirements, select the most suitable contractors and co-operate with them to obtain the best value for money.

Advice on scientific and technological matters is provided to the Secretary of State for Education and Science by the Advisory Board for the Research Councils and to the Prime Minister by the Advisory Council for Applied Research and Development (ACARD). A committee of Chief Scientists, under the chairmanship of the Chief Scientific Adviser, Cabinet Office, is responsible for co-ordination among departments. These three bodies ensure that scientific questions are brought before ministers as appropriate and that scientific priorities reflect those of the Government as a whole.

ACARD (whose members include senior industrialists and academics) produces reports on applied research, design and development in Britain; the application of research and technology, developed in Britain and elsewhere, for the benefit of both the public and private sectors in accordance with national economic needs; the co-ordination (in collaboration with the Advisory Board for the Research Councils) of these activities with research supported through the Department of Education and Science; and advice on the annual review of government-funded research and development. It also advises on Britain's role in international collaboration in applied research, design and development related to technology.

Research and Development Expenditure

Total government expenditure on research and development in 1986–87 is estimated to be some £4,800 million. The largest departmental research and development budget is that of the Ministry of Defence. The main civil departments involved are the Department of Education and Science, which supports the research councils and the universities; the Department of Trade and Industry; the Department of Energy; the Ministry of Agriculture, Fisheries and Food and the Department of Agriculture and Fisheries for Scotland; the Department of the Environment; and the Department of Transport.

The Ministry of Defence

Research and development in the Ministry of Defence is aimed at meeting the needs of the Armed Services. The research programme is undertaken both in the Ministry's research establishments and as funded research in industry, universities and other institutions of higher education. In 1986–87 the Ministry plans to spend some £2,300 million, of which some £400 million will be for research and £1,900 million for development. An increasing emphasis is placed on research funded jointly with industry, and initiatives are also being taken to promote 'spin-off' from defence technology to the civil market.

The Department of Trade and Industry

Although most industrial research and development is financed by industry, the Department of Trade and Industry provides support, some £440 million in 1985–86, to stimulate activities which would bring economic benefits but would not otherwise be undertaken by industry. The main areas of expenditure are aeronautics and space (some £185 million in 1985–86), while a wide range of industrial projects, and technology transfer, awareness, training and advisory activities is also undertaken. The Department has four research establishments: the National Physical Laboratory, the National Engineering Laboratory, the Laboratory of the Government Chemist and the Warren Spring Laboratory.

The Department of Education and Science

The Department of Education and Science discharges its responsibilities for basic and applied civil science mainly through the five research councils, to which it allocates funds from its science budget (£615 million in 1986–87). The councils and their allocations are: the Science and Engineering Research

Council (£315·5 million), the Medical Research Council (£128·3 million), the Natural Environment Research Council (£70·3 million), the Agricultural and Food Research Council (£52·7 million) and the Economic and Social Research Council (£23·6 million). Science budget grants are also made to the British Museum (Natural History), the Royal Society and the Fellowship of Engineering. The allocations provide support for research in the form of grants and contracts to universities, polytechnics and elsewhere, research units and other establishments of the research councils, postgraduate support and subscriptions to international scientific organisations. The Department is also responsible for some aspects of international scientific relations and helps to co-ordinate government policy regarding scientific and technical information.

The Department is also the main source of funding for the universities, whose allocations are determined by the University Grants Committee. Although individual universities decide upon the allocation of their resources between teaching and research, the proportion committed to research is generally believed to be between 25 and 30 per cent.

The Advisory Board for the Research Councils

The Advisory Board for the Research Councils advises the Secretary of State on civil science, particularly with regard to the research council system, on the support of postgraduate students, on the proper balance between national and international scientific activities, and on the allocation of the science budget among research councils and other bodies. It also promotes close liaison between the councils and users of their research. Its membership includes the chairman or secretary of each of the research councils, the chairman of the University Grants Committee, the Chief Scientists from departments with a major interest in the work of the research councils, the Chief Scientific Adviser, Cabinet Office, and independent members drawn from universities, industry and the Royal Society.

THE RESEARCH COUNCILS

Each of the five research councils is an autonomous body established under Royal Charter with membership drawn from the universities, professions, industry and the Government. They conduct research through their own research establishments and by supporting selected research, study and training in universities and other higher education establishments. They also receive income for research commissioned by departments under the customer–contractor principle and from the private sector. Income from commissioned research is particularly important for the Agricultural and Food Research Council and the Natural Environment Research Council.

In 1985 the Government announced new arrangements intended to make it easier for educational establishments to exploit research carried out with the support of grants from the research councils. Under the arrangements the rights and responsibility of exploitation will rest with the institution receiving the grant, subject to the existence of procedures agreed with the sponsoring research council.

Science and Engineering Research Council

The Science and Engineering Research Council (SERC) is responsible for the support of basic research work and postgraduate training in pure and applied science (including engineering) outside the areas of agriculture, medicine and the environment. It encourages active collaboration between higher education establishments and industry, particularly in areas of national importance, including the award of studentships to suitable graduates for training in methods of research or a specialised branch of science or engineering of importance to British industry.

Research Establishments	SERC maintains four research establishments: the Daresbury Laboratory at Warrington (Cheshire), the Royal Greenwich Observatory at Herstmonceux (East Sussex), the Royal Observatory, Edinburgh, and the Rutherford Appleton Laboratory at Chilton (Oxfordshire). The establishments are centres of specialised research, and are also used for the development and operation of central experimental facilities beyond the resources of an academic institution. They provide support for scientists whose research needs access to facilities run by international research organisations, such as the powerful particle accelerators at the European Centre for Nuclear Research (CERN) near Geneva and the high-flux neutron source at the Institut Laue-Langevin (ILL) at Grenoble.
International Collaboration	SERC provides national contributions to CERN and the European Incoherent Scatter Facility, and part of Britain's contribution to the European Space Agency (see p 394). It also contributes to the European Science Foundation, and shares with its French and Federal German partners the control of the ILL nuclear reactor at Grenoble. In addition, SERC encourages scientists and engineers to initiate or extend collaborative projects with colleagues overseas by using its fellowships, studentships and grant schemes.
Engineering	Developments in engineering research and training related to the needs of industry are major concerns of SERC. Some special programmes are being supported within a general effort to develop research and postgraduate training in university and polytechnic engineering departments. Among subjects receiving major support are information technology (including software engineering, intelligent knowledge-based systems and device fabrication), radio communications, the application of computers to manufacturing, biotechnology, marine technology, polymer engineering, materials, particulate technology, medical engineering, combustion engines and coal technology. The Teaching Company Scheme, jointly sponsored by SERC and the Department of Trade and Industry, supports collaborative ventures between academic engineering departments and industrial companies to improve their manufacturing methods and performance. A network providing an interactive computing facility to universities is serviced at the Rutherford Appleton Laboratory.
Astronomy	Britain has a leading position in most major branches of astronomy including radio astronomy, infra-red astronomy, X-ray astronomy and theoretical research. In optical astronomy (carried out in university departments and, within SERC, at the Royal Greenwich Observatory and the Royal Observatory, Edinburgh) it is expected to regain its leadership as a result of three optical telescopes which form the basis of a new international observatory on the island of La Palma in the Canary Islands. Two telescopes (the Isaac Newton Telescope, 2·5 m in diameter, and the 1-m Jacobus Kapteyn Telescope) are in use, while the 4·2-m William Herschel Telescope comes into operation in 1987. On Mauna Kea, Hawaii, SERC has a 3·8-m infra-red telescope, the largest telescope in the world designed specifically to make infra-red observations, and the 15-m James Clerk Maxwell radio telescope (which has been built in collaboration with the Netherlands and is scheduled to open in 1987) for observing wavelengths of less than a millimetre. Much of the observation will eventually be carried out under remote control from Britain and the Netherlands using computer communications networks. Cambridge and Manchester universities are the main centres for research in radio astronomy, with substantial support from SERC.

The Starlink network of computer systems, centred at Chilton and located at many centres of astronomical research in Britain, provides and co-ordinates image processing and data reduction facilities for use by British astronomers.

Nuclear Physics SERC establishments concerned with the provision of facilities for university research in nuclear physics are at Chilton, which supports university teams engaged in experiments in particle physics at CERN and other overseas centres, and the Daresbury Laboratory, where there is a 20-million-volt tandem accelerator for research into nuclear structure. Projects using these and other facilities are funded through research grants to universities.

Natural Sciences Support is provided for high-quality research in biological and natural sciences, and mathematics. Where experimental facilities are too expensive to be financed by individual universities and polytechnics, central facilities have been provided. For example, the Daresbury Laboratory operates a synchrotron radiation facility which provides high-intensity electromagnetic radiation used in a wide range of experiments in materials science, surface physics, crystallography and molecular biology. Other central facilities include a high-powered laser facility at Chilton, which is used to study plasmas, and a spallation neutron source, also at Chilton, to provide a pulsed beam of neutrons.

Medical Research Council The Medical Research Council (MRC) is the main government agency for the support of biomedical research, both at its own centres and by means of grants. Its major research establishments are the National Institute for Medical Research at Mill Hill, London, which carries out fundamental research relevant to medicine, the Clinical Research Centre at Northwick Park Hospital, London, and the Laboratory of Molecular Biology at Cambridge. The Council also has 53 research units, mostly located in university departments, medical schools and hospitals in Britain. Its primary objective is to advance knowledge that will improve the level of health. Major areas of activity include neurosciences, molecular and cell biology, reproduction and development, and cancer.

The MRC is assisted by four advisory boards: the Neurosciences and Mental Health Board; the Cell Biology and Disorders Board; the Physiological Systems and Disorders Board; and the Tropical Medicine Research Board.

Natural Environment Research Council The Natural Environment Research Council (NERC) has responsibility for research in the physical and biological aspects of the natural environment. The work is divided among three directorates: Earth Sciences, Marine Sciences, and Terrestrial and Freshwater Sciences. The Council's research institutes are: the British Antarctic Survey, the British Geological Survey, the Institute of Hydrology, the Institute for Marine Environmental Research, the Institute of Oceanographic Sciences, the Institute of Terrestrial Ecology, the Institute of Virology and the Sea Mammal Research Unit. The Council also operates a research vessel base and maintains a central computing service in support of all its institutes.

Research institutes aided by council grants are: the Freshwater Biological Association, the Marine Biological Association of the United Kingdom and the Scottish Marine Biological Association. Units based at universities include the NERC Unit for Thematic Information Systems at the University of Reading, and the Unit of Comparative Plant Ecology at Sheffield University.

Commissioned research accounts for about one-third of NERC's income. Contract research is carried out for public authorities, industry and commerce, both in Britain and overseas, and NERC is able to supply experienced personnel and material facilities across the spectrum of environmental science. Many applied projects are in progress overseas, for example, on biological pest control, regeneration of tropical hardwoods and drip irrigation techniques for tropical crops.

Agricultural and Food Research Council

The Agricultural and Food Research Council (AFRC), together with the Department of Agriculture and Fisheries for Scotland, supports a network of research institutes in Britain collectively known as the Agricultural and Food Research Service. The Service is involved with research into a wide range of topics relevant to the agricultural, horticultural and food industries: animals, plants, soils, engineering, nutrition and food. The results of this research are applied to increase the efficiency of these industries and those that support them, including the chemical and engineering industries. However, under the AFRC's long-term strategy, greater emphasis is being given to those areas of science related to agriculture and food, especially human food and nutrition research. Organisational changes have been implemented to consolidate research work into eight new institutes, each responsible for one area of research.

Economic and Social Research Council

The Economic and Social Research Council (ESRC) supports research, mainly in universities, polytechnics and research institutes. Among the research interests of its standing committees are the competitiveness of British industry, social change and economic life, information technology and education, efficiency in government, and the changing urban and regional system. The Council acts as agent for the Advisory Board for the Research Councils in preparing a programme of research on science policy, and for the Department of Trade and Industry in commissioning studies of public acceptance of new technologies.

UNIVERSITY RESEARCH

Of the total estimated university expenditure on scientific research in the academic year 1984–85 (£700 million), the largest government contribution (£360 million) was through the University Grants Committee.

Scientific research in the universities and other institutions of higher education is also supported through the research councils. This support takes two forms. First, almost half of the postgraduate students in science and technology receive maintenance awards from the research councils, through postgraduate studentships. These awards are in some cases for periods of up to three years of training in research work and in others for shorter periods for advanced studies. Secondly, grants and contracts are given to the universities and other institutions by the research councils for specified projects, particularly in new or developing areas of research. The AFRC, MRC and ESRC maintain a number of research units within universities. In addition, the research councils provide central facilities in their own establishments for use by university research workers. The other main channels of support for scientific research in the universities are various government departments, the Royal Society, industry and the independent foundations.

A number of universities in industrial centres have acquired outstanding reputations in studies relating to their local industries, and on a national scale close relationships are fostered between the universities, industry and the Government in numerous joint projects.

Science Parks

Of special interest are science parks, sites containing science-based industries, which have been designed to facilitate advanced technology through collaboration between university and industrial scientists and technologists. Britain's first science park was established in 1972 at Heriot-Watt University in Edinburgh. At the end of 1985 there were some 20 university-based science parks in Britain, with a further six in various stages of planning. In addition, there were more than 20 non-university high technology developments similar to science parks.

There are some 300 tenants on Britain's science parks, employing about

3,800 people. The parks vary widely in size, scope and management. The Listerhills high-technology development at Bradford University, on a site of only 6,000 sq m (64,000 sq ft), provides accommodation for 28 businesses, most of which are involved in microelectronics and computing, which together employ some 200 people. The Cambridge Science Park occupies a 53-hectare (130-acre) site, and the 65 tenants are engaged in a wide range of activities including the manufacture of ultra-violet light sources and pharmaceuticals, and services such as oil exploration consultancy and venture capital funds. Some 1,700 people are employed by companies on the science park.

CHARITABLE FOUNDATIONS

Charitable foundations sponsoring research in Britain include: the Cancer Research Campaign, the Chester Beatty Institute for Cancer Research, the Ciba Foundation, the Imperial Cancer Research Fund, the Institute for Cancer Research, the Leverhulme Foundation, the Nuffield Foundation, the Wellcome Trust and the Wolfson Foundation.

PROFESSIONAL INSTITUTIONS

There are numerous technical institutions and professional associations, many of which promote their own disciplines or are interested in the education and professional well-being of their members. The Council of Science and Technology Institutes has 15 member institutes representing, among others, biologists, chemists, mathematicians, metallurgists, physicists and geologists.

The Fellowship of Engineering

The Fellowship of Engineering, formed from distinguished engineers in the Royal Society and the leading chartered engineering institutions, advises the Government and other relevant bodies on all aspects of engineering. It also arranges lectures, seminars and conferences on matters of national importance in engineering. The Fellowship was incorporated by Royal Charter in 1983. Up to 60 leading engineers from industry, the academic world and the public service in Britain are elected each year and there were 660 Fellows in 1986.

THE LEARNED SOCIETIES

More than 300 learned societies in Britain play an important part in the promotion of science and technology. Through meetings, publications and recognition by the scientific community, they help to maintain high academic and professional standards and facilitate the spread of knowledge. The Royal Society, the oldest of these societies, is also the national academy of science, while the Royal Colleges in the various fields of medicine and the Fellowship of Engineering have similar leading roles in their areas. In addition, the Royal Society of Arts, the Royal Institution and the British Association for the Advancement of Science are also broadly concerned with the promotion of science and technology. In Scotland the Royal Society of Edinburgh, founded in 1783, is concerned with the promotion of science and literature.

Royal Society

The Royal Society, or, more fully, the Royal Society of London for Improving Natural Knowledge, founded in 1660, occupies a unique place in Britain's scientific affairs and is equivalent to national academies of sciences in other countries. It is the oldest such academy in the world to have enjoyed continuous existence. There are today three main categories of Fellowship: Royal Fellows; Foreign Members, of whom there are about 90; and the main body of Fellows numbering over 1,000. Election to the Fellowship, which is for life, is restricted to 40 people a year. The Royal Society is governed by a council of 21 members. The President of the Society is consulted on scientific appointments to research councils (other than the Economic and Social Research Council) and Fellows serve on most of the governmental advisory councils and committees concerned with research. The Society is financed through a parliamentary grant

(£6 million in 1985–86) and through funds from private sources (£3 million in 1985–86).

The Royal Society recognises the highest standards of scientific and technological achievements through its elections to the Fellowship and the award of its medals and endowed lectureships. It awards 15 medals (not all annually) including the Copley Medal (its highest award) and three Royal Medals, while there are eight endowed lectureships. The Society encourages research through the award of grants and research appointments. It administers 18 research professorships, of which four are supported from private funds and the remainder from its parliamentary grant. In addition, over 130 senior research fellowships and research fellowships are supported in British universities. Grants for research are made from its private funds and from its parliamentary grant, and particular funds are available for field research overseas, for travel by individual scientists, for studies in the history of science and for scientific publications. The dissemination of scientific knowledge is encouraged by a programme of scientific discussion meetings and through its publications. It has an extensive library of works relating to the history of science. The council gives advice to the Government and other bodies on matters relating to science and technology and their application, and study groups on particular aspects of science are established at intervals to prepare reports which are widely distributed to the scientific community. The Society, jointly with the Fellowship of Engineering, established in 1986 a Science and Engineering Policy Studies Unit to undertake detailed studies in areas important to national science policy. A number of committees of the council, some of them jointly with other bodies, promote improvements in education in science subjects and links between industry and higher education.

The international relations of the Royal Society are extensive. As the national academy of science, it represents Britain in all but two of the 19 international unions comprising the International Council of Scientific Unions. It is a member of the European Science Foundation and certain other organisations, and also plays a leading part in international scientific programmes. It has agreements for exchange visits by scientists and co-operative research with many academies throughout the world, and maintains informal relations to promote scientific co-operation with many other countries; some 3,000 visits abroad for periods ranging from a few days to two years are supported annually. The largest formal scheme is the European Science Exchange Programme, which provides for fellowships (usually of one year) and study visits (lasting about two months) with 15 other countries in Western Europe.

Royal Society of Arts

The Royal Society of Arts (properly, the Royal Society for the Encouragement of Arts, Manufactures and Commerce) is concerned with arts, architecture and design, science and technology, industry and commerce, the environment and education. Since its foundation in 1754, one of the Society's principal objects has been to promote the progress of all branches of practical knowledge, chiefly by means of lectures and conferences, and by the publication of a monthly journal designed to enable leading authorities to report on developments of public as well as specialist interest.

Royal Institution

The Royal Institution was founded in 1799 as a public body for facilitating the introduction of useful mechanical inventions and improvements, and for teaching the application of science to everyday life. It has extensive laboratories which undertake research on subjects including photophysics, photochemistry, photobiology, crystal structure and catalysis. Lectures are given to members and schoolchildren on recent developments in science and other branches of knowledge; the Institution has an extensive programme of educational activities, with particular emphasis on encouraging young people to take an interest in science.

British Association

The British Association for the Advancement of Science was founded in 1831 to promote general interest in science and its applications. One of its chief activities is the Annual Meeting, attended by many young students as well as by eminent scientists. In addition, the Association plans special lectures, exhibitions, conferences and discussions, appoints study groups and publishes pamphlets. The Association has 16 branches and five lectureships for young scientists (dealing with the physical, biological and social sciences) to encourage scientists to make their activities known to wider audiences.

Zoological Gardens

The Zoological Society of London, an independent scientific body, runs the world-famous London Zoo, which occupies 14 hectares (36 acres) of Regent's Park, London. The Society also runs Whipsnade Park Zoo near Dunstable (Bedfordshire) where some 2,000 animals roam a 200-hectare (500-acre) park. The Society is responsible for the Institute of Zoology, which carries out research in conservation and comparative medicine. It also organises scientific meetings and symposia for zoologists, publishes scientific journals and maintains one of the largest zoological libraries in the world. Other well-known zoos include those at Edinburgh, Bristol, Chester, Dudley, Chessington, Marwell (near Winchester) and Jersey. There are also a number of 'safari parks' containing wild animals; the public can drive through the parks in closed motor cars.

Botanical Gardens

The Royal Botanic Gardens (founded in 1759) cover 121 hectares (300 acres) at Kew (west London) and a 187-hectare (462-acre) estate at Wakehurst Place, Ardingly (West Sussex). They contain the largest collections of living and dried plants in the world. The Herbarium is primarily concerned with research into the classification of plants and the preparation of floras and plant lists as well as the identification of about 50,000 specimens a year from overseas. A Conservation Unit gathers and provides information on endangered species of plant on a world-wide basis. The study of plant anatomy, plant biochemistry, cytology and genetics is undertaken in the Jodrell Laboratory at Kew. The laboratory's plant physiology section is based at Wakehurst Place where research is being carried out into seed germination and storage, and a seed bank of temperate and tropical species is maintained. A wide range of living plants, comprising some 50,000 plant species representing most families, is displayed at Kew.

The Royal Botanic Garden at Edinburgh was founded in 1670. The Garden has three outstations, at Benmore (near Dunoon), at Logan (near Stranraer) and at Dawyck (near Peebles). The large collection of living plants, both out of doors and in greenhouses, is used for taxonomic (plant classification) and related research. An important botanical library with over 75,000 volumes is maintained at Edinburgh.

Scientific Museums

The British Museum (Natural History) is one of the world's principal centres for the general study of natural history, particularly for specialised research into taxonomy. It has five scientific departments: botany, entomology, mineralogy, palaeontology and zoology. It possesses extensive collections of extant and fossil animals and plants and of minerals, rocks and meteorites. The Science Museum illustrates the development of pure and applied science in all countries, but chiefly in Britain. The geology of Britain is probably known in more exact detail than that of any other country in the world, and there is an outstanding collection of exhibits in the Geological Museum. These three museums are in South Kensington, London. Other important collections include the Museum of

ALTERNATIVE ENERGY

The 'wind-energy farm' at Altamont Pass, California, is the world's largest collection of wind turbines, and was designed and built by the James Howden Group of Scotland. The 86 turbines produce about 30 MW of energy.

Right: BP Solar Systems Ltd has supplied over 5,000 33-watt solar modules to produce power for 38 microwave repeater stations in Peru's telecommunications network.

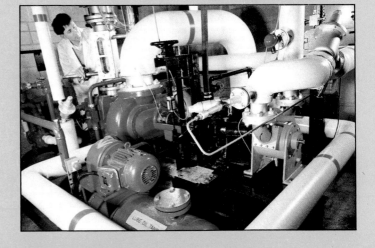

The City University, London, has developed a system to recover energy from geothermal hot water, hot rocks or industrial waste heat, and which is claimed to be able to recover twice the amount of energy than systems now in use.

SCIENTIFIC RESEARCH

Bulk monoclonal antibody production fermenter at Celltech. Set up by the British Technology Group in 1980, the company markets diagnostic kits based on monoclonal antibodies, used, for instance, to help in the diagnosis of viral diseases including AIDS.

The main synchrotron ring of the Spallation Neutron Source – a £100 million research project at the Rutherford Appleton Laboratory – designed to be the world's most powerful source of pulsed neutron beams, and one of the major international scientific facilities for which Britain is host nation.

"Green glue plants, now being studied at the Royal Botanic Gardens, Kew, could help to prevent the advance of desert in arid and semi-arid areas.

Right: British scientists carrying out research into diseases affecting clove trees in Zanzibar. Cloves are Zanzibar's main export.

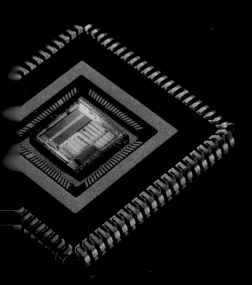

Above: The transputer, developed in Britain by Inmos, and claimed to be the world's first computer on a single chip, can process, on average, 10 million instructions per second.

MEDICAL TECHNOLOGY

Developed in Britain, this new anatomy teaching device combines video discs and detailed films in an interactive system for medical students. It can be used to differentiate tissue, study blood supply to particular organs or show the progression of disease, and is designed to reinforce practical anatomy work.

The first computerised system for the production of texts in Moon, an embossed language which is easier to read than Braille, has been developed by Brunel University's Research Unit for the Blind. By typing in the English text, documents can be produced in Moon, as well as Braille and large-print.

Science and Industry, in Birmingham, the Museum of the History of Science, at Oxford, and the Royal Scottish Museum, Edinburgh.

INTER-NATIONAL SCIENTIFIC RELATIONS

Britain is fully involved in the European Community committees concerned with the co-ordination of national policies on scientific and technological research and the implementation of joint projects of interest to the Community. It is also an active member of the Committee for Scientific and Technological Policy of the Organisation for Economic Co-operation and Development. Other intergovernmental organisations involved in scientific co-operation with which Britain is concerned include: specialised agencies of the United Nations such as the International Atomic Energy Agency; European Co-operation in Science and Technology; the Nuclear Energy Agency and the International Energy Agency; the European Centre for Nuclear Research; the European Space Agency; the European Molecular Biology Laboratory; the International Agency for Research on Cancer; the Institut Laue-Langevin; and the North Atlantic Treaty Organisation Science Committee. Britain is the host nation for a number of major international scientific facilities, such as the European Atomic Energy Community's Joint European Torus nuclear fusion project at Culham (Oxfordshire) and the Spallation Neutron Source at Chilton.

Among non-governmental organisations Britain is represented in the international unions comprising the International Council of Scientific Unions (see p 391). The five research councils, the Royal Society and the British Academy were founder members of the European Science Foundation in 1974. Since 1968 Britain has signed over 35 intergovernmental agreements with other countries on co-operation in science and technology or technical co-operation. These agreements are usually intended to promote mutually beneficial exchanges and are administered by various government departments. Britain has also played an active part in the Eureka initiative to promote collaborative projects by European companies in high technology sectors.

There are science and technology sections in the British Embassies in Washington, Paris, Bonn, Tokyo and Moscow, while staff in other British Embassies and High Commissions also promote contacts in science and technology between Britain and the countries to which they are accredited. They serve all central government departments concerned in overseas scientific affairs, as well as research councils and the Royal Society, which is the main representative of Britain in areas of non-governmental scientific collaboration. Substantial use of their services is made by industrialists. Reports from the embassies on overseas science and technology are disseminated to over 1,000 British companies. Administrative support for the overseas scientific network is provided by the Department of Trade and Industry's Overseas Technical Information Unit.

The British Council (which promotes an understanding of Britain overseas through cultural, educational and technical co-operation) fosters co-operation between British scientists and those of overseas countries to promote among overseas specialists a better understanding and knowledge of Britain and its scientific achievements, and, in the developing countries, to identify and manage development projects in the technological, scientific and educational sectors. The Council helps British scientists to visit other countries, makes its own awards for postgraduate study in Britain by scientists from overseas and supervises programmes for senior specialists and students who come to Britain through United Nations agencies or bilateral technical co-operation schemes.

Space Activities

The main tasks of the British National Space Centre (BNSC), established in 1985, are to produce a national space plan, to co-ordinate British space efforts and to foster the development of space technology. Its staff are drawn from the

Department of Trade and Industry, the Ministry of Defence, the Science and Engineering Research Council, the Natural Environment Research Council and industry. Government expenditure on civil space research amounts to about £100 million a year.

Britain is a member of the European Space Agency (ESA) together with Belgium, Denmark, France, the Federal Republic of Germany, the Irish Republic, Italy, the Netherlands, Spain, Sweden and Switzerland, while Austria and Norway will become members in 1987. The BNSC is responsible for leading the British delegation to the ESA. In the ESA's space applications programmes, British industry has led the consortia which have developed all of the satellites for the International Maritime Satellite Organisation and the European Communications Satellite series leased to the European telecommunications satellite authority (EUTELSAT). A much larger satellite, Olympus, is under development and is expected to be launched in 1987. This series of developments has been complemented by a national space programme administered by the BNSC which leads a British industry with advanced and wide-ranging capabilities, particularly in telecommunications.

In the ESA's other applications programmes, Britain is developing the main microwave instrument for an earth observation satellite, ERS-1, to be launched in 1989. Britain is also participating in the Ariane 4 launcher programme and in the Columbus preparatory programme. The latter, started in 1985, is designed to define the European contribution to the international space station proposed by the United States, and Britain is leading the studies on astronaut-tended platforms.

The BNSC is also responsible for Britain's space science programme, funding British experimenter groups and representing British interests in the ESA's science programme. British groups have been selected to participate in all but one of the ESA's science missions. The most recent was the mission to observe Halley's Comet – Giotto, which used a British-built spacecraft. British groups have been selected to participate in the ESA's infra-red observatory satellite project, which has recently been approved.

Participation in ESA missions is complemented by bilateral arrangements for space research with other countries, notably the United States through its National Aeronautics and Space Administration (NASA). British groups have participated in several NASA space science missions, and are currently developing a payload for NASA's Upper Atmosphere Research Satellite. Other collaborations include the development of the wide field camera for the Federal Republic of Germany's X-ray satellite ROSAT.

Through these programmes, British experimenter groups have gained an international reputation for their scientific work, especially in astronomy, geophysics and climate research.

21 Promotion of the Arts

Artistic and cultural activity in Britain ranges from the highest standards of professional performance to the enthusiastic support and participation of amateurs. London is one of the leading world centres for drama, music, opera and dance, and festivals held in towns and cities throughout the country attract much interest. Many British playwrights, composers, film-makers, sculptors, painters, writers, actors, singers, choreographers and dancers enjoy international reputations. Television and radio play an important role in bringing a wide range of artistic events to a large audience. At an amateur level, activities which make use of local talent and resources take many forms: choral, orchestral, operatic, dramatic and other societies for the arts abound, and increasing numbers of people take an interest in crafts such as pottery, weaving and woodwork. Arts activities introduced by the ethnic minorities are also flourishing, and range from Indian dance to Pakistani poetry and Caribbean steel bands.

Policies

The broad objectives of the Government's policies for the arts are to assist the provision and development of the performing and visual arts; maintain and enhance the collections of the national museums and art galleries; help preserve objects of importance to the national heritage; and sustain and develop national collections of literary material, archive and information stores. The general aim underlying these objectives is to meet the need for public access to, and enjoyment and appreciation of, the nation's cultural heritage and talents. The Government is maintaining existing levels of support for arts activities; encouraging private funding of the arts by various means including sponsorship; and making the arts more available to people in the regions. National museums and galleries are encouraged by the Government to increase their receipts either through trading activities or by making admission charges. An important concept in its funding policy is the 'arm's length principle' by which government funds are distributed to arts organisations indirectly, through bodies such as the Arts Councils and the British Film Institute; this helps to safeguard against political interference in arts activities.

Administration

Promotion and patronage of the arts are the concern of both official and unofficial bodies. The Government and local authorities play an active part, and a substantial and increasing amount of help also comes from private sources, including trusts and commercial concerns.

The Minister for the Arts, a Minister of State at the Privy Council Office, is responsible for general arts policy and heads the Office of Arts and Libraries which administers government expenditure on national museums and art galleries in England, the Arts Council, the British Library and other national arts and heritage bodies. Responsibility for the upkeep of ancient monuments and historic buildings is exercised by the Department of the Environment; the Historic Buildings and Monuments Commission for England (known as English Heritage) manages 400 ancient monuments and buildings on behalf of the

Secretary of State for the Environment. The regulation of the film industry and of broadcasting is conducted by the Department of Trade and Industry and the Home Office, respectively. The Secretaries of State for Wales and Scotland are responsible for the national museums, galleries and libraries in their countries, and for other cultural matters. In Northern Ireland the Department of Education has responsibility for these affairs.

Local authorities support a wide range of artistic and cultural activities. They maintain more than 1,000 local museums and art galleries, and some 4,000 public libraries; provide grant aid for professional and voluntary organisations including orchestras and theatre, opera and ballet companies; and undertake direct promotions through local arts councils. They also contribute to the cost of new or converted buildings for the arts.

Arts education in schools, colleges, polytechnics, evening institutes and community centres is the responsibility of central government education departments, in partnership with local education authorities and voluntary bodies.

Finance

Planned central government expenditure through the Office of Arts and Libraries amounts to some £320 million in 1986–87. About one-third of current expenditure is being spent on nine national galleries and museums in England, about a fifth on the British Library and two-fifths channelled through the Arts Council to support the performing and visual arts throughout Britain. Grants are also made to bodies including the British Film Institute, the Crafts Council, certain other museums, and to the National Heritage Memorial Fund. The Fund provides assistance to organisations wishing to acquire, for the public benefit, land, buildings, works of art and other objects associated with the national heritage. Additional central government expenditure on arts and libraries in Scotland, Wales and Northern Ireland amounts to over £100 million.

Planned spending on the arts and libraries by local authorities in 1986–87 is about £500 million. Some 80 per cent of current expenditure by the authorities in England is on the public library service, and the remainder on local museums and art galleries. Following the abolition of the upper tier of local government in Greater London and the metropolitan counties in April 1986, extra central government funding totalling £43 million in 1986–87 is being allocated to support the performing arts, films and museums to replace funding from these sources.

Industrial and commercial concerns offer a vital and growing source of sponsorship and patronage to a wide range of arts, including exhibitions, concerts and opera seasons, and are often advised by the Association for Business Sponsorship of the Arts and the Arts Councils. The Business Sponsorship Incentive Scheme was launched by the Office of Arts and Libraries in 1984, and in 1986–87 it has available £1·75 million to match new business sponsorships. The value of business sponsorship is currently some £20 million a year. Further support is encouraged by tax concessions announced in 1986 which will allow companies and individuals to obtain tax relief on donations to arts charities.

Two of the most generous acts of private patronage in recent years were made in 1985: an endowment of £20 million, to be followed by a further £30 million in subsequent years, was made to the National Gallery by Mr J. Paul Getty II, KBE, of the United States, and a gift to the nation of a new extension to the gallery (which is likely to cost in the region of £20 million) was made by the Sainsbury family.

Arts Councils

The independent Arts Council of Great Britain, established by Royal Charter in 1946, is the main channel for government aid to the performing and visual arts.

Its main objects are to develop and improve the knowledge, understanding and practice of the performing and visual arts, increase their accessibility to the public, and advise and co-operate with government departments, local authorities and other organisations. The Council gives financial help and advice to organisations ranging from the major opera, dance and drama companies, orchestras and festivals, to small touring theatres and experimental groups. It encourages such interests as contemporary dance, mime, jazz, literature, photography and art films, and helps professional creative writers, choreographers, composers, artists and photographers through a variety of schemes. It also promotes art exhibitions and tours of opera, dance and drama companies and of contemporary music groups, and provides funds for some specialist training courses in the arts.

Under a development programme for the next decade, launched in 1984, the Council is increasing its funding of the arts in the regions. In the first five years support for new activities is being concentrated in five main areas of the arts—art, dance, drama, music and education—focusing on 13 main centres of population throughout England. Increased funding and responsibilities are also being given to the regional arts associations (see below).

Organisations in Scotland and Wales receive their subsidies through the Scottish and Welsh Arts Councils, which are committees of the Arts Council of Great Britain with a large measure of autonomy. Northern Ireland has an independent Arts Council with aims and functions similar to those of the Arts Council of Great Britain.

Following the abolition of the Greater London Council, the Arts Council of Great Britain assumed responsibility for London's South Bank arts centre.

Regional Arts Associations

Regional co-operation in development of the arts is encouraged through 15 regional arts associations in England and Wales, which bring together all those in a region, ranging from local authorities and private companies to local artists, with an interest in improving the artistic life of their area. Their aim is to ensure that the arts are more widely available and that artists receive support at regional as well as national level. They offer financial assistance to artists and arts organisations, and advise on, and in some cases promote, activities. They are financed mainly by the Arts Council, the British Film Institute, the Crafts Council and local authorities, and these interests are represented on their governing bodies. Business sponsorship is also an increasingly important source of regional funds.

Arts Centres

About 220 arts centres in Britain provide opportunities for enjoyment of and participation in a range of arts activities. Amateur activities are supported by resident professional staff. The centres are supported mainly by regional arts associations and local authorities with some help from the Arts Council and other organisations. Many theatres and art galleries also provide a focal point for the community by offering facilities for other arts.

Local Arts Councils

Local arts councils in towns and communities throughout Britain, some of them founded and supported by local authorities, seek to promote and co-ordinate arts activities in their localities. Industrial and commercial interests also give financial help.

British Council

The British Council promotes knowledge of British culture and literature overseas and maintains libraries in many of the 80 or so countries in which it is represented. The Council may initiate or support overseas tours by British theatre companies, orchestras, choirs, and opera and dance companies, as well as by individual actors, musicians and artists. It promotes fine arts and other exhibitions overseas, organises British participation in international exhibitions and film festivals, maintains film libraries in many of the countries in which it works, and encourages professional interchange in all cultural fields between Britain and other countries.

Broadcasting Organisations

Both BBC radio and television and the independent television companies broadcast a wide variety of drama (including adaptations of novels and stage plays), opera, ballet, and music, and general arts magazine programmes and documentaries. These have won many international awards at festivals such as the Prix Italia and Montreux International Television Festivals. Independent television companies also make grants for the promotion of the arts in their regions.

The BBC has orchestras employing many of Britain's full-time professional musicians, and each week it broadcasts nearly 100 hours of classical and other music (both live and recorded) on its Radio 3 channel. Radios 1 and 2 broadcast popular and light music. The BBC regularly commissions new music, particularly by British composers, and sponsors concerts, competitions and festivals.

Festivals

Considerable interest and enthusiasm is shown for the 240 professional arts festivals which take place in Britain each year. The Edinburgh International Festival, featuring a wide range of different arts, is the largest of its kind in the world and celebrated its fortieth anniversary in 1986. Well-known festivals concentrating on music include the Three Choirs Festival, which has taken place annually for more than 250 years in Gloucester, Worcester or Hereford; the Cheltenham Festival, largely devoted to contemporary British music; and the Aldeburgh and Bath festivals. Among others catering for a number of art forms are the Royal National Eisteddfod of Wales, the Llangollen International Musical Eisteddfod and the festivals in Belfast, Buxton, Malvern, Chichester, Harrogate, Salisbury, Windsor and York.

DRAMA Professional Theatre

Britain is one of the world's foremost countries for theatre, and has a long and rich dramatic tradition. As well as companies based in London and other major cities and towns, numerous touring companies visit a wide range of theatres, festivals and other venues throughout Britain including arts and sports centres and working men's clubs. Contemporary British playwrights who have received international recognition include Harold Pinter, Tom Stoppard, Alan Ayckbourn, Caryl Churchill and David Edgar. The musicals of Andrew Lloyd Webber, such as *Cats* and *Evita*, have enjoyed considerable success both in Britain and overseas. Among the best-known directors are Sir Peter Hall, Trevor Nunn, Peter Brook, John Schlesinger and Terry Hands, while the many British performers who enjoy international reputations include Dame Peggy Ashcroft, Lord (formerly Sir Laurence) Olivier, Sir John Gielgud, Sir Alec Guinness, Vanessa Redgrave, Ian McKellen, Derek Jacobi, Jeremy Irons and Glenda Jackson. British designers such as John Bury, Ralph Koltai and Carl Toms are internationally recognised.

Britain has about 300 theatres intended for professional use which can seat between 200 and 2,300 people. Some are privately owned, but most are owned either municipally or by non-profit-distributing organisations. About 50 of these house resident theatre companies which receive subsidies from the Arts Council. London is the main focus with a hundred or so West End and suburban theatres, 12 of which are permanently occupied by subsidised companies. These include the National Theatre, which stages a wide range of modern and classical plays in its three auditoria in the South Bank arts centre; the Royal Shakespeare Company, which, while also performing in Stratford upon Avon, produces plays mainly by Shakespeare and his contemporaries, as well as modern work, in its two auditoria in the City's Barbican Centre; and the English Stage Company at the Royal Court Theatre, which produces the work of the most talented new playwrights.

Outside London most cities and many large towns have at least one theatre; some, like the Palace Theatre, Manchester, and the Theatre Royal, Nottingham, date from the nineteenth century and have been handsomely restored. Others, like the Crucible Theatre, Sheffield, and the Theatre Royal, Plymouth, have been built to the latest designs. Some universities such as those in Aberystwyth, Exeter and Newcastle upon Tyne have theatres which house professional companies playing to the general public. Most regional repertory companies mount about eight to ten productions a year; some also have studio theatres in addition to the main auditorium, where they present new or experimental drama and plays of specialist interest. Repertory theatres also frequently serve the function of a social centre and meeting place by offering a wide range of events such as concerts, poetry recitals and exhibitions, and by providing restaurants, bars and theatre shops. Successful productions from regional theatre companies often transfer to London's West End, while the largest regional theatres receive visits from the National Theatre or the Royal Shakespeare Company.

Theatre for Young People

A number of companies provide theatre for young audiences. Unicorn Theatre for Young People and Polka Children's Theatre, both in London, produce plays specially written for children, and the Whirligig Theatre tours throughout the country. The Young Vic Company in London and Contact Theatre Company in Manchester produce plays for young people. There are numerous Theatre-in-Education companies which perform in schools for all age ranges and abilities. Some of these companies operate independently (such as Theatre Centre, which plays in London and tours further afield), while others are attached to regional repertory theatres such as the Belgrade in Coventry and the Playhouse in Leeds. Most regional repertory theatres also mount occasional productions aimed at younger audiences, and concessionary ticket prices for those at school, college or university are generally available. There are also a number of puppet companies.

Both the National Youth Theatre in London and the Scottish Youth Theatre in Edinburgh offer early acting opportunities to young people.

Dramatic Training

Training for actors and stage managers is provided mainly in drama schools, among which the best known are the Royal Academy of Dramatic Art, the Central School of Speech and Drama, the London Academy of Music and Drama, and the Drama Centre (all in London), and the Bristol Old Vic School, the Royal Scottish Academy of Music and Drama (Glasgow) and the Manchester Polytechnic School of Drama. There are a number of theatre design courses, often based in art schools, which train designers for the stage. Several universities, polytechnics and other colleges offer courses in drama.

Amateur Theatre

There are several thousand amateur dramatic societies throughout Britain. Their work is encouraged by a number of bodies, such as the British Theatre Association, the Central Council for Amateur Theatre, the National Drama Conference, the Scottish Community Drama Association and the Association of Ulster Drama Festivals. Amateur companies sometimes receive financial support from local government, regional arts associations and other bodies.

MUSIC, OPERA AND DANCE

The widespread interest in classical music in Britain is reflected in the large audiences at choral and orchestral concerts and at performances of opera, dance and chamber music. Rock and pop music are extremely popular, especially among younger people, while folk music, jazz, light music and brass bands also have substantial followings.

Music

Orchestral and Choral

Seasons of orchestral and choral concerts are promoted every year in many of the large towns and cities. The principal concert-halls in central London are the Royal Festival Hall, next to which are the Queen Elizabeth Hall and the Purcell Room accommodating smaller-scale performances; the Barbican Hall (part of the Barbican Centre for Arts and Conferences); the Royal Albert Hall, where the world-famous seasons of BBC Promenade Concerts are given each summer; the Wigmore Hall, a recital centre; and St John's, Smith Square.

The leading symphony orchestras are the London Philharmonic, the London Symphony (resident at the Barbican Centre), the Philharmonia, the Royal Philharmonic, the BBC Symphony, the Royal Liverpool Philharmonic, the Hallé (Manchester), the City of Birmingham Symphony, the Bournemouth Symphony, and the Ulster and the Scottish National Orchestras. The BBC's six orchestras provide broadcast concerts which are often open to the public. There are also specialised string and chamber orchestras such as the English Chamber Orchestra, the Academy of St Martin-in-the-Fields, the Academy of Ancient Music, the Bournemouth Sinfonietta, the Northern Sinfonia (Newcastle upon Tyne), the Scottish Ensemble and the Scottish Chamber Orchestra. The London Sinfonietta specialises in performing contemporary music. Groups playing authentic early instruments attract interest throughout the country.

British conductors such as Sir Colin Davis, Sir Neville Marriner and Simon Rattle reach a wide audience through their recordings as well as by their performances, and the works of living composers such as Sir Michael Tippett and Peter Maxwell Davies enjoy international acclaim. The Master of the Queen's Music, Malcolm Williamson, holds an office within the Royal Household with responsibility for organising and writing music for state occasions.

Choirs

The principal choral societies include the Bach Choir, the Royal Choral Society, the Cardiff Polyphonic Choir, the Edinburgh Choral Union and the Belfast Philharmonic Society. Almost all the leading orchestras have close links with particular choirs. The English tradition of church singing is represented by choirs such as those of King's College Chapel, Cambridge, and Christ Church Cathedral, Oxford. There are many male-voice choirs in Wales and in certain parts of England.

Pop and Rock Music

Among the characteristics of modern pop and rock music are the diversity of styles, the frequency with which new styles and stars emerge, and the short lifespan of many groups. Electric guitars and drums usually provide the instrumental basis, but there has been an increasing use of brass instruments, while many groups have adopted synthesisers. In the 1960s and 1970s groups such as The Beatles, The Rolling Stones, The Who, Led Zeppelin and Pink Floyd achieved international success. British groups continue to have enormous appeal to audiences throughout the world and often set new trends in music; some of the more recent groups to have achieved renown are Dire Straits, Culture Club, Duran Duran and Simple Minds. Well-known performers include David Bowie, Elton John and Paul McCartney. In recent years black British musicians have made a large contribution to the development of popular music.

Jazz

Jazz has an enthusiastic following in Britain and is played in numerous clubs and public houses. British musicians such as Barbara Thompson, Stan Tracey, John Surman and Kenny Wheeler have established strong reputations throughout Europe. Festivals of jazz music are held annually at Camden (London) and Bracknell (Berkshire) and at a number of other places.

Opera and Dance

Regular seasons of opera and ballet are given at the Royal Opera House, Covent Garden, London. The Royal Opera and Royal Ballet, which rank among the world's finest companies, are supported by a permanent orchestra. Seasons of opera in English are given by the English National Opera at the London Coliseum and their wide range of productions receive much critical acclaim. Sadler's Wells Theatre is the home of Sadler's Wells Royal Ballet and the New Sadler's Wells Opera Company, and stages many of the London performances of visiting opera and dance companies. Scottish Opera has regular winter seasons at the Theatre Royal in Glasgow, and tours mainly in Scotland and northern England. Welsh National Opera has seasons in Cardiff and other cities and, with Kent Opera and Opera 80, provides most of the touring productions in England. Opera North, based in Leeds, undertakes tours in the north of England. Opera in Northern Ireland is promoted by Opera, Northern Ireland.

An opera season for which international casts are specially assembled is held every summer at Glyndebourne in Sussex; this is followed by an autumn tour by Glyndebourne Touring Opera using different casts.

Dance and Mime Companies

Dance companies also include: London Festival Ballet, which divides its performances almost equally between London and the regions; Ballet Rambert (Britain's oldest ballet company, which re-formed in 1966 as a leading modern dance company); Scottish Ballet, based in Glasgow; London Contemporary Dance Theatre (which provides regular seasons of contemporary dance in London besides touring extensively); and Northern Ballet Theatre, based in Manchester, which also tours widely throughout England. A number of modern dance groups are supported by regional arts associations and about 30 small dance and mime groups by the Arts Council. The three Arts Councils also support individuals and offer commissions to small groups.

Training in Music, Opera and Dance

Professional training in music is given mainly at colleges of music. The leading London colleges are the Royal Academy of Music, the Royal College of Music, the Guildhall School of Music and Drama and Trinity College of Music. Outside London the main centres include the Royal Scottish Academy of Music and Drama in Glasgow, the Royal Northern College of Music in Manchester, the Welsh College of Music and Drama, Cardiff, and the Birmingham School of Music. The National Opera Studio provides advanced training courses. The leading dance schools are the Royal Ballet School, the Ballet Rambert School and the London School of Contemporary Dance which, with many private schools, have helped in raising British dance to its present high standard. Dance is now a subject for degree studies at the Laban Centre, the University of Surrey and Dartington College.

Youth and Music, an organisation affiliated to the international Jeunesses Musicales, encourages attendance by young people at opera, dance and concert performances. Special performances of orchestral music for children include the Robert Mayer Concerts, held in London on Saturday mornings. Ludus Dance in Education Company and Outreach (in the north of England) work mainly with young people. Scottish Ballet Steps Out works in schools throughout Scotland.

Many children learn to play musical instruments at school, and some take the examinations of the Associated Board of the Royal Schools of Music. The National Youth Orchestras of Great Britain, of Scotland and of Wales and other youth orchestras are noted for their high standards. Nearly a third of the players in the European Community Youth Orchestra come from Britain. There is also a National Youth Jazz Orchestra.

FILMS

The British film industry is widely acknowledged to have undergone a revival in the early 1980s. British films, actors and the creative and technical services which support them have been achieving notable successes commercially and in international film festivals and other events. Besides feature films, including co-productions with other countries, the industry produces films for television as well as promotional, advertising, industrial, scientific, educational and training films.

There are about 1,300 cinema screens in Britain and estimated attendances in 1985 amounted to some 64 million. Cinema attendance figures declined rapidly between the mid-1950s and the early 1980s: in 1954 the average weekly cinema audience was some 25 million, but by 1984 it was about 4 per cent of that figure. Major reasons for the general decline have been competition from television viewing, the rapid rise in the use of home video-cassette recorders, and the effect of the economic recession on the spending power of a predominantly young cinema-going public. Attendances have started to rise again, however, since 1984. There has been a growth in recent years in the number of grant-aided regional film theatres and film societies offering alternative programmes to those of the commercial cinema chains.

British Film Year, a major initiative by the film industry, fully supported by the Government, was launched in April 1985. Its main aims were to encourage cinema-going as the best way to see films, develop the use of films as a medium of education, highlight Britain's great national assets as a film-making country and promote British films and film-making ability overseas. During the year attendances at cinemas increased by more than one-third.

Government Support for the Film Industry

Following a wide-ranging review of the film industry, measures were taken by the Government in 1985 to remove certain statutory controls on cinemas which had become outdated and which were no longer contributing to the industry's development. The Eady levy, a statutory levy raised from exhibitors on revenues received from cinema admissions, was abolished and future funding was secured for the various bodies which had benefited from the proceeds of the levy in recent years.

The National Film Finance Corporation, which had been funded from the Eady levy, was replaced by a private body, the British Screen Finance Consortium, whose members are drawn from the film, television and video industries. The consortium, investing its own money together with contributions from the Government amounting to £10 million over five years, part-finances the production of low- and medium-budget films involving largely British talent and encourages the early stages of film project development and the production of short films.

An annual government grant of some £9 million is also made to the British Film Institute.

British Film Institute

The development of film and television as an art form is promoted by the British Film Institute, founded in 1933, and in Scotland by the Scottish Film Council. The Institute offers direct financial and technical help through its Film Production Board to new and experienced film-makers who cannot find support elsewhere, and helps to fund film and video workshops in liaison with the Channel Four Television Company. It administers the National Film Theatre in London and the National Film Archive, and has a library from which films and video-cassettes may be hired. The Institute's Information Division has extensive international collections of books, periodicals, scripts, stills and posters. It offers an information service on all aspects of film and television, and produces a range of publications, including the British National Film and Video Catalogue, which records films and video-cassettes available in Britain, and a quarterly journal, *Sight and Sound.* The Education Department produces study materials and offers an advisory service to the growing number of teachers of film and television at all levels of formal education and in adult education.

The National Film Archive contains over 75,000 films, including newsreels and other miscellaneous items, and over 10,000 television programmes. The National Film Theatre has two cinemas showing films of outstanding historical, artistic or technical interest, and is unique in offering regular programmes unrestricted by commercial considerations or by the age or nationality of the films. Each autumn it mounts the London Film Festival, at which about 150 of the finest new films from all over the world are screened.

The British Film Institute has promoted and helps to fund the development of some 40 regional film theatres, and is involved in establishing film and television centres with a range of activities and facilities in a number of major cities. It also co-operates with the regional arts associations and grant-aids their film activities. In Wales, the Welsh Arts Council acts as the Institute's agent. In Scotland, the Scottish Film Council supports regional film theatres, administers the Scottish Film Archive, and promotes and provides material for media education. Together with the Scottish Arts Council, it set up the Scottish Film Production Fund, which makes grants towards film production in Scotland. Grants in Northern Ireland are made by the Arts Council of Northern Ireland.

Children's Films

The Children's Film and Television Foundation produces and distributes entertainment films specially designed for children. In view of the rapid decline of the children's matinee movement (only some 50 cinemas now provide programmes for children on Saturday mornings) the Foundation's films are increasingly shown through the medium of video and television.

Training in Film Production

The National Film and Television School, financed jointly by the Government and the film and television industry, offers courses for writers, directors, producers and camera technicians. Training in film production is also given at the London International Film School, the Royal College of Art, and at some polytechnics and other institutions.

Cinema Licensing and Film and Video Classification

Cinemas showing films to the public must be licensed by local authorities, which have a legal duty to prohibit the admission of children under 16 to unsuitable films, and may prevent the showing of any film. In considering the suitability of films the authorities normally rely on the judgment of an independent body, the British Board of Film Classification, to which films and also videos offered to the public must be submitted. The Board was set up on the initiative of the cinema industry to ensure that a proper standard was maintained in films offered to the public. It does not use any written code of censorship, but may require cuts to be made before granting a certificate; very rarely, it refuses a certificate. Films passed by the Board are put into one of five categories: U meaning universal—suitable for all; PG, meaning parental guidance, in which some scenes may be unsuitable for young children; 15 and 18, for people of not less than 15 and 18 years of age respectively; and Restricted 18, for restricted showing only at segregated premises to which no one under 18 is admitted—for example, licensed cinema clubs. There is a similar system of classification for videos.

VISUAL ARTS

State support for painting and sculpture mainly takes the form of maintenance and purchase grants for the national museums and galleries, purchase grants for municipal museums and galleries, funding for living artists channelled through the Arts and Crafts Councils, and grants towards the cost of art education. The Government also encourages high standards of industrial design and craftsmanship through grants to the Design Council.

All national museums and galleries are financed mainly from government funds. They are free to levy entrance charges to their permanent collections, special exhibitions and outstations at their discretion. Government policy is to give priority to the conservation of the buildings and collections of the national institutions rather than to increasing purchase grants for acquisitions. All the national collections in England, Scotland and Wales are administered by independent trustees. Museums and art galleries maintained by local authorities, universities and private benefactions may receive help in building up their collections through annual government grants administered by the Museums and Galleries Commission (for England and Wales) and the National Museums of Scotland. Financial and practical assistance to both national and local museums and galleries is also given by the Arts Council and by trusts and voluntary bodies including the Calouste Gulbenkian Foundation, the National Art-Collections Fund and the Contemporary Art Society. Pre-eminent works of art accepted by the Government in place of capital transfer tax are allocated to public galleries. Financial help may also be available from the government-financed National Heritage Memorial Fund; in recent years, the Fund has made important contributions towards pictures purchased by the Birmingham, Leeds and Manchester City Art Galleries, and by the national galleries and museums.

The Arts Council maintains its own collection of contemporary British art, and organises or offers grants or guarantees for a variety of exhibitions throughout the country. It runs the Hayward and Serpentine galleries in London and supports a number of art and photography galleries in London and the regions, such as the Arnolfini in Bristol and the Museum of Modern Art in Oxford. The Council also provides support for artists and photographers through purchasing, and commissioning fellowships and residences. Grant aid is also available to support art and photography books and magazines. Similar support is given by the Scottish Arts Council to galleries in Scotland such as the Fruitmarket Gallery in Edinburgh. The Welsh and Northern Ireland Arts Councils have galleries in Cardiff and Belfast respectively.

A number of modern British sculptors and painters have high international reputations, and have received many international prizes and commissions for major works in foreign cities. Among the best known are Henry Moore, Elisabeth Frink, Francis Bacon and David Hockney.

Museums and Art Galleries

Over 1,000 museums and art galleries are open to the public, including the major national collections and a wide variety of municipally and independently owned institutions. Nearly 18 million people visited the national galleries and museums in England in 1985.

The Government is advised on policy matters by the Museums and Galleries Commission, which also promotes co-operation between national and provincial institutions. Nine area museum councils provide technical services and advice on conservation, display, documentation and publicity.

Museums Association

The independent Museums Association, to which museums and art galleries and their staffs belong and which also has many overseas members, is a focus for the collection of information and discussion of matters relating to museum administration, and a training and examining body for professional qualifications.

National Collections

The national museums and art galleries, which are mostly located in London, contain some of the world's most comprehensive collections of objects of artistic, archaeological, scientific, historical and general interest. They are the British Museum (including the Museum of Mankind), the British Museum (Natural

History), the Victoria and Albert Museum, the Science Museum, the National Gallery, the Tate Gallery, the National Portrait Gallery, the Imperial War Museum, the National Army Museum, the Royal Air Force Museum, the National Maritime Museum, the Wallace Collection, the Geological Museum and a group of museums and galleries on Merseyside. Some of the museums in London have branches outside London, examples being the National Railway Museum (York) and the National Museum of Photography, Film and Television (Bradford) which are part of the Science Museum.

New developments planned or in progress at the Tate Gallery include the building of an extension to house the large collection of paintings bequeathed to the nation by the nineteenth-century artist J. M. W. Turner, and the opening of an outstation in Liverpool, to be called Tate in the North. An extension to the National Gallery, to be financed by private funds (see p 396), has also been announced. A national theatre museum is to be opened in 1987 in Covent Garden, London.

In Scotland the national collections are the National Museums of Scotland (formed by the bringing together in October 1985 of the Royal Scottish Museum and the National Museum of Antiquities of Scotland, and embracing the Scottish United Services Museum in Edinburgh Castle) and the National Galleries of Scotland (comprising the National Gallery of Scotland, the Scottish National Portrait Gallery and the Scottish National Gallery of Modern Art). The National Museum of Wales, in Cardiff, has a branch at St Fagan's Castle where the Welsh Folk Museum is housed, an Industrial and Maritime Museum in Cardiff's dockland, the Museum of the Woollen Industry at Drefach Felindre, and the North Wales Quarrying Museum at Llanberis. Northern Ireland has two national museums: the Ulster Museum in Belfast and the Ulster Folk and Transport Museum in County Down.

Other Collections

Other important collections in London include the Royal Armouries in the Tower of London, the Museum of London, Sir John Soane's Museum, the Courtauld collection and the London Transport Museum. The Queen's Gallery in Buckingham Palace has exhibitions of pictures from the extensive royal collections.

Most cities and towns have museums devoted to art, archaeology and natural history, usually administered by the local authorities but sometimes by local learned societies or by individuals or trustees. Both Oxford and Cambridge are rich in museums, many of them associated with the universities, such as the Ashmolean Museum in Oxford, founded in 1683, the oldest in the world, and the Fitzwilliam Museum in Cambridge. Many private art collections in historic family mansions, including those owned by the National Trusts, are open to the public, while an increasing number of open air museums depict the regional life of an area or preserve early industrial remains (for example, the Weald and Downland Museum in Sussex, the North of England Open Air Museum in Durham, and the Ironbridge Gorge Museum in Shropshire). Among the newest museums to have been established are the National Horseracing Museum at Newmarket, the Jorvik Viking Centre, a reconstruction of the Viking settlement in York, and a new maritime museum in Portsmouth, housing the restored wreck of the *Mary Rose*, the flagship of Henry VIII, which sank in 1545 and was raised in 1982. The new Burrell gallery in Glasgow houses a world-famous collection of tapestries, paintings and *objets d'art*. A new Museum of the Moving Image, due to open on the South Bank of the Thames in 1987, will feature exhibitions of moving images ranging from ancient shadow plays, through television and video, to images produced using optic fibres and lasers.

Apart from their permanent collections, most museums and galleries stage temporary exhibitions on particular themes. There are also a number of national art exhibiting societies, the most famous of which is the Royal Academy of Arts at Burlington House. The Academy holds an annual Summer Exhibition, in which the works of hundreds of professional and amateur artists are included, and important exhibitions of foreign art. The Royal Scottish Academy holds annual exhibitions in Edinburgh. There are also children's exhibitions, including the National Exhibition of Children's Art.

Crafts

Government aid for the crafts, amounting to almost £2 million in 1986–87, is administered in England and Wales by the Crafts Council. The Council holds regular exhibitions at its London gallery (which also houses a crafts resource centre, including a slide library) and publishes *Crafts* magazine, books on crafts subjects, and slides. It runs a number of grant, loan and bursary schemes to help people at different stages in the development of their art and is involved in promotional and marketing schemes. The Council runs activities in education and manages a British crafts shop at the Victoria and Albert Museum. Funding is given to the Welsh Arts Council and the regional arts associations in England for the support of crafts activities, and also to the British Crafts Centre, a membership organisation for craftsmen and craftswomen which holds exhibitions and sells work through its London gallery.

Scotland receives a separate government grant which is administered by the Crafts Consultative Committee of the Scottish Development Agency.

Training in Art and Design

Most practical education in art and design is provided in colleges of art (of which the most famous are the Slade School and the Royal College of Art, both in London), further education colleges and private art schools. Four art colleges in London were merged in January 1986 with other colleges to form the London Institute. Degrees at postgraduate level are awarded by the Royal College of Art. Art is also taught at an advanced level at the four Scottish Central (Art) Institutions.

Courses at universities and polytechnics concentrate largely on academic disciplines such as the history of art. The leading institutions include the Courtauld and Warburg Institutes of the University of London and the Department of Classical Art and Archaeology at University College, London. Art has a place in all school curricula, and the Society for Education through Art encourages, among other activities, the purchase by schools of original works of art by organising an annual Pictures for Schools exhibition.

The Art Market

London is a major centre for the international art market, and sales of works of art take place in the main auction houses (two of the longest established being Sotheby's and Christie's), and through private dealers. Certain items are covered by export control. These are: works of art and collectors' items over 50 years old and worth £16,000 or more (£4,000 or more in the case of British historical portraits); and photographic material over 60 years old and worth £400 or more apiece. A licence is required before such items can be exported, but this is granted automatically in the case of objects imported into Britain within the last 50 years. The application for a licence is considered by the Department of Trade and Industry, and, if the Department's expert advisers recommend the withholding of a licence, the matter is referred to the Reviewing Committee on the Export of Works of Art. If the Committee considers a work to be of national importance it can advise the Government to withhold the export licence for a specified time to give a public museum or art gallery an opportunity to buy at a fair price.

LITERATURE AND LIBRARIES

The study of literature is included in the curricula of all schools and of most colleges and universities. There are free public libraries throughout the country, private libraries and several private literary societies. Book reviews are featured in the press and on television and radio and there are numerous periodicals concerned with literature. Recognition of outstanding literary merit is provided by a number of awards, including the Booker, W. H. Smith & Son, and Whitbread prizes. Awards to encourage young writers include those of the Somerset Maugham Trust Fund and the E. C. Gregory Trust Fund. Many British writers are internationally recognised and in 1983 the Nobel prize for literature was awarded to the novelist William Golding. Other well-known living authors are Graham Greene, Anthony Burgess, Margaret Drabble and Iris Murdoch, while distinguished British poets include Ted Hughes, Seamus Heaney and Gavin Ewart. Ted Hughes is Poet Laureate, a member of the Royal Household who writes verse to mark royal occasions in return for a small stipend.

A public lending right scheme, introduced in 1982, gives registered authors the right to receive payment from a central fund (totalling £2·75 million in 1986–87) for the use of their books borrowed from public libraries.

Authors' Copyright

The author of any original literary, dramatic, musical or artistic work is automatically protected by the Copyright Act 1956 and its related international conventions[1] from the unauthorised reproduction of the work both before and after publication. The author of the work is the first owner of the copyright, and the normal term of copyright in published original works is the life of the author and a period of 50 years after his or her death.

Literary and Philological Societies

Societies to promote literature include the English Association and the Royal Society of Literature. The British Academy for the Promotion of Historical, Philosophical and Philological Studies (the British Academy) is the leading society for humanistic studies.

Other specialist societies include the Early English Text Society, the Bibliographical Society, the Harleian Society, the Saltire Society, and several societies devoted to particular authors, the largest of which is the Dickens Fellowship. A number of societies, such as the Poetry Society, sponsor poetry readings and recitals. There are also a number of clubs and societies, such as the Poetry Book Society, which distribute selected new books to their members.

Libraries

The British Library is the national library of the United Kingdom and ranks with the National Library of Congress in Washington and the Bibliothèque Nationale in Paris as one of the world's greatest libraries. Publishers have a legal obligation to supply the Library with a copy of each new book, pamphlet or newspaper published in Britain. The Humanities and Social Sciences division provides comprehensive information and reference services based on its world-famous collections of some 12 million items of monographs, manuscripts, maps, stamps, newspapers and recorded sound. The Library's exhibition galleries are housed in the British Museum building, where many of the Library's greatest treasures are on permanent display and temporary exhibitions are regularly mounted.

The British Library Science, Technology and Industry division comprises the Document Supply Centre in West Yorkshire and the Science Reference and Information Service in London. The former operates a rapid postal inter-library lending service of journals and photocopies and satisfies some 3 million requests each year. It also has access to many millions of books in other libraries and is the national centre for inter-library lending within Britain and between

---

[1] A copyright work first published in Britain has automatic copyright in all countries which are members of the Berne Copyright Convention and the Universal Copyright Convention. The law on copyright is under review.

Britain and countries overseas. The Science Reference and Information Service is Western Europe's most comprehensive collection of material on modern science and technology and holds patent specifications. It provides a referral service for company, product and market information. The Library's Bibliographic Services division processes the material deposited with the Library for inclusion in its catalogues, and publishes the British National Bibliography (which lists all new books and new editions published in Britain) and other bibliographic records. It also provides automated information services for bibliographic data for libraries and their users. The Research and Development Department is a major source of funding for research and development in library and information services.

A new building at St Pancras, to be occupied from 1991, will eventually house in one unit most of the Library's London-based operations.

The National Libraries of Scotland and of Wales, the Bodleian Library of Oxford University and the Cambridge University Library can claim copies of all new British publications under copyright legislation.

Some of the national museums and government departments have important libraries. The Public Record Office contains the records of the superior courts of law and of most government departments, as well as famous historical documents. The Scottish Record Office in Edinburgh serves the same purpose.

Besides a number of great private collections, such as that of the London Library, there are the rich resources of the learned societies and institutions. Examples are the libraries of the Royal Institute of International Affairs, the Royal Commonwealth Society, the Royal Geographical Society, the British Theatre Association, the Royal Academy of Music, the National Library for the Blind and the National Book League.

University Libraries

The university libraries of Oxford and Cambridge are unmatched by those of the more recent foundations, although the combined library resources of the colleges and institutions of the University of London total some 9 million volumes, the John Rylands University Library in Manchester contains some 3·4 million volumes, Edinburgh some 2 million, Leeds some 1·8 million, and Birmingham, Glasgow, Liverpool and Aberdeen each have over 1 million volumes. Many universities have important research collections in special subjects; examples include the Barnes Medical Library at Birmingham and the British Library of Political and Economic Science at the London School of Economics.

Special Libraries

Many associations and commercial and industrial organisations operate library and information services. Although most of these are primarily intended for use within the organisation, many special libraries can be used, by arrangement, by people interested in the area covered, and the specialist publications held are often available for inter-library lending.

Public Libraries

Local library authorities have a duty to provide a free lending and reference library service in their areas. Britain's network of libraries, consisting of 5,500 service points, has a total stock of some 137 million books. About one-third of the total population are members of public libraries. Some areas are served by mobile libraries, and domiciliary services cater for people unable to visit a library. Many libraries have collections of records, audio- and video-cassettes, and musical scores for loan to the public, while a number also lend from collections of works of art, which may be originals or reproductions. Most libraries hold documents on local history, and nearly all provide children's departments, while reference and information sections and art, music, commercial and technical departments meet the growing and more specific demands in these fields. The information role is one of increasing importance for many libraries, and they are making greater use of information technology including microcomputers and reference databases.

The Government is advised on library and information matters by four Library and Information Services Councils or Committees, representing England, Wales, Scotland and Northern Ireland, respectively.

Books

In 1985 British publishers issued almost 53,000 separate titles. Of these about 41,000 were new titles and the remainder reprints and new editions. The British publishing industry devotes much effort to the development of overseas markets, and exports of British books in 1985 amounted to over £470 million. The industry is also distinguished for its interest in new technological developments, including electronic publishing and the development of software for educational and other purposes.

Among the leading organisations representing publishing and distribution interests are the Publishers Association, which has 400 members, and the Booksellers' Association. The Publishers Association, through its associated body the Book Development Council, has been active in promoting the export of British books world-wide.

The British Council publicises British books overseas through its 116 libraries in over 60 countries, participation in international book fairs and a programme of travelling exhibitions. The Council also publishes a monthly periodical, *British Book News.*

The National Book League, whose membership includes authors, publishers, booksellers, librarians and readers, encourages an interest in books and arranges exhibitions throughout Britain.

22 The Press

More daily newspapers, national and regional, are sold per person in Britain than in most other developed countries. On an average day nearly three out of four people over the age of 15 read a national morning newspaper and about one in three reads an evening newspaper. Three out of four adults regularly read a paid-for regional or local newspaper. National papers have a total circulation of 14·6 million on weekdays and 17·6 million on Sundays though the total readership is considerably greater.

There are about 130 daily (Monday to Saturday) and Sunday newspapers, 1,300 weekly newspapers (including business, sporting and religious newspapers) and some 7,000 periodical publications.

The press caters for a variety of political views, interests and levels of education. There is no state control or censorship of the press, but it is subject to the general laws on publication (see p 419). Newspapers are almost always financially independent of any political party; where they express pronounced views and have obvious political leanings, these derive from traditional, proprietorial and other non-party influences. In order to preserve their character and traditions, a few newspapers and periodicals are governed by various trustee-type arrangements. Others have management arrangements to ensure their editors' authority and independence.

In discussions on a 'new world information order' and other communications questions, Britain has opposed measures designed to increase governmental regulation of the media or to limit the free flow of information. At the same time, it has reaffirmed its willingness to support efforts to improve communications systems in the developing world.

Unlike most of its European counterparts the British press receives no subsidies and relatively few tax and postal concessions. Newspaper and magazine sales (but not advertising receipts) are zero-rated for value added tax. Registered newspapers receive a concession on postal rates, and there are concessions on 'per-word' rates for international press telegrams and photo-telegrams. Like all postal customers, publishers can obtain reductions in charges for regular bulk postings.

Newsprint, about two-thirds of which is imported, forms roughly 30 per cent of average national newspaper costs; labour represents about 40 per cent but this proportion is likely to fall with the growing use of new technology (see p 415). Revenue from sales accounts for varying proportions of income; many newspapers and periodicals derive considerable earnings from their advertising.

Newspaper Ownership

Ownership of the national, London-evening and regional daily newspapers is concentrated in the hands of a number of large press publishing groups (the groups controlling the national press are listed in Table 43). There are, in addition, some 200 independent regional and local newspaper publishers.

Although most enterprises are organised as limited liability companies, individual and partner proprietorship survives. The large national newspaper and periodical publishers are major corporations with interests ranging over the whole field of publishing and communications; some have shares in independent television and radio companies while others are involved in industrial and commercial activities.

The law provides safeguards against the risks inherent in undue concentration of the means of communication. For instance, if it appears that newspaper shareholdings in independent television or independent local radio companies have led or are leading to results contrary to the public interest, the Independent Broadcasting Authority can, with the consent of the Home Secretary, notify the companies that their programmes may cease to be transmitted. There are similar controls over newspaper interests in cable television services. In addition, it is unlawful to transfer a newspaper or newspaper assets to a proprietor whose newspapers have an average daily circulation amounting, with that of the newspaper to be taken over, to 500,000 or more copies without the written consent of the Secretary of State for Trade and Industry. Except in certain limited cases, consent may be given only after the Secretary of State has referred the matter to the Monopolies and Mergers Commission and received its report.

Table 43: National Newspapers

Title and foundation date	Controlled by	Circulation[a] average Jan.–June 1986
National dailies		
'Populars'		
Daily Express (1900)	United Newspapers	1,855,627
Daily Mail (1896)	Associated Newspapers Group	1,801,317
The Star (1978)	United Newspapers	1,421,085
Morning Star (1966)	The People's Press Printing Society	29,000
Daily Mirror (1903)	Pergamon Press	3,048,963
The Sun (1964)	News International	4,061,781
Today (1986)	Lonrho International	not available
'Qualities'		
Daily Telegraph (1855)	Telegraph Newspaper Trust	1,156,304
Financial Times (1888)	Pearson Longman	251,554
The Guardian (1821)	The Guardian and Manchester Evening News	524,264
The Times (1785)	News International	471,483
National Sundays		
'Populars'		
The Mail on Sunday (1982)	Associated Newspapers Group	1,616,860
News of the World (1843)	News International	4,849,507
Sunday Express (1918)	United Newspapers	2,376,475
Sunday Mirror (1963)	Pergamon Press	3,052,817
Sunday People (1881)	Pergamon Press	3,056,445
Sunday Today (1986)	Lonrho International	not available
'Qualities'		
The Observer (1791)	George Outram & Co	778,207
Sunday Telegraph (1961)	Telegraph Newspaper Trust	678,233
Sunday Times (1822)	News International	1,149,116

[a] Circulation figures are those of the Audit Bureau of Circulations (founded in 1931 and consisting of publishers, advertisers and advertising agencies) and are certified average daily or weekly net sales for the period. The circulation figure of the Morning Star is otherwise audited.

The National Press

Eleven morning daily papers and nine papers published on Sunday (see Table 43) circulate throughout most parts of the country, and are known as national newspapers. They are mainly produced in London (where Fleet Street has been the traditional centre for the press), but six of the dailies and five of the Sundays also print northern editions in Manchester (accounting for about a quarter of the total production of the national press). An edition of the *Financial Times* is printed in the United States using facsimile pages sent by satellite. *Today*, a new national newspaper launched in March 1986, is published seven days a week. It is printed at Poyle (Middlesex), Manchester and Birmingham. A number of proposals for new national newspapers were under discussion during 1986.

Several newspapers have had very long and distinguished histories: for example, *The Observer*, first published in 1791, is the oldest national Sunday newspaper in the world, and *The Times*, one of the most influential of all newspapers and Britain's oldest daily national newspaper, celebrated its two-hundredth anniversary in 1985.

The leading Scottish papers, *The Scotsman* and the *Glasgow Herald*, have a considerable circulation outside Scotland.

National newspapers are often thought of as either 'quality' or 'popular' papers on the basis of differences in style, content and format (broadsheet or tabloid, though this is not a rigid distinction). Four dailies and three Sundays are usually described as quality newspapers. The three Sunday qualities and three of the Sunday populars produce colour supplements as part of the paper.

The slow decline in newspaper circulations as a whole was reversed in 1983 and circulation totalled 33 million in 1985 (compared with 36 million in 1973). This figure conceals the fact that the circulation of some newspapers has remained generally steady, while that of others has increased.

Regional Newspapers
England

The regional newspapers of England (outside London, over 70 morning or evening dailies and Sundays and some 550 newspapers appearing once or twice a week) provide mainly regional and local news. The daily newspapers also give coverage of national and international affairs. Generally, regional evening newspapers are non-political, while the morning newspapers adopt a more positive political stance and tend to be independent or conservative in outlook.

Of the morning papers the *Yorkshire Post* (Leeds) and the *Eastern Daily Press* (Norwich) have circulations of 93,000 and 91,000 respectively, and two provincial Sunday papers—the *Sunday Sun* (Newcastle upon Tyne) and the *Sunday Mercury* (Birmingham)—sell 125,000 and 168,000 copies, respectively. Circulation figures of evening papers start at about 11,000 and most are in the 20,000 to 100,000 range; those with much larger sales include the *Manchester Evening News* (311,000), the *Birmingham Evening Mail* (279,000), Wolverhampton's *Express and Star* (240,000), and the *Liverpool Echo* (211,000). Weekly papers are of mainly local appeal and are also a valuable medium for local advertising. Most have circulations in the 5,000 to 30,000 range.

There is currently one London evening newspaper, *The London Standard*, with a circulation of some 523,000. A number of evening newspapers are published in the outer metropolitan area. The hundred or so local weeklies include papers for every district in Greater London, often in the form of local editions of an individual paper.

Wales

Wales has one daily morning newspaper, the *Western Mail*, published in Cardiff; its circulation of 78,000 is mainly in south Wales. In north Wales the *Daily Post*, published in Liverpool, gives wide coverage to events in the area. Evening papers published in Wales are the *South Wales Echo*, Cardiff; the *South Wales Argus*, Newport; the *South Wales Evening Post*, Swansea; and the *Evening Leader*, Wrexham. Their circulation range is between 28,000 and 101,000. North Wales is also served by the *Liverpool Echo*, while the *Shropshire Star* covers parts of north and mid-Wales, and there is coverage to a smaller extent by the *Manchester Evening News*.

The weekly press (some 60 publications) includes English-language papers, some of which carry articles in Welsh, bilingual papers and Welsh-language papers. Welsh community newspapers receive an annual grant as part of the Government's wider financial support for the Welsh language.

Scotland

Scotland has six morning, six evening and three Sunday newspapers. The morning papers, with circulations of between 99,000 and 764,000, are *The Scotsman*, published in Edinburgh; the *Glasgow Herald*; the *Daily Record* (sister paper of the *Daily Mirror*); the Dundee *Courier and Advertiser*; the Aberdeen *Press and Journal*; and the *Scottish Daily Express* (printed in Manchester). The evening papers have circulations in the range of 13,000 to 192,000 and are the *Evening News* of Edinburgh, Glasgow's *Evening Times*, Dundee's *Evening Telegraph*, Aberdeen's *Evening Express*, the *Paisley Daily Express* and the *Greenock Telegraph*. The Sunday papers are the *Sunday Mail*, the *Sunday Post* and the *Scottish Sunday Express* (printed in Manchester).

Weekly and local newspapers number about 130, and there are some 35 free weekly newspapers.

Northern Ireland

Northern Ireland has two morning newspapers, one evening and one Sunday paper, all published in Belfast with circulations ranging from 42,000 to 149,000. They are the *News Letter* (unionist) and the *Irish News* (nationalist), the evening *Belfast Telegraph* and the *Sunday News*. There are 42 weeklies. Newspapers from the Irish Republic, as well as the British national press, are widely read in Northern Ireland.

Ethnic Minority Publications

More than 70 newspapers and magazines are produced by members of the ethnic minorities, 40 of which are printed in Asian languages and the rest in English. Most are published weekly or monthly. They include the Asian newspapers *New Life* and *Asian Times*, *The Weekly Gleaner*—a local edition of the *Jamaican Gleaner*, and *West Indian Digest*. *The Voice* and *Caribbean Times* are aimed at the black population in general as is the magazine *Root*. An Arabic daily, *Al-Arab*, is also produced in Britain.

Free Distribution Newspapers

Some 840 free distribution newspapers (mostly weekly and financed largely by advertising) are now published in Britain, just over half of them produced by established newspaper publishers. They have enjoyed rapid growth in recent years and now have an estimated total weekly circulation of some 36 million.

Europe's first daily free distribution paper, the *Daily News*, was launched in Birmingham in 1984.

The Periodical Press

The 7,000 periodical publications are classified as 'consumer general', 'specialised', 'trade', 'technical' and 'professional'. There are also several hundred 'house magazines' produced by industrial undertakings, business houses or public services for the benefit of their employees and/or clients. The 'alternative' press comprises several hundred further titles, most of them devoted to radical politics, community matters, religion, the occult, science or ecology.

Consumer general and specialised periodicals include magazines for a wide range of interests: women's magazines; publications for children; religious periodicals; fiction magazines; magazines dealing with sport, motoring, gardening, pop music, hobbies and humour; computer magazines; and the publications of learned societies, trade unions, regiments, universities and other organisations.

The weekly periodicals with the highest sales are: *Radio Times* and *TV Times Magazine*, which carry details of the week's television and radio programmes on BBC and independent television, respectively, each of which has a circulation of about 3 million, and *Woman's Weekly*, *Woman's Own*, *Woman*, *Weekly News* (which sells mainly in Scotland) and *My Weekly*, with circulations in the 640,000 to 1·3 million range. The leading journals of opinion are *The Economist*, a politically independent publication covering a wider range of topics than its title implies; the *New Statesman*, which reviews politics, literature and the arts from an independent socialist point of view; the *Spectator*, which covers much the same subjects from an independent conservative standpoint; *Tribune*, which represents certain left-wing views within the Labour Party; *New Society*, covering the sociological aspects of current affairs; and *New Scientist*, which reports on science and technology in terms which the non-specialist can understand. Articles and features relating largely to BBC television and radio programmes appear in *The Listener*. *Punch*, traditionally the leading humorous periodical, and *Private Eye*, a satirical fortnightly, also cover public affairs. *Financial Weekly* and *Investors Chronicle* are periodicals for people with business and investment interests.

Weekly 'listings' magazines including *Time Out* and *City Limits* provide details of cultural and other events in London and other large cities.

Literary and political journals and those specialising in international and Commonwealth affairs, published monthly or quarterly, generally appeal to the more serious reader.

Trade, technical, business, scientific and professional journals, publication of which ranges from twice weekly to quarterly, are an important aspect of British publishing and business communication, many having a considerable circulation overseas. There are about 500 publications of significant size covering business and industrial affairs.

Periodicals published in England circulate throughout Britain. In Wales there are also several monthly and quarterly journals published in both Welsh and English; in Scotland there are three monthly illustrated periodicals, a weekly paper devoted to farming interests, a number of literary journals and numerous popular magazines; and Northern Ireland has weekly, monthly and quarterly publications covering business, professional and leisure interests.

New Printing Technology

The heavy production costs of newspapers and periodicals continue to encourage publishers to look for ways of reducing these costs, often by using computer systems to control editing and production processes. The 'front end' or 'single stroking' system, for example, allows journalists or advertising staff to input 'copy' directly into a video terminal, and then by pressing a button to transform it automatically into computer-set columns of type. These columns can then be assembled electronically on a page-sized screen, turned into a full page, and made automatically into a plate ready for transfer to the printing press. Such systems present opportunities for reorganisation which have implications throughout a newspaper office and often give rise to disputes over manning levels and other industrial relations problems. Generally, and most recently in the case of national newspapers, the introduction of computerised systems has led to substantial reductions in workforces, particularly, but not solely, among print workers.

About half of the national newspapers now use some computer technology, while its use in the provincial press, which has generally led the way in adopting new techniques, is more widespread. The national newspaper, *Today*, is produced by a fully computerised system: journalists type articles directly into and edit them on computer terminals, while colour pictures and graphics are entered into the same system electronically by scanners. News International, publisher of two daily and two Sunday papers, uses at its new east London headquarters more than 500 computer terminals, one of the largest systems ever installed at one time anywhere in the world. Other national papers are also building new computer-based printing plants outside Fleet Street.

Other technological developments include the introduction of full-colour printing, and a switch from traditional letterpress printing to the web-offset litho process.

News Agencies

The three principal news agencies in Britain are: Reuters, an international news organisation registered in London, The Press Association Ltd and The Exchange Telegraph Company Limited.

Reuters is a publicly owned company, employing some 5,400 full-time staff in 81 countries. Of its 890 journalists, nearly 700 work outside the United Kingdom. The company's world-wide communications network makes use of satellites, cables and microwave radio, and is connected to computerised message-handling systems and data banks located around the world. Services include general news for the media delivered by teleprinter or fed directly into clients' computers, and specialised economic news and information services for business delivered through video terminals, by teleprinter or by direct computer feed. Reuters serves subscribers in 158 countries including financial institutions, commodities houses, traders in currencies, equities and bonds, newspapers, radio and television stations and news agencies.

In 1985 Reuters launched its own world service of news pictures, having in the previous year acquired the news pictures business outside the United States of United Press International, the American news agency.

The Press Association Ltd, the British national news agency, is co-operatively owned by the principal daily newspapers of the United Kingdom outside London, and of the Irish Republic. It provides to national and regional newspapers and broadcasting services a complete service of home news, including general and parliamentary news, legal reports, and all types of financial, commercial and sports news, and includes in its services to regional papers the world news of Reuters and Associated Press. News is teleprinted from London, certain items being available in teletypesetting form. Its 'Newsfile' service provides general home news on screen to non-media as well as media clients by means of telephone and viewdata terminals. Also available on screen is the 'Esmerk' service, an international digest of business information. The photographic department provides newspapers and broadcasters with a daily service of pictures from Britain and overseas; these are wired to the regional press. The Special Reporting Service supplies reports of local or special interest. Press Association Features provides exclusive rights to syndicated articles and visual features.

The Exchange Telegraph Company Limited supplies financial and sporting news services and transmits specialist racing services by telephone and video terminals from offices throughout Britain.

The British press and broadcasting organisations are also served by Associated Press Ltd and United Press International, which are British subsidiaries of United States news agencies.

A number of other British, Commonwealth and foreign agencies and news services have offices in London, and there are minor agencies in other cities, mostly specialising in various aspects of newspaper and periodical requirements. Syndication of features is not as common in Britain as in some countries, but a few agencies specialise in this type of work.

Training for Journalism

The National Council for the Training of Journalists (NCTJ), which represents the principal regional press organisations, sets and conducts examinations, and organises short training courses for journalists.

The two methods of entry into newspaper journalism are selection for a one-year NCTJ pre-entry course at a college of further education or direct recruitment by a regional or local newspaper. Both categories of entrant take part in an apprenticeship scheme consisting of 'on-the-job' training, and block-release courses are provided for those who have not attended a pre-entry course. There are similar courses for press photographers. Postgraduate courses in journalism are provided at University College, Cardiff, and at the City University (London), and courses are provided by the Newspaper Society Training Service for regional newspapers in such subjects as newspaper sales, advertising, industrial relations and management.

Specialist training courses for senior journalists from developing countries are run by the Thomson Foundation in London. The Foundation also conducts training courses in developing countries and provides consultants to assist newspapers and magazines in such areas as advertising, management, circulation and the introduction and operation of new technology. It runs an international training centre in collaboration with Xinhua News Agency in Peking.

The Periodical Training Trust is the official training organisation in periodical publishing. It offers a wide range of short courses covering editorial work, advertisement sales and circulation sales. It has special responsibility for editorial training and administers an industry-wide editorial training scheme for those already in employment. The postgraduate courses in journalism at Cardiff and the City University offer periodical journalism options, and the London College of Printing provides postgraduate courses and General Certificate of Education Advanced-level courses in periodical journalism. Business Press International Limited, one of the largest publishing companies, has an in-company training course for suitable candidates from the general public.

Under the Harry Brittain Memorial Fellowship Scheme, administered by the Commonwealth Press Union, several young Commonwealth journalists each year spend three months working and studying in Britain, while the Reuter Foundation, established in 1982, awards six fellowships each year to journalists from developing countries to study at Oxford, Stanford and Bordeaux universities.

Annual Student Media Awards are presented jointly by *The Guardian* newspaper and the National Union of Students to students in higher education who have excelled in college press, television and radio journalism.

Press Institutions

The most important employers' organisations are the Newspaper Publishers Association, whose members publish national newspapers in London and Manchester; the Newspaper Society, which represents the regional, local and London suburban press; the Scottish Daily Newspaper Society, which represents the interests of daily and Sunday newspapers in Scotland; the Scottish Newspaper Proprietors' Association, which represents the owners of weekly newspapers in Scotland; Associated Northern Ireland Newspapers, whose members are the proprietors of weekly newspapers in Northern Ireland; and the Periodical Publishers Association, whose membership embraces the majority of independent publishers of business, professional and consumer journals.

Organisations representing journalists are the National Union of Journalists, with some 32,500 members, and the Institute of Journalists, with about 2,500 members. Two main printing unions are concerned with the press: the Society of Graphical and Allied Trades (SOGAT) '82, with 207,000 members, and the National Graphical Association 1982, with 132,000 members, about one-third of whom work on newspapers.

The Guild of British Newspaper Editors is the officially recognised professional body for newspaper editors. It has approximately 450 members and aims to maintain the professional status and independence of editors, defend the freedom of the press, and improve the education and training of journalists. The British Association of Industrial Editors is the professional organisation to which most editors of house journals belong. The Association of British Editors, representing the whole range of media including radio, television, newspapers and magazines, was established in 1984.

The main aim of the Foreign Press Association, founded in 1888, is to help the correspondents of overseas newspapers in their work by arranging press conferences, tours, briefings and a range of other facilities.

The Press Council

The Press Council is a voluntary and non-statutory body founded by the newspaper industry in 1953 on the recommendation of the first Royal Commission on the press to safeguard the freedom of the press and to ensure that it conducts itself responsibly. It comprises equal numbers of press and non-press members, including members of the public, with an independent chairman. Its full aims are to preserve the established freedom of the press; maintain the character of the press in accordance with the highest professional and commercial standards; keep under review any developments likely to restrict the supply of information of public interest and importance; deal with complaints about the conduct of the press or the conduct of individuals and organisations towards the press; report on developments in the press which may tend towards greater concentration or monopoly; make representations on appropriate occasions to the Government, the United Nations and press organisations abroad; publish its adjudications and periodic reports recording its work; and review from time to time developments in the press and the factors affecting them.

Dealing with complaints from the public about the content and conduct of the press is the Council's best-known function. It has no power to impose penalties on publications which it has found guilty of malpractice, but relies on the sanction of adverse publicity. It can censure newspapers, magazines, editors and journalists, and issues adjudications which the editor of the newspaper or magazine criticised by the Council has a moral obligation to publish in full. The Council sometimes initiates inquiries into aspects of press conduct without first receiving public complaints. Its annual reports include press statistics and articles on the structure of leading press groups.

Advertising Practice

Advertising practice in the press (and in the cinema and on posters) is regulated and controlled by the Advertising Standards Authority, an independent body which aims to promote and enforce the highest standards of advertising in the interests of the public and the industry, in particular through the British Code of Advertising Practice. The objects of the code are to ensure that advertisements are legal, decent, honest and truthful; that they are prepared with a sense of responsibility to the consumer; that they conform to the principles of fair competition as generally accepted in business; and that no advertisement brings advertising into disrepute or reduces confidence in advertising as a service to industry and the public.

The Authority's main activities are monitoring advertisements for their compliance with the code; initiating modifications to the code; and dealing with complaints received direct from members of the public. Its main sanction is the recommendation to media that advertisements considered to be in breach of the code should not be published. It also publishes regular reports on the results of its investigations, naming the companies involved.

The Press and the Law

The press has generally the same freedom as the individual to comment on matters of public interest.

Apart from legal requirements to register newspapers and periodicals and to reproduce 'the printer's imprint' (the printer's name and place of publication), there are no specific press laws, but certain statutes include sections which apply to the press. These relate to such matters as the extent of newspaper ownership in television and radio companies; the transfer of newspaper assets; restrictions on the reporting of certain types of court proceedings and on publishing material likely to stir up racial hatred; the right of press representatives to be admitted to meetings of local authorities; restrictions on the publication of advertisement and investment circulars (which are governed by Acts dealing with the publication of false or misleading descriptions of goods and services and with fraud) and of advertisements for remedies for certain diseases, which are covered by public health legislation; agreements between British Telecom and newspaper proprietors on telegraphic communications, which must comply with telegraphs legislation; restrictions on certain types of prize competition; and copyrights, which come under copyright laws.

Of particular relevance to the press are laws such as those on contempt of court, official secrets, libel and defamation. A newspaper may not publish comments on the conduct of judicial proceedings which are likely to prejudice the courts' reputation for fairness before or during the actual proceedings, nor may it publish before or during a trial anything which might tend to influence the result. The unauthorised acquisition and publication of information of a confidential or security nature from state and official sources is an offence under the Official Secrets Act 1911. Newspapers are also liable to proceedings for seditious libel and incitement to disaffection. The majority of legal proceedings against the press are libel actions brought by private individuals. In such cases, the editor, proprietor, publishers, printer and distributor of the newspaper, as well as the author, may all be held responsible.

In certain circumstances, where the defence authorities and press representatives in the Defence, Press and Broadcasting Committee[1] agree that publication of information on particular topics would harm the national interest, defence notices ('D' notices) are circulated to the news media requesting that such information should not be published. Compliance with these requests is expected, but they have no legal force; the final responsibility for the decision whether to publish lies solely with the editor or publisher concerned.

---

[1] A committee, under the chairmanship of the Permanent Under-Secretary of State for Defence (a senior civil servant), composed jointly of officials from government departments concerned with national security and representatives of the press and broadcasting organisations.

23 Television and Radio

Broadcasting is based on the tradition that it is a public service accountable to the people through Parliament. Two public bodies—the British Broadcasting Corporation (BBC) and the Independent Broadcasting Authority (IBA)—provide television and radio services throughout the country. In Wales the Welsh Fourth Channel Authority is responsible for programmes on one channel. The authorities work to broad requirements and objectives defined by Parliament, but are otherwise independent in the day-to-day conduct of business.

This independence carries with it certain obligations over programmes and programme content. Programmes must display, as far as possible, a proper balance and wide range of subject matter, impartiality in matters of controversy and accuracy in news coverage, and must not offend against good taste. Codes of guidance on violence in television programmes, particularly during hours when large numbers of children are likely to be viewing, are operated by both authorities. A code of advertising standards and practice is also operated by the IBA. (The BBC does not broadcast advertisements.) A complaints commission deals with allegations of unfair treatment or infringement of privacy in programmes. Publicly available video recordings are classified according to their suitability for different audiences.

The Home Secretary regulates broadcasting generally, is answerable to Parliament on broad policy questions, and may issue directions on a number of technical and other matters.

Television viewing is by far the most popular leisure pastime in Britain: about 95 per cent of the population watch television, average viewing time per person being about 25 hours a week. Some 35 per cent of households have two or more receivers. The growth in use of video-cassette recorders and equipment (including home computers) for playing television games has for many people increased the choice of entertainment available in the home. (About 30 per cent of households rent or own a video-cassette recorder.) Practically every home also has a radio set, and car radios and portable sets have made radio a major daytime diversion.

Households with television must buy an annual licence costing £18 for black and white or £58 for colour. Over 18·6 million licences were current in March 1986, about 15·9 million for colour.

The British Broadcasting Corporation

The constitution and finances of the BBC are governed by Royal Charter and by a Licence and Agreement. The Corporation of 12 governors including the Chairman (each appointed by the Queen on the advice of the Government and including separate governors for Scotland, Wales and Northern Ireland) is finally responsible for all aspects of broadcasting. Committees advise them on a wide range of matters including the social effects of television, religious broadcasting, music, agriculture, schools broadcasting, further education, programmes for ethnic minorities, science and engineering, and charitable appeals. The governors appoint the Director-General, the Corporation's chief executive officer, who heads the BBC's board of management, which is in charge of the daily operation of the services.

The National Broadcasting Councils for Scotland, Wales and Northern Ireland control the policy and content of television and radio programmes intended primarily for reception in their areas. Local radio councils, representative of the local community, advise on the development and operation of the BBC's local radio stations.

The domestic services of the BBC are financed principally from the sale of television licences. This is supplemented by profits from trading activities, including television programme exports, sale of recordings and publications connected with BBC programmes, hire and sale of educational films, film library sales, and exhibitions based on programmes. Nearly three-quarters of expenditure on domestic services relates to television. The BBC meets the cost of its local radio stations while some local education authorities help to make educational programmes.

The BBC's External Services are financed by a grant-in-aid from the Foreign and Commonwealth Office.

Recommendations on the financing of the BBC's domestic services were made by a government-appointed committee under the chairmanship of Professor Alan Peacock whose report was published in July 1986. The report made proposals for radical changes in the structure of broadcasting. Its central recommendation was that British broadcasting should move towards a sophisticated market system based on freedom of consumer choice with viewers and listeners having the option of purchasing broadcasting services from as many alternative sources of supply as possible. Public finance would, however, continue to be needed for programmes of a public service nature. The report rejected the idea that the BBC should at present be funded by advertising.

The Independent Broadcasting Authority

The IBA's constitution and finances are governed by statute. Its 12 members (three of whom have responsibility for Scotland, Wales and Northern Ireland) are appointed by the Home Secretary. The IBA does not produce radio or television programmes; these are provided by independent programme companies and by the Channel Four Television Company (a wholly owned subsidiary of the IBA) for Channel 4 (see p 423). The IBA's main functions are to appoint the companies, supervise programme arrangements, control advertising, and build, own and operate transmitting stations. Its chief executive officer, the Director-General, is supported by a headquarters and regional office staff covering all technical and administrative services.

The IBA is advised by a General Advisory Council, by Scottish, Northern Ireland and Welsh committees, and by committees on educational broadcasting, religious broadcasting, charitable appeals and advertising. A specialist panel advises on advertisements of a medical nature. Local committees advise on local radio services.

The IBA's finance comes from annual rental payments made by the television and radio programme companies. The television programme companies are also liable to pay to the IBA, for transfer to government funds, a levy related to their profits.

The Programme Companies

Fifteen television programme companies hold contracts to provide programmes in the 14 independent television regions (two companies share the contract for London, one providing programmes during the week and the other at the weekend). A contract to provide a national early morning television service, transmitted on the ITV network, is held by an additional company. The companies operate on a commercial basis, deriving most of their revenue from the sale of advertising time. The financial resources, advertising revenue and programme production of the companies vary considerably, depending largely on the size of population in the areas in which they operate. Although newspapers can acquire an interest in programme companies, there are safeguards to protect the public interest.

In consultation with the IBA, each company plans the content of the programmes to be broadcast in its area. These are produced by the company itself and by other programme companies or bought from elsewhere. The five largest companies, serving London, north-west England, East Midlands, West Midlands and Yorkshire, provide more programmes for broadcast elsewhere on the national network than do the smaller ones. A common news service is provided by Independent Television News Ltd, a non-profit-making company in which all the programme companies are shareholders. Negotiations for the supply, exchange and purchase of programmes and their co-ordinated transmission through the independent television network take place largely on the Network Programme Committee, which consists of representatives of all the programme companies and of the IBA.

Similar principles apply to independent local radio. The programme companies are under contract to the IBA, operate under its control and are financed by advertising revenue. News coverage is supplied as a common service by Independent Radio News.

Television

Four television channels are in operation. BBC 1 and BBC 2 are owned by the BBC; ITV (Independent Television) is controlled by, and Channel 4 is owned by, the IBA; all four channels broadcast on 625 lines ultra-high frequency (uhf). About 99 per cent of the population live within range of transmission.

Apart from a break during the second world war the BBC has been providing regular television broadcasts since 1936. About 100 hours of programmes are transmitted by each of the two BBC channels every week; all BBC 2 programmes and the vast majority of those on BBC 1 are broadcast on the national network. Approximately 70 per cent of the BBC's network programmes for 1985–86 were produced in London and 30 per cent elsewhere in Britain.

Through co-ordinated planning on its two services the BBC caters simultaneously for people of different interests. While both services cover the whole range of television output, BBC 1 presents more programmes of general interest, such as light entertainment, sport, current affairs, children's programmes and outside broadcasts, while BBC 2 places greater emphasis on minority interests, but also provides documentaries, travel programmes, serious drama, music, programmes on pastimes and international films. An early morning television service on BBC 1 provides about 2½ hours a day of news, information and light entertainment. The service runs from Monday to Friday.

The first regular independent television programmes began in London in 1955. On average each of the 14 ITV areas transmitted over 100 hours of television programmes a week in 1985–86, nearly two-fifths of them comprising informative programmes—including news, documentaries, and programmes on current affairs, education and religion. Almost three-quarters of the programmes are produced by the programme companies. A national early morning television service on ITV provides about three hours of news, information, current affairs and light entertainment daily.

Channel 4, which began broadcasting in 1982, provides a national television service throughout Britain, except in Wales which has a corresponding service (Sianel 4 Cymru—S4C—see below). The IBA must ensure that programmes on Channel 4 are complementary to those of ITV, catering for tastes and interests not normally provided for by the original independent service. It must provide a suitable proportion (about 15 per cent) of educational programmes, encourage innovation and experiment, and include a substantial proportion of programmes from independent producers. Channel 4 broadcasts for approximately 70 hours a week, about half of which is devoted to informative programmes. The service, both nationally and in Wales, is financed by subscriptions from the programme companies in return for advertising time in fourth channel programmes broadcast in their own regions. In Wales, programmes on the fourth channel are run and controlled by the Welsh Fourth Channel Authority appointed by the Home Secretary. The Authority is required to ensure that a substantial proportion (in practice some 23 hours a week) are in Welsh and that those broadcast between 18.30 and 22.00 hours are mainly in Welsh. At other times the Welsh fourth channel shows national Channel 4 programmes.

Britain is one of the world's foremost exporters of television productions, exporting in 1984 programmes worth roughly £91 million. In 1985 British productions won a number of international awards, including first prizes in four of the five programme categories in the International Emmy Awards in the United States.

Cable Services

Until recently, about 12 per cent of households with television sets have received their television services by cable. The vast majority of cable systems have been used solely to relay broadcast television and radio services in order to improve reception quality, to avoid 'screening' by buildings or the local topography, or because external aerials are not allowed on some residential buildings.

Legislation has been passed to allow a much more general expansion of cable television. It is intended that cable investment should be privately financed (the Government is, however, providing £5 million to the cable television industry to encourage the development of advanced interactive services such as home banking and shopping over broadband cable systems); that regulation should be as light as possible to allow the development of a wide range of services and facilities, and flexible enough to adapt to changing technology; and that there should be certain safeguards for existing broadcasting services. A new national Cable Authority has been established to issue licences, supervise programme services and promote cable development. In 1983, licences were awarded to 11 cable systems to serve as pilot projects, and some existing cable operators, formerly relaying broadcast services, have been licensed to offer additional services on their existing systems. By August 1986 the Cable Authority had awarded a further nine cable franchises.

In January 1986 the number of homes capable of receiving non-broadcast cable services was 975,000. The number of homes receiving such services was 127,000. Cable operators are represented by the Cable Television Association.

Radio

BBC Radio has four national channels. Radio 1 broadcasts rock and pop music, while Radio 2 provides music and light entertainment as well as being the principal channel for the coverage of sport. Radio 3 broadcasts mainly classical music as well as drama, poetry and short stories, talks and documentaries, and Test Match cricket (on medium wave only). Radio 4 is the main speech network, providing the principal news and current affairs service, as well as drama, comedy, documentaries and panel games; it also carries parliamentary coverage and live relays of major public events. At present, there is no independent national radio service, but legislation passed in 1984 gave the IBA power to build a transmitter network for such a service.

There are 32 BBC local radio stations serving England and the Channel Islands, and regional and community radio services in Scotland, Wales and Northern Ireland, as well as 44 ILR (independent local radio) contractors throughout Britain. Further BBC and ILR stations are planned. About 90 per cent of the population is served by BBC or ILR stations. Broadcasts provide a comprehensive service of local news and information, music and other entertainment, education, consumer advice and coverage of local events, and offer listeners a chance to air their views, often by using the phone-in technique.

There are also some 200 hospital and 20 university closed-circuit radio stations.

Educational Broadcasting

Both the BBC and the IBA broadcast educational programmes for children and students in schools of all kinds, as well as for pre-school children, and for adults in colleges and other institutions and in their homes. Broadcasts to schools cover most subjects of the curriculum, while education programmes for adults cover many fields of learning, vocational training and recreation. Supporting material in the form of books, pamphlets, filmstrips, computer software, and audio and video cassettes, is available to supplement the programmes. The BBC broadcasts television and radio programmes made specially for students of the Open University, most of whose 130 or so undergraduate courses contain video and audio components, some of them available on cassette for use with correspondence texts. The BBC Open University Centre also produces educational and training audio-visual materials in collaboration with external agencies such as the Department of Trade and Industry, the Department of Education and Science and the Engineering Industry Training Board.

BBC External Services

The BBC External Services broadcast by radio world-wide, using English and 36 other languages, for over 730 hours a week. The main objectives are to give unbiased news, reflect British opinion and project British life, culture and developments in science and industry. News bulletins, current affairs programmes, political commentaries and topical magazine programmes form the main part of the output, with a full sports service, music, drama and general entertainment.

The languages in which the External Services broadcast and the length of time each is on the air are prescribed by the Government. Apart from this the BBC has full responsibility and is completely independent in determining the content of news and other programmes. A plan to improve audibility is in progress.

The BBC World Service broadcasts by radio for 24 hours a day in English and is supplemented at peak listening times by programmes of special interest to Africa, South Asia and the Falkland Islands. Plans to broadcast a televised service are being considered by the BBC.

BBC news bulletins and other programmes are re-broadcast by the radio services of many countries. Re-broadcasting involves direct relays from BBC transmissions and the use of recorded programmes supplied through the BBC Transcription Service. There are some 3,000 re-broadcasts weekly of World Service programmes in about 150 countries. The Transcription Service offers programmes to over 100 countries.

The BBC's English by Radio and Television Service is the most extensive language teaching undertaking in the world. English lessons are broadcast weekly by radio with explanations in 30 other languages, and recorded lessons are supplied to 300 stations in over 100 countries free of charge. English by Television programmes are also shown in more than 100 countries. There is a wide range of printed and audio material accompanying these programmes.

Another part of the External Services, the Monitoring Service, listens to and reports on foreign broadcasts, supplying a daily flow of significant news and comment from overseas to the BBC, the press and the Government.

Radio for overseas is also produced by the radio services of the Central Office of Information (COI). A wide range of recorded material is sent to radio stations in about 100 countries. COI television services provide material such as documentary and magazine programmes for distribution to overseas stations.

Advertising

The BBC does not give publicity to any firm or organised interest except when it is necessary to provide effective and informative programmes. It must not broadcast any commercial advertisement or any sponsored programme.

Advertisements are broadcast on independent television but advertisers can have no influence on programme content or editorial control. Advertisements must be clearly distinguishable and separate from programmes, and the time given to them must not be so great as to detract from the value of the programmes as a medium of information, education or entertainment. Advertising is normally limited to seven minutes in any one hour of broadcasting time, and averaged over the day's programmes must not exceed six minutes per hour. The independent local radio stations are normally limited to a maximum of nine minutes of advertising each hour. The IBA has a code governing standards and practice in advertising on television and radio and giving guidance on the types and methods of advertisement which are prohibited; this includes advertising with a political or religious object or on behalf of cigarettes or betting. Advertisements may not be inserted in certain types of programme, such as broadcasts to schools. A comparable code has been adopted by the Cable Authority, which is responsible for advertising control and policy on cable television. The IBA has endorsed the Principles for Advertising by Direct Satellite Broadcasting which have been drawn up by the European Broadcasting Union.

The Government has no general privileged access to radio or television but government publicity material to support non-political campaigns may be broadcast on independent radio and television. This is prepared through the COI and broadcast and paid for on a normal commercial basis. Short public service items, concerning health, safety and welfare, are also produced by the COI for free transmission by the BBC and independent television and radio.

Parliamentary and Political Broadcasting

Parliamentary reporting includes a daily factual and impartial account of proceedings in Parliament. Proceedings, including those of committees, are broadcast on radio, some live and others in recorded form in radio and television news and current affairs programmes. The House of Commons is not televised. The issue has arisen on a number of occasions, with members voting against it, most recently in 1985. However, an experiment in televising the House of Lords began in 1985 and members decided in 1986 that it should continue on a permanent basis.

Ministerial and party political broadcasts are transmitted periodically on radio and television, under rules agreed between the major political parties, the BBC and the IBA, and there are special arrangements for the period following the announcement of a general election.

Audience Research

Both the BBC and the IBA are required to keep themselves informed on the state of public opinion about the programmes (and, in the case of the IBA, the advertising) they broadcast. This is done through the continuous measurement of the size and composition of audiences and their opinions of programmes. For television, this work is undertaken through the Broadcasters' Audience Research Board, which is owned jointly by the BBC and the IBA. Information is collected from a panel of about 3,000 homes throughout the country designed to be representative of all private households in Britain with a television set. Meters attached to each television set and linked to a central computer are used to record times of viewing, numbers of viewers and programmes watched. Regular surveys and questionnaires are conducted by both the BBC and the IBA to gauge audience opinion on television and radio services, and public opinion is further assessed by both bodies through the work of their many advisory committees, councils and panels (whose members are drawn from a wide cross-section of the public); the regular holding of public meetings to debate the services provided; and careful consideration of correspondence and telephone calls from listeners and viewers.

Technical Developments

One of the most important recent developments has been the introduction of smaller, lighter cameras and video recorders for use on location. Electronic news-gathering equipment, whereby pictures can be transmitted directly to a studio or recorded on video tape on location, reduces significantly the time before an item can be broadcast. Other developments include the use of new types of video tape recorders, the increasing use of computers to generate graphical shapes such as captions and credits, and the improvement of the quality of video tape pictures.

Among recent developments by the BBC are the ACE digital television standards converter, probably the most advanced in the world, which is used to convert pictures between the European and American standards, and the NICAM system used to carry high-quality sound programme signals across the country. Both of these systems have been licensed to commercial manufacturers. The BBC has also developed a data-labelling system for sound programmes which will make programme and station selection much easier. Research includes investigations into stereo sound for television, digital transmission of signals over fibre-optic cables, improved picture displays, and many aspects of satellite broadcasting. IBA engineers were the first in the world to introduce a fully digital field rate standards converter to improve the interchange of programmes between areas using the 525-line system and those using the 625-line system. The IBA is at present engaged in the further development of digital techniques for studio applications and inter-city links, and a study of the future use of satellites for broadcasting which has included the development of a new C-MAC transmission system for use on future direct broadcast satellites. C-MAC has been accepted by the Government as the United Kingdom satellite transmission standard, and has been recommended by the European Broadcasting Union as the standard for Europe.

Another IBA development has been an enhanced C-MAC system for satellite transmission capable of providing wide-screen pictures at a subjective definition of about 1,000 lines, fully compatible with C-MAC transmissions and capable of being transmitted in a single 27-MHz satellite channel.

It is hoped that by 1990 direct broadcasting by satellite, by which television pictures are transmitted directly from space into people's homes, will be available throughout Britain. The IBA is seeking programme contractors for three of the five satellite channels allocated to the United Kingdom by international agreement. The service will be a commercial one funded by advertising or subscriptions.

The BBC and IBA have co-operated in the development of a teletext system, known by the BBC as CEEFAX and the IBA as ORACLE. The use of teletext allows the television signal to carry additional information which can be selected and displayed as 'pages' of text and graphics on receivers equipped with the necessary decoders. The system is also used to provide programme subtitles, which are of great benefit to the deaf and hard of hearing. Over 2 million teletext-equipped sets are in use in Britain. More than 95 per cent of teletext sets throughout the world are based on the British system, and working services operating to the British standard are in use or on trial in 13 countries, including Australia, the Federal Republic of Germany and the United States. British Telecom's public viewdata service, 'Prestel', offers a wide range of information which is transmitted via the telephone and viewed on the screen of a television receiver.

International Relations

The BBC and the IBA (together with the Independent Television Companies Association) are active members of the European Broadcasting Union. This body manages Eurovision, the international network of television news and programme exchange, and is responsible for the technical and administrative arrangements for co-ordinating the exchange of programmes and news over the Eurovision network and intercontinental satellite links; it also maintains a technical monitoring station where frequency measurements and other observations on broadcasting stations are carried out. The Union provides a forum linking the major public services and national broadcasters of Western Europe and other parts of the world and co-ordinates co-operation in radio and television.

The BBC is a shareholder in Visnews, which supplies world newsfilm to 425 television stations in 100 countries and is the most widely used newsfilm agency in the world. Worldwide Television News is owned by Independent Television News, the American Broadcasting Company and Channel 9 in Australia, and supplies services to over 500 broadcasters in 75 countries via the Eurovision network, and by satellite.

The BBC and the IBA are associate members of the Asian Pacific Broadcasting Union, and the BBC also belongs to the Commonwealth Broadcasting Association (CBA), whose members extend to one another such facilities as the use of studios, recording channels and programme contributions. The BBC provides technical aid, particularly in training the staff of other broadcasting organisations throughout the world; members of its staff are seconded for service overseas.

The Government finances a number of overseas students on broadcasting training courses at the BBC, the British Council (which aims to promote a wider knowledge of Britain and the English language abroad and to develop closer cultural relations between Britain and other countries) and the Thomson Foundation Television College in Glasgow, which sends lecturers and arranges courses overseas.

The BBC and the IBA participate in the work of the International Telecommunications Union, the United Nations agency responsible for regulating and controlling all international telecommunications services (including radio and television), allocating and registering all radio frequencies and promoting and co-ordinating the international study of technical problems in broadcasting. The BBC and the IBA are also represented on the United Kingdom Committee of the International Special Committee on Radio Interference. The BBC maintains a number of offices overseas.

24 Sport and Recreation

The British invented and codified the rules of many of the sports and games which are now played all over the world, and there is widespread interest in most kinds of sport throughout the country. Large crowds attend occasions such as the association football and rugby league challenge Cup Finals at Wembley Stadium, the international rugby union matches at Twickenham, Murrayfield and Cardiff Arms Park, the Wimbledon lawn tennis championships, the classic horse races, Grand Prix motor racing and the cricket Test matches. Extensive coverage of sport on television has helped to generate interest in a wide variety of sports including basketball, darts, snooker, ice skating, skiing and athletics.

Levels of participation in sport have been rising due mainly to the increases in leisure time and facilities, greater mobility and rising living standards. A growing awareness of the importance to good health of regular exercise has been reflected in the upsurge of interest in jogging and marathon running. It has been estimated that about one-third of the adult population regularly takes part in outdoor sport, and about a quarter in indoor sport. Men greatly outnumber women in active sport.

The Government has long recognised the importance of physical recreation for the general welfare of the community; the social role that sport can play has become more important at a time of high unemployment and rapid change in work and leisure patterns. The ten-year strategy for the development of sport in England drawn up by the Sports Council in 1982 is to encourage further increases in participation, particularly among young people and those nearing retirement; to provide adequate facilities for the whole community, especially in the inner cities and in deprived rural areas; and to continue to encourage high standards of performance. Similar strategies are being followed by the Sports Councils for Scotland, Wales and Northern Ireland. In January 1985 the four Sports Councils mounted a two-year campaign, 'Ever thought of Sport?', jointly financed by the Government and private commercial interests, which is aimed at boosting participation in sports among the 13 to 24 age group. The 'Action Sport' programme, which has been supported by the Manpower Services Commission, is designed to encourage young people in inner cities to take up sport and recreation; the programme is to be expanded in 1986–87. 'What's Your Sport?', a new campaign to increase participation in sports, will be launched by the Sports Councils in 1987.

Gleneagles Agreement

In accordance with the statement on apartheid in sport, agreed by the Commonwealth heads of Government at Gleneagles in Scotland in 1977, the Government seeks to discourage sporting contacts with South Africa and withholds any form of support for such contacts; in a democratic society, however, it cannot prevent these contacts if an individual sportsman or the governing body of the sport concerned chooses to ignore its advice.

ORGANISATION AND PROMOTION

Government policy on sport, active recreation and children's play is co-ordinated in England by the Minister for Sport (a Parliamentary Under-Secretary of State at the Department of the Environment). The Secretaries of State for Wales, Scotland and Northern Ireland have similar responsibilities in their countries.

Responsibility for the organisation and promotion of sport is largely decentral-ised, and most sports and recreation facilities are provided by local authorities.

The Government provides financial and other assistance through a number of official bodies and schemes. This 'arm's length' principle of funding safeguards the long-established independence of sports organisations in Britain. Some of these bodies, such as the Sports Councils and the Countryside Commissions, have specific responsibilities for sport and recreation, and help other public and private bodies to provide facilities. Others, like the Forestry Commission, the British Waterways Board, the Nature Conservancy Council and the regional water authorities, provide recreational amenities in addition to their main functions.

Individual sports are run by over 260 independent governing bodies whose functions usually include drawing up rules, holding events, regulating mem-bership, selecting and training national teams and promoting international links. There are also organisations representing people who take part in more informal physical recreation, such as walking and cycling.

A National Coaching Foundation has been established to improve the knowledge and practice of coaching in Britain. The work of the foundation complements that of the four Sports Councils and the governing bodies of sports.

Sports Councils Government assistance for the development of sport in Great Britain is channelled through three independent bodies—the Sports Council (for England and for general matters affecting Britain as a whole), the Sports Council for Wales and the Scottish Sports Council. In Northern Ireland the Department of Education makes direct grants towards the capital cost of facilities to local authorities and voluntary sports bodies; the Sports Council for Northern Ireland has limited grant-making powers. The Councils will allocate government funds amounting to some £45 million in 1986–87. They make grants for sports development, coaching and administration to the governing bodies of sports and other national organisations, and administer the national sports centres. Grants and loans are also made to voluntary organisations and local authorities (and, in some cases, to commercial organisations) to assist the provision of sports facilities. In all, the Councils supported over 1,000 projects in 1985–86. The Sports Council assists British representatives at international sports meetings and encourages links with international and overseas organisations. All four Councils have information centres providing data on a wide range of sports topics. The Sports Council consults with the Central Council of Physical Recreation, comprising members of the national governing and representative bodies of sport and physical recreation in England; the equivalent bodies in Scotland, Wales and Northern Ireland are the Scottish and Welsh Sports Associations and the Northern Ireland Council of Physical Recreation.

Ten regional councils for sport and recreation in England, on each of which sporting, countryside and local authority interests are represented, advise on investment in and the planning of sporting and recreational facilities.

Countryside Commissions The Countryside Commissions are responsible for encouraging the development of facilities for open-air recreation in the countryside. These include the provision, by public and private bodies and by voluntary groups, of country parks and picnic sites as well as recreational paths.

Private Sponsorship Increasing numbers of sports receive financial sponsorship from commercial organisations, and its importance as a source of funding is recognised by the Government and the Sports Council. The estimated value of commercial sponsorship was some £120 million in 1985. Sponsorship may take the form of financing specific events, or of grants to individual sports organisations or sportsmen and sportswomen. The Sports Aid Foundation and Sports Aid Trust raise and distribute funds from industry, commerce and private sponsors in order to assist the training of talented individual sportsmen; grants are awarded on the recommendation of the governing bodies of sport. The Scottish and Welsh Sports Aid Foundations and the Ulster Sports and Recreation Trust fulfil similar functions. Sponsorship advisory services are also run by the Sports Councils and the Central Council of Physical Recreation.

To encourage private sector investment in sporting projects and facilities, the Sports Council runs a scheme which matches contributions from the private and voluntary sectors to provide facilities in designated areas. Following the success of the scheme in Merseyside and Bristol, it has been extended to London, the West Midlands, and Tyne and Wear.

Successive governments have negotiated voluntary agreements with the tobacco industry to regulate tobacco companies' sponsorship of sport, the last one having been negotiated in 1986.

PROVISION OF FACILITIES

Local authorities are the main providers of land and large-scale facilities for community recreation: their total planned expenditure on sport and recreation amounts to some £900 million in Britain in 1986–87. Provision of facilities was substantially increased in the 1970s to meet the increasing demand and to encourage further expansion of participation. The facilities provided include parks, lakes, playing fields, sports halls, tennis courts, golf courses, swimming pools (of which there are nearly 1,200 throughout Britain) and sports centres catering for a wide range of activities.

Increased emphasis is being placed on the need to provide new and improved sports facilities in areas of urban stress. A wide range of sports and recreational projects in urban areas are supported under the Government's urban programme, while the Derelict Land Grant scheme provides funding towards sports and recreational facilities on reclaimed sites. In 1984–85 total urban programme and Derelict Land Grant scheme support for sports and recreational projects amounted to £35 million.

In addition to the recreational facilities provided by public authorities, many facilities are made available by local sports clubs. Some cater for indoor recreation, but more common are those providing sports grounds, particularly for games such as cricket, association and rugby football, hockey, tennis and golf. Clubs linked to business firms often cater for a wide range of activities. Commercial facilities include tenpin bowling centres, ice and roller-skating rinks, squash courts, golf courses and driving ranges, curling rinks and riding stables.

Publicly maintained schools must provide for the physical education of their pupils. All (except those solely for infants) are expected to have a playing field or the use of one, and most secondary schools have a gymnasium. Some have other amenities such as swimming pools, sports halls and halls designed for dance and movement. Sports and recreation facilities are also provided at institutions of higher and further education (some of which have departments of physical education), and there are 'centres of sporting excellence', often at universities and other colleges, which enable selected young athletes to develop their talents and which provide, where appropriate, for their educational needs.

In order to achieve the maximum use of existing sports facilities, the Government is encouraging greater community use of sports centres and other facilities owned by schools, colleges and other public and private sector institutions, including football clubs. In 1985, together with the Sports Council, the Government launched an initiative under the title 'Opening Doors' to encourage the shared use of school and other sports facilities at times when they would otherwise lie empty.

Safety at sports grounds and stadia is governed by legislation, but, following the fire at Bradford City Football Ground in 1985, in which 56 people died, and the subsequent findings of a committee of inquiry, safety standards are being strengthened.

Sports Centres

Six national sports centres, five in England and one in Wales, are run by the Sports Council, and provide a range of competition and training facilities. As well as offering residential courses for national teams, coaches and enthusiasts from all over Britain, the centres are used extensively by local sports clubs and the local community. Combined facilities for a range of sports are provided at three of the centres: Crystal Palace in south-east London, Bisham Abbey in Buckinghamshire and Lilleshall in Shropshire. Crystal Palace provides major competition venues for athletics and swimming and a variety of indoor sports, and Lilleshall houses the training school of the Football Association. The other three are specialist centres: the National Sailing Centre, Cowes, Isle of Wight; the National Water Sports Centre at Holme Pierrepont, Nottinghamshire, which caters for rowing, canoeing and water-skiing; and the Plas-y-Brenin National Centre for Mountain Activities in north Wales. The Sports Council for Wales runs the National Sports Centre for Wales in Cardiff and the National Outdoor Pursuits Centre at Plas Menai in north Wales.

The Scottish Sports Council operates three national sports training centres: Glenmore Lodge near Aviemore for outdoor pursuits, Inverclyde at Largs for general sports, and a national water sports training centre on Great Cumbrae Isle in the Firth of Clyde. The Sports Council for Northern Ireland operates one national facility, the Northern Ireland Mountain Centre at Tollymore in County Down.

Some 600 purpose-built indoor sports centres and 1,000 sports halls serve local rather than national needs; in Northern Ireland there has been a major development of multi-purpose centres. Several privately run centres cater for specialised interests, such as the National Equestrian Centre, run by the British Equestrian Federation, and the Ludwig Guttmann Sports Centre for the Disabled, Stoke Mandeville.

Children's Play

The Minister for Sport has responsibility for co-ordinating policy on children's play. The Department of Education and Science is concerned with play in schools, and the Department of Health and Social Security with play for the under-fives. Play Board—the Association for Children's Play and Recreation Ltd—is an independent national organisation, funded by the Department of the Environment, which promotes facilities and opportunities for children's play in England, Wales and Northern Ireland.

The National Playing Fields Association is a charity which has for many years encouraged the provision of playing fields and recreational facilities, specialising in the needs of children and young people, including the young disabled. There are affiliated associations in Scotland and Northern Ireland and in the counties of England and Wales.

The British Olympic Association

The British Olympic Association, founded in 1905, organises the participation of British teams in the Olympic Games. The Association's committee consists of representatives of the 29 sports in the programme of the Olympic Games (summer and winter). It determines the size of the British teams, raises funds, makes all the arrangements and provides a headquarters staff for the management of the teams.

SPORT AND RECREATION

Sport for Disabled People

The British Sports Association for the Disabled, founded in 1961, is the co-ordinating body of sport and recreation for all disabilities. The Association, which receives an annual Sports Council grant, encourages disabled people to take part in physical recreation and sport for pleasure and as an aid to rehabilitation and integration with the able-bodied community. It also seeks to secure the provision and improvement of facilities in consultation with national and local authorities.

Sports clubs for the disabled throughout Britain are affiliated to the Association, which helps to organise sporting and physical activities at all levels, including national and international meetings. As well as offering advice to local clubs and groups, the Association arranges conferences, seminars and coaching courses, and acts as co-ordinating body for the various disability groups. It serves as the focal point for national team management and selection at world and Paralympic levels, and organises world events on behalf of international bodies. In Scotland the Scottish Sports Association for the Disabled has a co-ordinating role.

The first sports stadium in the world designed for the disabled was opened at Stoke Mandeville, Buckinghamshire, in 1969, and is owned and maintained by the British Paraplegic Sports Society. Annual national games organised by several of the associations for the disabled take place at Stoke Mandeville, Crystal Palace in London and at other locations; the Seventh World Wheelchair Games (or Paralympics) were held at Stoke Mandeville in 1984.

Drug Abuse

The growing problem of drug-taking in sport in order to achieve unfair improvements in performance has been a cause of concern both to the Sports Councils and to the governing bodies of sport. A campaign to tackle the problem, launched by the Sports Council, includes the introduction in 25 sports of random drug-testing procedures which can lead to a life ban for offending competitors. In Scotland the governing bodies of over 90 per cent of competitive sports have voluntarily introduced testing. The Sports Council continues to fund research into methods of detection for new drugs that unfairly aid performance.

The Government and the Sports Council have also taken firm action at international level by supporting the adoption of a European Anti-Doping Charter and by chairing an international working party to examine ways of promoting effective anti-doping measures.

POPULAR SPORTS AND RECREATIONS

Some of the major sports and recreations in Britain are described below. The increased provision of sports centres has improved opportunities for participation in indoor sports such as basketball, volleyball, fencing, judo and other martial arts, gymnastics, squash, table tennis and shooting. Almost all outdoor sports have continued to gain in popularity, including the 'high-risk' activities such as rock-climbing and sub-aqua diving. The number of people enjoying the recreational amenities of the countryside, rivers and coastline is similarly growing. Two sports introduced from overseas in the 1970s which have gained rapidly in popularity are windsurfing and hang-gliding; the flying of microlight aircraft is one of the newest sports to achieve a keen following.

Sportsmen may be professionals (paid players) or amateurs. Some sports, such as rugby union, hockey and rowing, are amateur but in others the distinction between amateur and professional status is less strictly defined, or does not exist. The British Amateur Athletic Board, for example, allows payments to be made into trust funds held by many top-ranking athletes.

Association Football

The largest spectator sport and one of the most popular participation sports, association football was first developed and codified in England during the nineteenth century, and is controlled by separate football associations in England, Wales, Scotland and Northern Ireland. In England over 350 clubs are affiliated to the English Football Association (FA) and some 40,000 clubs to regional or district associations. The full-time professional clubs in England and Wales belong to the Football League (92 clubs) and in Scotland to the Scottish Football League (38 clubs); the clubs play in four divisions in England and Wales and three in Scotland. In Northern Ireland, 14 semi-professional clubs play in the Irish Football League. During the season, which lasts from August until May, attendances at over 2,000 English league matches total about 18 million. The Football Association, founded in 1863, and the Football League, founded in 1888, were both the first of their kind in the world.

The annual competitions for the FA Challenge Cup, the Littlewoods Challenge Cup (formerly the League Cup), the Scottish FA Cup, the Skol Cup (formerly the Scottish League Cup), the Irish Cup and the Welsh FA Cup are organised on a knock-out basis, and the finals are played at Wembley Stadium, London, at Hampden Park, Glasgow, at Windsor Park, Belfast, and on a two-match home and away basis in Wales. British clubs were European club champions (Liverpool three times, Nottingham Forest twice and Aston Villa once) for six consecutive years between 1977 and 1982, and Liverpool became champions again in 1984. Aberdeen won the European Cup-Winners Cup in 1983, as did Everton in 1985; Ipswich Town and Tottenham Hotspur won the Union of European Football Associations (UEFA) cup competition in 1981 and 1984 respectively.

The Sports Councils, using specially allocated funds, have made grants to a number of clubs and local authorities to enable them to modernise or expand football facilities in areas of urban deprivation. Grants for various improvements such as all-weather pitches are also made throughout Britain by the football associations and the Football Trust, a body financed by the football pools (see p 443) companies; its sister body, the Football Grounds Improvement Trust, is specifically concerned with ground safety.

Spectator violence associated with football both in Britain and overseas has been a subject of growing concern, and the Government has worked closely with the football authorities and the governments of other European countries to combat the problem. After serious disturbances involving English supporters at the European Cup Final in Brussels in May 1985 which led to the deaths of 38 spectators, English clubs were withdrawn from European competitions for the 1985–86 season by the Football Association; an indefinite ban on the clubs was subsequently imposed by UEFA and, on a world-wide basis, by FIFA (the International Federation of Football Associations), though the latter was later rescinded. Britain has signed a Council of Europe Convention, adopted in 1985, which is designed to eliminate spectator violence at all sporting events, including football. The Government has restricted the sale of alcohol in football grounds and banned its sale on transport to matches, and it is an offence to take cans or bottles into grounds.

Under public order legislation at present before Parliament the courts would be given power to ban convicted hooligans from football matches, and a new offence of disorderly conduct would be created covering behaviour which, while not in itself violent, causes unnecessary distress to others. Possession of smoke bombs and fireworks at or on entry to a football ground would also become an offence. Greater use is being made of closed-circuit television at football grounds, and the introduction of club membership schemes for supporters is under discussion.

Athletics   Amateur athletics is governed in England by the Amateur Athletic Association (which, formed in 1880, was the first national governing body for athletics) and by the Women's Amateur Athletic Association. Scotland, Wales and Northern Ireland have their own associations. International athletics and the selection of British teams are the concern of the British Amateur Athletic Board, which also administers coaching schemes. For the Olympic Games and the world and European championships one team represents the United Kingdom.

Athletics is attracting increasing numbers of participants, both men and women, in part because of the success of British competitors and the wide coverage of athletics events on television.

Many British athletes, especially middle-distance runners, have enjoyed distinguished reputations: in 1954, for example, Dr Roger Bannister became the first man to run a mile in under four minutes. More recently, Britons won 15 medals at the 1986 European Athletics Championships in Stuttgart, including gold medals in the 100 metres (Linford Christie), 400 metres (Roger Black), 800 metres (Sebastian Coe), 1,500 metres (Steve Cram), 5,000 metres (Jack Buckner), 4 × 400 metres relay (Derek Redmond, Kriss Akabusi, Brian Whittle and Roger Black), decathlon (Daley Thompson) and the women's javelin (Fatima Whitbread). At the 1984 Olympic Games held in Los Angeles British athletes won 16 medals including three gold medals. Eight world records were held by Britons in August 1986: the 800 metres and the 1,000 metres by Sebastian Coe; the mile and the 2,000 metres by Steve Cram; the 4 × 800 metres relay by Peter Elliott, Gary Cook, Steve Cram and Sebastian Coe; and the decathlon by Daley Thompson; the women's 5,000 metres by Zola Budd; and the women's javelin by Fatima Whitbread.

The thirteenth Commonwealth Games were held in Scotland in July and August 1986 at venues in Edinburgh and elsewhere.

Highland Games

Scottish Highland Games, at which sports (including tossing the caber, putting the weight and throwing the hammer), dancing and piping competitions take place, attract large numbers of spectators from all over the world. Among better-known Highland Games are the annual Braemar Gathering, which is traditionally attended by the royal family, the Argyllshire and Cowal Gatherings and the meeting at Aboyne.

Badminton

The origins of badminton are not clear, but the Badminton Association of England, which together with the Scottish, Welsh and Irish Badminton Unions today organises the sport in Britain, was formed in 1893 and the first tournament was promoted five years later. Badminton expanded rapidly in the 1970s and is played in a variety of locations from sports centres to village halls; some 2 million people are estimated to play the game in Britain, about 1 million of them regularly. Over 5,000 clubs and as many schools are affiliated to the Badminton Association of England, which organises the All England Championships each year. British women players have done particularly well in the sport: Nora Perry and Jane Webster of England were world champions in 1982. The England women's team won a silver medal, and the men's a bronze, at the 1984 world team championships. The English team (men and women) are reigning Commonwealth Games champions.

Basketball

Basketball is played in Britain both indoors and outdoors. There are about 900 registered clubs and the sport is played in most secondary schools and many other institutions; in all, over 1 million people participate and its popularity has been increasing rapidly. The English Basket Ball Association is the governing body of the sport in England, and there are similar associations in Wales, Scotland and Northern Ireland. The leading English clubs play in a national league and the main events of the year are the National Championship Finals, held at Wembley Arena in London, and the men's National Cup Final, staged at the Royal Albert Hall.

Billiards and Snooker

The character of the present game of billiards was established in Britain at the end of the seventeenth century. Snooker, a more varied game invented by the British in India in 1875, has greatly increased in popularity and become a major spectator sport as a result of widespread television coverage of the professional tournaments. It is estimated that between 5 and 6 million people now play the game. British players have an outstanding record in snooker and the major professional championships have been largely dominated by them. The main tournament is the annual Embassy World Professional Championship, held in Sheffield; British winners of this event include Ray Reardon (six times), John Spencer (three times), and more recently Joe Johnson (1986), Dennis Taylor (1985), Alex Higgins (1972 and 1982) and Steve Davis (1981, 1983 and 1984). Northern Ireland won the world team championship in 1984 and 1985, as did England in 1981 and 1983.

The controlling body for the world professional game is the Billiards and Snooker Control Council, which holds the copyright of the rules. The World Professional Billiards and Snooker Association is responsible for professional players, and it organises professional events.

Bowls

Bowls has been played in Britain since the thirteenth century. The game of lawn bowls is played on a flat green; in the midlands and north of England and in North Wales a variation called crown green bowls is played, so named because the centre of the green is higher than its boundaries. Lawn and crown green bowls are mainly summer games; in winter indoor bowls, played on synthetic greens, is growing in popularity. At one time regarded as a pastime for the elderly, bowls is increasingly played by adults of all ages. Over 2,600 lawn bowling clubs are affiliated to the English Bowling Association, which, together with the Bowling Associations of Scotland, Wales and Ireland and the English Women's Bowling Association, play to the rules of the International Bowling Board. Other associations, including the English Bowling Federation, are not under the Board's control. The British Crown Green Bowling Association is the governing body of crown green bowls, and has nearly 2,000 affiliated clubs.

Boxing

Boxing as a British sport is one of the oldest, probably originating in Saxon times. Its modern form, also adopted in many overseas countries, dates from 1865 when the Marquess of Queensberry drew up a set of rules eliminating much of the brutality that had characterised prize-fighting and making skill the basis of the sport. Boxing is both amateur and professional, and in both strict medical regulations are observed.

All amateur boxing in England, including schoolboy, club and association boxing, and boxing in the armed services, is controlled by the Amateur Boxing Association. There are separate associations in Scotland and Wales; Northern Ireland forms part of the Irish Boxing Association. The associations organise various amateur boxing competitions, and teams from England, Wales, Scotland and Northern Ireland take part in international competitions such as the Commonwealth Games and the European and world championships; a British team competes in the Olympic Games.

Professional boxing is controlled by the British Boxing Board of Control. The Board appoints inspectors, medical officers and representatives to ensure that regulations are observed and to guard against overmatching and exploitation. British boxing has a distinguished record and at various times British boxers have held European, Commonwealth and world championship titles; Dennis Andries holds the World Boxing Council light-heavyweight world title.

Chess

Chess has increased greatly in popularity and England now ranks among the top chess-playing nations (Scotland, Wales and Northern Ireland are separately represented). There are local chess clubs and leagues throughout the country and the game is widely played in schools and colleges. Important domestic competitions include the Kleinwort Grieveson British Championships, the Peterborough Software National Club Championships, the Leigh Grand Prix, the Pergamon British Lightning Championship and *The Times* British Schools Chess Tournament. The best-known international event is the Foreign and Colonial Hastings Chess Congress. The governing bodies of the game are the British Chess Federation, the Scottish Chess Association (the oldest such body in the world, which celebrated its centenary in 1984) and the Welsh and Ulster Chess Unions.

At present England has 10 Grandmasters for over-the-board chess.

Cricket

Cricket is among the most popular of summer sports and is sometimes called the English national game, having been played as early as the 1550s. Among the many clubs founded in the eighteenth century was the Marylebone Cricket Club (MCC), which reframed the laws of the game. The Club is based at Lord's cricket ground in north London, the administrative centre of the world game. Men's cricket in Britain is now governed by the Cricket Council, consisting of representatives of the Test and County Cricket Board (representing first-class cricket), the National Cricket Association (representing club and junior cricket) and the MCC.

Cricket is played in schools, colleges and universities, and in most towns and villages amateur teams play weekly games from late April to the end of September. In England there is a network of league cricket contested by teams of Saturday afternoon players; in the midlands and the north of England these teams include a full-time professional. The game is also played to a lesser extent in Scotland and Wales.

The main competition in professional cricket is the Britannic Assurance County Championship of three-day games played by 17 county teams, which also take part in three one-day competitions—the Benson and Hedges Cup, the National Westminster Bank Trophy, and the John Player Special League played on Sundays. Some of the best supported games are the annual series of five-day Test matches played between England and a touring team from Australia, India, New Zealand, Pakistan, Sri Lanka or the West Indies. A team representing England usually tours one or more of these countries in the British winter. Texaco Trophy one-day international games also attract large crowds. A World Cup is played every four years, with some of the smaller cricketing nations as well as the major countries competing; India and Pakistan will jointly hold the next one in 1987.

Cricket is also played by women and girls, the governing body being the Women's Cricket Association, founded in 1926. Women's cricket clubs have regular weekend local fixtures and participate in an annual national club knockout competition. The game is also played at county level and Test match series are played by England against Australia, India, New Zealand and the West Indies. A women's World Cup, in which England competes, is held every four years.

Darts

Darts, an indoor game which has its origins in medieval archery, is played mainly in public houses as a casual recreation to accompany drinking. It has gained in popularity as a result of widespread television coverage of the professional game. As many as 9 million people at a time watch televised darts contests and it is estimated that over 5 million people play the game regularly. Darts is organised in Britain by the British Darts Organisation, which forms part of the World Darts Federation; its rules have become the code for the world sport. The Organisation arranges events in Britain which bring entrants from as many as 45 countries. Every two years a World Cup tournament is held, which England won in 1985 in Brisbane. The main individual title in the game is the Embassy World Professional Championship. British players have dominated the event and in 1986 the title was won by Eric Bristow of England.

Field Sports

British field sports include hunting (on horseback and on foot), fishing, shooting, stalking, falconry and hare coursing. The hunting seasons vary depending on the quarry. The fox hunting and hare hunting season lasts from November to April, while mink hunting takes place in the summer months. Fox hunting on horseback with a pack of hounds is the most popular British hunting sport, and there are over 400 packs of hounds of all kinds in Britain.

Game shooting as an organised sport probably originated in the early part of the nineteenth century, and takes place in many parts of Britain. Game consists of grouse, black-grouse, partridge, pheasant and ptarmigan, species which are protected by law during a close season when they are allowed to breed on numerous estates supervised by gamekeepers. It is necessary to have a licence to kill game and a certificate issued by the police to own a shot-gun. The Game Conservancy, formed by landowners, farmers and others interested in game conservation, collects information and studies factors controlling game populations.

The most popular country sport is fishing, and there are about 4 million anglers in Britain. Many fish for salmon and trout, particularly in the rivers and lochs of Scotland and in Wales, but in England and Wales the most widely practised form of fishing is for coarse fish such as pike, perch, carp, tench and bream. Angling clubs in England affiliate to the National Federation of Anglers (there are similar bodies in Scotland, Wales and Northern Ireland) and many clubs organise angling competitions. The National Federation of Anglers organises national championships and enters a team in the world angling championships. In 1985 England won both the world team and individual events. Freshwater fishing usually has to be paid for: most coarse fishing is let to angling clubs by private owners, while trout and salmon fishermen may rent a stretch of river, join a club, or pay for the right to fish by the day, week or month. Coastal and deep-sea fishing are free to all (apart from salmon and sea trout fishing which is by licence only).

The British Field Sports Society and the British Association for Shooting and Conservation look after the interests of all field sports. Public opposition to field sports is not inconsiderable and is organised through such bodies as the League Against Cruel Sports.

Golf

Golf originated in Scotland, where for centuries it has borne the title of the Royal and Ancient Game. The Royal Burgess Golfing Society of Edinburgh, the oldest club in the world, celebrated its 250th anniversary in 1985. The Royal and Ancient Golf Club, the ruling authority of the sport for most of the world, is situated at St Andrews on the east coast. Golf is played throughout Britain and there are golf courses in the vicinity of most towns, some of them owned by local authorities. The main event of the British golfing year, and considered by many to be the world's leading tournament, is the Open Golf Championship; other important events include the Walker Cup match for amateurs and the Ryder Cup match for professionals, which are played between Britain and the United States and Europe and the United States respectively. Among the leading British professional players are Sandy Lyle, Nick Faldo, Mark James, Brian Barnes, Bernard Gallagher and Sam Torrance.

Hockey (Field and Indoor)

Variants of hockey have been played in Britain for at least five centuries, and some, like hurling in Ireland and shinty in Scotland, are still played. The modern game was started in the nineteenth century by the Hockey Association (of

England), which was founded in 1886. There are similar associations in Scotland, Wales and Ireland. Some 1,000 men's hockey clubs are located throughout Britain, many of which have women's and junior sections; large numbers of boys' schools also play the game. Cup competitions and leagues are played at national, division or district, and club levels both indoors (six-a-side) and outdoors, and there are regular international matches.

The controlling body of women's hockey in England is the All-England Women's Hockey Association (founded in 1895) to which are affiliated some 1,000 clubs and about 2,400 schools; there are similar associations in Scotland, Wales and Ireland. County, club and school championships for both outdoor and indoor hockey are played annually in England. The first international women's hockey match took place in 1896; nowadays the main international match is played each year at Wembley Stadium.

Men's and women's hockey are Olympic sports, and the British men's team won a bronze medal at the 1984 Olympic Games.

The Hockey Association will host the sixth World Hockey Cup for men in October 1986 at the new national hockey centre in Willesden, north London.

Ice Skating

Ice skating became popular in Britain in the late nineteenth and early twentieth centuries and takes three main forms: ice dancing, figure skating and speed-skating. The governing body for the sport is the National Skating Association of Great Britain, founded in 1879. Participation in ice skating is concentrated among the under-25s. There are some 40 ice rinks in Great Britain, a small number compared with many other European countries. In spite of this, British couples have won the world ice dance championship 17 times in its 32-year history, and Jayne Torvill and Christopher Dean were world ice dance champions for four successive years between 1981 and 1984, European champions in 1981, 1982 and 1984, and gold medal winners at the Sarajevo winter Olympic Games in 1984. Robin Cousins was the Olympic gold medal winner for figure skating in 1980.

Judo

Judo, a modern combat sport derived from the ancient Japanese arts of ju-jutsu, is growing rapidly in popularity in Britain, both as a sport and general fitness training method and as a self-defence technique. Men and women take part in judo at all levels, and in the last four Olympic Games judo has been one of Britain's most successful sports. Recent leading British exponents of the sport include Brian Jacks, Neil Adams, Neil Eckersley, Karen Briggs and Diane Bell. More than 1,000 judo clubs are registered with the British Judo Association which is the official governing body of the sport throughout Britain.

Other martial arts, such as karate, kung fu and aikido, are attracting increasing numbers of participants.

Lawn Tennis

The modern game of lawn tennis originated in England in 1872 and the first championships were played at Wimbledon in 1877. The controlling body in Great Britain, the Lawn Tennis Association, was founded in 1888; Northern Ireland forms part of the Irish Lawn Tennis Association. The main event of the season is the annual Wimbledon fortnight, widely regarded as the most important tennis event in the world; this draws large crowds, with the ground at the All England Club accommodating over 30,000 spectators. There are also national and county championships and national competitions for boys' and girls' schools. International events include the Davis Cup and European Cup for men and the Federation Cup for women. Women from Britain and the United States compete annually for the Wightman Cup.

Motor Sports

Among the most popular spectator sports in Britain are motor racing and rallying, and motor-cycle racing. The governing body for four-wheeled motor sport is the RAC [Royal Automobile Club] Motor Sports Association. The Association issues competition licences for a variety of motoring competitions and organises both the RAC Rally, an event in the contest for the World Rally Championship, and the British Grand Prix, held annually at the Silverstone racing circuit as part of the Formula One World Motor Racing Championship.

British car constructors including Lotus, McLaren and Williams have enjoyed outstanding successes in Grand Prix racing, and Britain has had six world champion motor racing drivers; Nigel Mansell and Derek Warwick are among the most successful of current drivers. Other popular types of motor-car sport include autocross, drag racing and karting.

Motor-cycle sport, governed by the Auto-Cycle Union, caters for all forms of competition on two or three wheels, from speed trials to Grand Prix road racing. The major events of the year are the Isle of Man Tourist Trophy races, and the British Grand Prix at Silverstone; there are also many world championship events for trials, motocross, speedway and other sports.

Mountaineering and Rock-Climbing

The popularity of mountaineering and rock-climbing has increased steadily. Clubs in the British Mountaineering Council and the Mountaineering Council of Scotland, the representative bodies of the sport, number 330, ranging from national clubs such as the Alpine Club (founded in 1857, the oldest mountaineering club in the world) and the Scottish Mountaineering Club to small regional clubs with 20 to 30 members. The National Centre for Mountain Activities is at Plas-y-Brenin in north Wales, and climbing takes place at other centres managed by the Sports Councils at Plas Menai (north Wales), Glenmore Lodge near Aviemore in Scotland and Tollymore in Northern Ireland. A number of local education authorities and national bodies such as the Outward Bound Trust have also established mountaineering training centres. The most popular areas in Britain for climbing include the Peak District of Derbyshire, the Lake District, Snowdonia in north Wales and the Western Highlands of Scotland.

British mountaineers have taken a leading part in exploring mountain ranges and climbing many of the great mountains of the world, achieving, for example, the first ascent of the Matterhorn in 1865, Everest in 1953, Kangchenjunga in 1955, Everest by its south-west face in 1975, and the south face of Gosainthan (in the Himalayas) in 1982.

Racing

Horse-racing takes two forms—flat racing (from late March to early November) and steeplechasing and hurdle racing (from late August to early June). The Derby, run at Epsom, is the outstanding event in the flat racing calendar. Other classic races are: the Two Thousand Guineas and the One Thousand Guineas, both run at Newmarket; the Oaks, run at Epsom; and the St Leger, run at Doncaster. The most important steeplechase and hurdle race meeting is the National Hunt Festival Meeting held at Cheltenham in March. The Grand National, run at Aintree near Liverpool, is the world's best-known steeplechase and dates from 1837.

The Jockey Club administers all horse-racing in Britain. Its rules are the basis of turf procedure and it also licenses racecourses. Racing takes place on most days (excluding Sundays) throughout the year and about 12,500 horses are in training. British thoroughbreds continue to be a source of the world's best bloodstock.

The racing of greyhounds after a mechanical hare (one of Britain's most popular spectator sports) takes place at 98 tracks licensed by local authorities. Meetings are usually held two or three times a week at each track with at least ten races a meeting. The rules for the sport are drawn up by the National Greyhound Racing Club, the sport's judiciary body. The Stewards of the Club are also responsible for overall administration and organisation. The representative body is the British Greyhound Racing Board.

Riding

Horse riding takes a number of forms ranging from recreational riding to show jumping. The art of riding is promoted by the British Horse Society, which is concerned with the welfare of horses, road safety, bridleways and training. It also runs the British Equestrian Centre at Stoneleigh in Warwickshire where activities take place throughout the year. With some 38,000 members the Society is the parent body of the Pony Club and the Riding Club movements, which hold rallies, meetings and competitions culminating in annual national championships. Horse trials are held during the spring and autumn under the auspices of the Society. Three-day events (comprising dressage, cross-country riding and show jumping) held each year include those at Badminton (Avon) in April; Windsor (Berkshire) in May; Bramham (Yorkshire) in June; Burghley House (Lincolnshire) in September; and Wylye (Wiltshire) in October.

Show jumping is promoted by the British Show Jumping Association, which has over 14,000 members and some 1,650 shows affiliated to it. The major show jumping events each year include the Royal International Horse Show at the National Exhibition Centre, Birmingham, the Horse of the Year Show at Wembley in London, and the Olympia International Show Jumping Championships in London.

The authority responsible for equestrian competitions (other than racing) at international level is the British Equestrian Federation, which co-ordinates the events of the British Horse Society and the British Show Jumping Association. British equestrian teams have an outstanding record in international competitions: a British team won the three-day event world championship held in Australia in 1986, and Virginia Leng won the individual gold medal. Silver medals were won by both the three-day event and the show jumping teams at the 1984 Olympic Games, while Virginia Leng won the bronze medal in the three-day event individual competition. Well-known show jumpers include Lucinda Green, David Broome, Malcolm Pyrah, Harvey Smith and Nick Skelton.

Rowing

Oarsmanship is taught in many schools, colleges and rowing clubs (including women's clubs) throughout Britain. The governing body of the sport in England is the Amateur Rowing Association, and there are similar bodies in Scotland, Wales and Northern Ireland. There are about 480 rowing clubs, and each year about 250 regattas and head races are held in England, Wales and Scotland under Association rules.

The University Boat Race (between eight-oared crews from Oxford and Cambridge) originated in 1829 and has been rowed on the Thames almost every spring since 1836. The Head of the River Race in March (also on the Thames) is the largest assembly of racing craft in the world, with more than 420 eights racing in procession. At the Henley Regatta in Oxfordshire, founded in 1839, crews from all over the world compete each July in various kinds of race over a straight course of 1 mile 550 yards (about 2·1 km).

The National Water Sports Centre at Holme Pierrepont, near Nottingham, has a rowing course of Olympic 2,000-metre standard, as does Strathclyde Park in west-central Scotland. Britain won the gold medal in the coxed fours event at the 1984 Olympic Games.

Rugby Football

Rugby football takes its name from Rugby School, in Warwickshire, where it was first played in 1823. The game is played according to two different codes: rugby union (a 15-a-side game) is played by amateurs while rugby league (a 13-a-side game) is played by professionals as well as amateurs. Rugby union is played under the auspices of the Rugby Football Union in England and similar bodies in Wales, Scotland and Ireland. Important domestic competitions include the Divisional and County Championships in England, the national club knock-out competitions in England and Wales and the Scottish League Cup Championship. The Five Nations Tournament between England, Scotland, Wales, Ireland and France is played each year and there are overseas tours by the national sides and by the British Lions, a team representing Great Britain and Ireland. In 1987, teams representing 16 countries will compete for the first time for the Webb Ellis Trophy in a tournament to be held in Australia and New Zealand.

Rugby league is played mainly in the north of England. The governing body of the professional game is the Rugby Football League, which sends touring teams representing Great Britain to Australia and New Zealand; annual matches are also played against France. The Challenge Cup Final, the major club match of the season, is played at Wembley Stadium in London. The amateur game is governed by the British Amateur Rugby League Association; matches between England and France take place each year. A national league consisting of ten leading clubs is to be launched in autumn 1986.

Sailing

Sailing has always been popular in Britain, and the Royal Yachting Association (RYA) has more than 1,400 affiliated clubs. Over 1,000 practical or shore-based teaching centres, including the National Sailing Centre at Cowes in the Isle of Wight and the Scottish National Water Sports Training Centre in the Firth of Clyde, offer RYA courses in all branches of the sport. One of the world's principal regattas takes place each summer at Cowes, and major events are held at other sailing centres. British sailors have undertaken many notable voyages. Sir Francis Chichester was the winner of the first single-handed transatlantic race in 1960 and made a solo circumnavigation of the world in 1966–67. The first non-stop solo circumnavigation was achieved by Robin Knox-Johnston in 1968. In 1976 Clare Francis held the record for the fastest single-handed crossing of the Atlantic, as did Naomi James in 1980. Rodney Pattison won gold medals in the 'Flying Dutchman' class at the Olympic regattas of 1968 and 1972 with his crews Ian McDonald-Smith and Christopher Davies, and in 1976 Reg White, crewed by John Osborne, won the gold medal in the 'Tornado' catamaran class. Jo Richards and his crew Peter Allam won a bronze medal in the 'Flying Dutchman' class in the 1984 Olympics. In 1985 the World Women's Sailing Championship was held at Largs in Scotland.

Skiing

When there is sufficient snow, skiing takes place in several parts of Britain. The governing body of the sport is the British Ski Federation and there are separate national councils. Skiing in Scotland has become very popular, especially at the winter sports centres established in the Cairngorms, Deeside, Glencoe and Glenshee, where ski-runs equal to those in other areas of Europe have been developed. Ski-lifts, ski-tows and professional instruction of a high quality are now available. There are also some 100 artificial ski-slopes throughout Great Britain. Interest in cross-country skiing has been increasing. There are over 200 ski clubs in Britain, and it is estimated that about half a million people take part in the sport.

Squash Rackets

Squash rackets originated at Harrow School in the 1850s. The Squash Rackets Association was formed in 1929 to promote and organise the men's game and there are separate governing bodies for Scotland, Wales and Ireland. The governing body of women's squash in Britain is the Women's Squash Association, founded in 1934. Squash enjoyed a period of very rapid growth during the 1970s and remains a fast-developing sport. There are 9,000 squash courts in England, and the estimated number of players in Britain is about 3 million. The main tournament is the British Open Championship.

Sub-Aqua

Underwater activities are varied and include exploratory diving (for example, wreck and reef diving), snorkel diving and underwater photography. The British Sub-Aqua Club is the governing body for all underwater activities and promotes underwater exploration, science and sport. The Club is the largest of its kind in the world, with some 35,000 members and more than 1,000 clubs in Britain and overseas. The Scottish Sub-Aqua Club governs the sport in Scotland.

Swimming

Swimming is enjoyed by millions of people in Britain, many of whom learn to swim at public baths, schools or swimming clubs. Instruction and coaching are provided by qualified teachers who hold certificates awarded by the Amateur Swimming Association, to which over 1,700 clubs are affiliated. The Association also controls swimming, diving, synchronised swimming and water polo championships and competitions in England. Separate associations control the sport in Scotland and Wales. Northern Ireland forms part of the Irish Amateur Swimming Association. For major international competitions, such as the Olympic Games and the world and European championships, England, Scotland and Wales compete together as one team under the auspices of the Amateur Swimming Federation of Great Britain. A number of British swimmers have had great success and Duncan Goodhew won a gold medal at the 1980 Olympics. At the 1984 Olympics, Britons won a silver and four bronze medals.

Windsurfing

Windsurfing, or boardsailing, was introduced to Britain from the United States in 1974 and is one of the fastest-growing sports, with an estimated 100,000 participants. The sport takes place on the sea and on lakes and reservoirs throughout the country. Racing is increasingly popular, and regattas are organised by the governing body of the sport, the Royal Yachting Association, and by the United Kingdom Boardsailing Association, which controls racing for certain classes of boards. There are some 170 windsurfing schools recognised by the RYA. Windsurfing is now an Olympic sport.

GAMBLING

Various forms of betting and commercial gaming are permitted in Britain under strict regulations. Spending on gambling fell by about 14 per cent in real terms in the ten years to 1984; in 1984–85 the total money staked (excluding gaming machines) was about £6,000 million. It has been estimated that over 90 per cent of adults gamble at some time or another, some 40 per cent regularly.

Gaming includes the playing of casino and card games, gaming machines and licensed bingo, thought to be played by about 5 to 6 million people on a fairly regular basis. Betting takes place mainly on horse or greyhound racing, and on football matches (usually through football pools). Racing bets may be made at racecourses and greyhound tracks, or through some 11,000 licensed off-course betting offices which take nearly 90 per cent of the money staked. A form of pool betting (totalisator betting) is organised on, and off, course by the Horserace Totalisator Board (HTB). Bookmakers and the HTB contribute a levy to the Horserace Betting Levy Board, which promotes the improvement of horse racing and breeding and the advancement of veterinary science.

In addition, legislation allows local authorities and certain other bodies to hold lotteries.

Appendix 1

Currency
The unit of currency is the pound sterling divided into 100 new pence (p). There are seven coins: £1; 50p; 20p; 10p; 5p; 2p and 1p.
Bank of England notes are issued for sums of £5, £10, £20 and £50.

Metric Conversions for British Weights and Measures

Length

	1 inch	=	2·54 centimetres
12 inches	= 1 foot	=	30·48 centimetres
3 feet	= 1 yard	=	0·914 metre
1,760 yards	= 1 mile	=	1·609 kilometres

Area

	1 square inch	=	6·452 square centimetres
144 square inches	= 1 square foot	=	929·03 square centimetres
9 square feet	= 1 square yard	=	0·836 square metre
4,840 square yards	= 1 acre	=	0·405 hectare
640 acres	= 1 square mile	=	2·59 square kilometres

Capacity

	1 pint	=	0·568 litre
2 pints	= 1 quart	=	1·136 litres
4 quarts	= 1 gallon	=	4·546 litres
8 gallons	= 1 bushel	=	36·37 litres
8 bushels	= 1 quarter	=	2·909 hectolitres

Weight (Avoirdupois)

	1 ounce (oz)	= 28·35 grammes
16 oz	= 1 pound (1lb)	= 0·454 kilogramme
14 lb	= 1 stone (st)	= 6·35 kilogrammes
112 lb	= 1 hundredweight (cwt)	= 50·8 kilogrammes
20 cwt (2,240 lb)	= 1 long ton	= 1·016 tonnes
2,000 lb	= 1 short ton	= 0·907 tonne

Double Conversion Tables for Measures and Weights

(Use the figures in the central column with those to the left or right, depending on which conversion is required. For example, 1 centimetre = 0·394 inch, and 1 inch = 2·540 centimetres.)

Centi-metres		Inches	Metres		Yards	Kilo-metres		Miles	Hec-tares		Acres
2·540	1	0·394	0·914	1	1·094	1·609	1	0·621	0·405	1	2·471
5·080	2	0·787	1·829	2	2·187	3·219	2	1·243	0·809	2	4·942
7·620	3	1·181	2·743	3	3·281	4·828	3	1·864	1·214	3	7·413
10·160	4	1·575	3·658	4	4·374	6·437	4	2·485	1·619	4	9·884
12·700	5	1·969	4·572	5	5·468	8·047	5	3·107	2·023	5	12·355
15·240	6	2·362	5·486	6	6·562	9·656	6	3·728	2·428	6	14·826
17·780	7	2·756	6·401	7	7·655	11·265	7	4·350	2·833	7	17·298
20·320	8	3·150	7·315	8	8·749	12·875	8	4·971	3·237	8	19·768
22·860	9	3·543	8·230	9	9·843	14·484	9	5·592	3·642	9	22·239
25·400	10	3·937	9·144	10	10·936	16·093	10	6·214	4·047	10	24·711

Kilo-grammes		Av. Pounds	Litres		Pints	Litres		Gallons	Metric Quintals per Hectare		Hun-dred-weight per Acre
0·454	1	2·205	0·568	1	1·760	4·546	1	0·220	1·255	1	0·797
0·907	2	4·409	1·136	2	3·520	9·092	2	0·440	2·511	2	1·593
1·361	3	6·614	1·705	3	5·279	13·638	3	0·660	3·766	3	2·390
1·814	4	8·818	2·273	4	7·039	18·184	4	0·880	5·021	4	3·186
2·268	5	11·023	2·841	5	8·799	22·730	5	1·100	6·277	5	3·983
2·722	6	13·228	3·409	6	10·559	27·276	6	1·320	7·532	6	4·780
3·175	7	15·432	3·978	7	12·319	31·822	7	1·540	8·787	7	5·576
3·629	8	17·637	4·546	8	14·078	36·368	8	1·760	10·043	8	6·373
4·082	9	19·842	5·114	9	15·838	40·914	9	1·980	11·298	9	7·169
4·536	10	22·046	5·682	10	17·598	45·460	10	2·200	12·554	10	7·966

Thermometrical Table

0° Centigrade = 32° Fahrenheit

100° Centigrade = 212° Fahrenheit

To convert °Fahrenheit into °Centigrade: subtract 32, then multiply by $\frac{5}{9}$; °Centigrade into °Fahrenheit: multiply by $\frac{9}{5}$, then add 32.

Bank and Public Holidays in Britain, 1987

Thursday 1 January	New Year's Day
Friday 2 January	Bank Holiday (Scotland only)
Tuesday 17 March	St Patrick's Day (Northern Ireland only)
Friday 17 April	Good Friday
Monday 20 April	Easter Monday (England, Wales and Northern Ireland only)
Monday 4 May	Early May Bank Holiday
Monday 25 May	Spring Bank Holiday
Monday 13 July	Orangeman's Day (Northern Ireland only)
Monday 3 August	Bank Holiday (Scotland only)
Monday 31 August	Summer Bank Holiday (England, Wales and Northern Ireland only)
Friday 25 December	Christmas Day
Monday 28 December	Extra day because Boxing Day falls on a Saturday

Appendix 2

Guide to Sources
The principal official periodical sources used in the preparation of this edition are given below:

Chapter 1   Land and People
Social Trends, Population Trends, Regional Trends, General Household Survey, Family Expenditure Survey

Chapter 3   Overseas Relations
British Aid Statistics, British Overseas Aid, Arms Control and Disarmament Newsletter

Chapter 4   Defence
Statement on the Defence Estimates

Chapter 5   Justice and the Law
Criminal Statistics, England and Wales; Criminal Statistics, Scotland

Chapter 8   The Environment
General Household Survey, Housing and Construction Statistics, Digest of Environmental Protection and Water Statistics

Chapter 10   National Economy
United Kingdom National Accounts (the 'Blue Book')

Chapter 11   Framework of Industry
United Kingdom National Accounts (the 'Blue Book'), British business

Chapter 12   Manufacturing and Service Industries
Report on the Census of Production, Monthly Digest of Statistics, Employment Gazette, British business

Chapter 13   Energy and Natural Resources
Digest of United Kingdom Energy Statistics, Development of the Oil and Gas Resources of the United Kingdom (the 'Brown Book'), United Kingdom Mineral Statistics

Chapter 14   Agriculture, Fisheries and Forestry
Annual Review of Agriculture

Chapter 15   Transport and Communications
Transport Statistics, Great Britain

Chapter 16   Employment
Employment Gazette, New Earnings Survey

Chapter 17   Public Finance
Financial Statement and Budget Report, The Government's Expenditure Plans (the public expenditure White Paper)

Chapter 19   Overseas Trade
Monthly Review of External Trade Statistics, United Kingdom Balance of Payments (the 'Pink Book'), British business

Chapter 23   Television and Radio
BBC's *Annual Report and Handbook*, IBA's *Television and Radio* and *Annual Report and Accounts*

Full purchasing details of these and other British Government publications can be obtained from the annual list *Government Publications* issued by Her Majesty's Stationery Office (HMSO), which has agents overseas. The list includes all Bills and Acts of Parliament and the official parliamentary report *Hansard*, White Papers, annual reports, reports of official committees and most publications of government departments including the Central Statistical Office, which publishes a *Guide to Official Statistics*. HMSO also sells in Britain many titles published by international organisations such as the United Nations, the European Community and the Organisation for Economic Co-operation and Development.

A Catalogue of British Official Publications not published by HMSO, published by Chadwyck-Healey, lists the more specialised departmental publications. Details of this and other commercial publications are available from bookshops or, overseas, from the British Council.

Index

Items are indexed under England, Northern Ireland, Scotland or Wales only where they are matters peculiar to these countries; otherwise they are indexed under the relevant subject headings.

Bold type in a sequence of figures indicates main references.

N

Acknowledgment for photographs
Camera Press (facing p 40). Andy Williams (Little Moreton Hall), Richard Surman (Hadrian's Wall, Powis Castle), Alan North (Castle Coole) – all from The National Trust Photographic Library; The National Trust for Scotland (between pp 40 and 41). Duke of Edinburgh's Award Scheme (facing p 41). Peter McCormack Photography (facing p 136). Lloyd's Register of Shipping, Barclays Bank plc (between pp 136 and 137). Balfour Beatty Ltd, Intermediate Technology Group (facing p 137). Royal Agricultural Society; Institute of Horticultural Research, East Malling; National Institute of Agricultural Engineering (between pp 296 and 297). Macaulay Institute of Soil Research (facing p 297). British Petroleum (facing p 392). Infopress (between pp 392 and 393).

Printed for HMSO by Hazell Watson & Viney Ltd
11/86 Dd 739578

Major conservation and recreation areas

Orkney Islands

Shetland Islands

National parks

Forest parks

Areas of outstanding natural beauty (national scenic areas in Scotland)

Heritage coast (primary nature conservation zones in Scotland)

Tourist Board area boundaries

London	1
South East	2
Southern	3
West Country	4
Thames & Chilterns	5
Heart of England	6
East Anglia	7
East Midlands	8
North West	9
Yorkshire & Humberside	10
Cumbria	11
Northumbria	12
Wales	13
Scotland	14
Northern Ireland	15

Glen More Forest Park

SCOTLAND

Argyll Forest Park

Queen Elizabeth Forest Park

14

Galloway Forest Park

Border Forest Park

Northumberland

12

NORTHERN IRELAND

15

11

Lake District

Yorkshire Dales

North York Moors

10

9

Snowdonia Forest Park

Snowdonia

Peak District

8

ENGLAND

7

13

WALES

6

Dean Forest Park

5

Pembrokeshire Coast

1

Brecon Beacons

3

2

Exmoor

4

New Forest

Dartmoor

0 20 40 60 80 100 km

0 20 40 60 miles